Successful
Marriages and Families

Successful Marriages and Families

Proclamation Principles and Research Perspectives

Edited by
Alan J. Hawkins
David C. Dollahite
Thomas W. Draper

BYU STUDIES
and
SCHOOL OF FAMILY LIFE

Brigham Young University
Provo, Utah

Library of Congress Cataloging-in-Publication Data

Successful marriages and families : proclamation principles and research perspectives / edited by Alan J. Hawkins, David C. Dollahite, and Thomas W. Draper.

    p. cm.

    Includes index.

    ISBN 978-0-8425-2803-0 (hard cover : alk. paper)

1. Families—Religious aspects—Church of Jesus Christ of Latter-day Saints. 2. Church of Jesus Christ of Latter-day Saints. First Presidency. Family. 3. Marriage—Religious aspects—Church of Jesus Christ of Latter-day Saints. I. Hawkins, Alan J., editor. II. Dollahite, David C. (David Curtis), editor. III. Draper, Thomas, 1947–, editor.

    BX8643.F3S83 2011

    248.8'44—dc23

                2011030493

Printed in the United States of America
10 9 8 7 6 5 4 3 2 1

Contents

Section II:
Proclamation Principles and Research on Successful Parenting

Section III:
Proclamation Principles and Research on Successful Family Processes

Section IV:
Advocating Public Policies for Successful Marriages and Families

Section V:
Perspectives on the Proclamation

Section VI:
Applying, Sharing, and Defending Proclamation Principles

Introduction to
Successful Marriages and Families:
Proclamation Principles and Research Perspectives

Alan J. Hawkins, David C. Dollahite, and Thomas W. Draper

IN AUGUST 2000, TWO SIGNIFICANT EVENTS TOOK place in the School of Family Life at Brigham Young University: the publication of *Strengthening Our Families: An In-Depth Look at the Proclamation on the Family* (Dollahite, 2000) and the introduction of a new foundational course, "Strengthening Marriage and Family: Proclamation Principles and Scholarship."

These related events were a response to an apostolic charge. On September 10, 1998, President Boyd K. Packer spoke to the School of Family Life. He read to us "The Family: A Proclamation to the World," charging us to use it as our charter, and gave us an apostolic blessing. He urged us to produce textbooks that were worthy of the wisdom generated by secular scholarship as well as faithful to the moral and spiritual values revealed in the holy scriptures and through latter-day prophets. Furthermore, these texts should not only impart information, but should also be practical, capable of preparing our students to be good spouses and parents. President Packer acknowledged that writing such texts would be difficult. But his charge and blessing then were a powerful source of strength in the difficult task of producing a text and course that honored his charge to us.

We relied upon that strength to produce *Strengthening Our Families,* our first effort to bring together sacred principles and relevant secular scholarship to help readers understand proclamation principles. A few years later, the School of Family Life faculty produced a second volume, *Helping and Healing Our Families: Principles and Practices Inspired by "The Family: A Proclamation to the World"* (Hart, Newell, Walton, & Dollahite, 2005). Though grounded in proclamation principles, this second volume covered a wider variety of family-related topics not explicitly linked to the proclamation, and it was intended more for the general Latter-day Saint reader.

But while proclamation principles are timeless, these two texts are not. The chapters for *Strengthening Our Families* were written in 1998 and 1999, and those in *Helping and Healing Our Families* in 2003 and 2004. Prophets and apostles have spoken often on the family proclamation and its principles over the ensuing years. Moreover, secular debates and struggles over marriage and family issues have accelerated and intensified since the publication of these earlier volumes. Recent family research has provided even more perspective on proclamation principles. Over the past decade or so, family life worldwide has been subject to significant challenges and change. Consequently, a more up-to-date treatment of the proclamation was needed. *Successful Marriages and Families: Proclamation Principles and Research Perspectives* is our attempt to provide a current and more comprehensive exploration of "The Family: A Proclamation to the World" for a new decade of instruction and insight.

The overall objective for *Successful Marriages and Families* remains the same as it was for the earlier volumes:

1. Strengthen readers' testimony in the principles of the restored gospel of Jesus Christ as they relate to family life.
2. Increase readers' confidence in their abilities to live and implement proclamation principles.

3. Help readers share and defend proclamation principles more effectively in their various spheres of influence.

This work includes new chapters of topics not addressed in the original text (chapters 1, 3, 5, 6, 7, 8, 9, 11, 14, 15, 17, 19, 25, 28, 34). It also includes new treatments of topics addressed in the original text (chapters 2, 4, 10, 12, 13, 16, 18, 20, 22, 24, 26, 27, 32, 33). In addition, we commissioned a few new chapters that provide a broader perspective on the proclamation itself (chapters 29, 30, 31). Readers familiar with the original text will recognize only a handful of chapters in *Successful Marriages and Families* as updates (chapters 21, 23).

It is important to point out at the outset of this volume that the views expressed in each chapter are the views of the author(s) and do not necessarily reflect the position of The Church of Jesus Christ of Latter-day Saints or the editors. As editors, we worked with authors to provide a text that would be aligned with proclamation principles and consistent with the restored gospel of Jesus Christ. Yet our knowledge is imperfect, our wisdom limited, and on many topics there is room for reasonable differences. The reader then shares responsibility for determining whether the authors' views are well aligned with gospel truth.

The title of this new volume comes directly from paragraph seven of the proclamation, which states, "Successful marriages and families are established and maintained on principles of faith, prayer, repentance, forgiveness, respect, love, compassion, work, and wholesome recreational activities." There are no quick or easy paths to a successful marriage and family life. Rather it takes work and patience and constant effort. Of course, there are no perfect marriages or families. In our view, successful marriages and families are those in which family members are striving to live the gospel of Jesus Christ and apply gospel principles in their family relationships. This volume contains both prophetic counsel and perspectives from social science research to help readers establish and maintain those principles in their marriages and families.

A reader comparing this work to the previous volumes will likely notice an even greater emphasis on social science research. President Brigham Young (1983, p. 247) proclaimed that "all wisdom, and all the arts and sciences in the world are from God, and are designed for the good of his people." While social science evidence has its limits and must be interpreted carefully, we are convinced that much of the social science evidence supports proclamation principles and not only helps us to understand these principles better but also to share and defend them more effectively. As a result of an increased attention to social science scholarship, we thought it appropriate to ask BYU Studies Press, as an academic publisher, to publish *Successful Marriages and Families*. We are grateful to BYU Studies for their support and particularly to John W. Welch for his valuable guidance. Also, we are grateful to the Religious Studies Center at Brigham Young University for a small but helpful grant to assist us in completing this project.

In addition, the reader will notice that this new volume gives somewhat more attention to families outside of North America. President Gordon B. Hinckley noted: "Why do we have this proclamation on the family now? Because the family is under attack. *All across the world* families are falling apart" (Hinckley, 1997, p. 5, italics added). Individuals and families everywhere are experiencing serious challenges. Still, the vast majority of research on family life samples North American families, and as a result, the dominant lens in this work remains focused on family life in North America.

As an editorial team, we express our gratitude to Dr. Rick Miller, Director of the School of Family Life at Brigham Young University, for his support of our efforts to produce this new volume. In addition, we are grateful to the contributing authors for their efforts to make this volume successful; many of them are recognized as national and international leaders in their respective fields. And they are faithful and devoted to the restored gospel of Jesus Christ. We also express our gratitude to our student editors, Courtney Dixon and Sarah Pierce, who in many ways were equal partners in this endeavor with three seasoned social science professors. They provided valuable suggestions and unique perspectives to virtually every chapter. We are indebted to Lisa Hawkins and Kimberly Reid for their exceptional editorial skills and to Marny K. Parkin for layout design and indexing. Finally, we thank the students in the family proclamation classes over the last decade or so who have shared with us their bright faith in proclamation principles and eager dedication to living, sharing, and defending these principles. They are the reason that we undertook this challenging labor to produce an up-to-date text. We hope it will aid them and all who read it in their study and application of "The Family: A Proclamation to the World."

Alan J. Hawkins *is a professor in the School of Family Life at Brigham Young University. He and his wife, Lisa, are the parents of two children and they have two grandchildren.* David C. Dollahite *is a professor in the School of Family Life at Brigham Young University. He and his wife, Mary, are the parents of seven children and they have two grandchildren.* Thomas W. Draper *is a professor in the School of Family Life at Brigham Young University. He and his wife, Linda, are the parents of four children and they have nine grandchildren.*

References

Dollahite, D. C. (2000). *Strengthening our families: An in-depth look at the proclamation on the family.* [Provo, UT]: School of Family Life, Brigham Young University.

Hart, C. H., Newell, L. D., Walton, E., & Dollahite, D. C. (Eds.). (2005). *Helping and healing our families: Principles and practices inspired by "The Family: A Proclamation to the World."* Salt Lake City: Deseret Book.

Hinckley, G. B. (1997, August). Inspirational thoughts. *Ensign, 27,* 2–7.

Young, B. (1983). *Discourses of Brigham Young.* Salt Lake City: Deseret Book.

Section I:
Proclamation Principles and Research on Successful Marriage

CHAPTER 1

Young Adulthood and Pathways to Eternal Marriage

Jason S. Carroll

Marriage . . . is ordained of God. . . . God has commanded that the sacred powers of procreation are to be employed only between man and woman, lawfully wedded as husband and wife. . . . Marriage between man and woman is essential to His eternal plan.

IN PREVIOUS GENERATIONS, MARRIAGE WAS REGARDED as the definitive transition to adulthood (Schlegel & Barry, 1991). However, recent studies suggest that the majority of young people today no longer consider marriage and other social milestones (for example, completing school or becoming a parent) to be a necessary part of becoming an adult (Nelson & Barry, 2005). Instead, young people report more personally defined qualities, such as accepting responsibility for one's self, achieving financial independence, and becoming independent decision makers, as the contemporary markers of adulthood (Cheah & Nelson, 2004). With most young people no longer associating marriage with the transition to adulthood and a notable rise in the average age at which people first marry (U.S. Census Bureau, 2010), many people consider marriage to be a part of later adult life rather than an important feature of young adulthood. However, there is growing evidence that young people's views of marriage—such as their desired age for marriage and the importance they place on getting married—are associated with their lifestyle choices during young adulthood as well as the later success of their marriage and family lives (Carroll, Willoughby, Badger, Nelson, Barry, & Madsen, 2007).

Although societal attitudes are changing about marriage and the transition to adulthood, the Lord's prophets have always emphasized the importance of marriage according to God's plan. Moses recorded that after the Lord placed Adam in the Garden of Eden, He declared "that it was not good that the man should be alone; wherefore I will make an help meet for him" (Moses 3:18). The Apostle Paul taught, "Neither is the man without the woman, neither the woman without the man, in the Lord" (1 Corinthians 11:11). In a revelation given to the Prophet Joseph Smith, we learn that "marriage is ordained of God unto man. Wherefore, . . . they twain shall be one flesh" (D&C 49:15–16). In modern times, the proclamation on the family reaffirms these teachings, stating that marriage "is essential to His eternal plan" for "the eternal destiny of His children" (¶¶ 7, 1).

Despite the emphasis the Lord's prophets have always placed on forming celestial marriage relationships, we live in a time when many people see the path toward marriage in a different light. Current societal trends reveal that there are a number of pitfalls in today's dating and courtship culture that require young adults to approach marriage with an even greater degree of faith and steadfastness than was required in previous generations. In fact, for some Latter-day Saint young adults today, following prophetic counsel to form an enduring marriage may feel like a daunting task. This chapter discusses several of the pitfalls of current dating practices and reviews prophetic and scholarly principles that can help young adults move toward marriage with faith and confidence.

The Erosion of Traditional Dating and Courtship

One of the most dramatic changes influencing marriage preparation in the United States during the last quarter century has been the emergence of a new period in life between adolescence and adulthood that has been labeled "emerging adulthood" (Arnett, 2000). This life stage has emerged as a result of the substantial increase in the median age at first marriage for both men and women. Since 1950, the median age at first marriage in the United States has increased and is currently at a historic high of 26 years for women and 28 years for men (U.S. Census Bureau, 2010). This pattern of delayed marriage has created an extended period of nearly 10 years in the family life cycle where many young adults have left adolescence and are beginning to view themselves as adults, but have not yet entered into the commitments and lifestyle patterns of married adult life. The emergence of this new period of life raises an important question: What impact does this period of "extended singleness" have on young adults' preparation for marriage and family life?

One of the best ways to understand how this new period of emerging adulthood is influencing preparation for later marriage and family life is to look at the defining characteristics of the current dating and courtship culture. Numerous scholars have noted that the culture of dating that young adults experience today is markedly different from the one experienced by their parents and grandparents. In particular, these family professionals have noted an erosion of traditional courtship patterns and a dating culture that lacks socially defined norms, rituals, and relationship milestones to guide young people toward marriage. As a result of these changes, a number of pitfalls exist in our current dating and courtship culture, including (a) a growing pessimism about marriage and a focus on personal independence before and after marriage, (b) a primary focus on personal financial independence for both men and women, (c) widespread sexual permissiveness, and (d) high rates of couples living together before marriage.

Pessimism About Marriage

Despite the growing trend to delay marriage, recent research indicates that having a successful, lifelong marriage is still a highly valued goal for the majority of emerging adults. In fact, a recent study showed that 90 percent of young adults in the United States rate "having a good marriage and family life" as being "quite important" or "very important" to them (Bachman, Johnston, & O'Malley, 2009). However, having grown up in a society saturated with divorce, many young people have become pessimistic about their chances of having a happy marriage. The same study found that

more than one-third of emerging adults agreed with the statement, "One sees so few good or happy marriages that one questions it as a way of life." Simply put, when it comes to marriage, many young adults today have high aspirations but low expectations.

Pessimism about marriage and wariness of divorce among emerging adults is creating a culture of divorce preparation rather than a culture of marriage preparation. The emerging ethic of marriage preparation appears to be: "When you are ready to get divorced, you are ready to get married." In this context, "single life" is not only becoming a permissible period for emerging adults, but it is also regarded by some as a necessary period before a young person is ready to settle down and get married. Many emerging adults believe that they will be ready for marriage only when they are finished being single. In a recent study, more than half of young adults today rank having "fully experienced the single life" as an important criterion to achieve before getting married (Carroll, Badger, Willoughby, Nelson, Madsen, & Barry, 2009).

Getting Ahead Before Getting Wed

The central responsibilities of adulthood in past generations centered on caring for one's spouse, providing for a family, and nurturing children—all of which involve duties toward others. However, as noted previously, recent research suggests that young people today have new visions about what the focus of adult life should be. For the most part, these new markers of adulthood carry a theme of personal independence and self-reliance. Coupled with a sense of pessimism about their chances for marital success, many young people now see their young adult years as a time to pursue their personal interests and become independent financially. Simply put, the emerging adult culture today encourages young people to "get ahead before getting wed" and to be careful not to let marriage alter or interrupt one's educational and career plans.

Both young women and young men frequently identify becoming financially independent as a key to being ready for contemporary marriage. This ideology is an apparent shift from an interdependence ethic more widely accepted by their parents' and grandparents' generations, wherein individuals saw marriage as a foundation for financial stability. In a recent study, a considerable proportion of emerging adults reported that to be marriage-ready they not only needed to be financially independent from their parents (91 percent), but they also needed to be finished with their education (43 percent) and settled into a long-term career (51 percent). Also, a notable percentage of emerging adults believed they needed to be able to pay for their own wedding (33 percent) and to have purchased a house (24 percent) before they would feel ready to get married (Carroll et al., 2009). Given that these financial goals were typically viewed as milestones of married life by previous generations, the greater emphasis on financial criteria for marriage readiness may indicate a need to feel settled as an adult before taking on the responsibilities of marriage. At the same time, however, the "financial stability first" approach also may be an approach that hedges one's bets, in that emerging adults do not want to step into marriage until they are ready for the economic realities of a possible divorce.

Some people also believe that an ethic of personal independence will make marriages more stable because young people enter marriage with more resources and greater maturity. While research confirms that marrying after your teenage years and getting more education are associated with greater marital stability (Heaton, 2002), there is also strong evidence that an attitude of personal independence may weaken some marriages by undermining the need for mutual partnership among couples. This occurs in two ways. First, many young people today enter marriage with a built-in escape route that lessens the likelihood that they will stick with a marriage in periods of trouble that are common early in marriage. Second, emerging adults who endorse economic self-reliance before the wedding rather than building economic stability together after the wedding will most likely put off marriage in order to achieve this goal. As they delay marriage to their late twenties or thirties in an attempt to achieve economic stability, they will increase their chances of participating in risk factors for a future divorce, such as premarital sex and cohabitation (Carroll et al., 2007).

Hanging Out and Hooking Up

One of the biggest changes in the current young adult culture is the disappearance of dating. Several studies have found that traditional dating, where the man asks the woman out on a date and pays for the evening together, is becoming rare. Only 50 percent of college

women reported that they had been asked out on six or more dates, and a third said they had been asked on two or fewer dates (Glenn & Marquardt, 2001). Young women and men more often "hang out" rather than go on planned dates. Young adults often report finding that even when they have been hanging out with someone over a period of time, they still do not know if they are a couple. In the current dating culture, there are few widely recognized norms to help guide young adults in thinking about love, commitment, and marriage.

Even though premarital sexual behavior has been shown to be a significant risk factor for future marital success (Heaton, 2002), single life in modern culture has become synonymous with sexual experimentation in non-committed relationships. A study of college young women showed that a form of getting together, called "hooking up," is widespread and accepted. Hooking up occurs when a young man and woman get together for the sole purpose of some kind of sexual encounter with nothing further expected of the relationship (Glenn & Marquardt, 2001). Another research team characterized today's dating and mating culture as "sex without strings, relationships without rings" (Whitehead & Popenoe, 2000). One study of young men suggested several reasons why so many are unwilling to marry early: (a) they can get sex without marriage, (b) they fear that marriage will require too many changes and compromises, (c) they face few social pressures to marry, and (d) they want to enjoy single life as long as they can (Whitehead & Popenoe, 2002).

Acceptance of Cohabitation

Recent research also indicates that emerging adults are increasingly embracing the idea that a couple needs to live together before marriage to test their relationship and see if they are ready for marriage. In one study, 62 percent of young adults reported that they believe that living together before marriage is a good way to avoid eventual divorce; more than half of all marriages in America today are preceded by cohabitation (Whitehead & Popenoe, 2001). These young adults believe that cohabitation is a good way to take the risk out of marriage and reduce their odds of divorce. However, research shows that this belief is often an illusion. Studies on cohabitation and later marital success have consistently found that couples who cohabit before marriage are *more* likely to divorce than couples who do not cohabit before marriage (Jose, O'Leary, & Moyer, 2010). A recent study using a national sample found that couples who cohabited before engagement (43.1 percent of couples) reported lower marital quality and greater potential for divorce than those who cohabited only after engagement (16.4 percent of couples) or only after marriage (40.5 percent of couples) (Rhoades, Stanley, & Markman, 2009). This suggests that the negative effect of cohabitation comes primarily from pre-commitment cohabitation, although more research on this point is needed. However, it should be noted that research has identified no disadvantages for couples who follow the prophetically prescribed pattern for dating and mating and do not cohabit prior to marriage.

Approaches to Dating: Becoming a Right Person for Marriage

Within this new period of emerging adulthood, there are a variety of ideas about how successful marriages are formed. These ideas translate into varied approaches to coupling that emphasize different aspects of relationships and criteria for selecting a partner. In particular, there are two common approaches to mate selection during the emerging adult years—and the approach that young people take will make a difference in their dating experience and success.

The first approach to dating can be called the "finding Mr./Ms. Right" approach. This approach is very popular in the mainstream culture and is quite common among many Latter-day Saint young people, too. This approach is emphasized in commercials for dating websites that promise to help single adults find that "one special person" who is "waiting for you." The primary question at the core of this approach to dating is, "How do I find the one right person for me?" In sum, the focus in this style of dating is on finding or matching with the person you are meant to marry. This approach creates feelings of anxiety about dating, as young people feel overwhelmed by the prospect of finding their "perfect match."

By contrast, Elder David A. Bednar (2009) warns young people about embracing a finding-focused view to dating and counsels them to practice a different approach. He said:

As we visit with young adults all over the Church, often they will ask, "Well, what are the characteristics I should look for in a future spouse?" As

though they have some checklist of, "I need to find someone who has these three, or four, or five things." And I rather forcefully say to them, "You are so arrogant to think that you are some catch and that you want someone else who has these five things for you! If you found somebody who had these three or four or five characteristics that you're looking for, what makes you think they'd want to marry you?" The "list" is not for evaluating someone else—the list is for you and what you need to become. And so if there are three primary characteristics that [you] hope to find in an eternal companion, then those are the three things [you] ought to be working to become. Then [you] will be attractive to someone who has those things. . . . You are not on a shopping spree looking for the greatest value with a series of characteristics. You become what you hope your spouse will be and you'll have a greater likelihood of finding that person.

Within a "becoming" approach to dating, the primary question is, "How can I be prepared to form and nurture an enduring marriage?" The difference between the "finding Mr./Ms. Right" approach and this approach is that the "becoming" approach primarily emphasizes personal readiness, maturity, and growth. While a becoming-based approach to dating still recognizes the importance of finding a good person to marry, finding is not the primary focus. Rather, the main emphasis is on becoming ready for marriage and then committing to that relationship when you have made the decision to marry. The remainder of this chapter will discuss principles that can assist young adults in both becoming a right person and in finding a right person, two essential parts of forming a loving and lasting marriage.

Sacred Perspectives on Marriage Readiness

In our society today, marriage is viewed almost exclusively as a *couple relationship*. When viewed as a couple relationship, marriage is seen as a personal expression of love between two people who want to share their lives together. This view of marriage typically emphasizes personal happiness, emotional gratification, physical attraction, good communication, pleasurable intimacy, and couple compatibility as the essential elements of a good marriage. Most of us would agree that to some degree these are parts of the marriage relationship we hope to have someday. However, for many people this "couple relationship" view is as deep as their perspective of marriage goes. If young people think of marriage only as a couple relationship, they miss out on the sacred aspects of marriage that emphasize the need for commitment, sacrifice, selfless caring for one's spouse, and the benefits of marriage for children. Most important, when marriage is viewed as only a couple relationship, couples will lack the needed foundation of the *divine institution of marriage* that grounds the couple's relationship in the principles of discipleship, covenant making, cleaving, equal partnership, the sacred responsibilities of husbands and wives, and the eternal purposes of marriage.

To be clear, viewing marriage as a couple relationship is not wrong—it is just incomplete. Such a view lacks doctrinal foundation, emphasizing the "fruits" of marriage that we all desire to experience without tying these outcomes to the true "roots" that create loving and lasting marriages. As young adults strengthen their testimonies of marriage as a divine institution, they will have a deeper foundation of true doctrine upon which to build effective skills related to communication, intimacy, and other relational aspects of marriage.

When we view marriage as a divine institution, we understand that the practices and patterns of successful marriage are not created nor defined by the spouses themselves. This view teaches us that one of the keys to lasting marriage is to seek not just compatibility with one's spouse, but also to seek alignment with God. When spouses build their marriage according to the Lord's pattern and seek to contribute to His divine purposes, their relationship with each other is endowed with the Holy Spirit of Promise, which blesses them with a greater love for each other, a deeper meaning in their lives, and an enduring sense of oneness with God.

Faith and Discipleship in Marriage

For some young people, however, the thoughts of becoming ready for marriage, finding someone to marry, and making a marriage work evoke fears and concerns. Sometimes these fears are grounded in poor family experiences while growing up that leave individuals feeling unprepared or poorly taught about healthy marriage. Some young people understandably worry about repeating the pattern of their parents' divorce

(Wolfinger, 2005). Others have anxiety about attracting a high-quality spouse and fear that their efforts at dating will not be successful. Many young people focus on their personal faults and worry that no one will want to marry them. Others fear the responsibilities of marriage—particularly marriages entered into during the young adult years. Issues of schooling, employment, and finances create an anxiety suggesting that marriage must be pushed further and further down the life path. Whatever the reasons may be, there seems to be a growing fear among some young people that forming a loving and lasting marriage is something they may not be able to do.

Given the prevalence of these types of fears about dating and marriage, the starting point for becoming ready for marriage is to develop faith in the Lord Jesus Christ and His divine plan for marriage and families. In 1 Nephi 3:7 we read, "I will go and do the things which the Lord hath commanded, for I know that the Lord giveth no commandments unto the children of men, save he shall prepare a way for them that they may accomplish the thing which he commandeth them." Although this scripture is not typically viewed as a marriage-preparation scripture, its principles are applicable to the modern dating context. Through young adults' faithfulness, the Lord endows them with what they need in order to live His divine plan of happiness.

As young adults strive to become the people our Father in Heaven wants them to become, they will increase their readiness for marriage in the future. Elder Jeffrey R. Holland (2003, p. 8) has taught:

Do you want capability, safety, and security in dating and romance, in married life and eternity? Be a true disciple of Jesus. Be a genuine, committed, word-and-deed Latter-day Saint. Believe that your faith has everything to do with your romance, because it does. You separate dating from discipleship at your peril.

Social Science Perspectives on Marriage Readiness

Scholars have found that there are certain personal characteristics or traits that happily married spouses have developed (Carroll, Badger, & Yang, 2006). These personal characteristics begin to be developed during adolescence and young adulthood and continue to be refined during the transition to marriage. Scholars have found that young adults' readiness for marriage is largely determined by their ability to love and communicate.

The Ability to Love

The ability to love is defined by how one asserts, expresses, and defines his or her importance, and the importance of others, in intimate as well as non-intimate relationships (L'Abate, 1997, p. 4). *Love* is defined as the ability to be emotionally available to self and others, especially in times of need—that is, when loved ones are hurting or are fearful of being hurt—without requirements of performance, perfection, problem-solving, or production. Thus, the ability to love requires a combination of a sense of self-worth or personal security plus intimate regard for others.

The ability to love consists of two aspects—personal security and other-centeredness. The term *personal security* refers to a person's sense of self-importance, which involves perceptions of self-worth, the ability to regulate negative affect (for example, depression, anxiety, or anger), and feelings of secure attachment (Carroll, Badger, & Yang, 2006). Personally secure people rely on sources of internal validation (such as the love of God, a sense of personal worth, and personal optimism) rather than seeking external validation of their worth (for example, through accomplishment, physical appearance, material possessions, or unhealthy relationships). Personal security is the foundation for several key attributes that are needed in dating and marriage relationships. These include courage, vulnerability, and a willingness to trust other people. Without personal security, vulnerability in close relationships becomes threatening and the fear of rejection will often dictate how people behave in dating situations. When this happens, there is less authenticity, disclosure, and mutual reliance in couple relationships—all necessary ingredients to forming an intimate and supportive relationship. Thus, seeking a romantic relationship means having the courage to be open and even vulnerable to being hurt.

Other-centeredness reflects an orientation toward the importance of others and is embodied in traits such as kindness, commitment, fairness, sacrifice, forgiveness, and other personal virtues. Other-centeredness is the capacity to care for others and the maturity to allow others' needs to become equal or greater in priority than one's own. In recent years, marriage researchers have begun to conduct studies on forgiveness, sacrifice, commitment, and other aspects of marital relationships that were previously considered to be the content of Sunday School classes and sermons (see Fincham, Stanley, & Beach, 2007).

The Ability to Communicate

Communication is defined as "the ability to bargain, problem-solve, and make decisions" (L'Abate, 1997, p. 43). In particular, the ability to communicate involves interacting with others in a way that consensus can be reached while respecting the rights of each individual. Because of this, competence in communication is founded upon and becomes an outward expression of one's ability to love. Effective communication is a set of skills that is grounded upon the foundation of the first dimensions—personal security and other-centeredness. While the first two aspects of personal maturity (for example, personal security and mature love) typically influence our motives and intents in relationships, the third aspect, effective communication, deals more with our behaviors and actions. When our hearts are in the right place, we are ready to learn skills that can help us effectively express our love toward others.

Effective communication involves two primary skills—*empathetic listening* and *clear-sending communication*. As young adults develop these skills, they are better prepared to establish healthy and productive couple interactions in dating and marriage relationships. The goal of empathetic listening is to help another person feel understood and valued. It is a vital and necessary skill needed in dating, courtship, and marriage. To be an empathetic listener, young adults must communicate in ways that help others believe that they really want to listen to them. Those who are speaking must feel that when they tell you something, you really care about what they are saying. If we do not really care what others are saying, then there is no set of skills or techniques we can use to convince them that we do.

In addition to empathetic listening, effective communication is built upon clearly sent messages to others. This is the talking part of communication. However, most unclear communication in close relationships has very little to do with partners having actual difficulties in talking or forming words. Messages become unclear because of background issues that prevent people from being direct, open, and authentic in their statements to others. In order to be effective communicators, we have to be authentic in our conversations with others. Simply put, we have to say what we mean and mean what we say while still respecting the feelings and perspectives of others. In dating relationships, when young adults do not state their true feelings or perspectives or when they lie about them, trust and intimacy cannot develop or be maintained. When the purpose of communication is to cover up, mislead, deceive, intimidate, threaten, disapprove, hurt, fault-find, or make someone feel guilty, relationships are damaged. Furthermore, if young adults allow their emotions or personal insecurities to overwhelm them, they tend to communicate in less authentic ways—thus sending less clear messages.

Finding a Choice Eternal Companion

While both spiritual and scholarly perspectives emphasize the need for young people to become a right person for marriage, this does not mean that finding a proper person to marry is an unimportant part of establishing an eternal marriage. In fact, in a culture of eroded courtship where many young people lack clear guidance about how to date and form a lasting marriage, principles of how to find a right person for marriage are particularly needed. In recent years, the Lord's prophets have focused on these principles in their counsel to young adults. These "principles of finding" have centered primarily on teaching young people (a) *when* they should seek to get married, (b) *whom* they should seek as a marriage companion, and (c) *how* to date in ways that will most likely lead toward the formation of eternal marriages.

When?—The Timing of Marriage

Ultimately, designations of what is "early" and "late" are relative comparisons based on a standard of what is considered "on time." As noted previously, the median age at first marriage in the United States has risen from about 20 years for females and 22 for males in the 1950s, to 26 and 28 years for females and males, respectively (U.S. Census Bureau, 2010). The best data available shows that the average age at first marriage for Latter-day Saint men who serve missions is 22.9, while the average age for marriage for Latter-day Saint women who do not serve missions is 21.6 and for women who do serve missions is 24.3 (McClendon & Chadwick, 2005). Considered in this context, current Latter-day Saint courtship patterns may be "late" compared to

the average marital ages of their parents and grandparents. But compared to their national counterparts, some might consider current Latter-day Saint dating patterns and ages as "early" or perhaps even "too early."

So, which perspective is right? Is there a best age to get married? Does getting married during the early young adult years put marriage at risk? Is it true that older people in their late twenties and thirties are more mature and better prepared for marriage than people who are younger? Answers to these questions can be helpful to young adults as they prayerfully consider the timing of marriage in their own lives. To give some perspective on these issues, we will consider prophetic counsel on timing of marriage in the life course and scholarly research on the association between age at marriage and later marital outcomes.

Prophetic counsel on marital timing. When it comes to counsel about timing related to dating and marriage, our prophetic leaders teach us principles rather than provide precise recommendations. However, this does not mean that the ideal timing of marriage is relative to each person. Prophets and apostles have repeatedly emphasized the importance of marriage in God's plan and the priority that should be given to marriage as young people transition to adulthood. In a devotional with BYU students, President Gordon B. Hinckley (2006, p. 6) said,

> I remind you that the association you now enjoy as students is probably the best time of your lives to find your own "Beloved Eternal Companion." Do so with a prayer in your heart. It will be the most important decision you will ever make. It will influence your life from now through all eternity.

Elder Dallin H. Oaks (2006, p. 13) has also taught, "It's marriage time. That is what the Lord intends for His young adult sons and daughters."

When it comes to the timing and priority of marriage in their lives, it is helpful for young adults to remember that the Lord has a family ideal that they should strive to fulfill as they become adults. Elder Richard G. Scott taught:

> Throughout your life on earth, seek diligently to fulfill the fundamental purposes of this life *through the ideal family*. While you may not have

yet reached that ideal, do all you can through obedience and faith in the Lord to consistently draw as close to it as you are able. Let nothing dissuade you from that objective (2001, p. 7, italics in original).

Marriage may or may not come during young adulthood, but young people should prepare themselves so that they are ready when a right opportunity presents itself. Trusting in the Lord means that you should prepare yourself to live according to His plan—even if marriage comes into your life sooner or later than you anticipate. The Lord's servants have counseled young adults to put marriage as their highest priority in their preparations for adult life, placing it above education, career, and other very important pursuits. This counsel is not intended to make young adults rush the process of dating or to compromise their standards in order to marry at a younger age. President Gordon B. Hinckley (1990, p. 6) said, "I hope you will not put off marriage too long. . . . Don't go on endlessly in a frivolous dating game. Look for a choice companion, one you can love, honor, and respect, and make a decision."

Scholarly perspectives on marital timing. Marriage researchers have conducted several studies to examine whether age at marriage is associated with marital success. When properly understood, the findings of these studies do not confirm the popular notion that labels marriage in the young adult years as "too early" or "too young." The graph in Figure 1.1 (taken from Heaton, 2002) displays the association between age at marriage and the probability of later divorce. Studies have repeatedly found that age at marriage has a strong association with marriage outcomes until approximately the age of 21 or 22. This means that up until this age, the older people are when they get married, the lower their chances are of getting divorced. However, the association between age at marriage and divorce rate is virtually erased after the age of 22. This means that being 23 or 25 or 30 years of age does little to decrease your chances of divorce any more than being 21 or 22 does. Also, young adults and their parents should keep in mind that the pool of desirable marriage candidates is not static and diminishes over time, so the prospect of partnering with a spiritually mature and well prepared spouse may decrease over time as an individual gets older and these potential partners marry others.

FIGURE 1.1
PROBABILITY OF DIVORCE BY AGE AT MARRIAGE

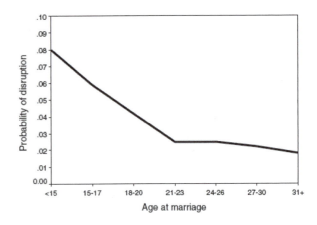

In sum, researchers have concluded that when it comes to age, the marriages that are most at risk for future divorce are the ones in which one or both of the partners are teenagers at the time of marriage. It is important to remember that these findings come from national data sets, and the findings for Latter-day Saint couples may differ. Age at marriage is best understood as a "proxy variable," which means that it stands as an indicator of other factors such as education, maturity, and family support (See Regnerus, 2009, for a detailed discussion of this issue). For Latter-day Saint couples, this means that if personal maturity and family support are higher, on average, for earlier marriages than in the national cohort, then the association between age at marriage and divorce may go flat at an earlier age. Thus, following prophetic teachings to make marriage a priority during young adulthood may not increase the risk of future divorce for mature Latter-day Saint young adults who marry in their early twenties.

Later Marriage. While I have primarily discussed the delay of marriage, for many people the trial of faith they experience related to the timing of marriage is that marriage does not happen as soon as they would like or expect. Our prophetic leaders have frequently addressed this topic. Elder Dallin H. Oaks (2003, p. 15) has stated:

Even our most righteous desires may elude us or come in different ways or at different times than we have sought to plan. For example, we cannot be sure that we will marry as soon as we desire. . . . We should commit ourselves to the priorities and standards we will follow on matters we do not control and persist faithfully in those commitments, whatever happens to us because of the agency of others or the timing of the Lord.

Elder Oaks (1993, p. 75) has also taught: "Singleness, childlessness, death, and divorce frustrate ideals and postpone the fulfillment of promised blessings. . . . But these frustrations are only temporary. . . . Many of the most important deprivations of mortality will be set right in the Millennium." Eternal life is best understood as "God-like life," which is a way of life centered on marriage and family relationships. The promise of the Lord is that eternal marriage will be a part of celestial glory for all true disciples of Jesus Christ. Therefore, all young adults can continue to prepare for marriage with the surety that it will be a part of their eternal destiny and future—even if the realization of that blessing does not happen according to their ideal timing in this life.

Who?—Eternal Companions versus Soul Mates

We live in the age of so-called "soul mate marriage," where love is frequently portrayed as a seamless matching with one's "other half" and couple relationships are seen as a pathway to personal happiness. In a recent national survey of single young adults, 94 percent agreed with the statement, "When you marry you want your spouse to be your soul mate, first and foremost," and 88 percent also agreed that "there is a special person, a soul mate, waiting for you somewhere out there" (Whitehead & Popenoe, 2001). The authors of this survey argue that marriage today, founded on the belief of predestined love, is often portrayed as a "super relationship"—an effortless and conflict-free union, filled with romantic intimacy and emotional togetherness—that can meet our every need and desire. Other important aspects of marriage, such as economic partnership or parenting, have generally disappeared from the popular culture's discussion of marriage.

While "soul mate love" may work for scripted Hollywood films or romance novels, most couples making marriage work in the real world will tell you that maintaining their relationship requires work, patience, personal growth, compromise, commitment, and sacrifice. They will tell you that marriage is definitely worth it, but that what they experience in marriage is not the type of relationship portrayed in popular culture. President Spencer W. Kimball (1976, p. 16) warned Latter-day

Saints to not get led astray by the soul mate culture of our day when he said,

Soul mates are fiction and illusion; and while every young man and young woman will seek with all diligence and prayerfulness to find a mate with whom life can be most compatible and beautiful, yet it is certain that almost any good man and any good woman can have happiness and a successful marriage if both are willing to pay the price.

Many young people like the idea of soul mate love and the idea of having a one and only. They resonate with the idea that they will be made complete in marriage and have a deep union with their spouse that is emotional, physical, and spiritual in nature. The good news is that none of us have to abandon our desires for any of these things. Desiring the type of couple unity portrayed in soul mate relationships is a good and righteous aspiration. However, while the goal or outcome of soul mate thinking is a good thing, the way that these relationships come about is wrongly presented in the soul mate thinking of our day. Our desire should be to become eternal companions with our spouse in this life. Eternal companions are different than soul mates. While soul mates are found, eternal companions are chosen and made. Two people become uniquely suited for each other as they go through the experience of life together and learn to adapt and grow in ways that make them a better fit with their spouse.

Unrealistic expectations. Some may ask, "Does believing in soul mates really do any harm?" There is some evidence that it does. The trouble lies in the unrealistic expectations and resulting consequences that arise from approaching marriage this way. When love in dating and marriage is portrayed as perfect and trouble-free, many couples are left grasping for answers when they have a major disagreement or when their partner's lack of responsiveness leaves them feeling hurt and alone. The romantic notions of soul mate love give spouses very little direction on ways to improve, restore, and maintain a marriage in the real world. Unrealistic expectations of one's spouse and married life in general can lead disillusioned partners to believe that their problems lie in having made a faulty match and that their only recourse is to unmatch and rematch again with someone else who must be their real soul mate. Even among Latter-day Saints, soul mate beliefs can lead to unrealistic expectations about marriage. In one study, Latter-day Saint marriage counselors listed "unrealistic expectations of marriage or spouse" as the most frequently reported issue they encountered in their work (Stahmann & Adams, 1997).

How?—A Pattern of Dating for Divine Purposes

Given the messages young people are receiving from the broader culture, and even at times from their families and friends, it is not surprising that many Latter-day Saint young adults are confused, afraid to make commitments, and too often turning to the patterns of the world. For example, a recent study of unmarried BYU students showed that "fear of making a mistake" was a factor influencing nearly 60 percent of those who are delaying marriage (Holman, Viveiros, & Carroll, 2005). Other studies have shown that hanging-out patterns have increased among Latter-day Saint young people, although such patterns are not as prevalent as they are among other samples of young adults (Carroll, 2010). There is also evidence that some Latter-day Saint young people are "hooking up" by engaging in NCMOs (non-committal make-outs) or other forms of non-committed physical intimacy prior to marriage (Carroll, 2010).

Similar to young people in the broader culture, Latter-day Saint young adults today must date and marry in a dating culture that lacks strong norms, rituals, and relationship milestones to guide young people toward marriage. Traditional dating is the most endangered part of the modern context of dating. Because of this, our prophetic leaders in recent years have warned young adults about the erosion of courtship in our society and have counseled them to follow a divinely directed approach to dating and courtship. Elder Dallin H. Oaks (2006) gave a landmark talk on this subject at a CES fireside. He encouraged young people to date rather than hang out. Dating involves planning ahead and pairing off. He urged young men to summon their courage and initiate dating. He counseled young women to be supportive by encouraging simple and inexpensive dates that foster greater frequency of dating. Above all, Elder Oaks encouraged young adults to resist cultural trends indicating that there are only two kinds of dating—hanging out or exclusive dating.

Specifically, he counseled young adults to engage in traditional dating patterns that can lead to exclusive dating, engagement, and marriage.

Traditional dating. One of the main risks in today's dating culture is that young people often lack much dating experience before they get involved in an exclusive dating relationship and, sometimes, even get quickly engaged. Proper mate selection and coupling needs the middle ground of traditional dating. In traditional dating, couples pair off for the duration of the evening or activity and may go out with one another on multiple occasions. While traditional dating involves one-on-one pairing and involvement, at this stage of dating young people still maintain a non-coupled status. To foster this type of dating culture, Elder Oaks encouraged frequent and simple dates. He also stressed that the goal in these dates is conversation and interaction, not entertainment. It is nice to have fun together and do things that are enjoyable, but traditional dating should also follow a pattern that allows for meaningful conversation and dialogue. Traditional dating experience provides young adults with greater self-awareness, greater appreciation of the range of potential partners, and greater preparation for marriage, which lead to wiser decision making about a marriage partner and increased confidence in later courtship.

Exclusive dating. When properly practiced, traditional dating patterns will lead eventually to exclusive dating, in which couples can explore a potential marriage relationship with a specific person and come to a decision whether they should move forward toward engagement or move back to traditional dating and explore relationships with other people. Exclusive dating is an important developmental milestone in a couple relationship that changes the social and developmental context of the relationship. This transition opens a new social reality that involves extended families, friends, and others. This transition should happen with open discussion between the partners and a clear understanding by both partners that the relationship has entered an exclusive stage of dating. This transition should not be entered lightly or unintentionally. Nor should the transition to exclusive dating be rushed.

While rushing into exclusivity can be problematic, so can unduly delaying or avoiding exclusivity when the relationship is ready for it. All relationships that appropriately progress toward marriage reach a point where they need to become exclusive in order to continue progressing. If this step does not happen at the right time, the relationship often stalls and anxiety replaces confidence. If this happens, even a very promising relationship can begin to falter.

Engagement. The purposes of engagement are to confirm a decision to marry someone, make wedding preparations, and strengthen new extended family relationships. When a couple becomes engaged, they promise to "forsake all others" as the couple finalizes their plans to marry. The practices of this stage involve strengthening relationships with extended family members, meeting regularly with priesthood leaders, preparing for a wedding, and making specific plans for early married life. President Spencer W. Kimball (1969, p. 242) has commented, "The successful marriage depends in large measure upon the preparation made in approaching it. . . . One cannot pick the ripe, rich, luscious fruit from a tree that was never planted, nurtured, nor pruned." By and large, couples will be better served by having longer periods of exclusive dating, followed by shorter engagements.

The exclusive dating stage is the primary period in which to make the decision whether or not to marry someone. However, engagement provides a chance to confirm the decision to marry, and any "red flags" that come up during engagement should be addressed before moving forward with the wedding. While engagement is an important relationship milestone that should be respected by the couple and others, it is not yet a stage of covenant. While it is common to experience some anxiety and nervousness as a wedding day approaches, engaged couples should not move forward with marriage if one or both of the partners has serious reservations and concerns about foundational aspects of the relationship. A pre-marriage break-up is always preferable to a post-marriage divorce. Even if arrangements have been made for a reception center or the invitations sent out, if there are serious and valid concerns about a partner or the relationship, these concerns should be resolved before going forward with the marriage. This is one reason why lavish spending on weddings is a problem. A sense that too much money would be lost by postponing or canceling the wedding can exist when a great deal is spent on wedding preparations.

Conclusion

The fundamental purposes of this life remain the same as they have always been—to receive a body, to believe in Christ, to progress spiritually, and to form an eternal marriage and family. As today's young adults prepare for eternal marriage, they must have faith that God will help them become ready for marriage, find a wonderful person, and establish a happy family—in His way and in His time. Despite the challenges of the modern dating context, young adults can find confidence in divine patterns of dating, courtship, and marriage. President Henry B. Eyring (1998, p. 10) promised:

> As we read what the [proclamation] tells us about the family, we can expect—in fact we must expect— impressions to come to our minds as to what we are to do. And we can be confident it is possible for us to do according to those impressions.

Elder Richard G. Scott (2004, p. 100) further advised, "You have a choice. You can wring your hands and be consumed with concern for the future or choose to use the counsel the Lord has given to live with peace and happiness." Although current dating trends may look discouraging, the Lord has provided the ways for young adults to form loving and lasting marriages.

Jason S. Carroll *is an associate professor in the School of Family Life at Brigham Young University. He and his wife, Stefani, are the parents of five children.*

References

Arnett, J. J. (2000). Emerging adulthood: A theory of development from the late teens through the twenties. *American Psychologist, 55,* 469–480.

Bachman, J. G., Johnston, L. D., & O'Malley, P. M. (2009). *Monitoring the Future: Questionnaire responses from the nation's high school seniors, 2008.* Ann Arbor, MI: Institute for Social Research.

Bednar, D. A. (2009). Mormon Channel, Conversations, Episode 001. Retrieved from http://radio.lds .org/eng/programs/conversations-episode-1

Carroll, J. S. (2010). *Dating patterns among Latter-day Saint young adults: Analyses from Project READY.* Unpublished results. Brigham Young University.

Carroll, J. S., Badger, S., & Yang, C. (2006). The ability to negotiate or the ability to love? Evaluating the developmental domains of marital competence. *Journal of Family Issues, 27*, 1001–1032.

Carroll, J. S., Badger, S., Willoughby, B. J., Nelson, L. J., Madsen, S. D., & Barry, C. M. (2009). Ready or not? Criteria for marriage readiness among emerging adults. *Journal of Adolescent Research, 24*(3), 349–375.

Carroll, J. S., Willoughby, B., Badger, S., Nelson, L. J., Barry, C. M., & Madsen, S. D. (2007). So close, yet so far away: The impact of varying marital horizons on emerging adulthood. *Journal of Adolescent Research, 22*, 219–247.

Cheah, C. S. L., & Nelson, L. J. (2004). The role of acculturation in the emerging adulthood of Aboriginal college students. *International Journal of Behavioral Development, 28*, 495–507.

Eyring, H. B. (1998, February). The family. *Ensign, 28*, 10–18.

Fincham, F. D., Stanley, S. M., & Beach, S. R. H. (2007). Transformative processes in marriage: An analysis of emerging trends. *Journal of Marriage and Family, 69*, 275–292.

Glenn, N., & Marquardt, E. (2001). *Hooking up, hanging out, and hoping for Mr. Right.* New York: Institute for American Values.

Heaton, T. B. (2002). Factors contributing to increasing marital stability in the United States. *Journal of Family Issues, 23*, 392–409.

Hinckley, G. B. (1990, March). Thou shalt not covet. *Ensign, 20*, 2–6.

Hinckley, G. B. (2006, October 31). Experiences worth remembering. BYU Devotional Address. Retrieved from http://speeches.byu.edu/reader/reader.php?id=11434&x=31&y=10

Holland, J. R. (2003, October). How do I love thee? *New Era, 33*, 4–8.

Holman, T. B., Viveiros, A., & Carroll, J. S. (2005). Progressing toward an eternal marriage relationship. In C. H. Hart, L. D. Newell, E. Walton, & D. C. Dollahite (Eds.) *Helping and healing our families* (pp. 44–49). Salt Lake City: Deseret Book.

Jose, A., O'Leary, K. D., & Moyer, A. (2010). Does premarital cohabitation predict subsequent marital stability and marital quality? A meta-analysis. *Journal of Marriage and Family, 72*, 105–116.

Kimball, S. W. (1969). *The miracle of forgiveness.* Salt Lake City: Bookcraft.

Kimball, S. W. (1976). *Marriage and divorce.* Salt Lake City: Deseret Book.

L'Abate, L. (1997). *The self in the family: A classification of personality, criminality, and psychopathology.* New York: John Wiley & Sons.

McClendon, R. J., & Chadwick, B. A. (2005). Latter-day Saint families at the dawn of the twenty-first century. In C. H. Hart, L. D. Newell, E. Walton, & D. C. Dollahite (Eds.) *Helping and Healing Our Families* (pp. 32–43). Salt Lake City: Deseret Book.

Nelson, L. J., & Barry, C. M. (2005). Distinguishing features of emerging adulthood: The role of self-classification as an adult. *Journal of Adolescent Research, 20*, 242–262.

Oaks, D. H. (1993, November). "The great plan of happiness." *Ensign, 23*, 72–75.

Oaks, D. H. (2003, October). Timing. *Ensign, 33*, 10–17.

Oaks, D. H. (2006, June). Dating versus hanging out. *Ensign, 36*, 10–16.

Regnerus, M. (2009). The case for early marriage. Retrieved from http://www.christianitytoday.com/ct/2009/august/16.22.html

Rhoades, G. K., Stanley, S. M., & Markman, H. J. (2009). The pre-engagement cohabitation effect: A replication and extension of previous findings. *Journal of Family Psychology, 23*, 107–111.

Schlegel, A., & Barry, H., III. (1991). *Adolescence: An anthropological inquiry.* New York: Free Press.

Scott, R. G. (2001, May). First things first. *Ensign, 31*, 6–8.

Scott, R. G. (2004, May). How to live well amid increasing evil. *Ensign, 34*, 100–102.

Stahmann, R. F., & Adams, T. R. (1997). *LDS counselor ratings of problems occurring among LDS premarital and remarital couples.* Unpublished manuscript. Brigham Young University.

U.S. Census Bureau. (2010). *Current population survey, March and annual social and economic supplements, 2009 and earlier.* Retrieved from http://www.census.gov/population/socdemo/hh-fam/tabMS-2.pdf

Whitehead, B. D., & Popenoe, D. (2000). Sex without strings, relationships without rings. In The National Marriage Project, *The State of Our Unions 2000: The Social Health of Marriage in America* (pp. 6–20). Piscataway, NJ: The National Marriage Project.

Retrieved from http://stateofourunions.org/pdfs/SOOU2000.pdf

Whitehead, B. D., & Popenoe, D. (2001). Who wants to marry a soulmate? In The National Marriage Project, *The State of Our Unions 2001: The Social Health of Marriage in America* (pp. 6–16). Piscataway, NJ: The National Marriage Project. Retrieved from http://stateofourunions.org/pdfs/SOOU2001.pdf

Whitehead, B. D., & Popenoe, D. (2002). Why men won't commit: Exploring young men's attitudes about sex, dating, and marriage. In The National Marriage Project, *The State of Our Unions 2002: The Social Health of Marriage in America* (pp. 6–16). Piscataway, NJ: The National Marriage Project. Retrieved from http://stateofourunions.org/pdfs/SOOU2002.pdf

Wolfinger, N. H. (2005). *Understanding the divorce cycle: The children of divorce in their own marriages.* New York: Cambridge University Press.

CHAPTER 2

The ABCs of Successful Romantic Relationship Development: Meeting, Dating, and Choosing an Eternal Companion

Thomas B. Holman, Frank Poulsen, and others

Marriage between a man and a woman is ordained of God.

"THE FAMILY: A PROCLAMATION TO THE WORLD" states that "marriage between a man and a woman is ordained of God" (¶1) and that "marriage between man and woman is essential to His eternal plan" (¶ 7). The importance of this solemn proclamation is not lost on Latter-day Saint single adults.

Indeed, Church presidents have noted the absolute importance of the decisions surrounding marriage. President Thomas S. Monson (2004, p. 4), speaking of his decision to ask his future wife for a date, said, "That decision, I believe, was perhaps the most important decision that I have ever made." Speaking of the marriage decision, President Gordon B. Hinckley (1999, p. 2) said, "This will be the most important decision of your life, the individual whom you marry." The difficulty for many single adults is how to do it!

The purpose of this chapter is to present research and prophetic and scriptural guidance to help young Latter-day Saints be successful in finding an eternal companion. We do so within the framework of the ABCs, or more correctly, the ABCDEs of mate selection. George Levinger (1983) postulated a five-phase development of heterosexual romantic relationships:

A. *Awareness* of or *Acquaintance* with another person;
B. *Buildup* of the relationship;
C. *Continuation* following *Commitment* to a long-term relationship (which may result in marriage for many couples);
D. *Deterioration* or *Decline* in the interdependence of the couple;
E. *Ending* of the relationship.

These phases are not always sequential, and few relationships go through all five phases. Many relationships don't even make it into the acquaintance phase, or if they do, they can quickly go straight to the ending (or E) phase. Relationships can terminate in any phase, and indeed most should. In some instances, couples double back to a previous phase because of unfinished business or because an event or new knowledge suggests that they need to back up.

The issue for single Latter-day Saints is how to enter into phase A and move progressively through phase A into phase B and then into phase C, with the end point being a temple marriage that will grow into an eternal and celestial marriage. Once in a relationship, another issue may arise when one becomes aware that a premarital relationship is not progressing or should not progress (phase D). One must then figure out how to move into phase E, while doing as little damage as possible.

Levinger's model neglects one essential phase—preparing for success, the pre-A phase. We turn first to this important phase.

Preparing for Success

President Thomas S. Monson (Monson, 2004, p. 4) noted, "Decisions determine destiny. That is why it is worthwhile to look ahead, to set a course, to be at least partly ready when the moment of decision comes." Thus, we must look ahead to the type of marriage we want, set a course toward that goal, and then "prepare every needful thing" (D&C 88:119; D&C 109:8) so when the opportunity for establishing a relationship that could lead to an eternal marriage arises, we are ready to move forward with faith.

Consistent with gospel principles, research suggests that our whole life plays a part in our preparation for marriage. Your family experiences; your relationships with significant other adults and peers; and your personality, attitudes, and emotional health are just a few of the factors that influence how well you master the ABCs of mate selection. (See chapter 1 of this volume for a discussion of other important factors).

Family Experiences: Coming to Terms with the Past, Moving Forward with Faith

Research shows that your family background has an influence on success in finding an eternal companion. However, the effect of family is not simple. Researchers like Sroufe, Egeland, Carlson, and Collins (2005) suggest that many experiences exert an influence on your success in meeting and choosing an eternal mate, including family experiences throughout childhood, adolescent experiences with other significant people in your life (such as teachers, Church leaders, or peers), and things that are happening in your current environment. They conclude that "nothing is more important in the development of the child than the care received, including that in the early years," and that "individuals are always impacted by the entire history of cumulative experience" (p. 19). However, these researchers note that "current circumstances" combine with cumulative history, and this allows for change. In other words, we are not condemned by our past. It is always there, but things that happen to us in the present and *what we choose, in the present, to do about the past* determine who we are and how we will do in the search for an eternal companion. For example, someone may have had a difficult childhood involving abuse and parental divorce. However, this doesn't mean the person is "doomed" to suffer from emotional problems, abuse their own children, or have a poor marriage. If the person, as a child, adolescent, and young adult has good friends, teachers, Church leaders and advisors, and so on, and develops a desire to change the path that seems laid out, the young person can look forward to a good marriage. But the poor childhood is still there and may have to be dealt with over and over again—depending on ongoing circumstances, such as stress in some part of life.

One set of researchers studied three groups of young adults—(a) those with healthy family background experiences, (b) those with unhealthy family background experiences who *had not* come to terms with those experiences, and (c) those with unhealthy family background experiences who *had* come to terms with those experiences (Martinson, Holman, Larson, & Jackson, 2010). The first group, who came from strong, healthy family backgrounds, had the highest quality premarital or marital relationships. The second group, those with unhealthy family backgrounds who *had not* come to terms with these negative experiences, had the lowest romantic relationship quality. But the most interesting results were that the individuals from the third group, those with unhealthy family backgrounds who *had* come to terms with these experiences, had romantic relationship quality scores very similar to those from healthy family backgrounds. This suggests that even if some negative things have happened to us in our families, we can recover and still build strong marriages.

How do we come to terms with negative experiences in our families? While therapy, good books, and good role models outside the family are helpful, ultimately, the doctrines of the gospel of Jesus Christ, especially the plan of salvation and the Atonement, are the most powerful agents of change (Packer, 2004). The power of Christ's Atonement works changes in our hearts that can come in no other way. One woman, whom we will call "Jenna," tells us how the Atonement worked in her life:

> After realizing all the different ways that my family of origin had altered the way I viewed the world and the things I was doing, I decided to make some changes. It was soon after that I realized that in order to really become the person that I wanted to be, I had to be able to use the Atonement of my Savior, but I had no idea how to use it. I went to a religion teacher, and he gave me the following two steps for applying the Atonement: Pray to get rid of all of the hurt and pain, and protect myself from further harm to allow for proper healing. He likened the Atonement process to the cleaning and healing of a bad scrape: First, I needed to get rid of all of the gravel and debris left in the injury; then I had to bandage the wound so that it could be restored. I struggled for some time with this concept; I knew the Lord

would take away my pain, but for some reason I was resisting. I was afraid that if my pain were gone, there would be nothing left and I would be empty. I finally decided to just trust God and give Him everything. When I did this, my pain was taken away and replaced with joy and love such as I had never felt. I had a purpose, and I knew the Lord would help me overcome every trial. . . . Above all the other things that I have tried (forming attachments, therapy, setting goals, etc.), it has always been the Lord who has helped me through.

Personality and Emotional Health: Taking Care of Mental Health Issues

In terms of preparing for success in mate selection and marriage, Mead (2005) found that negative expressions of personality, such as depression, anxiety, and immaturity in both partners, had negative effects on the relationship satisfaction of both partners. On the other hand, the more positive expressions of personality, like kindness and flexibility from each partner, the greater the satisfaction of both partners. Thus, being prepared for success in choosing an eternal companion should include taking care of tendencies toward common emotional challenges like depression, anxiety, panic attacks, and the like. These challenges are often treatable with individual or family therapy and prescription medications. Of course, as noted earlier, the best medicine is living the gospel of Jesus Christ.

So, after taking care of issues from your family and peer relationships and any personal emotional issues, what do you do next? You make efforts to initiate relationships with the opposite sex. How to do this is the topic of the next section of this chapter.

The Awareness and Acquaintance Phase

Most contemporary research on relationship formation suggests that *appraisal of attraction* is one of the first steps in the awareness and acquaintance phase (Bredow, Cate, & Hudson, 2008; Cunningham & Barbee, 2008). We ask ourselves a question like, "Is he/she attractive to me?" Certainly physical attractiveness is one of the things both men and women look for. And there is nothing wrong with that. Elder Bruce R. McConkie (1955, p. 13) said, "The right person [for you to marry] is someone for whom the natural and wholesome and normal affection that should exist does exist."

Although physical attractiveness is a necessary part of attraction (Li, Bailey, Kenrick, & Linsenmeier, 2002), it is not the most important factor. Researchers Buss, Shackelford, Kirkpatrick, and Larsen (2001) found that physical attractiveness was not even in the top five most important qualities people sought in a long-term relationship. "Jake," a research participant in a recent study, helps us see the importance of physical attractiveness in addition to other things:

I was actually a little bit infatuated with her. I remember listing some things off just after talking to her. . . . I guess in church when she would make comments, she was actually quite proficient in speaking. She showed a level of intelligence. I'm very, very attracted to intelligence. She has a beautiful face. That's actually one of the first things I look for. . . . She appeared a little bit shy. I don't know, I kind of like that. I'm [also] attracted to an open mind.

Beyond physical attraction, what are the qualities that people should look for in a long-term relationship and how do young people find them? In addition to temple worthiness, Elder Richard G. Scott (1999, p. 26) suggested several essential attributes that bring happiness that we should look for in a potential mate. A possible mate should have "a deep love of the Lord and His commandments [and] a determination to live them." A possible mate should also be "kindly understanding, forgiving of others, and willing to give of self, with the desire to have a family crowned with beautiful children and a commitment to teach them the principles of truth in the home."

One question young people may ask is, "How can I discern these qualities in others before I approach them and run the risk of embarrassment or failure?" Although these qualities might seem difficult to discern from a distance, there are means of gathering this information; most people do it intuitively. Berger and Perkins (1978) found that simple observation is an effective means of appraising these more important qualities of attractiveness. Furthermore, "the most information-rich environments for observing others are those in which the target person is interacting with others . . . and those that present relatively few social constraints on behavior" (Afifi & Lucas, 2008, p. 136).

However, attraction is not enough. Researchers find that unless the *probability of acceptance* is high, an approach is unlikely (Shanteau & Nagy, 1979). Thus, people often seek information to help them in assessing the probability of acceptance before making an approach. Factors that may heighten one's confidence that his or her overture will be accepted include similarity in perceived physical attractiveness (Huston, 1973), social status (for example, how people dress) (Huston & Burgess, 1979), and other observable attributes (Graziano & Bruce, 2008).

Once initial contact is made, other strategies may be used to assess mutual interest, and some are more effective than others. In research on "affinity testing," Douglas (1987) found that *approaching* (for example, touching or moving closer and then gauging response) was one of the most effective means of discerning someone's attraction to you. Other tactics were seen as ineffective and sometimes inappropriate, such as *diminishing the self* (for example, looking for agreement after acknowledging weaknesses in your character) or *networking* (for example, asking friends for information about someone's attraction to you). Although the risk may be seen as high, especially at this very early phase, the most effective strategy in Douglas's study was *confronting* (asking if a person would go out with you). No matter what the tactic, once there is an initial contact, Afifi and Lucas (2008) found that within minutes most individuals could gather sufficient information to determine whether another person was interested in further pursuing the relationship.

Confronting is easier if one has realistic and positive expectations and perceptions of others. These feelings and expectations develop over time when a person has a history of positive experiences with parents, peers, and others who are accessible and responsive to one's need for closeness and comfort. Those who question their own worth as a potential eternal companion or have negative evaluations of others will often avoid relationships for fear of being hurt, or, conversely, they may anxiously and inappropriately pursue relationships too vigorously (Mikulincer & Shaver, 2007). This points again to the importance of good-quality family and peer relationships while growing up or coming to terms with hurts and fears from the past.

Current research being conducted at BYU–Provo shows that this acquaintance/awareness stage is one of the particularly frustrating parts of dating. "Annette," one of our research participants, expressed that "the initial asking out, I can understand, can be hard for guys. So . . . that's frustrating, . . . like you're sending signals, 'It's okay if you ask me out,' . . . but it doesn't happen because they're not picking them up." And from a male perspective, "Joseph" says simply: "It would be nice if girls were clear about whether they like or don't like you." These real-life responses indicate that both males and females wish the other gender would be more straightforward in their dating strategies.

Whether or not individuals use effective approach tactics in large measure depends on how attraction appraisal and probability of acceptance add up. Figley (1979) found that when attraction is high and the probability of acceptance is high, individuals will typically present themselves as they really are without exaggerating their positive attributes or cloaking their negative ones. This typically leads to more success in making an initial approach. On the other hand, when attraction is high but probability of acceptance is low, individuals tend to try to appear the way they think the other person will find attractive (Figley, 1975). But this tactic often is obvious and typically diminishes a person's chances of success (Gordon, 1996).

Transition from Acquaintance to Buildup

How does one move from the acquaintance stage to building a relationship? This varies from person to person, from couple to couple, and from culture to culture. Most Americans find this transition confusing and ambiguous (Glenn & Marquardt, 2001, pp. 30–41), and Latter-day Saint young adults seem to feel the same way. In research being conducted at BYU–Provo, respondents speak of the difficulty of moving "to the next level." Guerrero and Mongeau (2008) discuss research showing that those who successfully progress in their relationships from acquaintance to buildup use prosocial maintenance behaviors. These behaviors include things like high levels of routine contact and activity (for example, calling, texting, going places together, and just spending lots of time together), providing emotional support and positivity (comforting each other, being optimistic), talking about the relationship (sharing feelings about the relationship and feelings of love), and instrumental support (such as sharing tasks or giving advice).

Some young men go straight to asking young women out for a date to accomplish these tasks, and this is encouraged by Latter-day Saint Church leaders (Oaks, 2006; 2007). For most Americans (Glenn & Marquart, 2001, pp. 24–29), and many Latter-day Saints, hanging out is a frequent way of going through the acquaintance process. Most Latter-day Saint young adults know that Church leaders discourage hanging out, and we have found in our current research that the kind of endless, making-no-progress-toward-a-relationship hanging out is indeed frustrating to both men and women. However, spending time together in the company of several potential eternal companions that (a) is clearly directed toward finding out if the person could be a good possibility for marriage, (b) has a short time limit, and (c) doesn't take advantage of anyone (for example, mooching free meals) is probably not the negative kind of hanging out that Church leaders discourage.

The Buildup Phase

Probably the best marker of having moved into the B or buildup phase is a first date. Elder Dallin Oaks (2006, p. 8) defines a date as: "(1) planned ahead, (2) paid for (by the man), and (3) paired off." Most people seem to prefer being friends before moving into a possible romantic relationship (Guerrero & Mongeau, 2008). Therefore, success in the buildup phase for Latter-day Saint young adults will include dates and will be entered into by two people who have developed a friendship, and especially a friendship that does not include any inappropriate expression of physical attraction (Pugmire, Martinson, & Holman, 2007).

In this section we will discuss two processes that, while occurring in other phases, are particularly salient in the relationship buildup phase and lead to successful mate selection: seeking mutual influence and developing mature love.

Seeking mutual influence. In a unique longitudinal study of Latter-day Saint women, Pugmire and others (2007) discovered a process they called "mutual influence."

Our LDS females . . . sought what we called "mutual influence," which is different from the 50–50 equality often sought in so-called equalitarian relationships. Their desire was to have an "equal" relationship in which they contributed fully to all aspects of the relationship, while expecting the same from their dates/fiancés/ husbands. . . . They sought a relationship in which both partners were contributing fully, caring wholly, and bringing their particular strengths to the relationship (p. 69).

The Latter-day Saint females interviewed in this study (Pugmire et al., 2007) noted that a mutual influence relationship was difficult if not impossible if the relationship started out as physical. However, once a friendship based on mutual influence was established, physical affection consistent with Latter-day Saint standards was a natural and beautiful part of relationship development. Pugmire and her colleagues also learned that women who were in relationships with men with whom they could have mutual influence had higher quality and more stable relationships than couples in more physically based relationships or unequal relationships (where power and control were exercised disproportionately by either the man or woman).

Developing mature love. Noller (1996) reviewed a great deal of the research on love and suggested that there are two types: mature and immature. Mature love leads to success in marriage and family life while immature love does not support success in marriage and family life. Love expresses itself through our emotions, beliefs, and behaviors. Noller identified immature and mature aspects of love within each of those categories. Table 2.1 summarizes her findings about immature and mature love.

Notice that Noller's mature love is similar to what Church leaders have said for years. For example, Elder Marvin J. Ashton (1975, p. 108) put it this way:

True love is a process. True love requires personal action. Love must be continuing to be real. Love takes time. Too often expediency, infatuation, stimulation, persuasion, or lust are mistaken for love. How hollow, how empty if our love is no deeper than the arousal of momentary feeling or the expression in words of what is no more lasting than the time it takes to speak them.

Many processes are involved in building up a new, budding relationship, but the development of respect as illustrated by developing mutual influence–type relationships and the development of mature love are two of the most important processes.

TABLE 2.1.
CHARACTERISTICS OF IMMATURE AND MATURE LOVE (BASED ON NOLLER, 1996)

Aspects of Love	Immature Love	Mature Love
Emotional Part of Love	Possessiveness Jealousy Infatuation Preoccupation Anxiety	Lasting Passion Desire for Companionship Warm Feeling of Contentment
Belief Part of Love	"Love Is Blind" Love Is External to Us "Cupid's Arrow" Love Is Beyond Our Control	Love Is Something You Have to "Decide" Love Means: Commitment Trust Sharing Sacrifice
Behavior Part of Love	Selfish Lustful Concern Only for Satisfying Own Needs Clinging Over-Dependent Demanding Obedience from Partner	Creates an Environment of Growth and Development Allows Partner Space for Growth

Dealing with Deterioration of and Ending a Relationship

Before our discussion of the transition to a serious relationship, engagement, and marriage, we think it is wise to discuss the deterioration and ending parts of most romantic relationships. Research shows that most people have several "break-ups" before finding the person they marry. Therefore, understanding these phases is just as important as understanding the process of progressing toward marriage. Furthermore, how people break up at whatever point in a relationship probably says a lot about how they will find, relate to, get serious with, and eventually marry their eternal companion.

The Deterioration and Ending phases of relationship development are possibly the most difficult to face. Relationships, of course, can deteriorate and end at any stage of development. But breaking up relationships where love was present and marriage was contemplated is particularly difficult. A study of premarital break-ups in which 70 percent of the sample were Latter-day Saints

is instructive (Holman, 2001). These seriously dating or engaged couples all completed questionnaires when they were dating and then about five years later. Those who broke up before marriage had poorer relationships with parents as children and as adults, lower levels of emotional health, and less support for the impending marriage from family and friends. Also, they had poorer communication, conflict resolution skills, and sense of couple identity than those who eventually married and had very satisfying marriages. Interestingly, their premarital scores on these factors were not much different from those who married but eventually divorced or who married but were very unhappy. Clearly, they were wise to break up their premarital relationships since they appeared to be on course to end up divorced or in unhappy marriages.

Research like that reported above and counsel from Church leaders suggests several reasons to break up. Church leaders counsel that when there is a lack of love (Widtsoe, 1944), temptations to break commandments and covenants (Tuttle, 1974), or partners who do not inspire the best in you (McKay, 1953), couples need to think seriously about ending the relationship. Certainly if one does not receive clear spiritual confirmation or if there are critical issues, one should seriously consider whether the relationship is viable.

If it is right to break off a relationship, how can that be done so as to cause the least hurt? The family proclamation principles that lead to successful marriages can be applied to relationships that do not proceed to marriage; the principles of prayer, repentance, forgiveness, respect, love, compassion, and work seem especially appropriate. The counsel given by the Lord contained in Doctrine and Covenants 121 also provides excellent instruction for not only strengthening but also ending a relationship. Especially helpful is the counsel contained in verses 41–44:

No power or influence can or ought to be maintained by virtue of the priesthood, only by persuasion, by long-suffering, by gentleness and meekness, and by love unfeigned; By kindness, and pure knowledge, which shall greatly enlarge the soul without hypocrisy, and without guile—Reproving betimes with sharpness, when moved upon by the Holy Ghost; and then showing forth afterwards an increase of love toward him whom thou hast reproved, lest he esteem thee to be his enemy; That he may know that thy faithfulness is stronger than the cords of death.

These verses suggest we should not attempt to continue a relationship by any unrighteous means. A partner should not be coerced into staying in a relationship, nor should we ever feel coerced. Furthermore, when a relationship should end, the principles articulated in these verses should be a guide for dealing with the hurt and emotion that may result. One may need to be long-suffering, gentle, meek, and kind with a partner who does not understand or resists change. The counsel given in verses 43 and 44 may seem extreme, but when considered carefully, it is some of the best counsel we can get for ending a relationship. To reprove means "to correct" and betimes means "early on." Thus, when "pure knowledge," received by the Holy Ghost, helps us understand a relationship must end, we should "correct" the situation (end the relationship) quickly, and not let it drag on. The word "sharply" can mean "with clarity" (think of a sharp image) rather than "with severity," as it is most often interpreted. Thus, while being as loving and kind as we can, we should make it clear that the relationship is ending and why, rather than "beating around the bush" and hoping the partner will get the message. Again, this should be done with kindness, meekness, and love unfeigned, recognizing that even if the partner has hurt us in some way, he or she is a beloved child of God and should be treated accordingly.

If one is the "breakee" rather than the "breaker," the same counsel applies. The breaking partner should not be coerced or forced in any way to continue if she or he does not want to continue. Even if the emotional hurt is strong, one needs to back off, not try to hurt the partner back in some way, and allow oneself time to heal. This healing is best accomplished when relying upon Him who was sent "to heal the brokenhearted" (Luke 4:18). However, gentle persuasion, when directed by the Spirit, can be appropriate if it seems the partner is simply getting the jitters. Gently reminding the partner of the good feelings and even spiritual confirmation that he or she has had about the relationship may soothe and calm a nervous partner.

Great learning and maturity can come from surviving a premarital break-up. If one initiates or goes through a break-up with as much Christlike behavior and feelings as possible, and allows oneself to be healed by the peace of the Spirit, that person is then better prepared to move on to a relationship that can result in an eternal marriage.

The Transition from B to C

During the transition from the buildup phase to the commitment phase, couples will be asking themselves and each other things like: Do we know enough about each other? Do we like what we have learned? Do we communicate well enough to want to spend more time together? As they think about and talk about their relationship, they find themselves becoming more future-oriented and imagining a joint future. They are moving out of initial "falling in love" and are developing characteristics of sincere, mature love. These kinds of behaviors and attitudes make the transition to deeply committed relationships possible.

Commitment and Continuation– Into a Successful Eternal Marriage

For many, the marriage decision is particularly anxiety-provoking because of our understanding of marriage as an eternal commitment coupled with the tugs and pulls of a secular world and the intense emotions associated with romantic relationships. Here we would like to offer some research-guided suggestions and some prophetic counsel as it applies to the decision to marry.

Sliding versus deciding. Stanley, Rhoades, and Markman (2006) found that people who make relationship transitions (such as dating exclusively or engaging in sexual intimacy) without thorough deliberation ran the risk of "sliding" into the next stage of a relationship rather than "deciding" to move forward. Without a deliberate discussion and decision, the couple is likely to slide through transitions into a marriage that they did not really commit to. Based on these research findings, individuals who do not thoroughly discuss the status of their relationship as it progresses and where they see the relationship going in the long run might be putting themselves at risk for an unhappy (if not short-lived) marriage.

Furthermore, Surra, Arizzi, and Asmussen (1988) found that those individuals who were frequently vacillating or indecisive about whether or not the relationship measured up to their standards were more likely to end up in an unhappy marriage. This research emphasized that in addition to deliberate communication about the relationship's progress, individuals should be open with each other about their doubts and insecurities. Otherwise they will likely find that their premarital doubts become marital regrets.

In addition to being decisive about the relationship and open about reservations, modern prophets have counseled individuals to seek guidance in this important decision. President Thomas S. Monson (2004, p. 4) counseled: "In making a decision as momentous as whom you will marry, I suggest you seek the help of your parents." He promised that "our Heavenly Father will also bless you and guide you in your decision." This final counsel to seek the guidance of our Heavenly Father identifies another area that is often disconcerting for Latter-day Saints as they progress in the relationship.

Spiritual confirmation. The scriptures and Church leaders demonstrate that in this most important decision of choosing an eternal companion, several factors need to be kept in mind as we seek spiritual confirmation. First, President Boyd K. Packer (1973, p. 11) reminds us that if we "desire the inspiration of the Lord in this crucial decision, [we] must live the standards of the Church." Second, Elder Bruce R. McConkie notes that we need to understand the balance between agency and inspiration. On the one hand, we have been given the power to choose and we are expected to exercise that right. But we have also been told to seek guidance from the Lord in all things. The fundamental principle, he says, is this: "We're supposed to learn correct principles and then govern ourselves. We make our own choices, and then we present the matter to the Lord and get his approving, ratifying seal" (McConkie, 1975, p. 38). Third, we must believe that the Lord answers such petitions. Oliver Cowdery was told that he would receive an answer if he asked in faith, with an honest heart, believing he would receive, and if he studied the matter out in his mind and then asked if the decision was right (D&C 9:7–9).

Some people expect this confirmation to come in a powerful way, but the typical workings of the Spirit are a still, small voice that whispers truth to our hearts and minds. One young man's experience illustrates this (Holman, 2000):

[As I prayed about marriage,] I didn't feel like I was getting a response. I prayed, "Heavenly Father, this is so important, I need to know whether or not it's right." Then toward the end of our courtship, I went to the temple. I was so frustrated because I wasn't getting an answer either way. After praying and waiting for an answer, I got more frustrated and gave up. That was when an impression came to me: "You already know the answer." Then I realized that God had answered my prayers. The decision to marry Becky always made sense and felt right. I can see now that God had been telling me in my heart and in my mind that it was a good decision. And later, at the time of the ceremony, I had another confirmation that what I was doing was right.

One last point is that the spiritual confirmation needs to come to both parties involved. A person should not feel that if his or her partner receives a confirmation, that he or she is therefore released from the necessity of seeking a similar confirmation. Elder Dallin H. Oaks (then a justice of the Utah Supreme Court) discussed this issue:

If a revelation is outside the limits of stewardship, you know it is not from the Lord, and you are not bound by it. I have heard of cases where a young man told a young woman she should marry him

---

BOX 2.1:

HOW LONG SHOULD THE ENGAGEMENT BE?

One question often asked is: How long should we date and be engaged? In two studies of BYU students (Holman, 2001; Schaalje & Holman, 2007), we found that the average time from first acquaintance to the temple marriage was between nine and ten months. For most couples, three to four months of that time they were engaged. When we asked couples if their engagements were too short, too long, or just right, the majority said "just right," but a substantial number felt they were "too long" and that once they had decided to get married, having to wait three to four months to plan the wedding was simply too long (Holman, 2001). The important principle here is that the couple should make the decision of when to get married, and if this conflicts with the desires of either set of parents, they need to lovingly help their parents understand that the marriage is an event of eternal consequence and should not be marred by postponements to satisfy parents' desires merely pertaining to wedding arrangements.

Some advice that was given to me by my bishop when I was engaged was to forget everything. Forget the world, forget that my mother wanted different flowers than I did, forget that my bridesmaids are fighting over what dresses to wear, forget that the reception center is overpriced, just forget everything. I had been under a tremendous amount of stress, and I realized after that conversation that I had lost my focus on the temple and I paid dearly for it. When I followed my bishop's advice, things started to go in the right direction.

Conclusion

We have shared some of the best research, counsel from Latter-day Saint Church leaders, and experiences of young adults on how to successfully prepare for a good relationship, initiate a relationship, build up a relationship, and perhaps appropriately end a relationship or move toward deeper commitment and marriage in the temple. The process of going from first acquaintance and attraction to making covenants together across the altar of the temple can be challenging, and at times, even a nightmare. But when done according to true principles, it can be a dream come true.

because he had received a revelation that she was to be his eternal companion. If this is a true revelation, it will be confirmed directly to the woman if she seeks to know. In the meantime, she is under no obligation to heed it. She should seek her own guidance and make up her own mind (Oaks, 1981).

Wedding Preparation versus Marriage Preparation

We began our discussion with the need to prepare for the process of finding your eternal companion and becoming someone else's eternal companion. We end with one last thought about preparation. In all the preparations to get acquainted, build up a relationship, commit to marriage, and especially to *get married*, do not forget to continue to *prepare for marriage*. Your temple marriage is infinitely more important than all that surrounds the wedding itself. Elder Richard G. Scott (1999, May, p. 26) said this: "Do not let receptions, wedding breakfasts, farewells, or other activities overshadow the sacred temple experience." A recently married young woman learned the truth of Elder Scott's counsel:

Thomas B. Holman *is a professor in the School of Family Life at Brigham Young University. He and his wife, Linda, are the parents of five children and they have eight grandchildren.* **Franklin O. Poulsen** *is pursuing a master's degree in marriage, family, and human development at Brigham Young University. He and his wife, Sara, are the parents of three children. This chapter was a major topic of discussion and writing in an advanced class of seniors in the School of Family Life at Brigham Young University in 2009. Their thinking and writing contributed to the direction and content behind this chapter. They are therefore noted as co-contributors and are listed here alphabetically: Kameron Barkle, Jeff Bentley, Allison Bills, Diane Browns, Melanie Brady, Matthew Call, Sarah June Carroll, Rhyll Croshaw, Eliza Diederich, Drew Eagan, Katie Gregson, Marissa Gutierrez, Jessica Hauser, Todd Jensen, Lauren Jones, Brianna Jones, Squire Kershaw, Heidi King, Andrea Kinghorn, Lindsay Lee, Ashley Literski, Stephen Mortensen, Mandy Owens, Stacie Pace, Camilla Paul, Lindsay Petersen, Noelle Pitcher, Kymee Redpath, Megan Rogers, Kevin Shirley, Kristy Smith, Brooke Stephenson, Teresa Stubbs, Lauren Wade, Carissa Wainwright, and Bill Walter.*

References

Afifi, W. A., & Lucas, A. A. (2008). Information seeking in the initial stages of relational development. In S. Sprecher, A. Wenzel, & J. Harvey (Eds.), *Handbook of relationship initiation* (pp. 135–151). New York: Psychology Press.

Ashton, M. J. (1975, November). Love takes time. *Ensign, 5,* 108–110.

Berger, C. R., & Perkins, J. W. (1978). Studies in interpersonal epistemology I: Situational attributes in observational context selection. In B. D. Ruben (Ed.), *Communication Yearbook 2* (pp. 171–184). New Brunswick, NJ: Transaction Books.

Bredow, C. A., Cate, R. M., & Huston, T. L. (2008). Have we met before? A conceptual model of first romantic encounters. In S. Sprecher, A. Wenzel, & J. Harvey (Eds.), *Handbook of relationship initiation* (pp. 3–28). New York: Psychology Press.

Busby, D. M., Holman, T. B., Taniguchi, N. (2001). RELATE: Relationship evaluation of the individual, family, cultural, and couple contexts. *Family Relations, 50,* 308–316.

Buss, D. M., Shackelford, T. K., Kirkpatrick, L. A., & Larsen, R. J. (2001). A half century of mate preferences: The cultural evolution of values. *Journal of Marriage and Family, 63,* 491–503.

Cunningham, M. R., & Barbee, A. P. (2008). Prelude to a kiss: Nonverbal flirting, opening gambits, and other communication dynamics in the initiation of romantic relationships. In S. Sprecher, A. Wenzel, & J. Harvey (Eds.), *Handbook of relationship initiation* (pp. 97–120). New York: Psychology Press.

Douglas, W. (1987). Affinity-testing in initial interactions. *Journal of Social and Personal Relationships, 4*(1), 3–15.

Figley, C. R. (1975). Tactical self-presentation in a dating decision-making context. *Dissertation Abstracts International, 36* (3), 1504B-1505.

Figley, C. R. (1979). Tactical self-presentation and interpersonal attraction. In M. Cook & G. Wilson (Eds.), *Love and attraction* (pp. 91–99). Oxford: Pergamon Press.

Glenn, N., & Marquardt, E. (2001). Hooking up, hanging out, and hoping for Mr. Right: College women on dating and mating today. New York: Institute for American Values. Retrieved from http://www.americanvalues.org/pdfs/hookingup.pdf

Gordon, R. A. (1996). Impact of ingratiation on judgments and evaluations: A meta-analytic investigation. *Journal of Personality and Social Psychology, 71*(1), 54–70.

Graziano, W. G., & Bruce, J. W. (2008). Attraction and the initiation of relationships: A review of the empirical literature. In S. Sprecher, A. Wenzel, & J. Harvey (Eds.), *Handbook of relationship initiation* (pp. 269–295). New York: Psychology Press.

Guerrero, L. K., & Mongeau, P. A. (2008). On becoming "more than friends": The transition from friendship to romantic relationship. In S. Sprecher, A. Wenzel, & J. Harvey (Eds.), *Handbook of relationship initiation* (pp. 175–194). New York: Psychology Press.

Hinckley, G. B. (1999, February). Life's obligations. *Ensign, 39,* 2–5.

Holman, T. B. (2000, August 1). The right person, the right place, the right time: guidelines for wisely choosing a spouse. BYU Devotional Address. Retrieved from http://speeches.byu.edu/reader/reader.php?id=1124&x=57&y=6

Holman, T. B. (2001). *Premarital prediction of marital quality or breakup.* New York: Kluwer Academic/Plenum.

Huston, T. L. (1973). Ambiguity of acceptance, social desirability, and dating choice. *Journal of Experimental Social Psychology, 9,* 32–42.

Huston, T. L., & Burgess, R. L. (1979). Social exchange in developing relationships: An overview. In R. L. Burgess & T. L. Huston (Eds.), *Social exchange and developing relationships* (pp. 3–28). New York: Academic Press.

Levinger, G. (1983). Development and change. In H. H. Kelley, E. Berscheid, A. Christensen, J. H. Harvey, T. L. Huston, G. Levinger et al. (Eds.) *Close relationships* (pp. 315–359). New York: W. H. Freeman & Co.

Li, N. P., Bailey, J. M., Kenrick, D. T., & Linsenmeier, J. A. W. (2002). The necessities and luxuries of mate preferences: Testing the tradeoffs. *Journal of Personality and Social Psychology, 82*(6), 947–955.

Martinson, V. K., Holman, T. B., Larson, J. H., & Jackson, J. B. (2010). The relationship between coming to terms with family-of-origin difficulties and adult relationship satisfaction. *The American Journal of Family Therapy, 38,* 207–217.

McConkie, B. R. (1955, October). Conference Report, Oct. 1955, 13.

McConkie, B. R. (1975, January). Agency or inspiration? *New Era, 5,* 38–47.

McKay, D. O. (1953). *Gospel ideals.* Salt Lake City: The Improvement Era.

Mead, N. (2005). Personality predictors of relationship satisfaction among engaged and married couples: An analysis of actor and partner effects. Unpublished master's thesis. Department of Marriage, Family, and Human Development, Brigham Young University, Provo, Utah.

Mikulincer, M., & Shaver, P. S. (2007). *Attachment in adulthood: Structure, dynamics, and change.* New York: Guilford Press.

Monson, T. S. (2004, October). The message: Whom shall I marry? *New Era, 34,* 4–7.

Noller, P. (1996). What is this thing called love? Defining the love that supports marriage and family. *Personal Relationships, 3,* 97–115.

Oaks, D. H. (1981). Revelation. BYU Devotional Address. Retrieved from http://speeches.byu.edu/reader/reader.php?id=6846&x=75&y=8

Oaks, D. H. (2006, June). Dating versus hanging out. *Ensign, 35,* 10–16.

Oaks, D. H. (2007, May). Divorce. *Ensign, 37,* 70–73.

Packer, B. K. (1973). *Eternal love.* Salt Lake City: Deseret Book.

Packer, B. K. (2004, May). Do not fear. *Ensign, 34,* 77–80.

Pugmire, E. M., Märtinson, V. K., & Holman, T. B. (2007). Seeking mutual influence: The experience of LDS females during heterosexual romantic relationships development. In M. J. Woodger, T. B. Holman, & K. A. Young (Eds.), *Latter-day Saint courtship patterns* (pp. 59–70). Lanham, MD: University Press of America.

Schaalje, G. B., & Holman, T. B. (2007). Courtship statistics for BYU students. In M. J. Woodger, T. B. Holman, & K. A. Young (Eds.), *Latter-day Saint courtship patterns* (pp. 41–58). Lanham, MD: University Press of America.

Scott, R. G. (1999, May). Receive the temple blessings. *Ensign, 29,* 25–27.

Shanteau, J., & Nagy, G. F. (1979). Probability of acceptance in dating choice. *Journal of Personality and Social Psychology, 37*(4), 522–533.

Sroufe, L. A., Egeland, B., Carlson, E. A., & Collins, W. A. (2005). *The development of the person: The Minnesota study of risk and adaptation from birth to adulthood.* New York: The Guilford Press.

Stanley, S. M., Rhoades, G. K., & Markman, H. J. (2006). Sliding versus deciding: Inertia and the premarital cohabitation effect. *Family Relations, 55,* 499–509.

Surra, C. A., Arizzi, P., & Asmussen, L. A. (1988). The association between reasons for commitment and the development and outcome of marital relationships. *Journal of Social and Personal Relationships, 5,* 47–63.

Tuttle, A. T. (1974, November). Your mission preparation. *Ensign, 4,* 71–72.

Widtsoe, J. A. (1944). *An understandable religion.* Salt Lake City: Deseret Book.

CHAPTER 3

Foundational Processes for an Enduring, Healthy Marriage

Stephen F. Duncan and Sara S. McCarty Zasukha

Husband and wife have a solemn responsibility to love and care for each other.

IN AN ADDRESS PRESIDENT SPENCER W. KIMBALL first delivered to BYU students at a devotional in September 1976 (2002, p. 42), he stated,

> While marriage is difficult, and discordant and frustrated marriages are common, yet real, lasting happiness is possible, and marriage can be more an exultant ecstasy than the human mind can conceive. This is within the reach of every couple, every person.

This prophetic statement creates a high ideal for all married couples to strive for in a world where marital distress and divorce are commonplace. In a consumer culture where "people have learned to discard everything from paper plates to spouses" (Bateman & Bateman, 2003, p. 7), many are understandably fearful of marriage. Fear of divorce, being an inadequate spouse, financial needs, and lifestyle changes may compound sufficiently to deter singles from marriage (Howell, 2006). They may doubt they can have the kind of exultant ecstasy in marriage envisioned by President Kimball. Still others may wonder: What are the tried-and-true tools needed to build the foundation of a successful marriage?

This chapter explores the work of leading scholars who study healthy marriages, and the teachings of Latter-day Saint Church leaders on these foundational processes. *Foundational processes* are actions couples take in relation to each other to help their marriage flourish. We first provide an overview of the current emphasis in marital processes research, and then follow with a discussion of several specific foundational processes important in a healthy marriage. The elements discussed in this chapter include personal commitment

to the marriage covenant, love and friendship, positivity, accepting influence, handling differences and conflict respectfully, and continued courtship.

Some of the most careful and influential research programs on what makes marriages work have been led by John Gottman, one of the world's leading marriage researchers. In addition to his scholarly work, he has published several books for the public based on this research, including the best-selling *The Seven Principles for Making Marriage Work* (1999). While we incorporate the work of other scholars, we acknowledge Gottman's influence in delineating several of the foundational processes.

Research on healthy marital processes has largely been conducted in North America using white, well-educated, middle-class couples. That reality may limit its application. However, aspects of the processes can be seen in multicultural marriage research (e.g., Sharlin, Kaslow, & Hammerschmidt, 2000). Church leaders, also, have added commentary about these processes that apply to everyone. We believe the principles involved are probably universal, but the processes manifest differently across cultures. For example, while the principle "Spouses need to feel loved by their partners" is likely true everywhere, how love is shown in Latin America will possibly be different in North America or the Orient. And even within the same culture, people will differ in how they show love.

Current Emphasis in Marital Processes Research

Marital processes research today essentially is three-fold. One aspect places emphasis on marital disruption and understanding the processes that lead to marital breakdown (e.g., Gottman, 1994). This area of research often focuses on communication processes, how conflict is managed, and how problems are addressed. A second major emphasis looks at the characteristics of individual spouses and positive couple processes in relation to establishing and maintaining a strong, healthy marriage. According to recent observations (Holman, Carroll, Busby, & Klein, 2008), evidence suggests that researchers increasingly are investigating these elements, often referred to as "marital virtues" or "spousal strengths." These virtues or strengths include positivity, friendship, generosity (Fowers, 2000; Hawkins, Fowers, Carroll, & Yang, 2007), and fairness (Fowers, 2001). A third major emphasis attends to elements some scholars call "transformative processes" in marriage (Fincham, Stanley, & Beach, 2007), which are efforts at self-change that spouses make to heal a relationship rift or forge a deeper connection. These elements include forgiveness (Fincham, 2000; McCullough, Rachal, Sandage, Worthington, Brown, & Hight, 1998), commitment (Fowers, 2000; Stanley, 2005), sacrifice (Whitton, Stanley, & Markman, 2002), and sanctification (Mahoney, Pargament, Murray-Swank, & Murray-Swank, 2003). Gottman (1999) has also begun to highlight individual aspects of couple interaction, such as fondness, admiration, affection, and respect. These factors within each person become the basis for couples' efforts to communicate well and handle issues between them respectfully (Carroll, Badger, & Yang, 2006).

Consistent with this view, this chapter focuses on key personal characteristics that lead to marital virtue-based interactions, as well as key interpersonal processes that bless marriages and prevent disruption. We will examine these processes through scholarly and gospel lenses and give suggestions for how couples can apply these elements in their marriages.

Foundational Process #1:
Personal Commitment to the
Marriage Covenant

"The Family: A Proclamation to the World" declares that "marriage between a man and a woman is ordained of God" (¶ 1), and that "husband and wife have a solemn responsibility to love and care for each other" (¶ 6). Furthermore, it emphasizes that "marriage . . . is essential to His eternal plan" (¶ 7). These statements make clear that marriage is a purposeful, divinely created relationship, not merely a social custom, and that couples

have God-given covenant obligations to one another. A correct understanding of these doctrines should set in motion the attitudes and behaviors that nurture covenant commitments (see Packer, 2004).

While serving as a member of the Seventy, Elder Bruce C. Hafen (2005, p. 76–77) clarified the nature of a covenant relationship by contrasting it with a contractual relationship:

> When troubles come, the parties to a *contractual* marriage seek happiness by walking away. They marry to obtain benefits and will stay only as long as they're receiving what they bargained for. But when troubles come to a *covenant* marriage, the husband and wife work them through. They marry to give and to grow, bound by covenants to each other, to the community, and to God. *Contract* companions each give 50 percent. But *covenant* companions each give 100 percent. Enough and to spare. Each gives enough to cover any shortfall by the other.

Successful covenant marriages are founded on the teachings of the Lord Jesus Christ and tied to our discipleship. Elder David A. Bednar (2006, p. 86) beautifully described how being focused on Jesus in a covenant marriage relationship influences marital progress:

> The Lord Jesus Christ is the focal point in a covenant marriage relationship. Please notice how the Savior is positioned at the apex of this triangle, with a woman at the base of one corner and a man at the base of the other corner. Now consider what happens in the relationship between the man and the woman as they individually and steadily "come unto Christ" and strive to be "perfected in Him" (Moroni 10:32). Because of and through the Redeemer, the man and woman come closer together.

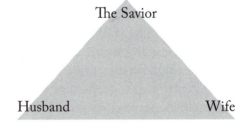

THE COVENANT MARRIAGE RELATIONSHIP
Elder David A. Bednar (2006)

Social Science Perspectives on Covenant Commitment

While not directly researching marriage as a covenant relationship, some scholars in the social sciences have also noted the importance of commitment in marriage. For example, marriage scholar Scott Stanley (2005) has identified two kinds of commitment: *constraint commitment* and *personal dedication*. Constraint commitment comprises a sense of obligation, "forces or costs that serve to keep couples together even if they would rather break up" (Stanley, Whitton, & Markman, 2004, p. 498). For example, couples may stay together because of social pressure, the high expense of divorce, or for the sake of the children. Personal dedication, on the other hand, is an intentional decision and desire to stay in a marriage for mutual benefit. You "sacrifice for [the relationship], invest in it, link it to personal goals, and seek the partner's welfare, not just your own" (Markman, Stanley, & Blumberg, 2001, p. 325). Each type of commitment is important, like epoxy glue: "Mixing the two components gives married couples a superstrong bond" (Stanley, 2005, p. 23). Constraint commitment is helpful for the stability of a relationship, and couples can lean on it to weather the storms that are a part of every marriage. However, personal dedication is essential for fulfillment in marriage. Research shows that personally dedicated couples show a greater priority for the relationship, feel greater satisfaction with giving, and are less likely to seek greener marital pastures (Stanley, 2005).

Marital Processes that Nurture Covenant Commitment in Marriage

What marital processes show a covenant commitment? Religious leaders and scholars are remarkably consistent in their suggestions. Here are some ideas:

Intentional personal dedication. To nurture their covenant commitments to one another and God, couples will wisely make a decision to be intentionally and personally dedicated. This involves a commitment to sacrifice for and organize one's life around the companion spouse; it also means a willingness to change any and all behaviors and attitudes for the good of the relationship. This might involve learning to resolve differences in a more healthy way, overcoming tendencies toward impatient listening, moderating unrealistic expectations, spending an evening alone together each week, or resolving personal problems. As marriage scholar

Blaine Fowers (2000) has observed, one of the basic ways for a person to have a good marriage is to be a good person. Couples who are personally dedicated will continually strive for individual improvement in their conduct as a partner, realizing that eternal marriage blessings are not automatic. Such conduct might also emphasize the active development of virtues that especially benefit marriage, such as being more tolerant and accepting of imperfections, being fair, or being more patient, courteous, kind, and generous. Elder Robert D. Hales (1996, p. 65) explained:

An eternal bond doesn't just happen as a result of sealing covenants we make in the temple. How we conduct ourselves in this life will determine what we will be in all the eternities to come. To receive the blessings of the sealing that our Heavenly Father has given to us, we have to keep the commandments and conduct ourselves in such a way that our families will want to live with us in the eternities.

Exclusive cleaving and unity. The Lord declared, "Thou shalt love thy wife with all thy heart, and shalt cleave unto her and none else" (D&C 42:22). In explaining this passage of scripture, President Spencer W. Kimball (1972, p. 143) taught:

The words *none else* eliminate everyone and everything. The spouse then becomes preeminent in the life of the husband or wife, and neither social life nor occupational life nor political life nor any other interest nor person nor thing shall ever take precedence over the companion spouse.

In a related verse, the Lord also states, "Therefore shall a man leave his father and his mother, and shall cleave unto his wife, and they shall be one flesh" (Genesis 2:24). President Henry B. Eyring (1998, p. 66) explained the importance of this verse:

At the creation of man and woman, unity for them in marriage was not given as hope; it was a command! . . . Our Heavenly Father wants our hearts to be knit together. That union in love is not simply an ideal. It is a necessity.

Practice spiritual patterns. When couples are involved in unifying spiritual activities, such as prayer and active religious involvement, they bring a number of benefits into their marriages. Couples who practice their faith together generally have less conflict, are more likely to reach a mutually satisfying resolution if there is conflict, and are more likely to remain committed to each other and the marriage when conflict does occur (Lambert & Dollahite, 2006). Shared religious faith aids in helping couples create a shared "inner life together—a culture rich with symbols" (Gottman & Silver, 1999, p. 243) that binds couples together. "The more you can agree about the fundamentals in life, the richer, more meaningful, and in a sense easier your marriage is likely to be" (Gottman & Silver, 1999, p. 245). Couples who pray together say they feel closer to God, have softer feelings, think about what is best for the couple, and receive help dealing with conflict (Butler, Gardner, & Bird, 1998).

President Kimball (2002, p. 44) taught the transcendent importance of spiritual patterns emerging from covenant commitments in marriage:

When a husband and wife go together frequently to the holy temple, kneel in prayer together in their home with their family, go hand in hand to their religious meetings, keep their lives wholly chaste—mentally and physically—so that their whole thoughts and desires and loves are all centered in the one being, their companion, and both work together for the upbuilding of the kingdom of God, then happiness is at its pinnacle.

Foundational Process #2: Love and Friendship

Beyond simply assuming that spouses know they love each other, "husband and wife have a solemn responsibility to love and care for each other" (¶ 6). The proclamation mentions the responsibility to love and care before any other marital obligation or virtue. Christlike love is the lodestar virtue in marriage—it lights the way and draws attention to other virtues couples may wish to foster in their marriage. The Lord said, "A new commandment I give unto you, That ye love one another; As I have loved you, that ye also love one another" (John 13:34). The command to love, by itself, was not the new commandment, for the commandment to "love thy neighbor" was given during Old Testament times (see Leviticus 19:18). The new commandment was to love as

Jesus loves, thus setting the standard for the pure love of Christ that should be sought in marriage.

In this dispensation the Lord commanded, "Thou shalt love thy wife with all thy heart" (D&C 42:22), applying equally to wives as well as husbands. In commenting about this verse, President Ezra Taft Benson (1987, p. 50) taught, "To my knowledge there is only one other thing in all scripture that we are commanded to love with all our hearts, and that is God Himself. Think what that means!" Parents have not been commanded to love their children with all their hearts, though undoubtedly they do. But marital love seems to occupy a high and holy status.

The love of which the Lord speaks is more than a feeling. Agency, or personal choice, is involved. The influential Christian writer C. S. Lewis, in his book *Mere Christianity* (1952, p. 99), taught:

Love as distinct from "being in love" is not merely a feeling. It is a deep unity, maintained by the will and deliberately strengthened by habit. . . . They can have this love for each other even at those moments when they do not like each other. . . . It is on this love that the engine of marriage is run: being in love was the explosion that started it.

Elder Lynn G. Robbins (2000, p. 22) emphasized this same idea when he said:

Agency plays a fundamental role in our relationships with one another. This being true, we must make the conscious decision that we will love our spouse and family with all our heart, soul, and mind; that we will build, not "fall into," strong, loving marriages and families.

True marital love emerges from profound friendship (Fowers, 2001). After surveying 25 years of research on marriage, Gottman and Silver stated simply, "Happy marriages are based on a deep friendship . . . a mutual respect for and enjoyment of each other's company" (1999, p. 19). This summary parallels gospel teaching of the role of friendship in marriage. Elder Marlin K. Jensen of the Seventy (1999, p. 64) emphasized that "a relationship between a man and a woman that begins with friendship and then ripens into romance and eventually marriage will usually become an enduring, eternal friendship."

Nurturing Love and Friendship

What can married couples do to nurture love and friendship? Here are several ideas:

Get in sync with your partner's love preferences. Find out how your partner likes to receive love and then do those things often. Different scholars and practitioners recommend different approaches for accomplishing this. Gottman and Silver (1999) recommend that couples build and use a "love map." A love map is like a mental (or possibly physical) notebook where we collect personal information about our spouse that we want to remember. This notebook includes the spouse's dreams, joys, fears, likes, dislikes, frustrations, and worries. The map helps us to identify different "points" about our spouse so we know how to love him or her better. For example, if you know your spouse's favorite food is lasagna, you might prepare that meal during an evening together. Therapist Richard Stuart (1980) recommends couples engage in "Caring Days," where couples identify sets of loving actions that they would like to receive from their partner. These actions must be specific ("Tell me you love me at least once a day"), positive (not "Don't do this" or "Stop doing that"), small enough to be done on a daily basis ("Call me at work during lunch, just to see how I'm doing"), and not related to any recent conflict. Experimental research shows that couples engaging in Caring Days significantly enhanced their marital satisfaction (LeCroy, Carrol, Nelson-Becker, & Sturlaugson, 1989). Regardless of which approach couples choose, the idea is for couples to talk openly about how they like to receive love and then agree to do those things often.

Talk as friends. Sometimes our couple conversation is all about the business of life: the job, the kids, problems. Of course, these things need to be handled, but it is also important to make time to simply talk as friends. These types of conversations were the kinds of discussions that drew couples close in the first place. Be sure to protect "friend time" from issues and conflict (Markman et al., 2001). Gottman and Silver (1999) recommend having daily stress-reducing, validating conversation as friends, not family business partners. When conversing as friends, we make sure to show genuine interest (look at our spouse, give full attention), take turns talking, avoid giving unsolicited advice, communicate our understanding on occasion, take our spouse's side, avoid interrupting or rebutting, express affection, and validate emotions.

Respond to bids for connection. Our best efforts to connect in marriage can be jeopardized as a result of the failure to respond to another's bids, which Gottman, Gottman, and DeClaire (2001, p. 4) call "the fundamental unit of emotional communication." A bid can be a question, a look, a gesture, a touch—any single expression that says, "I want to feel connected to you." Gottman's laboratory studies identified that couples responded to bids for connection in one of three ways: by turning away (such as ignoring), turning against (such as verbally attacking), or turning toward (actively responding to bids for attention, affection, humor, or support). How spouses responded to bids for connection affected the future of the relationships in a major way: husbands who eventually divorced disregarded their wives' bids for connection 82 percent of the time, whereas husbands in stable marriages did this only 19 percent of the time; wives headed for divorce disregarded their husbands' bids for connection 50 percent of the time, whereas wives in stable marriages did this only 14 percent of the time.

Set goals for couple interaction. Couples can turn toward each other in many ways every day (Gottman & Silver, 1999). To summarize the suggestions above:

1. Respond to bids for attention, affection, humor, or support. An announcement of "I've had a rotten day" can be met with an acknowledgement of feelings ("I'm sorry to hear that"), a hug, and an invitation to talk more about it.
2. Make an effort to do everyday activities together, such as reading the mail or making the bed.
3. Have a stress-reducing conversation at the end of the day. This involves reuniting at the end of a busy day to see how things went, and listening to and validating one another.
4. Do something special every day to communicate affection and appreciation.
5. Keep track of how well you are connecting emotionally with each other, and make enhancements when necessary.

Foundational Process #3: Positive Interaction

Positive emotions toward one's spouse are vital to a healthy marriage. Negative emotions, if they occur frequently and are allowed to deepen, can threaten a marriage. In the Gottman laboratory studies (1999), researchers observed couples during conflict situations and assessed the proportions of negative and positive interactions. For example, a negative interaction would be a hurtful argument about an overdraft in the checking account; a positive interaction would be a loving greeting to one another after returning home from work. The researchers discovered that for couples in stable marriages, the ratio of positive to negative interactions during conflict situations was at least 5 to 1, whereas in couples headed for divorce, the ratio was only 0.8 to 1. Thus couples doing well show at least five times more positives than negatives and far fewer negatives than couples headed toward divorce. Gottman and Silver (1999) call this "positive sentiment override" or the five to one ratio. In a nine-year longitudinal study of newlyweds, Gottman, Coan, Carrere, and Swanson (1998) found that positive emotions were the only predictor of marital stability or dissolution, as well as the long-term marital satisfaction of the newlyweds who remained married. This does not mean that negativity is always bad or that the goal is to eliminate any negativity (Gottman, 1999). Negativity can inform couples where change is needed for relationship enhancement. The important finding here is that the ratio of positive to negative interaction influences marital outcomes, and that the better the ratio of positivity to negativity, the better the marriage.

To enhance positive interaction in marriage, focus on your spouse's positive qualities. Humorist Jay Trachman once gave some sage advice: "The formula for a happy marriage? It's the same as the formula for living in California: when you find a fault, don't dwell on it." If spouses decide that negativity is their "dwelling place," they can become experts at identifying negative traits and minimizing or ignoring the positive ones. President Gordon B. Hinckley (2003, p. 59) taught a similar principle:

> I have witnessed much of the best and much of the worst in marriage. . . . Faultfinding replaces praise. When we look for the worst in anyone, we will find it. But if we will concentrate on the best, that element will grow until it sparkles.

Couples can focus on positive qualities by making and sharing lists of the things they admire and appreciate about each other. These things can be personal traits (she's intelligent, witty), talents (he's a good listener), something you especially like about him or her (I love the way she laughs), a feature of your relationship that you like (I like how we seem to finish each other's thoughts), or something positive your spouse has done (he rubbed my feet when I was tired). Doing this activity doesn't ignore the negative; it is an active decision to focus on the positive.

From your list, choose two or three qualities and rehearse them silently in your mind. Put them on an index card and in places where you can see them and think about them, such as on your car dashboard, in your front pocket or purse, or on your desk. Do this daily for up to two weeks. Rotate different qualities from the list and repeat the activity. This way couples can override the temptation to be negative toward one another. Couples who nurture their fondness and admiration for one another in this way are better able to accept each other's flaws and weaknesses and prevent them from threatening their relationship (Gottman & Silver, 1999).

Foundational Process #4: Accepting Influence from One's Spouse

In marriage, the process of sharing the decision-making power with one's spouse is referred to in some scholarly literature as accepting influence (Gottman et al., 1998). Accepting influence refers to counseling with and listening to one's spouse, respecting and considering his or her opinions as valid as one's own, and compromising when making decisions together. Elder Russell M. Nelson (1991, p. 23) taught, "Husbands and wives, learn to listen, and listen to learn from one another." For some, accepting influence from others comes naturally, but many have a harder time giving away some of their power.

Share influence in all family affairs. Part of the recipe for a happy, healthy marriage (and a sturdy marriage foundation) is for both partners to share equal ownership and influence in all family affairs (Gottman, 1999; Gottman, Gottman, & DeClaire, 2006). This research finding supports principles of the proclamation, which state that men and women are "obligated to help one another as equal partners," and that they "will be held accountable before God for the discharge of these obligations" (¶¶ 6–7). From his many studies, Gottman (1999) concluded that "marriages . . . work to the extent that men accept influence from, share power with, women" (Gottman, 1999, p. 52). Women, Gottman argues, are already well practiced at accepting influence from men, so it is critical for the well-being of marriage that men learn to do likewise.

Ways to accept influence. To help translate this knowledge into practical behavior, Gottman and others (2006) give a few suggestions of how to accept influence and respond to one's spouse. For example, we can accept influence by turning to our spouse for advice, being open to his or her ideas, listening to and considering his or her opinions, learning from our spouse, showing respect during disagreements, recognizing points we both agree on, compromising, showing trust in our spouse, and being sensitive to his or her feelings. Vocalizing these suggestions can be done in any of the following ways: "Explain your thinking to me, please." "What are your feelings about this issue?" "Please tell me why this is so important to you." "Please tell me how you would solve the problem." "What are your goals in regard to this issue?" Note that a kind tone of voice and the openness with which these questions are framed are critical in accepting the other's influence. Understanding, compromising, and unity are goals happily married couples constantly work toward.

Foundational Process #5: Respectfully Handle Differences and Solve Problems

Elder Bruce C. Hafen (2005, p. 76) tells the following story: "[A] bride sighed blissfully on her wedding day, 'Mom, I'm at the end of all my troubles!' 'Yes,' replied her mother, 'but at which end?'" Conflicts, disagreements, and challenges are a normal part of every marriage. When we read the prophet Lehi's words stating that there "must needs be . . . opposition in all things" (2 Nephi 2:11) for good things to be brought to pass, we usually don't think that he may also have included marriage. Couples may enter marriage expecting it to be idyllic, but the experience of differences and resolving them are conditions of mortality, perhaps eternity. Disagreements crop up in even the best marriages. How differences are handled is an important key to marital success or failure (Markman et al., 2001). While a member of the Seventy, Elder Joe J. Christensen (1995, p. 65) taught a similar principle: "Any intelligent couple will have differences of opinion. Our challenge is to be sure

that we know how to resolve them. That is part of the process of making a good marriage better."

What are some of the major areas in which couples may have differences and disagreements? In one study (Markman et al., 2001), money and children were the issues couples were most likely to report arguing about. However, it is possible to deal with the issues between partners without the discussion escalating into an argument. In addition to a covenant commitment, love and friendship, and other marital virtues and processes that bind a couple together, a good skill set is necessary to work through the challenges brought on by differences and conflict. These skills include prevention; eliminating destructive patterns; becoming calm; discussing issues softly, gently, and privately; making and accepting repair attempts; soothing one's self and each other; and reaching a consensus.

Prevention. Some issues may not need to be raised. Having charity, the pure love of Christ, may prevent some things from ever becoming an issue. For example, maybe we can let go of our deep concerns about trivial matters, such as the stereotypical uncapped toothpaste.

A second important aspect of prevention is the holding of regular couple councils (Markman et al., 2001). Unlike family councils, where the focus is on the entire family, couple councils provide couples with the opportunity to discuss issues directly related to their marriage relationship. Couples who regularly visit together about their relationship are more likely to nip marriage problems in the bud. While a member of the Seventy, Elder Robert L. Simpson (1982, p. 21) underscored the importance of couple councils:

Every couple, whether in the first or the twenty-first year of marriage, should discover the value of pillow-talk time at the end of the day—the perfect time to take inventory, to talk about tomorrow. And best of all, it's a time when love and appreciation for one another can be reconfirmed. The end of another day is also the perfect setting to say, "Sweetheart, I am sorry about what happened today. Please forgive me." You see, we are all still imperfect, and these unresolved differences, allowed to accumulate day after day, add up to a possible breakdown in the marital relationship—all for the want of better communication, and too often because of foolish pride.

Eliminate destructive interaction patterns. We need to work to eliminate destructive interaction patterns from our relationships so they don't creep in and influence the nature of our discussion of issues. Gottman (1994) has identified four of these and labeled them "the four horsemen of the apocalypse," as they progressively lead to the downfall of a relationship: criticism (attack on one's personality), contempt (criticism mixed with sarcasm, name-calling, eye-rolling), defensiveness (not taking responsibility for change), and stonewalling (unwillingness to discuss or withdrawal from an issue). Other major patterns (Markman et al., 2001) include escalation (upping the ante on a discussion), invalidation (putting down the other's opinions), and negative interpretations (assigning a more negative view than what was meant). Couples are wise to identify the degree to which any of these patterns are present in their current relationship and resolve to eliminate them.

Calm yourself first. When issues arise, couples need calm, respectful discussion. Before approaching your spouse on an issue, ask: "Am I in control of myself?" The Lord has made it clear that contention is of the devil (3 Nephi 11:29–30). Alma taught us to "bridle all [our] passions," including those leading to contention. Why? "That [we] may be filled with love" (Alma 38:12). Contention results in anger escalation, hostility, and hurt feelings that can seriously harm relationships. If you cannot approach an issue without contending about it, it is better to deal with it later, after you have calmed yourself. Do whatever calms you: pray, listen to peaceful music, walk around the block, take a shower.

Bring up the concern softly, gently, and privately. Set the stage for a discussion by bringing up issues softly, gently, and calmly, remembering that "a soft answer turneth away wrath" (Proverbs 15:1). Gottman's research (1999) labeled this the "softened start-up." Avoid negative, accusatory remarks, sarcasm, and critical or contemptuous statements. Complaining is okay, but don't blame. Speak for yourself. Use "I" statements to communicate your feelings ("I felt hurt when you left me alone at the party"), not "you" statements ("You are so inconsiderate"). Describe what is happening; don't evaluate or judge. Be clear. Be polite. Be appreciative. Don't store things up—remember D&C 121:43: "Reproving betimes [without delay] with sharpness [clarity, openness], when moved upon by the Holy Ghost." Bring up the issue privately with the person concerned "and not before the world" (see D&C 42:88–89).

Learn to make and receive repair attempts. When a discussion on an issue gets off on the wrong foot, put the brakes on before disaster strikes and things get contentious. Gottman (1999) calls this a "repair attempt." Ultimately, a repair attempt is anything in a discussion that de-escalates tension so discussion and problem solving can proceed. It might include apologies ("I'm sorry, please forgive me, I didn't mean that"), acknowledgment of actions ("Yes, you do help with the laundry on occasion"), or taking breaks ("Whoa! This is getting out of hand. Let's take ten minutes and cool off"). Because we love our spouse, we will want to work hard at receiving repair attempts rather than coldly rejecting them.

Soothe yourself and each other. Gottman (1999) observes that taking breaks may be essential if repair attempts are unsuccessful or if you begin to feel out of control ("flooded") physically and emotionally. Even if you calmed yourself prior to discussing an issue, you may need to continue to do so during the discussion. Self-soothing may be accomplished by using one or more relaxation techniques. After you've spent about 20 minutes calming down on your own, you can help soothe each other by talking about what produced the "flood" and what each of you can do to calm one another. Some people need a longer time to become calm enough to resume the discussion.

Reach a consensus about a solution. Most issues need only to be discussed and not solved (Markman et al., 2001); in fact, many issues are not solvable but perpetual (Gottman & Silver, 1999). However, after a full discussion of an issue has occurred and it is classified as a "solvable" problem, it is time to counsel together to find a solution that you both feel good about. Reaching a consensus is the ideal (see D&C 107:27–29). Let your spouse influence you as you arrive at a mutually agreeable solution. Steps to reaching agreement might include brainstorming possibilities, evaluating alternatives, choosing one you feel good about, putting the solution into action, and following up (Markman et al., 2001).

Foundational Process #6: Continuing Courtship through the Years

What is entropy? Yes, it is a physical science concept. So it may surprise you to learn that this concept has application in marriage, too. A good definition of entropy is "the tendency of a physical system to lose energy and coherence over time, such as a gas that expands and dissipates until there is little trace left" (Doherty, 1997, p. 9).

How does this apply in marriage? Years ago, President Spencer W. Kimball (2002, p. 44) taught that "many couples permit their marriages to become stale and their love to grow cold like old bread or worn-out jokes or cold gravy." More recently, scholar William Doherty (1997) commented about the *entropic family*, and by extension, the entropic couple who, through a lack of attention to their inner life, gradually loses a sense of cohesion over the years. Couples gradually drift apart because they lack infusions of bonding and intimacy. They become victims of the "cold gravy syndrome."

Research suggests that all marriages are subject to this kind of entropy, erosion, or disenchantment if neglected. The stress of unresolved issues and grievances and damaging communication and conflict resolution skills can pile up over time until couples have had enough and want their marriage to end (Gottman, 1994).

How does a couple keep their marriage "entropy-resistant" through the years? President David O. McKay (The Church of Jesus Christ of Latter-day Saints, 2003, p. 149) taught,

I should like to urge *continued courtship*, and apply this to grown people. Too many couples have come to the altar of marriage looking upon the marriage ceremony as the end of courtship instead of the beginning of an eternal courtship.

What are some things couples can do to keep courtship alive through the years?

Attend to the little things. President James E. Faust (2007, p. 8) taught,

In the enriching of marriage, the big things are the little things. There must be constant appreciation for each other and a thoughtful demonstration of gratitude. A couple must encourage and help each other grow. Marriage is a joint quest for the good, the beautiful, and the divine.

Be intentional about doing things every day to enrich the marriage. Couples who are continuing courtship have special activities they purposefully engage in to continue to build and maintain their relationship. Some scholars call these activities rituals. Doherty (1997) has

suggested three kinds of rituals to help couples: connection rituals (to maintain the bond between two people), love rituals (to keep the romance alive in marriage), and celebration rituals (to show honor, love, and respect for each other). An example of a connection ritual is time set aside for a couple's validating conversations, mentioned earlier; an example of a love ritual is an annual private getaway for the couple's wedding anniversary; a celebration ritual could be an exciting and creative gift each spouse gives the other on birthdays every year.

Spend at least five hours a week strengthening your relationship. In his studies, Gottman found that couples spending at least five hours a week on their relationship fared the best over time (Gottman & Silver, 1999). However, in order to succeed it is important for the couple to accomplish these four things during those five hours: (a) learn one thing that happened in your spouse's life each day, (b) have a stress-reducing conversation at the end of each day, (c) do something special every day to show affection and appreciation, and (d) have a weekly date.

Conclusion

With the various foundational processes of successful marriage working together, couples are more likely to experience the kind of marriage that President Kimball (2002, p. 42) described as "more an exultant ecstasy than the human mind can conceive." Deliberate, careful attention to these marital processes assures that marriage—a relationship central to Heavenly Father's plan—receives the care and attention it deserves. While a member of the Seventy, Elder F. Burton Howard (2003, p. 94, italics in the original) underscored the kind of treatment marriage deserves if it is expected to last indefinitely:

If you want something to last forever, you treat it differently. You shield it and protect it. You never abuse it. You don't expose it to the elements. You don't make it common or ordinary. If it ever becomes tarnished, you lovingly polish it until it gleams like new. It becomes special because you have made it so, and it grows more beautiful and precious as time goes by. Eternal marriage is just like that. We need to treat it just that way.

Stephen F. Duncan *is a professor in the School of Family Life at Brigham Young University. He and his wife,*

Barbara, are the parents of five children and they have one grandchild. **Sara S. McCarty Zasukha** *graduated with her bachelor's degree in marriage, family, and human development from Brigham Young University. She is currently an associate family teacher for the Utah Youth Village, and she and her husband have been married since August 2010.*

References

Bateman, M. J., & Bateman, M. S. (2003, January 14). Mortality and our eternal journey. BYU Devotional Address. Retrieved from http://speeches.byu.edu/reader/reader.php?id=486&x=67&y=7

Bednar, D. A. (2006, June). Marriage is essential to his eternal plan. *Ensign, 36,* 82–87.

Benson, E. T. (1987, November). To the fathers in Israel. *Ensign, 17,* 48–51.

Butler, M. H., Gardner, B. C., & Bird, M. H. (1998). Not just a time-out: Change dynamics of prayer for religious couples in conflict situations. *Family Process, 37,* 451–478.

Carroll, J. S., Badger, S., & Yang, C. (2006). The ability to negotiate or the ability to love? Evaluating the developmental domains of marital competence. *Journal of Family Issues, 27,* 1001–1032.

Christensen, J. J. (1995, May). Marriage and the great plan of happiness. *Ensign, 25,* 64–65.

The Church of Jesus Christ of Latter-day Saints. (2003). *Teachings of the Presidents of the Church: David O. McKay.* Salt Lake City: Author.

Doherty, W. J. (1997). *The intentional family: How to build family ties in our modern world.* Reading, MA: Addison-Wesley.

Eyring, H. B. (1998, May). That we may be one. *Ensign, 28,* 66–68.

Faust, J. E. (2007, April). Enriching your marriage. *Ensign, 37,* 4–8.

Fincham, F. D. (2000). The kiss of the porcupines: From attributing responsibility to forgiving. *Personal Relationships, 7,* 1–23.

Fincham, F. D., Stanley, S. M., & Beach, S. R. H. (2007). Transformative processes in marriage: An analysis of emerging trends. *Journal of Marriage and Family, 69*(2), 275–292.

Fowers, B. J. (2000). *Beyond the myth of marital happiness: How embracing the virtues of loyalty, generosity, justice, and courage can strengthen your relationship.* San Francisco: Jossey-Bass.

Fowers, B. J. (2001). The limits of a technical concept of a good marriage: Exploring the role of virtue in communication skills. *Journal of Marital and Family Therapy, 27,* 327–340.

Gottman, J. M. (1994). *Why marriages succeed or fail: And how you can make yours last.* New York: Simon & Schuster.

Gottman, J. M. (1999). *The marriage clinic: A scientifically based marital therapy.* New York: W. W. Norton.

Gottman, J. M., Coan, J., Carrere, S., & Swanson, C. (1998). Predicting marital happiness and stability from newlywed interactions. *Journal of Marriage and the Family, 60*(1), 5–22.

Gottman, J. M., & DeClaire, J. (2001). *The relationship cure: A five-step guide to strengthening your marriage, family, and friendships.* New York: Three Rivers Press.

Gottman, J. M., Gottman, J. S., & DeClaire, J. (2006). *Ten lessons to transform your marriage.* New York: Three Rivers Press.

Gottman, J. M., & Silver, N. (1999). *The seven principles for making marriage work.* New York: Crown Publishers.

Hafen, B. C. (2005). *Covenant hearts: Marriage and the joy of human love.* Salt Lake City: Deseret Book.

Hales, R. D. (1996, November). The eternal family. *Ensign, 26,* 64–66.

Hawkins, A. J., Fowers, B. J., Carroll, J. S., & Yang, C. (2007). Conceptualizing and measuring marital virtues. In S. L. Hofferth & L. M. Casper (Eds.), *Handbook of measurement issues in family research* (pp. 67–83). Mahwah, NJ: Lawrence Erlbaum Associates.

Hinckley, G. B. (2003, May). Loyalty. *Ensign, 33,* 58–60.

Holman, T. B., Carroll, J. S., Busby, D. M., & Klein, D. M. (2008). *Preparing, coupling, and marrying: Toward a unified theory of marriage development.* Unpublished manuscript.

Howard, F. B. (2003, May). Eternal marriage. *Ensign, 33,* 92–94.

Howell, M. (2006, February). Confidence to marry. *Ensign, 36,* 18–22.

Jensen, M. K. (1999, May). Friendship: A gospel principle. *Ensign, 29,* 64–65.

Kimball, S. W. (1972). *Faith precedes the miracle.* Salt Lake City: Deseret Book.

Kimball, S. W. (2002, October). Oneness in marriage. *Ensign, 32,* 40–45.

Lambert, N. M., & Dollahite, D. C. (2006). How religiosity helps couples prevent, resolve, and overcome marital conflict. *Family Relations, 55,* 439–449.

LeCroy, C. W., Carrol, P., Nelson-Becker, H., & Sturlaugson, P. (1989). An experimental evaluation of the caring days technique for marital enrichment. *Family Relations, 38,* 15–18.

Lewis, C. S. (1952). *Mere Christianity.* New York: Macmillan.

Mahoney, A., Pargament, K. I., Murray-Swank, A., & Murray-Swank, N. (2003). Religion and the sanctification of family relationships. *Review of Religious Research, 44*(3), 220–236.

Markman, H. J., Stanley, S. M., & Blumberg, S. L. (2001). *Fighting for your marriage: Positive steps for preventing divorce and preserving a lasting love.* San Francisco: Jossey-Bass.

McCullough, M. E., Rachal, K. C., Sandage, S. J., Worthington Jr., E. L., Brown, S. W., & Hight, T. L. (1998). Interpersonal forgiving in close relationships: II. Theoretical elaboration and measurement. *Journal of Personality and Social Psychology, 75,* 1586–1603.

Nelson, R. M. (1991, May). Listen to learn. *Ensign, 21,* 22–25.

Packer, B. K. (2004, May). Do not fear. *Ensign, 34,* 77–80.

Robbins, L. G. (2000, October). Agency and love in marriage. *Ensign, 30,* 16–22.

Sharlin, S. A., Kaslow, F. W., & Hammerschmidt, H. (2000). *Together through thick and thin: A multinational picture of long-term marriages.* New York: Haworth Press.

Simpson, R. L. (1982, May). A lasting marriage. *Ensign, 12,* 21–22.

Stanley, S. M. (2005). *The power of commitment: A guide to active, lifelong love.* San Francisco: Jossey-Bass.

Stanley, S. M., Whitton, S. W., & Markman, H. J. (2004). Maybe I do: Interpersonal commitment and premarital or nonmarital cohabitation. *Journal of Family Issues, 25,* 496–519.

Stuart, R. B. (1980). *Helping couples change: A social learning approach to marital therapy.* New York: The Guilford Press.

Whitton, S., Stanley, S., & Markman, H. (2002). Sacrifice in romantic relationships: An exploration of relevant research and theory. In A. L. Vangelisti, H. T. Reis, & M. A. Fitzpatrick (Eds.), *Stability and change in relationships* (pp. 156–182). West Nyack, NY: Cambridge University Press.

CHAPTER 4

Equal Partnership between Men and Women in Families

Valerie M. Hudson and Richard B Miller

By divine design, fathers are to preside over their families in love and righteousness and are responsible to provide the necessities of life and protection for their families. Mothers are primarily responsible for the nurture of their children. In these sacred responsibilities, fathers and mothers are obligated to help one another as equal partners.

The Doctrinal Concept of Equal Partnership between Men and Women

The restored gospel of Jesus Christ proclaims a doctrine that is not widely held in the fallen world, even among certain Christian sects, and that is the doctrine of sincerely equal partnership between men and women, here and in the eternities. Indeed, from our extensive research and reading over the past 15 years, we may go so far as to say that this doctrine, mentioned explicitly in "The Family: A Proclamation to the World," is revolutionary and distinguishes The Church of Jesus Christ of Latter-day Saints as a unique belief system.

What Is Meant by the Term *Equality*?

Before we delve into that rich doctrinal context, it is important to understand what Latter-day Saints mean by the term *equality*. Equality is all too often used to mean "identity"; that is, that two equal things must be identical to each other. Such usage represents a fallen and harmful understanding of equality that is espoused by Lucifer, who passionately wants all to be "like . . . himself" (2 Nephi 2:27). In contrast, Elder Joseph B. Wirthlin taught:

> The Lord did not people the earth with a vibrant orchestra of personalities only to value the piccolos of the world. Every instrument is precious and adds to the complex beauty of the symphony. All of Heavenly Father's children are different in some degree, yet each has his own beautiful sound that adds depth and richness to the whole (2008, p. 18).

Even though we all aspire to be of "one heart and one mind" (Moses 7:18), apparently that does not mean that we will all be identical. Since the proclamation teaches that gender is "an essential characteristic of individual premortal, mortal, and eternal identity and purpose" (¶ 2), gender or sex presents at least one way we will differ in the eternities. Indeed, as we will explore in a moment, without gender difference there could not be divinity. Yet Latter-day Saint theology does not teach that gender difference superimposes a hierarchy between men and women. Think of all we believe to be true about the equality, both here and in Zion, of men and women in God's kingdom: equal in blessings; equal in power, intelligence, wisdom, dignity, respect, giving counsel, giving consent, agency, value, potential, authority, exalted fullness, virtue, spirituality, and spiritual gifts; equal in temporal things in Zion; and equal heirs with Christ. When we read this list, do we unconsciously redefine "equality" as "identity" and thus struggle with these concepts? If so, it is time to work on a personal definition of *equal* that eschews both intimations of identity or hierarchy. One gender does not have greater eternal possibility than the other (Moses 2:26–27; 2 Nephi 26:28, 33). While serving as a member of the Seventy, Elder Earl C. Tingey said:

> You must not misunderstand what the Lord meant when Adam was told he was to have a helpmeet. A helpmeet is a companion suited to or equal to us. We walk side by side with a helpmeet, not one before or behind the other. A helpmeet results in an absolute equal partnership between a husband

and a wife. Eve was to be equal to Adam as a husband and wife are to be equal to each other (2008, n.p.).

As this passage suggests, without understanding the story of Adam and Eve in light of the restored gospel, much that we understand about God's plan for the equal relationship between the genders is apt to go awry. For this reason, we turn to the story of our first parents.

Eve and Adam and the Plan of Happiness

Adam and Eve and all their descendants were created spiritually and physically, male and female, in the image of our heavenly parents. The proclamation states: "All human beings—male and female—are created in the image of God. Each is a beloved spirit son or daughter of heavenly parents" (¶ 2). Indeed, the restored gospel teaches us that the term "God" means an exalted man and exalted woman united in the everlasting covenant of marriage. Heavenly Father is no bachelor; indeed, Heavenly Father could not be a god if he were unmarried (D&C 132:19–20). Therefore, Eve was not created in the image of a divine man and was no deformed or inferior version thereof: Eve was created in the image of a divine woman. The body, parts, and passions of a woman, then, are as divine as the body, parts, and passions of a man. A woman's body is no curse, but rather the fullest material expression of her divine potential.

Many religions and sects have interpreted the story of the Garden of Eden as the story of Eve's spiritual inferiority and venality (Young, 1993). However, the Latter-day Saint view rejects this interpretation in wholesale fashion. Indeed, as Elder Dallin H. Oaks has declared:

> Some Christians condemn Eve for her act, concluding that she and her daughters are somehow flawed by it. Not the Latter-day Saints! Informed by revelation, we celebrate Eve's act and honor her wisdom and courage in the great episode called the Fall (1993, p. 73).

To understand what Elder Oaks meant by this, we have to remember that Latter-day Saints do not view the Fall as a tragedy. Yes, the Fall brought the possibility of evil and affliction into the world, but, as the proclamation teaches, gaining a body and earthly experience are necessary for progression toward our eternal destiny to become like our heavenly parents. The only failure in the Garden of Eden would have been if Adam and Eve had *not* partaken of the forbidden fruit. When we picture our great ancestors Adam and Eve partaking of the fruit, with the whole host of heaven watching, likely we envision shouts of joy among that host, not tears of grief. Furthermore, Elder Oaks teaches that partaking of the fruit was not a sin, but a necessary transgression:

> [Eve's] act, whatever its nature, was formally a transgression, but eternally a glorious necessity to open the doorway toward eternal life. . . . [The Prophet] Joseph Smith taught that [Eve did not] "sin," because God had decreed it. (1993, p. 73).

As we step back and contemplate that there were two trees in the Garden of Eden, we might begin to see how this suggests a strong and equal complementarity between the divine responsibilities of men and women in the great plan of happiness. If the fruit of the tree of life represents those ordinances of salvation and exaltation that are given to the worthy sons and daughters of God by the sons of God, perhaps the fruit of the tree of knowledge of good and evil is a special gift as well, a special gift given to all worthy sons and daughters of God by God's daughters. If we view the fruit of the first tree as representing the passage of a soul into mortality and full material agency, we notice the similarity to the great gift of birth given by women to those who kept their first estate, as echoed in the Spanish phrase for giving birth, *dar la luz* ("to give the light").

Eve was not created second to show that she was an appendage or afterthought to the man Adam. Eve also had an essential role in inaugurating the plan of happiness. Only a daughter of God could open the door to mortal life for God's children. Eve was no airhead, no evildoer; no, Eve perhaps was the most courageous and wise of all God's daughters, and as Elder Oaks (1993) has said, she is to be "celebrated" for this wisdom and courage.

When viewed in the light of the restored gospel, we see that not only was God not unhappy with Eve's choice, but also we see that God approved her choice. And so God pronounced that, yes, she would enter mortality and she would have children. These are great blessings, just as were the blessings to Adam of having to work instead of having Eden provide for all his needs. And then God reassured Eve that Adam would play his role in administering the fruit of the second tree, by telling Eve that Adam would rule with her—meaning that he would prove himself worthy to be her equal companion. As Elder Bruce C. Hafen, a member of the Seventy at the time, and his wife, Marie, explained,

> Genesis 3:16 states that Adam is to "rule over" Eve, but this doesn't make Adam a dictator. . . . *Over* in "rule over" uses the Hebrew *bet,* which means ruling *with,* not ruling *over.* . . . The concept of interdependent, equal partners is well-grounded in the doctrine of the restored gospel. Eve was Adam's "help meet" (Genesis 2:18). The original Hebrew for *meet* means that Eve was adequate for, or equal to, Adam. She wasn't his servant or his subordinate (2007, p. 27).

Just as Adam hearkened first to Eve, accepted from her the fruit of the first tree, and entered into mortality, so Eve would hearken to Adam, accept from him the fruit of the second tree, and enter into eternal life. When viewing the entire plan of happiness, we see that the man and the woman play equally powerful and equally important roles in the plan. Each is to hearken to the other for the plan to work. Each stands before the other, and in the sight of God, as equals.

Equality and Love in Latter-day Saint Doctrine

In Latter-day Saint theology, there is a crucial relationship between equality and love, which we must not overlook. Think about the love of God and our Savior. We readily acknowledge that we are not their equals. But, heretical as it is to many other faiths, we believe that God ultimately hopes, plans, and acts to create a path for his children to become as He is. In the end, God hopes we will become His friends, not His servants or perpetual inferiors (D&C 84:77). The truest, most noble love is the love of a superior for an inferior where the superior makes every sacrifice so that the inferior might, if willing, rise to become an equal. And that is the wonder of the Savior's Atonement: He, a superior, suffered and died so that all who will, males and females, may become equal heirs with Him (D&C 88:107) and receive "all power" and the "fullness" of God

(D&C 76:54–56, 94–95; 132:20). In this highest realm, the Savior "makes them equal in power, and in might, and in dominion" (D&C 76:95). Parental love in mortality emulates godly love. Those with healthy parental love make sacrifices so that their children may one day stand as their equals, and be not only their children, but also their friends.

There are also relationships in which people come together not as superiors and inferiors with the hope that the inferiors might be made equal; there are relationships in which people are to come together as presumed equals. The terms used in the scriptures help us understand that equality is a *commandment:* "It must needs be that there be an organization of my people . . . that you may be equal in the bonds of heavenly things, yea, and earthly things also" (D&C 78:3, 5; see also 38:24–27). And why is the presumption of equality necessary? That we may truly love our neighbors, for if we cannot envision them as our equals—as ourselves—we cannot really love them. A Zion community lives the fullness of this commandment. Zion, as we know, is a place where the Saints are equal in both heavenly and temporal things, as noted above (D&C 70:14; 78:5–7). Zion must come together presuming the equality of each person and then acting on it to remove any discordance between the ideal and the lived situation.

Thus it is in the units of Zion—the marriages in that community. Spouses are to enter their marriage relationship convinced of each other's equality. They cannot form a relationship that will be blessed by God if they come to the marriage altar unsure of each other's equality, doubting it, or not even thinking about how it should order their relations. According to Latter-day Saint doctrine, the first utterance after God married Adam and Eve in the Garden of Eden was Adam's bold declaration of Eve's equality with him—that they would be "one flesh" (Genesis 2:24). (Adam even put in an injunction against patrilocal marriage, where wives live with their husband's family. Such a living situation has an inherent ability to turn a marriage into an unequal one favoring the husband [Genesis 2:24].)

Stewards in Equal Partnership

Family stewardships should be understood in terms of their responsibilities—obligations to one's spouse, not power over one's spouse. As we noted above, according to the Hebrew translation, Genesis 3:16 is more accurately understood to mean Adam "ruling *with*," not "ruling *over*" Eve. President Hunter said: "The Lord intended that the wife be . . . a companion equal and necessary in full partnership. . . . For a man to operate independent of or without regard to the feelings and counsel of his wife in governing the family is to exercise unrighteous dominion"(Hunter, 1994, p. 51). Gender equality is not some gratuitous element of God's vision of marriage: rather, we are commanded to presume the equality of our spouse as we approach the marriage altar, for otherwise we cannot truly love her or him. It is hoped that we then deepen that vision of our spouse's equality in the divine work that is procreation and parenthood. Indeed, given that we believe Adam and Eve lived this law, a marriage reflecting the equality of the spouses is *the ultimate traditional marriage.*

We acknowledge that different cultures across the globe and across time have viewed the relationship between husbands and wives in many different ways, often at odds with the true doctrine of equal partnership. But Latter-day Saint General Authorities have stated explicitly that priesthood holders must reject hierarchical marriage. In a conference address, Elder Richard G. Scott (2008, p. 46) made this plain:

> In some cultures, tradition places a man in a role to dominate, control, and regulate all family affairs. That is not the way of the Lord. In some places the wife is almost owned by her husband, as if she were another of his personal possessions. That is a cruel, mistaken vision of marriage encouraged by Lucifer that every priesthood holder must reject. It is founded on the false premise that a man is somehow superior to a woman. Nothing could be farther from the truth.

Tradition is not something to be blindly revered in the Latter-day Saint Church. The Book of Mormon is replete with the phrase "the foolish traditions of the fathers," lamenting their falseness and the lasting harm done thereby to societies. Where tradition is at odds with Latter-day Saint doctrine, the tradition must be relinquished. According to Elder Scott, there are traditions of marriage in the world that are wrong because they deny the equality of women.

Moreover, contrary to scripture and the teachings of latter-day prophets, some men and women have interpreted *presiding* to mean that after equal counsel, equal consent is not necessary because the presider (or husband) has the right of final say. But President Boyd K. Packer (1998, p. 73) explained: "In the Church there is a distinct line of authority. We serve where called by those who preside over us. In the home it is a partnership with husband and wife equally yoked together, sharing in decisions, always working together."

In considering the equal partnership envisioned by the proclamation on the family, Elder L. Tom Perry (2004, p. 71) puts it eloquently: "There is not a president or a vice president in a family." We have copresidents working "together eternally for the good of their family." In other words, "they are on equal footing. They plan and organize the affairs of the family jointly and unanimously as they move forward."

The stewardship of priesthood does not superimpose a hierarchical relationship over the God-ordained equality between husband and wife. President James E. Faust (1996, p. 6) taught that "every father is to his family a patriarch and every mother a matriarch as coequals in their distinctive parental roles." We emphasize that the patriarchal priesthood is not so called to imply a hierarchy between men and women. Instead, as President Ezra Taft Benson taught, it is called patriarchal because in ancient days it was handed down from faithful father to faithful son and frequently still is today (D&C 107:40–42). (*Patri* is Latin for father.) President Benson also taught that the patriarchal order is the family order of government, presided over by mothers and fathers (Benson, 1985). One of the most revolutionary aspects of the restored gospel is its ability to help us envision difference without hierarchy, distinctiveness without inequality. This is what the proclamation calls upon us to hold as the ideal relationship between husbands and wives.

A marriage of equal partners will also be one in which the partners help one another in their stewardships, indeed, are "obligated to help one another as equal partners" (¶ 7). This assistance includes help with housework and childcare. President Boyd K. Packer (1989, p. 75) has said, "There is no task, however menial, connected with the care of babies, the nurturing of children, or with the maintenance of the home that is not [the husband's] equal obligation." Likewise, women assist their husbands, directly and indirectly, with the burdens of supporting a family.

Of course, marriage is not only about responsibilities; it is also about dreams, both shared and individual. After his wife's death, President Gordon B. Hinckley shared some tender moments from their marriage. He described one of the most poignant moments this way: "In our old age my beloved companion said to me quietly one evening, 'You have always given me wings to fly, and I have loved you for it'" (2004, p. 85). There must be room enough in a marriage for the dreams of both the husband and the wife and sweet encouragement from each to the other to follow those dreams.

Thus, among the Latter-day Saints, marriages should not be built around the domination of one partner over the other, whether that domination be male over female or female over male. Such is not the vision of sincerely equal partnership to which we are called of God. Both husband and wife have a sacred obligation to refrain from thoughts and actions that might undermine an equal partnership. Thoughts or actions that tend toward the domineering or the subservient are to be avoided by both spouses.

The doctrine of equal partnership in marriage points powerfully and gloriously to truth. Thus, it should not surprise us that social science research, even with its limitations, confirms the importance and benefits of equal partnership in marital and family relationships. In this next section, we briefly review what social science scholars have learned about equal partnership.

Social Science Research Findings on Equal Partnership in Marriage

When addressing the issue of partnership in marriage, family scholars use the concept of relationship power, usually defined as the capacity to influence one's spouse (Gray-Little & Burks, 1983). In a marital relationship that is established on principles of partnership, both partners are able to mutually influence each other. A male-dominated relationship, on the other hand, is characterized by the husband having more influence in the relationship than the wife. A female-dominated relationship occurs when the wife has more influence than the husband.

Historically, most marriages were male-dominated. Women had few rights in society, and it was assumed that the husband had the right to exercise influence over his wife. Most people believed that part of the husband's role was to make important decisions in the family (Cott, 2000). As he often does, Satan took the divine

doctrine of the patriarchal order, which honors both men and women as equal partners, and twisted it so that it was used as a rationalization to oppress women, both in society and marriage. Thus, for most of human history, women lived in a fallen patriarchal society that subordinated them to men. Unfortunately this remains true for many today. The fallen patriarchal society was the prevailing attitude and norm until about 50 years ago, when societal changes in many nations began to impact the traditional power structure of marriages. The modern women's movement, which began in the 1960s and gained considerable momentum in the 1970s, had a major influence on the role of women in society as well as in marriage. This movement motivated many people to consciously question the justification for placing women in a subordinate role (Amato, Booth, Johnson, & Rogers, 2007). Outgrowths of the women's movement were the abilities of women to attain greater education and to work in a wider range of professions and occupations. As women became better educated, they were less willing to accept subordinated positions in their marital relationships. In addition, as women were able to work in more prestigious and higher-paying jobs, they were less dependent upon men for their financial well-being. Hence, women became less tolerant of male-dominated relationships, and they had the financial resources to leave relationships that were oppressive.

Societal attitudes about the power structure of marriage have continued to change over time, and today the majority of men and women in Western cultures believe that marriages should be characterized as a partnership, with both spouses having equal influence in the relationship (Thornton & Young-DeMarco, 2001). Even in the last few decades, there has been an increase in the proportion of U.S. marriages that are characterized as equal partnerships. A national study in the United States found the percentage of men who reported that they shared decision-making equally with their wives increased from 51 percent in 1980 to 63 percent in 2000. In the same study, 47 percent of women in 1980 reported that decision-making was equally shared in their relationship, while 64 percent reported equality in 2000 (Amato et al., 2007). And among those 36 percent who reported that decision-making was not shared, 20 percent of women reported that they more frequently had the final say, while 16 percent reported that their husbands more frequently had the final say.

Benefits of Equal Partnership

Research has demonstrated that couples who have an equal partnership have happier relationships, better individual well-being, more effective parenting practices, and better- functioning children. Researchers have consistently found that couples who share power are more satisfied and have better overall marital quality than couples where one spouse dominates (Gray-Little & Burks, 1983). An important reason for equal partners having greater satisfaction is that they have less negative interaction and more positive interaction in their relationship (Gray-Little, Baucom, & Hamby, 1996). In addition, couples that are equal partners are significantly less likely to experience verbal aggression and physical violence (Sagrestano, Heavey, & Christensen, 1999). Moreover, there is evidence that equal partners are more satisfied with the quality of the physical intimacy in their relationship (Brezsnyak & Whisman, 2004).

Research also indicates that the personal well-being of spouses is greatest in equal partnerships. There is substantial evidence that spouses who feel that they lack influence in their relationship—those who don't have a voice—are more likely to experience symptoms of depression (Halloran, 1998). This is especially true among women (Byrne & Carr, 2000).

Equal partners are generally better parents. Parents with less relationship equality are less likely to work together as a team in parenting their children (Hughes, Gordon, & Gaertner, 2004). They are less likely to support each other and form a united front when disciplining their children. They are more likely to triangulate their children, which entails bringing one or more children into the parent's struggles and having the children take sides (Lindahl, Malik, Kaczynski, & Simons, 2004). With research indicating that couples who have unequal partnerships have more stressful marriages and are less effective parents, it is not surprising that children who grow up in homes where the parents have an unequal relationship are at higher risk for depression, anxiety, drug abuse, and delinquency (Lindahl et al., 2004).

Assessing Equal Partnership

As we recognize the importance of equality in marital relationships, it is useful to be able to assess the balance of power in relationships. When assessing equality in a marital relationship, scholars have differentiated between *power processes* and *power outcomes* (Cromwell & Olson,

1975). Power processes are the patterns of interaction among couples, the communication techniques that they use with each other when they are discussing decisions to be made (Babcock, Waltz, Jacobson, & Gottman, 1993). These techniques include their level of assertiveness, listening to their spouse's point of view, domination, and control. A scale was recently developed to assess the degree to which a person perceives that his or her spouse tries to dominate the process of decision-making (Miller, Day, & Bogue, 2008; see Box 4.1). Notice that the statements refer to assessment of the spouse's behavior. That

---

BOX 4.1. ASSESSING POWER IN RELATIONSHIPS

Power Processes Scale

1. My partner tends to discount my opinion.
2. My partner does not listen to me.
3. When I want to talk about a problem in our relationship, my partner often refuses to talk with me about it.
4. My partner tends to dominate our conversations.
5. When we do not agree on an issue, my partner gives me the cold shoulder.
6. I do not feel free to express my opinion about issues in our relationship.
7. My partner makes decisions that affect our family without talking to me first.
8. My partner and I do not talk about problems until we both agree on a solution.
9. I feel like my partner tries to control me.

Power Outcomes Scale

1. When it comes to money, my partner's opinion usually wins out.
2. When it comes to children, my partner's opinion usually wins out.
3. It often seems my partner can get away with things in our relationship that I can never get away with.
4. I have no choice but to do what my partner wants.
5. My partner has more influence in our relationship than I do.
6. When disagreements arise in our relationship, my partner's opinion usually wins out.

is because family scholars have learned that people tend to give more honest answers when they are reporting on someone else's behavior rather than their own. We are often unaware of some of our own behavior and we often minimize our weaknesses. On the other hand, we are generally very aware of others' behavior and are quick to recognize their weaknesses. Agreeing with these statements indicates that a marriage (or dating relationship) is characterized by an imbalance of relationship power. Disagreement with these statements indicates an equal partnership in terms of power processes.

Power outcomes refer to which spouse typically makes the final decision when there are differing opinions between the spouses (Babcock et al., 1993). When there is a disagreement, who "wins"? Which spouse usually has the final say? In an equal partnership, spouses continue to discuss the issue and negotiate until they agree on a decision. They both have veto power, meaning that both have to agree on the decision. In an unequal relationship, on the other hand, one partner tends to have the final say and can make decisions without the spouse's consent or agreement. A power outcomes scale has been developed that assesses the distribution of power between spouses (Miller et al., 2008). Agreeing with the statements suggests an unequal relationship, while disagreeing with the statements indicates an equal partnership. Readers may want to use these scales to assess their own relationships.

Conclusions

Our heavenly parents wish us joy in our journey of becoming as they are. One of the most precious wellsprings of that joy is a sincerely equal partnership between husband and wife. As we have seen, the family proclamation's exhortation to equal partnership in marriage does not mean that husband and wife are identical, but it does mean that in a very real and meaningful sense they must stand as equals before each other to find the joy that is their heritage in marriage. For Latter-day Saints, equal partnership in marriage is a commandment, not an alternative lifestyle. The reason is simple: men and women are that they might have joy! (2 Nephi 2:25). Recent social science research findings confirm that better physical and emotional health, better marital relationships, and better parenting and outcomes for children are the fruits of equal partnership in marriage.

Valerie M. Hudson *is professor of political science at Brigham Young University. She and her husband, David, are the parents of eight children.* **Richard B Miller** *is professor and director of the School of Family Life at Brigham Young University. He and his wife, Mary, are the parents of six children.*

References

Amato, P. R., Booth, A., Johnson, D. R., & Rogers, S. J. (2007). *Alone together: How marriage in America is changing.* Cambridge, MA: Harvard University Press.

Ashton, M. J. (1992). *One for the money: Guide to family finance.* Salt Lake City: The Church of Jesus Christ of Latter-day Saints.

Babcock, J. C., Waltz, J., Jacobson, N. S., & Gottman, J. M. (1993). Power and violence: The relation between communication patterns, power discrepancies, and domestic violence. *Journal of Consulting and Clinical Psychology, 61,* 40–50.

Ballard, M. R. (2006, March). The sacred responsibilities of parenthood. *Ensign, 36,* 26–33.

Benson, E. T. (1985, August). What I hope you will teach your children about the temple. *Ensign, 15,* 6–10.

Brezsnyak, M., & Whisman, M. A. (2004). Sexual desire and relationship functioning: The effects of marital satisfaction and power. *Journal of Sex and Marital Therapy, 30,* 199–217.

Byrne, M., & Carr, A. (2000). Depression and power in marriage. *Journal of Family Therapy, 22,* 408–427.

Cott, N. F. (2000). *Public vows: A history of marriage and the nation.* Cambridge, MA: Harvard University Press.

Cromwell, R. E., & Olson, D. H. (1975). *Power in families.* New York: John Wiley & Sons.

Faust, J. E. (1996, May). The prophetic voice. *Ensign, 26,* 4–6.

Fowers, B. J. (2000). *Beyond the myth of marital happiness: How embracing the virtues of loyalty, generosity, justice, and courage can strengthen your relationship.* San Francisco, CA: Jossey-Bass.

Gilliland, T., Hawkins, A. J., Christiaens, G., Carroll, J. S., & Fowers, B. J. (2002). *Marriage Moments: Strengthening your marriage as you become parents.* Provo, UT: Family Life Education Institute. Retrieved from http://www.marriagemoments.org/index.php?s= content&p=fairness

Gottman, J. M., & Silver, N. (1999). *The seven principles for making marriage work*. New York: Crown Publishers.

Gray-Little, B., & Burks, N. (1983). Power and satisfaction in marriage: A review and critique. *Psychological Bulletin, 93*, 513–538.

Gray-Little, B., Baucom, D. H., & Hamby, S. L. (1996). Marital power, marital adjustment, and therapy outcome. *Journal of Family Psychology, 10*, 292–303.

Hafen, B. C., & Hafen, M. K. (2007, August). Crossing thresholds and becoming equal partners. *Ensign, 37*, 24–29.

Halloran, E. C. (1998). The role of marital power in depression and marital distress. *The American Journal of Family Therapy, 26*, 3–14.

Hinckley, G. B. (2004, November). The women in our lives. *Ensign, 34*, 82–85.

Hughes, F. M., Gordon, K. C., & Gaertner, L. (2004). Predicting spouses' perceptions of their parenting alliance. *Journal of Marriage and Family, 66*, 506–514.

Hunter, H. W. (1994, November). Being a righteous husband and father. *Ensign, 24*, 49–51.

Kimball, S. W. (1976, September 7). Marriage and divorce. BYU Devotional Address. Retrieved from http://speeches.byu.edu/reader/reader.php?id=6136&x=61&y=3

Lindahl, K. M., Malik, N. M., Kaczynski, K., & Simons, J. S. (2004). Couple power dynamics, systemic family functioning, and child adjustment: A test of a mediational model in a multiethnic sample. *Development and Psychopathology, 16*, 609–630.

Markman, H. J., Stanley, S. M., & Blumberg, S. L. (2010). *Fighting for your marriage*. (3rd ed.). San Francisco, CA: Jossey-Bass, 333–336.

Miller, R. B., Day, R., & Bogue, A. (2008, October). The development of a measure of couples relationship power. Poster presented at the annual conference of the American Association for Marriage and Family Therapy, Memphis, TN.

Oaks, D. H. (1993, November). The great plan of happiness. *Ensign, 23*, 72–75.

Packer, B. K. (1989, July). A tribute to women. *Ensign, 19*, 72–75.

Packer, B. K. (1998, May). The Relief Society. *Ensign, 28*, 72–74.

Perry, L. T. (2004, May). Fatherhood, an eternal calling. *Ensign 34*, 69–72.

Sagrestano, L. M., Heavey, C. L., & Christensen, A. (1999). Perceived power and physical violence in marital conflict. *Journal of Social Issues, 55*, 65–79.

Scott, R. G. (2008, November). Honor the priesthood and use it well. *Ensign, 38*, 44–47.

Thornton, A., & Young-DeMarco, L. (2001). Four decades of trends in attitudes toward family issues in the United States: The 1960s through the 1990s. *Journal of Marriage and Family, 63*, 1009–1037.

Tingey, E. C. (2008, January 13). The simple truths from heaven—the Lord's pattern. CES fireside for young adults, Brigham Young University. Retrieved from http://lds.org/library/display/0,4945,538-1-4399-1,00.html

Wirthlin, J. B. (2008, May). Concern for the one. *Ensign, 38*, 17–20.

Young, S. (Ed.). (1993). *An anthology of sacred texts by and about women*. New York: Crossroad.

BOX 4.2: ACHIEVING AN EQUAL PARTNERSHIP IN MARRIAGE
Courtney D. Dixon

As I neared the end of my undergraduate career, I reflected on the value of my degree in the School of Family Life. One thing I learned was the importance of prevention in striving for healthy family relationships. Applying correct principles and effective practices before marriage and during the early years of married life is by far preferable to mending a broken marriage down the road. As a student assisting in the editing of this textbook, I was intrigued by what I learned from reading drafts of the equal partnership chapter. This fascination became a motivation for me to interview two professors in the School of Family Life and research how to create an equal partnership. From that research sprang this essay, which will outline concrete ways couples can achieve an equal partnership, drawing on both spiritual and secular ideas.

Marry Your Equal
Marrying your equal does not mean finding a perfect match or a soul mate. President Spencer W. Kimball (1976, p. 146) declared, "'Soul mates' are fiction and an illusion." Yet Latter-day Saint Church leaders urge members of the Church to exercise great care in choosing a spouse. Specifically, President Kimball said that spouses should be selected who have "common backgrounds, common ideals and standards, common beliefs, hopes, and objectives" (Kimball, 1976, p. 143). Being similar on these fundamental levels is essential to forming an equal partnership. However, it is not enough to have the same beliefs if those beliefs are contrary to the patterns of righteousness. Equal partnership can only be established where there is no hierarchy (of gender or other factors) and where self-aggrandizement gives way to charity.

The Role of Expectations in Establishing an Equal Partnership
Although equal partnerships must be founded on the principles of righteousness, the specific practices of equal partnership are not universal but are unique to each person and couple. There are many "right" ways to do things, but when there is a discrepancy between the expectations of husband and wife, a sense of inequality in the relationship may exist. For example, in regard to decision-making, a husband might expect that he should manage all the financial decisions unilaterally. But Elder Marvin J. Ashton (1992) counseled against this. He suggests that "control of the money by one spouse as a source of power and authority causes inequality in the marriage" (p. 3). Furthermore, "if a marriage partner voluntarily removes himself or herself entirely from family financial management, that is an abdication of necessary responsibility" (p. 3). Similarly, a wife might expect that she should make all of the decisions regarding the children or her husband might passively abdicate his mutual obligation on child rearing matters.

As couples determine what constitutes an equal partnership, they must depend on correct principles as well as be sensitive to the personalities and backgrounds of each spouse. These differing views and backgrounds need to be understood so that a unified view may emerge. Marriage researchers Markman, Stanley, and Blumberg (2010) provide some guidelines to help couples overcome misaligned expectations that may impede the formation of an equal partnership, including: "(1) being *aware* of what you expect; (2) being *reasonable* in what you expect; and (3) being *clear* about what you expect" (p. 333).

Be aware of what you expect. Individuals cannot communicate expectations they do not realize they have. Many expectations are so deeply imbedded in us that we are unconscious of them. Markman, Stanley, and Blumberg (2010) suggest that feelings of disappointment mean an expectation has not been met. Recognizing areas of disappointment is the first step to helping couples address and resolve problems in positive, constructive ways.

Be reasonable in what you expect. Reasonable expectations are more likely to be fulfilled. Scholars suggest varying ways to assess whether or not expectations are reasonable. The noted marriage researcher and therapist John Gottman provides a list for couples to work through to determine who presently fulfills which tasks and who would ideally complete the tasks (Gottman & Silver, 1999, pp. 207–210). However, although it may be typical and even healthy for partners to reflect on and reassess the equity in their relationship, when they keep meticulous track records, a sense of inequality can easily result. Feelings of inequality will likely lead to resentment and conflict. One group of scholar-practitioners warns against such scorekeeping:

> If we get too caught up in our rights, prerogatives, and happiness as individuals, we will be tempted to practice a kind of "grocery-list justice": we mentally or even physically list everything that has to be done to run a household and try to divide it right down the middle. This approach to fairness tends to divide spouses rather than unite them, because it's virtually impossible to divide things evenly (Gilliland, Hawkins, Christiaens, Carroll, & Fowers, 2002, p. 26).

If one spouse expects perfection, the other may feel discouraged by an unrealistic ideal. Partners must therefore temper their expectations so they are reasonable and achievable.

Be clear about what you expect. Expectations are not likely to be met unless they are properly communicated. It is neither fair nor effective for one spouse to hope that the other will read his or her mind and intuitively perceive what is desired. When couples are clear about their expectations early on in the relationship, many misunderstandings, hurt feelings, and conflicts can be prevented. Ideally, the conversations regarding task distribution arise before marriage—generating a greater understanding of views, backgrounds, and expectations. With this communication in place early in the relationship, couples can come to an agreement on what equity will look like in their conjugal family. Couples may decide to adopt certain ways of doing things from each of their families of origin or may decide to establish new patterns and traditions, or both. As both partners contribute to the decision and feel that their own interests are understood, couples will be more prepared to set off on a course toward equal partnership.

Help with Complementary Responsibilities

A narrow and worldly view of equality is that spousal responsibilities are indistinguishable and the time allotted to these responsibilities is comparable. But this rigid view of equality differs from the Lord's perspective. As outlined in the proclamation, equal partnership means each person fills her or his special responsibilities as a mother or father, while also supporting and assisting each other in those divine duties.

Elder M. Russell Ballard (2006, p. 30) suggests that "on a day-to-day basis, fathers can and should help with the essential nurturing and bonding associated with feeding, playing, storytelling, loving, and all the rest of the activities that make up family life." Wives can assist their husbands in the provider role by being mindful of family finances. Wives are instructed to "recognize the difference between basic necessities and material wants, [which will] lessen family financial burdens" (Ballard, 2006, p. 31). As wives are careful with the expenditure of family funds, the money earned by their husbands will stretch further and both partners will be united in striving for financial stability. In addition, wives may be able to contribute to family finances, if needed, in ways that do not unduly interfere with their primary responsibility to nurture their children.

Do Your Best

Patience is vital, however. Fowers (2000) advocates flexible fairness by saying that partners "will contribute to their marriages in different ways and in differing degrees and that this balance will fluctuate over time" (p. 189). He further posits that flexible fairness takes shape when both husband and wife do their best and trust that the spouse is doing his or her best.

The Savior's teaching regarding the widow's mite (Mark 12:41–44) suggests that the Lord has a more sophisticated scale of equality. A spouse may not have a lot to give in a particular area or at a particular time. However, what matters most, rather than the precise quantity given, is that both parties are doing their best. As both spouses put in their full effort, are understanding of shortcomings, and are mutually supportive, they walk the path of equal partnership. Moreover, doing all that you can means not being complacent, self-satisfied, or idle. "Equal partnerships are not made in heaven—*they are made on earth,* one choice at a time, one conversation at a time . . . and getting there is hard work" (Hafen & Hafen, 2007, p. 28, italics in original).

Conclusion

For individuals such as myself who are not yet married, equal partnership begins by first selecting a mate who is equal on fundamental levels, then discussing backgrounds, beliefs, and expectations regarding roles and responsibilities. Those who are already married will inevitably discover that they are different in more ways than they realized on their wedding day. However, despite differences, equal partnership is an achievable ideal. As couples recognize and respect each other's contribution in the relationship, discuss their expectations, fulfill their complementary responsibilities and assist their spouses with theirs, and selflessly give their all, they will be able to enjoy a sense of unity and fulfillment in their relationship. Moreover, they will strengthen their testimonies of the reality that all are necessary and equal in the Lord's eyes and that "neither is the man without the woman, neither the woman without the man, in the Lord" (1 Corinthians 11:11).

Courtney D. Dixon recently graduated from Brigham Young University in the School of Family Life. She served as a student editor for Successful Marriages and Families.

CHAPTER 5

Marital Sexuality and Fertility

James M. Harper and Leslie Feinauer

We declare that God's commandment for His children to multiply and replenish the earth remains in force. We further declare that God has commanded that the sacred powers of procreation are to be employed only between man and woman, lawfully wedded as husband and wife. We declare the means by which mortal life is created to be divinely appointed.

A 13-YEAR-OLD DAUGHTER AND HER MOTHER WERE lying comfortably beside each other as the mother read aloud from a book. At a pause in the story, the daughter asked her mother, "Mom, is sex better than candy?" While most mothers might be taken aback by such a question unrelated to the story, this mother, without any hesitation, responded, "Oh yes, dear, with your husband in an eternal marriage, sex is far better than candy."

As an adult woman, this daughter related that her mother's answer had significant impact in shaping her attitudes about marriage and sexuality. Her mother conveyed at least three important attitudes in her answer: first, that a sexual relationship should occur in the proper context of marriage; second, that in this proper context, sex brings joy; and third, that it is okay to talk about sex with a parent.

A loving Heavenly Father reserved something divine, the physical union between husband and wife, for the heart of marriage. In the intimate, personal, and often vulnerable space of marriage, God drew bounds around sacred physical union as something to be experienced with each other as husband and wife. Sex within marriage potentially teaches Heavenly Father's deepest truths about oneness. In this sense, sex within marriage is sanctified and serves great spiritual and temporal purposes, but as with most divine opportunities, much depends on the attitudes, timing, and behaviors of the individuals involved.

LDS and Other Religions' Doctrines on the Purposes of Marital Sexuality

Marital sexuality serves several purposes for both husband and wife as individuals as well as for the couple relationship. These purposes include becoming one, connecting with God, strengthening the emotional and spiritual bonds in marriage, avoiding temptation, and continuing the generational chain by bringing children into a family. These purposes will now be explored in greater detail.

Becoming one. The first purpose, becoming one, while a doctrinal foundation of Christian belief, is only given lip service by many couples—the sexual aspect of their relationship is not always acknowledged. Elder David A. Bednar (2006, p. 83) taught, "The natures of male and female spirits complete and perfect each other, and therefore men and women are intended to progress together toward exaltation." Rabbi Shuley Boteach (1999, p. 55) identified physical intimacy of a husband and wife as something that symbolizes the tie between God and all of His creations. He stated that it is because of this symbolism "that Judaism has always identified sex as the most holy of all human endeavors." This belief that marital sexual expression serves a purpose of oneness is also shared by other religions. Representing a Latter-day Saint view of marital sexual intimacy and becoming one, Elder Jeffrey R. Holland (2001, pp. 17–18) said that sexual union is a "welding . . . in matrimony . . . [a] physical blending [symbolic of a] larger, more complete union of eternal purpose and promise . . . a symbol of total union . . . of their hearts, their hopes, their lives, their love, their family, their future, their everything."

H. B. Yusuf (2005, p. 3), speaking on the unity in marital intimacy, stated that in Islam, "the union of the man and his wife is traced to a common origin of equality because both are created from a single soul." The

Qur'an, the Islamic holy book, proclaims, "It is He who created you from a single soul and therefrom did he make his mate, that he might dwell in tranquility with her," meaning that marital sexual union helps build tranquil unity between spouses (Al A'raf sura 7:189). Gardner (2002, p. 15), a Christian author, summed up this purpose when he stated:

> Godly sex is so much more . . . than merely a physical act; it has a spiritual component. . . [A] deeper connection [within sexual relations] goes far beyond simply understanding how to overcome sexual dysfunction. . . . It goes way beyond technique and physique. This deeper dimension is experienced when we move past pleasure as a goal and instead seek intimate connection—not just with our bodies but also with our souls.

Connection with God. A second purpose of marital sexual intimacy, connection with God, is described again by representatives of various religious views. Latter-day Saint writers and other Christians describe the sexual union of husband and wife as a sacrament. Gardner (2002, p. 5) described sex in marriage as "an act of worship, a sacrament of marriage that invites and welcomes the very presence of God." Elder Holland (2001, pp. 27, 29) described this purpose of marital sexuality:

> Sexual intimacy is . . . symbolic of a union between mortals and deity, between otherwise ordinary and fallible humans uniting for a rare and special moment with God himself and all the powers by which he gives life in this wide universe of ours. . . . Indeed, if our definition of sacrament is that act of claiming, sharing, and exercising God's own inestimable power, then I know of virtually no other divine privilege so routinely given to us all—women or men, ordained or unordained, Latter-day Saint or non-Latter-day Saint—than the miraculous and majestic power of transmitting life, the unspeakable, unfathomable, unbroken power of procreation.

Strengthening bonds. The third purpose, strengthening emotional and spiritual bonds in marriage, is likewise explained in various religious views around the world. President Spencer W. Kimball taught that the intimacy

of sexual relations in marriage is a way of expressing love for one's partner in marriage (Kimball, E. L., 1982). He said, "There is nothing unholy or degrading about sexuality in itself, for by that means men and women join . . . in an expression of love" (p. 311). Husbands and wives can learn to share a view that marital sexual expression is designed to protect and strengthen emotional bonds, which in turn will influence marital sexuality and satisfaction.

From an Islamic point of view, the purpose of sexual intimacy is for the mutual pleasure and bonding of a wife to her husband. In Islam, M. Holland (1998) explained that one of the benefits of marriage is to obtain peace of mind. He goes on to state that the pleasure derived from sexual intercourse between a husband and wife is an example of happiness in the afterlife. The Qur'an states, "And among His signs is this, that He created for you mates from among yourselves, that you may dwell in tranquility with them, and He has put love and mercy between your (hearts)" (Qur'an 30:21).

Procreation. The last purpose of marital physical intimacy, procreation and continuing of the generations, is emphasized not only by the Latter-day Saint faith but also by numerous other religions around the world. According to Ghazzali (translated by Fazlul-Karim, 1996, pp. 17–18), an imam and author in the Islamic faith, the main purpose of marriage is to beget children. He further states, "The [wife's] uterus is the fertile field and both the male and female organs are the tools for cultivation. He [God] also created sexual passion in both the male and female for the bearing of children through the use of these organs."

Christianity, Judaism, and Islam point to the scriptural reference when God blessed Adam and Eve and told them, "Be fruitful, and multiply, and replenish the earth" (Genesis 1:28). Likewise, latter-day scripture confirms God's injunction to "multiply" (Moses 2:28), that "the Gods" caused men and women to be fruitful in the context of lawful marriage, and They blessed marriage and gave it to Adam and Eve to be holy as the gateway of premortal spirits into this phase of their eternal progression (see Abraham 4:27–28). For the continuation of generations, the marital act of procreation is the foundation of the bridge between ancestors and progenitors. For those married couples unable to have children, the promise of increase as part of the Abrahamic covenant is an eternal promise (Nelson, 1995), and of course, for those who choose to adopt, the sealing power will achieve this same purpose as though the adoptive parents had borne the child biologically.

In the plan of happiness, an important doctrine of the Latter-day Saint faith that is also referred to as the plan of salvation, individuals must be born into this world to receive a body, and receiving a physical body is an important step in the eternal progression of women and men. Lawful marriage between a man and a woman is the authorized channel through which premortal spirits enter this earthly experience (Bednar, 2006). According to President Spencer W. Kimball (Kimball, E. L., 1982, p. 311),

> The union of the sexes, husband and wife (and only husband and wife), was for the principal purpose of bringing children into the world. . . . We know of no directive from the Lord that proper sex experienced between husbands and wives need be limited totally to the procreation effort, but we find much evidence from Adam until now that no provision was ever made by the Lord for indiscriminate sex.

In summary, the doctrinal views of the Latter-day Saint Church as well as many major religions of the world identify several purposes of marital sexuality: becoming one, connecting with God, strengthening the bonds of marriage, and bringing children into a family. Unfortunately, couples often understand only one or two of these purposes and ignore the rest. The sex-saturated culture so prevalent in modernized societies worships bodies and only focuses on the erotic purpose of sex, which emphasizes individual pleasure. Only focusing on this purpose of marital sexuality leads to a focus on "technique" to create the greatest physical pleasure. Gardner (2002, p. 13) agrees that despite more available knowledge of technique, couples are "more sexually empty, more sexually frustrated, and more sexually lost than ever before." Alternatively, some couples may focus on the procreative purpose of their sexual union and forego the divinely appointed purposes of oneness and connection. By seeking to have a balance of all the divine purposes in their sexual relationship, husbands and wives together will experience not just satisfaction but more commitment, relationship growth, and connection with God.

Patterns in Marital Sexuality

One of the most studied aspects of marital sexuality is frequency of intercourse over the life course of the married couple. Numerous research studies (Call, Sprecher, & Schwartz, 1995; McNulty & Fisher, 2008) have shown that the frequency of intercourse declines with age and over the duration of a marriage. Call and colleagues (1995) found that married persons in a national sample reported an average sexual intercourse of 6.3 times per month, which is about 1.5 times per week. Those married couples who were younger than 24 reported an average frequency of 11.7 times per month, which is about 3 times per week. Those older than 75 reported an average frequency of slightly less than once per month. Smith (1994) found that average frequency of intercourse was highest among those married less than three years.

There is a scarcity of studies that have examined marital sexuality in countries other than the United States, let alone a global perspective. Cheung, Wong, Liu, Yip, Fan, and Lam (2008) studied marital sexual satisfaction among 1,124 married couples living in Hong Kong. Married persons under the age of 30 reported average frequency of sexual intercourse of about 6 times per month. In this early married group, 4 percent of married women and 9 percent of married men reported that they had no sexual intercourse during the previous month. Spouses in their thirties reported average frequency of intercourse as about 4.5 times per month, and those in their forties reported frequency as 4 times per month, or about once a week. The majority of couples over the age of 50 reported a frequency of about 2 times per month. Apparently, the trend of intercourse frequency data is similar in Hong Kong and the United States in that early married couples report having sexual intercourse more frequently than longer married couples, and the average frequency of older couples is about 1 to 2 times per month in both countries. Unfortunately, specific studies on sexuality *in marriage* in other countries have not been reported in the literature. What little is reported usually lumps marital sexual behavior with sexual behavior of men and women in general, so it is difficult to determine how marital sexual activity differs.

One surprising finding is the percentage of marriages that are considered nonsexual. In the Hong Kong study, approximately 8 percent of persons under the age of 40 reported having no sex in the previous month.

Approximately 20 percent of married couples in the United States have a nonsexual marriage, meaning that they report having no sexual relationship in the last year (Michael, Gagnon, Laumann, & Kolata, 1994).

In the United States, a good marital sexual relationship accounts for about 15 to 20 percent of the differences in marital satisfaction for both husbands and wives. However, a poor or nonexistent marital sexual relationship plays an inordinately powerful role, accounting for 50 to 70 percent of the differences in marital satisfaction between husbands and wives (McCarthy, 1998, 2003).

Sexual problems are a major cause of divorce in the first two years of marriage. Anticipatory anxiety, awkward and unsuccessful sexual experiences, and a cycle of avoiding sexual interaction contribute to early marital sexual problems (McCarthy, 1998). According to McCarthy (2003), an expert in marital and sex therapy, approximately 1.5 percent of marriages are not consummated in the first year, and husbands and wives typically avoid marital discussions about their sexual interaction when they are having sexual problems. A marriage becomes devitalized if a couple experiences these kinds of problems in the first three years of marriage.

McCarthy and McCarthy (2003) listed attitudes that help promote positive marital sexuality as including the beliefs that:

1. Sexual interaction is a healthy component of marriage that need not be a source of negative feelings or guilt.
2. Married persons deserve to feel good about their bodies and to view sexual expression as a normal, healthy part of their marriage.
3. A primary component of marital sexuality is giving and receiving pleasure-oriented touching in the context of an intimate, committed, and divinely supported relationship. As such, it requires relaxation and focus on the other person as well as on one's own pleasure.
4. Sexuality should be expressed in a way that enhances your intimate, marital relationship and bonds you together.
5. Couples should strive to create a "we" relationship, where both partners' sharing and pleasure is important as opposed to one person individually focused on what she or he will get out of the experience.

In a marriage, not all affectionate touching should proceed to sexual intercourse. Couples should be physically affectionate with each other separate and apart from sexual interaction. If a wife begins to feel that physical touch from her husband is always a prelude to sexual interaction ending in intercourse, she will learn over time to avoid any kind of touching when she does not desire to be sexual. This affects couple attachment and interferes with good couple bonding, which is partly built on marital affection. Holding hands, hugging, kissing, and cuddling should all be part of a marital relationship—without these shared behaviors always leading to sexual interaction.

A developmental task of early marriage is to make a transition from romantic love to an emotionally intimate, interactive sexual style (McCarthy & McCarthy, 2009). A good prescription for marital sexuality is integrating emotional closeness, pleasuring, excitement or eroticism, and spirituality. One way of thinking about these different dimensions of sexual experience in marriage is to consider recent neuroscience advances. Fisher (2004) studied the brain activity of both men and women in love and discovered that initial attraction and romance involve the brain releasing dopamine, a neurotransmitter related to feeling elated and ecstatic, part of the passion dimension of sexuality. The erotic dimension of marital sexuality is associated with the hormones testosterone and estrogen in both men and women. The romantic dimension not only involves dopamine but norepinephrine and serotonin as well. The emotional closeness dimension involves the release of the hormones oxytocin and vasopressin. If any of these dimensions of sexual experience are missing in the interaction of husbands and wives, then they are likely also missing the release of the associated chemicals in their brains.

Over time, successful marriages shift from romanticism as a time-limited binding force to companionship and attachment as a stable, enduring force (Schnarch, 2009). President Spencer W. Kimball (The Church of Jesus Christ of Latter-day Saints, 2006, pp. 191) observed,

> We need an unspoiled companion who will not count our wrinkles, remember our stupidities nor remember our weaknesses; . . .we need a loving companion with whom we have suffered and wept and prayed and worshipped; one with whom we

have suffered sorrow and disappointments, one who loves us for what we are or intend to be rather than what we appear to be in our gilded shell.

Such a positive perspective on the part of a spouse can contribute to the making of a stable, enduring relationship.

Realistic expectations that are mutually acceptable and shared between partners help establish a good foundation. Some research findings may help couples develop realistic expectations of their sexual relationship. Among happily married couples who report they are highly satisfied with their sexual relationship, slightly less than half of their experiences involve equal desire, arousal, orgasm, and satisfaction (Frank, Anderson, & Rubinstein, 1978). According to Schnarch (2009), one fact about sexual desire that transcends all relationships is that husbands' and wives' sexual desire do not usually vary together. He states that "there is *always* a low desire partner, just as there is *always* a high desire partner— and there is one of each in *every* relationship" (p. 9, italics in original). According to Schnarch, even when both want the same thing, one will want it more than the other. Being the low desire partner does not mean that sexual desire is low in general. Rather, it means that sexual desire is lower than a partner's desire at most times. While a husband and wife may change these roles from time to time, the low desire partner typically controls the frequency of their sexual interaction.

The "good enough sex" approach. The fact that husbands and wives are not usually at the same level in terms of desire, arousal, or satisfaction is related to what McCarthy and Metz (2008; Metz & McCarthy, 2007) have coined "good enough sex" for marriage. Relying on a career of more than forty years of counseling couples with sexual problems, McCarthy argues that equal desire, arousal, and satisfaction are unrealistic expectations and will interfere with positive marital sexuality (2003).

The central aim of the "good enough sex" approach for marriage is that husband and wife become emotionally close, erotic friends, who can accept marital sexuality as a variable and flexible experience and not be anxious when sexual interaction does not flow to intercourse. In this approach, desire and satisfaction are far more important than arousal and orgasm. In this sense, marital sex and pleasure belong together, but marital

sex combined with expectations that the experience will always be 100 percent satisfactory results in unrealistic demands of marriage. In the "good enough" approach, the couple is an "intimate team" who work together to create relaxation for both, which is a crucial foundation for pleasure and sexual function. Both spouses value abandoning a goal of "perfect performance," which helps them overcome fears and pressures associated with sexual performance. Metz and McCarthy (2007) encourage married couples to adopt the "85 percent approach." Research (Laumann, Paik, & Rosen, 1999; Laumann, Gagnon, Michael, & Michaels, 1994) shows that well-functioning, satisfied couples experience their sexual relationship as very good about 20 to 25 percent of the time, good about 40 to 60 percent of the time, fair but unremarkable about 20 to 25 percent of the time, and dissatisfying or dysfunctional 5 to 15 percent of the time. A realistic expectation, then, is that marital sexual experience for both husbands and wives will be good to very good about 60 to 85 percent of the time. This expectation helps partners accept each other, allows them to avoid fear and panic when a problem occurs, and prevents sexual problems associated with aging. The "good enough" approach promotes sex in marriage as playful and even spiritual and also encourages the belief that marital sexuality grows and evolves throughout life. In contrast, the "always great" approach often portrayed by media and culture results in disappointment, as experiences fail to match high expectations.

Sexual desire may present challenges to some couples, including Latter-day Saint married couples. Both partners may understand that sexual interaction is expected in marriage, but they both might experience inhibitions early in marriage due to poor body image, reluctance to initiate sexual interaction with their spouse, fear of relaxing and letting go with the spouse present, embarrassment with nudity in front of their partner, awkwardness in talking about sex with each other, and embarrassment in seeking information (McCarthy & McCarthy, 2003). These inhibitions are counter to the idea that married partners need to be honest, disclose deep feelings and experiences, and create safety for one another that leads to optimal relaxation during marital sexual interaction. The antidote to all of these inhibitions is being able to talk about them together, and in the moments of sexual interaction to be able to disclose what is happening rather than closing down emotionally and backing out of sexual interaction, which will likely be experienced as rejection by a partner. Some suggestions for talking about sex include finding a convenient time, making sure that both partners have opportunity to talk about what they like and what they don't like, making sure that statements aren't blaming but stated in terms of wants. For example, a wife might say to her husband, "I want us to spend more time leading up to intercourse" rather than, "You always move too quickly to intercourse."

Who initiates sexual interaction in marriage is often a source of conflict for married couples. A good attitude to develop about this is that both husband and wife should feel free to initiate sexual sharing with each other. The "good enough" approach would guide couples to expect that the initiation aspect of a couple's sexual relationship may vary from time to time, but it also encourages couples to work together to share initiation so that one partner does not feel like he or she is always initiating and the other partner is always accepting or rejecting. Rigid patterns where husbands are always the initiator often develop into desire problems. Husbands and wives need to work together to achieve a pattern of equal participation in order to avoid getting into rigid patterns of high-desire partner versus low-desire partner. Both spouses need to value and set aside time for physical intimacy, engage in affectionate touching, and establish a rhythm of sexual sharing (McCarthy, 1998).

Sexual problems that can occur early in marriage include "honeymoon cystitis," a female bladder infection that is associated with sexual intercourse and premature ejaculation, a problem that some men experience early in marriage. Of course, more serious sexual problems can arise. When any sexual dysfunctions occur, a couple should seriously consider seeking reliable information and possibly professional help. While such problems are often embarrassing to a couple, early intervention usually alleviates the problem quickly, whereas waiting may make it more difficult to resolve.

Sex is one of the areas married couples may argue about (Chethik, 2006). Usually such arguments occur when one person is focused on his or her personal needs and desires rather than the couple working together to achieve the attitudes and practices of the "good enough sex" approach for marriage. Disagreements about frequency of sexual intercourse typically involve men wanting to have sex more frequently than their wives.

When initiation of sex in marriage seems compulsive and there is a large discrepancy in desire between a husband and wife, working on emotional bonding and disclosure of vulnerable feelings often helps reduce the discrepancy in desires. Men who feel inadequate, unwanted, or "bound up with stress" are likely to pursue sex as a way of managing these feelings. Sharing such feelings with a spouse often helps relieve the feelings and the associated sexual tension. On the other hand, a married partner who has little or no desire to have sex should also work with her or his spouse to determine if they can together, as intimate friends, build a bridge to desire for the lower desire spouse.

Conflict between couples about sexual practices usually creates a drain on the vitality of marriage. If a wife is uncomfortable with a sexual practice that her husband is obsessed with, she may shut him out. Such conflicts ignore the multidimensional aspect and purposes of marital sexuality. Rather than focusing on a balance of emotional closeness, eroticism, and spirituality, the person becomes increasingly more focused on the erotic dimension, assuming that the sexual practice would lead to greater sexual satisfaction. The result is disappointing primarily because all of the principles of the "good enough" approach become violated. Sexual practice is not as strongly linked to desire and arousal as to relational dynamics of attachment and mutual closeness. When marital partners can focus on their emotional connection (attachment) and work toward both feeling emotionally close, they will find that their sexual satisfaction increases, whereas being focused only on the eroticism of arousal does not necessarily lead to enduring marital sexual satisfaction. Married couples who frequently experience arguments about practices would be better served by talking together, working toward a mutually acceptable solution, rather than engaging in polarizing conversations that entrench a rigid pursue-withdraw pattern.

In summary, the "good enough sex" approach was developed as a result of research finding that happily married people experience their sexual relationship as good about 60 to 85 percent of the time and that even the happiest married couples' experiences do not fit an "always great" approach. Couples who are flexible enough to adapt their attitudes and expectations to the principles of the "good enough sex" approach will likely experience greater overall marital satisfaction.

The Decision to Bear and Rear Children

Speaking to married couples in our time, President Hinckley (The Church of Jesus Christ of Latter-day Saints, 2004, p. 26) said, "If you are married, you and your spouse should discuss your sacred responsibility to bring children into the world and nurture them in righteousness." For those married couples who are physically able, it is a spiritual obligation as well as a joy with subsequent blessings to bear and rear children. Some married couples will be physically unable to bear children. However, they are still entitled to the blessings and joy of having children through adoption. The Abrahamic blessing of eternal increase is a promise that extends beyond the boundaries of this earth life (Nelson, 1995).

For couples who are able to have children, agency appears to be an important principle in determining when to have children and how many children to have. *The Church Handbook of Instructions* (The Church of Jesus Christ of Latter-day Saints, 2010b, p. 195) states, "The decision as to how many children to have and when to have them is extremely intimate and private and should be left between the couple and the Lord. Church members should not judge one another in this matter." *Private* in this sense means that spouses should be careful in discussing these matters with others. Sometimes it is a temptation to discuss such matters more with a parent, sibling, or friend than with one's partner. This principle implies that family members should not pry, judge, nor interfere in a couple's decisions about timing and the number of children to have.

Elder Dallin H. Oaks (1993, p. 75) counseled:

How many children should a couple have? All they can care for! Of course, to care for children means more than simply giving them life. Children must be loved, nurtured, taught, fed, clothed, housed, and well started in their capacities to be good parents themselves.

Married couples are required to exercise their agency by applying divine principles, considering their own circumstances, and seeking inspiration. In this sense, these sacred decisions about having children occur within the uniqueness of each marriage rather than being guided by precise "yes-and-no" guidelines in scripture or Church handbooks (Ellsworth, 1979, 1992). President Gordon B.

Hinckley (1984, p. 6) said, "The Lord has told us to multiply and replenish the earth that we might have joy in our posterity. . . . But he did not designate the number, nor has the Church. That is a sacred matter left to the couple and the Lord."

Homer Ellsworth (1979, p. 23), an LDS gynecologist, relates a Church president's experience of visiting his daughter after her miscarriage. As a mother of eight children, in her forties, she asked him if she could stop having children now. He replied, "Don't ask me. That decision is between you, your husband, and your Father in Heaven."

What principles can a married couple use to determine when and how many children to have? Ellsworth (1979, 1992) identified principles that will help guide husbands and wives in making this decision. The first principle is to study the matter carefully. The Church (The Church of Jesus Christ of Latter-day Saints, 2004; Hinckley, 1984) teaches that married couples consider the sanctity and meaning of life and the joy that children bring to the home. Husbands and wives might also ponder the plan of salvation and the necessity within the plan for Heavenly Father's spirit children to come to earth to receive bodies. While the world moves in the direction of declining in population by encouraging fewer children (Eberstadt, 2000), married couples in the Church may partake of the privilege of replenishing the earth. These principles provide a gospel foundation and context for studying the matter further. Ellsworth (1979, 1992) suggested an additional principle—that married couples should weigh the consequences of their choices. In this regard, the physical and mental health of mother and father are important considerations for a married couple in deciding when and how many children to have. A couple's capacity to provide basic necessities is another consideration (The Church of Jesus Christ of Latter-day Saints, 2010a). In weighing these matters, Ellsworth (1979, p. 23) suggested that it is important to examine motivations. The measuring stick of "Is it selfish?" causes husbands and wives to consider not only their individual motivations but also their priorities and motivations as a couple. Ellsworth points out that having luxuries is not a legitimate consideration in the context of these principles.

Counseling together is an important principle. In this regard, neither husband nor wife should seek to coerce the other to a particular point of view. Instead they should respectfully and patiently listen and try to understand the principles that underlie differing points of view. If selfishness is kept in check, counseling together should bring couples closer to a mutual decision.

Finally, married couples should seek the inspiration of the Lord throughout their decision-making process. They should seek His help as they study the doctrines and the plan of salvation and consider their circumstances. They should seek His help in counseling together and arriving at a decision.

Implementing principles. How might a couple implement these principles as they determine when and how many children to have? Jonathan and Elizabeth were recently married and were both attending a university. They had discussed the possibility of using contraceptives with a physician prior to getting married and had decided to use birth control. As is true of most college students, they had little money and struggled to make ends meet. They had prayed several times together about their decision to practice birth control and both felt they had spiritual confirmation to do so. After being married for a few months, Elizabeth asked Jonathan what he thought about the commandment to "multiply and replenish the earth." He suggested that they study what the apostles and prophets have said about it during their next family home evening. They continued to counsel together by sharing thoughts about what they were reading and by openly sharing feelings and seeking spiritual guidance. Through this counseling together, they both felt strongly that they should have a child, but Elizabeth felt that she should get pregnant soon and Jonathan felt that they should wait. He was worried about their finances and the fact that they were both in school. Elizabeth felt that it was important for her to listen carefully to all of Jonathan's worries and concerns. This helped him to listen to her feelings as well. They learned that it is important to consider the physical and mental health of both the mother and father, but both of them were healthy. The main consequence they could identify is that they weren't sure how they would be able to afford having a child and whether they could adequately support a baby under their present circumstances. Over the next several weeks, they continued to pray and seek spiritual guidance. In their discussions, they decided to openly express in their prayers their concerns and desires. In his prayers, Jonathan asked

for help in opening any doors he hadn't considered for funding the medical costs of having a baby. He later discovered an insurance company that provided affordable maternity coverage and shared this information with Elizabeth. Up to that time, neither Jonathan nor Elizabeth had talked with their parents about the possibility of having a baby. That was appropriate, since such matters are intimate and private. However, they decided together that they would approach his parents and share their worries about having adequate finances to have a baby. His parents gave them both loving counsel, ending with President Hinckley's statement that the decision is ultimately between them and the Lord. Through this process, which took them several months, Jonathan and Elizabeth studied scriptures and talks by General Authorities, began saving money to have a baby, found affordable maternity insurance, and sought divine inspiration about how soon to stop using contraceptives. With mutual respect, they worked together to make this important decision. They felt it was important not to be selfish in their desires to accumulate possessions, and they turned to the Lord to help them decide when the time was right. When they decided together that it was time, it took a few months for Elizabeth to become pregnant, but they were then blessed with their first child. Couples of childbearing years will be faced numerous times with the question of how many children to have and when or if to add another member to their family.

A different couple, Michael and Raquel, had four children and wanted more. She began having difficulties with varicose veins and developed a blood clot in her leg. She recovered, but her gynecologist later discovered that she also had difficulties with varicosity in the veins surrounding her uterus and ovaries. He told Michael and Raquel that it would be life threatening to her to have another baby and suggested that she have a hysterectomy. She was so distressed that she consulted a second specialist, who said that while a hysterectomy was not necessary, she should not have another child. As this couple counseled together, they decided to consult their bishop in the matter. He lovingly told them that they should take the advice of the physicians seriously and then reminded them that the blessings of the Abrahamic covenant are eternal. Michael and Raquel decided not to have more children and not to have a hysterectomy and then sought confirmation from the

Lord. They received the sweet assurance that they had made the right decision, but then they were faced with how to keep from getting pregnant, since Raquel was still of childbearing age. As should all couples whose decision has been confirmed by the Spirit, they sought competent medical advice on the method of birth control that would be most appropriate for them. As they sought medical input, they continued to counsel together and pray for inspiration and confirmation. They eventually adopted their fifth child and felt their family was complete.

In conclusion, marital sexuality serves many purposes that are part of the divine plan of a loving Heavenly Father. A sexual relationship is symbolic of the total union of husband and wife working together as "we" and "us" rather than individually. Husbands and wives should strive together to develop good attitudes about the sexual aspect of their relationship. One of the important purposes of sexuality in marriage is to express love to each other, "to bind husband and wife together in loyalty, fidelity, consideration, and common purpose" (The Church of Jesus Christ of Latter-day Saints, 2004, p. 26). An added purpose is to provide physical bodies for God's children, which is a sacred matter and should receive serious attention regarding when and how many children to have. Couples who turn to the Lord for spiritual guidance to make proper use of the choices and challenges that come with the wonderful gift of marital sexuality will find comfort and eternal blessings.

James M. Harper is a Zina Young Williams Card professor in the School of Family Life at Brigham Young University. He and his wife, Colleen, are the parents of five children and they have seven grandchildren. Leslie Feinauer *is a professor of marriage and family therapy at Brigham Young University.*

Recommended Books for Married and Engaged Couples about Marital Sexuality

Brotherson, L. M. (2004). *And they were not ashamed: Strengthening marriage through sexual fulfillment.* Boise, ID: Inspire Book.

Lamb, S. E., & Brinley, D. E. (2008). *Between husband and wife: Gospel perspectives on marital intimacy.* Salt Lake City: Covenant Communications.

Stahmann, R. F., Young, W. R., & Grover, J. G. (2004). *Becoming one: Intimacy in marriage.* American Fork, UT: Covenant Communications.

References

Bednar, D. A. (2006, June). Marriage is essential to His eternal plan. *Ensign, 36,* 82–87.

Boteach, S. (1999). *Kosher sex: A recipe for intimacy and passion.* New York: Doubleday.

Call, V., Sprecher, S., & Schwartz, P. (1995). The incidence and frequency of marital sex in a national sample. *Journal of Marriage and the Family, 57,* 639–652.

Chethik, N. (2006). *VoiceMale: What husbands really think about their marriages, wives, sex, housework, and commitment.* New York: Simon & Schuster.

Cheung, M. W.-L., Wong, P. W.-C., Liu, K. Y., Yip, P. S.-F., Fan, S. Y.-S., & Lam, T.-H. (2008). A study of sexual satisfaction and frequency of sex among Hong Kong Chinese couples. *Journal of Sex Research, 45,* 129–139.

The Church of Jesus Christ of Latter-day Saints. (2004). *True to the faith: A gospel reference.* Salt Lake City: Author.

The Church of Jesus Christ of Latter-day Saints. (2006). *Teachings of the Presidents of the Church: Spencer W. Kimball.* Salt Lake City: Author.

The Church of Jesus Christ of Latter-day Saints. (2010a). Birth control. Retrieved from http://lds.org/study/topics/birth-control?lang=eng

The Church of Jesus Christ of Latter-day Saints. (2010b). *Church Handbook of Instructions, Book 1, Stake Presidents and Bishops.* Salt Lake City: The Church of Jesus Christ of Latter-day Saints.

Eberstadt, N. (2000, April). The problem isn't overpopulation and the future may be depopulation. *Marriage and Families,* 9–10.

Ellsworth, H. (1979, August). I have a question: Questions of general gospel interest answered for guidance, not as official statements of Church policy. *Ensign, 9,* 23–25.

Ellsworth, H. (1992). Birth control. In Daniel H. Ludlow (Ed.), *Encyclopedia of Mormonism* (pp. 116–117). New York: Macmillan.

Fazlul-Karim, A. M. (Trans.) (1996). *Imam Gazzali's Ihya Ulum-id-Din: The book of religious learnings.* New Delhi: Islamic Book Services.

Fisher, H. (2004). *Why we love: The nature and chemistry of romantic love.* New York: Henry Holt.

Frank, E., Anderson, C., & Rubinstein, D. (1978). Frequency of sexual dysfunction in "normal" couples. *New England Journal of Medicine, 299,* 111–115.

Gardner, T. A. (2002). *Sacred sex: A spiritual celebration of oneness in marriage.* Colorado Springs, CO: Water Brook Press.

Hinckley, G. B. (1984). *Cornerstones of a happy home* [pamphlet]. Salt Lake City: The Church of Jesus Christ of Latter-day Saints.

Holland, J. R. (2001). *Of souls, symbols, and sacraments.* Salt Lake City: Deseret Book.

Holland, M. (Trans.) (1998). *The proper conduct of marriage in Islam (*Adab an-Nikah*): Book 12 of* Ihya'Ulum al-Din. Hollywood, FL: Al-Baz Publishing.

Kimball, E. L. (Ed.). (1982). *The teachings of Spencer W. Kimball.* Salt Lake City: Bookcraft.

Laumann, E. O., Gagnon, J. H., Michael, R. T., & Michaels, S. (1994). *The social organization of sexuality: Sexual practices in the United States.* University of Chicago Press.

Laumann, E. O., Paik, A., & Rosen, R. C. (1999). Sexual dysfunction in the United States: Prevalence and predictors. *Journal of the American Medical Association, 281,* 537–544.

McCarthy, B. W. (1998). Sex in the first two years of marriage. *Journal of Family Psychotherapy, 9,* 1–11.

McCarthy, B. (2003). Marital sex as it ought to be. *Journal of Family Psychotherapy, 14,* 1–12.

McCarthy, B., & McCarthy, E. (2003). *Rekindling desire: A-step-by-step program to help low-sex and no-sex marriages.* New York: Brunner-Routledge.

McCarthy, B. W., & Metz, M. E. (2008). The "good enough sex" model: A case illustration. *Sexual and Relationship Therapy, 23,* 227–234.

McCarthy, B. W., & McCarthy, E. (2009). *Discovering your couple sexual style: Sharing desire, pleasure, and satisfaction.* New York: Routledge.

McNulty, J. K., & Fisher, T. D. (2008). Gender differences in response to sexual expectancies and changes in sexual frequency: A short-term longitudinal study of sexual satisfaction in newly married couples. *Archives of Sexual Behavior, 37,* 229–240.

Metz, M. E., & McCarthy, B. W. (2007). The "good-enough sex" model for couple sexual satisfaction. *Sexual and Relationship Therapy, 22,* 351–362.

Michael, R. T., Gagnon, J. H., Laumann, E. O., & Kolata, G. (1994). *Sex in America: A definitive survey.* Boston: Little, Brown.

Nelson, R. M. (1995, May). Children of the covenant. *Ensign, 25,* 32–35.

Oaks, D. H. (1993, November). "The great plan of happiness." *Ensign, 23,* 72–75.

Schnarch, D. (2009). *Intimacy and desire: Awaken the passion in your relationship.* New York: Beaufort Books.

Smith, T. W. (1994). *The demography of sexual behavior.* Menlo Park, CA: Kaiser Family Foundation.

Yusuf, H. B. (2005). *Sexuality and the marriage institution in Islam: An appraisal.* Understanding Human Sexuality Seminar Series 4. Lagos, Nigeria: Africa Regional Sexuality Resource Centre.

CHAPTER 6

Honoring Marital Vows with Complete Fidelity

Scott Gardner and Christian Greiner

We further declare that God has commanded that the sacred powers of procreation
are to be employed only between man and woman lawfully wedded as husband and wife.

PRESIDENT EZRA TAFT BENSON ONCE SAID, "THE plaguing sin of this generation is sexual immorality. This, the Prophet Joseph said, would be the source of more temptations, more buffetings, and more difficulties for the elders of Israel than any other" (Benson, 1988, p. 277).

In our day the First Presidency and Quorum of the Twelve Apostles declared in "The Family: A Proclamation to the World" that "God has commanded that the sacred powers of procreation are to be employed only between man and woman, lawfully wedded as husband and wife" (¶ 4). We live in a world that struggles with keeping the seventh commandment, "Thou shalt not commit adultery" (Exodus 20:14). As Elder Neal A. Maxwell (1979, p. 36) has pointed out, "The seventh commandment is one of the least heeded but most needed laws of God."

The proclamation goes on to explain that a husband and wife should "honor marital vows with complete fidelity" (¶ 7). A misconception in the world today is that infidelity involves solely the commission of sexual acts outside of marriage. However, being completely faithful to one's spouse requires more than avoiding adultery.

President Spencer W. Kimball (1962) taught, "Marriage presupposes total allegiance and total fidelity" (p. 57). We marry with the understanding that we will give ourselves completely to our spouse and that any divergence is sin. We show our faithfulness to God by loving him with all our "heart, might, mind and strength" (D&C 4:2). We show fidelity to our spouse in the same ways. Indeed, our spouse is the only other being besides

God whom we are commanded to love with all our heart. We are commanded to love our spouse with all our heart and cleave unto none else (D&C 42:22).

In this chapter we will discuss the incidence of infidelity, the different types of infidelity, the impact of infidelity, and the overall causes of infidelity. We then offer suggestions on how to prevent infidelity and make our marriages less vulnerable to acts of infidelity. Finally, we discuss recovery and how to repair a marriage if an act of infidelity has taken place.

The Prevalence of Marital Infidelity

One might think that infidelity is rampant in our world today. This is not surprising given the pervasive news coverage of the indiscretions of politicians, athletes, and celebrities. Similarly, television shows often tout affairs as commonplace.

Based on the best sources, the numbers of unfaithful spouses are much lower than the media portrays. According to research from the National Marriage Project (2009), 21 percent of married men and 14 percent of married women in 2000 report ever being unfaithful to their spouse. Although these numbers represent far too many traumatized families, this research also indicates that this number has not increased over the past 20 years. In terms of the percent of currently unfaithful married couples, Smith (2006, p. 8) reports, "The best estimates are that about 3–4 percent of currently married people have a sexual partner besides their spouse in a given year" (see also Allen, Atkins, Baucom, Snyder, Gordon, & Glass, 2005). Another encouraging statistic is that during the past three decades, the percent of U.S. adults reporting that marital infidelity is "always wrong" has steadily increased from 63 percent of men and 73 percent of women in 1970 to 78 percent of men and 84 percent of women in 2000 (Smith, 2006). One particular age group, however, has increased their infidelity rate from 1991 to 2006: for those over 60 years of age, men have an increased incidence of infidelity from 21 percent to 28 percent and women have an increased incidence from 5 percent to 15 percent (Atkins, Furrow, & Yang, under review).

A Typology of Infidelity

Researchers and therapists identify different kinds of infidelity. In summary, infidelity can be categorized based on the type of involvement (emotional or physical) and the level of relational attachment (attached or detached). Based on these dichotomies, there appear to be four general types of infidelity: fantasy, visual, romantic, and sexual (see Table 6.1). It is important to point out that it does not take two people for infidelity to occur. Many times infidelity is committed within the mind or heart of a married individual with no other participating party.

TABLE 6 .1. TYPES OF INFIDELITY

Type of Relational Attachment	Type of Involvement	
	Emotional	*Physical*
Detached	Fantasy	Visual
Attached	Romantic	Sexual

Fantasy Infidelity

Fantasy infidelity (emotional/detached) is characterized by having an emotional affair with someone who has no knowledge about what is taking place, or with someone who is anonymous (such as a person in a chat room) or will likely never be encountered in person (such as a celebrity), or all three. This type of infidelity involves fantasizing romantically about someone other than a spouse. When we let ourselves imagine what life would be like with another person, we are not being fully faithful to our spouse. Although this type of infidelity can take place entirely within one's imagination, more and more emotional infidelity is being committed online through emails, chat rooms, or social networking sites.

One survey showed that online sexual activities (which can range from flirting to sharing emotional intimacies or sexual scenarios) were the stated cause of separation and divorce in more than 22 percent of those surveyed (Subotnik, 2007). Many justify their thoughts by claiming their love for their spouse is dead (p. 60). However, President Kimball (1962) taught that when love wanes or dies, "it is often infidelity of thought or act which gave the lethal potion" (p. 60). "There must be no romantic interest, attention, dating, or flirtation of any kind with anyone [outside the bounds of marriage]" (Kimball, 1969, p. 70).

President Harold B. Lee (1974, p. 37) taught that a

> thought is the father of an act. No man ever committed murder who did not first become angry. No one ever committed adultery without a preceding immoral thought. The thief did not steal except he first coveted that which was his neighbor's.

It is important to remember, "For as [a man] thinketh in his heart, so is he" (Proverbs 23:7).

One female married college student reported this tender and powerful story:

> One principle that really pricked my mind was the idea of being emotionally unfaithful. This really hit home to me. I have a certain guy friend, "Jake," who has been a big influence in my life and will always be important to me. I could have married him, but chose not to. I love and cherish my husband, "Chad," and don't doubt that I made the right decision in marrying him, but I have found myself still wanting that friendship with Jake from my past. I found myself thinking, "Why can't Chad be more like Jake?" I looked forward to running into Jake on campus. I spoke to him occasionally on the computer. As I read the chapter on purity in our text, I was horrified, and tears filled my eyes when I realized that I was in those beginning stages of an emotional affair. The thought of being unfaithful to my sweetheart is disgusting to me, and yet in a way I was playing with emotional infidelity. I really loved the quote, "The grass is greener . . . on the side of the fence you water!" (Goddard, 2007, p. 89). It is so true! My friendship was not bad, but what was bad was that I was

putting energy into it, which should have been put into my marriage. I made a strict commitment to myself and the Lord that I would not share my heart with anyone but my husband. I had been thinking about "Jake," worrying a lot about him, and I decided this was the end and I cut it out of my mind. . . . I changed my usual route walking to class because I knew that sometimes walking that way I would run into Jake. I stopped talking to him on the computer. All that energy, the thoughts, the time on the computer, everything, I turned over to my husband plus more. I am again looking for little acts of service I can do to show Chad how much I do totally adore him. I am doing the things to build our relationship spiritually and to give God his place in our marriage. I want to have the greenest, most beautiful grass on the side of the fence where my husband is, and I will not let anything in to harm that.

Visual Infidelity/Pornography

Visual infidelity (detached/physical), such as pornography, is perhaps the most common type of unfaithfulness. And the physical aspect of pornography involves the common practice of self-stimulation while viewing pornography. The Lord has warned us that we should not look upon anyone lustfully (Matthew 5:27–28). President Kimball (1962, p. 58) said,

> There are those married people who permit their eyes to wander and their hearts to become vagrant, who think it is not improper to flirt a little, to share their hearts, and have desire for someone other than the wife or the husband. . . . Many acknowledge the vice of physical adultery, but still rationalize that anything short of that heinous sin may not be condemned too harshly; however, the Lord has said many times: "Ye have heard that it was said by them of old times, Thou shalt not commit adultery: But I say unto you, that whosoever looketh on a woman to lust after her hath committed adultery with her already in his heart" (Matthew 5:27–28).

Romantic Infidelity

Romantic infidelity (emotional/attached) occurs when an individual becomes emotionally involved with a

specific person other than his or her spouse. Romantic infidelity is characterized by a "second life" and commonly is a result of trying to escape the monotony of everyday life (VanderVoort & Duck, 2004).

While a member of the Seventy, Elder Bruce C. Hafen and his wife, Sister Marie K. Hafen, noted that while romance in marriage is wonderful, "Lucifer, the enemy of our desire for fullness, tries to convince us that we must escape our dull routines and seek the dramatic gestures of 'romance' *outside the home,* because he claims that life's petty burdens and chores impede" desire and love (1994, p. 310, italics added). They go on to suggest that Satan wants us to believe that every marriage should be like a Shakespearean love story, never asking us to imagine Romeo and Juliet dealing with household clutter, unpaid bills, and crying children.

Research by VanderVoort and Duck (2004, p. 12) confirms that there is often a "utopian edge" to infidelity. They believe that one reason this type of affair is so tempting is that it offers an escape from everyday life. An adulterer might feel like he or she is empowered and reinventing his or her life. However, research by Duncombe and Marsden (2004) suggests that those who are unfaithful as a way to escape everyday life will be disappointed over time, since everyday life has a way of catching up with us. Initially infidelity can seem spontaneous, romantic, and thrilling. Over time, the exciting romantic target "ceases to be a stranger and routine becomes the enemy of spontaneity" (p. 144).

Sexual Infidelity

"Whoso committeth adultery with a woman lacketh understanding: he that doeth it destroyeth his own soul" (Proverbs 6:32). In contrast to romantic infidelity, sexual infidelity (physical/attached) occurs when a person engages in sexual acts outside the bonds of marriage with or without emotional attachment. In some instances, sexual infidelity can be detached, such as infidelity with a prostitute. In some instances, visual affairs or fantasies will lead a person into committing the more serious sin of physical, sexual infidelity. What begins as a detached fantasy or romantic affair can lead to physical infidelity. Veon Smith (1975, p. 58), professor and marriage counselor, warned, "Infidelity is a subtle process. It does not begin with adultery; it begins with thoughts and attitudes. Each step to adultery is short, and each is easily taken; but once the process starts, it is difficult to stop." In other words, what may start off as fantasy or visual infidelity can evolve into more serious types of infidelity, such as romantic or sexual infidelity, which involves other people directly.

Satan will try to convince us that we can find happiness in infidelity. Even though it may seem for a time that everything is wonderful, President Benson (1988, p. 285) warned, "Quickly the relationship will sour. Guilt and shame set in. We become fearful that our sins will be discovered. We must sneak and hide, lie and cheat. Love begins to die. Bitterness, jealousy, anger, and even hate begin to grow."

Consequences of Infidelity

There are spiritual consequences associated with all types of infidelity. Elder Richard G. Scott (1994, p. 38) has warned, "Intimate acts are forbidden by the Lord outside . . . of marriage because they undermine His purposes. . . . When experienced any other way, they are against His will. They cause serious emotional and spiritual harm."

Apart from the spiritual impacts, infidelity has other negative consequences. Infidelity is one of the leading factors in divorce (Amato & Previti, 2003); infidelity produces traumatic impacts on the spouse who was cheated on and turns one's world upside down (Baucom, Snyder, & Gordon, 2007). The spouse often feels nauseated, repulsed, depressed, undesirable, insecure, helpless, abandoned, anxious, and even suicidal (Hall & Fincham, 2006). Children whose parents have been unfaithful also tend to be confused and disillusioned, and at times also experience despair (Lusterman, 2005).

Infidelity has also become a significant public health issue. With the rapid spread of sexually transmitted diseases, individuals who engage in sex outside of marriage not only risk exposing themselves but also their spouse to these diseases. With the constant threat of HIV, infidelity can "literally become a matter of life and death" (Hall & Fincham, 2006, p. 155).

Use of pornography results in distinctive negative impacts, including the objectification of people, overemphasis on the visual, overemphasis on sex, and the expectation of instant gratification (Valentine, 2005).

Objectification

We are constantly being bombarded with messages that it is normal to treat people as objects. Women especially

are depersonalized, sexualized, and exploited to sell products. Objects are not alive; their job is to please us. Objects do not speak up, challenge us, or walk away. We control objects, and when they do not satisfy us, we get rid of them. When we objectify people, we falsely believe that they are there only to please and gratify us, not to challenge or disagree with us. We stop seeing their humanness and uniqueness. In turn, we begin to lose the ability to notice and respect the needs and feelings of real people in our lives.

Overemphasizing the Visual

The exaggeration of visual stimulation creates dysfunctions in the way males relate to women's bodies. "When women are presented as visually perfect, compliant sex objects, real women with real personalities become less appealing" (Valentine, 2005, p. 29). Some men may begin to believe in a false sense of entitlement and have distorted expectations about how all women should look. Instead of relating to real women, these men fantasize about over-idealized body types. This fantasizing may lead these men to become emotionally absent and unavailable to a real wife.

Overemphasizing Sex

The Savior taught that lusting after someone to whom you are not married is a form of adultery (Matthew 5:27–28). "Lust is defined in the dictionary as the strong physical desire to have sex with somebody, usually *without associated feelings of love or affection*" (Valentine, 2005, p. 31, italics in original). When people view pornography, it is likely done without feelings of love, delight, generosity, consideration, sympathy, and kindness. The end result is a state of numbness, isolation, and loneliness. Elder Maxwell (1979, p. 39) stated,

> When we lose our capacity to feel, it is because we have destroyed the tastebuds of the soul. We have blunted our capacity to appreciate those refinements, that graciousness and empathy that belong to that better world toward which we are pointed.

One reason sexual immorality is so dangerous is because it is so desensitizing. Elder Maxwell pointed out,

> Lasciviousness can, ironically, move people who wrongly celebrate their capacity to feel to a point

where they lose their capacity to feel! They become, in the words of *three* different prophets in *three* different dispensations, "past feeling" (1 Nephi 17:45; Ephesians 4:19; Moroni 9:20) (p. 38, italics in original).

Instant Gratification and Instant Solutions

Over time, consumers of pornography are conditioned to believe that they are entitled to instant sexual gratification. This runs counter to the Christlike attributes of persuasion, long-suffering, gentleness, meekness, love unfeigned, and kindness (D&C 121:41–42) and is contrary to our Heavenly Father's plan of happiness for us. When times are stressful, pornography can be seen as a "quick fix," but it allows only a temporary escape at best. Valentine (2005, p. 33) asserts, "The best sexual relationship is the result of a loving, respectful relationship carried out in the many aspects of everyday life." Thus real intimacy in real marriage takes time, patience, and sensitivity as the two endeavor to become "one flesh" (Genesis 2:24).

Factors Associated with Infidelity

Factors associated with greater likelihood of infidelity can be broken down into intrapersonal, interpersonal, and contextual categories. Research suggests that intrapersonal factors include: being male, ever being divorced, using drugs and alcohol, having permissive attitudes about extramarital relationships (Allen et al., 2005; Smith, 2006), being narcissistic (Atkins, 2003; Atkins, Yi, Baucom, & Christensen, 2005), and having low religiosity and low church attendance (Atkins & Kessel, 2008; Atkins, Baucom, & Jacobson, 2001; Smith, 2006). Interpersonal factors include: marital instability, inequality in marital relations, cohabiting before marriage, personality differences (Allen et al., 2005; Smith, 2006; Treas & Giesen, 2000), dishonesty, arguments about trust, and less time spent with one's spouse (Atkins, 2003; Atkins, Yi, et al., 2005). Contextual factors include working with others of the opposite sex and peer/colleague acceptance of extramarital relationships (Allen et al., 2005; Atkins et al., 2001; Treas & Giesen, 2000).

With regard to the interpersonal factors, it is important to realize that dissatisfaction in marriage does not by itself result in infidelity. A common myth is that affairs occur only because of a bad marriage (Snyder, Baucom, & Gordon, 2007a). This belief is simply untrue. President Kimball (1962, p. 59) stated, "Spouses are sometimes inconsiderate, unkind, and difficult, and they must share the blame for broken homes, but this never justifies the other spouse's covetousness and unfaithfulness and infidelity." There are many people in troubled marriages who do not commit adultery just as there is plenty of infidelity that occurs even when spouses are generally satisfied with their marriages (Allen et al., 2005). A troubled marriage neither causes nor justifies infidelity.

Infidelity has less to do with the state of a marriage and more to do with the individual. It is often a result of a personal transformation that has taken place within an individual's nature. Elder Bruce C. and Sister Marie K. Hafen (1994, p. 310) explained:

> When men or women are true to the deepest instincts of their natures, they will nurture sensitivity and kindness as part of their marital fidelity. But when their motives darken toward betrayal or a quest for power, they cast away their human kindness in ways that deny the link between true sexuality and fidelity.

Preventing Marital Infidelity

Infidelity is easier to prevent than to remedy. In addition to working to strengthen our marriages, we can prevent affairs by being on guard and being fiercely loyal.

Boundaries: Being on Guard

Often we think that infidelity primarily happens when spouses do not love each other enough, when the marriage is bad, when sexual intimacy is suffering, or when a more attractive alternative comes along. But infidelity is not primarily about love, sex, or attraction; it is about boundaries—where we draw the line. Therapist and author Dr. Shirley Glass (2003) points out that infidelity is more about boundaries than anything else. She uses the analogy of walls and windows. In an extramarital affair, people put up walls in their own marriage and open the window to others outside the marriage. Instead, we must know how to put up appropriate walls to protect our marriages from outside influences and open the window of love and communication within our marriage. Consider the suggestions in Box 6.1.

BOX 6.1:
WISE WALLS FOR PREVENTING INFIDELITY
(Broderick, 1991; Glass, 1999; Goddard, 2007)

• Resist the desire to rescue an unhappy soul who pours his or her heart out to you.
• Don't share the most painful things of your soul with an attractive alternative. This develops deep levels of intimacy.
• If a conversation makes light of marriage, respond with something positive about your own marriage.
• Discuss marital issues with your spouse. Work on the problems at home. If you do need to talk to someone else about your marriage, be sure he or she is a friend of the marriage.
• Don't have lunch or take work breaks with the same person all the time.
• Don't have lunch alone with an old flame.
• If an old boyfriend or girlfriend is going to be at a class reunion, make sure you bring your spouse along.
• When you travel with a coworker, meet only in public places.
• Don't flirt with anyone other than your spouse.
• Don't travel together with someone of the opposite sex when going to meetings for work, church, or in other circumstances.

Fiercely Loyal

Another myth is that if we love our spouse enough, we are immune to infidelity (Smith, 1975). Fidelity is a process and is measured by the degrees of loyalty, allegiance, and commitment between husband and wife. Any action that allows inappropriate relationships to grow erodes fidelity.

Many situations in work, society, and church assignments involve men and women working closely together. All of these situations can be opportunities for emotional involvement to develop (Treas & Giesen, 2000). The task for every married couple is to maintain complete fidelity and loyalty to the spouse and none other. President Hinckley (1999, p. 2–4) counseled: "Determine that there will never be anything that will come between you that will disrupt your marriage. . . . Be fiercely loyal one to another."

Modern subtlety. Satan attacks us with subtle and indirect means. He tempts us to become inappropriately close to someone who is not our spouse under the guise of mentoring, friendship, or helpfulness. He subtly tempts us to build inappropriate emotional bonds while quieting our consciences with weak rationalizations. Perhaps this is Satan's favorite ploy with those who desire goodness and are filled with compassion. The Book of Mormon describes his strategy:

And others will he pacify, and lull them away into carnal security, that they will say: All is well in Zion; yea, Zion prospereth, all is well—and thus the devil cheateth their souls, and leadeth them away carefully down to hell (2 Nephi 28:21; see Goddard, 2007, p. 83).

Controlling thoughts. Part of being fiercely loyal is controlling our thoughts. In their summary of the research on extramarital relationships, Allen and colleagues (2005, p. 115) suggest that some cognitive processes increase one's likelihood of infidelity, such as "minimization of the impact of [extra-marital involvement]." They report that other thought processes protect us from infidelity, such as reinforcing commitment to our spouse, devaluing extramarital alternatives, and suppressing thoughts and feelings about others outside our marriage.

In Doctrine and Covenants 121:45, the Lord counseled us to "let virtue garnish thy thoughts unceasingly." This applies to marriage as well. President Kimball (1969, p. 250) counseled that when a couple is faithful to each other, "eyes will never wander and thoughts will never stray toward extra-marital romance. In a very literal sense, husband and wife will keep themselves for each other only, in mind and body and spirit." Elder Maxwell (1979, p. 42), while discussing temptation, stated, "Temptation expands so as to fill the time and space available to it. Keep anxiously engaged in good things, for idleness has a way of wrongly insisting, again and again, that it is ourselves we must think of pleasing."

Putting our spouse first. All of our relationships with others will be considered secondary when our spouse is foremost in our lives. We all know the commandment, "Thou shalt love thy wife with all thy heart, and shalt cleave unto her and none else" (D&C 42:22). This allows for no sharing, dividing, nor depriving. President Kimball (1962, p. 57) related,

The words none else eliminate everyone and everything. The spouse then becomes preeminent in the life of the husband or wife, and neither social life nor occupational life nor political life nor any other interest nor person nor thing shall ever take precedence over the companion spouse.

As we construct appropriate boundaries, are fiercely loyal, control thoughts, and put our spouse first, it is unlikely our marriage will ever be traumatized by infidelity.

Repairing Marriage after Infidelity

Although most spouses initially see infidelity as a sure sign of the death of a marriage, research has shown that this is often not the case. Snyder, Baucom, and Gordon (2007a) indicate that the majority of couples, about 70 percent, stay together and attempt to work it out, despite one of them being unfaithful. Nearly half of those who choose to stay together end up building a strong relationship. Research also suggests that when couples attend counseling to recover from infidelity, these couples tend to improve quickly (Atkins, 2003; Atkins, Eldridge, Baucom, & Christensen, 2005; Atkins, Marin, Lo, Klann, & Hahlweg, 2010).

How then are such marriages repaired? Is there life and hope after such trauma? Five important steps are necessary to successfully overcoming infidelity. These include: rebuilding trust, gaining perspective, repentance and forgiveness, overcoming addiction, and making the choice to stay together (Snyder et al., 2007a).

Step 1—Rebuild Trust

Becoming Accountable

Even if others do not know of the infidelity, the first step to rebuilding trust is to become accountable. Accountability means being responsible for your actions. And this means breaking the secrecy that has been taking place, which helps relieve the feeling of being an imposter. Elder Richard G. Scott (1995, p. 77) related that cover-ups will never solve the problem nor save us from the spiritual consequences of our actions. Our Heavenly Father sees every act. The adversary only persuades us to procrastinate repentance so we will suffer these consequences of sin longer or so he can make public our most embarrassing acts at the most harmful

time. In the words of Elder Scott, one who takes comfort in the fact that his transgressions are not known by others is like "an ostrich with his head buried in the sand. He sees only darkness and feels comfortably hidden. In reality he is ridiculously conspicuous."

Chamberlain, Gray, and Reid (2005) point out that after disclosing the infidelity, an unfaithful spouse may need to give his or her spouse time to deal with the emotions precipitated by the disclosure. This is part of taking responsibility for the pain the offending spouse has caused. This time is best spent focusing on personal behaviors and what changes need to be made.

Establishing Boundaries

After full disclosure, the next step of rebuilding trust involves setting boundaries. Snyder, Baucom, and Gordon (2007b) suggest that a couple begin by discussing how often and what aspects of the infidelity they will talk about. They will also need to set clear boundaries on interactions with the outside offender, since trust is seldom regained quickly when any contact continues.

Rebuilding the Trust Bank Account

According to Snyder and colleagues (2007a), trust is often one of the last things to return after infidelity. Most couples enter marriage with high levels of trust. Once an affair has occurred, that same level of trust is hard to recover. Rebuilding trust takes time, and progress typically is made only in small steps.

In this way, trust is much like a bank account. At the beginning of a marriage, the trust bank account is full. However, an act of infidelity will wipe out the trust bank account and leave a gaping deficit. The bank account will need to be rebuilt by making large and small deposits repeatedly over a period of time—perhaps years.

The partner that has wiped out the account can best make deposits through actions such as eliminating secrecy, honoring relationship boundaries, and keeping agreements made with his or her spouse about specific issues in their relationship (Snyder et al., 2007a).

Step 2—Gain Perspective

The next step is for both partners to understand how the infidelity came about, exploring aspects of the marriage that made it more susceptible to infidelity. Possible factors might have included high amounts of conflict, lack of emotional connectedness, lack of physical intimacy, high amounts of stress, and other influences. Once again, it is important to remember that reasons are not excuses (Snyder et al., 2007b, p. 112). There is no justification for infidelity, but examining the relationship will help the couple locate factors that made their marriage more vulnerable to it. A couple should then regain a "big picture" view of each other and their relationship, acknowledging the strengths and assessing areas for improvement, rather than just focusing on the infidelity.

Gaining a better perspective also includes realizing that one person is not responsible for the sins of another. For example, an innocent wife may believe that if she were more attractive or more alluring, her husband would not have viewed images of other women on the Internet or have had an affair. This is simply untrue. If a man's satisfaction with his wife just depended on her physical attractiveness, men married to supermodels and movie stars would be the most faithful husbands (Snyder et al., 2007a); observation suggests otherwise.

Finally, during this step, Snyder and colleagues (2007a) advise couples to refrain from making big decisions about the marriage, since right after an affair has occurred can be a very stressful time full of turmoil and conflict. The emotions experienced during this time are often not an accurate sample of what the marriage was like before the infidelity or could be like over time if the couple decides to work through the challenge.

Step 3—Repentance and Forgiveness

Sins of sexual impurity, although very serious, are forgivable. The first part of repentance involves determining how serious the Lord finds our transgression. President Kimball (1969, p. 62) reminds us that "the Lord apparently rates adultery close to premeditated murder, for he said: 'And again, I command thee that thou shalt not covet thy neighbor's wife; nor seek thy neighbor's life' (D&C 19:25)." Studying and pondering the Lord's commandments concerning the sin of infidelity after it has been committed will bring feelings of sorrow and remorse. Although painful, these are necessary and will help develop a sincere desire for change and repentance (Scott, 1995).

Confession

One of the greatest resources members of the Church have is the ability to receive priesthood help after a transgression. Davidson (1999) points out that Satan wants nothing more than for the transgressor to be cut off from the love and concern of priesthood leaders. This enables the adversary to continue the work of destruction that has already begun. Instead, the offender should confess to and counsel with his or her bishop or branch president.

Forsaking Sin

Forsaking a habit is not an easy thing to do, but it is possible. Elder Scott (1990, p. 75) outlined the process by explaining:

> Decide to stop what you are doing that is wrong. Then search out everything in your life that feeds the habit, such as negative thoughts, unwholesome environment, and your companions in mischief. Systematically eliminate or overcome everything that contributes to that negative part of your life. Then stop the negative things permanently.
>
> Recognize that you'll go through two transition periods. The first is the most difficult. You are caging the tiger that has controlled your life. It will shake the bars, growl, threaten, and cause you some disturbance. But I promise you that this period will pass. How long it takes will depend upon the severity of your transgression, the strength of your determination, and the help you seek from the Lord. But remember, as you stand firm, it will pass.
>
> The second period is not as intense. It is like being on "battle alert" so that you can fend off any enemy attack. That too will pass, and you will feel more and have increased control of your life. You will become free.

Finding Forgiveness

"He that has committed adultery and repents with all his heart, and forsaketh it, and doeth it no more, thou shalt forgive" (D&C 42:25). Sometimes when we realize the seriousness of our sins, we tend to wonder if the Lord will ever be able to forgive us. Although it may seem impossible, President Kimball (1982, p. 5) stated, "In the matter of sexual sin and adultery . . . repentance can bring forgiveness if that repentance is sufficiently 'all-out' and total."

Forgiving an Unfaithful Spouse

Forgiving an unfaithful spouse can be one of the most difficult tasks in a couple's healing process; it is also one of the most necessary. According to Snyder and colleagues (2007a), when the injured partner decides to forgive an unfaithful spouse, he or she is choosing not to let feelings of hurt and anger dominate life. Furthermore, he or she gives up the right to continue punishing the unfaithful partner or demanding further restitution.

Although it is difficult and seems unfair, forgiveness is the only way the injured spouse can find healing. Snyder and colleagues (2007a, p. 286) explain that being the injured partner up to this point has permitted the person "to claim the moral high ground by having been wronged." Forgiveness is difficult because it requires letting go of the role of victim and its benefits. But while vengeance may feel satisfying in the short run, it will keep the injured spouse stuck in the past.

These authors (Snyder et al., 2007a) also point out that forgiving does not mean condoning the behavior or ceasing to feel hurt by what happened. Forgiveness, as defined by Dr. Sidney Simon (Faust, 2007, p. 68), means

> freeing up and putting to better use the energy once consumed by holding grudges, harboring resentments, and nursing unhealed wounds. It is rediscovering the strengths we always had and relocating our limitless capacity to understand and accept other people and ourselves.

Step 4—Overcoming Addiction

When infidelity has occurred as a result of an addiction, overcoming that addiction is an important step to repairing the marriage. Addiction does not make a person bad. A husband who views pornography can be a good person, but one who has fallen into a deep pit and needs help to climb out. When infidelity has occurred in the form of a visual affair, it is important to realize that it is not simply a bad habit, but more similar to an illness.

Overcoming an addiction is a process that requires a great change to take place. Even a strong desire to stop and long periods of abstinence are not signs the addiction is gone. It is similar to trying to kill a dandelion plant by mowing off the top. As long as the roots are

still present, the addiction is guaranteed to resurface (Chamberlain et al., 2005). Counseling by a professional trained in helping people to overcome addiction may be needed.

Step 5—Making the Choice to Stay Together

The final step in the recovery process is for both spouses to decide whether to continue the marriage. As mentioned earlier, about 70 percent of married couples affected by a spouse's affair remain married. And about half of these couples emerge from the wreckage of the infidelity reporting an even stronger marriage than before (Snyder et al., 2007a).

When a couple chooses to stay together, Snyder and colleagues (2007a) emphasize that this means the choice is also being made to commit to, strengthen, and maintain the relationship. They offer these suggestions about moving on together as a couple.

Healing the Past

Discussing and acknowledging hard feelings to each other in a caring way may be the most critical step toward moving beyond the deep hurt from the infidelity.

Strengthening the Present

Instead of trying to get back to where they were, a couple should focus on making the most of where they are. They should make efforts to reduce conflict and create opportunities for intimacy and joy. They should make continuing efforts to build a secure and loving relationship, even when they do not feel like it.

Enriching the Future

Couples should talk about their dreams of moving forward together and what they are willing to do to make those dreams a reality. This will help them remain emotionally connected and help prevent the problem of remaining together physically, but being emotionally apart.

Through hard work, couples can and do rebuild their lives by building trust, gaining perspective, repenting and forgiving, overcoming any addictions, and making the courageous choice to stay together. Of course, there are situations in which spouses decide not to try to repair a relationship broken by infidelity, and instead divorce. The scriptures clarify that infidelity may be a just cause for divorce (Matthew 19:8–9).

"The Family: A Proclamation to the World" provides concise counsel to protect us from the spiritual and relational consequences of infidelity. There is safety and peace in following these commands. The children of the world are blessed and protected when they are "reared by a father and a mother who honor marital vows with complete fidelity."

Scott P. Gardner *is a professor in the Department of Home and Family at Brigham Young University–Idaho, and a marriage and family therapist. He and his wife, Brenda, have three sons.* Christian F. Greiner *is a graduate of the College of Education and Human Development at Brigham Young University–Idaho. He and his wife, Tiffany, are the parents of two young boys.*

References

Allen, E. S., Atkins, D. C., Baucom, D. H., Snyder, D. K., Gordon, K. C., & Glass, S. P. (2005). Intrapersonal, interpersonal, and contextual factors in engaging in and responding to extramarital involvement. *Clinical Psychology: Science and Practice, 12,* 101–130.

Amato, P. R., & Previti, D. (2003). People's reasons for divorcing: Gender, social class, the life course, and adjustment. *Journal of Family Issues, 24,* 602–626.

Atkins, D. C. (2003). Infidelity and marital therapy: Initial findings from a randomized clinical trial. Unpublished doctoral dissertation. University of Washington, Seattle. Retrieved from *Dissertation Abstracts International: Section B: The Sciences and Engineering, 64,* 2377.

Atkins, D. C., Furrow, J. L., & Yang, Y. (under review). A diminishing double-standard: Gender differences in occurrence of infidelity.

Atkins, D. C., & Kessel, D. E. (2008). Religiousness and infidelity: Attendance, but not faith and prayer, predict marital fidelity. *Journal of Marriage and Family, 70,* 407–418.

Atkins, D. C., Baucom, D. H., & Jacobson, N. S. (2001). Understanding infidelity: Correlates in a national random sample. *Journal of Family Psychology, 15*(4), 735–749.

Atkins, D. C., Eldridge, K. A., Baucom, D. H., & Christensen, A. (2005). Infidelity and behavioral couple therapy: Optimism in the face of betrayal. *Journal of Consulting and Clinical Psychology, 73,* 144–150.

Atkins, D. C., Marin, R. A., Lo, T. T. Y., Klann, N., & Hahlweg, K. (2010). Outcomes of couples with infidelity in a community-based sample of couple therapy. *Journal of Family Psychology, 24,* 212–216.

Atkins, D. C., Yi, J., Baucom, D. H., & Christensen, A. (2005). Infidelity in couples seeking marital therapy. *Journal of Family Psychology, 19,* 470–473.

Baucom, D. H., Snyder, D. K., & Gordon, K. C. (2007). Treating infidelity: An integrative approach to resolving trauma and promoting forgiveness. In P. R. Peluso (Ed.), *Infidelity: A practitioner's guide to working with couples* (pp. 99–126). New York: Routledge.

Benson, E. T. (1988). *The teachings of Ezra Taft Benson.* Salt Lake City: Bookcraft.

Broderick, C. (1991). *One flesh, one heart.* Salt Lake City: Shadow Mountain.

Chamberlain, M. D., Gray, D. D., & Reid, R. C. (2005). *Confronting pornography: A guide to prevention and recovery for individuals, loved ones, and leaders.* Salt Lake City: Deseret Book.

Davidson, R. (1999). *I, the Lord, have seen thy sorrow: An LDS guide to dealing with the pain of infidelity.* Sandy, UT: Camden Court Publishers.

Duncombe, J., & Marsden, D. (2004). From here to epiphany . . . : Power and identity in the narrative of an affair. In J. Duncombe, K. Harrison, G. Allan, & D. Marsden (Eds.), *The state of affairs: Explorations in infidelity and commitment* (pp. 141–166). Mahwah, NJ: Lawrence Erlbaum Associates.

Faust, J. E. (2007, May). The healing power of forgiveness. *Ensign, 37,* 67–69.

Glass, S. (1999, July). *Not just friends.* Paper presented at the annual Smart Marriages Conference, Washington, D.C.

Glass, S. (2003). *Not "just friends": Protect your relationship from infidelity and heal the trauma of betrayal.* New York: The Free Press.

Goddard, H. W. (2007). *Drawing heaven into your marriage.* Fairfax, VA: Meridian Publishing.

Hafen, B. C., & Hafen, M. K. (1994). *The belonging heart: The Atonement and relationships with God and family.* Salt Lake City: Deseret Book.

Hall, J. H., & Fincham, F. D. (2006). Relationship dissolution following infidelity. In M. A. Fine & J. H. Harvey (Eds.), *Handbook of divorce and relationship dissolution* (pp. 153–168). Mahwah, NJ: Lawrence Erlbaum Associates.

Hinckley, G. B. (1999, February). Life's obligations. *Ensign, 29*, 2–6.

Kimball, S. W. (1962, October). *Conference Report,* 55–60.

Kimball, S. W. (1969). *The miracle of forgiveness.* Salt Lake City: Bookcraft.

Kimball, S. W. (1982, March). God will forgive. *Ensign, 12*, 2–8.

Lee, H. B. (1974). *Stand ye in holy places.* Salt Lake City: Deseret Book.

Lusterman, D. (2005). Helping children and adults cope with parental infidelity. *Journal of Clinical Psychology, 61*, 1439–1451.

Maxwell, N. A. (1979, June). The stern but sweet seventh commandment. *New Era, 9*, 36–43.

National Marriage Project (2009). Figure 1: Percent of Ever-Married U.S. Adults (18–60) Reporting Sexual Infidelity, by Gender and Decade. Retrieved from http://www.virginia.edu/marriageproject/pdfs/research_stats.pdf

Scott, R. G. (1990, May). Finding the way back. *Ensign, 20*, 74–76.

Scott, R. G. (1994, November). Making the right choices. *Ensign, 24*, 37–38.

Scott, R. G. (1995, May). Finding forgiveness. *Ensign, 25*, 75–77.

Smith, T. W. (2006). *American sexual behavior: Trends, sociodemographic differences, and risk behavior.* (GSS Topical Report No. 25, National Opinion Research Center).

Retrieved from http://www.norc.org/GSS+Website/Publications/GSS+Reports/Topical+Reports/Topical+Reports.htm

Smith, V. G. (1975, January). Warning signs of infidelity. *Ensign, 5*, 58–61.

Snyder, D. K., Baucom, D. H., & Gordon, K. C. (2007a). *Getting past the affair: A program to help you cope, heal, and move on—together or apart.* New York: Guilford.

Snyder, D. K., Baucom, D. H., & Gordon, K. C. (2007b). Treating infidelity: An integrative approach to resolving trauma and promoting forgiveness. In P. R. Peluso (Ed.). *Infidelity: A practitioner's guide to working with couples in crisis* (pp. 99–126). New York: Routledge.

Subotnik, R. (2007). Cyber-infidelity. In P. R. Peluso (Ed.). *Infidelity: A practitioner's guide to working with couples in crisis* (pp. 169–190). New York: Routledge.

Treas, J., & Giesen, D. (2000). Sexual infidelity among married and cohabiting Americans. *Journal of Marriage and the Family, 62*, 48–60.

Valentine, L. (2005). How our sex-saturated media destroys our ability to love. In M. D. Chamberlain, D. D. Gray, & R. C. Reid (Eds.), *Confronting pornography: A guide to prevention and recovery for individuals, loved ones, and leaders* (pp. 26–40). Salt Lake City: Deseret Book.

VanderVoort, L., & Duck, S. (2004). Sex, lies, and . . . transformation. In J. Duncombe, K. Harrison, & D. Marsden (Eds.), *The state of affairs: Explorations in infidelity and commitment* (pp. 1–14). Mahwah, NJ: Lawrence Erlbaum Associates.

CHAPTER 7

The Warm, Happy Marriage: Cold, Hard Facts to Consider

Elizabeth VanDenBerghe and Alan J. Hawkins

Marriage between a man and a woman is ordained of God.

"WE GREW UP IDEALIZING MARRIAGE," WROTE SINgle mother Lori Gottlieb in the *Atlantic* (Gottlieb, 2008, p. 4), her voice joining the increasing ideological battle over marriage that, one decade into the 21st century, engaged social scientists, writers, and pop-culture observers. They pronounced marriage everything from crucial to irrelevant. For writer Gottlieb and her friends, marriage turned out to be far more important and vital than they had imagined. "If we'd had a more realistic understanding of its cold, hard benefits," she bemoaned, "we might have done things differently" (p. 4). She, for one, would have married before having a child, even settling for "Mr. Good Enough," a stable husband who might not share a passion for the same movies, but who would nevertheless join her in the trenches of diaper-changing, bill-paying, sickness-and-health married life. Instead, Gottlieb confessed, she remained oblivious to those practical and often mundane benefits: "I truly believed, 'I can have it all—a baby now, my soul mate later!'" Her reaction now to those who think marriage is no longer necessary for happy family life? "Well . . . ha! Hahahaha. And ha" (p. 6).

Other voices in the fray differed, calling marriage not only dispensable, but passé, unrealistic, and downright stifling. They pointed fingers at high divorce statistics, reality TV couples splitting, and scandalous politicians and sports figures incapable of married fidelity. Sandra Tsing Loh emerged in the *Atlantic*'s skirmishes over marriage with her own essay (Tsing Loh, 2009), a divorce-memoir entitled "Let's Call the Whole Thing Off," that relied on "evidence" from her broken union and similar stories from dinner-group friends to reach a shocking

conclusion: Do away with marriage altogether. "How about the tribal approach?" she asked, with "children between the ages of 1 and 5 . . . raised in a household of mothers and their female kin" (p. 8), after which "nurturing superdads" could become the custodial parents. That suggestions like these, however flippant, made it to the pages of erudite magazines with flimsy anecdotal data for backup reveals the extent to which public perceptions of marriage have became battered and scarred in the 21st century.

Marriage researchers stood quietly in the background of the saga, softly beating the drums of their findings. They began serious scholarly reflection on marriage during the 1990s, and at first many viewed alternatives to marriage empathetically. Maybe divorce really wasn't so hard on kids. Maybe marriage really had run its course, as the popular historian Stephanie Coontz (2005) asserted, to be replaced with a liberating menu of new-age family alternatives anchored in "the sexually based primary relationship" (Scanzoni, Polonko, Teachman, & Thompson, 1989).

But interestingly, the cold, hard evidence of marriage's benefits began piling up and gradually amounted to Everest-like proportions. All kinds of studies contributed to the findings: longitudinal research over decades (Wallerstein, 2000), cross-national surveys comparing multiple countries (Stack & Eshleman, 1998; Scott et al., 2009), and rigorous syntheses drawing together the data from economists, medical scientists, sociologists, and more (Waite & Gallagher, 2000; Wood, Goesling, & Avellar, 2007). At some point, the accumulating evidence made data-driven academics stop and scratch their heads and follow the facts to a more sanguine picture of marriage. They had to conclude it was good. A stable marriage corresponded with happiness, health, prosperity, and the well-being of offspring and communities.

This chapter features evidence on the benefits of marriage, drawing primarily on research, but also comparing comments from the public foray with data. Public discussions and depictions of marriage—whether in Internet articles, movies, or public radio—form the 21st century zeitgeist of how the young, the unmarried, and even the married perceive the institution of marriage and its alternatives. The commentators involved rarely pay heed to academic findings. But fortunately, some in the discussion are, knowingly or unknowingly, aligning themselves ideologically with what researchers have been concluding for years. Others continue advocating alternatives to marriage, especially cohabitation, that dismiss reams of studies showing deleterious results. The more columnists, bloggers, screenwriters, and the public at large can intersect with rigorous research, the more the cold, hard facts will influence policies and personal lives for the better, helping all involved understand that marriage underlies the optimal family structure for men, women, children, neighborhoods, and the world at large. Marriage fully merits the sacrifices required for lifelong commitment and, as a whole, rewards those who accept its boundaries.

The Benefits

"Marriage is sexless, boring, and oppressive," declares the headline of a blogger who goes on to declare that marriage is failing people as an institution (Marcotte, 2009, p. 1). While this invective bears little resemblance to objective reality, the writer's sentiments in some ways accurately depict the cultural lens through which many view marriage. Movies, more often than not, portray sterile married couples desperate to break free of constraints; Internet confessions boast of marital liberation; and influential writers like Elizabeth Gilbert offer destructive praise for the institution in their bestsellers. In *Eat, Pray, Love*, Gilbert's (2006) journey begins with an emotional escape from marriage and husband, while her latest bestseller, *Committed* (Gilbert, 2010), spends most of its pages excoriating the institution that throughout history, she claims, has destroyed women's freedom. Hordes of women, particularly those in their twenties, embraced Gilbert's reluctance to marry as

empowering, believing a strong woman is one who doesn't need marital compromise and entanglement. As for "coming to terms" with marriage and commitment, which the book's blurbs and title promise, one reviewer found that "the 'peace and contentment' at which Gilbert abruptly arrives in the final chapter of the book is a little suspicious, given the hundreds of pages of panic that have preceded it" (Levy, 2010, p. 3). Gilbert, the screenwriters, and the bloggers may or may not be winning over the public perception of marriage, but their conclusions in no way mirror extensive academic research across multiple disciplines. Research reveals that marriage gets far from a failing grade and that married couples, including wives, are far from oppressed.

An extensive body of evidence documents that married adults are clearly healthier than their non-married counterparts (for a summary, see Waite & Gallagher, 2000; Wood, Goesling, & Avellar, 2007). They have lower rates of morbidity and mortality, and their health benefits persist even when factors such as race, income, and health status prior to marriage are taken into account. This means that married couples living in poverty have better physical health compared to other low-income unmarried people, and that marital health benefits extend across all major ethnic groups. A man's or woman's marital status at age 48 strongly predicts his or her chances of surviving to age 65, with those not married more likely to die prematurely. Divorced men experience health risks akin to smoking a pack of cigarettes a day, while a woman's risk of dying prematurely decreases with the duration of her marriage. At older ages, married people are significantly healthier and experience fewer physical limitations in daily activities than their non-married counterparts. Married people also recover better from illness and surgery. Perhaps blogging marriage-naysayers need to examine data on better health and longevity before giving a failing grade to marriage as an institution.

As for being unfulfilled and stifled, married people are generally happier, the studies find, with greater life satisfaction, lower risk for depression, and greater economic stability, all contributing to better mental health (Scott et al., 2009; Stack & Eshleman, 1998; Wood, Goesling, & Avellar, 2007). Interestingly, when young adults marry, they experience an immediate reduction in depressive symptoms, and higher life satisfaction levels hold true for the married across incomes, ethnic groups, and gender (Staton & Ooms, 2008). Recent research in 30 European countries even confirms a significant happiness gap between married and cohabiting individuals except in those countries where approval of cohabitation is deeply embedded in legal and social norms (Soons & Kalmijn, 2009).

While some speculate that marriage makes men happier than women, research suggests that both reap mental benefits from the union (Stack & Eshleman, 1998; Scott et al., 2009; Waite & Gallagher, 2000). A significant study published in *Psychological Medicine* (Scott et al., 2009) concludes that marriage reduces the risk of mental disorders for both men and women; however, gender differences exist. For men, marriage lowers their risk for depression and panic disorder. For women, it reduces their risk of substance abuse. For both genders, marriage offers higher levels of social integration as well as a source of emotional support from which spouses draw a sense of being esteemed, valued, and cared about.

While mutual support and emotional security might not be a young adult's idea of bliss, they are the aspects of marriage that "Mr. Good Enough" writer Lori Gottlieb went on to explore after her *Atlantic* article spawned a near-tumult of public discussion on television, public radio, and the Internet. The resulting book, *Marry Him,* details Gottlieb's (2010) extensive discussions with marriage researchers, neurobiologists, behavioral economists, historians, matchmaking experts, the happily married, and still-searching singles—all of whom enabled Gottlieb to create a new paradigm of what matters in marriage. Passion, physical chemistry, and love: yes, they're important, but must be considered alongside crucial qualities that predict a lasting union. "What I didn't realize when I chose to date only men who excited me from the get-go (without considering the practical side of things)," Gottlieb writes, "is that what makes for a good marriage isn't necessarily what makes for a good romantic relationship" (p. 227).

And just what makes a good marriage, according to Gottlieb's diverse assortment of experts? Distinguishing "needs" from "wants" certainly helps foster wiser choices in a marriage partner, with qualities in the "needs" category like selflessness, humility, maturity, sense of humor, and the ability to commit taking precedence over those in the "wants" category, like height, college pedigree, type of career, hair color, and social status. Gottlieb's trajectory leads her to view a great spouse not only as an appealing romantic companion but also as a steady partner with whom "to run a very small, mundane nonprofit business," which, among its many perks, includes "having a solid, like-minded teammate in life" (pp. 227–228). Yes, emotional and physical chemistry are certainly part of the ideal benefits package; however, as a professional dating coach in her book cautions, those looking for a lasting marriage "should look for a chemistry that's a six or seven and a compatibility that's a nine. . . . People are consistently steering themselves into a ditch because of the all-consuming pursuit of chemistry" (p. 259).

In making the marriage decision, Gottlieb's survey concludes, couples should consider shared values and life goals as paramount. These two factors just happen to be the ultimate foundation for a strong marriage, according to noted marriage researcher and therapist, Blaine Fowers (2000). Research confirms that a marriage founded on realistic expectations as opposed to fantasy manages to satisfy the deep, human need for emotional and physical closeness throughout life's ups and downs. "Committed couples hunker down and stay the course together," writes prolific researcher Scott Stanley. "Although they may experience pain, they may also know the great joy of overcoming challenges and loss together" (Stanley, 2005, p. 200).

"I know there's deep drama in the little moments," confirms none other than John Gottman, perhaps the world's most influential marriage researcher (Gottman & Silver, 1999, p. 80). He hails the value of the small, ordinary indications of a successful marriage, and explains that these quiet moments run counter to Hollywood's distorted concepts of passion and romance: "Watching Humphrey Bogart gather teary-eyed Ingrid Bergman into his arms may make your heart pound, but real-life romance is fueled by a far more humdrum approach to staying connected" (pp. 79–80). According to Dr. Gottman, "comical as it may sound, romance actually grows when a couple are in a supermarket and the wife says, 'Are we out of bleach?' and the husband says, 'I don't know. Let me go get some just in case,' instead of shrugging apathetically" (p. 80). Filming and analyzing interactions between hundreds of married couples has enabled Dr. Gottman to predict which marriages will thrive and which are in trouble. A high indicator of success consists of the mundane moments, which, he writes, "any Hollywood film editor would relegate to the cutting room floor" (p. 80).

Further contributing to a sense of security for married couples are well-documented economic benefits. Married couples, even those with lower incomes, report greater financial security and, as a result, have greater access to better housing, food, and services like health care than the never-married, divorced, or widowed (Stack & Eshleman, 1998). Economists have postulated that much of the financial instability of minorities living in poverty can be attributed to low levels of marriage and high levels of cohabitation and children born to unmarried mothers (Currie, 2009). Whatever the theories, solid research proves that married people in general are better off financially as well as physically and mentally. So, some bloggers are correct in accusing marriage of lacking excitement, if by that they mean it consists of economic stability, less stress, and fewer doctor visits.

The 21st century zeitgeist also keeps telling us that married people are missing out on sex. What could be more obvious? Among writer Sandra Tsing Loh's dinner-group friends, she tells us, only the single woman is sexually fulfilled, with her multiple partners "toppled behind her in ditches like crashed race cars" (2009, p. 6). But faithfully married people report being well satisfied with their sex lives, more so than any other category of sexually active people (Laumann, Gagnon, Michael, & Michaels, 1994). The studies also find that married men and women are the least likely to lack interest in sex or to consider it lacking in pleasure, and are also least likely to associate sex with feelings of fear, anxiety, or guilt (Laumann et al., 1994; Laumann, Paik, & Rosen, 1999). Even unexpected voices in the public foray back up the research claiming that sexual expression within committed marriage may not be so stifling. Feminist writer Naomi Wolf (2003, p. 1) observes that "the ubiquity of sexual images does not free eros but dilutes it." She bemoans a generation of porn-saturated men and women whose sex lives seem compulsive, Internet-driven, and profoundly lonely. She writes that the "power and charge of sex are maintained when there is some sacredness to it, when it is not on tap all the time," and she points out that more traditional cultures "know that a powerful erotic bond between parents is a key element of a strong family" (p. 1). When Ms. Wolf visits an Orthodox Jewish wife in an Israeli settlement, she compares the shrouded sanctity of the marital bedroom (in which the kids are not allowed) to the atmosphere back home in which "our husbands see naked women all day—in Times Square if not on the Net," and writes of her friend, "She must feel, I thought, so hot" (p. 2).

Wouldn't marriage, then—one based on fealty and devotion, and void of adultery in both real and cyber worlds—provide the remedy for sexual satiety and dissatisfaction? Contrary to soap-opera and tabloid mythology, research finds that married men and women typically remain faithful to each other (Laumann et al., 1994; Mosher, Chandra, & Jones, 2005). And two economists who studied a random sample of 16,000 men and women in the United States further bolstered support for marital fidelity by establishing that the greatest happiness comes in a monogamous marital relationship (Blanchflower & Oswald, 2004).

On Further Inspection

Of course, marriage researchers are always asking more questions about the benefits of marriage, wondering if they diminish with finer-grained examination. For example, do marriage benefits apply more to Americans than those in other countries, since Americans divorce more and possibly avoid unhappy long-term situations (Cherlin, 2009)? What about other relationships—could strong social networks and deep friendships produce the benefits found in marriage? Does the state of marriage itself actually cause benefits to occur in the lives of married people or do the people who marry just have better lives in the first place? And what about the quality of the marriage—how good does it have to be to achieve the benefits, and just what constitutes a beneficial marriage and what constitutes an unhappy one? The following studies attempt, fairly successfully, to answer these probing questions, while the writers and cultural observers offer practical applications and philosophical implications for the results.

One unique and extensive study (Stack & Eshleman, 1998) explored the United States versus other countries with data collected on 18,000 adults in 17 nations, carefully controlling for sociodemographic differences. "The results," summarize the study's authors, "offer perhaps the most sweeping and strongest evidence to date in support of the relationship between marital status and happiness" (p. 534). In 16 of the 17 countries, the married displayed significantly higher levels of happiness than their single, divorced, or widowed counterparts. The study further investigated the possibility of a marriage-like relationship, cohabitation, compensating for the real thing. Living together not only failed to compensate for marriage, but was also associated with *decreased* chances of happiness, health, and financial security.

Yet another study (Holt-Lunstad, Birmingham, & Jones, 2008), this one in behavioral medicine, probed whether relationships like friendship could replicate the benefits of marriage, asking as part of its title, "Is there something unique about marriage?" The authors researched whether an above-average social network of family and friends could compensate, in terms of psychological and cardiovascular health, for not being married. Interestingly, "there does appear to be something unique about the spousal relationship," conclude the authors, "as other relationships did not compensate for the lack of a satisfying marriage" (p. 243). The researchers found that the spousal relationship, with its intimacy, time involvement, and especially commitment level, exerted a much stronger positive influence on health than other relationships.

Mutual commitment, writes University of Denver marriage and cohabitation expert Scott Stanley, is what distinguishes marriage from other relationships. Yet contemporary culture, particularly in the United States, remains deeply afraid of limiting choices. Having it all and keeping your options open, just in case something better comes along, has become almost a mantra of modern life. But Stanley points out that "loss of freedom outside the boundaries of the marriage union actually creates new opportunities for a profound level of freedom within them" (Stanley, 2005, p. 44). In other words, by giving up other choices in order to fully commit to marriage, spouses find that barriers within the relationship collapse and the couple feels a freedom unique to marriage—an emotional, psychological, and sexual safety unmatched by any other relationship.

Writer and cultural observer Caitlin Flanagan (2009) calls a good marriage "the one reliable shelter in an uncaring world" (p. 2), an awareness stemming not only from the data, but also from her descent into cancer and chemotherapy, during which her husband took over the household through sickness and very little health. That reliable shelter aspect of marriage—the comfort found in someone nurturing you through cancer or just running for the bleach in the grocery store—lies at the core of questions regarding the nature and influence of

marriage. Does marriage itself actually cause good physical or mental health and create the shelter (the causal theory)? Or are already physically and mentally healthy people more apt to marry (the selection theory) and bring the shelter along with them? A rigorous synthesis of the research, which brought together studies from various fields with diverse methodologies, finds evidence of both cause and selection entangled in the marriage-benefit results (for a summary, see Wood, Goesling, & Avellar, 2007). Yes, happier and healthier people are more likely to marry and stay married. But studies arguing for the causal explanation use longitudinal data that show changes in health as people enter and exit marriage: being married definitely affects human behavior such as smoking, diet, exercise, and access to health care. Marriage also seems to reduce depressive symptoms for both men and women and affects many aspects of mental health. Conversely, depressive symptoms remain elevated years after a divorce, which evidence, again, gives credence to the idea that marriage itself has something to do with good health and positive emotions. These benefits also extend intergenerationally. Married couples' children, whether black, white, or Hispanic, enjoy better physical health and longevity. The causes lie in better education, healthier behaviors, and more stable economic conditions associated with marriage.

The evidence for so many marital benefits brings up one of the most compelling questions of all: Do such benefits result from holding any membership card in the institution of marriage, or do you need to be a member in good standing with a loving, healthy marriage? According to the National Healthy Marriage Resource Center and its own rigorous synthesis of the research, "a good-enough, or healthy marriage—one that is low in negativity—will provide cumulative, lifelong protection against chronic illness and premature death for both men and women, as well as greatly increasing the chances that their children will grow up healthy. These benefits seem only to increase as couples grow old together" (Staton & Ooms, 2008, pp. 13–14).

Obviously, abusive marriages won't offer any immune boosts or stress reduction, and children of stressed couples actually have higher levels of stress hormones (Staton & Ooms). But how bad does a marriage have to be to erase the benefits? And how good does a marriage have to be to be "good enough"? Paul Amato, one of the most respected marriage and divorce researchers in the world, has studied these shades-of-gray marriages and has drawn some conclusions. Children of highly conflicted marriages tend to do better if the parents divorce; however, children of low-conflict, less-than-happy marriages do worse if the parents divorce (Amato & Booth, 1997). The same holds true for the not-so-blissful couple themselves, for Amato has shown there really is such a thing as a "good enough" marriage. The adults and children involved reap most of the benefits of marriage even when the spouses don't always feel fulfilled and even when they wish they had married someone else (Amato, 2001; Amato & Booth, 1997). There must be something powerful about an institution that can produce such positive benefits despite its members' flaws and lackluster performance.

In this context, it shouldn't be surprising that many married people admit they have considered divorce, yet of those who have considered divorce, more than 90 percent say that they are glad to still be married to their spouse (Johnson et al., 2002; Schramm et al., 2003). Marriage researcher Scott Stanley uses a stock market analogy to explain this phenomenon, calling marriage a long-term investment with satisfaction levels going up and down over time. "Some couples' satisfaction level bounces around a lot more than others," he observes. "But long-term commitment will carry you through the ups and downs of married life. . . . Most who consistently invest in their marriages will do very well *over the long term*" (2005, p. 215, italics added). "A lasting marriage is the reward, usually, of hard work and self-sacrifice," writes Flanagan. "We recognize that it is something of great worth, but we are increasingly less willing to put in the hard work and personal sacrifice to get there" (2009, p. 5).

Ironically, as expectations for sacrifice spiral downward, expectations for our "soul mate" spouse ascend higher and higher. Stanley bemoans what he calls the modern obsession with "soul-mate-ism" as a phenomenon that saddles both the married and unmarried with completely unrealistic expectations of a union devoid of irritation, personality differences, and the need to compromise. "Soul-mate-ism," Stanley argues, "conveys an expectation of heavenly connection that makes earthbound relationships more difficult" (2005, p. 147). Cold, hard benefits aside, once married, there are no guarantees that one won't undergo mental or physical health problems or economic troubles. What the evidence makes clear is that marriage is a unique and powerful relationship that positively contributes to individuals, families, and the greater good in crucial ways. As we look into its alternatives, we find that there are no real alternatives—none that even come close to providing the same benefits, anyway, from a statistical perspective.

Variations on the Marriage Theme

Nevertheless, most couples today choose to "test-drive" their relationships by living together before choosing to marry. Young men and women usually move in together without understanding the realities of premarital cohabitation (for a summary, see Popenoe & Whitehead, 2002). Couples who live together before marriage have higher rates of divorce and lower levels of marital quality (Jose, O'Leary, & Moyer, 2010). They report more negative communication in their marriages and have lower levels of marital satisfaction than married couples who did not live together. Infidelity is more common among marriages preceded by cohabitation, and physical aggression is also more common. Many, many studies back up these findings, writes marriage and cohabitation researcher Stanley, who has worked to understand the links between cohabitation and marital success and failure. Why does living together profoundly affect the chances of marital success and its accompanying benefits?

Or does it? Once again, a "selectivity" theory exists, positing that there's just something about the kind of people who live together before marriage that draws them into cohabitation arrangements: they are less religious, less educated, less well off, less traditional in their family values, and more likely to have experienced the divorce of their parents. As a result, cohabiting couples are already at higher risk to begin with. Other researchers lean toward an "experience" theory, which suggests that something inherent in the experience of living together before marriage changes the couple. They become less interested in commitment, marriage, and having children. Or, writes Stanley (2005, p. 153), "they develop a mind-set in which they think, 'Well, if this doesn't work out, I can easily get out,'" a mindset that doesn't necessarily reverse itself if the couple ends up marrying.

But after careful consideration of experience and selection theories, both of which show some support from research, Stanley puts more weight on his own "inertia" theory. In cohabitation, Stanley finds an increasing weight of forces that favor couples' staying together when they move in together. Shared cars, homes, time spent living together, and even children born to the union contribute to a sense of inevitability. It's much harder to break off a relationship in which possessions and time commitments are involved, so marriage often "just happens" without the conscious decisions that true commitment requires. Living together, far from being the no-risk way to test-drive the relationship, can bring hidden, fine-print clauses in the unread cohabitation contract that trap couples into marriage. For this reason, Stanley advises dating couples to choose "low cost" tests of compatibility: read books and work on projects together; get to know the other person very well and carefully observe how he or she treats close friends and relatives; figure out how closely he or she shares your deeply held beliefs, religious and otherwise; ask for the opinions of family and friends. At the very least, wait until there is a formal commitment—an engagement ring—to move in together. Research suggests that couples who move in together after an engagement do not experience quite the risk for eventual divorce that couples who cohabit before engagement do (Jose, O'Leary, & Moyer, 2010; Rhoades, Stanley, & Markman, 2009).

The costs of cohabitation, divorce, and single parenthood are expensive—and not just for the couples involved. The societal ramifications of marital alternatives, represented by yet another voluminous stack of studies, are substantial. The fallout on children, especially, is well documented. According to Amato (2005), being raised by divorced or single parents negatively affects children academically, socially, and psychologically, and also correlates with a greater incidence of risky behaviors. And remarriage, while a valid option for many families, proves problematic as a whole with its complexities of re-adjustment, blended families, and even higher divorce rates. In his treatise on American marriage-divorce-remarriage habits, deftly titled *The Marriage-Go-Round*, Andrew Cherlin (2009) concludes that second, third, and fourth marriages inflict all the more damage on children as adults go from one relationship to the next in pursuit of individual fulfillment. Researchers like Amato, Cherlin, and others belong to that group of scholars who have connected the research dots to a sometimes uncomfortably honest assessment of the data.

Of course, like the data on marriage benefits, statistics on children of divorce, single parenthood, and blended families do not determine how each individual life will play out. People raised by parents in a less-than-ideal or nonexistent marriage can and often do overcome the odds. But what the long-term findings offer is a corrective to wishful notions like those of Tsing Loh, who says of her children's adjustment to divorce: "Their most ardent daily fixations continue to be amassing more Pokémon cards and getting a dog named Noodles to add to their menagerie of five fish and two cats" (2009, p. 5). Like most parents who yearn for the effects of family dissolution to bypass their children, she ignores the overwhelming evidence concerning single parenthood and its long-term repercussions.

She isn't alone in her ignorance, for childbearing trends outside of marriage have taken a precipitous upward climb over the past half century, with the steepest incline recently consisting of the rise in births to unmarried women in their twenties. Four in ten births in the United States are to unmarried mothers, with women between ages of 20 and 29—not teenagers—accounting for most of them (Ventura, 2009). The economic implications of nonmarital births have been well documented and have hit the most disadvantaged the hardest. Perhaps wanting to bring greater attention to such cold, hard facts, President Obama, the first African American President of the United States, told a recent Father's Day audience, "Children who grow up without a father are five times more likely to live in poverty and commit crime, nine times more likely to drop out of schools, and 20 times more likely to end up in prison" (Currie, 2009, p. 27).

Research fellow Mary Eberstadt waxes impatient with some of her academic colleagues who intellectually refuse to get on board the marriage train despite the undeniable record attesting to the economic, social, and moral disaster wrought by sexual promiscuity. "The minority of scholars who have amassed the empirical record and drawn attention to it," she writes, "have been rewarded, for the most part, with a spectrum of reaction ranging from indifference to ridicule to wrath" (2009, p. 30). University of Virginia sociologist Brad Wilcox notes in the *Wall Street Journal* that the tendency to explain away the facts results in scholars who "provide intellectual cover to contemporary young adults' laissez-faire approach to childbearing and marriage" (2009, p. 1).

But science is not on their side. In the academic world, the research goes on, delving ever deeper into the intricacies and nuances of marriage. And in the culture at large, softer evidence emerges as well to support the value of marital commitment: a successful film endearingly depicts the middle-aged, affectionate, and devoted union of Paul and Julia Child; bloggers call for Jay-Z to rap about his marriage to Beyoncé; and books like Gottlieb's *Marry Him* are published, with a movie in the making. Antagonists vehemently attacked Gottlieb for promoting the message that many would be happier in fulfilling but realistic marriages, but supporters gratefully acknowledged her insight into the qualities of a lasting marriage.

Both the soft stories and the hard evidence attest to the fact that good marriages are undeniably worth the work, sacrifice, and dedication they require. The benefits of marriage are unique; the disadvantages of alternative family forms are real, profound, and all too common. The benefits begin at the marriage ceremony; extend into the lives of husbands, wives, and their children across time; then stretch out to bolster neighborhoods, communities, and the world at large.

Elizabeth VanDenBerghe *is a writer specializing in marriage and family issues. She and her husband, Jed, are the parents of John, William, Christian, Grace, Anika, Benjamin, Samuel, and Andrew.* **Alan J. Hawkins** *is a professor in the School of Family Life at Brigham Young University. He and his wife, Lisa, are the parents of two children and they have two grandchildren.*

References

Amato, P. R. (2001). Good-enough marriages: Parental discord, divorce, and children's well-being. *Virginia Journal of Social Policy and the Law, 9,* 71–94.

Amato, P. R. (2005). The impact of family formation change on the cognitive, social, and emotional well-being of the next generation. *The Future of Children, 15*(2), 75–96.

Amato, P. R., & Booth, A. (1997). *A generation at risk.* Cambridge, MA: Harvard University.

Blanchflower, D. G., & Oswald, A. J. (2004, May). *Money, sex, and happiness: An empirical study.* NBER Working Paper No. W10499. Retrieved from http://ssrn.com/abstract=552104

Cherlin, A. J. (2009). *The marriage-go-round: The state of marriage and the family in America today.* New York: Knopf.

Coontz, S. (2005). *Marriage, a history: From obedience to intimacy or how love conquered marriage.* New York: Viking.

Currie, D. (2009, June 8). The parent problem. *National Review, 61*(10), 27–28.

Eberstadt, M. (2009, February). The will to disbelieve. *First Things* (issue 190), 29–33.

Flanagan, C. (2009, July 2). Is there hope for the American marriage? *Time,* 1–8. Retrieved from http://www.time.com/time/printout/0,8816,1908243,00.html

Fowers, B. J. (2000). *Beyond the myth of marital happiness: How embracing the virtues of loyalty, generosity, justice, and courage can strengthen your relationship.* San Francisco: Jossey-Bass.

Gilbert, E. (2006). *Eat, pray, love: One woman's search for everything across Italy, India, and Indonesia.* New York: Penguin.

Gilbert, E. (2010). *Committed: A skeptic makes peace with marriage.* New York: Viking.

Gottlieb, L. (2008, March). Marry Him! *The Atlantic.* Retrieved from http://www.theatlantic.com/doc/200803/single-marry

Gottlieb, L. (2010). *Marry him: The case for settling for Mr. Good Enough.* New York: Dutton.

Gottman, J. M., & Silver, N. (1999). *The seven principles for making marriage work.* New York: Crown.

Holt-Lunstad, J., Birmingham, W., & Jones, B. Q. (2008). Is there something unique about marriage? The relative impact of marital status, relationship quality, and network social support on ambulatory blood pressure and mental health. *Annals of Behavioral Medicine, 35,* 239–244.

Johnson, C. A., Stanley, S. M., Glenn, N. D., Amato, P. R., Nock, S. L., Markman, H. J., et al. (2002). *Marriage in Oklahoma: 2001 baseline statewide survey on marriage and divorce.* Stillwater: Oklahoma State University Bureau for Social Research.

Jose, A., O'Leary, K. D., & Moyer, A. (2010). Does premarital cohabitation predict subsequent marital stability and marital quality? A meta-analysis. *Journal of Marriage and Family, 72,* 105–116.

Laumann, E. O., Gagnon, J. H., Michael, R. T., & Michaels, S. (1994). *The social organization of sexuality.* Chicago: University of Chicago.

Laumann, E. O., Paik, A., & Rosen, R. C. (1999). Sexual dysfunction in the United States: Prevalence and predictors. *JAMA, 281,* 537–544.

Levy, A. (2010, January), Hitched: In her new memoir, Elizabeth Gilbert gets married. *The New Yorker.* Retrieved from http://www.newyorker.com/arts/critics/books/2010/01/11/100111crbo_books_levy

Marcotte, A. (2009). For many, marriage is sexless, boring and oppressive: Time to rethink the institution? Retrieved from http://www.alternet.org/story/141024/

Mosher, W. D., Chandra, A., & Jones, J. (2005). Sexual behavior and selected health measures: Men and women 15–44 years of age, United States, 2002. *Advance data from vital and health statistics*, no. 362. Hyattsville, MD: National Center for Health Statistics. Retrieved from http://www.cdc.gov/nchs/data/ad/ad362.pdf

Popenoe, D., & Whitehead, B. D. (2002). *Should we live together? What young adults need to know about cohabitation before marriage—a comprehensive review of recent research*, 2nd ed. Piscataway, NJ: The National Marriage Project, Rutgers University.

Rhoades, G. K., Stanley, S. M., & Markman, H. J. (2009). The pre-engagement cohabitation effect: A replication and extension of previous findings. *Journal of Family Psychology, 23,* 107–111.

Schramm, D. G., Marshall, J. P., Harris, V. W., & George, A. (2003). *Marriage in Utah: 2003 baseline statewide survey on marriage and divorce.* Salt Lake City: Department of Workforce Services.

Scanzoni, J., Polonko, K., Teachman, J., & Thompson, L. (1989). *The sexual bond: Rethinking families and close relationships.* Newbury Park, CA: Sage.

Scott, K. M., Wells, J. E., Angermeyer, M., Brugha, T. S., Bromet, E., Demyttenaere, K., et al. (2009). Gender and the relationship between marital status and first onset of mood, anxiety and substance use disorders. *Psychological Medicine, 39*(12), 1–11.

Soons, J. P. M., & Kalmijn, M. (2009). Is marriage more than cohabitation? Well-being differences in 30 European countries. *Journal of Marriage and Family, 71,* 1141–1157.

Stack, S., & Eshleman, J. R. (1998). Marital status and happiness: A 17-nation study. *Journal of Marriage and the Family, 60,* 527–536.

Stanley, S. M. (2005). *The power of commitment: A guide to active lifelong love.* San Francisco: Jossey-Bass.

Staton, J., & Ooms, T. (2008). *Making the connection between healthy marriage and health outcomes: What the research says.* Oklahoma City: National Healthy Marriage Resource Center.

Tsing Loh, S. (2009, July/August). Let's call the whole thing off. *The Atlantic.* Retrieved from http://www.theatlantic.com/doc/200907/divorce

Ventura, S. J. (2009, May). Changing patterns of nonmarital childbearing in the United States. *NCHS Data Brief*, no. 18, National Center for Health Statistics, Centers for Disease Control and Prevention, U.S. Department of Health and Human Services. Retrieved from http://www.cdc.gov/nchs/data/databriefs/db18.pdf

Waite, L. J., & Gallagher, M. (2000). *The case for marriage: Why married people are happier, healthier, and better off financially.* New York: Doubleday.

Wallerstein, J. S., Lewis, J. M., & Blakeslee, S. (2000). *The unexpected legacy of divorce: A 25-year longitudinal study.* New York: Hyperion.

Wilcox, W. B. (2009, May 22). The real pregnancy crisis. *Wall Street Journal.* Retrieved from http://online.wsj.com/article/SB124294779002345281.html

Wolf, N. (2003, October 20). The porn myth. *New York Magazine.* Retrieved from http://nymag.com/nymetro/news/trends/n_9437/index1.html

Wood, R. G., Goesling, B., & Avellar, S. (2007, June). The effects of marriage on health: A synthesis of recent research evidence. *ASPE Research Brief*, Office of Human Services Policy, Office of the Assistant Secretary for Planning and Evaluation, U.S. Dept of Health and Human Services. Retrieved from http://www.aspe.hhs.gov/hsp/07/marriageonhealth/rb.htm

Should I Keep Trying to Work It Out? Sacred and Secular Perspectives on the Crossroads of Divorce

Alan J. Hawkins and Tamara A. Fackrell

Marriage between man and woman is essential to [God's] eternal plan.

VIRTUALLY EVERYONE DESIRES A HEALTHY, STABLE marriage, but when a person's marriage does not fit that description, he or she may consider divorce. Researchers have estimated that 40 to 50 percent of first marriages—and about 60 percent of remarriages—are ending in divorce in the United States (Bramlett & Mosher, 2002; Popenoe & Whitehead, 2007). And although the United States unfortunately has one of the highest divorce rates in the world, it is common in many other countries, as well (Popenoe, 2008).

Faithful Latter-day Saints are hardly immune to divorce. Precise estimates of the Latter-day Saint divorce rate are difficult to obtain. One estimate is that 25 to 30 percent of Latter-day Saint couples who regularly attend Church experience a divorce (Heaton, Bahr, & Jacobson, 2004). Other researchers estimate that the lifetime divorce rate for returned missionary men was about 12 percent and for women about 16 percent (McClendon & Chadwick, 2005). While it is heartening to know that the divorce rate for faithful Latter-day Saints is much lower than the national average, still many Latter-day Saints face difficult decisions regarding serious problems in their marriages at one time or another. Some will find themselves at a crossroads, pondering whether their marriages can be repaired or would best be ended. The purpose of this chapter is to provide spiritual principles and secular wisdom pertaining to the decision to divorce or stay together.

After seeing a lot of divorce around them and perhaps even experiencing their parents' divorce, young people today probably already sense what researchers are finding about the impact of divorce on children.

While many children are resilient (Emery, 2004), still the process of family dissolution is associated with about twice the risk for various social and emotional problems in children of divorce (Amato, 2005; Hetherington & Kelly, 2002). Feelings of loneliness are more common for children who experience family breakdown (Wallerstein, Lewis, & Blakeslee, 2000). They are much more likely to experience financial hardship (Waite & Gallagher, 2000), not only in the United States but also in European countries that have more generous social welfare systems than the United States (Andreß & Hummelsheim, 2009). Children who experience their parents' divorce are less likely to graduate from high school, go to college, or graduate from college once they start (Amato, 2005; Wallerstein et al, 2000). They are twice as likely to doubt their parents' religious beliefs and less likely to attend church services (Marquardt, 2005). They are at greater risk for early sexual behavior and pregnancy (Woodward, Fergusson, & Horwood, 2001). And they are much more likely to experience a divorce when they marry (Wolfinger, 2005). One prominent divorce researcher described children's experience with their parents' divorce this way:

For a young child, psychologically, divorce is the equivalent of lifting a hundred-pound weight over the head. Processing all the radical and unprecedented changes—loss of a parent, loss of a home, of friends—stretches immature cognitive and emotional abilities to the absolute limit and sometimes beyond that limit (Hetherington & Kelly, 2002, p. 112).

Spiritual Counsel on Divorce

Marriage is ordained of God and central to our spiritual and temporal well-being. Accordingly, ancient and modern prophets have provided important counsel on marriage and divorce. Though our actions often fall short, the celestial law treats the bonds of marriage as permanent. The Lord taught:

> But from the beginning of the creation God made them male and female. For this cause shall a man leave his father and mother, and cleave to his wife. . . . What therefore God hath joined together, let not man put asunder (Mark 10:6–9).

That God intended from the beginning for us to cleave to our spouse and not separate is evident in Adam's response to God's inquiry of whether he had partaken of the fruit of knowledge of good and evil: "The woman thou gavest me, and commandest that she should remain with me, she gave me of the fruit of the tree and I did eat" (Moses 4:18). In the celestial law of marriage, God has commanded us to remain together and keep our marriages strong, even when that means we must partake of some of the bitter fruits of life together.

In our day, latter-day prophets and apostles have provided valuable clarifications and counsel regarding divorce. First, President Gordon B. Hinckley (2000, p. 134) said: "There is now and again a legitimate cause for divorce. I am not one to say that it is never justified. But I say without hesitation that this plague among us . . . is not of God." Referring directly to the doctrine of marriage, Elder Dallin H. Oaks (2007, p. 70) explained: "Because 'of the hardness of [our] hearts' (Matthew 19:8–9), the Lord does not currently enforce the consequences of the celestial standard [of marriage]. He permits divorced persons to marry again." Like the ancient Israelites whom Moses suffered to divorce (see Deuteronomy 24:1), Latter-day Saints too struggle to live the higher law. Thus, a loving God gives us a law more aligned with mortal capabilities and circumstances.

In addition, Elder Oaks (2007, p. 71) taught that "when a marriage is dead and beyond hope of resuscitation, it is needful to have a means to end it." For Latter-day Saint couples, it would be wise to make this determination in consultation with a bishop. Elder Oaks also explained that when one spouse abandons the other, the option of divorce allows an innocent spouse to remarry. He adds that this is not an available option in some places, for example the Philippines, and in those situations the civil law prevents abandoned spouses from moving forward with their lives. In other cases there is complete psychological abandonment, as well.

Although the Lord permits divorce and remarriage, the standard for divorce is still high. President James E. Faust addressed this issue directly (2004, p. 6; italics added):

> In my opinion, any promise between a man and a woman incident to a marriage ceremony rises to the dignity of a covenant. . . .
>
> Over a lifetime of dealing with human problems, I have struggled to understand what might be considered "just cause" for breaking of covenants. I confess I do not claim the wisdom nor authority to definitely state what is "just cause." Only the parties to the marriage can determine this. They must bear the responsibility for the train of consequences which inevitably follow if these covenants are not honored. In my opinion, "just cause" should be nothing less serious than *a prolonged and apparently irredeemable relationship which is destructive of a person's dignity as a human being.*
>
> At the same time, I have strong feelings about what is not provocation for breaking the sacred covenants of marriage. Surely it is not simply "mental distress" nor "personality differences," nor "having grown apart," nor "having fallen out of love." This is especially so where there are children.

President Faust's humble statement is striking in that he does not claim to possess "the wisdom [or] authority to definitively state what is 'just cause.'" His statement underlies an important principle—circumstances surrounding each marital breakdown are unique and perhaps cannot be fully understood by others. Thus only the individuals involved—and an omniscient and all-loving God—can determine "just cause."

President Faust provides some counsel, however, on the decision to divorce. He gives a three-part "test" for those seeking to determine if ending a marriage is justified: "just cause" should be nothing less serious than "a prolonged and apparently irredeemable relationship which is destructive of a person's dignity as a human being." In the sections that follow, we explore President Faust's counsel. Then, from a secular perspective, we show how social science research supports this counsel. Finally, we address the question of how we are to act when the possibility of divorce presents itself.

Prolonged difficulties. The first part of President Faust's test is that only prolonged marital difficulties should lead a couple to contemplate divorce. By this we believe President Faust counsels that spouses should not seek a divorce without a lengthy period of time to attempt to repair or reduce serious problems. The standard does not require that couples spend the decision-making time living together, and in cases where a spouse's or child's personal safety is at stake, a separation likely is necessary while determining whether repentance, forgiveness, and change are possible. For obvious reasons, President Faust does not specify how long is long enough to meet the "prolonged" standard, and indeed behavior that places family members at risk may require immediate separation from the perpetrating spouse. But the principle President Faust sustains is that a determination of just cause for divorce requires a substantial period of problems, time for potential change to occur, and an unrushed, careful decision. Elder Oaks (2007, p. 73) counseled: "Even those who think their spouse is entirely to blame should not act hastily," noting that most unhappy marriages become happy again if couples hang on and work to resolve their problems.

As professionals, we strive to promote this counsel not to be hasty about a divorce decision. We encourage people at the crossroads of divorce to do everything possible to correct the problem: get rid of the computer (if Internet pornography is an issue), go to counseling, move (if needed)—whatever it takes. At the end of this process, a person can look her or his children—and God—in the eyes and honestly say, "I tried everything possible." The process of trying everything to keep the marriage covenant is as important as the outcome of staying married. One case involved a man who had been having an affair for several months. His wife had small promptings that led to the discovery of the sinful secret. Upon her discovery, instead of being brash and advertising the offense to many others, she was wise and kept the issue from her children and others except for the closest friends and family. She began slowly and decided she would try everything possible to save her marriage. The road was extremely difficult, but through the repentance process, the support of ecclesiastical leaders, and the gift of forgiveness, the couple was able to repair their marriage. Several years later, the couple is thriving and both are extremely grateful they made the decision not to act hastily.

Apparently irredeemable relationship. The second part of the test is directly related to the first. The marital relationship must reach the point where it is apparently irredeemable. By this we believe President Faust means that there appears to be little hope for repairing the marital relationship. This determination requires that sincere and sustained efforts have been made to understand and fix the problems. If one spouse is unwilling or unable to make such an effort, this does not excuse the other spouse from determining his or her part in any problems and making needed change. Elder Oaks (2007, p. 73) reassures us that the Lord will "consecrate [our] afflictions for [our] gain" (2 Nephi 2:1–2) in difficult circumstances such as these, and promises, "I am sure the Lord loves and blesses husbands and wives who lovingly try to help spouses struggling with such deep problems as pornography or other addictive behavior or with the long-term consequences of childhood abuse." While a member of the Seventy, Elder Bruce C. Hafen (2005) taught that we have a shepherd's covenant in our marriages, not a hireling's contract: "The good shepherd giveth his life for the sheep; but he that is an hireling . . . seeth the wolf coming, and leaveth the sheep and fleeth" (John 10:11–12). Even in the face of serious problems, Elder Hafen urges us to do all that we can to protect the marriage.

In one case, a marriage survived one spouse's addiction. After surgery, a spouse became addicted to prescription drugs and later other drugs, which adversely affected the marriage. Further, the addicted spouse incurred large debts to purchase the drugs. The husband lost his employment because of the drug problem. The wife needed to learn to set limits within the marriage and attended the Latter-day Saint 12-step program (Addiction Recovery Program, 2010). She felt tremendous support through this program. After a time, a separation, and rehabilitation for the addicted spouse, the family was reunited. Many years later, both spouses are grateful that they made the decision to work together on the issue.

Destruction of human dignity. The third part of the test is that the relationship has deteriorated to the point that it threatens to destroy the dignity of one or both spouses. By this we believe President Faust means that the marital problems have become serious enough over a period of time that an individual begins to lose his or her sense of worth. Although this may be a difficult standard to discern, certainly abuse or repeated infidelity can threaten a victim's sense of worth. President Faust's counsel suggests that feeling unhappy or unfilfilled in the marriage does not meet this standard. Nor do feelings of emotional or psychological distance or growing apart. Irritations or conflicts brought on by personality differences and other personal preferences rarely rise to the level of threatening our sense of worth. Indeed, these kinds of problems motivate us to pursue changes and improvements that affirm our agency, good desires, and skills that, in turn, reinforce our personal dignity. If this appears to be the hardest course, we can take strength in knowing that we are on the right path. Elder Bruce C. Hafen (2005, p. 86), again referring to the parable of the shepherd, the sheep, and the wolf, taught that "life is hard and full of problems—wolves. Dealing with the wolves is central to life's purpose. For a husband and wife to deal with the wolves together is central to the purpose of marriage."

In a case of a couple confronting the serious challenge of adultery, the husband also was insulting to his wife and belittled her often in front of friends and family. Not surprisingly, the wife's sense of worth eventually hit rock bottom. Nevertheless, the couple was able to work through this difficult time through tears and counseling. Many years later, however, the husband again had multiple affairs. At this point, the wife knew that the marriage needed to end. Later the wife remarried a good man. She was confident she made the right choice to divorce. Another couple began the divorce process because of a pornography addiction, but with the aid of professional counseling, the couple overcame the problem and eventually reconciled.

The three-part test that President Faust offers to determine just cause for ending our marital covenants is a high standard by contemporary secular ethics. Such a high standard is best understood in light of God's eternal plan for His children. In "The Family: A Proclamation to the World," the Lord's anointed proclaim that marriage is "ordained of God," it is "essential to His eternal plan," and it is "central to the Creator's plan for the eternal destiny of His children" (¶¶ 1, 7). In this context we can fully understand the spiritual significance of marriage and God's commandment not to "put asunder" (Mark 10:6–9) the marital bonds that God ordains for his purposes.

Secular Perspectives on the Crossroads of Divorce

A strong case for a high standard in determining just cause for divorce can also be made with secular research. In the next section, we review the secular case for a high bar on the decision to divorce. We believe reviewing this research provides more insight into the wisdom of President Faust's counsel.

Allowing time for deciding about divorce. The first test President Faust gave was that serious marital problems should exist for a prolonged period of time before one can determine if there is just cause for ending a marriage. (Although if there are safety issues, then a separation is likely necessary while assessing whether change can occur.) There is not much research on how long people experience problems before seeking a divorce. However, research documents that the first five years of a marriage are the years with the highest risk of divorce, and these risks are even higher for remarriages (Bramlett & Mosher, 2002). Apparently, then, many who divorce are married for a relatively short period of time. In our own professional work, we have learned that unfortunately many people divorce after a short period of problems and make their decision quickly, based almost solely on emotion.

Some research suggests that many who divorce have regrets about the divorce later. Divorce scholar Robert Emery reports that ambivalent or mixed feelings about a divorce are common (Emery & Sbarra, 2002). A handful of surveys from various states in the United States estimate that perhaps half of individuals wished they had worked harder to try to overcome their differences (see Hawkins & Fackrell, 2009, 65–74). A study that followed divorced individuals over a long period of time found that in 75 percent of divorced couples at least one partner was having regrets about the decision to divorce one year after the breakup (Hetherington & Kelly, 2002). If feelings of regret are common, this suggests that the decision to divorce may not have been fully considered. One divorced woman remarked:

Now that I'm older and more mature, I look back and I think, "Oh my goodness, the issues were really not as big as we made them out to be." And truly, I wish I would have done things differently to maybe work on that relationship further.

Trying to resolve problems before deciding to divorce. The second part of President Faust's test of just cause is that the marriage is "apparently irredeemable," or that there is little hope of repairing the relationship. Related to this point, researchers estimate that only about 30 percent of U.S. couples who divorce make an attempt to reconcile before the divorce (Wineberg, 1995). Other research suggests that most couples do not seek counseling before they divorce. A survey of Utah adults found that only about half of couples who divorced first sought either secular or religious counseling (Schramm, Marshall, Harris, & George, 2003; see p. 22). This is unfortunate because researchers have estimated that about 80 percent of couples may see improvement in their relationship after visiting a marriage counselor (Ward & McCollum, 2005) and, over the short term, almost half say all of their major problems were resolved (Bray & Jouriles, 1995; Ward & McCollum, 2005). One Latter-day Saint couple said: "One of the things we've worked on since [we decided to try to save our marriage], we've actually gone to counseling a lot. . . . It's been really helpful. . . . I think [counseling provided] a backbone of stability for us." A final determination of whether problems are "irredeemable" rests with each spouse. However, we should seek help from various sources, including religious leaders and professional counselors who provide needed perspective and who help distressed couples develop the skills to resolve their problems.

Many people seem to believe that once a marriage has gone "bad," it is like bruised fruit that cannot be restored, but instead needs to be thrown out and new fruit bought. But research shows that a high percentage of people who say they are unhappy in their marriage, but persevere for several years, later report that their marriages are happy again (Waite & Gallagher, 2000). More than 75 percent of individuals in Waite and Gallagher's study who gave the lowest rating on a marital satisfaction scale but persisted reported a few years later that they were happy or very happy. This study suggests that long-lasting marital unhappiness is uncommon; unhappy marriages often improve significantly over time for those who are patient and keep trying to work things out. Thus, we think there

should be a presumption that current unhappiness in a marriage will diminish, problems will be resolved, and happiness will return. Patience and perserverance can make a real difference.

Perhaps this intriguing research finding can be better understood in the context of the common reasons that people give for divorce. A national study documented that the most common reason people gave for their divorce was a lack of commitment; nearly 75 percent said it was a major factor (National Fatherhood Initiative, 2005). Other common reasons given were too much arguing (56 percent), infidelity (55 percent), unrealistic expectations (45 percent), lack of equality in the relationship (44 percent), and lack of effective preparation for marriage (41 percent). A survey in Utah found a similar pattern of common reasons (Schramm et al., 2003). Most of these reasons seem amenable to patience and effort. People can learn better communication and problem-solving skills; they can establish more realistic expectations; they can learn to treat each other with greater respect and act as equal partners. Also, many good resources are available for engaged couples who want to work before their marriage to prepare better for the challenges that lie ahead. (See www.twoofus.org/engaged/preparing-for-marriage/index.aspx and beforeforever.byu.edu for resources.) There are ways to strengthen commitment to each other and to the marriage before and after the wedding (Stanley, 2005). While infidelity is one of the most difficult marital injuries to heal, therapists devoted to helping couples recover from infidelity report significant success (Snyder, Baucom, & Gordon, 2007). While most (63 percent) Americans say they would not forgive their spouse and would get a divorce if they discovered he or she had been unfaithful (Jones, 2008), in actuality, researchers have found that about half of men and women who have been unfaithful are still married to their same spouse (Allen & Atkins, under review).

Another interesting finding that sheds light on whether marriages can be repaired is that most divorces come from marriages that were not experiencing abuse or high levels of conflict. One set of researchers estimated that half to two-thirds of divorces come from couples who were not having a lot of serious arguments or experiencing abuse (Amato & Booth, 1997; Amato & Hohmann-Marriott, 2007). Instead these divorces seem to result from other problems, such as one or both spouses having unrealistically high expectations about the marriage. Also noteworthy is the finding that the children of these divorces are generally the ones who have the hardest time adjusting to divorce (Amato & Booth). In high-conflict marriages, the children likely are aware of the problems, and divorce may be an expected and even welcome resolution. But in low-conflict marriages that end in divorce, the children likely are surprised and bewildered. A key foundation of their world has been cracked, and they struggle to deal with these unwanted and, from their perspective, unwarranted changes in their family.

One Latter-day Saint couple was married for decades before divorcing because of solvable irritations. The wife was mad at her husband because she felt he was not a good provider; she had grudgingly worked most of their married lives. They experienced serious friction regarding the cleanliness of the home and the undefined roles of each spouse. The children, although all adults, were furious about the divorce. Some of the children have refused to talk to their mother, who initiated the action.

In our professional work, we see that family and friends often encourage a struggling couple to bail out. They see the pain these struggles are causing and instinctively want to end the pain. But instincts are often shortsighted. Again, we acknowledge that there are situations in which divorce is justified and family and friends should support the difficult choice to end such marriages. But as a general principle, we believe that family and friends should encourage their loved ones to work hard to repair their marriage.

Divorce, dignity, and well-being. The third, interrelated part of President Faust's test of just cause for divorce is that the marital relationship has become destructive to a person's basic human dignity. Certainly there is ample evidence that the process of marital breakdown, the aftermath of divorce, and struggles to rebuild a life and meet daily challenges can leave people feeling exhausted, lost, beaten down, lacking confidence, and depressed (Hetherington & Kelly, 2002; Wallerstein et al., 2000). Of course, for some adults, divorce, despite its difficulties, can be the beginning of a new, energizing, and exciting path (Hetherington & Kelly). But for most, marital breakdown and divorce carry with them difficult adjustments that challenge our personal resources to adapt (Amato, 2000; Hetherington & Kelly, 2002). In this body of research findings, it is difficult to separate the effects of marital breakdown from the effects of adjustment to divorce. Most likely both contribute to adjustment difficulties. That is, problems in the marriage make people unhappy and contribute to lower self-esteem, for instance, but problems adjusting to divorce exacerbate these problems and likely spawn additional ones. Moreover, research finds little evidence that, overall, those who divorce rather than stay together are able to rebuild a greater sense of well-being and happiness (Waite et al., 2002; Waite, Luo, & Lewin, 2009). Specifically, those who were unhappy in their marriage and divorced did not end up having greater emotional well-being a few years down the road compared to unhappily married individuals who stayed together. This was true even for those who remarried (or repartnered) after the divorce. Evidently, for most, divorce is not a reliable path to improving one's well-being over time.

However, it is important to acknowledge that this is only a general statement. Certainly there are far too many instances when one's basic human dignity or safety—as well as children's well-being—is put in jeopardy by a destructive marital relationship. Spousal abuse carries with it a high risk of destructive consequences, including poor mental and physical health (Afifi et al., 2009; Campbell, 2002). Similarly, the discovery of infidelity, especially a pattern of repeated infidelity, can produce feelings of traumatic stress, anger, depression, anxiety, disorientation, and psychological paralysis (Snyder et al., 2007). Furthermore, when children are witnesses to ongoing high levels of marital conflict, research suggests that most are better off if their parents divorce (Amato & Booth, 1997).

One challenge associated with this third principle is that sometimes individuals struggling in a destructive marriage get so worn down that they lose a sense of self-efficacy and an ability to trust their own judgment. Hence they may be unable to make a difficult but correct decision to divorce. In these instances, caring family and friends may need to help. As we said earlier, generally we believe family and friends should encourage loved ones at the crossroads of divorce to act with faith and do all they can to repair the marriage. But there may be times when a family member or close friend will need to prayerfully and carefully intervene to help a loved one see that the marriage has become destructive or unsafe and strengthen them to make a difficult decision to divorce.

One situation that can cause great marital pain occurs when one spouse rejects or questions his or her faith while the other remains devout. We do not believe that a spouse's spiritual wanderings are just cause for divorce. With the right perspective, this situation does not constitute a threat to human dignity. Instead, we should offer compassion, love, and patience as a light to attract our spouse back onto the path of full righteousness. One Latter-day Saint husband left the Church early in the marriage. The wife remained devoted to the Church and her husband, even during his struggle with addiction. She raised her children in the Church and all of her children were married in the temple. After more than 25 years of inactivity, the husband again embraced his faith.

The Best Course

The Lord's standard for just cause for a divorce is a high one, even if God mercifully allows us to live by something less than the celestial law. In no way do we want to imply that adhering to this standard is easy. Without question, it takes courage and discipline to stay in an unhappy marriage for a prolonged period of time to attempt change and improvement. It takes wisdom (and perhaps seeking some wise counsel) to evaluate whether a highly troubled marriage can be redeemed, plus skill and effort and humility to repair the relationship. And it takes spiritual insight to discern if an unhappy marriage is becoming destructive of one's basic human dignity. But because marriage is "central to the Creator's plan for the eternal destiny of His children," the bar should be set high, encouraging couples to work to preserve the marriage. Moreover, from a secular perspective, research suggests that a wise course includes patient efforts to repair the relationship, if possible, and that there is wisdom in carefully considering the potential consequences of divorce for all in the family.

Then what is the best course if we come to the crossroads of divorce? Echoing similar, earlier teachings from President Gordon B. Hinckley (2000), Elder Dallin H. Oaks (2007, pp. 71–72) provided challenging but needed counsel:

Now I speak to married members, especially to any who may be considering divorce.

I strongly urge you and those who advise you to face up to the reality that for most marriage problems, the remedy is not divorce but repentance. Often the cause is not incompatibility but selfishness. The first step is not separation but reformation. . . . Under the law of the Lord, a marriage, like a human life, is a precious living thing. If our bodies are sick, we seek to heal them. We do not give up. While there is any prospect of life, we seek healing again and again. The same should be true of our marriages, and if we seek Him, the Lord will help us and heal us.

Latter-day Saint spouses should do all within their power to preserve their marriages.

Some divorces are necessary and just, and may actually serve to clarify the moral boundaries of marriage by identifying behavior that seriously violates marriage covenants. But both spiritual principles and secular learning should motivate us to do all we can to keep our marital covenants. If we find ourselves at the crossroads of divorce, the best path usually is to seek divine help to change course and repair the marriage.

Prayer can be invaluable in this process. There is social science evidence that personal and couple prayer and the faith that motivates it can soften hearts and help strengthen marital relationships (Butler, Gardner, & Bird, 1998; Lambert & Dollahite, 2006). Seeking spiritual guidance from priesthood leaders can also be helpful, even though it is difficult for some because they do not want to reveal their personal struggles to others. Similarly, it can be helpful to seek out trusted family members or friends who have overcome struggles in their marriages and gain strength, perspective, and support from them. In addition, it is important for those at the crossroads of divorce to surround themselves with a network of friends and family who will support their efforts to repair and strengthen their marriage rather than urge them to abandon the marriage. It is more effective to work on repairing the relationship together, but if only one spouse is willing to do so, there is still hope that the actions of one can create positive change in the relationship and spur the other spouse to action (Davis, 2001). We also recommend three excellent books for those at the crossroads of divorce to give them perspective and guidance. *The Seven Principles for Making Marriage Work* (Gottman & Silver, 1999) and *The Divorce Remedy* (Davis, 2001) take a secular approach while *Covenant Hearts* (Hafen, 2005) has a sacred focus.

Whatever sincere actions are taken, we know that a loving God will support those efforts to help couples preserve a union that is essential to his plan for the eternal welfare of his children. And if those efforts ultimately prove unfruitful, then couples can know that they have done all they could to honor a relationship ordained of God.

Alan J. Hawkins *is a professor in the School of Family Life at Brigham Young University. He and his wife, Lisa, are the parents of two children and they have two grandchildren.* **Tamara A. Fackrell** *is an attorney and a Ph.D. candidate in marriage, family, and human development at Brigham Young University. She and her husband, Jacob, are the parents of six children.*

References

Addiction Recovery Program. (2010). Accessed July 24, 2010, from http:// www.providentliving.org/content/display/0,11666,6629-1-3414-1,00.html

Afifi, T. O., MacMillan, H., Cox, B. J., Asmundson, G. J. G., Stein, M. B., & Sareen, J. (2009). Mental health correlates of intimate partner violence in marital relationships in a nationally representative sample of males and females. *Journal of Interpersonal Violence, 24,* 1398–1417.

Allen, E. S., & Atkins, D. C. (under review). The likelihood of divorce given extramarital sex.

Amato, P. R. (2000). The consequences of divorce for adults and children. *Journal of Marriage and the Family, 62,* 1269–1287.

Amato, P. R. (2005). The impact of family formation change on the cognitive, social, and emotional well-being of the next generation. *The Future of Children, 15*(2), 75–96.

Amato, P. R., & Booth, A. (1997). *A generation at risk.* Cambridge: Harvard University.

Amato, P. R., & Hohmann-Marriott, B. (2007). A comparison of high- and low-distress marriages that end in divorce. *Journal of Marriage and Family, 69,* 621–638.

Andreß. H, & Hummelsheim, D. (2009). When marriage ends: Results and conclusions. In H. Andreß & D. Hummelsheim (Eds.), *When marriage ends: Economic and social consequences of partnership dissolution* (pp. 286–329). Cheltenham, UK: Edward Elgar.

Bramlett, M. D., & Mosher, W. D. (2001). First marriage dissolution, divorce, and remarriage: United States. Advance data from vital and health statistics, no. 323. Hyattsville, MD: National Center for Health Statistics.

Bray, J., & Jouriles, E. N. (1995). Treatment of marital conflict and prevention of divorce: *Journal of Marital and Family Therapy, 21,* 461–473.

Butler, M. H., Gardner, B. C., and Bird, M. H. (1998). Not Just a Time Out: Change Dynamics of Prayer for Religious Couples in Conflict Situations. *Family Process 37,* 451–478.

Campbell, J. C. (2002). Health consequences of intimate partner violence. *The Lancet, 359,* 1331–1336.

Davis, M. W. (2001). *The Divorce Remedy: The Proven Seven-Step Program for Saving Your Marriage.* New York: Simon and Schuster.

Emery, R. E. (2004). *The truth about children and divorce: Dealing with the emotions so you and your children can thrive.* New York: Viking.

Emery, R. E., & Sbarra, D. A. (2002). Addressing separation and divorce during and after couple therapy. In A. S. Gurman & N. S. Jacobson (Eds.), *Clinical handbook of couple therapy,* 3rd ed. (pp. 508–530). New York: Guilford.

Faust, J. E. (2004, August). Fathers, mothers, marriage. *Ensign, 34*(8), 3–7.

Gottman, J. M., & Silver, N. (1999). *The Seven Principles for Making Marriage Work.* New York: Crown.

Hafen, B. C. (2005). *Covenant hearts: Marriage and the joy of human love.* Salt Lake City: Deseret Book.

Hawkins, A. J., & Fackrell, T. A. (2009). *Should I keep trying to work it out? A guidebook for individuals and couples at the crossroads of divorce (and before).* Salt Lake City: Utah Commission on Marriage.

Heaton, T. B., Bahr, S. J., & Jacobson, C. K. (2004). *A statistical profile of Mormons: Health, wealth, and social life.* Lewiston, NY: Edwin Mellen Press.

Hetherington, E. M., & Kelly, J. (2002). *For better or for worse: Divorce reconsidered.* New York: W. W. Norton.

Hinckley, G. B. (2000). *Standing for something: Ten neglected virtues that will heal our hearts and homes.* New York: Times Books.

Jones, J. M. (2008, March 25). Most Americans not willing to forgive unfaithful spouse. Gallup Poll. Retrieved from www.gallup.com/poll/105682/Most-Americans -Willing-Forgive-Unfaithful-Spouse.aspx.

Lambert, N. M., & Dollahite, D. C. (2006). How Religiosity Helps Couples Prevent, Resolve, and Overcome Marital Conflict. *Family Relations, 55,* 439–449.

Marquardt, E. (2005). *Between two worlds: The inner lives of children of divorce.* New York: Crown.

McClendon, R. J., & Chadwick, B. A. (2005). Latter-day Saint families at the dawn of the twenty-first century. In C. H. Hart, L. D. Newell, E. Walton, & D. C. Dollahite (Eds.) *Helping and healing our families* (pp. 32–43). Salt Lake City: Deseret Book.

National Fatherhood Initiative. (2005). *With this ring… A national survey on marriage in America.* Gaithersburg, MD: The National Fatherhood Initiative.

Oaks, D. H. (2007, May). Divorce. *Ensign, 37*(5), 70–73.

Popenoe, D. (2008). Cohabitation, marriage and child wellbeing: A cross-national perspective. Pistacaway, NJ: The National Marriage Project. Retrieved from http://www.virginia.edu/marriageproject/pdfs/NMP2008CohabitationReport.pdf

Popenoe, D., & Whitehead, B. D. (2007). The state of our unions 2007: The social health of marriage in America. Piscataway, NJ: The National Marriage Project. Retrieved from http://www.virginia.edu/marriageproject/pdfs/SOOU2007.pdf

Schramm, D., Marshall, J., Harris, V., & George, A. (2003). *Marriage in Utah: 2003 baseline statewide survey on marriage and divorce.* Salt Lake City: Utah Department of Workforce Services. Retrieved from http://utahmarriage.org/files/uploads/UtahMarriage-2.pdf

Snyder, D. K., Baucom, D. H., & Gordon, K. C. (2007). *Getting past the affair: A program to help you cope, heal, and move on—together or apart.* New York: Guilford.

Stanley, S. M. (2005). *The power of commitment.* San Francisco: Jossey-Bass.

Waite, L. J., & Gallagher, M. (2000). *The case for marriage.* New York: Doubleday.

Waite, L. J., Browning, D., Doherty, W. J., Gallagher, M., Luo, Y., & Stanley, S. M. (2002). *Does divorce make people happy? Findings from a study of unhappy marriages.* New York: Institute for American Values. Retrieved from http://www.americanvalues.org/UnhappyMarriages.pdf

Waite, L. J., Luo, Y, & Lewin, A. C. (2009). Marital happiness and marital stability: Consequences for psychological well-being. *Social Science Research, 38,* 201–212.

Wallerstein, J., Lewis, J. M., & Blakeslee, S. (2000). *The unexpected legacy of divorce: A 25- year landmark study.* New York: Hyperion.

Ward, D. B., & McCollum, E. E. (2005). Treatment effectiveness and its correlates in a marriage and family therapy training clinic. *The American Journal of Family Therapy, 33,* 207–223.

Wineberg, H. (1995). An examination of ever-divorced women who attempted a marital reconciliation before becoming divorced. *Journal of Divorce and Remarriage, 22*(3/4), 129–146.

Wolfinger, N. H. (2005). *Understanding the divorce cycle: The children of divorce in their own marriages.* New York: Cambridge University.

Woodward, L., Fergusson, D. M., & Horwood, L. J. (2001). Risk factors and life processes associated with teenage pregnancy: Results of a prospective study from birth to 20 years. *Journal of Marriage and Family, 63,* 1170–1184.

CHAPTER 9

Marriage in the Later Years

Jonathan G. Sandberg, James M. Harper, James G. Strait, and Carly D. Larsen LeBaron

The family is ordained of God. Marriage between a man and a woman is essential to His eternal plan. . . .
The divine plan of happiness enables family relationships to be perpetuated beyond the grave.

IN HIS BEST-SELLING BOOK *TUESDAYS WITH MORRIE*, Mitch Albom describes an interchange with his old professor, Morrie Schwartz, as they discuss keys to a good marriage:

> [Morrie:] "I've learned this much about marriage," he said. "You get tested. You find out who you are, who the other person is, and how you accommodate or don't."
> [Mitch:] Is there some kind of rule to know if a marriage is going to work?
> Morrie smiled. "Things are not that simple, Mitch."
> [Mitch:] I know.
> [Morrie:] "Still, there are a few rules I know to be true about love and marriage. If you don't respect the other person you're gonna have a lot of trouble. If you don't know how to compromise, you're gonna have a lot of trouble. If you can't talk openly about what goes on between you, you're gonna have a lot of trouble. And if you don't have a common set of values in life, you're gonna have a lot of trouble. Your values must be alike.
> "And the best one of those values, Mitch?"
> [Mitch:] Yes?
> [Morrie:] "Your belief in the *importance* of your marriage" (Albom, 1997, 149, italics in original).

Whether a couple is newly married or celebrating a 50th wedding anniversary, creating and maintaining a mutually satisfying, stable, vibrant marital relationship takes time, effort, and a shared commitment about the importance of marriage. "The Family: A Proclamation to the World" succinctly and powerfully states, "The family is ordained of God. Marriage between a man and a woman is essential to His eternal plan. . . . The divine plan of happiness enables family relationships to be perpetuated beyond the grave" (1995, ¶¶ 7, 3). Because marriage is meant to be eternal, its centrality and importance among human relationships does not decrease over time. Yet in scholarly and religious literature, mature marriages have not received the attention afforded the newly married or couples raising children. The tendency to over-focus on the young is curious, considering the fastest-growing segment of the world's population is over age 65, or will be within the next 20 years, with explosive growth in developing, non-European countries such as Singapore, Malaysia, Colombia, and Costa Rica (Kinsella & Velkoff, 2001). The over-focus on the young has spiritual consequences as well. The purpose of this chapter is to highlight some of the challenges and opportunities facing couples as their marriages mature over time, as well as to provide practical suggestions for dealing with those challenges and maximizing opportunities in the last third of life.

Principles Underlying Successful Marriages

Over the last few decades, researchers from around the world have sought to identify principles and practices that contribute to high-quality marital relationships (Zao-huo, Xiao-hong, & Lin-xiang, 2005; Johns, 2005). In their attempts to identify these keys, some researchers have focused on the way couples communicate

(Markman, Renick, Floyd, Stanley, & Clements, 1993). Others have highlighted couples' attempts to address conflict and resolve problems (Gottman & Gottman, 2008). Some have stressed the importance of the emotional bond or attachment between partners (Johnson & Whiffen, 2003), while a few have articulately described a couple's relationship with God and its impact on marital functioning (Butler & Harper, 1994).

A clear, comprehensive summary of key processes underlying successful marriages is included in chapter 3 of this book. In their chapter, Duncan and McCarty highlight the need for (a) personal commitment to the marriage covenant, (b) love and friendship, (c) positivity, (d) the ability to accept influence from one's spouse, (e) the respectful handling of differences and the ability to solve problems, and (f) continual courtship throughout the years. This excellent summary of key processes includes an integration of scholarly and prophetic writings that can guide couples at any stage of the life cycle toward healthier interaction and closer connection.

Of particular importance to the discussion of mature marriage in this chapter is attachment theory (Bowlby, 1988; Mikulincer & Shaver, 2007). Attachment theory suggests that there is an innate, motivating force hardwired in the brain that compels all humans, at all points in the life cycle, to seek contact and connection to others (Johnson, 2004). When securely and safely connected to others, both men and women are more confident; are healthier physically, mentally, and emotionally; and are able to more effectively cope with life's stresses and challenges. When isolated, abandoned, or in a conflictual relationship, both partners suffer (Kiecolt-Glaser & Newton, 2001; Johnson, 2004; Sandberg, Miller, Harper, Robila, & Davey, 2009). Thus, developing and maintaining a secure base and safe haven within marriage becomes the great challenge across the life cycle for all couples (Johnson, 2008).

Because of the potential for decline, loss, unresolved conflict, and forced transitions in the last third of life, older couples are particularly vulnerable to isolation, distance, and long-standing wounds in their marital relationships. Researchers and clinicians have begun to draw attention to the clear need for secure attachments in later life, highlighting greater adjustment following bereavement, healthier transition to illness and caregiving, and better overall well-being for older adults with attachment security (Bradley & Palmer, 2003). Therefore, older couples with secure and safe marital bonds

(that is, accessible, responsive, and engaged partners) will likely be better prepared to adapt successfully to the challenges of aging and thrive in later life. In the end, forming and maintaining a strong marital bond in the last third of life serves as both *preventative* and *curative* medicine for most common ills of later life.

There is an abundance of both scholarly research and inspired counsel from Church leaders to help couples practice general principles leading to satisfying marriages. But there is less direction on how to maintain a high-quality marriage across the life cycle or to rebuild and fortify a mature marriage that lacks strength and stability. Could it be that there are particular challenges and opportunities in marriage during the last third of life that require special attention, above and beyond the outstanding principles mentioned previously? Are there some normal developmental transitions (such as empty nesting, retirement, loss of loved ones, forced change of residence, health issues, and caregiving) that will likely tax and strain even the strongest marriages? Are there practices and principles particular to this stage of married life that, if applied, could make the journey more manageable and even enjoyable for mature couples? Because we believe the answer to these three questions is a resounding *yes,* we feel it is crucial that couples consider the distinctive challenges, opportunities, and coping strategies that correspond to mature marriage.

Challenges Facing Mid- and Later-Life Couples

A number of mid- and later-life transitions pose obstacles for mature couples seeking to repair or strengthen marital bonds (Bradley & Palmer, 2003). A review of these transitions and challenges can help couples to, first, recognize that such struggles are normal, and second, develop a plan to address them. These events and experiences do not cause marital conflict or distance in and of themselves; it is likely the way couples prepare for and respond to the challenges that determines these obstacles' overall impact on marriage (Johnson, 2008).

Empty nest. A wife married for 33 years said, "It's important to build a good relationship with your spouse so that when the children leave, you have the underlying joy of focusing on each other and not your adult children" (Arp & Arp, 1996, p. 68).

The natural process of launching children can cause strain and uncover marital difficulties for many couples because they have allowed distance and differences to grow over time. Research suggests that the empty nest period is a transition that can be successfully navigated by couples if they understand and address the issues uncovered at this time of marriage (Mitchell & Lovegreen, 2009).

The launching of children can require several major shifts for older couples. First, the empty nest transition often necessitates a role change (Arp & Arp, 1996). If our lives are no longer driven by the activities and daily needs of children, what is our purpose? This shift can be particularly difficult for mothers who have been actively engaged in mothering for many years and find themselves alone for long stretches of the work week or with unwanted free time. Second and closely related, older adults, particularly mothers, may face an identity crisis as they adjust to this new stage of life (Owen, 2005). They may ask, "Who am I now that I am no longer a full-time parent?" If either partner is retired or has not worked outside the home, the identity crisis may be more pronounced.

The great question of this period therefore becomes, "What are some things [we] can do to develop a partner-focused [versus child-focused] marriage?" (Arp & Arp, 1996, p. 83). At this point in marriage, couples must draw together, rekindle romance, and begin to redefine themselves as marital partners as well as parents or individuals. This transition can be challenging because many couples have let their relationship slip to the back burner for many years, giving career and children perhaps too high a priority. Such relational neglect, although common, is curable, even avoidable. Because forming a strong bond with one's partner and developing a solid support network seem to facilitate better adjustment to the empty nest stage of marriage, mid-life couples would do well to shore up these key relationships before, during, and after they begin to launch children (Arp, Arp, Stanley, Markman, & Blumberg, 2000).

Retirement. "People need to prepare emotionally for retirement," advises one who has experienced this stage of life. "People planning to retire need to retire to something," not just from something, because "adjusting to less money and being home all the time is a real change." A recently retired man stated, "The first year [after retirement] was absolutely terrible, I didn't know what to do with myself. . . . I still get edgy now and then and want to go and do things and get out of the house." An older woman observed, "When you have a man who

has worked all his life and is now home and doesn't have any real hobbies or anything, [he's] always there. You take a step backwards and you're going to step on his toes; I mean it's been seven years [since his retirement] and we still have that" (transcripts of interviews with older couples, Sandberg, 1998, p. 66–67).

Whereas the empty nest transition seems to be particularly challenging for women, retirement struggles are most often linked to men. Perhaps many men view their role as provider as primary among the "three P's"—provide, preside, protect—whereas women are focused on their primary role as nurturers in the family (see ¶ 7). As a result, the role transition and identity re-formation required at retirement may represent bigger obstacles for retiring men, particularly those with little practical experience with day-to-day household labor. In any case, retirement clearly impacts marriage for both partners as both face major role changes.

Research has shown that for well-adjusted couples, retirement can simply mean more of something that is good, such as increased time together and shared household labor (Davey & Szinovacz, 2004). However, for couples with pre-existing marital problems, retirement can mean more of the not-so-good as conflict results from those same areas of more time together and shared household labor, particularly if the husband's presence at home represents an intrusion into the wife's domain (Davey & Szinovacz, 2004). Coping strategies relevant to the empty nest stage include building a secure bond in marriage, developing interests outside of work, retiring to something and not just from something, and becoming partner-focused. These strategies apply also to the post-retirement stage of married life.

Physical decline. President Gordon B. Hinckley quipped:

More and more we are living longer, thanks to the miracle of modern science and medical practice. But with old age comes a deterioration of physical capacity and sometimes mental capacity. I have said before that I have discovered that there is much of lead in the years that are called golden" (Hinckley, 2002, p. 54).

On a more serious note, President Boyd K. Packer said, "When your body begins to deteriorate, the patterns of revelation will be augmented and magnified" (Packer, 2003a, p. 5).

It is natural for the physical body to decline over time (Viña, Borrás, & Miquel, 2007). Normative aging processes impact mobility, memory, stamina, strength, sexual functioning, sight, hearing, and many other physical and cognitive processes (Cavanaugh & Blanchard-Fields, 2010). The challenge of facing and accepting the changes that accompany aging and eventually precede death may begin to surface at what some call the "midlife crisis" (Becker, 2006). The struggle to see positively the exchange of physical vitality and youth for the gifts of aging (wisdom, stability, transcendence) can influence both individuals and marriages. This may be especially true when decline requires major changes in the way partners relate to each other and in their overall quality of life, which can lead to other mental and emotional health problems if not addressed. These specific challenges will be discussed in greater detail in the caregiving section that follows.

Importantly, the aforementioned physical changes alone do not pose the greatest threat to marriage in the last third of life. As western culture has become obsessed with youth, beauty, sex appeal, productivity, and physical strength, many middle-aged and older adults have moved from working toward peaceful acceptance to intensely fighting the aging process (Cox, 2010). This hyper-focus on youth has implications for couples. Individual partners may become increasingly self-focused—causing partners to withdraw into isolation as the losses and pains of aging set in—at a time when a focus on others (family, community, and service) could bring peace. In addition to providing loving encouragement and support as decline marches on, partners will likely need to help each other accept the changes that accompany aging. For example, couples can work to broaden their definition of adult romantic love to include stability and serenity in addition to the passion they developed as young lovers.

Caregiving. President Packer related the following insights regarding his family's experience with caregiving:

My wife and I have seen our grandparents and then our parents leave us. Some experiences that we first thought to be burdens or trouble have long since been reclassified as blessings. My wife's father died in our home. He needed constant care. Nurses taught our children how to care for our bedridden grandpa. What they learned is of great

worth to them and to us. How grateful we are to have had him close to us. We were repaid a thousand times over by the influence he had on our children. That was a great experience for our children, one I learned as a boy when Grandpa Packer died in our home (Packer, 2003b, pp. 83–84).

Caregiving, whether for a parent or a spouse, is truly a tension of opposites where a person can feel isolation and connection, burden and joy, sorrow and peace. Midlife couples often find themselves in a double caregiving position: they may still be looking after children as they begin providing care for an aging parent. These couples are often referred to as the "sandwich" or "bridge" generation because they simultaneously provide care for the generations before and after themselves. They seem to experience more strain and live less healthy lives than others in their cohort (Chassin, Macy, Seo, Presson, & Sherman, 2010). In terms of marriage, these bridge generation couples will have to work hard to foster and maintain a strong bond in marriage during this period of increased demands on their time and resources. Marital struggles in the face of stress and strain are both normal and understandable. The key is for couples to identify overload and growing distance or conflict between them early on and address those issues as they arise, before they become problematic. If problems are not easily resolved, couples can and may wish to seek outside help (Sandberg, 2006).

One major challenge for couples is the requirement to provide care for a spouse with significant limitations. Caregivers in general experience lower levels of subjective well-being and physical health as well as greater levels of stress and depression than non-caregivers (Pinquart & Sorensen, 2003), all of which can tax relationships. However, spousal caregivers seem to experience a more personal burden than other caregivers, particularly when aspects of spousal intimacy are decreased due to cognitive, physical, or other types of impairment. The loss of connection to one's spouse, although he or she is still living, is referred to as a type of ambiguous loss, which is difficult to name and overtly mourn (Boss, 1999). Although providing care can bring a sense of satisfaction, joy, and fulfillment to some caregivers (Sandberg, 2006), it comes at great cost to spousal caregivers who are forced to give up a sense of partnership, unity, and true companionship as limitations increase over time.

The sense of loss and unwanted change can be exacerbated if couples are required to change residences or even be physically separated as the ill partner requires increased care or a specialized living environment. Not all families will choose or are able to provide in-home care for parents or partners as President Boyd K. Packer described previously. The inability to age in a familiar and self-selected environment represents another loss that some face, often without the support and understanding of a declining spouse (Cox, 2010). In such cases, where one partner is still highly functioning and the other is not, support from extended family, friends, and others becomes crucial (Zarit & Zarit, 1998). Managing these difficult times in the marital life cycle with some sense of dignity will likely require all the resources a spouse has developed over the years (such as wisdom, patience, and long-suffering), as well as the consistent support of additional loved ones. In the end, such soul-stretching sequences in life's journey will require divine help, as suggested by Elder Dallin H. Oaks:

> [The Savior] knows of our anguish, and He is there for us. . . . [His] healing blessings come in many ways, each suited to our individual needs, as known to Him who loves us best. Sometimes a "healing" cures our illness or lifts our burden. But sometimes we are "healed" by being given strength or understanding or patience to bear the burdens placed upon us. [Alma and his people] . . . did not have their burdens removed, but the Lord strengthened them so that "they could bear up their burdens with ease, and they did submit cheerfully and with patience to all the will of the Lord" (Mosiah 24:15). This same promise and effect applies to you . . . caregivers who are burdened (Oaks, 2006, pp. 7–8).

Loss of loved ones. In the following passage, a novelist describes one husband's feelings after the loss of a child:

> For three nights he hadn't known how to touch [his wife] or what to say. Before, they had never found themselves **broken together.** Usually, it was one needing the other but not both needing each other, and so there had been a way, by touching, to borrow from the stronger one's strength. And they had never understood, as they did now, what

the word *horror* meant (Sebold, 2002, pp. 20–21, boldface added, italics in original).

Loss of loved ones can pose problems for mature couples. A simple yet painful fact is that with aging comes the greater likelihood that our dear ones (parents, siblings, even children) will precede us in death. Mourning, grief, and suffering are natural byproducts of a loving relationship severed, although temporarily, by death. As Elder Russell M. Nelson said,

> The only length of life that seems to satisfy the longings of the human heart is life everlasting. Irrespective of age, we mourn for those loved and lost. Mourning is one of the deepest expressions of pure love. It is a natural response in complete accord with divine commandment: "Thou shalt live together in love, insomuch that thou shalt weep for the loss of them that die" (D&C 42:45). Moreover, we can't fully appreciate joyful reunions later without tearful separations now. The only way to take sorrow out of death is to take love out of life (Nelson, 1992, p. 72).

Grieving and sorrow are natural, even healthy (Lindstrom, 2002). Nevertheless, even healthy mourning and grieving can lead to distance and separation in marriage if partners fail to connect or bond during grieving. In the initial quote of this section, Alice Sebold (2002), author of *The Lovely Bones,* wrote eloquently of the distance that can grow between parents after the death of a child. Couples in such situations must work to find shared coping mechanisms that unite them, especially when silent withdrawal into hurt and depression may feel more natural and less painful (Ungureanu & Sandberg, 2010).

But what if the loss is the death of one's spouse? What do widows and widowers—those who consider themselves married, yet alone for a season—do in times of struggle? Because widowhood is a near-majority experience for older women across the world and for a sizeable number of men, it is important to address the impact of spousal death after long-term marriage. Cattell (2009) notes that more than 50 percent of women age 60 and older are widows in Egypt, Ethiopia, China, India, and Russia. In one study of recently widowed women, the author reported that participants appeared to be adjusting well despite high levels of grief. For these women, high levels of retrospective marital quality were positively related to self-esteem, with higher self-esteem acting as a significant predictor of greater life satisfaction and lower levels of depression (Howard, 2000). Apparently, a perceived strong marital connection, even after the death of a partner, is linked to positive outcomes, further highlighting the need for strong marital bonds across the life cycle (Johnson, 2008).

Even those widows and widowers with positive feelings toward their deceased partner will be required to face potentially troubling decisions related to living arrangements, finances, social commitments, and possible remarriage (O'Bryant & Hansson, 1995). Certainly social support from family and other loved ones can play a crucial role in helping widows or widowers make important decisions regarding the future. Other research notes that one's church community (Stuckey, 1997) can also provide support and combat isolation and depression, as can volunteerism (Li, 2007). Both academic and religious literature suggest that engagement with life, especially after the loss of one's partner, can provide needed emotional and physical health benefits as well as purpose and meaning in life. President Ezra Taft Benson taught:

> The key to overcoming aloneness and a feeling of uselessness for one who is physically able is to step outside yourself by helping others who are truly needy. We promise those who will render this kind of service that, in some measure, you will be healed of the loss of loved ones or the dread of being alone. The way to feel better about your own situation is to improve someone else's circumstances (Benson, 1989, p. 6).

Remarriage brings with it a separate set of blessings and challenges. There are numerous perceived benefits that can lead a widow or widower to remarry, including companionship, financial security, shared intimacy, increased quality of life, and opportunities to serve (O'Bryant & Hansson, 1995). Certainly the response of two mature, larger, extended families to the requirement of "sharing mom or dad" can prove problematic as new role requirements are introduced into both families. In addition, there are a number of practical (financial and legal) issues around the globe that prevent some older adults from remarrying after death or divorce in mid- to

later life. Blending families at any stage of the life cycle is not a job for the faint of heart; yet there is a great deal of research and practical information available to families as they attempt to make this transition and do it well (Gonzales, 2009; Wells, 1997).

Addressing old wounds. While a member of the Seventy, Elder Hugh W. Pinnock shared the following story:

> A couple . . . married later in life; the wife had been married before, but it was the husband's first marriage. After several months of marital bliss, a serious disagreement erupted that so hurt the husband emotionally that he could not function at his daily tasks. As he reeled from the impact of this confrontation, he stopped to analyze the problem and realized that at least a part of the problem had been his. He went to his bride and stammered awkwardly several times, "I'm sorry, Honey." The wife burst into tears, confessing that much of the problem was hers, and asked forgiveness. As they held each other, she confessed that in her experience those words of apology had not been used before, and she now knew that any of their future problems could be worked out. She felt secure because she knew they both could say, "I'm sorry"; "I forgive" (Pinnock, 1981, p. 36–37).

We have saved perhaps the most difficult process for last in our discussion of mid- to later-life marital challenges. Over time in any marriage there are likely to be numerous wounds, both intentional and unintentional. In their fine book *The Second Half of Marriage*, Arp and Arp (1996) describe the need to "let go of past marital disappointments, forgive each other, and commit to making the rest of your marriage the best" it can be (p. 51). Numerous authors, teachers, and clinicians, both secular (Fincham, Hall, & Beach, 2006) and religious (Sorensen, 2003; Faust, 2007) have made a powerful case for the need for forgiveness in life and especially in marriage (Miller, 2010). In cases of more significant injuries involving abandonment, betrayal, and abuse, couples may need overt healing conversations and rituals that require time, consistent effort, and sometimes outside help (Johnson, 2004). In all cases, divine help is needed to truly repent and forgive (Packer, 1979).

One approach to forgiveness and healing, as proposed by Hargrave and colleagues (Hargrave & Anderson,

1992, 1997; Hargrave & Hanna, 1997), comprises forgiveness in later life as two distinct processes: exoneration and forgiveness. *Exoneration* means the victim can come to understand the frailties and humanity of the victimizer, without necessarily resolving the injury, "whereas forgiveness means that the victim and victimizer are actually able to restore a loving and trustworthy relationship" (Hargrave & Anderson, 1997, p. 68). They propose that the work of forgiveness involves two steps: giving the opportunity for compensation and the overt act of forgiveness.

Giving the opportunity for compensation is a process whereby the victim allows the victimizer to demonstrate trustworthiness and show love in an attempt to address and erase past injustice (Hargrave & Anderson, 1992). During this process, the hurt party can test, in stages, the trustworthiness of the one who has inflicted pain. The theory states that only as trustworthiness is rebuilt can a true healing connection be re-established.

The overt act of forgiveness occurs when both the victim and victimizer directly address past wrongs, and apologies are offered and received. During this process, the victim and victimizer agree what the hurt is, acknowledge that the wrongdoer is responsible for the wounds inflicted, and facilitate an apology that demonstrates regret and a sincere desire to do better (Hargrave & Hanna, 1997). This process, though intense and only possible with two willing parties, can provide tremendous healing. In some situations, the help of a qualified and competent professional or clergy member may be required to accomplish this last step. Yet healing and forgiveness are possible even when addressing longstanding and painful issues in mid- and later-life marriages.

Taking Advantage of Distinctive Opportunities Facing Mature Couples

Perhaps while reviewing any list of common struggles in the last third of life, couples, families, and professionals may overlook the numerous opportunities that are only afforded those experiencing the gifts of aging. President Ezra Taft Benson spoke of the Lord's appreciation for the wisdom and other contributions of the more experienced among us:

> The Lord knows and loves the elderly among His people. It has always been so, and upon them He has bestowed many of His greatest responsibilities.

In various dispensations He has guided His people through prophets who were in their advancing years. He has needed the wisdom and experience of age, the inspired direction from those with long years of proven faithfulness to His gospel. . . . How the Lord knows and loves His children who have given so much through their years of experience! (Benson, 1989, p. 4).

Perspective and the ability to share and teach. With age comes experience and perspective. President Packer said, "Life's lessons, some of them very painful, qualify [older adults] to counsel, to correct, and . . . try to teach the practical things [they] have learned over the years to those who are younger—to . . . family and to others" (Packer, 2003b, p. 84). Because of life's lessons, older adults are often in a better position to know what really matters, what brings happiness and what does not. Robert Butler described one process that further amplifies older adults' understanding of the true meaning of life. In his 1963 landmark article, Butler coined the phrase "life review," which describes the naturally occurring period of reflection about the purpose and meaning of existence as one draws nearer to death. This life review is not a global or theoretical process; instead each individual will be prompted to evaluate the purpose, meaning, and efficacy of his or her own life. This review often leads to a shift in priorities and sincere attempts to reconcile past mistakes. As a result, older adults are in a position to teach, share wisdom, and help others avoid the mistakes they have made. There are many outlets for this type of sharing and teaching. Some older couples gather family and friends regularly to create formal teaching moments; others write weekly letters and blogs filled with wisdom and perspective; others volunteer in local schools or work with children and youth. Such sharing of wisdom by older adults is a blessing to all.

Increased discretionary time. When the daily demands of childrearing and the work force have subsided, many older adults find themselves with extra time, a luxury previously unknown to them (Lee & King, 2003). This opportunity can turn into a detriment if couples withdraw from social, mental, or physical activity as relational roles and expectations shift (Rowe & Kahn, 1997). For the first time in many years, post-retirement and post-childrearing couples may pursue hobbies, interests, or projects long relegated to the back burner. An increasing number of grandparents are actively raising grandchildren (Pinazo-Hernandis & Tompkins, 2009). This contribution to the next generation represents a selfless use of discretionary time by many older couples. Other older couples turn to service and volunteerism to fill discretionary time.

Service. Because older couples have both wisdom to share and the time to make a difference in families, churches, and communities, many turn to service and volunteerism in the last third of life (Morrow-Howell, Hinterlong, Rozario, & Tang, 2003). Research and inspired declarations have long shown that volunteer service enhances well-being on many levels for older adults (Benson, 1989; Thoits & Hewitt, 2001). Of particular interest to many older couples, and dear to their hearts, is church service. Church service and participation has been linked not only to increased well-being and decreased depression (Stuckey, 1997), but also to increased life expectancy (Hummer, Rogers, Nam, & Ellison, 1999).

Particular to Latter-day Saint culture is the emphasis on missionary service as a couple in the last third of life (Hales, 2005; Nelson, 2004). Not only does this type of service yield many benefits for couples and those they serve, but it also has the potential to enhance marital bonds as couples work together as companions in a common cause. Many of the challenges facing later-life couples (marital distance, lack of common interests and goals, lack of meaningful work after active parenting and full-time work) can be addressed and resolved prior to or even during missionary or temple service. Arp and Arp (1996), married counselors who work with elderly couples, describe the need to "evaluate where you are in your spiritual pilgrimage, grow closer to each other and to God, and together serve others" (p. 171). Both secular and religious insights suggest that spiritual, couple-based service (such as missionary work) is a great way for couples to draw together and make a positive difference in the world during the last stages of their lives (see Hales, 2005).

A Multitude of Experiences: A Focus on Global Experiences of Aging Couples

Much of the research on marriage in the later years has examined older couples in the United States, and even much of the conceptualization about what married couples experience in later years occurs through a Western/

European lens in which nuclear families live separately and sometimes long distances from their extended families. For example, the concept of an "empty nest" makes sense when the typical pattern is living in a nuclear family in which parents raise children, children grow up and move away, and the primary emphasis is placed again on marriage and one's marital partner.

In some cultures, however, such as those in the South Pacific, extended family often are more involved in each others' lives, even in raising children. In many Asian cultures, one of the governing Confucian principles is a child's allegiance to parents. This emphasis sometimes makes marriage less of a focus than the parent–child relationship. In these countries, parents traditionally move in with adult children and their families when the parents reach a certain age. For example, when adults reach their 60th birthday in Korea, tradition encourages a ceremonial celebration because the person is viewed as entering a "second childhood," and traditionally parents move in with the oldest child and his or her family. Sung (1998) described how filial piety (dutiful respect for parents) influences how extended family relate to an elderly married couple even when the older couple does not live with adult children. Kamo and Zhou (1994) found that elderly Chinese and Japanese in the United States were more likely to live in extended-family households. For these couples, the "empty nest" phenomenon as the beginning of a period where they turn more toward each other may be an alien concept.

Many Latino families also share the perspective that "we take care of our own." This strong sense of family, or *familismo,* leads many Latino families to provide care in the home for older adults, even in the face of disability (Gonzalez-Sanders, 2007). The tendency to rely on families for support and services (Talamantes, Lawler, & Espino, 1995) makes it less likely that older Latino couples will experience or desire an "empty nest" stage. Economic pressures facing older immigrants also can make retirement more of a dream than a reality.

In Asian cultures, the idea of "saving face" and talking more indirectly flavors the communication patterns of elderly couples (Ling, Wong, & Ho, 2008). The style of direct communication in the United States, where openness and assertiveness are valued and perhaps sought after as an ultimate marital accomplishment for older couples, would not be valued by more traditional Asian couples. In such cases, deep emotional disclosure and the direct resolution of problems may not be seen as healthy processes.

An additional contextual force that affects later marriages is how religious or how secularized the country in which they live has become. For example, in Muslim and Jewish cultures, elders have major significance in families, which results in both married couples and their children viewing later life as a time for being involved with extended family. Lavee and Katz (2003) found that the majority of elderly Israeli citizens, both Jews and Arabs, live close to children and have daily physical or telephone contact. While we know very little about later-life marriage and living arrangements for Africans, the pattern of living in extended family groups is probably similar, especially in African nations with Muslim influence.

Physical changes and the need for caregiving as life moves on are universal in all cultures and nations. The lens through which married persons view caring for their spouses in later life may differ, depending on whether they live in a culture that values extended-family caregiving or a culture where the burdens of caregiving fall mainly on a married partner. Cultures that value extended-family involvement in elderly care are more likely to find positive meaning and experience the blessings that come from involving multiple family members in caregiving.

Conclusion

The last third of marriage can be a time of strengthening marital bonds and solidifying spiritual resolve. Abraham and Sarah serve as an example of an elderly couple faced with a particular physical and spiritual challenge: The Lord had promised Abraham that his seed would be as numerous as the stars (Genesis 15:5), and yet they grew old, past the age of childbearing for Sarah, and still did not have any children. Nevertheless, Sarah gave birth to Isaac in keeping with God's covenant with Abraham (Genesis 21:1–3). Even in the face of Sarah's doubts, an angel admonished, "Is any thing too hard for the Lord?" (Genesis 18:14). As we mature in our marriages, we can have faith that "with God all things are possible" (Matthew 19:26). Commitment, tenacity, and faith are required to confront successfully (in a unifying and supportive way) the many challenges faced by mature married couples. The rewards of such "works of righteousness, . . . including peace in this life

and eternal life in the world to come" (D&C 59:23), are within the reach of all older couples who are willing to consistently apply principles that lead to the formation of a safe haven and a secure bond in marriage.

Jonathan Sandberg *is a professor of marriage and family therapy at Brigham Young University. He and his wife, Sharon, are the parents of four children.* James M. Harper *is a Zina Young Williams Card university professor in the School of Family Life at Brigham Young University. He and his wife, Colleen, are the parents of five children and they have seven grandchildren.* James G. Strait *has a master's in marriage and family therapy and works with the Utah Division of Child and Family Services. James and his wife, Lydia, are the parents of three children.* Carly D. Larsen LeBaron *is a doctoral student in marriage and family therapy at BYU and a licensed associate marriage and family therapist. She married her husband, Kevin, in June 2011.*

References

Albom, M. (1997). *Tuesdays with Morrie: An old man, a young man, and life's greatest lesson.* New York: Doubleday.

Arp, D., & Arp, C. (1996). *The second half of marriage: Facing the eight challenges of every long-term marriage.* Grand Rapids, MI: Zondervan.

Arp, D. H., Arp, C. S., Stanley, S. M., Markman, H. J., & Blumberg, S. L. (2000). *Fighting for your empty nest marriage: Reinventing your relationship when the kids leave home.* New York: Jossey-Bass.

Becker, D. (2006). Therapy for the middle-aged: The relevance of existential issues. *American Journal of Psychotherapy, 60*(1), 87–99.

Benson, E. T. (1989, November). To the elderly in the Church. *Ensign, 19,* 4–8.

Boss, P. (1999). *Ambiguous loss: Learning to live with unresolved grief.* Cambridge, MA: Harvard University Press.

Bowlby, J. (1988). *A secure base: Parent-child attachment and healthy human development.* New York: Basic Books.

Bradley, J. M., & Palmer, G. (2003). Attachment in later life: Implications for intervention with older adults. In S. M. Johnson & V. E. Whiffen (Eds.), *Attachment processes in couple and family therapy* (pp. 281–299). New York: The Guilford Press.

Butler, M. H., & Harper, J. M. (1994). The divine triangle: God in the marital system of religious couples. *Family Process, 33*(3), 277–286.

Butler, R. N. (1963). The life review: An interpretation of reminiscence in the aged. *Psychiatry, 26,* 65–76.

Cattell, M. G. (2009). Global perspectives on widowhood and aging. In J. Sokolovsky (Ed.), *The cultural context of aging: Worldwide perspectives* (3rd ed.) (pp. 155–172). Westport, CT: Praeger.

Cavanaugh, J. C., & Blanchard-Fields, F. (2010). *Adult development and aging* (6th ed.) Belmont, CA: Wadsworth Cengage Learning.

Chassin, L., Macy, J. T., Seo, D.-C., Presson, C. C., & Sherman, S. J. (2010). The association between membership in the sandwich generation and health behaviors: A longitudinal study. *Journal of Applied Developmental Psychology, 31*(1), 38–46.

Cox, H. (Ed.). (2010). *Annual editions: Aging 09/10.* New York: McGraw-Hill.

Davey, A., & Szinovacz, M. E. (2004). Dimensions of marital quality and retirement. *Journal of Family Issues, 25*(4), 431–464.

Faust, J. E. (2007, May). The healing power of forgiveness. *Ensign, 37,* 67–69.

Fincham, F. D., Hall, J., & Beach, S. R. H. (2006). Forgiveness in marriage: Current status and future directions. *Family Relations, 55*(4), 415–427.

Gonzales, J. (2009). Prefamily counseling: Working with blended families. *Journal of Divorce and Remarriage, 50,* 148–157.

Gonzalez-Sanders, D. J. (2007). Familismo and resilience in latino family caregivers of demential-afflicted relatives: An ethno-cultural cross-sectional study. Doctoral dissertation. Retrieved from *Dissertation Abstracts International* (AAI3271230).

Gottman, J. M., & Gottman, J. S. (2008). Gottman method couple therapy. In A. S. Gurman (Ed.) *Clinical handbook of couple therapy* (4th ed.) (pp. 138–164). New York: Guilford.

Hales, R. D. (2005, May). Couple missionaries: Blessings from sacrifice and service. *Ensign, 35,* 39–42.

Hargrave, T. D., & Anderson, W. T. (1992). Finishing well: Aging and reparation in the intergenerational family. New York: Brunner/Mazel.

Hargrave, T. D., & Anderson, W. T. (1997). Finishing well: A contextual family therapy approach to the aging family. In T. D. Hargrave & S. M. Hanna (Eds.), *The aging family: New visions in theory, practice, and reality.* (pp. 61–80). New York: Brunner/Mazel.

Hargrave, T. D., & Hanna, S. M. (Eds.). (1997). *The aging family: New visions in theory, practice, and reality.* New York: Brunner/Mazel.

Hinckley, G. B. (2002, May). Personal worthiness to exercise the priesthood. *Ensign, 32,* 52–59.

Howard, S. P. (2000). Spousal bereavement in older women: The impact of self-esteem and retrospective reports of marital satisfaction and marital support on adjustment. Doctoral dissertation. Retrieved from *Dissertation Abstracts International* (AAI9941636).

Hummer, R. A., Rogers, R. G., Nam, C. B., & Ellison, C. G. (1999). Religious involvement and U.S. adult mortality. *Demography, 36*(2), 273–285.

Johns, A. L. (2005). The role of affect in the marital satisfaction of monoethnic Latino, biethnic Latino, and European-American newlywed couples. Doctoral dissertation. Retrieved from *Dissertation Abstracts International* (AAI3155428).

Johnson, S. (2008). *Hold me tight: Seven conversations for a lifetime of love.* New York: Little, Brown.

Johnson, S. M. (2004). *The practice of emotionally focused couple therapy (2nd ed.): Creating connection.* New York: Brunner-Routledge.

Johnson, S. M., & Whiffen, V. E. (Eds.). (2003). *Attachment processes in couple and family therapy.* New York: Guilford.

Kamo, Y., & Zhou, M. (1994). Living arrangements of elderly Chinese and Japanese in the United States. *Journal of Marriage and the Family, 56,* 544–558.

Kiecolt-Glaser, J. K., & Newton, T. L. (2001). Marriage and health: His and hers. *Psychological Bulletin. 127*(4), 472–503.

Kinsella, K., & Velkoff, V.A. (2001). *An aging world: 2001.* U.S. Census Bureau, Series P95/01-1. Washington, DC: U.S. Government Printing Office.

Lavee, Y., & Katz, R. (2003) The family in Israel: Between tradition and modernity. *Marriage and Family Review 35*(1–2), 193–217.

Lee, R. E., & King, A. C. (2003). Discretionary time among older adults: How do physical activity promotion interventions affect sedentary and active behaviors? *Annals of Behavioral Medicine, 25*(2), 112–119.

Li, Y. (2007). Recovering from spousal bereavement in later life: Does volunteer participation play a role? *Journals of Gerontology: Series B: Psychological Sciences and Social Sciences, 62B*(4), S257–S266.

Ling, D. C. Y., Wong, W. C. W., & Ho, S. C. (2008). Are post-menopausal women "half-a-man"?: Sexual beliefs, attitudes and concerns among midlife Chinese women. *Journal of Sex and Marital Therapy, 34*, 15–29.

Lindstrom, T. C. (2002). "It ain't necessarily so" . . . Challenging mainstream thinking about bereavement. *Family Community Health, 25*(1), 11–21.

Markman, H. J., Renick, M. J., Floyd, F. J., Stanley, S. M., & Clements, M. (1993). Preventing marital distress through communication and conflict management training: a 4- and 5-year follow-up. *Journal of Consulting and Clinical Psychology, 61*(1), 70–77.

Mikulincer, M., & Shaver, P. R. (2007). *Attachment in adulthood: Structure, dynamics, and change.* New York: Guilford.

Miller, R. (2010, January 19). Repentance and forgiveness in marriage. BYU Devotional Address. Retrieved from http://speeches.byu.edu/reader/reader.php?id=12957&x=61&y=2

Mitchell, B. A., & Lovegreen, L. D. (2009). The empty nest syndrome in midlife families: A multimethod exploration of parental gender differences and cultural dynamics. *Journal of Family Issues, 30*(12), 1651–1670.

Morrow-Howell, N., Hinterlong, J., Rozario, P. A., & Tang, F. (2003). Effects of volunteering on the well-being of older adults. *Journal of Gerontology: Series B: Psychological Sciences and Social Sciences, 58B*(3), S137–S145.

Nelson, R. M. (1992, May) Doors of death. *Ensign, 22*, 72–74.

Nelson, R. M. (2004, November). Senior missionaries and the gospel. *Ensign, 34*, 79–82.

Oaks, D. H. (2006, November). He heals the heavy laden. *Ensign, 36*, 6–9.

O'Bryant, S. L., & Hansson, R. O. (1995). Widowhood. In R. Blieszner & V. H. Bedford (Eds.), *Handbook of aging and the family.* (pp. 440–458). Westport, CT: Greenwood.

Owen, C. J. (2005). The empty nest transition: The relationship between attachment style and women's use of this period as a time for growth and change. Doctoral dissertation. Retrieved from *Dissertation Abstracts International* (AAI3139014).

Packer, B. K. (1979, August). The balm of Gilead. *New Era, 9*, 36–43.

Packer, B. K. (2003a, February 2). The instrument of your mind and the foundation of your character. BYU Devotional Address. Retrieved from http://speeches.byu.edu/reader/reader.php?id=478&x=55&y=4

Packer, B. K. (2003b, May). The golden years. *Ensign, 33*, 82–84.

Pinazo-Hernandis, S., & Tompkins, C. J. (2009). Custodial grandparents: The state of the art and the many faces of this contribution. *Journal of Intergenerational Relationships, 7*(2–3), 137–143.

Pinnock, H. W. (1981, September). Making a marriage work. *Ensign, 11*, 33–37.

Pinquart, M., & Sorensen, S. (2003). Differences between caregivers and noncaregivers in psychological health and physical health: A meta-analysis. *Psychology and Aging, 18*(2), 250–267.

Rowe, J. W., & Kahn, R. L. (1997). Successful aging. *Gerontologist, 37*(4), 433–440.

Sandberg, J. G. (1998). A qualitative study of depression and marital process in mature marriages. *Dissertation Abstracts International: Section B: The Sciences and Engineering, 59(5-B)*, 2433.

Sandberg, J. G. (2006). Interventions with family caregivers. In D. R. Crane & E. S. Marshall (Eds.), *Handbook of families and health: Interdisciplinary perspectives.* Thousand Oaks, CA: Sage.

Sandberg, J. G., Miller, R. B., Harper, J. M., Robila, M., & Davey, A. (2009). The impact of marital conflict on health and health care utilization in older couples. *Journal of Health Psychology, 14*(1), 9–17.

Sebold, A. (2002). *The lovely bones.* New York: Little, Brown.

Sorensen, D. E. (2003, May). Forgiveness will change bitterness to love. *Ensign, 33*, 10–12.

Stuckey, J. C. (1997). A community of friends : The Sunday school class as a conduit for social contacts and social support among older women. *Journal of Religious Gerontology, 10*(3), 53–71.

Sung, K.-T. (1998). An exploration of actions of filial piety. *Journal of Aging Studies, 12*(4), 369–386.

Talamantes, M. A., Lawler, W. R., & Espino, D. V. (1995) Hispanic American elders: Caregiving norms surrounding dying and the use of hospice services. *Hospice Journal, 10* (2), 35–49.

Thoits, P. A., & Hewitt, L. N. (2001). Volunteer work and well-being. *Journal of Health and Social Behavior, 42,* 115–131.

Ungureanu, I., & Sandberg, J. G. (2010). "Broken together": Spirituality and religion as coping strategies for couples dealing with the death of a child: A literature review with clinical implications. *Contemporary Family Therapy, 32,* 302–319.

Viña, J., Borrás, C., & Miquel, J. (2007). Theories of ageing, *IUBMB Life, 59*(4–5), 249–254.

Wells, R. E. (1997, August). Uniting blended families. *Ensign, 27,* 24–29.

Zao-huo, C., Xiao-hong, L., & Lin-xiang, T. (2005). An investigation of marital satisfaction among Chinese couples. *Chinese Journal of Clinical Psychology, 13*(3), 282–284.

Zarit, S. H., & Zarit, J. M. (1998). Mental disorders in older adults: Fundamentals of assessment and treatment. New York: Guilford.

Section II:
Proclamation Principles and
Research on Successful Parenting

Parenting with Love, Limits, and Latitude: Proclamation Principles and Supportive Scholarship

Craig H. Hart, Lloyd D. Newell, and Julie H. Haupt

Parents have a sacred duty to rear their children in love and righteousness.

AFTER ADAM AND EVE WERE PLACED IN THE GARden of Eden, "the first commandment that God gave . . . pertained to their potential for parenthood as husband and wife" (¶ 4). Parents bringing children into this world and then rearing them in love and righteousness is essential to the great plan of happiness (Alma 42:8). In the course of teaching and nurturing children in a family setting, parents can learn and grow by practicing godly virtues that lead to sanctification. In the earth's first family, Adam and Eve discovered the importance of agency as they dealt with family members with different personalities and proclivities who chose to use their agency for good and for ill. Our wise first parents applied gospel principles in teaching their children about the commandments of God. They learned firsthand about the spiritual guidance that God grants to parents as they fulfill their sacred responsibilities, encouraging their growth and happiness (Moses 5:10–12).

To assist parents in meeting their family responsibilities, the Lord has given commandments, guiding principles, and helpful examples in the scriptures, along with the counsel of modern-day prophets and apostles. Joseph Smith said, "I teach the people correct principles, and they govern themselves" (quoted in Young, 1865, *Journal of Discourses,* 10:57–58). In parenting, mothers and fathers have the challenge and opportunity to apply general principles derived from inspired sources and adapt them to their individual and family circumstances as they diligently strive to meet their children's physical, emotional, and spiritual needs (see D&C 68:25–28; 75:28; 83:4–5; Mosiah 4:14; 1 Timothy 5:4).

Despite many similarities among modern-day families, each family has unique circumstances that affect the way parents raise their children. Family members' individual talents and personality traits, coupled with intergenerational influences, family structure, living arrangements, and cultural norms and expectations make it impossible to prepare a handbook for parenting that addresses every situation. President Ezra Taft Benson (1974, p. 381) said:

> Usually the Lord gives us the overall objectives to be accomplished and some guidelines to follow, but he expects us to work out most of the details and methods. The methods and procedures are usually developed through study and prayer and by living so that we can obtain and follow the promptings of the Spirit.

Thus, this chapter emphasizes inspired, eternal parenting principles that are based on the proclamation and supported by empirical and conceptual scholarship. These principles can guide parents in developing individualized child rearing practices.

Spiritual Personality and Genetic Traits

Latter-day Saint theology includes a remarkable wealth of information about the influence of a premortal life. For example, the First Presidency stated, "All people who come to this earth and are born in mortality, had a pre-existent, spiritual personality, as the sons and daughters of the Eternal Father" (Statement of the First Presidency, 1912, p. 417). President Joseph F. Smith (1916,

p. 426) noted, "Notwithstanding this fact that our recollection of former things was taken away, the character of our lives in the spirit world has much to do with our disposition, desires and mentality here in mortal life." Accordingly, President Brigham Young said, "There is the same variety in the spirit world that you behold here, yet they are of the same parentage, of one Father, one God" (The Church of Jesus Christ of Latter-day Saints, 1997, p. 295).

Regarding the cultivation of spiritual gifts, Elder Bruce R. McConkie (1979, vol. 1, p. 23) stated,

> Being subject to law, and having their agency, all the spirits of men, while yet in the Eternal Presence, developed aptitudes, talents, capacities, and abilities of every sort, kind, and degree. During the long expanse of life which then was, an infinite variety of talents and abilities came into being.

Certainly the way individual children respond to their earthly environments is greatly influenced by their spiritual identity and the spiritual gifts cultivated in the premortal realm (D&C 46; Alma 13:3–5; Abraham 3:22–23; Moroni 10; Moses 5:24; 1 Corinthians 12–14).

Indeed, each individual displays different interests, personalities, and behavior, which come from biological blueprints provided by parents as well as each child's own spiritual predispositions, talents, and desires. These spiritual traits interact with genetic individuality in ways that have not yet been revealed, but are often observed in daily interactions in the home (Hart, 2008). An individual's characteristics are further refined by environmental factors in and out of the home (for example, parents, peers, siblings, school, and culture) and by the ways that each child responds to them (Hart, Newell, & Olsen, 2003). Even among children in the same family, some children may be more difficult or easy to rear due, in part, to inherent personality characteristics that stem from spiritual personality and predispositions.

Beyond spiritual personality influences, a growing body of evidence suggests that biological characteristics play a role in children's dispositions and temperaments in ways that interact with environmental influences. (See Bornstein & Lamb, 2011; Hart et al., 2003; Eisenberg, 2006; Kuczynski, 2003; and Smith & Hart, 2011, for scientific support for the principles that follow.) These characteristics include tendencies toward inhibition or shyness, sociability, impulsiveness and "thrill-seeking," activity level (degree of lively energetic behavior and perpetual motion), aggression, cognition and language acuity, behavior problems stemming from psychiatric disorders, emotionality (for example, intensity of arousal related to fear, anger, or elation), and religiosity. Evidence also indicates that different genetically based characteristics can turn on or off at different points in development in ways that may be partially influenced by environmental factors. Thus, it may be that some children cycle in and out of easier and more difficult developmental periods as they grow.

Research exploring genetic contributions to children's development suggests that children may select, modify, and even create their own environments according to their biological predispositions. For example, a more sociable child may by nature seek out opportunities to interact with peers, but may be less academically motivated. Alternatively, a more socially passive child in the same family may actively avoid social gatherings and prefer to spend time in solitary activities (such as reading) and be more academically inclined.

In the same way, some children with more spirited dispositions (that show aggressive, highly emotional, or thrill-seeking tendencies) may raise concerns and evoke more formal intervention by parents in terms of rules, redirection, punishment, and monitoring than children who are "easier" to rear. This can be particularly true when child behavior falls outside cultural norms and family expectations. Thus, even though there are shared parenting influences, children by their natures can foster different parenting behaviors for different siblings in the same family. Or they may respond to similar parenting practices in different ways, depending on how experiences are filtered through their perceptions. Even children recognize that parents adjust their styles to different needs and personality characteristics of their siblings.

As President James E. Faust (1990, p. 34) observed, "Child rearing is so individualistic. Every child is different and unique. What works with one may not work with another." Whatever the nature and disposition of a given child, wise parents work to adjust, relate to, and rear each child in a manner that is somewhat tempered to individual needs as parents and children learn from each other. How this bidirectional parent–child interaction process plays out across development for each child varies according to his or her individual nature. Although children are differentially susceptible to child-rearing influences, scientific studies suggest that parents can help children reach their potential. This comes as parents do their best to emphasize positive child characteristics while providing opportunities for growth in areas where behaviors arising from the expression of particular spiritual and genetic attributes may be less desirable (Hart et al., 2003). As we know from the scriptures, weaknesses can foster humility and can eventually become strengths (Ether 12:27). Parents can play a supportive role by helping children overcome weaknesses and building upon natural strengths in ways that enhance "individual premortal, mortal, and eternal identity and purpose" (¶ 2).

Rearing Children in Love and Righteousness

Important principles found in the scriptures and the proclamation have been taught throughout the ages to assist parents to "rear their children in love and righteousness" (¶ 6) and adapt to child individuality. The proclamation admonishes respect for the divine and individual nature of children as parents love, teach, and guide them with an emphasis on teaching and preparing children rather than unrighteously controlling their wills. As Brigham Young suggested,

> Parents should never drive their children, but lead them along, giving them knowledge as their minds are prepared to receive it. Chastening may be necessary betimes, but parents should govern their children by faith rather than by the rod, leading them kindly by good example into all truth and holiness (Widtsoe, 1978, p. 208).

Righteous parenting emphasizes charity, gentleness, kindness, long-suffering, persuasion, and appropriate discipline in a warm and nurturing relationship (D&C 121:39–46). It invites children to adopt the parent's perspective on many issues. By contrast, unrighteous dominion centers on coercion, dominion, and compulsion "upon the souls of the children of men" (D&C 121:36–37).

In order to promote optimal development and to rear children in love and righteousness, the following are crucial elements for each child, although specific implementations and approaches may be individualized based upon the needs and personality of the particular child:

- Love, warmth, and support
- Clear and reasonable expectations for competent behavior
- Limits and boundaries with some room for negotiation and compromise
- Reasoning and developmentally appropriate consequences and punishments for breaching established limits
- Opportunities to perform competently and make choices
- Absence of coercive, hostile forms of discipline, such as harsh physical punishment, love withdrawal, shaming, and inflicting guilt
- Models of appropriate behavior consistent with self-control, positive values, and positive attitudes

The foregoing bulleted list constitutes some of the characteristics of the authoritative style of child rearing that will be elaborated upon later. Of each of the several parenting styles identified by scholarly research, the authoritative style of parenting is most consistent with the proclamation and the words of modern prophets and scripture (Hart, Newell, & Sine, 2000; Haupt, Hart, & Newell, 2005). Diana Baumrind (1971) reported a now widely accepted, research-based parenting style typology, which has established that authoritative parenting, in contrast to coercive parenting and permissive parenting, increases the probability of positive child developmental outcomes (Baumrind, Larzelere, & Owens, 2010). Scientific support for the following principles can be found in Barber and Olsen (1997), Baumrind and others (2010), Eisenberg (2006), Hart and others (2003), Kuczynski (2003), and Smith and Hart (2011).

The coercive parenting style. The coercive/hostile or authoritarian style of parenting is characterized by parents who deride, demean, or diminish children and teens by continually putting them in their place, putting them down, mocking them, or holding power over them via punitive or psychologically controlling means. It takes place in homes where there is a climate of hostility manifested by frequent spanking, yelling, criticizing, and forcing, and has been linked to many forms of antisocial, withdrawn, and delinquent behaviors in children and adolescents (Hart et al., 2003; Hart, Nelson, Robinson, Olsen, & McNeilly-Choque, 1998). Authoritarian parenting has also been associated with children believing they will get their way by using force with peers.

Likewise, psychological control designed to manipulate children's mental and emotional experience and expression has been associated with children's and adolescents' "externalizing," or aggressive, disruptive, or delinquent behavior; and "internalizing," or developing problems such as anxiety or depression (Barber, 2002). Psychologically controlling behaviors by parents communicate disinterest in what a child is saying; invalidate or discount a child's feelings; attack the child in a condescending or patronizing way; and use guilt induction, love withdrawal, shaming, or erratic emotional behavior as means of control and manipulation. Love withdrawal (for example, angrily refusing to talk to or look at a child after he or she misbehaves) in particular runs contrary to ways that God deals with His disobedient children and is damaging to the delicate parent–child relationship (Nelson, Hart, Yang, Olsen, & Jin, 2006). Wise parents follow the Lord's example as He assures His people: "[My] hand is stretched out still" (Isaiah 5:25).

From the beginning, unrighteous dominion has centered on control, dominion, and compulsion (D&C 121). In gospel terms, it was Satan who wanted to destroy agency and achieve obedience through compulsion (Moses 4:3). His motivation for doing so was pride and self-aggrandizement by bringing honor unto himself (Moses 4:1). Although parents' exclusive reliance on coercion may result in immediate or short-term compliance in children, it often comes with a cost to children's long-term abilities to learn how to self-regulate their own behavior. Certainly coercive parenting shows little respect for the divine nature and individual characteristics of the child.

Parenting practices that include physical punishment ("the rod") have been advocated on the basis of biblical interpretations (MacArthur, 1998). However, Brigham Young (1865, *Journal of Discourses,* 10:360), disagreed, stating, "I will here say to parents, that kind words and loving actions toward children will subdue their uneducated nature a great deal better than the rod, or, in other words, than physical punishment." President Gordon B. Hinckley (1994, p. 53) echoed President Young's words and those of other prophets when he said, "I have never accepted the principle of 'spare the rod and spoil the

child.' . . . Children don't need beating. They need love and encouragement." Brigham Young (1862, *Journal of Discourses,* 9:196) further stated, "Let the child have a mild training until it has judgment and sense to guide it. I differ with Solomon's recorded saying as to spoiling the child by sparing the rod."

In support of this view, the scriptural metaphor of a good shepherd and the importance of his rod reminds us that he guides his sheep by gathering the lambs in his arms, carrying them in his bosom, and gently leading them along (Isaiah 40:11). The shepherd's rod is never used for beating sheep, else the passage "thy rod and thy staff . . . comfort me" (Psalm 23:4) makes little sense. The shepherd's staff is used instead to ward off intruders; to count sheep as they "pass under the rod" (Leviticus 27:32; Ezekiel 20:37); to part the wool to examine for defects, disease, or wounds; and to nudge sheep gently from going in the wrong direction. The rod is viewed as a protection and is also translated from the Hebrew in other places as "the word of God" or "the rod or voice of his mouth" (see Micah 6:9 and Isaiah 11:4; see also 1 Nephi 15:23–24 and Psalm 23:4).

Accordingly, there are alternate ways one can choose to read the scriptures that appear to support the view that sparing the rod will spoil the child. For example, Proverbs 13:24, which reads, "He that spareth his rod hateth his son: but he that loveth him chasteneth him betimes," might be read as, "He who withholds the word of God hateth his son: He who loveth his son, corrects (or teaches) him early on (when he is young)." Proverbs 23:13–14, which reads, "Withhold not correction from the child: for if thou beatest him with the rod, he shall not die. Thou shalt beat him with the rod, and shalt deliver his soul from hell," might be read as, "Withhold not correction from a child; for if you regulate him with the word of God, he will not die. Regulate him with the word of God, and you will deliver his soul from hell."

Parents are often confused by the contradictory evidence for and against spanking that is reported in the national media. On one side, Diana Baumrind (1996a, p. 828), a leading researcher in the study of parenting effects on children, states that "a blanket injunction against disciplinary spanking . . . is not scientifically supportable." A body of scientific literature suggests that "nonabusive" spanking, consisting of one or two mild slaps on the buttocks in limited situations (for example, in cases of out-of-control child behavior that poses danger to the child or others) can be beneficial as a last resort, but only for children between 2 and 6 years of age (Baumrind, Larzelere, & Cowan, 2002). It can be particularly beneficial when backing up other discipline measures that have already been tried and have failed (such as reasoning with the child or withdrawing privileges), or when conducted infrequently in the context of a warm and responsive relationship (Baumrind, 1996b; Baumrind et al., 2010). The child's personality should be taken into account. Whereas a more spirited youngster may benefit at times from stronger measures, a more sensitive child who comes to tears from a single disapproving word may not require such discipline at all.

Another body of sophisticated research supports the notion that even though limited spanking may immediately stop a child from misbehaving and willfully defying in the short term, it actually increases the likelihood of greater disobedience and antisocial behavior later on (Gershoff & Bitensky, 2007; Straus, Sugarman, & Giles-Sims, 1997; Strassberg, Dodge, Pettit, & Bates, 1994) and is also more likely to be done in anger (Holden, Coleman, & Schmidt, 1995). As Brigham Young observed, "I have seen more parents who were unable to control themselves than I ever saw who were unable to control their children" (The Church of Jesus Christ of Latter-day Saints, 1997, p. 338). Due to the inherent limitations associated with the scientific studies supporting both sides of the argument, the debate over spanking will likely continue. As will be noted later in the section on authoritative parenting, there are usually better alternatives to physical punishment (see, for example, Hyman, 1997).

The permissive parenting style. Permissive parenting is characterized by parents who overindulge children or neglect them by leaving them to their own devices. This style includes a shirking of sacred parental rsponsibilties as parents fail to provide guidance and constraint when it is required for the child's good. Modern-day prophets counsel parents to provide and enforce reasonable limits to teach their children the clear bounds of acceptable and unacceptable behavior.

In contrast to coercive parenting, where adult authority dominates excessively, Baumrind (1996b) notes that in the permissive style, children are essentially considered parental equals in terms of rights, but not in terms of responsibilities. Although permissive parents exert a degree of control over their children, they do so to a much lesser degree than coercive and authoritative parents.

Permissive parents tend to avoid using their authority to control their children's behavior, tolerate children's impulses (including aggression), encourage children to make their own decisions without providing necessary parameters, and refrain from imposing structure on children's time (such as establishing bedtime, mealtime, or limits on computer usage). They also keep restrictions, demands for mature behavior, and consequences for misbehavior at a minimum.

Social science research suggests that children raised by permissive parents may have greater difficulty respecting others, coping with frustration, delaying gratification for a greater goal, and following through with plans. Unlike coercive parenting, in which child outcomes are predominately negative, permissive parenting produces mixed results. Children of permissive parents have often been found to be quite social and to have low rates of depression and anxiety, but they tend to do less well academically, are more defiant of authority, and have a higher rate of adolescent sexual activity and drug and alcohol use.

Overindulging children is a form of permissiveness that requires careful consideration. As a member of the Seventy, Elder Joe J. Christensen (1999, p. 9) counseled:

We should avoid spoiling children by giving them too much. In our day, many children grow up with distorted values because we as parents overindulge them.... One of the most important things we can teach our children is to deny themselves. Instant gratification generally makes for weak people.

Elder Neal A. Maxwell (1999, p. 2) taught:

A few of our wonderful youth and young adults in the Church are unstretched—they have almost a free pass. Perks are provided, including cars complete with fuel and insurance—all paid for by parents who sometimes listen in vain for a few courteous and appreciative words. What is thus taken for granted . . . tends to underwrite selfishness and a sense of entitlement.

In summary, permissive parenting does not fit well with proclamation principles. As has been noted, parents are charged with the responsibility to guide and teach the principles of the gospel to their children by example and precept (see D&C 68:25–28). As President

David O. McKay (1955, p. 26) observed, "Children are more influenced by sermons you act than by the sermons you preach."

The authoritative parenting style. The optimal parenting style is the authoritative parenting style. Authoritative parenting fosters a positive emotional connection with children, provides for regulation that places fair and consistent limits on child behavior, and allows for reasonable child autonomy in decision making. This style creates a positive emotional climate that helps children be more open to parental input and direction, and allows for parents to individualize child rearing as encouraged by Brigham Young when he enjoined parents to "study their [children's] dispositions and their temperaments, and deal with them accordingly" (Widtsoe, 1978, p. 207). Some children, for example, may require more limits, while others may respond better to more latitude, depending on their predispositions.

Children and adolescents reared by authoritative parents tend to be better adjusted to school; are less aggressive and delinquent; are less likely to abuse drugs; are more friendly and accepted by peers; are more communicative, self-motivated, and academically inclined; and are more willing to abide by laws. They are also more capable of moral reasoning and are more self-controlled (Hart et al., 2003). For Latter-day Saint families, the implication is that such children are more willing to abide by and reap the blessings of spiritual laws as well. Positive parenting styles are likely more effective when parents are unified in their parenting efforts. In sum, authoritative parenting consists of three well-defined and researched characteristics: connection, regulation, and autonomy. These characteristics might also be referred to as love, limits, and latitude (Hart, Newell, & Haupt, 2008).

Research has shown that Latter-day Saint parents who take the time to become emotionally connected with their teens, set regulatory limits, and foster autonomy in ways described later are far more likely to have adolescents who are careful in their selection of peers, regardless of what part of the country they live in. Children reared in these types of family environments, where prayer, scripture study, and religious values are stressed, were also more likely to internalize religiosity. Personal prayer and scripture study, as well as private spiritual experiences, were found to be a deterrent to delinquent behavior (Top & Chadwick, 1998).

Love

The first of the three characteristics of authoritative parenting is love, or connection. President Gordon B. Hinckley (1997b, p. 416) stated:

> Every child is entitled to grow up in a home where there is warm and secure companionship, where there is love in the family relationship, where appreciation one for another is taught and exemplified, and where God is acknowledged and His peace and blessings invoked before the family altar.

Brigham Young (1864, p. 2) counseled, "Kind looks, kind actions, kind words, and a lovely, holy deportment toward them will bind our children to us with bands that cannot easily be broken; while abuse and unkindness will drive them from us." Prophetic statements such as these, supported by research, suggest that warm and responsive parenting tends to promote lasting bonds between parents and children and "felt security" within children (Hart et al., 2003). This, in turn, has been linked to better behavior now and in the future. Warm and responsive child rearing also helps to mitigate hostility, resentment, and anger in children, all of which have been reproved in holy writ through the ages: "Provoke not your children to wrath: but bring them up in the nurture and admonition of the Lord" (Ephesians 6:4).

Specifically, research has documented that children are less aggressive and more sociable and empathetic if they have parents (particularly fathers) who are more loving, patient, playful, responsive, and sympathetic to children's feelings and needs. President Gordon B. Hinckley (1997a, p. 52) stated, "Fathers, be kind to your children. Be companionable with them." Similarly, mothers who take the time to engage in mutually enjoyable activities with their children more effectively convey values and rules to them (Kochanska, 1997). President Ezra Taft Benson (1990, p. 32) counseled parents:

> Take time to be a real friend to your children. Listen to your children, really listen. Talk with them, laugh and joke with them, sing with them, play with them, cry with them, hug them, honestly praise them. Yes, regularly spend unrushed one-on-one time with each child. Be a real friend to your children.

Children are less likely to push limits and seek attention through misbehavior when they feel that they are a high priority in their parents' lives. Sister Marjorie Hinckley was an excellent example. Speaking of her mother-in-law, Kathleen H. Hinckley writes,

> When I called her for advice, she verbalized something I would say over and over to myself for many years to come, "Just save the relationship." I believe those words are the most simple and powerful parenting principle I have ever learned (Pearce, 1999, p. 56).

All this takes significant time and energy. Elder M. Russell Ballard (2003, p. 6), speaking to mothers, advised:

> Mothers must not fall into the trap of believing that "quality" time can replace "quantity" time. Quality is a direct function of quantity—and mothers, to nurture their children properly, must provide both. To do so requires constant vigilance and a constant juggling of competing demands. It is hard work, no doubt about it.

Limits

The second element of authoritative parenting is limits, known in the scholarly literature as regulation. Finding ways to effectively help children learn how to regulate their own behavior in noncoercive ways is one of the most challenging parts of authoritative parenting. Determining how and when to tighten or loosen the reins requires considerable creativity, effort, and inspiration. In all cases, discipline or correction should be motivated by a sincere interest in teaching children correct principles rather than merely to exert control, exercise dominion, or vent anger. As they apply limits to a child's behavior, authoritative parents must again make a conscious effort and use good judgment by taking into consideration the developmental level of the child and the child's individual temperament.

In authoritative homes, parents are clear and firm about rules and expectations. Unlike coercive parents who administer harsh, domineering, arbitrary punishments, authoritative parents are confrontive by proactively explaining reasons for setting rules and by administering corrective measures promptly when children do not abide by the rules (Baumrind et al., 2010). In an effort to make the home a place of security, parents build a safety net of appropriate limits for their children, generously communicate their approval of desirable behavior, and help children understand how to regulate themselves. These lessons are taught within friendly parent–child interactions where tutoring and discipline occur when necessary. Research has shown that when firm habits of good behavior are established early in life through parental regulatory practices that include limit-setting, a judicious use of punishment, positive reinforcement, and reasoning, parents are better able to relax control as their children grow older (Baumrind, 1996b).

Setting limits and following through with pre-established consequences when rules are violated is one way that parents can help children learn to be self-regulating. Just as the rod is used to gently nudge sheep away from dangerous places, setting limits around potentially harmful influences (for example, inappropriate media and early dating) helps children feel safer and more secure. The careful monitoring of adolescents' whereabouts and behavior as well as encouragement to adhere to parental expectations is a form of limit-setting that can go far in reducing delinquent activity (Laird, Pettit, Bates, & Dodge, 2003).

Authoritative parents take responsibility for setting the appropriate number of rules that can be realistically remembered and enforced. Some children may require more and varying types of rules and punishments than others, depending on their individual natures. Some rules may be implicit and just part of the family routine (for example, family prayer is daily at 7:00 a.m.). Others may be more explicit with consequences attached (for example, rollerblading in the house will result in the roller blades being put away for several days). When rules and their accompanying consequences have been explained in advance and a sufficient number of warnings adapted to the child's ability for self-regulation have been given, authoritative parents are firm and consistent in following through in a calm and clear-headed manner when violations occur. Examples could include temporarily suspending teen driving privileges for traffic violations, calmly showing up at a teen son's or daughter's party when curfew is violated, withholding a privilege until chores or homework is completed, or enforcing time-out when a child hurts others out of anger, then discussing alternative methods for dealing with anger. Authoritative strategies might include reproving, withdrawing privileges, setting up opportunities to make restitution, or following through on predetermined consequences for breaking rules. Consistency in administering corrective discipline provides opportunities for children to experience the negative consequences of poor choices. Consistency allows subsequent opportunities for children to "rehearse" better behavior by arming them with new tools and information about how to handle the situation more appropriately in the future. President Spencer W. Kimball (1982, p. 341) noted, "Setting limits to what a child can do means to that child that you love him and respect him."

Regulation strategies can also include more subtle approaches that maintain a positive tone and do not require imposing penalties. For example, young children sometimes respond better to simply being redirected to more acceptable behaviors (for example, being shown how to gently pet a cat rather than inadvertently mishandling it). Planning ahead can also eliminate problems before they occur, like putting safety latches on cupboards for curious toddlers, providing a watch with a beeper alarm so children won't forget to come home in the midst of play with friends, and teaching and reminding children about behavior in social settings before arriving—such as helping them whisper in a library or being sensitive to an elderly grandparent's physical limitations.

While there are times when chastisement and other forms of punishment are necessary (see D&C 121:43; Hebrews 12:5–11), it is crucial that these be carried out in a spirit of love and under the guidance of the Holy Spirit (see D&C 121:41–46). Indeed, punishment is an eternal principle (see, for example, Alma 42:16, 18–21; 2 Nephi 2:13). To be most effective, punishments should be logically tied to the misbehavior, accompanied by reasoning, and administered in a prompt, rational manner (Baumrind et al., 2010). Seeking guidance from the Spirit will assist parents in finding ways to discipline in a context of love, respect, consistency, justice, and sensitivity to the child's developmental level and individual personality.

When consequences need to be enforced, the scriptures teach the principle of "showing forth afterwards an increase of love toward him whom thou hast reproved" (D&C 121:43). When the child has been corrected in a calm, controlled manner, that same Spirit that prompted such correction can create a sense of compassion, charity, and forgiveness toward the child. These are moments when children have a particularly intense and immediate need to feel the strength of parental love. Authoritative parents will take action to assure the child of their love and genuine concern in a way that is suited to the age and individual needs of the child. For example, physical affection may assist a young child with a quivering lip to restore a sense of inner security: "Maybe you can sit here on my lap for a while until you feel like playing with your sister again." Affirming verbal statements are important at all ages to keep relationships strong during times of reproof: "Although I am disappointed that you did not obey, I love you very much." At times, humor can be used to break the tension: "Okay, enough of this serious stuff. Time for a group hug!" A change in activity may help, particularly when it gives children a chance to positively interact with the parent: "Will you be my helper in the kitchen? I need a junior chef to help me whip up some cornbread." Finally, expressing confidence in the child can help alleviate his or her concerns: "I know it's been a hard day. We all make mistakes. I know you'll do better next time."

Although consequences are important to the learning process, punishment is not always the answer to misbehavior. Seeking to understand the underlying causes of the misbehavior can help parents treat the core problem and not just react to symptoms. For example, challenging behavior can be tied to an unfulfilled need (like being tired, hungry, or lacking necessary parental attention), a stage of growth (such as teething or natural striving for autonomy during the wonderful twos and threes and again during the teenage years), something going awry in the present environment (like friends being mean or fear of the dark), or a child simply not knowing better (for example, animals get hurt when mistreated; friends are not happy when one refuses to share). Ignoring misbehavior that is not harmful to self or others may be an appropriate strategy at times when followed up by love and acceptance (for example, calmly ignoring whining and then responding positively to the child's normal speech). It should be noted that chronic conditions associated with a biologically based mood, thought, behavioral, or learning disorder may require professional assistance to resolve.

While confrontations and conflicts are inevitable in family life, parents can work diligently to nurture relationships and keep a positive tone in the home. Rewarding good behavior and framing expectations in a positive manner can go far in inviting children to regulate their behavior in desirable ways. Periodically surprising a child with extra privileges or providing ways to earn benefits associated with desirable behavior can also encourage good performance: "You have worked so hard on your piano practicing over the last month that I'd like go on a daddy–daughter date with you to the concert this weekend." (See the entry "Reward," pp. 430–431 in the Topical Guide of the Latter-day Saint scriptures, to gain a sense of the eternal principle of rewards.)

The use of induction or reasoning also helps keep parenting methods positive. As noted earlier, prophets have emphasized that reason and persuasion are important when working with children. President Joseph F. Smith (1963, pp. 316–317) counseled,

> Use no lash and no violence, but . . . approach them with reason, with persuasion and love unfeigned. . . . The man that will be angry at his boy, and try to correct him while he is in anger, is in the greatest fault; . . . You can only correct your children by love, in kindness, by love unfeigned, by persuasion, and reason.

For example, when guiding behavior, a parent may help a child who has trouble being bossy with friends by talking through some strategies before a friend comes over: "If you do only what you want to do when playing with Johnny, he probably won't want to play with you anymore. What things do you think he would like to do when you two get together?" Induction is also important in pointing out more socially acceptable ways of handling situations: "I can understand why you are angry, but it's not okay to hit Jenny. Remember next time to use your words to ask her for your tricycle back."

Induction is effective because it does more than simply correct behavior; it can also potentially teach the child reasons for socially acceptable behavior, communicate clear limits, acknowledge the emotions being felt, emphasize consequences to others for hurtful behavior, and present more acceptable strategies for dealing with conflict. Following up with role plays, perhaps in a family home evening, can go far in helping children rehearse acceptable behavior. Research shows that consistent efforts to provide simple rationales that are often repeated eventually sink in and can win voluntary obedience even in 2- to 3-year-old children. Numerous studies have documented positive ways that reasoning with children (especially in advance of a problem) can help them willingly regulate their own behavior, resulting in more confident, empathetic, helpful, and happy children (Hart et al., 2003).

For adolescents and older children, if not carefully worded, induction can come across as preachments and may provoke more opposition and testiness. Also, wise parents remember that the tone of voice, a loving touch, and the sincere feeling behind the parents' words often communicate much more than the words themselves. Playing a "consultant role" often works better (Cline and Fay, 1990; Cline and Fay, 1992). This involves (a) reflective listening (for example, saying something like, "So it sounds like you're feeling angry because your teacher doesn't explain math very well and you are suffering for it"), (b) using less directive "I" rather than more intrusive "you" statements ("I am confused about why you want to drop algebra. You've seemed really excited about a career in electrical engineering," rather than, "You will never be an electrical engineer without algebra"), (c) musing and wondering aloud about potential consequences and alternatives (for example, saying, "I am just wondering how you are going to graduate from high school if you drop algebra," rather than saying, "You need to take algebra in order to graduate"), and (d) leaving more ownership for problem-solving to the child (for example, "What do you want to have happen here?" or "What are you planning to do about it and is there a way I can be helpful?").

In summary, as parents reason with their children and guide them to more appropriate behavior, it is important to remember that, ultimately, they are teaching children to live by the simple truths of the gospel embodied in the proclamation, such as love, respect, repentance, forgiveness, and compassion. President Boyd K. Packer (1986, p. 17) has said, "True doctrine, understood, changes attitudes and behavior. The study of the doctrines of the gospel will improve behavior quicker than a study of behavior will improve behavior." As parents focus on emulating, teaching, and helping children internalize the eternal truths of the great plan of happiness (Alma 42:16), children will be more likely to embrace the correct principles of their parents. Through parents' loving reassurance and gentle persuasion as well as children's participation in personal and public religious experiences, children will more likely "lay hold upon the word of God" (Helaman 3:29) and remain faithful (Top & Chadwick, 1998).

Latitude

The third component of authoritative parenting is latitude, or autonomy. Children benefit from being given choices and appropriate levels of latitude to make their own decisions in a variety of domains. Children learn and grow by learning how to make choices within limits that are acceptable to parents (for example, allowing a child the option of taking the trash out in the evening or in the morning before school; asking whether the child would prefer hot or cold cereal). Whenever possible, supporting children's autonomy in this manner helps children view adults as providers of information and guidance rather than as deliverers of messages of control. When children have been taught principles of truth, internalize correct principles, and have many opportunities to make choices within an environment of love and concern, they are more likely to learn to choose wisely. Elder M. Russell Ballard (2003, p. 8) taught:

> Helping children learn how to make decisions requires that parents give them a measure of autonomy, dependent on the age and maturity of the child and the situation at hand. Parents need to give children choices and should be prepared to appropriately adjust some rules, thus preparing children for real-world situations.

Authoritative parents teach with warmth and responsiveness, which allows a give-and-take relationship with their children. Differences are respected and valued. Parental communication is open and nonjudgmental, with more emphasis on listening to understand rather than on talking. Respect for authority and independent thinking and feeling are valued, rather than being seen as conflicting principles. Research has shown that children are more likely to be respectful to parents and others when there is reciprocity and a degree of power sharing in their relationships with parents. These positive interactions are conducive to building strong relationships. For example, research demonstrates that parents who maintain at least a 5- or 6-to-1 ratio of positive to negative interactions with their children and teens have more stable and adaptive relationships with them (Cavell & Strand, 2003).

Developmental stages and needs are also considered in reciprocal relationships. As children grow older and more mature, they are granted more autonomy and a greater share in family decision making. Provided that a pattern of giving choices, setting limits, following through, and reasoning is established early in children's lives, parent–child relationships and positive child development will more likely be enhanced. Reciprocity comes into play in areas where firm rules and restrictions are deemed unnecessary or unreasonable and parents model and encourage negotiation and compromise (for example, allowing the child's input into clothing choice, while restraining choice in less negotiable areas, such as modesty). Research shows that the developmental forces that tug at older children and teens will require some compromise to create patterns of interaction that both parent and child can live with (Kuczynski, 2003).

Finding ways to say "yes" more often than "no" to a child's request lends more credence when a parent has to say no. Sister Marjorie Hinckley said,

> My mother taught me some basic philosophies of rearing children. One is that you have to trust children. I tried hard never to say "no" if I could possibly say "yes." I think that worked well because it gave my children the feeling that I trusted them and they were responsible to do the best they could (Pearce, 1999, p. 55).

A daughter of President Heber J. Grant shared the following insights:

> In matters of small importance, father seldom said "No" to us. Consequently, when he did say "No," we knew he meant it. His training allowed us to make our own decisions whenever possible. He always explained very patiently just why he thought a certain procedure was unwise and then he would say, "That's the way I feel about it; but of course, you must decide for yourself." As a result, our decision was usually the same as his. He was able somehow to motivate us to *want* to do the right thing rather

than to be forced to do it (The Church of Jesus Christ of Latter-day Saints, 2002, p. 200).

By contrast, minimizing opportunities for autonomy can have serious consequences for children. For example, recent studies show that temperamentally shy and inhibited children are more likely to withdraw from peer-group interaction when their parents are overprotective (Nelson, Hart, Wu, Yang, Roper, & Jin, 2006). Parents often have a natural tendency to "protect" their children from failure in social relationships when they perceive their child is having difficulty engaging in ongoing peer-group activities. However, this usually has the opposite effect in that it does not allow children opportunities to develop critical social skills that can only be developed through interactions with peers.

When children and teens are given latitude for decision making in areas that matter less, they are more likely to feel trusted and empowered to choose rightly and conform to parental expectations that matter more. Elder Robert D. Hales (1999, p. 34) counseled,

Act with faith; don't react with fear. When our teenagers begin testing family values, parents need to go to the Lord for guidance on the specific needs of each family member. This is the time for added love and support and to reinforce your teachings on how to make choices. It is frightening to allow our children to learn from the mistakes they may make, but their willingness to choose the Lord's way and family values is greater when the choice comes from within than when we attempt to force those values upon them. The Lord's way of love and acceptance is better than Satan's way of force and coercion, especially in rearing teenagers.

Unfortunately, some children, despite gospel-centered teaching in the home, will use their agency to make decisions that take them far from parental values. In these cases, good judgment is needed to strike the right balance between love and law. Elder Dallin H. Oaks (2009, pp. 28) said:

If parents have a wayward child—such as a teenager indulging in alcohol or drugs—they face a serious question. Does parental love require that these substances or their consumption be allowed in the home, or do the requirements of civil law or the seriousness of the conduct or the interests of other children in the home require that this be forbidden? To pose an even more serious question, if an adult child is living in cohabitation, does the seriousness of sexual relations outside the bonds of marriage require that this child feel the full weight of family disapproval by being excluded from any family contacts, or does parental love require that the fact of cohabitation be ignored? I have seen both of these extremes, and I believe that both are inappropriate. Where do parents draw the line? That is a matter for parental wisdom, guided by the inspiration of the Lord. There is no area of parental action that is more needful of heavenly guidance or more likely to receive it than the decisions of parents in raising their children and governing their families.

Because authoritative parenting implies flexibility, this style is more effective than the others in dealing with children, since each child has unique characteristics and varying temperamental dispositions. In other words, each child is guided in a balanced style of connection, regulation, and autonomy that best matches his or her set of strengths and weaknesses. For example, some teenagers are self-motivated to engage in appropriate activities, do not require curfews, and are home at reasonable hours. Other teens lose control of their lives and wander into dangerous paths without restrictions. Some rebel when locked into tightly controlled curfews and expectations and do better when parents take the time to talk through the constraints of each new situation that arises (such as the use of a new cell phone).

Providing latitude may include parents developing a middle-of-the-road approach that balances granting autonomy with regulation. This especially works well for more spirited teenagers. These teens often become surprisingly responsible when the general expectation is that they learn to inform parents about their whereabouts and plans and have confidence that their parents will consider compromises when there is a difference of opinion (Chapman, 2000). Surely, creativity and inspiration are required to know how to work best with each child and teen. Parents will find frequently that they need direction and insight into approaching their child authoritatively in any given situation and should humbly seek the guidance of the Spirit.

Even the most wonderful, responsive parents will, from time to time and under difficult circumstances, lose patience with demanding children (Holden, 1995). Parents who admit mistakes and say they are sorry model sincere efforts to change and overcome human weaknesses. At one moment parents may be more permissive because of various external and internal factors, and at another moment more coercive. However, most parents tend to be more one way than another. It is the pattern of interaction, or the climate the parenting style creates in the home, that makes the difference. When parents try to be unified and consistent in employing an authoritative style with balancing characteristics of love, limits, and latitude, children have more chance at optimal growth and joy, and there will be more peace in spousal and parental relationships. When children are reared in a home where parents are striving to lead and guide with love, patience, and humility, children will more likely respond in positive ways.

As the proclamation declares, parents should maintain a high priority on teaching children the principles of righteousness (¶ 7). Sound scholarship confirms that this is best done in authoritative rather than coercive or permissive ways. By studying their children's individual temperaments, which stem from each child's genetic and spiritual natures, parents can create the best environment for optimal growth and development. Where better than in a righteous home that is imbued with the Spirit for children to learn to discern between good and evil (see Moroni 7:13–19; D&C 84:44–46) and to develop in optimal ways? Living in harmony with proclamation principles maximizes the possibilities that children will make choices that help them "return to the presence of God" (¶ 3).

Maintaining a Strong and Positive Influence on Children

Parents often wonder how they might maintain a strong and righteous influence on their children in a world where there are many other influences seeking for their time, attention, and loyalty. In the context of authoritative parenting, research suggests that it is within the moral and spiritual domains where parents can have the most influence (e.g., Leman, 2005), even though schools, culture, the media, and peer interaction can play major roles as well (e.g., Comunian & Gielen, 2006; Gibbs, Basinger, Grime, & Snarey, 2007; Speicher,

1994). For example, studies have shown that while peers have influence, they seem to matter more in superficial aspects of behavior like hair and clothing styles, the use of slang, and transient day-to-day behaviors, all of which can shift frequently with changes in friendships. Parents are more likely to have influence on core values that are reflected in religiosity, political persuasion, and educational plans, to name a few (Collins, Maccoby, Steinberg, Hetherington, & Bornstein, 2000; Sebald, 1986). For example, it is the quality of the parent–child relationship that more often determines the type of peers that teenagers choose and whether they accept and adhere to parental values (Furman, Simon, Shaffer, & Bouchey, 2002; Laird et al., 2003; Zhou et al., 2002). When parents neglect the active teaching of strong core values by precept and example in the context of a coercive or permissive parent–child relationship, children will be more likely to gravitate to peers and adopt their value systems, for good or ill.

One of the most powerful tools that parents have in teaching positive values to their children is their religious faith (Smith, 2005). Research indicates that adolescents who embrace a religious community are more likely to exhibit behavior that is consistent with positive moral values. Compared to nonaffiliated youth, they are more involved in activities that help the less fortunate and in community service that reflects a concern for others (Kerestes, Youniss, & Metz, 2004). Religious involvement also fosters better academic performance and prosocial behavior, as well as discourages misconduct (Dowling et al., 2004). Religiosity is also associated with less delinquent behavior, including lower levels of sexual activity and drug and alcohol use (Bahr & Hoffmann, 2010; Smith, 2005; Regenerus, Smith, & Fritsch, 2003).

In short, religious practices and traditions create conditions that engender greater moral maturity. Youth activities and religious education provide opportunities for moral discussion and civic engagement in ways that help youth think beyond themselves and consider the needs of others (King & Furrow, 2004). They also provide young people with expanded networks of exemplary, religiously oriented adults and peers—conditions that also provide opportunities for internalizing important values that help children and teens override temptations that stem from biological urges or negative peer group pressure (Bridges & Moore, 2002; Jang

& Johnson, 2001). Encouragement of and support for religious involvement begins with parents in the home and is maintained as parents teach religious precepts in the home to their children and youth.

Rearing children in love and righteousness, as the proclamation admonishes, requires the best effort parents have to offer. Nevertheless, the rewards of such well-placed time and attention are eternal. President Gordon B. Hinckley (1997b, p. 421) said,

Of all the joys of life, none other equals that of happy parenthood. Of all the responsibilities with which we struggle, none other is so serious. To rear children in an atmosphere of love, security, and faith is the most rewarding of all challenges. The good result from such efforts becomes life's most satisfying compensation.

Craig H. Hart is a professor in the School of Family Life and the associate academic vice president for faculty at Brigham Young University. He and his wife, Kerstine, are the parents of four children and they have two grandchildren. Lloyd D. Newell is a professor of religious education at Brigham Young University. He and his wife, Karmel, are the parents of four children. Julie H. Haupt has taught for many years as an adjunct faculty member in the School of Family Life at Brigham Young University. She and her husband, Bob, are the parents of three children.

References

Bahr, S. J., & Hoffman, J. P. (2010). Parenting style, religiosity, peers, and adolescent heavy drinking. *Journal of Studies on Alcohol and Drugs, 71*, 539–543.

Ballard, M. R. (2003, August 19). The sacred responsibilities of parenthood. BYU Devotional Address. Retrieved from http://speeches.byu.edu/reader/reader.php?id=8397&x=62&y=6

Barber, B. K. (2002). *Intrusive parenting: How psychological control affects children and adolescents.* Washington, DC: American Psychological Association.

Barber, B. K., & Olsen, J. A. (1997). Socialization in context: Connection, regulation, and autonomy in the family, school, and neighborhood, and with peers. *Journal of Adolescent Research, 12*, 287–315.

Baumrind, D. (1971). Current patterns of parental authority. *Developmental Psychology Monograph, 4*, 1–103.

Baumrind, D. (1996a). A blanket injunction against disciplinary use of spanking is not warranted by the data. *Pediatrics, 98*(4, part 2), 828–831.

Baumrind, D. (1996b). The discipline controversy revisited. *Family Relations, 45*, 405–414.

Baumrind, D., Larzelere, R. E., & Cowan, P. A. (2002). Ordinary physical punishment: Is it harmful? Comment on Gershoff (2002). *Psychological Bulletin, 128*, 580–589.

Baumrind, D., Larzelere, R. E., & Owens, E. B. (2010). Effects of preschool parents' power assertive patterns and practices on adolescent development. *Parenting: Science and Practice, 10*, 157–201.

Benson, E. T. (1974). *God, family, country: Our three great loyalties.* Salt Lake City: Deseret Book.

Benson, E. T. (1990). To the mothers in Zion. In E. T. Benson (Ed.), *Come, listen to a prophet's voice.* Salt Lake City: Deseret Book.

Bornstein, M. H., & Lamb, M. E. (2011). *Developmental science: An advanced textbook* (6th ed.). New York: Psychology Press.

Bridges, L. J., & Moore, K. A. (2002). Religious involvement and children's well-being: What research tells us (and what it doesn't). *Child Trends Research Brief.* Retrieved from http://www.childtrends.org/files/ReligiosityRB.pdf

Cavell, T. A., & Strand, P. S. (2003). Parent-based interventions for aggressive children. In L. Kuczynski (Ed.), *Handbook of dynamics in parent-child relations* (pp. 395–415). Thousand Oaks, CA: Sage Publications.

Chapman, D. (2000, February). The three questions. *New Era, 30*, 26–27.

Christensen, J. J. (1999, May). Greed, selfishness, and overindulgence. *Ensign, 29*, 9–11.

The Church of Jesus Christ of Latter-day Saints. (2002). *Teachings of presidents of the Church: Heber J. Grant.* Salt Lake City: Author.

The Church of Jesus Christ of Latter-day Saints. (1997). *Teachings of presidents of the Church: Brigham Young.* Salt Lake City: Author.

Cline, F. W., & Fay, J. (1990). *Parenting with love and logic: Teaching children responsibility.* Colorado Springs: Pinon Press.

Cline, F. W., & Fay, J. (1992). *Parenting teens with love and logic: Preparing adolescents for responsible adulthood.* Colorado Springs: Pinon Press.

Collins, W. A., Maccoby, E. E., Steinberg, L., Hetherington, E. M., & Bornstein, M. H. (2000).

Contemporary research on parenting: The case for nature and nurture. *American Psychologist, 55*, 218–232.

Comunian, A. L., & Gielen, U. P. (2006). Promotion of moral judgment maturity through stimulation of social role-taking and social reflection: An Italian intervention study. *Journal of Moral Education, 35*, 51–69.

Dowling, E. M., Gestsdottir, S., Anderson, P. M., von Eye, A., Almerigi, J., & Lerner, R. M. (2004). Structural relations among spirituality, religiosity, and thriving in adolescence. *Applied Developmental Science, 8*, 7–16.

Eisenberg, N. (Ed.). (2006). *Handbook of child psychology: Social, emotional, and personality development* (vol. 3, 6th ed.). Hoboken, NJ: John Wiley & Sons.

Faust, J. E. (1990, November). The greatest challenge in the world—Good parenting. *Ensign, 20*, 32–35.

First Presidency of The Church of Jesus Christ of Latter-day Saints. (1912). Statement concerning premortal life. *Improvement Era, 15*, 417.

Furman, W., Simon, V. A., Shaffer, L., & Bouchey, H. A. (2002). Adolescents' working models and styles for relationships with parents, friends, and romantic partners. *Child Development, 73*, 241–255.

Gershoff, E. T., & Bitensky, S. H. (2007). The case against corporal punishment of children: Converging evidence from social science research and international human rights law and implications for U.S. public policy. *Psychology, Public Policy, and Law, 13*, 231–272.

Gibbs, J. C., Basinger, K. S., Grime, R. L., & Snarey, J. R. (2007). Moral judgment development across cultures: Revisiting Kohlberg's universality claims. *Developmental Review, 27*, 443–500.

Hales, R. D. (1999, May). Strengthening families: Our sacred duty. *Ensign, 29*, 32–34.

Hart, C. H. (2008, August 5). Our divine nature and life decisions. BYU Devotional Address. Retrieved from http://speeches.byu.edu/?act=viewitem&id=1799

Hart, C. H., Nelson, D. A., Robinson, C. C., Olsen, S. F., & McNeilly-Choque, M. K. (1998). Overt and relational aggression in Russian nursery-school-age children: Parenting style and marital linkages. *Developmental Psychology, 34*, 687–697.

Hart, C. H., Newell, L. D., & Haupt, J. H. (2008, August). Love, limits, and latitude. *Ensign, 38*, 60–65.

Hart, C. H., Newell, L. D., & Olsen, S. F. (2003). Parenting skills and social-communicative competence in childhood. In J. O. Greene & B. R. Burleson (Eds.), *Handbook of communication and social interaction skills* (pp. 753–800). Mahwah, NJ: Lawrence Erlbaum.

Hart, C. H., Newell, L. D., & Sine, L. L. (2000). Proclamation-based principles of parenting and supportive scholarship. In D. C. Dollahite (Ed.), *Strengthening our families: An in-depth look at the Proclamation on the Family* (pp. 100–123). [Provo, UT]: School of Family Life, Brigham Young University.

Haupt, J. H., Hart, C. H., & Newell, L. D. (2005). Rearing children in love and righteousness. In C. H. Hart, L. D. Newell, E. Walton, & D. C. Dollahite (Eds.), *Helping and healing our families: Principles and practices inspired by "The Family: A Proclamation to the World"* (pp. 141–151). Salt Lake City: Deseret Book.

Hinckley, G. B. (1994, November). Save the children. *Ensign, 24*, 52–54.

Hinckley, G. B. (1997a, November). Some thoughts on temples, retention of converts, and missionary service. *Ensign, 27*, 49–52.

Hinckley, G. B. (1997b). *Teachings of Gordon B. Hinckley.* Salt Lake City: Deseret Book.

Holden, G. W. (1995). Parental attitudes toward childrearing. In M. H. Bornstein (Ed.), *Handbook of parenting, vol. 3: Status and social conditions of parenting* (pp. 359–392). Mahwah, NJ: Lawrence Erlbaum.

Holden, G. W., Coleman, S. M., & Schmidt, K. L. (1995). Why 3-year-old children get spanked: Parent and child determinants as reported by college-educated mothers. *Merrill-Palmer Quarterly, 41*, 431–452.

Hyman, I. A. (1997). *The case against spanking: How to discipline your child without hitting.* San Francisco: Jossey-Bass.

Jang, S. J., & Johnson, B. R. (2001). Neighborhood disorder, individual religiosity, and adolescent use of illicit drugs: A test of multilevel hypotheses. *Criminology, 39*, 109–143.

Kerestes, M., Youniss, J., & Metz, E. (2004). Longitudinal patterns of religious perspective and civic integration. *Applied Developmental Science, 8*, 39–46.

Kimball, E. L. (Ed.). (1982). *The teachings of Spencer W. Kimball: The twelfth president of the Church of Jesus Christ of Latter-day Saints.* Salt Lake City: Bookcraft.

King, P. E., & Furrow, J. L. (2004). Religion as a resource for positive youth development: Religion, social capital, and moral outcomes. *Developmental Psychology, 40*, 703–713.

Kochanska, G. (1997). Mutually responsive orientation between mothers and their children: Implications for early socialization. *Child Development, 68,* 94–112.

Kuczynski, L. (Ed.). (2003). *Handbook of dynamics in parent–child relations.* Thousand Oaks, CA: Sage Publications.

Laird, R. D., Pettit, G. S., Bates, J. E., & Dodge, K. A. (2003). Parents' monitoring-relevant knowledge and adolescents' delinquent behavior: Evidence of correlated developmental changes and reciprocal influences. *Child Development, 74,* 752–768.

Leman, P. J. (2005). Authority and moral reasons: Parenting style and children's perceptions of adult rule justifications. *International Journal of Behavioral Development, 29,* 265–270.

MacArthur, J. (1998). *Successful Christian parenting.* Nashville: Word Publishing.

Maxwell, N. A. (1999, January 12). Sharing insights from my life. BYU Devotional Address. Retrieved from http://speeches.byu.edu/?act=browse&speaker=Maxwell%2C+Neal+A.&topic=&type=&year=1999&x=8&y=6

McConkie, B. R. (1979). *The mortal Messiah book I: From Bethlehem to Calvary, 4 vols.* Salt Lake City: Deseret Book.

McKay, D. O. (1955, April). In *Conference Report,* 26.

Nelson, D. A., Hart, C. H., Yang, C., Olsen, J. A., & Jin, S. (2006). Aversive parenting in China: Associations with child physical and relational aggression. *Child Development, 77,* 554–572.

Nelson, L. J., Hart, C. H., Wu, B., Yang, C., Roper, S. O., & Jin, S. (2006). Relations between Chinese mothers' parenting practices and social withdrawal in early childhood. *International Journal of Behavioral Development, 30*(3), 261–271.

Oaks, D. H. (2009, November). Love and law. *Ensign, 39,* 26–29.

Packer, B. K. (1986, November). Little children. *Ensign, 16,* 16–18.

Pearce, V. H. (Ed.). (1999). *Glimpses into the life and heart of Marjorie Pay Hinckley.* Salt Lake City: Deseret Book.

Regenerus, M., Smith, C., & Fritsch, M. (2003). *Religion in the lives of American adolescents: A review of the literature.* Chapel Hill, NC: National Study of Youth and Religion.

Sebald, H. (1986). Adolescents' shifting orientation toward parents and peers: A curvilinear trend over recent decades. *Journal of Marriage and the Family, 48,* 5–13.

Smith, C. (2005). *Soul searching: The religious and spiritual lives of American teenagers.* New York: Oxford University Press.

Smith, J. F. [Joseph F.]. (1916, March). Is man immortal? *Improvement Era, 19,* 425–431.

Smith, J. F. [Joseph Fielding]. (1963). *Gospel doctrine* (3rd ed.). Salt Lake City: Deseret Book.

Smith, P. K., & Hart, C. H. (2011). *The Wiley-Blackwell handbook of childhood social development* (2nd ed.). Oxford, UK: Wiley-Blackwell Publishers.

Speicher, B. (1994). Family patterns of moral judgment during adolescence and early adulthood. *Developmental Psychology, 30,* 624–632.

Strassberg, Z., Dodge, K. A., Pettit, G. S., & Bates, J. E. (1994). Spanking in the home and children's subsequent aggression toward kindergarten peers. *Development and Psychopathology, 6,* 445–461.

Straus, M. A., Sugarman, D. B., & Giles-Sims, J. (1997). Spanking by parents and subsequent antisocial behavior of children. *Archives of Pediatrics and Adolescent Medicine, 151,* 761–767.

Top, B. L., & Chadwick, B. A. (1998, Summer). Raising righteous children in a wicked world. *BYU Magazine.* Provo, UT: Brigham Young University.

Widtsoe, J. A. (Ed.). (1978). *Discourses of Brigham Young: Second president of the Church of Jesus Christ of Latter-day Saints.* Salt Lake City: Deseret Book.

Young, B. ([1862,1865] 1956). *Journal of Discourses.* G. D. Watt & J. V. Long (Reporters). Los Angeles: Gartner Printing.

Zhou, Q., Eisenberg, N., Losoya, S. H., Fabes, R. A., Reiser, M., Guthrie, I. K. , Murphy, B. C., Cumberland, A. J., & Shepard, S. A. (2002). The relations of parental warmth and positive expressiveness to children's empathy-related responding and social functioning: A longitudinal study. *Child Development, 73,* 893–915.

CHAPTER 11

Parenting in Gospel Context: Practices Do Make a Difference

David A. Nelson

Parents have a sacred duty to rear their children in love and righteousness,
to provide for their physical and spiritual needs, to teach them to love and serve one another,
to observe the commandments of God, and to be law-abiding citizens wherever they live.

THE PRIOR CHAPTER BY HART AND COLLEAGUES (chapter 10) gives an excellent overview of parenting research and how it relates to gospel teaching, including the proclamation. Chapter 10 particularly shows how conceptions of authoritative parenting are consistent with gospel-based advice for parents. The purpose of this chapter is to provide greater depth by visiting some of the most recent and significant debates and theoretical innovations in parenting research. First, I describe recent debates over the influence of parents, and the studies that suggest parenting influence interacts with genetic predisposition and peer influences in complex ways. Second, I discuss the important distinction between parenting styles and practices and apply that information to recent debates over parenting in different cultures. Some flexibility exists in the definition of the various styles—similar parents can vary somewhat in their practices and still fall under the umbrella of a particular style (with similar effects on child development). Third, I contrast the concept of psychological control with behavioral control, giving examples of the former in order to better elucidate what the Lord may mean when He cautions us against unrighteous dominion. I conclude with some parting thoughts about keeping parenting in proper perspective.

Parenting, Genes, and Peers

The family proclamation makes clear that Heavenly Father expects parents to have significant influence in the lives of their children. God's plan for His children may be ideally characterized as the placement of children into homes where parents are committed to their development and proclamation principles are practiced. No other arrangement is as effective, as demonstrated by the First Presidency's call to parents

to devote their best efforts to the teaching and rearing of their children in gospel principles which will keep them close to the Church. The home is the basis of a righteous life, and no other instrumentality can take its place or fulfill its essential functions in carrying forward this God-given responsibility (First Presidency of The Church of Jesus Christ of Latter-day Saints, 1999, p. 3).

As further evidence of the inspired and timely nature of the family proclamation, at the time of its pronouncement a new controversy regarding parental influence was emerging. Specifically, social scientists debated the relative influence of parents, with some defending substantial parental influence while others argued that parents in fact have little influence on child outcomes (Harris, 1998; Scarr, 1992). Advocates of the latter position believe the primary determinants of child outcomes are in the child's DNA or peer group influence.

The genetic emphasis may be expected as such research has accelerated in recent decades. Like in any new realm of research, however, there is a tendency to overstate and oversimplify the issues; in this case, genetic influence on behavior (Collins, Maccoby, Steinberg, Hetherington, & Bornstein, 2000). Many are also strongly tempted to attribute even complex behaviors to inborn traits, saying, "He was just born that way." In overemphasizing genetic influence, parents may feel less pressure to intervene when their children veer off into less desirable habits. Parents may also be encouraged to affirm an emerging behavior, although evidence of genetic predisposition does not provide an argument for or against the desirability of any given behavior (biology is inherently amoral). Parenting researcher Diana Baumrind (1993, p. 1300) has summarized the potential danger of such an approach to childrearing:

> Causal attributions that assign primary responsibility for child outcomes to genetic factors, the effect of which parents believe they cannot change, undermine parents' beliefs in their own effectiveness, whereas parents' attribution of responsibility for their children's outcomes to parents' own actions is associated with more effective caregiving, which in turn is associated with more positive child outcomes.

Nonetheless, due to belief in predominant genetic influence on human development, some have argued that parents only need to be "good enough" in child rearing. In other words, as long as parents are not abusive and otherwise provide the essentials of life, there may be little difference in parenting influence, as genes fundamentally shape behavior. For example, Scarr (1992, p. 15) has stated,

> Ordinary differences between families have little effect on children's development, unless the family is outside of a normal, developmental range. Good enough, ordinary parents probably have the same effects on their children's development as culturally defined super-parents. . . . Children's outcomes do not depend on whether parents take children to the ball game or to a museum so much as they depend on genetic transmission, on plentiful opportunities, and on having a good enough environment that supports children's development to become themselves.

In contrast, Baumrind (1993, p. 1299) argues that different parenting practices bring about varied child outcomes, and parents should thus be conscientious. In particular,

> the "exact details and specifications of the socialization patterns" are crucial to an understanding of normal development. All nonabusive environments above the poverty line are not equally facilitative of healthy development, so that the self a child will become in one kind of "normal" rearing environment is not the same self that child would become in another kind of rearing environment.

Baumrind's perspective mirrors that of the proclamation, which gives a substantial list of principles and practices parents should follow in seeking to establish a happy family and successfully rear their children. Each word in proclamation counsel denotes a world of possibilities; the details do matter. Moreover, the proclamation also suggests that significant teaching is required to bring about positive outcomes (for example, teaching children to love and serve one another). Such counsel implies that children may otherwise struggle to develop positive tendencies and, by extension, to abandon less desirable tendencies. Parents may turn to gospel teachings to classify child behaviors that are desirable and should be fostered as compared to undesirable behaviors that should be counteracted. As noted earlier, biology by itself cannot tell us what to reinforce or counter in child development.

Several fascinating adoption studies demonstrate the power of parenting to moderate genetic predispositions. For example, Tienari and colleagues (2004) demonstrated that a genetic predisposition for mental illness may be manifest or not, depending on whether family conditions act as a trigger or not. Consistent with the idea of genetic risk, they generally found that adopted children who had a schizophrenic biological parent were more likely over time to develop a range of psychiatric disorders (including schizophrenia) than children whose biological parents did not exhibit schizophrenia. However, this association was only evident if at-risk children were adopted into dysfunctional families. Children adopted into functional families largely demonstrated healthy development. Similarly, adopted children who are genetically at risk for criminality are far less likely to develop adult criminality if they are adopted into well-functioning rather than low-functioning homes (12 percent versus 40 percent risk; Bohman, 1996). Accordingly, the processes that lead from genotype to phenotype are not fixed; parenting can buffer children from genetic risk. In regard to many genetic vulnerabilities, therefore, parents may essentially conduct "gene therapy" on their children by the way they parent. Genes matter, but they do not function in a vacuum; gene-by-environment interaction is the norm (see also Reiss, Neiderhiser, Hetherington, & Plomin, 2000).

Additional insights regarding the importance of parenting are evident in the domain of parenting intervention, where studies consistently show that positive changes in parenting lead to more appropriate child behaviors beyond the family environment. The latest research by Patterson, Forgatch, and DeGarmo (2010), who have sought to reduce antisocial behavior in boys, suggests that these positive changes endure in unexpected ways. In particular, "strengthening parenting sets in motion an avalanche of enduring effects that generalize throughout and beyond the family" (p. 949). Better parenting by mothers leads to reductions in deviant behavior in sons, which correspondingly gives a lift to mothers as they see positive change. As relationships improve in the home, both mother and son find new opportunities for positive interaction beyond the home, since they are both learning better ways to interact socially. Thus, the impact of the parenting intervention actually becomes stronger and more expansive over time.

Peers also undoubtedly influence child development, as children are anxious to develop friendships and be generally accepted. Nonetheless, some researchers and cultural commentators exaggerate peer influence. Harris (1998) famously argued that youth shed parental influence as soon as they step outside the front door of their house, "as easily as the dorky sweater their mother made them wear" (p. 12). Peers are presumed to immediately take over the out-of-home socialization process. In contrast, significant evidence suggests that parents provide standards whereby children select appropriate friends, and parental monitoring is a key deterrent to negative behavior, even when such behavior is common to peers. For example, studies show that when parents teach their children to avoid illicit drug use, they are indeed less likely to use drugs. Recent studies by BYU sociologists further confirm that a combination of parental warmth

and effective monitoring tends to limit drug use among teens, even among those who have best friends who abuse drugs (Dorius, Bahr, Hoffman, & Harmon, 2004). Accordingly, parental influence substantially moderates peer pressure to use illicit drugs. Teenagers who have a good relationship with their parents and recognize their parents' willingness to monitor are usually sensitive to keeping their parents happy. This desire to please loving parents begins early in life (Kochanska, 2002).

Thus, in the midst of confusion generated by differing theoretical perspectives, extant empirical evidence readily asserts that parental influence can significantly interact with genetic predispositions and other environmental influences to help shape behavior. Hence, parents should follow Brigham Young's counsel to "study their children's dispositions and temperament, and deal with them accordingly" (1998, p. 2007). Parents must realize that they have the opportunity to proactively help their children develop positive traits or overcome undesirable tendencies. Children will be most open to instruction when they feel loved and accepted by their parents. They will act to maintain positive interactions. In addition to love and warmth, parents must also provide significant instruction in the morals and values that a child must learn in order to effectively self-regulate. This learning often occurs in the context of parental reactions to child behavior and misbehavior as parents seek to either praise or correct.

Elder David A. Bednar (2010) further explains that parents should also create opportunities "to be watchful and discerning concerning their children" (p. 41). Meaningful interaction with children provides context for "a spiritual early warning system," where parents may sense emerging problems and realize the need for prayerful and deliberate intervention. Parents should also wisely choose the neighborhoods, wards, and schools where their children will find desirable peers and friends. With appropriate teaching, guidance, and monitoring, parents can promote better friendships and effectively respond to destructive peer trends and messages. In this sense, parents directly influence children's developing peer relationships.

Parenting Styles versus Practices

Chapter 10 in this volume overviews Diana Baumrind's (1971) long-accepted and empirically supported parenting model, in which she defined authoritarian (coercive), permissive, and authoritative forms of parenting. In addition to these typologies, a fourth, the uninvolved/disengaged parent (who is neither loving nor demanding), has also been added. Of these four forms of parenting, empirical research has generally found that authoritative parenting is ideal in supporting positive child and adolescent outcomes (Steinberg, Lamborn, Darling, Mounts, & Dornbusch, 1994). In addition, this finding generally seems to hold for all racial and ethnic groups studied in the United States (Collins & Steinberg, 2006; Glasgow, Dornbusch, Troyer, Steinberg, & Ritter, 1997) as well as in a variety of cultures outside the United States (e.g., Hart, Nelson, Robinson, Olsen, & McNeilly-Choque, 1998; Vazsonyi, Hibbert, & Snider, 2003).

Parenting styles have been defined as "constellations of behaviors that describe parent–child interactions over a wide range of situations and that are presumed to create a pervasive interactional climate" (Mize & Pettit, 1997, p. 312). Authoritative parents are presumed to create a positive interactional climate based on an optimal balance of high warmth and high expectations, which environment in turn leads children and adolescents to be most receptive to parental influence. Elder Robert D. Hales has taught, "The key to strengthening our families is having the Spirit of the Lord come into our homes" (1999, p. 33). In essence, authoritative parenting creates an interactional climate that not only promotes positive parent–child relationships but also invites the Spirit of the Lord.

Despite research clearly favoring authoritative parenting, significant debate continues about the appropriateness of promoting certain parenting practices. Disagreement also exists on how various practices fit into parenting style categories. For example, does the Western description of authoritative parenting adequately capture good parenting in all cultures and families? Alternatively, does authoritarian parenting always lead to negative child adjustment, or only in cultures where such practices are not the norm? Is it possible for parents to be mostly authoritative in childrearing, yet engage in a few authoritarian practices? Some argue, for example, that occasional spanking is a hallmark of a good parent. A related issue is that parents may be discouraged by what appears to be an overly high standard embodied in the ideals of authoritative parenting (also referred to as "positive discipline"). Being the perfect balance of both warm and demanding is not an easy

standard to emulate. Is it enough to be "authoritative-like," coming close to the standard?

Answers to these questions are partially informed by differentiating between parenting styles and practices. Parenting practices are "strategies undertaken by parents to achieve specific academic, athletic, or social competence goals in specific contexts and situations" (Hart et al., 1998, p. 688). Strategies and goals are therefore linked together, and both may vary across families or cultures or both. Darling and Steinberg (1993) suggest the possibility that "authoritative parenting as a style is equally effective in socializing children across all cultural contexts, but that the goals toward which children are socialized, and thus parents' practices, vary across these very same ecologies" (p. 494). Even similar goals may yield different practices across families and cultures.

In other words, certain practices tend to come together in defining a parenting style, but there is room for some flexibility in the practices that determine the overall feel (or style) of parenting. For example, parents express warmth to children in myriad ways. One family may emphasize appropriate humor to promote parent–child communication, while another may do so with gentle, hushed conversations at bedtime. The net effect of either, in terms of child competence, may be quite similar, particularly when such practices accompany more common authoritative practices.

Parents may also tailor their parenting to children of different temperaments or challenges and still be congruent in style with all their children. For example, relative to their siblings, some children may require more frequent conversations with their parents about how to solve behavior problems. Furthermore, in these conversations, parents can allow children to give input regarding how to resolve an issue. Different children may suggest varying consequences or solutions which, if considered appropriate by the parent, may allow for some diversity in discipline strategies.

This discussion ties in with recent debates over culture and parental style (particularly in regard to variations in parental control). For example, cross-cultural studies find that Asian parents are generally more strict and controlling (that is, authoritarian) than Caucasian parents in the United States. Yet Asian children tend to do well academically. Chao (1994) has argued that what appear to be authoritarian practices might arguably be more suitable for proper child development in Asian rather than Western cultures. This has led some to question whether authoritative parenting is really ideal across all cultures. If practices that are typically considered to be authoritarian (that is, strict) are perceived by children in another culture to be reflective of parental involvement and concern, perhaps no damage is done. In other words, can aversive parenting yield negative outcomes in one culture and positive or neutral outcomes in another?

Ronald Rohner has proposed a theory emphasizing that parenting practices are likely to be similarly perceived by children across cultures, ethnicities, races, genders, and socioeconomic backgrounds, and therefore yield similar outcomes. Rohner's parental acceptance–rejection theory (PARTheory; Khaleque & Rohner, 2002) posits that children's psychological adjustment depends on the degree to which they perceive parental acceptance or rejection. Thus, a child's perceptions of acceptance or rejection by the parent may define healthy parenting practices, even if those specific practices vary across cultures. PARTheory has been particularly put to the test in studies that assess the effects of spanking across cultures. Results of these studies generally support PARTheory but also provide evidence for culture-specific associations.

For instance, corporal punishment is associated with children's perceptions of parental rejection and negative psychological adjustment even in cultures where most parents and children endorse its regular use and describe it as evidence of good parenting (Rohner, Kean, & Cournoyer, 1991). Nonetheless, the correlation between spanking and negative child outcomes is less pronounced (though not neutral) in cultures where spanking is more normative (Lansford et al., 2005). Therefore, whereas relatively mild authoritarian practices (like strictness) may blur the distinction between authoritarian and authoritative practices, harsh, rejecting practices (like consistent use of corporal punishment) appear more commonly to produce negative child outcomes across cultures (See Nelson, Hart, Yang, Olsen, & Jin, 2006, for a review).

Another issue mentioned earlier is whether authoritative parents may feel permission at times to be more directive in the supervision of their children, including the occasional use of corporal punishment. Is it possible to be authoritative if you spank on occasion? Some research suggests that nonabusive spanking (not overly harsh or frequent in use), in the context of an otherwise warm relationship, may indeed yield few negative effects. McLoyd and Smith (2002) analyzed the longitudinal connections between maternal spanking and problem behavior over a six-year period (using the National Longitudinal Survey of Youth). Results showed that spanking predicted increases in problem behavior over time, but only when maternal emotional support was low. In the context of high emotional support, spanking was not connected to problem behavior. This pattern held for European American, African American, and Hispanic children. Baumrind, Larzelere, and Owens (2010) have also studied different variants of parental control in preschool and their long-term (adolescent) correlates. They found, consistent with previous research, that authoritarian and permissive parenting predicted significant maladjustment in adolescence. However, "normative physical punishment" (spanking that is not overly harsh or frequent) appeared to be neutral in its long-term effects, and was not practiced exclusively by authoritarian parents (consistent with surveys showing that most American parents spank their children, at least infrequently). This idea of "normative physical punishment" clashes with the views of other researchers who consider a blanket injunction against the use of spanking to be the best policy. Gershoff and Bitensky (2007) argue, for example, that

> the primary goal of any socialization should be to promote children's internalization of the reasons for behaving appropriately rather than to behave solely to avoid punishment. . . . The research to date indicates that physical punishment does not promote long-term, internalized compliance (p. 234).

Accordingly, the debate rages on.

As noted by Hart and colleagues (Chapter 10), Latter-day Saint prophets have counseled against the use of physical punishment with children. For example, President Gordon B. Hinckley (1994, p. 53) taught, "I have never accepted the principle of 'spare the rod and spoil the child.' . . . Children don't need beating. They need love and encouragement." Parents should understand, therefore, that infrequent, nonabusive spanking, in the context of an otherwise warm and responsive relationship, may not cause lasting harm, but it is not likely to be a teaching (and internalization) moment. Similarly, permissive or uninvolved/disengaged parents who do not actively teach their children or confront them when they act inappropriately may find that their children will not learn important principles or learn to exercise proper self-governance.

Parents should therefore seek to abandon coercive or permissive parenting in favor of what Baumrind and colleagues (2010) call confrontive discipline, which involves "firm, direct, forceful, and consistent" responses to child misbehavior (p. 158). Authoritarian parents, although capable of confrontive discipline, tend to consistently resort to coercive discipline, which Baumrind and colleagues define as "peremptory, domineering, arbitrary, and concerned with retaining hierarchical family relationships" (p. 158). Power assertion, psychological control, severe physical punishment, and hostile criticism all signify coercion. The escalation to coercive discipline often stems from frustration and anger in parenting moments, and this escalation is often swift if parents do not feel significant warmth toward their children. In contrast, authoritative parents effectively balance giving high demands (being confrontive in response to child misbehavior) with being highly responsive (warm) while actively promoting appropriate child autonomy (rather than maintaining hierarchies and child subservience). In layman's terms, authoritative parents optimally balance love, limits, and latitude in the parent–child relationship.

Is such a balance achievable or an overly high standard? According to Baumrind and colleagues (2010), parents can take comfort in being "authoritative-like," in that they may not optimally balance warmth, demands, and autonomy, but nonetheless come close. These parents are generally composed of two groups. The first group, directive parents, are those who are more demanding than they are warm (tilting a bit toward the more directorial nature of authoritarian parents), but they generally avoid the coercive practices of the authoritarian style. Given their emphasis on demands, these parents may be a bit less likely to grant sufficient child autonomy. Democratic parents, in contrast, are more warm and supportive of child autonomy than they are demanding (tilting a bit toward the lenient nature of permissive parents). Yet they do not allow child autonomy to outweigh the need for adequate discipline. In Baumrind's longitudinal research, the children of directive or democratic parents fare long-term just as well as children of the more optimally balanced authoritative parents.

Hence, parents need not despair if they do not feel that they are the perfect balance of being both responsive and demanding in their parenting approach. A parent who is not "bubbly" in his or her expression of warmth, yet is appropriately demanding, can do well in child rearing, so long as that parent provides sufficient amounts of warmth so that the child feels adequately accepted and not rejected (consistent with PARTheory). Similarly, favoring warmth and autonomy over being demanding need not provoke significant problems as long as the child experiences sufficient restraint when it is deemed necessary. The problems emerge when parents become too imbalanced in their behavior along these dimensions. For instance, the overemphasis on giving demands leads authoritarian parents into tragically rejecting forms of parenting (coercion), which quickly dissipate any semblance of warmth in the parent–child relationship.

Psychological Control versus Behavioral Control

An important distinction has also been emphasized in parenting research in recent years: behavioral versus psychological control. Behavioral control is generally what is meant by the term "demandingess," in which parents monitor child behavior and hold children accountable when they misbehave. Appropriate behavioral control is necessary for positive child outcomes. Authoritarian parents engage in excessive behavioral control via coercive strategies, whereas permissive parents fail to provide adequate behavioral control. The tone and level of behavioral control are important to positive child development. In contrast, psychological control is generally considered to be deleterious, regardless of its tone or level. Barber (1996) has defined psychological control as

a rather insidious type of control that potentially inhibits or intrudes upon psychological development through manipulation and exploitation of the parent–child bond (e.g., love-withdrawal and guilt induction), negative affect-laden expressions and criticisms (e.g., disappointment and shame), and excessive personal control (e.g., possessiveness, protectiveness) (p. 3297).

Psychological control has long been neglected in parenting research, so a brief description and some examples of constituent practices are in order. Before launching into a discussion, however, it is important to note that this area of research is new enough that many questions exist as to the full meaning of psychological control and whether all practices under this umbrella are similarly detrimental. Generally speaking, psychologically controlling practices are consistent with the rejecting nature of the authoritarian style. But not all dimensions of psychological control may communicate rejection. Debate exists over whether practices such as guilt induction or love withdrawal might actually be productive in helping children learn social responsibility and appropriate feelings of guilt. Among clinicians, disappointment is clearly differentiated from shaming in its potential influence. Showing disappointment may be an appropriate way to "get in a child's head" and trigger self-reflection and greater self-control without communicating rejection.

Also not entirely clear is how a discussion in which a parent shares disappointment over a child's behavior is different from an episode of parental induction (an essential part of authoritativeness), in which the parent digs deeply into why a child chooses to act inappropriately and then comes up with potential solutions for future behavior. Finally, there is also the issue of magnitude, with more extreme (manipulative) forms of psychological control likely to be the most damaging. It may be that infrequent or mild manifestations of psychological control are less likely to be detrimental, much like Baumrind and colleages have argued with regard to "normative physical punishment." In short, there are many unanswered questions in this area of research, and our understanding of psychological control is therefore fairly narrow.

Nonetheless, the focus on psychological control is welcome in that our discussions of inappropriate parenting usually focus on traditional authoritarian practices, such as spanking. Evidence exists that parental psychological control is enacted from early childhood (Nelson et al., 2006) all the way through adulthood, as parents may struggle to keep even adult children subordinate to their wishes. The following examples concern young adults, but the same behaviors can easily be imagined with earlier age groups.

Love withdrawal, guilt induction, and shaming are some of the essential elements of this type of control, in which the child's psychological world and personal identity are manipulated as parents seek to force compliance with parental wishes. Love withdrawal is evidenced in the behavior of parents who cease talking with a child or become less affectionate when the child has displeased the parent (such as giving the cold shoulder, usually over extended periods). For example, a college-age woman visits home at Thanksgiving time and somehow offends her mother. Her mother starts to give her the silent treatment. The daughter, not certain what she did to offend, asks her mother for an explanation. Her mother, speaking through her father (as moderator), tells him to explain that the daughter knows what she did to offend and that the mother will not speak to her until she has apologized. No reconciliation occurs as the daughter does not know what to apologize for. This unreasonable situation continues all the way through Christmas break and well into the next year.

Guilt induction, in its worst manifestations, is about guilt trips that are gradually ratcheted up until compliance is met. For example, a daughter in her mid-twenties tells her mother that she plans to visit friends in another state for Thanksgiving. The mother values the entire family being together at Thanksgiving and immediately feels distressed. Rather than talking productively about her feelings, she chooses to exercise psychological control and seeks to manipulate her daughter into changing plans. The mother responds to the daughter by saying, "So, you love your friends more than your family?" The daughter is taken aback and deeply hurt by the accusation and the guilt it naturally induces. If the daughter decides to follow through with her plans, she may not be able to shake the feeling of guilt during her time away. She has "betrayed" the family. Notably, in this situation, guilt induction focuses on a direct personal attack on the goodness of the child. If such tactics fail to induce compliance, parents in such situations may grow more disaffected and prepare to level greater attacks in the future. The relationship will continue to sour, gradually replacing the good relationship experiences of the past.

As these examples should demonstrate, control is often the driving force behind such practices. Shaming, in particular, aims to keep the child psychologically subservient, even if that comes at the price of the child's self-esteem and the parent–child relationship. Through these manipulative tactics, parents demean and belittle children, adolescents, and young adults, communicating distrust in the child's ability to make proper choices.

Consistent with PARTheory, these behaviors communicate parental rejection. Anxiety and low self-esteem plague some children of such parents, whereas others respond to rejection with anger, rebellion, and estrangement. As hinted above, one of the most striking aspects of psychological control is that it is often employed in the service of otherwise worthy goals, such as desire for family unity.

For example, two young adults meet, begin to date, and decide to marry. They approach their parents with the great news. They have already decided on a date, the temple of choice, and how to arrange the wedding dinner. Both sets of parents are taken aback by the sudden news, but only the young man's parents react with psychological control. They tell the engaged couple that they do not like the date, the temple they selected, or the wedding dinner plans. They insist on a different date, a different temple, and a wedding luncheon rather than a dinner, which leaves the young woman feeling bewildered and confused. They restrict their son, who is still living at home, from seeing his fiancée more than once a week, telling him that he will have to move out if he does not comply. The young woman learns that the pattern in the family is for all the children to work for their father, who can then wield continued economic power over them (in case it is needed for compliance). Thus, the young couple is expected to live close to home and the business, and any plan to pursue other educational or work opportunities is automatically out of the question. These parents know best, even concerning the most minute details of their children's lives, and even if the wedding plans should normally recognize the reasonable wishes of those who are being married. Seeking to compromise, the young woman changes some of her plans but refuses to change the choice of temple. This is sufficient cause for the young man to be pressured by his parents to cancel the engagement. Unfortunately, he complies. Fortunately, the young woman does not step further into this web of inappropriate control.

I hope it goes without saying that such techniques are inappropriate. Not all psychological control tactics are as harsh as those shared in these examples. All such tactics, however, will cause damage to the parent–child relationship and the child's sense of self. There is evidence that shaming tactics, sometimes described as "wounding words" that demean or belittle, are actually more predictive of child maladjustment than physical punishment (Baumrind et al., 2010). Therefore, the campaign to reduce corporal punishment should be matched with a greater focus on ways to replace psychological control with healthier practices. As noted earlier, harsh parenting is often driven by intense anger and frustration on the part of parents. Parents would do well, then, to seek to better regulate themselves emotionally so their child does not feel rejected by them. In this vein, Brigham Young observed, "I have seen more parents who were unable to control themselves than I ever saw who were unable to control their children" (1870, p. 2). In contrast, the more positive we are, the better our relationships will tend to be. President Hinckley (1990, p. 70) taught this precept:

As children grow through the years, their lives, in large measure, become an extension and a reflection of family teaching. If there is harshness, abuse, uncontrolled anger, disloyalty, the fruits will be certain and discernable, and in all likelihood they will be repeated in the generation that follows. If, on the other hand, there is forbearance, forgiveness, respect, consideration, kindness, mercy, and compassion, the fruits again will be discernible, and they will be eternally rewarding. They will be positive and sweet and wonderful. . . . I speak to fathers and mothers everywhere with a plea to put harshness behind us, to bridle our anger, to lower our voices, and to deal with mercy and love and respect one toward another in our homes.

Some Parting Words

Baumrind (1978) appropriately captured the complexity of parenting when she described parents as having "the complex task of adjusting their demands and disciplinary methods flexibly to the developing capacities of the child so as to encourage social responsibility without discouraging independence and individuality" (p. 249). Striking the right balance between love, limits, and latitude in parenting is not a simple enterprise for most parents, particularly those who were not raised themselves in authoritative households. In addition, although authoritative parenting enhances the chances of parenting success, it does not guarantee that children will be compliant. Even the best parents sometimes have difficult children to raise due to no fault of their own. Parents who struggle with parenting at whatever level should be encouraged to constantly add potential tools to their "parenting tool-box" by turning to positive discipline books, the examples of family and friends, and gospel teachings. With time, parents can improve as they implement sound principles. Parents should also remember that their own development did not end with adolescence; individuals continue to develop through their parenting experiences. A portion of adults' collective wisdom is gained through the experience of parenthood.

The Latter-day Saint approach to teaching children, particularly through avenues such as family home evening and scripture study, is most essential to promoting understanding and internalization of important values that will guide behavior. Similarly, prayer encourages children's sense of accountability to their Heavenly Father for their lives and actions. Elder David A. Bednar (2010) has given numerous insights into the value of gospel teaching, both for promoting positive child outcomes as well as for helping parents sense impending problems. In addition to standard venues such as family home evening, Elder Bednar also encourages the numerous opportunities parents have to informally share gospel insights and testimony with their children (for example, at the dinner table in informal conversation). In short, the family that embraces multiple opportunities to teach will generally find that they need to discipline their children less often as their children internalize principles and gradually evidence greater ability for self-control. Speaking of the exemplary society the Prophet Joseph Smith helped form in Nauvoo, he explained, "I teach them correct principles and they govern themselves" (quoted in Young, 1965, *Journal of Discourses*, 10:57–58). This principle can be applied to parenting, with the recognition that the teaching must be adjusted to the developmental readiness of the child, and that teaching sometimes takes much time, even years, to fully sink in with the young (as well as the old). Parents should not be discouraged by the need to repeat themselves; the same principle is regularly practiced in our church meetings, as well as in our own parent–child relationship with Heavenly Father.

David A. Nelson *is an associate professor in the School of Family Life at Brigham Young University. He and his wife, Emily, are the parents of four children: Jessica, Joshua, Christian, and Sarah.*

References

Barber, B. K. (1996). Parental psychological control: Revisiting a neglected construct. *Child Development, 67,* 3296–3319.

Baumrind, D. (1971). Current patterns of parental authority. *Developmental Psychology Monograph, 4,* 1–103.

Baumrind, D. (1978). Parental disciplinary patterns and social competence in children. *Youth and Society, 9,* 239–276.

Baumrind, D. (1993). The average expectable environment is not good enough: A response to Scarr. *Child Development, 64,* 1299–1317.

Baumrind, D., Larzelere, R. E., & Owens, E. B. (2010). Effects of preschool parents' power assertive patterns and practices on adolescent development. *Parenting: Science and Practice, 10,* 157–201.

Bednar, D. A. (2010, May). Watching with all perseverance. *Ensign, 40,* 40–43.

Bohman, M. (1996). Predisposition to criminality: Swedish adoption studies in retrospect. In G. R. Bock & J. A. Goode (Eds.), *Genetics of criminal and antisocial behavior, Ciba Foundation Symposium 194* (pp. 99–114). Chichester, England: John Wiley & Sons.

Chao, R. K. (1994). Beyond parental control and authoritarian parenting style: Understanding Chinese parenting through the cultural notion of training. *Child Development, 65,* 1111–1119.

Collins, W. A., Maccoby, E. E., Steinberg, L., Hetherington, E. M., & Bornstein, M. H. (2000). Contemporary research on parenting: The case for nature and nurture. *American Psychologist, 55,* 218–232.

Collins, W. A., & Steinberg, L. (2006). Adolescent development in interpersonal context. In W. Damon & R. M. Lerner (Series Eds.) & N. Eisenberg (Vol. Ed.), *Handbook of child psychology: Vol. 3. Social, emotional, and personality development* (6th ed., pp. 1003–1067). New York: Wiley.

Darling, N. & Steinberg, L. (1993). Parenting style as context: An integrative model. *Psychological Bulletin, 113,* 487–496.

Dorius, C. J., Bahr, S. J., Hoffman, J. P., & Harmon, E. L. (2004). Parenting practices as moderators of the relationship between peers and adolescent marijuana use. *Journal of Marriage and Family, 66,* 163–178.

First Presidency of The Church of Jesus Christ of Latter-day Saints, Letter of February 11, 1999, cited in *Church News*. (February 27, 1999), 3. Retrieved from http://lds.org/hf/statements/0,16955,4232-1,00.html

Gershoff, E. T., & Bitensky, S. H. (2007). The case against corporal punishment of children: Converging evidence from social science research and international human rights law and implications for U.S. public policy. *Psychology, Public Policy, and Law, 13,* 231–272.

Glasgow, K. L., Dornbusch, S. M., Troyer, L., Steinberg, L., & Ritter, P. L. (1997). Parenting styles, adolescents' attributions, and educational outcomes in nine heterogeneous high schools. *Child Development, 68,* 507–529.

Hales, R. D. (1999, May). Strengthening families: Our sacred duty. *Ensign, 29,* 32–34.

Harris, J. R. (1998). *The nurture assumption: Why children turn out the way they do; Parents matter less than you think and peers matter more.* New York: Free Press.

Hart, C. H., Nelson, D. A., Robinson, C. C., Olsen, S. F., & McNeilly-Choque, M. K. (1998). Overt and relational aggression in Russian nursery-school-age children: Parenting style and marital linkages. *Developmental Psychology, 34,* 687–697.

Hinckley, G. B. (1994, November). Save the children. *Ensign, 24,* 52–54.

Hinckley, G. B. (1990, May). Blessed are the merciful. *Ensign, 20,* 68–70.

Khaleque, A., & Rohner, R. P. (2002). Perceived parental acceptance-rejection and psychological adjustment: A meta-analysis of cross-cultural and intracultural studies. *Journal of Marriage and Family, 64,* 54–64.

Kochanska, G. (2002). Committed compliance, moral self, and internalization: A meditational model. *Developmental Psychology, 38,* 339–351.

Lansford, J. E., Chang, L., Dodge, K. A., Malone, P. S., Oburu, P., Palmérus, K., . . . Quinn, N. (2005). Physical discipline and children's adjustment: Cultural normativeness as a moderator. *Child Development, 76,* 1234–1246.

McLoyd, V. C., & Smith, J. (2002). Physical discipline and behavior problems in African American, European American, and Hispanic children: Emotional support as a moderator. *Journal of Marriage and Family, 64,* 40–53.

Mize, J., & Pettit, G. S. (1997). Mothers' social coaching, mother–child relationship style, and children's

peer competence: Is the medium the message? *Child Development, 68,* 312–332.

Nelson, D. A., Hart, C. H., Yang, C., Olsen, J. A., & Jin, S. (2006). Aversive parenting in China: Associations with child physical and relational aggression. *Child Development, 77,* 554–572.

Patterson, G. R., Forgatch, M. S., & DeGarmo, D. S. (2010). Cascading effects following intervention. *Development and Psychopathology, 22,* 949–970.

Reiss, D., Neiderhiser, J. M., Hetherington, E. M., & Plomin, R. (2000). *The relationship code: Deciphering genetic and social influences on adolescent development.* Cambridge, MA: Harvard University Press.

Rohner, R. P., Kean, K. J., & Cournoyer, D. E. (1991). Effects of corporal punishment, perceived caretaker warmth, and cultural beliefs on the psychological adjustment of children in St. Kitts, West Indies. *Journal of Marriage and the Family, 53,* 681–693.

Scarr, S. (1992). Developmental theories for the 1990s: Development and individual differences. *Child Development, 63,* 1–19.

Steinberg, L., Lamborn, S. D., Darling, N., Mounts, N. S., & Dornbusch, S. M. (1994). Over-time changes in adjustment and competence among adolescents from authoritative, authoritarian, indulgent, and neglectful families. *Child Development, 65,* 754–770.

Tienari, P., Wynne, L. C., Sorri, A., Lahti, I., Laksy, K., Moring, J., . . . Wahlberg, K. E. (2004). Genotype-environment interaction in schizophrenia-spectrum disorder: Long-term follow-up study of Finnish adoptees. *British Journal of Psychiatry, 184,* 216–222.

Vazsonyi, A. T., Hibbert, J. R., & Snider, J. B. (2003). Exotic enterprise no more? Adolescent reports of family and parenting processes from youth in four countries. *Journal of Research on Adolescence, 13,* 129–160.

Young, B. ([1862, 1865] 1965). *Journal of discourses.* G. D. Watt & J. V. Long (Reporters). Los Angeles: Gartner Printing.

Young, B. (1870, July 12). *Deseret News Semi-Weekly.*

Young, B. (1998). *Discourses of Brigham Young* (John A. Widtsoe, Ed.) Salt Lake City: Deseret Book.

CHAPTER 12

Mothers as Nurturers

Jenet J. Erickson

Mothers are primarily responsible for the nurture of their children.

I AWOKE EARLY THIS MORNING AND COULD NOT go back to sleep. It must be that my 60 years is finally leading me to those days when you can't sleep in. But most of all I was awakened by a profound sense of overwhelming joy. Those feelings seem to come upon me more and more—and they are always accompanied by images and pictures of our children. As I picture them—their lives, their spouses, their children—I marvel at what has come of the union of Jim and me. What a remarkable journey! What a remarkable gift! There have been seasons of sorrow and seasons of struggle— those too I remember. But the joy in what God has enabled through us seems to eclipse those struggles that seemed and sometimes even now seem so difficult. As I see it all in a picture before me, I can't help but simply feel gratitude—gratitude for the precious privilege of being a nurturer, a mother.
—LaDawn Jacob, personal interview

In 1978, President Spencer W. Kimball spoke prophetically of women in the latter days. His words entered a world of loud and clamoring voices raising questions about the purpose of womanhood and the meaning of motherhood. In response to this challenging confusion, he declared:

To be a righteous woman is a glorious thing in any age. To be a righteous woman during the winding up scenes on this earth, before the second coming of our Savior, is an especially noble calling. The righteous woman's strength and influence today can be tenfold what it might be in more tranquil times (p. 103).

Teachings from the living prophets clarify and bring truth to the confusion and distortions that surround womanhood and motherhood. President Kimball's prophetic declaration suggested that by adhering to these truths, righteous women of the latter days would have the potential to be a remarkable influence. The purpose of this chapter is to respond to some of the questions and dilemmas women are likely to experience in fulfilling their divine role as nurturers. Responses to these questions draw on scientific theories and research, clarified by revealed truths in the restored gospel.

Questions about the Importance of Motherhood

Yesterday my husband called a little bit before lunchtime to check on how we were doing at home. The conversation was more brief than usual because he had a lunch appointment held at a nice restaurant near his office. But it was also interrupted because the toddler sitting at the table in his booster seat knocked a cup of apple juice over, sending juice flying all over himself, the floor— and all over me. When I hung up the phone I began the task of cleaning him off, wiping the sticky juice off the table and floor, and finally changing out of the now sticky sweat pants I had not been able to change out of since early that morning. While kneeling on the floor with a rag in my hand I couldn't help but reflect on the differences between the work my husband was doing and the work I so often did as a mother. I knew in my mind that caring for children mattered, but honestly, it was hard to see what could possibly be so important about changing diapers, wiping noses, cleaning muddy feet, and all the other hundreds of mundane chores that seemed to make up my daily life. I reflected on the bachelor's and master's degrees I had received and couldn't help but wonder how after all that preparation I ended up on the floor with a rag in my hand wiping up juice spilled by a toddler. Hadn't I been prepared to do something more significant? Something that would really make a lasting difference? (Personal communication with the author.)

Although scientific evidence has continued to demonstrate the importance of a mother's care, motherhood has been questioned and devalued in the broader culture. A survey of a nationally representative sample of mothers in the United States in 2005 found that fewer than half of mothers (48 percent) felt appreciated most of the time, and almost 20 percent said they felt less valued by society when they became a mother (M. F. Erickson & Aird, 2005). Many mothers feel that society does not value the kind of self-sacrificing work motherhood requires. As a result, they may feel pressured to invest their talents and energies in work that they perceive to be more valued by the larger culture. While a member of the Seventy, Elder Bruce C. Hafen explained, "For most of our history, the word motherhood meant honor, endearment, and sacrifice. . . .Yet this spirit of self-sacrifice has become a contentious issue in recent years, making contentious the very idea of motherhood" (2005, p. 181).

In 1968, Betty Friedan released *The Feminine Mystique,* her report from the "trenches" of marriage and motherhood. Friedan's book was in many ways an expansion of efforts to bring awareness to the often invisible experiences of women in dealing with challenges of unequal power and opportunity, where men had greater privilege. In the developed world, these unequal privileges were expressed in political, educational, and employment opportunities; economic benefits; and occurrences of domestic violence and rape. Similarly, in less-developed countries, where 80 percent of the women of the world

live, these inequities have expressed themselves in significant restrictions politically, economically, and educationally. But there are also dramatically higher rates of female infanticide, controlling customs that prevent women from choosing their spouses, a normalization of battery and assault of wives by husbands, and forced prostitution of women (see summary, Sorensen & Cassler, 2004).

Friedan's work reacted to the problems of these inequities in the modern world by advocating the expansion of women's opportunities in educational and professional work. But it also seriously questioned the meaning and contribution of a woman's life when she is mainly engaged in child rearing. According to the feminist reaction advocated by Friedan, the caring labor of motherhood was harmful because it made women "dangerously vulnerable to exploitation" (Whisnant, 2004, p. 201). The demands of caring for children full time meant that women would be dependent on men economically, and hence have less access to the economic, political, and societal power Friedan perceived mattered most.

Speaking to the many women who primarily cared for their children at home, Friedan asked, "Why should women accept this picture of a half-life, instead of share in the whole of human destiny?" For Friedan, meaningful achievements depended on doing "work that is of real value to society—work for which, usually, our society pays." From this point of view, the family—including motherhood and marriage—was a "risky proposition" for women because it "ranked lowest in terms of prestige" and obligated women "to subordinate their personal objectives, . . . putting the needs of others first, devoting themselves to the day-to-day well-being of other family members," which may be deemed "virtuous," but is not a path to power and success (Polatnik, 1983, p. 35).

The result of Friedan's book among middle-class women was a "divide through the country," separating women from one another (Roiphe, 1996, p. 13). Mothers heard radical feminist slogans such as "Renounce your martyrdom. Become a liberated mother—a woman, not a mom." These expressions engendered conflict between the feelings of love and responsibility in caring for children and the fear that such care may be a source of enslavement. On the one hand there was motherhood, which by definition requires the sacrifice of some wishes to care for a helpless human being. In contrast was the assertion that women should demand more attention to the self—the full humanity, wishes, desires, and capacities of the self (Roiphe, 1996). A series of dilemmas emerged for women: "Must creativity clash with motherhood? Are passion and love and beauty irreconcilable with domestic life? Is maternity keeping us from our destiny as creative people? Is the home a shelter or a prison?" (p. 38).

Historical Causes for Questions about the Importance of Motherhood

In some ways, these dilemmas were a predictable response to the dramatic changes of industrialization and urbanization in the 19th century. Prior to industrialization, mothers and fathers worked side by side to build their household economy, represented in the family farm or small artisan shop. With industrialization, the work of production moved outside the home, creating a split between work and home (Griswold, 1993). Mothers alone became the primary socializers, educators, and caregivers of their children. Fathers were moved to the periphery of family life as they went out into "the world" to establish themselves as earners (Blankenhorn, 1995). Among middle- and upper-class whites, an entire code of conduct for women emerged, reinforcing the division between men and women. Household labor became more burdensome and isolating as tasks that had once been shared by family members were now assigned to women, reinforcing a strong divide between the work lives and worlds of fathers and mothers.

This meant that women's role in the home would be inflexibly defined. Because their property and earnings belonged to their husbands, married women could not pursue personal economic interests. As one author concluded, women "lacked the means and motive for self-seeking" (Cott, 1977, p. 70–71). Further, cultural ideals around womanhood prescribed women's appropriate attitude to be selflessness—so that they could absorb and even redeem the home from the strains that resulted from the "evils" of the business world. Women were "to live for others" by giving up all self-interest—and in that way save the home (Cott, 1977, p. 71).

In the words of Elder Bruce C. Hafen, those who have criticized these ideas have an important point. This model of motherhood viewed women as "excessively dependent on their husbands." Some mothers were exploited in their "willingness to accept relentless demands." And many women experienced "undue pressure to conform to rigid roles that deny a woman's sense of self" (2005, p. 182). But, as Elder Hafen continues,

"The critics have swung the pendulum too far." Quoting an article from *Newsweek,* Elder Hafen said that they "sometimes crossed the line into outright contempt for motherhood" (p. 182).

The family came to be viewed as inherently repressive, the institution to be blamed most for women's oppression. According to Elshtain (1982, p. 444), "early feminist rhetoric [had] a dramatic insistence that the family was 'the enemy.'" Feminist writers argued that the social assignment of women to mothering had to be challenged because women's oppression and male domination was connected to mothering.

At the same time, the modern era valued an orientation toward individualism and consumerism that also devalued women's role of nurturing children. Rearing children inherently demanded a surrendering of self-interest and independence. As a result, children came to be viewed as a liability—expensive, inconvenient, and an encroachment on personal fulfillment. These attitudes further devalued motherhood, the work of nurturing children, and the virtues of femininity and selflessness that had been identified with motherhood. Feminist ideas that had intended to elevate women then became self-defeating, because they required that women embrace a view of the meaning of life that "had rejected or devalued the world of the traditionally 'feminine'" (Elshtain, 1982, p. 447). Rather than challenging the attitudes that had devalued women, the new woman advocated by feminism looked more like "the old man" feminists had criticized (p. 447).

Prophetic Teachings about the Importance of Motherhood

Teachings of the restored gospel provide clarity in resolving the complexity of these issues and establishing the significance of motherhood. A First Presidency statement in 1942 declared: "Motherhood is near to divinity. It is the highest, holiest service to be assumed by mankind. It places her who honors its holy calling and service next to the angels" (James R. Clark, 1935–1951, p. 178). The calling of motherhood has been identified as the most ennobling endowment God could give His daughters, "as divinely called, as eternally important in its place as the priesthood itself" (J. Reuben Clark Jr., 1946, p. 801). This endowment enables women to have a unique influence in the lives of those around them, particularly their children.

In the words of President Spencer W. Kimball,

Mothers have a sacred role. They are partners with God, as well as with their own husbands, first in giving birth to the Lord's spirit children, and then in rearing those children so they will serve the Lord and keep his commandments (1976, p. 72).

President Thomas S. Monson eloquently added, "May each of us treasure this truth: . . . One cannot remember mother and forget God. Why? Because these two sacred persons, God and mother, partners in creation, in love, in sacrifice, in service, are as one" (1998, p. 6). These statements give motherhood an unparalleled position of significance in Heavenly Father's plan of happiness.

Prophets of the restored gospel have also been clear in declaring that demeaning women or their divine roles as wives and mothers is a diabolical tactic that takes from women and men the true sources of happiness. Elder Richard G. Scott explained,

Satan has unleashed a seductive campaign to undermine the sanctity of womanhood, to deceive the daughters of God and divert them from their divine destiny. He well knows women are the compassionate, self-sacrificing, loving power that binds together the human family. . . . He has convinced many of the lie that they are third-class citizens in the kingdom of God. That falsehood has led some to trade their divinely given femininity for male coarseness (2000, p. 36).

The countless acts of selfless service mothers perform are recognized as expressions of the highest love and noblest of womanly feelings (Faust, 1986). Wendell Berry (1987, p. 10) asserted that such tasks as feeding, tending, bathing, clothing, wiping, and cleaning become holy works; "only in such ways can love become flesh." Through such sacrificing love, a mother creates a foundation from which self-confidence and integrity are woven into the fabric of her children's character (Scott, 1996). As Elder Bruce C. Hafen and Sister Marie K. Hafen explain,

Just as a mother's body may be permanently marked with the signs of pregnancy and childbirth, [the Savior] said, "I have graven thee upon the palms of my hands" (1 Nephi 21:15–16). For both a mother and the Savior, those marks memorialize a wrenching

sacrifice—the sacrifice of begetting life—for her, physical birth; for him, spiritual rebirth (1994, p. 29).

In response to questions about motherhood keeping women from personal growth, Elder Robert D. Hales further clarified,

The world would state that a woman is in a form of servitude that does not allow her to develop her gifts and talents. Nothing, absolutely nothing, could be further from the truth. Do not let the world define, denigrate, or limit your feelings of lifelong learning and the values of motherhood in the home (Hales, 2008, n.p.).

He added,

Motherhood is the ideal opportunity for lifelong learning. A mother's learning grows as she nurtures the child in his or her development years. They are both learning and maturing together at a remarkable pace. It's exponential, not linear. . . . In the process of rearing her children, a mother studies such topics as child development; nutrition; health care; physiology; psychology; nursing with medical research and care; and educational tutoring in many diverse fields such as math, science, geography, literature, English, and foreign languages. She develops gifts such as music, athletics, dance, and public speaking. The learning examples could continue endlessly (n.p).

An Exploration of Effective Mothering

Research studies exploring influences on children's development support statements of the prophets regarding the significant influence of women as mothers. Findings from these studies confirm what President David O. McKay declared:

Motherhood is the greatest potential influence either for good or ill in human life. The mother's image is the first that stamps itself on the unwritten page of the young child's mind. It is her caress that first awakens a sense of security; her kiss, the first realization of affection; her sympathy and tenderness, the first assurance that there is love in the world (1953, p. 452).

Love:
The Foundation of Effective Mothering

The significance of mothers' influence is first grounded in the relationship she forms with her child. Because motherhood is part of a woman's divine identity, her role as mother is defined by a relationship more than a set of tasks. Dorothy Lee, an anthropologist, clarified this when she explained,

> I like the way a Wintu [tribe] in reference to his mother will say, 'she-whom-I-made-into-mother,' even though he is the fourth child. I like it because it gives recognition to the fact that this is not a repetition of the same event. A new mother has been born, mother-to-this-child, and a new relationship of motherness has come into being. When this is recognized, the mother is helped to sense the particularity of her child, and the peculiar flavor, the peculiar quality of the relationship that she can have with each child (1966, p. 134).

A mother's attentive love in this new relationship becomes the foundation by which all of the other tasks of mothering become effective.

John Bowlby's attachment theory (1944, 1982) provides scientific understanding for the influence of the relationship between mother and child from infancy (Belsky, 2001). Bowlby's exploration of the importance of this bond started after he observed a consistent pattern of disrupted mother–child relationships and later adult psychopathology. Children who had been deprived of maternal care during extended periods in their early lives seemed to develop into individuals who "lacked feeling, had superficial relationships, and exhibited hostile or antisocial tendencies" (Kobak, 1999, p. 23). This led Bowlby to conclude that the attachment between mother and child is critical for a child's healthy social–emotional development.

Margaret Ainsworth expanded on Bowlby's ideas by exploring how the quality of the attachment between mother and child influenced the child's development. She found that children seemed to thrive when they had an emotionally secure attachment with their mothers. The security of the attachment was related to how mothers interacted with their children, which Ainsworth labeled maternal sensitivity. According to Ainsworth, maternal sensitivity is a measure of how a mother detects, interprets, and responds appropriately to her child's needs; how positive and kind she is in her interactions; and how much she respects her child's autonomy in exploring and growing (Ainsworth, Blehar, Waters, & Wall, 1978).

When a mother is consistently available and supportive, the child receives the physical and psychological security necessary to foster playing, exploring, and appropriate social behaviors (Bretherton & Munholland, 1999). If this security is threatened, fear activates the attachment system to help restore access to the attachment figure. Fear that is not appropriately addressed seems to lead to feelings of depression, anxiety, aggression, and defensive distortions of vulnerable feelings (Kobak, 1999). In contrast, a secure attachment enables a child to develop feelings that he or she deserves love, feelings that help him or her learn to appreciate, understand, and empathize with the feelings of others and appropriately regulate relationship closeness and conflict resolution (Bretherton & Munholland, 1999). These findings did not suggest that every child with an insecure attachment necessarily experienced problems. But the insecure attachment seemed to initiate pathways associated with later pathology (Sroufe, Carlson, & Shulman, 1993).

These findings led researchers to conclude that the way a mother interacts with her child, her maternal sensitivity, is the strongest, most consistent predictor of her child's cognitive, social, and emotional development (NICHD, 2003). Neuropsychological studies of infant brain development provided additional evidence supporting the importance of mothers' interactions. Mothers seem to have a special ability to sensitively modify the stimulation they give to their infants. Through finely tuned perceptions, they match their infants' intellectual and emotional state and provide the optimal "chunked bits" of positive interaction needed for the child's developing brain (Schore, 1994). In speaking of this finely tuned process, three scholars from the University of California at Berkeley concluded,

> Whether they realize it or not, mothers use the universal signs of emotion to teach their babies about the world. . . . Emotionality [love] gives the two of them a common language years before the infant will acquire speech. . . . It isn't just his mother's beaming countenance but her synchrony that he requires—their mutually responsive interaction (Lewis, Amini, & Lannon, 2000, pp. 61–62).

Such attentive, loving interactions are not only important during infancy. Numerous studies have demonstrated that the quality of a mother's relationship with her child is associated with her child's social interactions and behaviors across development (Buehler, 2006; Guilamo-Ramos, Jaccard, Dittus, & Bouris, 2006). Children seem to do best when mothers show love by communicating about and being aware of their activities and behaviors. Expressing love through listening, communicating, and monitoring enables a mother to be warm and supportive while setting and enforcing appropriate limits. Studies consistently indicate that adolescents who report telling their mothers where they are going and what they will be doing after school and on weekends also report lower rates of alcohol misuse, drug use, sexual activity, and delinquency (Barnes, 2006). Children's academic success and healthy behaviors have also been tied to their mothers' involvement in talking with them, listening to them, and answering their questions (Luster, Bates, Vandenbelt, & Nievar, 2004).

The Goals of Effective Mothering

The relationship formed through a mother's attentive love provides the foundation for all of the other major tasks of motherhood. Mothering scholar Sara Ruddick identified a number of central tasks for which attentive love provides the foundation, including: (a) preserving children's lives and wellbeing, and (b) fostering children's growth and development (1983).

Preserving life. From the moment of her child's birth, a mother faces the realization that a fragile life depends on her (Stern & Bruschweiler-Stern, 1998). The physical connection inherent in the biological relationship between mother and child seems to make mothers particularly sensitive to responsibility for the child's protection and well-being (Doucet, 2006). Her fear for the baby's survival and growth may also make her vigilant and attentive to finding the best food, care, and medical help, and avoiding possible dangers. These natural attunements, especially when shared with the father, serve important constructive and protective functions for a child (Stern & Bruschweiler-Stern, 1998). Studies consistently indicate that mothers have a significant role in influencing their children's health and well-being throughout their development.

Nurturing growth and development. The desire to sustain the life of the child is part of the second central task of mothering, that of nurturing growth and development. Research findings suggest that the ways mothers nurture their children's individual growth is the critical influence on their development. Although men can and do take on this work of nurturing, there appear to be important and useful differences between men and women. Further, much of the day-to-day work and responsibility for this nurturing care continues to "rest with women." As a result, mothers are more often identified in research studies as central to these nurturing processes (Doucet, 2006, p. 111).

One of the primary ways mothers nurture growth and development is through helping create an environment of safety, peace, and learning. A central part of creating that environment is through organizing the home and family so that routines and rituals are carried out effectively. A range of studies indicate that having ordered and predictable routines (waking up, getting dressed, taking vitamins or medications, brushing teeth, going to school, doing homework, eating dinner, going to bed) is central to children's healthy development (Fiese, 2006). Further, mothers have the primary role in carrying out family rituals and traditions (such as Christmas, Easter, family celebrations including birthdays, and distinctive family traditions such as Sunday night sing-alongs or periodic service projects).

For preschool and school-age children, routines and rituals are especially important in helping with self-regulation, skill development, problem solving, and development of good academic habits. For adolescent children, routines and rituals have been associated with a sense of identity and family belonging, warmth in relationships with parents, fewer risk behaviors, and better psychological health (Fiese, 2006). Mothers significantly influence the environment in which their children grow and develop through the routines and rituals they ensure are carried out (Ring, 2006).

A second critical way that mothers influence development is through the emotion work they perform to maintain and strengthen individual well-being and family relations. Mothers do this emotion work by facilitating conversations about feelings, listening carefully to family members' feelings, recognizing the importance of feelings and offering encouragement, expressing appreciation, and asking questions to elicit family members' sharing of feelings. For many mothers, providing this kind of emotion work is integral to their efforts to nurture the growth and development of children (R.

Erickson, 2005). Where a father may be oriented toward fixing the problem that arises, mothers seem particularly adept at helping children to express feelings and to feel better (Doucet, 2006).

Mothers' emotion work may be especially effective if mothers are available when children are most willing to share their thoughts and feelings. Research findings suggest that the hours after school may be particularly important for mothers in sharing experiences and monitoring children (Aizer, 2004). During these moments at "the crossroads" (see Monson, 1992, p. 5), children may be more inclined to share their thoughts and feelings. Children also seem to be more inclined to open up and share when working alongside parents in household responsibilities. Washing dishes, preparing food, folding laundry, and other household tasks provide opportunities for thoughts and feelings to be shared while hands are busy working (see Chapter 21, this volume).

A third critical way in which mothers influence development is through teaching. Mothers are the most important influence on intellectual development and children's learning because they often spend the most time with the child. During a child's infancy, the cognitive stimulation and emotional support mothers provide lay the foundation for intellectual and linguistic functioning throughout development. As mothers talk to their infants, direct their attention to objects in the environment, and label the objects they see, they provide cognitive stimulation that enhances their infant's language skills and intellectual abilities (Tamis-LeMonda & Bornstein, 1989).

As children grow, mothers provide essential stimulation when they ask questions or give suggestions that invite the child's thinking, or when they provide conceptual links among objects, activities, locations, persons, or emotions (Hubbs-Tait, Culp, Culp, & Miller, 2002). Mothers continue to provide cognitive stimulation for pre-school and school-age children when they read to their children and teach them concepts; encourage them in hobbies; take them to libraries, museums, and theaters; and expose them to books and other sources of learning in the home (Votruba-Drzal, 2003). Dinnertime conversations, car rides, and shared work also provide important opportunities for engaging children in important developmental processes. The significant influence of this cognitive stimulation is enhanced through the emotional support she provides by being positive, particularly when a child is trying to learn a

task or solve a problem. Her expression of positive emotions, without inappropriately intruding or restraining, fosters a secure environment for children to learn and grow (Hubbs-Tait et al., 2002).

Even more significant than the cognitive stimulation a mother provides is her teaching of wisdom and truth to guide her children's development. Research findings consistently indicate that children whose mothers openly discuss the risks of behaviors such illicit sexual activity, alcohol and substance abuse, and smoking are less likely to engage in dangerous behaviors (Guilamo-Ramos et al., 2006). Further, children whose mothers transmit their religious beliefs and facilitate their children's involvement with religion report the lowest levels of delinquency among adolescents (Pearce & Haynie, 2004). These findings indicate that her teachings become a key ingredient in preparing her children to live fulfilling and contributing lives.

In summary, research findings have supported the truth that a mother's loving, attentive relationship with each child becomes the foundation by which all other mothering tasks become effective. From the foundation of love, mothers significantly influence children's development by creating an environment in which children can flourish. Mothers significantly influence development through establishing consistent routines and strengthening emotional well-being and relationships among family members. Finally, research indicates that mothers are a critical influence on children's development through the cognitive stimulation and teaching they provide.

Gaining Strength for the Challenges of Motherhood

The other day I ran into another mother who asked me how I was doing. Within a few minutes I was crying—how could I possibly explain the complexity of my feelings?! Hadn't I always wanted to be a mother? And yet, why do I sometimes feel like all I want to do is escape? How is it possible that I can love my children so much and yet at the same time feel like I am too tired to be able to take the responsibility any more? I have to admit that sometimes I feel like my wings have been clipped—I wake up in the morning and there the dirty dishes are again, and the messy diapers, and the dirty high chair, and noses that have to be wiped, and I don't know if I have the energy to face it again. And yet I feel guilty even expressing those thoughts. Is motherhood really supposed to be this way? (Personal communication with the author.)

Research on motherhood has consistently revealed that motherhood is full of "dialectical tensions." Mothers will feel profound joy and meaning in loving and caring for children and at the same time an immense burden of responsibility. Mothers naturally filled with great love for their children face the relentless tasks of identifying and responding to each child's needs while fostering each child's development. The amount of energy exerted in the process can tax the physical stamina of any mother, leading her to struggle emotionally as well as physically. Mothers may come to feel that the reality of their experience as mothers is dramatically different than their idealization of what motherhood would be like.

Mothers who are feeling exhausted and stressed are less likely to feel they are able to mother the way they think would be best. Dr. Wally Goddard captures this reality when he explains,

> We have all seen the effect that stress and exhaustion can have on our parenting. We overreact. We are harsh. We fail to use good sense. We lose sight of the child's motives and needs. When we're not happy and balanced, our parenting suffers (Goddard, 2011, n.p.).

In response, mothers may feel guilt, which may lead them further into a cycle of exhaustion and perceived failure in parenting. The experiences of burnout and depression are more likely for mothers when they have "shoulds" that are unattainable, hold themselves responsible for things they cannot control, have a hard time setting limits and saying no, or feel that they would be continually satisfied if they were a better person and mother. Many mothers learn that mothering requires aligning of expectations with reality rather than putting unneeded "shoulds" on the list of essentials, setting priorities so they can do well the things they most care about, and structuring their lives to include activities that replenish (Tannenhauser, 1985).

It is critical that mothers care for themselves and nurture their own minds, hearts, and bodies as they consecrate their minds, hearts, and bodies to mothering.

They must be nurtured in order to be able to nurture those to whom they are consecrated. Elder M. Russell Ballard counseled mothers to

> find some time for yourself to cultivate your gifts and interests. Pick one or two things that you would like to learn or do that will enrich your life, and make time for them. Water cannot be drawn from an empty well, and if you are not setting aside a little time for what replenishes you, you will have less and less to give to others, even to your children (2008, p. 110).

When they see motherhood as a relationship rather than a set of tasks, mothers will also recognize the dangers in comparing their mothering with others. A mother will understand that her mothering will be individual because she is giving her best, unique self to her children. The one thing that she has to offer is her individual person. Her interests, talents, mind, and all that she has developed become her offering to the relationship she has with each of her children. As Elder Ballard taught,

> There is no one perfect way to be a good mother. Each situation is unique. Each mother has different challenges, different skills and abilities, and certainly different children. The choice is different and unique for each mother and each family. . . . What matters is that a mother loves her children deeply and, in keeping with the devotion she has for God and her husband, prioritizes them above all else (May, 2008, p. 108).

In addition, husbands and fathers play a crucial role in enabling mothers to be nurtured and strengthened. As one author wrote, the greatest work of any man is "the endowment of motherhood" (Carver, 1913, p. 293). As a husband "endows" his wife with motherhood, he does all that he can to enable her work as a mother to flourish, because she is the central nurturer of their greatest treasure.

Perhaps most important, mothers and fathers who are honest with themselves will recognize that in every relationship they will fail their children in some important way. That is part of being mortal in a fallen world. No mother or father is good enough to care perfectly for God's children. The only true solution is to be changed—to have our natures changed so that we can draw inspiration from heaven and become fit parents. The promise of the Savior's Atonement is that we can receive His image by humbly bringing our tattered, weak selves to Him for healing. In that place of dependence, we will feel His transforming mercy bless us to become more like Him in our parenting.

A recent study of a large sample of Latter-day Saint parents found that a mother's private religious behaviors—including fasting, personal prayer, scripture study, study of other religious materials, and thinking about religion—were a more significant influence on the quality of her parenting than the family's religious behaviors. Mothers who spent more time in these activities were more likely to feel close to their children and to be effective in providing warmth, love, and support, while setting clear and appropriate boundaries and expectations. They were also less likely to resort to physical coercion, verbal hostility, unreasonable punishing, indulgence, or psychological control—all unhealthy patterns of discipline in parenting. The findings suggest that humbly seeking for the Savior's influence and help enables us to become the kinds of mothers we desire to become (Behling, 2010).

Individual Circumstances that Necessitate Adaptation

It's been five years since my former husband chose to leave our marriage and the covenants that had kept us close in the early years of our marriage. Though I have been blessed with peace during this period of being single, I have also faced the recurring thought that I am a failure in the thing that matters most on earth and eternity. It is painful for me to hear the ideals of motherhood that I treasure talked about in church because those ideals are not possible for me. The stay-at-home mom who can be available whenever her children are home, the ability to ensure my children are in the best environment for their growth when they are staying with their dad, the opportunity to provide an example of a loving husband and wife who work together to rear their children in love and righteousness, etc., are all ideals of motherhood I cannot fully give. Where do I fit in this gospel of ideals around motherhood and family? (Personal communication with the author.)

Teachings from the living prophets about the most crucial priorities for mothers are particularly important as many mothers find themselves in family circumstances that are not ideal. Whatever the specific circumstances, many situations necessitate individual adaptation, as specified by the proclamation. The guidance provided by the restored gospel will help mothers prioritize and focus on the most important things they can do to bless their families.

Research findings support the priorities emphasized by living prophets. Studies have consistently indicated, for example, that children do better under the challenging circumstances of divorce, poverty, and a parent's mental or emotional disability when rituals and routines such as family dinner, family prayer, assigned chores and responsibilities, and consistent wholesome recreation are in place (Fiese, 2006). Further, the emotional support and connectedness mothers facilitate may become more directly influential when circumstances are not ideal. Her efforts to ensure that she builds a strong relationship with her children through spending focused time, being available, listening to them, and being aware of their experiences and feelings help children thrive even when there are difficult challenges. Finally, her love and teachings, expressed through example and verbal communication, become the critical threads by which confidence and peace are woven into children's hearts, regardless of the challenge.

A large body of research addresses the effects on children when mothers have to spend many hours away from them in employment. These studies provide evidence for the importance of mothers spending time with their children, but they also indicate that it is the way a mother interacts with her children when she is with them that is most important. Extensive hours of non-mother childcare (30 hours per week) during the early years of a child's life have been associated, on average, with less social competence and cooperation, more problem behaviors, negative mood, aggression, and conflict in children. Negative effects have been identified in caregiver reports of children's behavior at age 4 and through the first, third, and sixth grades, particularly for children who spent long hours in day-care centers (Jacob, 2009).

But the way a mother interacted with her children—her maternal sensitivity—was the strongest, most consistent predictor of children's social–emotional development and behavior, even when she was away from them for long periods of time (Jacob, 2009). Further, childcare that was more like a nurturing home than a childcare center, with a higher adult-to-child ratio that allowed children to receive consistent, responsive nurturing, was not associated with negative effects over the long term. Negative effects that might ensue because of a mother's absence seem to be ameliorated when a mother is able to provide consistent, sensitive nurturing, and to coordinate a form of childcare that is more like a child would experience if the mother were present.

Some circumstances may require that the father becomes the primary caretaker and nurturer of children for a season. A recent study of stay-at-home fathers concluded that many men learn to nurture in ways that are similar to mothers when they are given primary responsibility for their children. But even then, men differed from women in their style of nurturing, with most fathers emphasizing fun, playfulness, physical activities, the outdoors, practicality in the emotional response, and the promotion of independence and risk taking with older children (Doucet, 2001). Men are very nurturing in caring for their children, but the complementarity of men and women in nurturing their children's development is important.

Finally, some women may not experience motherhood in this life, or may experience a long period of waiting before the opportunity comes. In this circumstance, understanding the true definition of motherhood will allow women to recognize their call to nurture life. As Sister Sheri Dew, who has not had the opportunity to marry or bear children, explained:

> Of all the words they could have chosen to define her role and her essence, both God the Father and Adam called Eve "the mother of all living"—and they did so *before* she ever bore a child. . . . Motherhood is more than bearing children. . . . It is the essence of who we are as women. It defines our very identity, our divine stature and nature, and the unique traits our Father gave us (2001, p. 96, italics in original).

In their divine identity as mothers, all women have been called to partner with God in doing all they can to help guide children home to Him. Recognizing that, Sister Dew explained:

Every one of us can show by word and by deed that the work of women in the Lord's kingdom is magnificent and holy. I repeat: *We are all mothers in Israel,* and our calling is to love and help lead the rising generation through the dangerous streets of mortality (2001, p. 97).

As women engage in the work of motherhood, whatever their circumstances, they will find that their greatest source of strength will come from knowing and following the doctrines of Christ and relying on Him for help. In speaking of this great effort, Sister Barbara B. Thompson of the General Relief Society Presidency said:

> Remember the great love of our Savior. He said in Isaiah 41:10, "Fear thou not; for I am with thee: be not dismayed; for I am thy God: I will strengthen thee; yea, I will help thee." Then in verse 13 He says again, "I will help thee." And once more in verse 14 He says, "I will help thee." Believe the Savior. He will help us. He loves us (2007, p. 117).

There is no work in which the Lord takes greater interest than in the nurturing and rearing of our children. Because of that, we can be assured that He will strengthen mothers in their holy calling. Truly, motherhood places her who honors its holy work next to the angels, for nothing could be of greater significance to God than the nurturing of His little ones—His precious children.

Jenet J. Erickson is a former assistant professor in the School of Family Life at Brigham Young University. She and her husband, Michael, currently are the parents of one young daughter.

References

Ainsworth, M. D. S., Blehar, M. C., Waters, E., & Wall, S. (1978). *Patterns of attachment: A psychological study of the Strange Situation.* Hillsdale, NJ: Lawrence Erlbaum Associates.

Aizer, A. (2004). Home alone: Supervision after school and child behavior. *Journal of Public Economics, 88,* 1835–1848.

Ballard, M. R. (2008, May). Daughters of God. *Ensign, 38,* 108–110.

Barnes, G. (2006). Effects of parental monitoring and peer deviance on substance use and delinquency. *Journal of Marriage and Family, 68*, 1084–1104.

Behling, S. (2010, September). The impact of religiosity on parenting behaviors in Latter-day Saint families. Dissertation submitted to the Department of Psychology: College of Liberal Arts and Sciences. DePaul University, Chicago, IL.

Belsky, J. (2001). Emanuel Miller lecture: Developmental risks (still) associated with early child care. *Journal of Child Psychology and Psychiatry and Allied Disciplines, 42*, 845–859.

Berry, W. (1987, July). Men and women in search of common ground: Personal growth requires strong roots. *Sunstone, 11*, 8–12.

Blankenhorn, D. (1995). *Fatherless America: Confronting our most urgent social problem.* New York: Basic Books.

Bowlby, J. (1944). Forty-four juvenile thieves: Their characters and home-life. *International Journal of Psychoanalysis, 25*, 19–52, 107–127.

Bowlby, J. (1982). *Attachment* (2nd ed.). In J. Bowlby (Series Ed.), Attachment and loss series: Vol. 1. New York: Basic Books.

Bretherton, I., & Munholland, K. A. (1999). Internal working models in attachment relationships: A construct revisited. In J. Cassidy & P. R. Shaver (Eds.), *Handbook of attachment: Theory, research, and clinical applications* (pp. 89–111). New York: Guilford Press.

Buehler, C. (2006). Parents and peers in relation to early adolescent problem behavior. *Journal of Marriage and Family, 68*, 109–124.

Carver, T. N. (1913). Home economics from a man's point of view. *Journal of Home Economics, 5*, 291–300.

Clark, James R. (Comp.). (1935–1951). *Messages of the First Presidency of The Church of Jesus Christ of Latter-day Saints,* 6 vols. (vol. 6), Salt Lake City: Bookcraft.

Clark, J. Reuben. Jr. (1946, December). Our wives and our mothers in the eternal plan. *Relief Society Magazine, 33*, 795–804.

Cott, N. F. (1977). *The bonds of womanhood.* New Haven, CT: Yale University Press.

Dew, S. L. (2001, November). Are we not all mothers? *Ensign, 31*, 96–98.

Doucet, A. (2001). "You see the need perhaps more clearly than I have": Exploring gendered processes of domestic responsibility. *Journal of Family Issues, 22*, 328–357.

Doucet, A. (2006). *Do men mother?* Toronto: University of Toronto Press.

Elshtain, J. B. (1982, Fall). Feminism, family, and community. *Dissent, 29*, 442–449.

Erickson, R. J. (2005). Why emotion work matters: Sex, gender, and the division of household labor. *Journal of Marriage and Family, 67*, 337–351.

Erickson, M. F., & Aird, E. G. (2005). The motherhood study: Fresh insights on mothers' attitudes and concerns. New York: Institute for American Values. Executive summary retrieved from http://www.americanvalues.org/pdfs/motherhoodexsumm.pdf

Faust, J. E. (1986, September). A message to my granddaughters: Becoming "great women." *Ensign, 16*, 16–21.

Fiese, B. H. (2006). *Family routines and rituals.* New Haven, CT: Yale University Press.

Griswold, R. L. (1993). *Fatherhood in America: A history.* New York: Basic Books.

Goddard, W. (2011, January 3). Godly parenting: Getting our hearts right. Retrieved from http://www.ldsmag.com/index.php?option=com_zine&view=article&Itemid=3&ac=1&id=7134

Guilamo-Ramos, V., Jaccard, J., Dittus, P., & Bouris, A. M. (2006). Parental expertise, trustworthiness, and accessibility: Parent–adolescent communication and adolescent risk behavior. *Journal of Marriage and Family, 68*, 1229–1246.

Hafen, B. C. (2005). *Covenant hearts.* Salt Lake City: Deseret Book.

Hafen, B. C. & Hafen, M. K. (1994). "Eve heard all these things and was glad": Grace and learning by experience. In D. H. Anderson & S. F. Green (Eds.), *Women in the covenant of grace: Talks selected from the 1993 Women's Conference* (pp. 16–33). Salt Lake City: Deseret Book.

Hales, R. D. (2008, August 19). The journey of lifelong learning. BYU Devotional Address. Retrieved from http://speeches.byu.edu/reader/reader.php?id=12394&x=83&y=4

Hubbs-Tait, L., Culp, A. M., Culp, R. E., & Miller, C. E. (2002). Relation of maternal cognitive stimulation, emotional support, and intrusive behavior during Head Start to children's kindergarten cognitive abilities. *Child Development, 73*, 110–131.

Jacob, J. I. (2009). The social-emotional effects of nonmaternal child care on children in the USA: A critical review of recent studies. *Early Child Development and Care, 179,* 559–570.

Kimball, S. W. (1976, March). The blessings and responsibilities of womanhood. *Ensign, 6,* 70–73.

Kimball, S. W. (1978, November). Privileges and responsibilities of sisters. *Ensign, 8,* 102–106.

Kobak, R. (1999). The emotional dynamics of disruptions in attachment relationships: Implications for theory, research, and clinical intervention. In J. Cassidy & P. R. Shaver (Eds.), *Handbook of attachment* (pp. 21–43). New York: Guilford Press.

Lee, D. (1966). To be or not to be: Notes on the meaning of maternity. In S. M. Farber & R. H. L. Wilson (Eds.), *The challenge to women.* New York: Basic. Reprinted in K. Bahr, A. Hawkins, & S. Klein (Eds.), *Readings in family science 371* (pp. 133–138). Dubuque, IA: Kendall/ Hunt Publishing.

Lewis, T., Amini, F., & Lannon, R. (2000). *A general theory of love.* New York: Random House.

Luster, T., Bates, L., Vandenbelt, M., & Nievar, M. A. (2004). Family advocates' perspectives on the early academic success of children born to low-income adolescent mothers. *Family Relations, 53,* 68–77.

McKay, D. O. (1953). *Gospel ideals: Selections from the discourses of David O. McKay.* Salt Lake City: Deseret News Press.

Monson, T. S. (1992, May). Memories of yesterday, counsel for today. *Ensign, 22,* 4–5.

Monson, T. S. (1998, April). Behold thy mother. *Ensign, 28,* 2–6.

NICHD. (2003). Does amount of time spent in child care predict social–emotional adjustment during the transition to kindergarten? *Child Development, 74,* 976–1005.

Pearce, L. D., & Haynie, D. L. (2004). Intergenerational religious dynamics and adolescent delinquency. *Social Forces, 82,* 1553–1572.

Polatnick, M. R. (1983). Why men don't rear children: A power analysis. In J. Trebilcot (Ed.), *Mothering: Essays in feminist theory* (pp. 21–40). Totowa, NJ: Rowman and Allanheld.

Ring, K. (2006). What mothers do: Everyday routines and rituals and their impact upon young children's use of drawing for meaning making. *International Journal of Early Years Education, 14*(1), 63–84.

Roiphe, A. (1996). *Fruitful: A real mother in the modern world.* Boston: Houghton Mifflin.

Ruddick, S. (1983). Maternal thinking. In J. Trebilcot

(Ed.), *Mothering: Essays in feminist theory* (pp. 213–231). Totowa, NJ: Rowman and Allanheld.

Schore, A. N. (1994). *Affect regulation and the origin of the self: The neurobiology of emotional development.* Hillsdale NJ: Lawrence Erlbaum Associates.

Scott, R. G. (1996, November). The joy of living the great plan of happiness. *Ensign, 26,* 73–75.

Scott, R. G. (2000, May). The sanctity of womanhood. *Ensign, 30,* 36–38.

Sorensen, A. D. & Cassler, V. H. (2004). *Women in eternity, women of Zion.* Springville, UT: Cedar Fort.

Stern, D. N., & Bruschweiler-Stern, N. (1998). *The birth of a mother.* New York: Basic Books.

Sroufe, L. A., Carlson, E., & Shulman, S. (1993). Individuals in relationships: Development from infancy through adolescence. In D. C. Funder, R. D. Parke, C. Tomlinson-Keasey, & K. Widaman (Eds.), *Studying lives through time: Personality and development* (pp. 315–342). Washington, D. C.: American Psychological Association.

Tamis-LeMonda, C. S., & Bornstein, M. H. (1989). Habituation and maternal encouragement of attention in infancy as predictors of toddler language, play, and representational competence. *Child Development, 60,* 738–751.

Tannenhauser, L. (1985, December 26). Motherhood stress. *Woman's Day,* 54–62. Reprinted in K. Bahr, A. Hawkins, & S. Klein (Eds.), *Readings in family science 371* (pp. 116–120). Dubuque, IA: Kendall/Hunt Publishing.

Thompson, B. (2007, November). I will strengthen thee; I will help thee. *Ensign, 37,* 115–117.

Votruba-Drzal, E. (2003). Income changes and cognitive stimulation in young children's home learning environments. *Journal of Marriage and Family, 65,* 341–355.

Whisnant, R. (2004). Woman centered: A feminist ethic of responsibility. In P. DesAutels & M. U. Walker (Eds.), *Moral psychology: Feminist ethics and social theory* (pp. 201–217). Lanham, MD: Rowman & Littlefield.

CHAPTER 13

"Honor Thy Father":
Key Principles and Practices in Fathering

Sean E. Brotherson

FROM SINAI LONG AGO RANG A SACRED INVITATION from the God of Israel: "Honour thy father and thy mother" (Exodus 20:12). There is much to consider in this invitation and divine command. A perspective of fathering that embraces the divine injunction to "honor thy father" suggests a set of high ideals for men in family life. Indeed, if men wish to receive honor in their efforts as fathers, then it is essential that they be worthy of honor. In his address on being a righteous husband and father, President Howard W. Hunter (1994) set forth clear standards of moral behavior and caring involvement that defined a father's primary responsibilities in family life. "The teaching and governance of the family," he observed, "must not be left to [a man's] wife alone, to society, to school, or even the Church" (p. 50). To father a child is more than a biological act or fulfillment of a social role. To father a child is to accept a divine calling, a moral stewardship, and a lasting commitment across generations. President Ezra Taft Benson taught that a father's calling "is an eternal calling from which [he is] never released" (1987, p. 48).

Debate over the roles of men in family life or academic efforts to document father involvement should not cloud our attention to two fundamental realities:

- Parenting is a work of vital, even eternal, importance to children, families, and communities.
- Fathers make a fundamental difference in parenting across generations.

Some think and write about fathers from a perspective of skepticism, wondering whether fathers are even essential to children's healthy development or productive family life (e.g., Silverstein & Auerbach, 1999). However, President Howard W. Hunter taught that a father's "leadership of the family is [his] most important and sacred responsibility" and the "family is the most important unit in time and in eternity and, as such, transcends every other interest in life" (1994, p. 50). Thus, it is of vital importance to define the doctrines that underlie the sacred work of fathering and outline the dimensions of father involvement that make a difference for children, families, and communities.

Key Principles and Practices in Fathering

What are the essential principles and key practices that characterize healthy fathering and contribute to positive outcomes for children, women, and men in family life? In searching for truth and meaning in both sacred and secular approaches to knowledge, we can discover and define key principles that carry lasting value for humanity. Both sacred and secular approaches are useful and often complementary in defining such lasting principles.

A vital definition of the term *principle* was given by President Boyd K. Packer (1996, p.17), who taught that "a principle is an enduring truth, a law, a rule that you can adopt to guide you in making decisions." Elder Richard G. Scott (1993, p. 86) further taught, "Principles are concentrated truth, packaged for application to a wide variety of circumstances."

The search for key principles through a spiritual or religious approach tends to focus on ideas based on *revealed* truths—doctrines or key concepts that have been revealed to humanity by God through spiritual means. The search for key principles through a secular or scientific approach tends to focus on concepts that are *discovered* or *accumulated*, concepts that have been deemed lasting and significant based on repeated investigation through scientific means. In this chapter I have purposefully sought to integrate sacred doctrines that pertain to fathering with overlapping scholarly findings on father–child relationships, thus identifying key principles and practices essential in fathering.

Organizing Principles of Fathering

Fatherhood can be conceptualized as a parental stewardship that links generations and is defined by those caring activities that nurture family relationships, foster growth, and enable the transmission of values between generations. While family scholars have used varying theoretical perspectives to frame the relationship between fathers and children, the definition stated above most closely links to the conceptual model of *fathering as generative work* (Dollahite & Hawkins, 1998). Generative work is generational work and embraces the understanding that the father–child relationship asks for a morally committed, actively involved effort over a lifetime from a father. Fathering as generative work, in essence, recognizes that fathering is spiritual work. As President Harold B. Lee (1972, p. 52) so eloquently summarized, "The most important of the Lord's work you and I will ever do will be within the walls of our own homes."

Both sacred and secular perspectives on fathering suggest that "the challenge facing most fathers today, as in the past, is to develop the skills and insights necessary to nurture the rising generation" (Brotherson & White, 2007, p. 17). Even more important, the decisions and behaviors of fathers in their family relationships have long-lasting and fundamental consequences. John Snarey, who investigated the contributions of fathers to children across generations in a multi-decade research project, summarized this tremendous body of research in saying: "Good fathering, it seems, really does matter. It matters over a long time, over a lifetime, and even over generations" (1993, p. 356). Thus, fathers matter, their choices matter, and the work they do in raising the next generation matters immensely.

The scholarly formulation of generative fathering fits well with sacred perspectives on fathering. The generative fathering framework outlines several primary domains of generative work that fathers engage in as they raise children. Although this framework is not meant to be exhaustive, it is a useful conceptual tool for organizing principles about fathering. It also fits well with other scholarly findings and spiritual truths that pertain to fathers and their families. Based on this approach, I will focus here on five fundamental principles of fathering: to *preside, partner, be present, provide,* and *protect.*

To Preside

"The Family: A Proclamation to the World" (¶ 7) states, "By divine design, fathers are to preside over their families in love and righteousness." A brief examination of this statement makes clear three fundamental realities regarding fatherhood. First, fathers are directed to take upon themselves the responsibility of spiritual leadership in family life as part of a loving Eternal Father's plan for family functioning. Second, a father's responsibility to preside occupies the first and foremost duty among the varied obligations that rest upon men in family life. Third, the manner in which a father is to exercise spiritual guidance among family members is explicitly articulated: "in love and righteousness." These words emphasize that perhaps it is only through the gentle application of love and the consistent example of personal spiritual attentiveness that spiritual persuasion can be appropriately exercised (see D&C 121:41–42).

President Ezra Taft Benson (1984, p. 6) reinforced this key principle of fathering in a conference address: "God established that fathers are to *preside* in the home. Fathers are to provide love, teach, and direct" (italics added). Abraham Heschel (1975), a leading Jewish philosopher, identified the father as a powerful spiritual figure in the family circle with a moral responsibility to teach and care for his children. He suggested that fathers are meant to be teachers and holy figures in the lives of their children. Before the patriarch Jacob died, he called his children to him and said, "Gather yourselves together, and hear, ye sons of Jacob; and hearken unto Israel your father" (Genesis 49:2). He bestowed counsel and blessings upon each of his children. In him was the power to bless generations. He exercised a holy influence upon his children as he blessed them and uplifted them; this is part of what it truly means to preside.

The concept of blessing future generations does not belong only to scriptural imperatives or cultural traditions. Indeed, a concept known as *generativity* has become a bedrock principle of lifespan developmental theory and research (Erikson, 1950). Generativity is defined, simply, as the "challenge to adults . . . to create, care for, and promote the development of others, from nurturing the growth of another person to shepherding the development . . . of a broader community" (Snarey, 1993, p. 19). Erikson (1964, p. 130) further summarized the place of parenting relative to generativity, stating, "Parenthood is, for most, the first, and for many, the prime generative encounter." For fathers, then, the fundamental task of parenthood is to be generative, to bless generations, to preside. Involved fathers bless children from the time of birth onward. For example, preschool children whose fathers are involved and interact positively with them display greater cognitive ability, more individual control, and more empathy than other children (Pleck, 1997). As children grow older, positive involvement by fathers is strongly associated with fewer behaviors involving externalizing (negative actions) and internalizing (negative emotions). Both boys and girls who have positively involved fathers show higher social competence and experience fewer problems in school (Mosley & Thomson, 1995). Snarey's (1993) landmark study of fathers and generativity showed that fathers' generative engagement with children accounted for a significant portion of their educational and occupational attainment in young adulthood. Generativity can also involve compensating for the mistakes of past generations, as some fathers indicate they often attempt to make up for a difficult, fatherless past by acting generatively in their fathering efforts (Roy & Lucas, 2006).

The aspects of generative fathering most closely aligned with the principle of presiding in family life are the domains of *spiritual work* and *ethical work*. Dollahite (2003, p. 241), in studying the spiritual commitments of fathers to special needs children, has argued that "generative spirituality meaningfully binds a father to his child and inspires him to meet his child's needs through responsible and responsive involvement." Generativity assumes a moral commitment to nurture and guide the next generation and transmit lasting values. Thus, it is linked with presiding in family life and blessing family members through love, warmth, and guidance (Marks & Dollahite, 2007; Snarey, 1993). For many men, a spiritual or moral focus provides an anchor that motivates their parental commitment and encourages

generative care of their children (Latshaw, 1998; Marks & Dollahite, 2007). Fathering practices that flow from spiritual and ethical commitments vary widely, ranging from a long-term personal commitment to be present in a child's life to modeling good behavior and engaging in positive spiritual practices with children (Marks & Dollahite, 2007). Most important, however, fathers who embrace the principle that fathering means "to preside . . . in love and righteousness" have an anchoring principle and a spiritual focus for their fathering efforts designed to bless the children and families they love.

To Partner

Parenthood is a partnership. In other words, when any individual becomes a parent, he or she also enters into a community of relationships. Raising a child is an individual journey, but it is also a community journey, a relational partnership across generations as fathers and mothers, grandparents, aunts and uncles, teachers, coaches, pastors, and parents' friends all work together in rearing a child to responsible adulthood. For fathers, being aware of and attentive to these relationships is critical to raising a child. As parents, mothers and fathers decide how to partner and whether they include or exclude other individuals in a child's life and upbringing. Thus, another fundamental principle in fathering is to partner with others in raising a child, including the child, the child's mother, extended family members, and the larger community.

It is instructive to note that God the Father's first commandment, given to Adam and Eve in the Garden of Eden, pertained to their relationship as partners in parenthood. In "The Family: A Proclamation to the World," latter-day prophets teach that the "first commandment that God gave to Adam and Eve pertained to their potential for parenthood as husband and wife" (¶ 4). In other words, parenthood was framed as a joint partnership within the context of a committed relationship between husband and wife, as father and mother. What is the divine principle upon which men and women are to enter this parental union? The proclamation further states, "In these sacred responsibilities, fathers and mothers are obligated to help one another as equal partners" (¶ 7). Thus, to partner in fathering is to accept the responsibility of rearing a child in cooperation with others, particularly the child's mother, and to assist and give support in doing the work of nurturance, love, and guidance in a child's upbringing.

The domain of generative fathering most closely linked with the principle of partnering in family life is *relationship work*. Relationship work is fundamental in father–child relationships because individuals experience meaning and the formation of identity primarily through their involvement in human relationships (Dollahite, Hawkins, & Brotherson, 1997). Brotherson, Dollahite, and Hawkins (2005, p. 5) have suggested that "relationship work involves both the sense of feeling emotionally and psychically connected with a son or daughter and the father's efforts to create and maintain healthy bonds between the child, himself, and others in the child's environment." In our home, evening routines with Dad include brushing teeth, reading stories, saying prayers together, and giving bedtime hugs. While I am involved directly in these tasks, my wife also guides and encourages these interactions. These daily interactions foster lasting feelings of connection that occur in a family setting where we partner together in creating healthy family relationships.

Partnering with the child's mother. A key article on responsible fathering suggests that "fathering cannot be defined in isolation from mothering, [or] mothers' expectations" (Doherty, Kouneski, & Erickson, 1998, p. 278). While many factors affect a father's motivation and involvement, research suggests that the quality of a father's relationship with a child's mother is perhaps the "secret ingredient" that makes the fathering recipe work best for most men and their children (Cowan & Cowan, 2000; Holmes, Duncan, Bair, & White, 2007). The optimal environment for this fathering partnership to take place is a healthy marriage. Research indicates that a healthy, satisfying marriage is a fathering "force multiplier" for men, which helps fathers to be more involved with their children, more confident in their parental skills, more satisfied in their paternal efforts, and more sensitive to the needs of children (Holmes et al., 2007). Doherty and colleagues (1998, p. 286) further emphasize the value of a healthy marriage in their declaration that "the family environment most supportive of fathering is a caring, committed, and collaborative marriage." For fathers, then, a key element of fathering involves maintaining a positive working relationship with a child's mother, whether they are married to each other or not. Vital strategies for fathers and mothers in working together to raise children include maintaining a positive emotional relationship, appreciating each other, offering instruction and accepting help, and making parenting decisions together (Holmes et al., 2007).

Partnering with the child. Becoming a father necessarily means entering into a continuing relationship of care and involvement with a child. Children come into life with their own personalities and preferences, and thus it is important to remember that this is a two-way relationship in which children and fathers mutually influence each other in their development, not simply a relationship in which all influence flows from the father to the child (Pardini, 2008). Thus, fathers and children are essentially engaged in a relational partnership in which children are nurtured to form their individual identities, master life skills, build relationships with others, acquire knowledge and moral understanding, and develop their full potential as human beings and children of a loving earthly father and Heavenly Father.

President Howard W. Hunter (1994, p. 51) advised that fathers should "earn the respect and confidence of [their] children through [their] loving relationship with them," and suggested also that fathers should give children "time and presence in their social, educational, and spiritual activities and responsibilities" and provide "tender expressions of love and affection toward children." In this process, fathers partner with their children from birth forward and the relationship becomes a continuing influence over a lifetime and beyond. The quality of the father–child relationship makes a lasting difference for children beginning in the earliest years (Parke, 1996). Fathers who involve themselves and connect with young children facilitate greater cognitive development, increased social competence, and empathy toward others (Lamb, 1997). Research has further indicated that "it is not his mere presence, per se, but his connection to children that is pivotal," and that "strong connections can have beneficial effects" while "poor connections can have adverse effects" (Brotherson, Yamamoto, & Acock, 2003, p. 208).

Partnering with others in the child's life. Beyond partnering with a child's mother and the child, fathers conduct the generative work of fathering within a broader system of relationships. Children are born into the world with many family ties: father, mother, sibling, and grandparent, among others. These extended family ties are critical in providing support to fathers, as it has been suggested that fathering is more sensitive to contextual and relationship influences than mothering (Doherty et al., 1998). In particular, social support in extended family relationships is helpful as fathers benefit from "a threshold of support from inside the family and from the larger environment" (Doherty et al., 1998, p. 287). Fathers who care for children under more challenging family conditions, such as divorce or widowhood, suggest that their own parenting and the well-being of their children improve substantially when they work in partnership with extended family support (DeGarmo, Patras, & Eap, 2008). Further, children find their lives enriched as parents help them develop positive associations with extended family members.

Finally, fathering thrives when it is supported by local and spiritual communities and men link themselves in partnership with those communities. Fathers and their children benefit as linkages are built between fathers and mentors, teachers, and others to facilitate healthy outcomes for children. Community institutions ranging from educational institutions to the business community can act in ways that support responsible fatherhood (White, 2007). Fatherhood scholar Ken Canfield (2007, pp. 384–385) has argued that fathering improves most for "dads in groups, gathering for mutual support, wisdom, and encouragement," and that such community groups "offer men three vital elements: companionship, assistance and insight, and accountability."

To Be Present

Parenting requires presence. While a parent does not need to be constantly present to care for children, a parent's presence is a fundamental requirement if he is to meet children's needs and build a lasting parent–child bond. The longing of any individual for home, especially the longing of a child, is partly the longing for the presence of family members who furnish security and love. The longing for home, a universal aspect of human history and psychology, is a longing for presence, for parental connection, for companionship in family living (Seiden, 2009). A fundamental principle of fathering that meets this need is to *be present* in a child's life and consciousness, to be available and aware of a child's needs such that he or she develops in an atmosphere of security and love.

The power of the ideal of presence is affirmed in the proclamation, which states that our eternal goal is "to return to the presence of God and for families to be united eternally" (¶ 3). President Howard W. Hunter

(1994, p. 50) has explained that a father's leadership in family life "requires both quantity and quality time" and that fathers give their "time and *presence* in their social, educational, and spiritual activities and responsibilities" (italics added). In our understanding, to be present in fathering is to act on the obligation to be there for one's children with your physical presence and availability, mental awareness and engagement, and practical involvement in their lives and activities.

In generative fathering, the elements that correspond with the principle of being present in family life are *ethical work* and *relationship work*. Ethical work embraces the recognition that a long-term father–child relationship is fostered through a lasting altruistic commitment, a sense of "obligation and duty to ensure that necessary nurturance and care of family members continues even when such activities are neither pleasant to do nor personally rewarding in the short run" (Bahr, 1992, p. 289). In essence, it involves a continuing moral commitment to be present for the work of meeting needs and providing care in a lifelong relationship with a child. Such efforts cannot occur in the vacuum of a father's absence. For my 3-year-old daughter, being present means reading books together and giving her a piggyback ride at bedtime. Being present with my teenage son is more likely to involve listening to his descriptions of scientific projects and providing positive affirmation when he has personal doubts. In either case, being present is a continuing commitment.

A primary reason that being present is crucial to responsible fathering is that, simply, children need the presence and support of caring adults from the time of birth onward. A child's dependence, both physically and psychologically, on parents fashions a relationship in which fathers must willingly accept the moral obligation to provide their children a secure atmosphere and be responsive to daily needs and desires (Pruett, 1998). What is a child's greatest need? Though there are many things a child needs, the greatest need of any child is security. A sense of security is perhaps the most fundamental of all human needs in a variety of ways, but it is primary and intensive for children (Webster-Stratton, 1999). The central answer to this primary need in children is parental presence. Food, warmth, shelter, affection, and attention, all of which a child needs, cannot be provided without such presence. Writing on responsible fatherhood, Doherty and colleagues (1998,

p. 280) assert that "the bedrock of fathering is presence in the child's life."

Research on the phenomenon of father absence shows that the two most common pathways to fathers' diminished presence and involvement are nonmarital childbearing and divorce (Doherty et al., 1998). Further, research on the consequences of father absence for children is compelling. A careful review of the research literature on father absence indicates that, in general, children and youth who do not experience the benefits of a father's presence and engagement are likely to score lower on measures of academic achievement and more likely to drop out of school and to display behavioral problems. In addition, such children are more likely to use illegal substances, become sexually active at a younger age, experience psychological health difficulties in adulthood, and struggle with satisfaction and permanence in their own adult relationships (Blankenhorn, 1995; Sigle-Rushton & McLanahan, 2002). It is important to note that children and youth raised in diverse family situations may do well and thrive, and that a father's presence does not guarantee positive outcomes; however, it would be inaccurate to suggest that father presence is not a significant influence that can dramatically impact the well-being of children and youth while growing up and beyond (Doherty et al., 1998).

What precisely does it mean for fathers to "be present" in the lives of their children and families? Simply, presence can be organized into three related dimensions: to be there (physical), to be aware (psychological), and to give care (practical). Physical presence (or being there) involves what has been called "accessibility" in the fathering literature, or physical availability to a child (Pleck, 1997). A father who is physically present or otherwise available to a child (for example, via cell phone) can be responsive to needs or concerns. This might be called the first level of father presence, a dimension that is necessary but not sufficient.

Psychological presence (or being aware) involves cognitive and emotional availability to a child, a mental sensitivity to children and their needs, as well as appropriate responsiveness (Pruett, 1998). As an example, such presence means putting down a newspaper or turning off a television show when a child wishes to ask an involved question and listening carefully. Fathers that are physically absent for long periods of time (like a soldier deployed abroad) or even fathers who have passed away can have a powerful psychological presence, and mothers are key figures in supporting fathers' psychological presence (Krampe & Fairweather, 1993). Critiques that too often fathers are physically present but functionally absent are complaints about fathers not being psychologically present for their children (Hawkins & Dollahite, 1997).

Practical presence (or giving care) involves a father's larger presence in a child's life through giving direct care, teaching, and otherwise guiding a child.

To Provide

One of the fundamental aspects of life in mortality is that we as human beings have material needs (food, clothing, shelter) and that we must manage limited resources, time, and energy. Fathering in contemporary society occurs within the context of extreme demands and expectations upon men and families, both in the marketplace and the domestic arena of the home (Hill, Martinengo, & Jacob, 2007). To be a good father is often equated with being a good provider (Christiansen & Palkovitz, 2001). This context of material demands and management of resources in raising a family furnishes another fundamental principle of fathering, which is to meet a child's temporal needs and make opportunities for him or her to grow and develop.

The archetypal pattern for family life that God set forth in His instructions to Adam and Eve emphasizes work to provide for one's family, as God told Adam that "in the sweat of thy face shalt thou eat bread," and sent him "to till the ground from whence he was taken" (Genesis 3:19, 23). The latter-day prophets emphasize in the proclamation that in rearing children, parents are to "provide for their physical and spiritual needs" (¶ 6), and fathers in particular are "responsible to provide the necessities of life and protection for their families" (¶ 7). Additional scriptural emphasis is given to this paternal responsibility in the Doctrine and Covenants, as the Lord instructs, "Verily I say unto you, that every man who is obliged to provide for his own family, let him provide, and he shall in nowise lose his crown" (D&C 75:28). In essence, then, to provide in fathering is to assume the stewardship of meeting children's needs and offering opportunities for their development, as well as dedicating one's time, energy, and resources for the benefit of the next generation.

The generative fathering domain that overlaps most clearly with the principle of providing in family life is *stewardship work*. Stewardship work acknowledges the task of providing in family life for men and also that children's needs must be met through producing resources and managing them with wisdom (Christiansen & Palkovitz, 2001). Dollahite, Hawkins, and Brotherson (1997, p. 28) wrote, "Stewardship work involves creative, dedicated effort to provide resources for children and family and provide opportunities for children to develop and learn to care for their own and others' physical and psychosocial needs."

The task of men's providing for family members is strongly supported across social and cultural contexts and also carries significant weight in how men define themselves as fathers. Doherty and colleagues (1998, p. 287) affirm, "One aspect of responsible fathering, that of economic support, is nearly universally expected of fathers by their cultures." For example, Latino fathers identify the challenge of providing for their families as a key concern in their fathering efforts (Behnke & Allen, 2007). Scholars accurately suggest that the "energy, sacrifice, and labor extended in order to provide" should be understood as complementary to other aspects of father involvement rather than necessarily competitive with other dimensions (Christiansen & Palkovitz, 2001, p. 86). The generative fathering paradigm suggests that one way in which fathers demonstrate their love in family life is by working for the benefit of others, and despite changing gender ideologies, women still expect fathers to be good providers (Wilcox & Nock, 2006).

Historical research on fatherhood shows that once-positive images of providing by fathers in family life transformed somewhat to suggest the father-as-provider model was cold, distant, or removed from family life (LaRossa, 1996). However, recent work has aided in reclaiming fathers' efforts at provision as "active, responsible, emotionally invested, demanding, expressive, and measured real devotion" (Christiansen & Palkovitz, 2001, p. 88). A useful conceptualization of providing includes three key aspects: financial and resource capital, human capital, and social capital. In this formulation, financial and resource capital involves fathers' efforts to generate money and material resources to be invested in supporting the healthy development of children. The human capital aspect involves fathers' efforts to contribute their skills and knowledge to children and invest their time and energy in assisting children to develop knowledge and skills

to support themselves and others. Finally, the social capital dimension of providing involves giving time and energy to relationships and opportunities that will benefit and guide a child (Christiansen & Palkovitz, 2001). The principle of providing for one's family as a father recognizes that each man is "a steward over his own property," is "accountable unto [God]" for that stewardship, and should administer those resources in a manner that "is sufficient for himself and [his] family" (D&C 42:32).

To Protect

Each person born into the world begins a journey that is often attended by confusion, challenges, and personal risks. The external world of stresses and threats to well-being sometimes intrudes upon the immediate world of family life. For fathers, a primary task involves welcoming children to the realm of family life and preparing them over time for the external world that they will have to navigate as they grow. One commentator has framed this aspect of fathering as "the job of preparing children to possess competencies to independently take on adult challenges in the world outside . . . the family" (Hall, 2007, p. 322). The context of preparing a child for the outside world and instilling a child with needed skills and knowledge sets up yet another fundamental principle of fathering, to protect a child from harm and also equip him or her to both avoid and manage life challenges.

The image of a father figure as a protective figure is common in scriptural symbolism. Indeed, the ultimate protective figure is the Savior, Jesus Christ, who protects and heals His children from death, sin, and suffering as they come unto Him (see Mosiah 4:6–8). As articulated in the proclamation, "fathers are responsible to provide . . . protection for their families" (¶ 7). One definition of protecting in fathering might be to arouse one's sense of responsibility and actively work to ensure that children avoid risks or personal harm by modeling positive behaviors, mentoring children in personal abilities, and monitoring their behaviors and environments.

The mentoring work and spiritual work aspects of generative fathering align well with the principle of protecting in family life. Mentoring work addresses the complexities and burdens of life for children and advocates aiding children through sharing wisdom and support. Spiritual work further concerns assisting children in acquiring the values and character virtues needed to transition well through adolescence into adulthood (Dollahite & Hawkins, 1998). Both of these types of work and the activity of protecting one's children center around the idea of preparing children to deal with life's obligations and challenges and protecting them from risks or harm.

Perhaps the most important aspect of protecting children occurs as fathers model appropriate and righteous behavior in their own actions and choices. A variety of protective benefits accrues to children as fathers behave well and model positive choices. First, as modeling is perhaps the most powerful method of teaching young people, children are able to learn and acquire habits of behavior that will protect them as they follow a father's positive example. For example, children who adopt a father's example in avoiding usage of cigarettes or tobacco will be protected from the harmful health effects of tobacco use. Second, fathers can model moral living and kindness to others so that children accept sacred covenants and qualify for the protective umbrella of divine favor under such covenants. President Howard W. Hunter (1994, p. 51) counseled that fathers should lead in family life so that their children "will know the gospel and be under the protection of the covenants and ordinances." Third, fathers who choose moral living protect their children and families from the negative consequences of their own sins or poor behavioral choices. Children suffer when fathers fail to model righteous choices and inflict the difficulties associated with infidelity, abuse, or addiction upon their families. The proclamation states "that individuals who violate covenants of chastity, who abuse spouse or offspring, or who fail to fulfill family responsibilities will one day stand accountable before God" (¶ 8). A primary avenue of protection for children thus comes from fathers' living and modeling positive and righteous behaviors.

Another important aspect of protecting children takes place as fathers mentor them to develop skills and knowledge needed for making their own wise choices in life. Children are not born to permanently remain dependent. Instead, they must develop their own skills and patterns of independent living. Fathers are central to this process. Fathering research generally agrees that "many fathers play the role that encourages the child to push, explore, and take more risks in order to grow" (Hall, 2007, p. 322; Pruett, 2000). Exploration invites risks and consequences. So fathers face the twin tasks of protecting children from harmful outcomes while equipping them with skills and knowledge to handle diverse challenges and consequences. For example, teaching a child to swim invites the risks of fear of water, failure for the child, and even drowning, yet it also offers the possibility of mastery (learning to swim) and confidence (new ability). I remember teaching my second son to swim in a swimming pool in Canada while on vacation, balancing efforts to equip him with sufficient skills to swim with being protective and calming his fears. Mentoring efforts involve teaching skills and knowledge in a tutoring relationship that leads to personal development (Pleban & Diez, 2007).

Yet another important aspect of protecting children flows from fathers' efforts to monitor the environments and behaviors of their children. Parental efforts in monitoring behavior have been recognized as a key pattern of influence that is protective to children and their well-being (Barber, Olsen, & Shagle, 1994). Fathers' efforts to monitor children and their environments exert a protective influence in a variety of ways. Most fundamentally, a father's presence and protective attention can warn away outside threats. For example, fathers in the home environment tend to limit the intrusion of other negative influences that can affect children, such as gang culture or criminal invitations (Letiecq & Koblinsky, 2003). Also, fathers who monitor their children can limit the risky behaviors that children might attempt or choose to pursue. Hawkins and others (2000) explain that fathers can "actively protect their children by helping them to make wise choices about the literature they read, the movies they see, the television programs they watch, the Internet sites they visit, and the friendships they establish" (p. 69).

Conclusion

Fathers have the ability, for good or ill, to exercise great power and influence in the lives of their children and families. Power alone, however, is not what a father truly needs, nor does he need only the ability to influence and direct a child's life, thoughts, and feelings. A father needs the power to bless, which might be called "power in righteousness." Men do not bless by the mere exercise of power. They bless only by the exercise of power in righteousness. This is especially true of the exercise of priesthood power. To be a holy figure in the life of a child, in the life of a family, requires an association with powers that exist beyond our own mortal abilities.

Power in righteousness comes only as we associate ourselves through prayer and sacred living with the powers of heaven. The Doctrine and Covenants teaches that "the powers of heaven cannot be controlled nor handled only upon the principles of righteousness" (D&C 121:36).

This chapter has summarized the importance of fatherhood in shaping men and children and its link with our Father's divine plan of happiness. The divine pattern for human development establishes that family life is the primary context for the unfolding of our eternal potential. The journey that each child of God undertakes in the plan of salvation is a developmental journey, a journey of progression, designed to help us acquire spiritual knowledge and character virtues that allow us to grow toward perfection. Palm (2007) has written encouragingly of the "developmental journey" and argues that fathers may engage differing aspects of care and involvement at different developmental periods in a child's life, such as playmate and nurturer during infancy and interpreter of the outside world during middle childhood. The importance of fathers nurturing and supporting each child's potential through each phase is affirmed in President James E. Faust's observation that the bonds of parents and children are revealed "in family relationships, in attributes and virtues developed in a nurturing environment, and in loving service" (1993, p. 37). As fathers practice these essential principles in their lives and relationships, they fulfill their own potential and guide the rising generation toward achieving the divine potential that resides in each of us as "a beloved spirit son or daughter of heavenly parents" (¶ 2).

Sean E. Brotherson *is an associate professor and extension family science specialist in the Department of Human Development and Family Science at North Dakota State University. He and his wife, Kristen, are the parents of seven children.*

References

Bahr, K. S. (1992). Family love as a paradigmatic alternative in family studies. *Family Perspectives, 26*, 281–303.

Barber, B. K., Olsen, J. E., & Shagle, S. C. (1994). Associations between parental psychological and behavioral control and youth internalized and externalized behaviors. *Child Development, 65*(4), 1120–1136.

Behnke, A. O., & Allen, W. D. (2007). Beating the odds: How ethnically diverse fathers matter. In S. E. Brotherson & J. M. White (Eds.), *Why fathers count: The importance of fathers and their involvement with children* (pp. 227–246). Harriman, TN: Men's Studies Press.

Benson, E. T. (1984, May). Counsel to the Saints. *Ensign, 14*, 6–8.

Benson, E. T. (1987, November). To the fathers in Israel. *Ensign, 17*, 48–50.

Blankenhorn, D. (1995). *Fatherless America: Confronting our most urgent social problem*. New York: Basic Books.

Brotherson, S. E., Dollahite, D. C., & Hawkins, A. J. (2005). Generative fathering and the dynamics of connection between fathers and their children. *Fathering, 3*(1), 1–28.

Brotherson, S. E., & White, J. M. (Eds.). (2007). *Why fathers count: The importance of fathers and their involvement with children*. Harriman, TN: Men's Studies Press.

Brotherson, S. E., Yamamoto, T., & Acock, A. C. (2003). Connection and communication in father–child relationships and adolescent child well-being. *Fathering: A Journal of Theory, Research, and Practice about Men as Fathers, 1*(3), 191–214.

Canfield, K. R. (2007). The big benefits of small groups for fathers. In S. E. Brotherson & J. M. White (Eds.), *Why fathers count: The importance of fathers and their involvement with children* (pp. 383–394). Harriman, TN: Men's Studies Press.

Christiansen, S. L., & Palkovitz, R. (2001). Why the "good provider" role still matters. *Journal of Family Issues, 22*, 84–106.

Cowan, C. P., & Cowan, P. A. (2000). *When partners become parents: The big life change for couples*. Mahwah, NJ: Lawrence Erlbaum Associates.

DeGarmo, D. S., Patras, J., & Eap, S. (2008). Social support for divorced fathers' parenting: Testing a stress-buffering model. *Family Relations, 57*, 35–48.

Doherty, W. J., Kouneski, E. F., & Erickson, M. F. (1998). Responsible fathering: An overview and conceptual framework. *Journal of Marriage and the Family, 60*, 277–292.

Dollahite, D. C. (2003). Fathering for eternity: Generative spirituality in Latter-day Saint fathers of children with special needs. *Review of Religious Research, 44*, 237–251.

Dollahite, D. C., & Hawkins, A. J. (1998). A conceptual ethic of generative fathering. *Journal of Men's Studies, 7(1)*, 109–132.

Dollahite, D. C., Hawkins, A. J., & Brotherson, S. E. (1997). Fatherwork: A conceptual ethic of fathering as generative work. In A. J. Hawkins & D. C. Dollahite (Eds.) *Generative fathering: Beyond deficit perspectives* (pp. 17–35). Thousand Oaks, CA: Sage.

Erikson, E. H. (1964). *Insight and responsibility: Lectures on the ethical implications of psychoanalytic insight.* New York: Norton.

Faust, J. E. (1993, May). Father, come home. *Ensign, 23,* 35–37.

Hall, J. M. (2007). Strong fathers as strong teachers: Supporting and strengthening a child's education. In S. E. Brotherson & J. M. White (Eds.), *Why fathers count: The importance of fathers and their involvement with children* (pp. 319–333). Harriman, TN: Men's Studies Press.

Hawkins, A. J., & Dollahite, D. C. (1997). Beyond the role-inadequacy perspective of fathering. In A. J. Hawkins & D. C. Dollahite (Eds.), *Generative fathering: Beyond deficit perspectives* (pp. 3–16). Thousand Oaks, CA: Sage.

Hawkins, A. J., Spangler, D. L., Hudson, V., Dollahite, D. C., Klein, S. R., Rugh, S. S., . . . Hill, E. J. (2000). Equal partnership and the sacred responsibilities of mothers and fathers. In D. C. Dollahite (Ed.), *Strengthening our families: An in-depth look at the proclamation on the family* (pp. 63–82). [Provo, UT]: School of Family Life, Brigham Young University.

Heschel, A. J. (1975). *The wisdom of Heschel.* New York: Farrar, Straus, & Giroux.

Hill, E. J., Martinengo, G., & Jacob, J. (2007). Working fathers: Providing and nurturing in harmony. In S. E. Brotherson & J. M. White (Eds.), *Why fathers count: The importance of fathers and their involvement with children* (pp. 279–292). Harriman, TN: Men's Studies Press.

Holmes, E. K., Duncan, T. B., Bair, S., & White, A. M. (2007). How mothers and fathers help each other count. In S. E. Brotherson & J. M. White (Eds.), *Why fathers count: The importance of fathers and their involvement with children* (pp. 43–58). Harriman, TN: Men's Studies Press.

Hunter, H. W. (1994, November). Being a righteous husband and father. *Ensign, 24,* 49–51.

Krampe, E. M., & Fairweather, P. D. (1993). Father presence and family formation: A theoretical reformulation. *Journal of Family Issues, 14(4),* 572–591.

Lamb, M. E. (Ed.) (1997). *The role of the father in child development* (3rd ed.) New York: John Wiley & Sons.

LaRossa, R. (1996). *The modernization of fatherhood: A social and political history.* University of Chicago Press.

Latshaw, J. S. (1998). The centrality of faith in fathers' role construction: The faithful father and the *axis mundi* paradigm. *Journal of Men's Studies, 7(1),* 53–70.

Lee, H. B. (1972, February). Maintain your place as a woman. *Ensign, 2,* 48–56.

Letiecq, B. L., & Koblinsky, S. A. (2003). African-American fathering of young children in violent neighborhoods: Paternal protective strategies and their predictors. *Fathering, 1(3),* 215–237.

Marks, L. D., & Dollahite, D. C. (2007). Turning the hearts of fathers to their children: Why religious involvement can make a difference. In S. E. Brotherson & J. M. White (Eds.), *Why fathers count: The importance of fathers and their involvement with children* (pp. 335–351). Harriman, TN: Men's Studies Press.

Mosley, J., & Thomson, E. (1995). Fathering behavior and child outcomes: The role of race and poverty. In W. Marsiglio (Ed.), *Fatherhood: Contemporary theory, research, and social policy* (pp. 148–165). Thousand Oaks, CA: Sage.

Packer, B. K. (1996, May). The Word of Wisdom: The principle and the promises. *Ensign, 26,* 17–19.

Palm, G. (2007). The developmental journey: Fathers and children growing together. In S. E. Brotherson & J. M. White (Eds.), *Why fathers count: The importance of fathers and their involvement with children* (pp. 163–175). Harriman, TN: Men's Studies Press.

Pardini, D. A. (2008). Novel insights into longstanding theories of bidirectional parent–child influences: Introduction to the special section. *Journal of Abnormal Child Psychology, 36,* 627–631.

Parke, R. D. (1996). *Fatherhood.* Cambridge, MA: Harvard University Press.

Pleban, F. T., & Diez, K. S. (2007). Fathers as mentors: Bridging the gap between generations. In S. E. Brotherson & J. M. White (Eds.), *Why fathers count: The importance of fathers and their involvement with children* (pp. 307–318). Harriman, TN: Men's Studies Press.

Pleck, J. H. (1997). Paternal involvement: Levels, sources, and consequences. In M. E. Lamb (Ed.), *The role of the father in child development* (3rd ed., pp. 66–103). New York: John Wiley & Sons.

Pruett, K. D. (1998). Role of the father. *Pediatrics, 102*(5), 1253–1261.

Pruett, K. D. (2000). *Fatherneed: Why father care is as essential as mother care for your child.* New York: Free Press.

Roy, K. M., & Lucas, K. (2006). Generativity as second chance: Low-income fathers and transformation of the difficult past. *Research in Human Development, 3*(2), 139–159.

Scott, R. G. (1993, November). Acquiring spiritual knowledge. *Ensign, 23,* 86–88.

Seiden, H. M. (2009). On the longing for home. *Psychoanalytic Psychology, 26,* 191–205.

Sigle-Rushton, W., & McLanahan, S. (2002). Father absence and child well-being: A critical review. Working Paper #02-20. Princeton, NJ: Center for Research on Child Well-Being.

Silverstein, L. B., & Auerbach, C. F. (1999). Deconstructing the essential father. *American Psychologist, 54,* 397–407.

Snarey, J. (1993). *How fathers care for the next generation: A four-decade study.* Cambridge, MA: Harvard University Press.

Webster-Stratton, C. (1999). *How to promote children's social and emotional competence.* Thousand Oaks, CA: Sage Publications.

White, J. M. (2007). Fatherhood in the community context: A grassroots approach to engaging communities to support responsible fathering. In S. E. Brotherson & J. M. White (Eds.), *Why fathers count: The importance of fathers and their involvement with children* (pp. 367–382). Harriman, TN: Men's Studies Press.

Wilcox, W. B., & Nock, S. L. (2006). What's love got to do with it? Equality, equity, commitment, and women's marital quality. *Social Forces, 84,* 1321–1345.

CHAPTER 14

Modern Fertility Patterns and God's Commandment to Multiply and Replenish the Earth

E. Jeffrey Hill, Sarah June Carroll, and Kaylene J. Fellows

The first commandment God gave to Adam and Eve pertained to their potential for parenthood as husband and wife. We declare that God's commandment for His children to multiply and replenish the earth remains in force.

WHEN PRESIDENT HINCKLEY ANNOUNCED "The Family: A Proclamation to the World," Juanita and I (Jeffrey) were the parents of eight children. Our youngest would soon be entering kindergarten, and we were looking forward to greater freedom after two decades of young children in the home. We also had four energetic teenagers and, as we tried to keep up with them, we appreciated not having any babies to care for. We did not miss the constant feeding, changing, and lack of sleep that always accompany infants. We had prayerfully decided our family was complete.

Soon after its introduction, I memorized the proclamation. I recited it frequently and received many impressions that blessed my family (See chapter 33, Drawing Specific Inspiration from the Proclamation). One unforgettable morning I recited the proclamation while jogging along the wide avenues of Logan, Utah. As the words "We declare that God's commandment for His children to multiply and replenish the earth remains in force" (¶ 4) flowed through my mind, I had the unmistakable impression that this commandment applied to Juanita and me. I clearly felt that we should consider inviting one more soul to join our family. When we discussed it, I found that Juanita had been similarly touched in her own way. As a result, our ninth child, a beautiful baby boy, came into the world. With the help of the Spirit, we made a decision about human life that will affect our family, our community, our nation, and the world for generations.

In this chapter, we examine how modern fertility patterns match up with God's commandment, reiterated in the proclamation, to "multiply and replenish the earth." We specifically look at present and projected fertility trends around the world, possible reasons for these trends, and the consequences these trends are likely to have for individuals, communities, and nations. We conclude the chapter by examining the blessings of keeping the commandment to bear children.

Multiply and Replenish: A Command from the Lord

On the sixth day of creation, God created Adam and Eve in His image, blessed them, and gave them the commandment to "be fruitful, and multiply, and replenish the earth, and subdue it" (Genesis 1:28). In essence, God commanded Adam and Eve to have children in order to fill the earth "with the measure of man" (D&C 49:17) and bring it under productive cultivation.

The commandment to multiply and replenish the earth was given "that the earth might answer the end of its creation" (D&C 49:16). The earth was designed to be a habitation for spirit children of our Heavenly Father as they come from the premortal existence, are clothed with an earthly tabernacle, and "gain earthly experience to progress toward perfection" (¶ 1). As men and women employ "the sacred powers of procreation . . . lawfully wedded as husband and wife" (¶ 4), they invite children into their homes. Caring for and nurturing infants, toddlers, young children, and teenagers enables mothers and fathers to obtain greater "faith, hope, charity and love" (D&C 4:5) as well as "virtue, knowledge, temperance, patience, brotherly kindness, godliness, humility, [and] diligence" (D&C 4:6). Parenthood is the ideal apprenticeship for our duties and responsibilities as exalted beings. Thus, it appears that the whole gospel plan hinges on being willing to keep this commandment.

Modern fertility patterns reveal that men and women around the world are choosing to have much smaller families, and much more frequently choosing to have no children at all. These decisions not to "multiply and replenish the earth" have significant consequences for generations to come.

Current Fertility Trends

Global fertility rates. The Total Fertility Rate (TFR), or the average number of children a woman bears in her lifetime, is a telling demographic statistic. For any society to persist, women must have enough babies to replace the population. In societies with lower infant mortality rates and access to modern health care, the TFR to achieve stasis should be 2.1 children per woman (2.0 to replace the population and 0.1 to account for children who do not live to maturity). However, where infant mortality is higher and access to modern health care is limited, replacement TFR is higher. In some parts of the less-developed world, replacement-level TFR may be as high as 3.5. It is estimated that overall, the average TFR required to replenish the earth's population is presently about 2.3 (Espenshade, Guzman, & Westoff, 2003).

The current world TFR in 2010 is estimated to be 2.49 (United Nations, 2009). However, this rate has been reduced by more than 50 percent in the last 50 years (down from 4.91 in 1960), indicating an unprecedented decline in global birthrates (see Table 14.1). With birthrates plummeting so far, so fast, the global TFR is projected to dip below replacement levels by about 2045 (United Nations, 2009). Latest demographic projections also indicate that by 2050, deaths will outnumber births and the earth will begin to see depopulation—continued population losses (United Nations, 2009). In many countries, TFRs have already fallen below the replacement level. In fact, 113 of 223 countries, including the United States, have TFRs below the replacement level of 2.3 (CIA World Factbook, 2009). Having approximately half the countries above and half the countries below the replacement level does not mean that some countries will become overcrowded as others become vacant. But it does mean that the cultural diversity of

the countries below the replacement level will change (Draper, Holman, White, & Grandy, 2007).

Table 14.1.
World Historical and Predicted Total Fertility Rates (TFR) (1950–2050)

Years	TFR	Years	TFR
1950–1955	4.92	2000–2005	2.67
1955–1960	4.81	2005–2010	2.56
1960–1965	4.91	2010–2015	2.49
1965–1970	4.78	2015–2020	2.40
1970–1975	4.32	2020–2025	2.30
1975–1980	3.83	2025–2030	2.21
1980–1985	3.61	2030–2035	2.15
1985–1990	3.43	2035–2040	2.10
1990–1995	3.08	2040–2045	2.15
1995–2000	2.82	2045–2050	2.02

Replacement level fertility rates:
World TFR: 2.3
Developed World TFR: 2.1

Fertility rates by nation. Although fertility rates are decreasing worldwide, it is interesting to note that rates still vary dramatically among nations. On the average, women in the country with the highest TFR (Niger, in Africa) have *eight times* as many babies as women in the country with the lowest TFR (Macau, a special administrative urban island district of the People's Republic of China). Other countries are distributed in between (CIA World Factbook, 2009).

In general, the countries with the highest fertility rates are the poorest and least educated countries with the highest infant and maternal mortality rates and the least access to modern health care. The eleven countries with the highest TFRs are all impoverished African countries. In contrast, greater wealth and education are associated with lower fertility rates. Although, according to one controversial work, family size in America was positively correlated with intelligence (Herrnstein & Murray, 1994). Bright people had larger families, sometimes jeopardizing their educational attainments. Economically advantaged countries in Asia have particularly low fertility rates. European nations also have extremely low fertility rates, well below the replacement level TFR. Among wealthy nations, only the United States, with a TFR of 2.05, approaches replacement.

Why Fertility Rates Are Decreasing

Decreasing economic value of children. Throughout most of human history, societies and civilizations have been organized to maximize human reproduction to assure survival. Even with fertility rates averaging eight or more children per woman, population growth was slow and sporadic until the last century. High levels of maternal and infant mortality, disease, poverty, poor nutrition, persistent local warfare, dangerous living conditions, and accidents all contributed to the need to maximize fertility in order to simply replace the population (Livi-Bacci, 2007). With such bleak prospects for family growth, children in almost all cultures were considered a blessing from God, "an heritage of the Lord" (Psalm 127:3).

Additionally, for most of its existence humankind has lived in rural areas with economies based on subsistence agriculture. In this setting, children, in addition to their intangible worth, were also economic assets. They could help their families to survive by being involved in planting, harvesting, and raising livestock. However, since the industrial revolution, increasing numbers of families live in urban environments and work in non-agricultural settings. Thus, for the majority of parents in developed countries, children have become economic liabilities rather than assets (Day, 2003). This may have contributed to lower fertility rates.

Fear of overpopulation. Modern culture and media have caused many to believe that overpopulation is a real and imminent danger—that we are quickly overrunning the planet, using up its resources and spoiling the natural environment. Common wisdom is that the earth needs fewer babies, not more. For example, Paul R. Ehrlich (1968) published the best-selling book *The Population Bomb* in which he warned that the increase in population was quickly outpacing the ability of the planet to produce enough food and that millions would soon be starving. He and others advocated extreme measures to move toward a stable and sustainable world population. Indeed, many policymakers, particularly in the United Nations, have strongly advocated the proliferation of family planning, contraceptives, and reproductive rights (such as abortion) in order to reduce the birthrate and enhance economic prosperity (Eberstadt, 2007b). However, recent United Nations population projections have revealed that high birthrates are of less concern to international economic policymakers (United Nations, 2009).

Government pressure. In certain parts of the world, governments enforce low fertility rates. For example, in the 1970s, China launched its one-child policy in order to curb population growth. Although this complex, intrusive policy has been criticized for violating human rights (Liu & Zhang, 2009), it generally remains in force. Those who violate these policies and have multiple children forfeit economic benefits, employment, and other opportunities provided by the state. Due to these policies and other social trends in China, the drop in fertility has been astounding. The TFR has dropped from 5.9 in 1970, to 2.9 in 1979, to 1.7 in 1995 (Hesketh, Lu, & Zhu, 2005). Policies like this create a host of additional problems, such as unbalanced sex ratios (Hudson & den Boer, 2004). Chinese mothers prefer to have their only child be a boy so that they have someone to carry on the family name and care for them in their old age.

Hence, they sometimes choose to abort female fetuses, causing younger generations to have a significant gender imbalance (Hudson & den Boer, 2008).

More are choosing to remain childless. In previous generations, about 95 percent of women became mothers. Typically, women who did not become mothers were not childless by choice, but because of infertility. In today's world, more women are remaining childless by choice (Wattenberg, 2004). For example, by the end of their childbearing years, more than a quarter (26 percent) of German women have had no children. Rates of childless women in other countries include Finland (21 percent), United Kingdom (21 percent), Netherlands (19 percent), Italy (19 percent), Switzerland (16 percent), and the United States (16 percent) (Wattenberg, 2004). It has been suggested that some of those who choose not to have children have lower levels of intergenerational and cultural adult attachments (Draper et al., 2007).

Widespread contraceptive use. Perhaps the greatest contributor to lower birth rates is increased contraceptive use. Modern birth control methods are relatively safe, effective, and available. It is estimated that 69 percent of married or partnered women of child-bearing age in the developed world use one or more methods of artificial contraception (United Nations, 2002a). In addition, a more severe form of birth control—abortion—is gaining acceptability. It is estimated that of approximately 200 million pregnancies that occur annually worldwide, about 20 percent, or approximately 40 million, end in abortion (Guttmacher Institute, 2009). From an ecclesiastical perspective, abortion can only be justified in the most rare and extreme circumstances. However, the use of milder contraceptive measures is a matter to be prayerfully considered by each couple and not subject to the opinions of others (The Church of Jesus Christ of Latter-day Saints, 2010).

Potential Consequences of Low Fertility Rates

This section considers possible demographic consequences of sub-replacement fertility rates around the world, specifically depopulation and the aging of the population that would result from depopulation. These possible consequences are necessarily speculative, because long-term population projection is difficult.

Depopulation. An eventual demographic consequence of sub-replacement TFRs would be depopulation. After only a few decades of sub-replacement TFRs, the number of deaths each year may exceed the number of babies born, and the population may begin to decrease (perhaps rapidly). For example, some project that the population of Germany may shrink from 82.5 million in 2005 to as low as 62.6 million in 2050 (United Nations, 2009). That represents a loss of approximately 25 percent of the population, which is equivalent to the entire population of the former East Germany. By 2050, deaths in Western Europe may far outnumber births and immigration, leading to a net population loss of up to one million per year (United Nations, 2009). However, these declines pale in comparison to China, which may be losing more than four million in population annually by 2050 (United Nations, 2009) and could lose 20 to 30 percent of its population *every* generation if current fertility rates are maintained. This would equate to a net loss of 300 to 450 million people between 2050 and 2080. In addition to those in the developed world, sub-replacement fertility rates are common in the developing world as well, and countries such as Thailand, Burma, Cuba, Uruguay, and Brazil will also begin losing population by 2015 (United Nations, 2009). One ancillary issue is that since depopulation seems to occur more readily among the educated than the uneducated, the overall education level of the world's population may decrease.

Aging. Another consequence of declining fertility and increasing longevity is global population aging; that is, the average age of the population is increasing. The United Nations Population Division (2002b) identified four major global aging trends. First, population aging is unprecedented, without parallel in human history—and the 21st century will witness more rapid increases in the average age than did the century just past. Second, population aging is pervasive—a global phenomenon affecting every man, woman, and child. Third, population aging is enduring; we will not return to the young populations that our ancestors knew. Finally, population aging has profound implications for many facets of human life.

Some telling demographic statistics illustrate this aging trend from the mid-20th century projected through the mid-21st century. In 1950, there were 206 million people in the world over the age of 60. This number increased by 323 percent to 871 million by 2000. This is much higher than the increase of 138 percent in the overall world population. The population over age

60 is expected to increase another 125 percent to 1,964 million by 2050—almost 2 billion people. What is truly surprising is the increase in the number of people in the world age 80 or older, those considered to be the "old old." In 1950, there were only 14 million octogenarians in the world. This number increased by 393 percent to 69 million by 2000. It is expected that by 2050 there will be 379 million individuals over age 80, representing an increase of 449 percent since 2000. Of course, long-term population projections are necessarily speculative, and unforeseen events may affect these numbers. Still, it is likely there will be a much greater proportion of elderly people in the near future.

Potential Worldwide Consequences of Depopulation and Aging

The potential consequences of failing to multiply and replenish the earth are thought-provoking. Here are a few of the economic, societal, familial, and individual consequences of depopulation that we may experience.

Economic consequences. Patterns of fertility and population growth have spiritual as well as temporal consequences. Scholars and policymakers are just starting to realize the serious long-term negative consequences that failing to multiply and replenish the earth may have on the global economy. Recently, the United Nations Population Division (2002b) has warned that depopulation and the resultant aging population will result in the widespread decrease of what is called the *potential support ratio* on a global basis. Simply put, this is the ratio of the number of workers in the labor force to the number who are not in the labor force. When the potential support ratio decreases, it creates an environment where an increasing number of economically dependent individuals are supported by a relatively smaller number of contributors, mainly those in the economically active ages of 18 to 64. Almost always, taxes need to increase in order to fund the benefits enjoyed by the older groups (such as healthcare benefits and pensions). Unless dramatic increases in productivity occur, the standard of living will decrease over time, or retirement ages will increase, or both.

It is true that for one generation, having fewer children may lead to greater prosperity because of a temporary reduction in this dependency ratio. For example, during their working years, a couple that chooses not to have children will be better off economically than the couple that chooses to have children. Because the childless couple does not have all of the expenses associated with raising children, they have more for themselves now—at least while they are working and probably during retirement, relative to other people who are spending their means raising children and saving less for retirement. The country in which they live temporarily has more Gross Domestic Product (GDP) per capita because there are fewer nonproductive children in the economic equation. However, in the next generation both the voluntarily childless couple and the society in which they live suffer serious economic setbacks because of their choice to remain childless. After they retire, the childless couple will not have the benefit of support from children in their old age. Also, they have foregone the creation of human capital to generate economic benefit in future generations.

Let's look at this scenario in dollars and cents. It is estimated that parents in the United States spend between $160,000 and $370,000 to raise a child to productive economic life (Lino, 2010). That same child, on average, will contribute approximately $4,000,000 to $8,000,000 to the GDP of the United States during the 40 to 50 years of his or her economically productive life. That means that a couple who chooses to remain childless will save $320,000 to $740,000 in child expenses; this will increase their standard of living during the short run of 20 to 25 years. However, compared to the contribution of a couple with two children, the national economy loses $8 million to $16 million in the next generation because of the absence of the childless couple's children as adults in the labor force. Short-term economic gain turns into massive long-term economic loss.

China, the most populous nation on earth, provides an example of potentially detrimental economic consequences of sub-replacement fertility rates. China's contemporary economic success has been created to a great degree because of its young, inexpensive, plentiful, educated workforce (Eberstadt, 2007a). Because of China's one-child policy and its dramatic lowering of fertility rates, the pool of children who will become future workers is now much smaller. During the next generation, China's workforce will begin to contract. By mid-century, hundreds of millions of Chinese will be retiring. With the advent of capitalism in China, old communist pension schemes have been eliminated without adequate replacements. This means that each working young adult may potentially be responsible for two parents approaching retirement years, four retired dependent grandparents, and, with increasing longevity, potentially eight dependent great-grandparents. In China, the oldest son has the responsibility to care for aged parents. Yet, with the one-child policy, about a third of women approaching retirement will have no son at all to care for them (Eberstadt, 2007a).

Historically, economic growth has been closely tied to the increase in the labor force accompanying population growth (Weiss, 1995). It is also reasonable to suppose that economic decline will be associated with population decline. With a greater proportion of retirees, and the lag effect of lower fertility rates 20 to 50 years ago, the number of working-age individuals in the world is forecast to decline by 40 percent by mid-century (Longman, 2004). This may result in smaller GDPs for countries with lower populations. This will first be of significant concern in Europe, where there have been sub-replacement TFRs for 30 years. When baby-boomers are ready for retirement, there will not be enough workers to finance their pensions. Meyer points out, "Recent strikes and demonstrations in Germany, Italy, France and Austria over the most modest pension reforms are only the beginning of what promises to become a major sociological battle between Europe's older and younger generations" (2009, p. 3). The elderly do not want their benefits reduced and the young do not want their contributions to increase.

Failure to replenish the earth may have deleterious economic consequences to Japan as well. Matsutani (2006) predicts that because of Japan's depopulation, national income will shrink by 15 percent by 2030. And what happens in Japan may also affect the global economy. The Japanese have legendary savings habits, which have enabled the West to borrow hundreds of billions of dollars of Japanese capital to fuel economic growth. It is sobering to think what might happen when an aging Japanese population retires and needs to recall its investments to provide for living expenses. Matsutani (2006) also speculates that the decrease in taxes paid by an aging population may make it necessary for the Japanese government to cut back on services.

Population decline inevitably leads to an aging population. The elderly are more likely to suffer from a host of physical maladies, including cardiovascular disease, strokes, and cancer. Thus, a rising proportion of the GDP of the world will be consumed by medical expenses. For example, medical expenses in the United States in 1950 represented just 4 percent of the GDP. By 2000 the percentage had risen to 8 percent of the GDP and it is projected to increase to 20 percent of GDP in 2017 (Keehan, Sisko, Truffer, Smith, Cowan, Poisal, & Clemens, 2008). To put that in perspective, the cost will be greater than all other federal outlays currently in place. And because there will be fewer workers, the tax burden will be heavier.

Societal and political consequences. Failure to multiply and replenish the earth may have far-reaching societal and political consequences. In Europe, the economic consequences of fewer labor market entrants and an ageing workforce ultimately may be problematic for the political bases of the welfare states there. The graying of these democracies will mean that more and more political power will be held by those in older-middle-age and older-age groups. The political power of younger citizens who are still in their economically productive years will be in decline because of their relatively scarce numbers at the polls. Adjustments to the generous benefits of the welfare state may become necessary, but the elderly, who hold the majority of the political power, will be likely to oppose such measures. The alternative will be to increase taxes on the younger workers. The shifting demands of the various age groups may create political pressures, fueling conditions that may give rise to intergenerational conflict and even undermine the political system (Walker, 1990; United Nations, 2002b).

China's one-child policy and attendant imbalanced sex ratio creates a situation that could be problematic for its political stability (Hudson & den Boer, 2008). It is estimated that there are currently 32 million more young men than young women in China. The Chinese government has openly expressed concerns about the security and stability of the nation with large numbers of unmarried men (Zhu, Lu, & Hesketh, 2009). Some have worried about the historical correlation between nations having excess men and being more warlike (Hudson & den Boer, 2004). Imbalanced sex ratios have also been noted in other countries, most notably South Korea and India (Liu & Zhang, 2009).

What tends to happen when there is a large sex ratio imbalance is that wealthier, more educated, and higher-status men tend to get married, while lower-status, less educated, and lower-income men tend to remain single. Already, it has been noted that these disadvantaged single men tend to be more involved in gangs, violence, crimes, and political protests (Hudson & den Boer, 2004).

Potential Individual and Familial Consequences

Up to this point we have discussed the potential consequences of failure to multiply and replenish the earth on nations and the earth as a whole. The microlevel consequences to individuals and families may also be significant.

Consequences for couples. The transition to parenthood is considered to be a normative stage in marriage (White, 1991). Foregoing that stage may affect the stability and satisfaction in the marriage. Married couples who choose to be childless possibly may be more likely to separate and divorce when marital satisfaction wanes. The idea that people are "staying together for the sake of the children" is sometimes true.

In addition, from a gospel perspective, choosing to remain childless or unduly limit family size may reduce the potential for earthly couples to become like their heavenly parents. It is in the daily trials and sacrifices required to nurture and provide for one's offspring that the characteristics of godliness are acquired (The Quorum of the Twelve Apostles, 2002). Parenthood provides the opportunity for adults to learn to be patient, exercise faith, look forward with hope, and show forth compassion to God's children. Over their lifetime, couples with children have more opportunities for experience upon which to develop these attributes of Deity.

Consequences for children. We are moving toward a world where having just one child is more and more common. Many children will grow up without brothers or sisters, without cousins, without aunts and uncles, without nieces and nephews. Children without siblings or extended family may have a less than optimal environment for development. All of these kin relationships have traditionally provided a rich context for social development (Berk, 2003). Also, Wattenberg (2004) speculates that "compared to parents with three children, parents with one child might not allow their child to take the reasonable risks associated with learning about the world" (p. 44).

The research, however, is equivocal. Having fewer children tends to mean that each child gets more parental attention. Children from smaller families generally receive better nutrition (Desai, 1995) and are more likely to attend college (Blake, 1981). However, other evidence indicates that family size is not a relevant factor in the academic achievement of children (Steelman, 1985).

Consequences for individuals. Choosing to remain childless or severely curtail the number of offspring may affect adult development. Erikson (1980) enumerates eight stages of psychosocial development over the lifespan. In middle adulthood (approximately ages 35 to 65), the required developmental task is *generativity*, or making meaningful contribution to the next generation. Generally this is accomplished through bearing and raising children. Erikson speculated that "individuals who do not develop generativity often begin to indulge themselves as if they were their own one and only child" (Erikson, 1980, p. 103). Therefore, an individual consequence of pervasive failure to multiply and replenish the earth may be the absence or reduction of opportunities to provide care for the next generation. This may lead to legions of adults who are developmentally stuck in self-absorption and stagnation (Hawkins, Christiansen, Sargent, & Hill, 1993).

Depopulation may adversely affect elderly individuals. The reduction in potential support ratios puts into question the long-term viability of intergenerational social support systems that are particularly crucial for the well-being of the aged (Grundy, 1999). The "old old," ages 80 and older, often require care to meet basic human needs such as feeding, bathing, and clothing. In the past, the relatively few numbers of "old old" people were often cared for by numerous children and grandchildren. However, an important consequence of fertility decline is "a progressive reduction in the availability of kin to whom future generations of older persons may turn for support. This process may have a significant impact on the well-being of older persons" (United Nations, 2002b, p.1). In proclamation terms, extended family will be less able to "lend support when needed" (¶ 7). In addition, some fear that the "young old," ages 60 to 80, will increasingly have significant elder care responsibilities and will be less able to devote time and resources to their children and grandchildren.

Blessings of Multiplying and Replenishing the Earth

This chapter has demonstrated that "multiplying and replenishing the earth" is no longer a cultural norm. And yet, the First Presidency recently reasserted in the proclamation, "God's commandment for His children to multiply and replenish the earth remains in force." Regardless of current trends and ideologies, God has not relinquished His commandment, but has instead reminded us of it.

We have detailed calamities that may potentially befall individuals, families, nations, and the world when we fail to multiply and replenish the earth. There are, however, promised blessings for those who are willing to invest in the next generation. And there are those who continue, primarily for religious reasons, to have children in sufficient numbers to replenish the population. For example, the United States is the only developed nation of the world that has a near replacement-level TFR of 2.05, and it is one of the most religious nations on earth. Within the United States, Utah has the highest TFR of 2.63, well above replacement level of 2.1. And Utah has the highest proportion of members of The Church of Jesus Christ of Latter-day Saints, who are taught to subscribe to the proclamation and the commandment to "multiply and replenish the earth" (Willoughby, 2009).

Multiplying and replenishing the earth yields the blessing of more stability for society as a whole. Article 16.3 of the Universal Declaration of Human Rights states, "The family is the natural and fundamental group unit of society and is entitled to protection by society and the State" (United Nations, 1948). A global society consists of nations of communities of families. Society as a whole is stronger when the family is placed as the natural and fundamental group. It follows that citizens who are parents are more invested in the well-being of their community.

As mentioned in the previous section, Erikson (1980) also theorized that bearing and caring for children is a blessing that contributes to adult development by facilitating generativity. In a sample of fathers of young children, generativity was positively related to their self-esteem, locus of control, and instrumentality (Bailey, 1992). The feelings of productivity and accomplishment are natural consequences of a significant investment in the care and teaching of the next generation.

Prophets and apostles have also associated parenting with the blessing of joy. President James E. Faust noted that "while few human challenges are greater than that of being good parents, few opportunities offer greater potential for joy" (1990, p. 32). A second witness of this principle was offered by Elder Russell M. Nelson: "God has revealed the eternal nature of celestial marriage and the family as the source of our greatest joy" (2001, p. 71). President Gordon B. Hinckley proclaimed:

> Of all the joys of life, none other equals that of happy parenthood. Of all the responsibilities with which we struggle, none other is so serious. To rear children in an atmosphere of love, security, and faith is the most rewarding of all challenges. The good result from such efforts becomes life's most satisfying compensation (1994, p. 54).

These are prophetic promises that result from obeying God's commandment. We invite the reader to consider the significance of bearing and raising children in light of our desire to be like our Father in Heaven. Exaltation is a state of perfection, in which we act like God and raise spirit children as He does (The Church of Jesus Christ of Latter-day Saints, 2009). And parenthood is preparation for exaltation. The work of the Father now, in His exalted state, is to raise His spirit children. He declared: "For behold, this is my work and my glory—to bring to pass the immortality and eternal life of man" (Moses 1:39). Therefore, He has ordained the family as a training ground for godhood. "The home is to be God's laboratory of love and service" (Nelson, 2008, p. 8).

The sacrifices that parents make for their children are one example of how parenthood is preparation for godhood. Elder Dallin H. Oaks noted:

> Mothers suffer pain and loss of personal priorities and comforts to bear and rear each child. Fathers adjust their lives and priorities to support a family. The gap between those who are and those who are not willing to do this is widening in today's world. . . . We rejoice that so many Latter-day Saint couples are among that unselfish group who are willing to surrender their personal priorities and serve the Lord by bearing and rearing the children our Heavenly Father sends to their care (2009, p. 93).

The unselfish acts of service rendered by parents are effective preparations for eternal life.

It should be noted that the interpretation of "multiply and replenish" is determined by husband and wife united in counsel with the Lord. There is no mandated quota assigned to members of the Church. President Hinckley taught:

> The Lord has told us to multiply and replenish the earth that we might have joy in our posterity, and there is no greater joy than the joy that comes of happy children in good families. But he did not designate the number, nor has the Church. That is a sacred matter left to the couple and the Lord (Hinckley, 1984, p. 6).

Conclusion

We started this chapter with a personal story about one fertility decision that resulted in the birth of Jeffrey's son. Many other decisions have had the opposite effect—reducing dramatically the number of children born. As a result, within his son's lifetime, the world will become a very different place. This chapter has examined modern-day fertility patterns and how the earth as a whole is not attending to the commandment to "multiply and replenish the earth." As we examine evidence that birth rates are often far below those needed to replace the population, we cite both Church and scholarly authorities who make the case that in today's world we must heed this commandment, or else the earth will soon begin to rapidly depopulate with potentially dangerous consequences. This chapter sounds a warning that the earth is approaching many "calamities foretold by ancient and modern prophets" (¶ 8) precisely because so many throughout the world are unwilling to be fruitful and have children in sufficient numbers so that the earth can fulfill its purpose. It is our hope that more couples will determine how the Lord would have them keep the commandment to "multiply and replenish the earth" so we might find more joy in our posterity.

E. Jeffrey Hill *is an associate professor in the School of Family Life at Brigham Young University. He and his wife, Tammy, are the parents of twelve children and they have twelve grandchildren.* Sarah June Carroll *is pursuing a master's degree in marriage and family therapy from Brigham Young University.* Kaylene J. Fellows *is pursuing a master's degree in marriage, family, and human*

BOX 14.2
LDS CHURCH GUIDELINES ON PERSONAL FERTILITY CONTROL
The official website of The Church of Jesus Christ of Latter-day Saints (http://lds.org/study/topics/birth-control?lang=eng) presents the following under the heading "Birth Control: An Introduction."

Children are one of the greatest blessings in life, and their birth into loving and nurturing families is central to God's purposes for humanity. When husband and wife are physically able, they have the privilege and responsibility to bring children into the world and to nurture them. The decision of how many children to have and when to have them is a private matter for the husband and wife.

God has a plan for the happiness of all who live on the earth, and the birth of children in loving families is central to His plan. The first commandment He gave to Adam and Eve was to "be fruitful, and multiply, and replenish the earth" (Genesis 1:28). The scriptures declare, "Children are a heritage of the Lord" (Psalm 127:3). Those who are physically able have the blessing, joy, and obligation to bear children and to raise a family. This blessing should not be postponed for selfish reasons.

Sexual relations within marriage are not only for the purpose of procreation, but also a means of expressing love and strengthening emotional and spiritual ties between husband and wife.

Husband and wife are encouraged to pray and counsel together as they plan their families. Issues to consider include the physical and mental health of the mother and father and their capacity to provide the basic necessities of life for their children.

Decisions about birth control and the consequences of those decisions rest solely with each married couple. Elective abortion as a method of birth control, however, is contrary to the commandments of God.

development at Brigham Young University. She and her husband, Steven, recently married.

References

Bailey, W. T. (1992). Psychological development in men: Generativity and involvement with young children. *Psychological Reports, 71*, 929–930.

Berk, L. E. (2003). *Child development* (6th ed.). Boston: Allyn & Bacon.

Blake, J. (1981). Family size and the quality of children. *Demography, 18*(4), 421–442.

CIA World Factbook. (2009). *Country comparison: Total fertility rate.* Retrieved from https://www.cia.gov/library/publications/the-world-factbook/rankorder/2127rank.html

The Church of Jesus Christ of Latter-day Saints. (2009). In *Gospel principles* (pp. 275–280). Salt Lake City: Author.

The Church of Jesus Christ of Latter-day Saints. (2010). *Handbook 2: Administering the Church.* Salt Lake City: Author.

Day, R. D. (2003). *Introduction to family processes* (4th ed.). Mahwah, NJ: Lawrence Erlbaum Associates.

Desai, S. (1995). When are children from large families disadvantaged? Evidence from cross-national analyses. *Population Studies, 49*, 195–210.

Draper, T. W., Holman, T. B., White, W., & Grandy, S. (2007). Adult attachment and declining birthrates. *Psychological Reports, 100*, 19–23.

Eberstadt, N. (2007a, September 17). China's one-child mistake. *Wall Street Journal*, A17.

Eberstadt, N. (2007b). *Too many people?* London: International Policy Press.

Ehrlich, P. R. (1968). *The population bomb.* New York: Ballantine Books.

Erikson, E. H. (1980). *Identity and the life cycle.* New York: W. W. Norton.

Espenshade, T. J., Guzman, J. C., & Westoff, C. F. (2003). The surprising global variation in replacement fertility. *Population Research and Policy Review, 22*, 575–583.

Faust, J. E. (1990, November). The greatest challenge in the world—Good parenting, *Ensign, 20*, 32–35.

Grundy, E. (1999). Changing role of the family and community in providing support for the elderly. In R. Cliquet & M. Nizamuddin (Eds.), *Population ageing: Challenges for policies and programmes in developed and developing countries* (pp. 103–122). New York: United Nations Population Fund.

Guttmacher Institute. (2009, October). *Facts on induced abortion worldwide.* Retrieved from http://www.guttmacher.org/

Hawkins, A. J., Christiansen, S. L., Sargent, K. P., & Hill, E. J. (1993). Rethinking fathers' involvement in child care: A developmental perspective. *Journal of Family Issues, 14*, 531–549.

Herrnstein, R. J., & Murray, C. (1994). *The bell curve: Intelligence and class structure in American life.* New York: Simon & Schuster.

Hesketh, T., Lu, L., & Zhu, W. X. (2005). The effect of China's one-child family policy after 25 years. *New England Journal of Medicine, 353*, 1171–1176.

Hinckley, G. B. (1984). *Cornerstones of a happy home* (pamphlet). Salt Lake City: The Church of Jesus Christ of Latter-day Saints.

Hinckley, G. B. (1994, November). Save the children, *Ensign, 24*, 52–54.

Hudson, V. M., & den Boer, A. M. (2004). *Bare branches: The security implications of Asia's surplus male population.* Cambridge, MA: MIT Press.

Hudson, V. M., & den Boer, A. M. (2008). China's security, China's demographics: Aging, masculinization, and fertility policy. *Brown Journal of World Affairs, 14*(2), 185–200.

Keehan, S., Sisko, A., Truffer, C., Smith, S., Cowan, C., Poisal, J., Clemens, M. K., & the National Health Expenditure Accounts Projection Team. (2008). Health spending projections through 2017: The baby-boom generation is coming to Medicare. *Health Affairs, 27*(2), w145–w155.

Lino, M. (2010). *Expenditures on children by families, 2009.* U.S. Department of Agriculture, Center for Nutrition Policy and Promotion. Miscellaneous Publication No. 1528-2009. Retrieved from http://www.cnpp.usda.gov/Publications/CRC/crc2009.pdf

Liu, T., & Zhang, X. (2009). Ratio of males to females in China. *British Medical Journal, 338*(b483), 899–900.

Livi-Bacci, M. (2007). *A concise history of world population* (4th ed.). Malden, MA: Blackwell Publishing.

Longman, P. (2004). *The empty cradle: How falling birthrates threaten world prosperity and what to do about it.* New York: Basic Books.

Matsutani, A. (2006). *Shrinking-population economics: Lessons from Japan.* Tokyo: International House of Japan.

Meyer, M. (2009, September 27). Birth dearth: Remember the population bomb? The new threat to the planet is not too many people but too few. How the new demography will shape the coming century. *Newsweek International.* Retrieved from http://www.religiousconsultation.org/News_Tracker/birth_dearth_Newsweek.htm.

Nelson, R. M. (2001, November). Set in order thy house. *Ensign, 31,* 69–71.

Nelson, R. M. (2008, May). Salvation and exaltation. *Ensign, 38,* 7–10.

Oaks, D. H. (2009, May). Unselfish service. *Ensign, 39,* 93–96.

The Quorum of the Twelve Apostles. (2002, June). Father: Consider your ways. *Ensign, 32,* 12–16.

Steelman, L. C. (1985). A tale of two variables: A review of the intellectual consequences of sibship size and birth order. *Review of Educational Research, 55*(3), 353–386.

United Nations. (1948, December 10). *Universal declaration of human rights.* General Assembly res. 217A (III). Retrieved from http://www.un.org/en/documents/udhr/

United Nations, Department of Economic and Social Affairs, Population Division. (2002a). *Levels and trends of contraceptive use as assessed in 2002.* Retrieved from http://www.un.org/esa/population/publications/wcu2002/WCU2002_Report.pdf

United Nations, Department of Economic and Social Affairs, Population Division. (2002b). *World population ageing: 1950–2050.* Retrieved from http://www.un.org/esa/population/publications/worldageing19502050/

United Nations, Department of Economic and Social Affairs, Population Division. (2009). *World population prospects: The 2008 revision.* Retrieved from http://esa.un.org/UNPP/

Walker, A. (1990). The economic "burden" of ageing and the prospect of intergenerational conflict. *Ageing and Society, 10,* 377–396.

Wattenberg, B. J. (2004*). Fewer: How the new demography of depopulation will shape our future.* Chicago: Ivan R. Dee.

Weiss, D. (1995). Ibn Khaldun on economic transformation. *International Journal of Middle East Studies, 27*(1), 29–37.

White, J. M. (1991). *Dynamics of family development: A theoretical perspective.* New York: Guilford Press.

Willoughby, R. (2009, January 19). *United States total fertility rate increases.* Retrieved from http://www.rickety.us/2009/01/united-states-fertility/

Zhu, W. X., Lu, L., & Hesketh, T. (2009). China's excess males, sex selective abortion, and one child policy: Analysis of data from 2005 national intercensus survey. *British Medical Journal, 338*(b1211), 1–6.

CHAPTER 15

LDS Family Services:
Assistance for
Unwed Parents and Prospective Adoptive Parents

Kenneth W. Matheson

Children are entitled to birth within the bonds of matrimony,
and to be reared by a father and a mother who honor marital vows with complete fidelity.

IN THIS CHAPTER, I FOCUS ON ASSISTANCE THAT LDS Family Services (LDSFS) can provide to unmarried women and men who learn that they have unexpectedly conceived a child. Also, this chapter describes the assistance LDS Family Services can provide to adoptive parents.

Most of us know individuals who have had children out of wedlock. In 2003, there were approximately 1.4 million children born to unmarried women in the United States, which accounted for one-third of the total births (U.S. Department of Health and Human Services, 2005). That figure has continued to rise; in 2007, 40 percent of children were born to unmarried women (McLanahan, Garfinkel, Mincy, & Donahue, 2010). When a woman realizes that she is having a child out of wedlock when she did not plan to do so,[1] she may be confronted with many conflicting emotions and decisions. She may wonder what would be best for herself and for the baby; whom she should tell about her situation and when; and whether she should choose to keep the child and rear it herself, place the child for adoption, or consider an abortion.

One option: Abortion. Abortion of the unborn child may seem to be an option that will erase any pending problems that unmarried parents anticipate. However, the proclamation "affirm[s] the sanctity of life and . . .

its importance in God's eternal plan" (¶ 5). Speaking of sexual intercourse outside marriage and the possibility of abortion, Elder Russell M. Nelson offered the following counsel:

> When a life is created by sinful behavior, the best way to begin personal repentance is to preserve the life of that child. To add another serious sin to a serious sin already committed only compounds the grief. Adoption is a wonderful alternative to abortion. Both the baby and the adoptive parents can be greatly blessed by the adoption of that baby into a home where the child will be lovingly nurtured and where the blessings of the gospel will be available (Nelson, 2008, p. 37).

LDS Family Services counsels unwed parents from the perspective that abortion is not acceptable for personal or social convenience.[2]

---

1. "Artificial insemination of single sisters is not approved. Single sisters who deliberately refuse to follow the counsel of Church leaders in this matter are subject to Church discipline" (The Church of Jesus Christ of Latter-day Saints, 2010, p. 195).

---

2. "The Lord commanded, 'Thou shalt not . . . kill, nor do anything like unto it' (D&C 59:6). The Church opposes elective abortion for personal or social convenience. Members must not submit to, perform, arrange for, pay for, consent to, or encourage an abortion. The only possible exceptions are when:
- Pregnancy resulted from forcible rape or incest.
- A competent physician determines that the life or health of the mother is in serious jeopardy.
- A competent physician determines that the fetus has severe defects that will not allow the baby to survive beyond birth.

Even these exceptions do not justify abortion automatically. Abortion is a most serious matter and should be considered

Another option: Keeping and rearing the baby. A pregnant woman may decide to keep and rear her child; few mothers today place their babies for adoption, and abortion rates are declining. Within our society, voluntary relinquishment of children by unwed parents is rare and steadily becoming more so. In the 1990s, less than 1 percent of all children born to unwed parents were placed for adoption, and in 2003, less than 14,000 babies were voluntarily relinquished (U.S. Department of Health and Human Services, 2005). Generally, African American unwed mothers have been more likely to parent their children than Caucasian unwed mothers, but the gap between the two groups is closing. Currently it seems that adoption is frowned upon; it is seen as "giving away your baby" and not accepting responsibility. A major reason that unwed parents are not placing their children for adoption may be that many are still romantically involved when the baby is born and hope someday to marry. Unfortunately, only a small proportion of these "fragile families" remain together; most break up within five years (McLanahan & Beck, 2010).

The decline in abortion rates, along with the decreasing number of adoptions, suggest that unwed mothers are choosing to keep the pregnancy and child or are giving the care of the child over to a family member or close friend. More unwed mothers may be parenting their children because it has become more socially acceptable and more financially viable (U.S. Department of Health and Human Services, 2005). Single mothers may be self-supporting or have family support, and public assistance funds are available to help single mothers. (For more information and statistics concerning keeping babies and adoptions, go to adoptionfacts.com.)

A pregnant woman who is considering keeping her baby may wonder how she will pay the medical and other expenses of pregnancy and childbirth. She may question where she and her child will live, how she will support herself and the child, what will happen to her plans for education and job opportunities, and what role the birth father will play. If she is in her teens or twenties, she may be concerned about the effect that motherhood will have on her processes of maturation and becoming an adult, as well as her prospects for marriage

in the future. A woman in her thirties or forties, even though she may be better established financially, may be concerned about the impact of single motherhood on her living arrangements, employment, and existing relationships.

A young man facing unexpected fatherhood may wonder how it will affect his plans for schooling, service as a missionary, and employment. He may ask whether he and the mother should marry, how he will support his child, and even if he is really the father of the child.

LDS Family Services wants to help those who choose to parent, because that will ultimately help improve the family situation for the children.

LDS Family Services and Adoption

LDS Church leaders provide the following counsel:

> When a man and woman conceive a child outside of marriage, every effort should be made to encourage them to marry. When the probability of a successful marriage is unlikely due to age or other circumstances, the unmarried parents should be counseled to work with LDS Family Services to place the child for adoption, providing an opportunity for the baby to be sealed to temple-worthy parents. Adoption is an unselfish, loving decision that blesses both the birth parents and the child in this life and in eternity (The Church of Jesus Christ of Latter-day Saints, 2010, p. 166).

From an LDS perspective, it is desirable for young birth parents to complete their physical and spiritual maturation before taking on the heavy responsibilities of parenting.

Ideally, one or both of the expectant parents will visit LDS Family Services (LDSFS) early in the pregnancy, regardless of what decision they have made or whether they have made a decision at all. LDS Family Services is, among other things, a licensed adoption agency sponsored by The Church of Jesus Christ of Latter-day Saints. Even though there are many excellent adoption agencies, and, in states where private adoptions are legal, there are also other individuals (often doctors or lawyers) who are able to assist a birth mother or father and potential adoptive parents, LDSFS is prepared to assist the individual or couple regardless of their decision; the

only after the persons responsible have consulted with their bishops and received divine confirmation through prayer" (The Church of Jesus Christ of Latter-day Saints, 2010, p. 195).

agency doesn't help only those who choose adoption. LDSFS staff can provide valuable resources and support during the decision-making process. A major advantage of working with LDS Family Services is that they serve birth parents of any religion, race, culture, or ethnicity.

Adoption has been shown to be a beneficial option for birth mothers. Research has indicated that teenage birth mothers who place their babies for adoption are more likely to graduate from high school (Namerow, 1997, as cited in Wiley & Baden, 2005, p. 32) and tend to enjoy better employment and income (Donnelly & Voydanoff, 1996; McLaughlin, Pearce, Manninen, & Winges, 1988, as cited in Zamostny, O'Brien, Baden, & Wiley, 2003). Even though outcomes vary, the results of placing a child for adoption can be extremely positive for many birth mothers. Many become advocates for adoption or volunteer to help other women through this important decision-making process.

Even though a mother may decide that it is right to place her baby for adoption in a good home, that decision does not insure she will be free of pain, depression, anxiety, or anguish (Wiley & Baden, 2005). Yet experiencing these feelings does not mean she made the wrong decision. I was asked on one occasion to go to the hospital and obtain from the birth mother the documents giving her permission for the adoption of her baby. As I was walking down the hall toward her room, I was overcome with the magnitude of what was about to happen. I was going to ask her to sign a paper indicating that she was willing to give up her rights to the baby she had carried for nine months. That decision, although difficult, requires a mature individual. One birth mother said, "Even though knowing that placing my baby was the right thing to do, it still didn't make the decision easy. It was the hardest decision of my life, but a day never goes by without thinking of her." Birth mothers who have placed a baby for adoption may experience a variety of emotions, especially at significant times in the child's development, such as when the child would be learning to walk or talk, when he or she would start school, on birthdays and holidays, at the age of baptism, or when the child would be participating in school activities and athletic events. Even with these varied emotions, birth mothers may also experience a calmness and peace concerning their decision to place their child for adoption.

The various emotions experienced by the birth mother can be less negative if she receives adequate counseling

about adoption prior to delivery, is involved in selecting the adoptive parents, and continues to receive counseling after the adoption. Birth parents, especially birth mothers, are naturally anxious to do the right thing for their child. They may worry that the adoptive family will not be loving enough or may even be abusive. However, the more knowledge, responsibility, control, and involvement birth parents have in the adoption process, the more confidence they will have that their child is safe and happy.

Counseling and participation in the adoption process are services available through LDSFS. When placing a child in a home, LDS Family Services makes a major effort to assure that couples are temple worthy, which means that each baby placed will be sealed to the adoptive parents in the temple. Each LDSFS agency has access to couples desiring to adopt throughout the United States.

Traditionally, adoptions have been sealed—that is, the identities of the birth parents were not available to the adopted child and the birth parents and child had no contact after the adoption. Many positive changes have occurred due to increased openness in the adoption process. In many situations, birth parents can maintain some contact with the adoptive parents and child through updates in the form of pictures, gifts, or invitations to attend special events (Wiley & Baden, 2005). LDS Family Services helps birth parents and adoptive parents to decide what degree of openness they should plan on for the future.

When birth parents desire assistance with their spiritual growth during and after the pregnancy, LDS Family Services is able to help. Through the Atonement of Jesus Christ, birth parents can repent of sexual sin and seek to form their own eternal families when they have reached the appropriate maturity and time in their life. LDSFS has the philosophy that, although the lives of both the birth parents and the child may ultimately be better because of adoption, the birth parents' mixed emotions are natural and need to be expressed and understood rather than dismissed. These emotions are not quickly or easily resolved. Accordingly, unwed parents should not be judged or condemned. Rather, understanding and sensitivity should be paramount in all conversations. The feelings and other issues facing the unwed couple should be a major focus. Above all, the encouragement and hope available through repentance and the Atonement should be the main focus of any spiritually oriented activity or discussion.

Further information concerning unwed pregnancy, marriage, single parenting, abortion, and adoption can be obtained from LDS Family Services at www.itsabout love.org.

LDS Family Services and Prospective Adoptive Parents

Some couples are unable to have their own biological children, and others who can bear children may desire to adopt additional children. Because not all married couples are able to conceive children, adoption is one of many opportunities that allow them to fulfill their divinely appointed parental roles. LDS Family Services is available to help these couples.

There are numerous variations of the terms *couple* and *parent*. There are single individuals, biracial couples, blended families, unmarried heterosexual couples, and same-sex couples. The question naturally arises, "Who can adopt a child?" (For more information, see the U.S. Department of Health and Human Services website at www.childwelfare.gov/systemwide/laws_policies/statutes/parties.cfm.) However, for the purposes of this chapter, "a couple" will be defined as a man and woman legally married and living together. The LDS Church's guidance for adopting couples is as follows:

Members who are seeking to adopt children . . . should strictly observe all legal requirements of the countries (and their governmental subdivisions) that are involved. They are encouraged to work through licensed, authorized agencies (The Church of Jesus Christ of Latter-day Saints, 2010, p. 180).

One study reported that there are about two million couples in the United States waiting to adopt a child. Furthermore, many of these couples would want two or three children, if they were available. Many will take hard-to-place children with special needs (Bachrach, London, & Maza, 1991).

Throughout the adoption process, adoptive parents will experience a variety of emotions, just as the birth parents do. Couples who discover they cannot have biological children may be in shock; they can't understand how such a thing could happen to them and know they

would be great parents. Some may believe that God is punishing them or that they will conceive if only they exercise sufficient faith. They may also feel anger, or intense sadness, to the point of mourning the loss of their fertility. One or both may feel they are responsible for the infertility and its effects on their spouse's life. Although infertile couples may be happy for others who are experiencing pregnancy and childbirth, they also may have difficulty watching others receive blessings they do not enjoy. Despite other blessings and happiness in their lives, the yearning to be a parent remains unfulfilled. Sometimes after considerable investments of time, money, emotions, and appointments with specialists and clinics, a couple may reach the point of accepting infertility as part of God's plan for them. They may then be ready to start thinking about adoption.

Some infertile couples may feel that seeking to adopt is giving up. They may fear that they will not be able to love an adopted child as much as their own, although from my experience as a social worker, for the large majority of adoptive couples this is not a problem. The restored gospel of Jesus Christ teaches us who our children are. President Gordon B. Hinckley (1997, p. 73) said:

Never forget that these little ones are the sons and daughters of God and that yours is a custodial relationship to them, that He was a parent before you were parents and that He has not relinquished His parental rights or interest in these His little ones. Now, love them, take care of them. . . . Rear your children in love, in the nurture and admonition of the Lord. Take care of your little ones. . . . Welcome them into your homes, and nurture and love them with all of your hearts.

Whether parents conceive and bear children or adopt them, these little ones are the Lord's children first. We are asked by Heavenly Father to be stewards over the children who come to us. In this light and by the power of temple ordinances, adopted children sealed to their parents in the temple are their children as much as if they had conceived them. One adoptive mother commented, "I was so devastated to learn after being married that I would not be able to have my own biological children. I thought I could never love someone else's child. How wrong I was. My husband and I have adopted two children, both of whom have been sealed to us in the temple. They have blessed our lives more than I can express."

LDS Family Services and Adjustments of Adopted Children

Adoptive parents are generally pleased with their choice to adopt even though there are challenges. Barth and Brooks (1997, as cited in Barth & Miller, 2000) studied adoptive families and found that child–parent relationships became strained during the teenage years, but significantly improved as the children reached early adulthood—a pattern typical of all families. They also found that 90 percent of adoptive parents had good relationships with their children and would adopt again. Feigelman found that:

> The adaptations of adoptees (are) much like those of adolescents in intact bio-parent families, with little evidence of problem behaviors. Both adopted males and females showed possible adjustment difficulties in only three aspects: higher frequencies of running away from home, in getting counseling help and in fewer wanting to go on to college. In most all other respects surveyed, adoptees were nearly evenly matched with adolescents living in two-parent biologic families (2001, p. 31).

Although most children's lives will be better overall because of adoption, an adopted child may still encounter psychological and behavioral problems associated with being adopted. Families may be referred by their bishops to LDSFS for counseling in these and other problematic family situations. Outcomes are different for children adopted as infants versus children adopted at later ages. For children adopted after infancy, problems in the adoptive home may stem from children's experiences prior to the adoption (such as abuse or neglect).

Nevertheless, the majority of children adopted when they are older do not have pervasive problems. For the adoptive child, peer relationships and social and academic self-concepts are positive. In addition, parents experience a high level of satisfaction with the adoption (Johnson, 2002). To some extent, emotional and social problems are a normal part of adolescence; some research suggests that many of the differences between

adopted children and non-adopted children disappear as they reach adulthood (Johnson, 2002).

Being in a healthy, two-parent family is the best way for adopted children to overcome their challenges. As one scholar summarized:

> Data collected over the past three decades continue to support adoption as a superior means of promoting normal development in children permanently separated from birth parents. For children suffering severe neglect or abuse in early life or exposure to illicit drugs in utero, an adoptive family is a remarkable environment for healing emotional and physical trauma and reversing developmental deficits (Johnson, 2002, p. 40).

LDS Family Services and Interracial or Interethnic Adoptions

In the United States, adoption of orphaned or neglected children from other countries is a growing trend and is generally viewed as positive. In contrast, there are conflicting points of view on interracial and interethnic adoptions. Some parents do not want a child who is of a different race or culture. Some parents worry that their children will have trouble fitting in with society if they are of a different race or background. Parents have different views about how much they should emphasize or de-emphasize their children's ethnic heritage. Some minority groups oppose adoption of their children by majority group couples because they believe the children will lose their cultural and racial heritage. LDS Family Services has not made any official statements on interracial adoption. However, they do facilitate interracial adoptions. They allow birth parents and adoptive couples to make their own decisions regarding these matters. They do not facilitate international adoptions; rather they refer couples to agencies that perform these services. More information on interracial and interethnic adoptions can be found at: http://www.americanadoptions.com/adopt/transracial_adoption.

In the United States, children from minority groups represent a majority of children in foster care (Lee, 2003). Because of this, some African American and Native American groups have encouraged efforts to place these children with members of their own ethnic groups. In 1978, Native American efforts succeeded when Congress passed the Indian Child Welfare Act, which stipulates that any Native child who needs to be placed in foster care or adopted be preferentially placed with Native Americans. Following this legislation, social service agencies began to practice similar policies with other minority groups (Lee, 2003). There are similar concerns about ethnic identity with international adoptions.

Even with the many obstacles of adopting internationally, one couple who did so stated:

> We were able to have our own biological children. We thought we were through. However, when the opportunity arose to adopt children from another country, both my wife and I concluded that we were financially able to provide a better situation than what these children are presently living in. It would be selfish on our part not to share the love that we have with others. Even though our adopted children are of a different nationality, my love for them is no less than for my biological children. They have been sealed to us and there is nothing that we would not do for them. The circle of our love keeps increasing—how blessed we are.

Additional Resources

The process of adoption is complicated, but there are resources available to birth parents who wish to place their children for adoption and couples who wish to adopt. More information concerning the legalities, processes, costs, types, and details of adoption can be found at government websites. For United States adoption, see the U.S. government's website: www.childwelfare.gov/adoption. The website is comprehensive and provides links to individual state websites, as adoption laws and processes vary according to state laws. State regulations about residency and who has the right to place a child for adoption can be located at the Child Welfare Information Gateway, *Who may adopt, be adopted, or place a child for adoption?* (http://www.childwelfare.gov/system wide/laws_policies/state/adoption/).

Other informative sites for assistance in adoption are: www.americanadoptions.com, www.parenting.adop tion.com, www.adoption.families.com, and informed adoptions.com.

Conclusion

Based on my years of experience in working with adoptions, I have found that the majority of unwed parents who place their child for adoption have a spiritual confirmation that their decision is correct. Making the decision to place a child for adoption takes considerable maturity, selfless thinking, and viewing the decision from an eternal perspective.

The primary concern for all children is their wellbeing, safety, and ability to grow and mature physically, emotionally, socially, mentally, and spiritually into healthy, well-adjusted, productive adults. While earthly identities are not trivial considerations, they are not permanent. Parents and children are equally children of God, brothers and sisters sent to earth to help each other return to Heavenly Father. That mission can be accomplished through a variety of family compositions.

In a general statement to the Church, the First Presidency commended all those who participate in adoption:

> We . . . express our support of unwed parents who place their children for adoption in stable homes with a mother and a father. We also express our support of the married mothers and fathers who adopt these children. Children are entitled to the blessing of being reared in a stable family environment where father and mother honor marital vows. Having a secure, nurturing, and consistent relationship with both a father and a mother is essential to a child's wellbeing. When choosing adoption, unwed parents grant their children this most important blessing. Adoption is an unselfish, loving decision that blesses the child, birth parents, and adoptive parents in this life and throughout the eternities. We commend all those who strengthen children and families by promoting adoption (First Presidency, 2006, as quoted in Nelson, 2008, p. 37).

Kenneth W. Matheson *is a professor in the School of Social Work at Brigham Young University. He and his wife, Marlene, are the parents of seven children and they have seven grandchildren.*

References

Bachrach, C. A., London, K. A., & Maza, P. (1991). On the path to adoption: Adoption seeking in the United States, 1988. *Journal of Marriage and the Family, 53,* 705–718.

Barth, R. P., & Miller, J. M. (2000). Building effective post-adoption services: What is the empirical foundation? *Family Relations, 49*(4), 447–455.

Child Welfare Information Gateway. (2006). Who may adopt, be adopted, or place a child for adoption? Retrieved from http://www.childwelfare.gov/system wide/laws_policies/statutes/parties.cfm

The Church of Jesus Christ of Latter-day Saints. (2010). *Handbook 2: Administering the Church.*

Feigelman, W. (2001). Comparing adolescents in diverging family structures: Investigating whether adoptees are more prone to problems than their non-adopted peers. *Adoption Quarterly, 5*(2), 5–37.

Hinckley, G. B. (1997, July). Excerpts from recent addresses of President Gordon B. Hinckley. *Ensign, 27,* 72–77.

Johnson, D. E. (2002). Adoption and the effect on children's development. *Early Human Development, 68,* 39–54.

Lee, R. M. (2003). The transracial adoption paradox: History, research, and counseling implications of cultural socialization. *Counseling Psychologist, 31*(6), 711–744.

McLanahan, S., & Beck, A. N. (2010). Parental relationships in fragile families. *Future of Children, 20*(2), 17–37.

McLanahan, S., Garfinkel, I., Mincy, R. B., & Donahue, E. (2010). Introducing the issue. *Future of Children, 20*(2), 3–16.

Nelson, R. M. (2008, October). Abortion: An assault on the defenseless. *Ensign, 38,* 32–37.

U.S. Department of Health and Human Services. (2005, March). *Voluntary relinquishment for adoption.* Washington, DC: Child Welfare Information Gateway. Retrieved from www.childwelfare.gov/pubs/s_adopted/index.cfm

Wiley, M. O., & Baden, A. L. (2005). Birth parents in adoption: Research, practice, and counseling psychology. *Counseling Psychologist, 33*(1), 13–50.

Zamostny, K. P., O'Brien K. M., Baden A. L., & Wiley, M. O. (2003). The practice of adoption: History, trends, and social context. *Counseling Psychologist, 31*(6), 651–678.

CHAPTER 16

They Cannot Be Lost: Temple Covenants Save Families

Kyle L. Pehrson, Ron Cook, and Nancy L. Madsen

The divine plan of happiness enables family relationships to be perpetuated beyond the grave.
Sacred ordinances and covenants available in holy temples make it possible
for individuals to return to the presence of God and for families to be united eternally.

A FATHER FILLED WITH OVERWHELMING GRIEF lamented:

I remember lying on the bed after work one day and sobbing that I wanted my child back, pure and innocent and part of the family again. I had to tell this daughter to leave our home because she would not live the rules and we were trying to protect her younger sisters. I sat in the closet for a long time that night crying, thinking over and over again, how can a father kick one of his daughters out of the home?

One need not look far to find a Latter-day Saint family with deep concern for some family member; the fear of losing a family member is frighteningly common. The stories of heartbroken families in this chapter, like the above one, are quite real. All are personal acquaintances of the authors and, with permission, we quote them directly.

Few family challenges are of more significance and have longer-term implications than when family members fall away from correct principles and eventually become involved in serious transgressions. There can be no assurance that individual family members will hold to the family ideals revealed in "The Family: A Proclamation to the World." This is true even in the most faithful of families. However, most Latter-day Saint parents would sacrifice their own resources, security, or well-being if it would assure their children's faithfulness. In this chapter, we explore the prophetic promises made to faithful parents who are struggling with straying children.

President Boyd K. Packer reminds us that "it is a great challenge to raise a family in the darkening mists of our moral environment" (1992, p. 68). Despite the efforts of loving and dedicated parents who want nothing more than to teach their children true principles, some of those children may stray and be drawn away by forces well beyond the control of their parents.

Thankfully, latter-day prophets and apostles assure us that the Atonement and sealing ordinances are sufficiently powerful to eventually bring salvation to the children of parents who diligently seek to keep their temple covenants. The Prophet Joseph Smith promised that "when a seal is put upon the father and mother, it secures their posterity, so that they cannot be lost, but will be saved by virtue of the covenant of their father and mother" (1976, p. 321). Of course, Latter-day Saints understand that exaltation is more than salvation; God will righteously and mercifully judge the ultimate reward of those who have strayed from the gospel path in this life (Faust, 2003). But as Elder Orson F. Whitney taught:

The Shepherd will find his sheep. They were his before they were yours—long before he entrusted them to your care; and you cannot begin to love them as he loves them. They have but strayed in ignorance from the Path of Right, and God is merciful to ignorance. Only the fullness of knowledge brings the fullness of accountability. Our Heavenly Father is far more merciful, infinitely more charitable, than even the best of his servants, and the Everlasting Gospel is mightier in power to save than our narrow finite minds can comprehend (1929, p. 110).

The scriptures teach that the Atonement is both infinite and eternal (Alma 34:10, 14). The infinite nature of the Atonement provides assurance that there is no limit to its capacity to cover sins of every type, severity, and frequency. The eternal nature of the Atonement means that it is in force both in this life and in the life to come, though we are warned that deliberately delaying our repentance places our individual eternal reward in jeopardy (Alma 34:31–35). Yet, understanding the danger of willful disobedience in this life, prophets and apostles still have promised that even the most wayward children can become heirs of salvation through eventual repentance by virtue of the Atonement. The diligent efforts of parents, sealed in the temple as an eternal family, who strive valiantly to keep their temple covenants, will one day be rewarded.

Before delving into the doctrine underlying that promise, perhaps it will be beneficial to consider just how far wayward children can stray.

Andrea's Story

Andrea entered the Young Women program of the LDS Church when she turned 12 years old and flowered into an enthusiastic young woman. She dreamed and planned for the day she would enter the temple and, thereafter, create a loving home where she would be honored as a wife and mother in a faithful family.

During Andrea's 15th year, however, she found new friends and spent increasing amounts of time away from home and family. She became defensive and argumentative. The slightest attempt to reach out and express love or concern was met with mistrust and anger. Much of her behavior, though of concern to her parents and family, was accepted as part of the adolescent struggle for independence and identity. Andrea's parents and siblings were among the last to learn that she was deeply involved in the use of illegal drugs and their associated lifestyle. By the time her family became aware of the extent of Andrea's serious problems, she had estranged herself from her home and the Church.

Her worried parents refused demands to stay out of Andrea's life and faced the realization that she needed medical and psychiatric help. At 16, Andrea was involuntarily hospitalized, which led to her commitment to change the direction of her life. Family, Church leaders, and friends in the Young Women program gathered around to provide love and support for Andrea's efforts to come back into full religious activity. However, in a relatively short time, Andrea returned to her previous friends and to a life of lies and secrecy. Married civilly at the age of 18 to a man of questionable character and dependability, Andrea believed she could find happiness outside of the Lord's appointed way.

During still another period of promised change, recommitment, and repentance, Andrea's husband was taught the gospel and baptized. Her family's hearts were filled with joy and hope when Andrea and her husband became parents themselves. They worked with a loving bishop and eventually entered the temple to receive their own endowments and to be sealed together as a family. Tremendous outpourings of love and affection for the return of the prodigal daughter were expressed. The fatted calf was figuratively prepared because the entire family was finally one.

Sadly, this is not the end of the story. Other children were eventually born to this union. Andrea's marriage was eventually plagued with conflict, unhappiness, separation, and divorce. Again, drug abuse was a prominent issue and neither parent lived a life worthy of the covenants previously made in the house of the Lord. Not only was Andrea's life seemingly out of control, but her family also felt increasing fear and anxiety for her children, who were growing up in a difficult environment.

Promises to change and go through drug rehabilitation were made and broken. Andrea continued to rear her children while living with a known drug abuser in a small home where illegal substances were reportedly used and sold. She continued to deny the substance abuse and the unsavory nature of her living environment to anyone she feared might be able to interfere in her life or take away her children. Eventually Andrea married the man she had been living with. The couple took the children and moved to another state, ending all contact with Andrea's family. Her family continued fasting and praying, often pleading with the Lord that they could simply find out where their daughter was and if the children were safe.

Years passed without contact. Then, one Mother's Day, Andrea called her surprised mother from a state on the other side of the country, where she was living. She related her story of the intervening years, in which she was loved and fellowshipped back into the Church. After months of soul-searching and feeling the enticings of the Holy Spirit, Andrea had been prepared spiritually and felt impressed to contact her family.

For years Andrea's story, like many others, had been an unfinished chapter in the book of life. And, like all of our stories, it is yet unfinished. However, today Andrea is a single mother of five daughters, she lives near her extended family, and her Church activity continues. She holds a temple recommend and all of her children are active in the Church.

Steven's Story

Steven was an obedient and loving child who desired to please his parents and teachers. He was baptized at age 8 and ordained to the Aaronic Priesthood at age 12. Home life during Steven's childhood and adolescent years exemplified Latter-day Saint standards. Later, Steven became a faithful, dedicated, and hardworking missionary. His mission president taught him that being a successful missionary requires total effort. That admonition would turn out to be the focus of Steven's entire future professional life.

Following his mission, Steven enrolled at BYU in pre-med coursework, which he approached with the same intensity and determination he had applied in the mission field. Within a year, he met and married a worthy young woman in the temple; they had two children prior to his college graduation. Although life was good, Steven's single-minded approach to education was not shared by his wife. The inherent pressures of medical school followed, and a spirit of contention invaded their home. Steven and his wife were divorced during his final year of medical school.

Continuing his drive toward excellence, Steven completed a residency and an advanced fellowship in his chosen specialty while spending little time with his children. Two more short-lived marriages and divorces followed, along with excommunication and eventual alienation from the Church due to poor and immoral choices. Steven's behavior caused a serious deterioration of his relationship with his parents and his children. Steven's father felt a responsibility, as patriarch of the family, to counsel and admonish him. It was soon obvious that those efforts were counterproductive and often created a wedge in their relationship. While his father acted in good faith, his efforts caused contention and

threatened the warm and loving bond that once existed between father and son. His parents realized they had done all that they could do. Only God could cure the ills from which their son suffered.

Steven's parents decided to place the matter in God's hands and trust in the infinite Atonement of Jesus Christ and in the power of their temple covenants. They began to show Steven a soft-hearted approach with unconditional love, and eventually their relationship began to improve. Steven's two children, now adults, have both graduated from BYU, and each has been married in the temple to a worthy companion. The children find it difficult to forgive their father and to welcome him into their lives; however, the recent birth of a grandson has helped bridge this gap.

Steven has become a world authority in his field. In that regard, he has reached a worthy goal, but he has paid a high price in other aspects of his life and in his family relationships. Now in his mid-fifties, having lost his membership in the Church, and estranged from his family, Steven continues to distance himself from the testimony that had been his foundation so many years ago. To his parents, the situation appears irresolvable— at least in this life.

Is There Really Hope?

For those families who have experiences like those of Andrea's and Steven's families, the terms *agency* or *going astray,* although accurate, do not capture the depth and severity of the damage that can come to families in such situations. Steven's story is disheartening, but not atypical of families in the Church where the choices of individual members tear at the fabric of the eternal nature of the family.

In ever-increasing numbers, families are experiencing similar heartaches, but they do not always reach a positive outcome even after a period of 10 or 20 years, or in some cases, not even in this life. Examples abound where poor individual choices bring long days and nights filled with pain, sorrow, and suffering to parents, spouses, children, siblings, and extended families. Sentiments from a distraught father echo the feelings of many such parents:

Why doesn't the Lord send an angel to [my children] as he did to Alma the Younger? Did Alma's father pray with more faith? Why aren't my prayers being answered? Doesn't the Lord love me or my children as much as he did Alma and his child?

As a member of the Seventy, Elder John K. Carmack explained:

Typical and normal parental reactions [to family problems with wayward children] include sorrow, despair, desperation, depression, feelings of guilt and unworthiness, and a sense of failure. In such circumstances, parents may also experience anger and withdrawal and may feel like simply giving up. These reactions usually make matters worse, deepening the problems they face (1997, p. 7).

Our Heavenly Father knows, far better than any mortal, the pain and sorrow associated with having children who exercise their moral agency to their condemnation rather than exaltation. Can there be any better parent than God? Children's decisions may bring us sorrow, no matter how faithfully we have taught our children. This consolation does not excuse families from their obligation to teach and model correct principles and try to lead their children to Christ, but it does bring a clearer perspective of the divine work of parents and families.

The fervent prayers of family members for their loved ones ring out in a seemingly endless chorus of fear, sadness, and frustration. Feeling helpless, families too often watch their loved ones use their God-given gift of agency to place themselves in bondage. For this reason, some loving and faithful parents are left feeling overwhelmed, realizing that their adult children are using their agency to make choices that they may not be able to recover from in this life. In their efforts to reclaim their children, parents may discover that their best path is to work diligently toward developing increased tenderness and less judgment in their hearts. Careful not to confuse their love with acceptance of sin, dedicated parents strive to attain the "pure love of Christ" in this life, believing that one day, even if it must be in the hereafter, a loving Father in Heaven will overrule evil and provide the way for repentance and a return to Him.

The scriptures include counsel to cultivate certain emotions, including love unfeigned, patience, and long-suffering (see Mosiah 3:19; D&C 121:41–42). The scriptures also warn against emotions such as anger, hate, resentment, envy, and jealousy (see 2 Nephi 26:32; 3 Nephi 30:2; Leviticus 19:17–18; Psalm 37:8; Ephesians 4:31). Active acceptance of such counsel must be integral

to the efforts of family members in addressing the difficult challenge of children who choose a wayward path.

A grateful and repentant daughter, thankful for involved parents and the covenant that binds her family for eternity, stated:

After retiring to my guest bed at their house after long hours of good conversation, I sat in wonder that conversation like that with my parents could still happen at all. I thought, "What if my parents hadn't been in a good place spiritually when I told them of all the horrible things I'd done? Would I still be able to sit in their living room till all hours of the night gleaning guidance and strength from their steadfastness?" I am so incredibly grateful that my parents continue to stay focused on Christ and the covenants they have made with Heavenly Father so that when I pushed them to their very limits of grace, they were still able to embrace me with a love that can only be described as Christlike. Having their love made all the difference in fortifying me along the long road of repentance on which I was about to embark.

It should be no surprise that in "The Family: A Proclamation to the World," love is virtually commanded and tied to moral commitment and obligation, even toward family members who seem committed to breaking God's commandments. The commands are: "Husband and wife have a solemn responsibility to love and care for each other and for their children" and "parents have a sacred duty to rear their children in love and righteousness, . . . to teach them to love and serve one another" (¶ 6). Success in family life is deemed to be grounded in honoring principles such as "forgiveness, respect, love, [and] compassion" (¶ 7). To observe such counsel, mothers and fathers would embrace and nurture forgiving attitudes, loving emotions, and compassionate feelings. That quality of experience requires a meek and lowly heart (see Matthew 11:29) as demonstrated by this mother's comment:

I don't think there is a greater influence than one that is fueled by love. I think that God created the family unit as part of the divine plan to have his children return to Him. I don't think it's to create a feeling of despair when a loved one strays from the gospel; I think it's to create a feeling of urgency on our part to help that son or daughter come back—to keep ourselves on high, firm ground, even holy ground, so that we can reach out to one who does not have as firm a footing on gospel ground. Although a connection to God might seem to be broken, a line of communication and love through us remains.

The Saving Power of Temple Covenants

There is every reason to believe that the wayward children of righteous parents will, in the end, receive salvation. Amid the anguished experiences of wandering children, abuse, addiction, and every other conceivable heartache, the words of the prophets are clear and unequivocal. From the teachings of Joseph Smith through the teachings of the prophets of our day, the message of hope is this: temple covenants save families.

A statement by Elder Orson F. Whitney, called to the Quorum of the Twelve Apostles on the same day as David O. McKay and a member of that quorum from 1906 until his death in 1931, contains the essence of the promise:

The Prophet Joseph Smith declared—and he never taught more comforting doctrine—that the eternal sealings of faithful parents and the divine promises made to them for valiant service in the Cause of Truth, would save not only themselves, but likewise their posterity. Though some of the sheep may wander, the eye of the Shepherd is upon them, and sooner or later they will feel the tentacles of Divine Providence reaching out after them and drawing them back to the fold. Either in this life or the life to come, they will return. They will have to pay their debt to justice; they will suffer for their sins; and may tread a thorny path; but if it leads them at last, like the penitent Prodigal, to a loving and forgiving father's heart and home, the painful experience will not have been in vain. Pray for your careless and disobedient children; hold on to them with your faith. Hope on, trust on, till you see the salvation of God (1929, p. 110).

Elder Whitney's remarks appear to be based on the following quote found in *Teachings of the Prophet Joseph Smith*: "When a seal [the everlasting covenant] is put upon the father and mother, it secures their posterity, so that they cannot be lost, but will be saved by virtue of the covenant of their father and mother" (1976, p. 321).

President Henry B. Eyring reaffirmed Elder Whitney's testimony in the October 2009 general conference:

The story of the prodigal son gives us all hope. The prodigal remembered home, as will your children. They will feel your love drawing them back to you. Elder Orson F. Whitney, in a general conference of 1929, gave a remarkable promise, which I know is true, to the faithful parents who honor the temple sealing to their children: "Though some of the sheep may wander, the eye of the Shepherd is upon them, and sooner or later they will feel the tentacles of Divine Providence reaching out after them and drawing them back to the fold" (2009, p. 72).

Speaking of families in which children are born under the new and everlasting covenant of marriage, President Joseph Fielding Smith said:

Being heirs [to the kingdom, through the sealing ordinance] they have claims upon the blessings of the gospel beyond what those not so born are entitled to receive. They may receive a greater guidance, a greater protection, a greater inspiration from the Spirit of the Lord; and then there is no power that can take them away from their parents. . . . Those born under the covenant, throughout all eternity, are the children of their parents. Nothing except the unpardonable sin, or sin unto death, can break this tie (Smith, J. F., as cited in McConkie, 1955, p. 90).

President Boyd K. Packer emphasized the binding power of the sealing ordinance in a 2008 Worldwide Leadership Training Meeting:

Now, sometimes there are those that are lost. We have the promise of the prophets that they are not lost permanently, that if they are sealed in the temple ordinances and if the covenants are kept [by the parents], in due time, after all the correction that's necessary to be given, that they will not be lost (2008, p. 9).

From the loving parents of one such young lady, the testimony of President Boyd K. Packer is reflected in their own personal experience:

> [Both my husband and I] felt that keeping the door open for our [unwed and pregnant] daughter to come home was the most important thing we could do. That involved not judging her, loving her as our daughter and as a daughter of God, allowing her to make her own decisions, and most importantly, being able to separate the sin from the sinner. Doing our best to keep our temple covenants from the day we made those covenants 23 years earlier, we believe, was the key to being able to love her with the Christlike love she needed. Through regular temple attendance, we were able to recognize her pregnancy as a stumbling block for her, not a dead end.

In a general conference talk dedicated to the principle of eternal hope for wandering children, President James E. Faust declared,

> Perhaps in this life we are not given to fully understand how enduring the sealing cords of righteous parents are to their children. It may very well be that there are more helpful sources at work than we know. I believe there is a strong familial pull as the influence of beloved ancestors continues with us from the other side of the veil. . . . To those brokenhearted parents who have been righteous, diligent, and prayerful in the teaching of their disobedient children, we say to you, the Good Shepherd is watching over them. God knows and understands your deep sorrow. There is hope (2003, pp. 62, 68).

President Faust further clarified:

> We remember that the prodigal son wasted his inheritance, and when it was all gone he came back to his father's house. There he was welcomed back into the family, but his inheritance was spent (Luke 15:32). Mercy will not rob justice, and the sealing power of faithful parents will only claim wayward children upon the condition of their repentance and Christ's Atonement. Repentant wayward children will enjoy salvation and all the blessings that

> go with it, but exaltation is much more. It must be fully earned. The question as to who will be exalted must be left to the Lord in His mercy (2003, p. 62).

We are blessed on this earth through righteous participation and commitment to covenants between a loving God and His mortal children. These covenants, by their nature, are intended to bring the sweetest blessings God has to offer to those who exercise faith in the gospel plan and prove themselves worthy through obedience.

Triumph Over Satan

How is it possible that the willful and wayward disobedient can be reclaimed? After all, the scriptures are very clear that "this life is the time for men to prepare to meet God; yea, behold the day of this life is the day for men to perform their labors" (Alma 34:32). Perhaps it is beneficial to consider how much we once knew, how clearly we once understood the choice between right and wrong, and that in the future, the same clear understanding will return to all of the children of God.

All those who come to this earth followed Christ in the premortal world and accepted His plan for our eternal progression. A third of God's children, however, rejected Christ and as a result did not receive mortal bodies and progress. For those who followed Christ in the premortal existence, earth life is known as the second estate. From the very beginning of the second estate—the creation of Adam—Satan has striven to expand his influence by recruiting the embodied children of Heavenly Father to follow him. Satan takes advantage of the fact that the events of premortality are erased from the minds of those who receive bodies on this earth. In addition, he knows that the pleasures and sensations available to embodied beings far exceed those that unembodied spirits can experience. Satan leads his forces throughout the earth to tempt and deceive the children of men away from the Church of the Lamb of God. To succumb to the enticing of Satan is to succumb to the best deceiver there is. For some on this earth, it appears easier and much more pleasurable to follow Satan than to follow God—at least in the short term.

In this life, the followers of Christ must rely on faith. Affirmation of the true path comes through the whisperings of a still, small voice instead of coming from Heavenly Father himself. The promptings are quiet. And stepping off the path—even if it's not very far nor intended to last very long—diminishes the most powerful tethering force there is: the Holy Spirit. False ideas form the foundations of many prominent earthly philosophies, from religion to politics and beyond. Any number of deceptions, misconceptions, addictions, and ailments can lead one from the path of true discipleship.

Yet the Atonement of Christ will rescue the wayward—which includes all of us. "For all have sinned and come short of the glory of God" (Romans 3:23). Indeed, we are assured that only a very small handful of those who came to earth and received a body will be cast into outer darkness; all others will be saved in a kingdom of glory (D&C 76:43–44). Gospel instruction will continue on the earth and in the spirit world through the end of the Millennium. By the end of the Millennium, every child of God who came to earth will have a sufficient understanding of the role of the Savior such that every knee shall bow and every tongue confess that Jesus is the Christ (Philippians 2:10–11).

> And this shall be the sound of his trump, saying to all people, both in heaven and in earth, and that are under the earth—for every ear shall hear it, and every knee shall bow, and every tongue shall confess, while they hear the sound of the trump, saying: Fear God, and give glory to him who sitteth upon the throne, forever and ever; for the hour of his judgment is come (D&C 88:104).

The fact that every knee will bow and every tongue confess suggests that everyone will have a full comprehension of the mission of the Savior at that point in time. Doctrinal understanding will return to where it was in the premortal existence. Every person who came to earth voted to follow the Savior's plan in the premortal existence. If, having a full comprehension of the choices, our children chose to follow Christ in premortality, it should not be difficult to believe that they will eventually choose Christ again at some point before the Final Judgment.

Having the reassurance of prophets and apostles that the sealing power of the holy priesthood is sufficient to allow righteous parents to reclaim their wayward children, we can do everything in our power to ensure that we merit exaltation, and leave the timing of our children's acceptance of the gospel to the Lord. Joseph Smith's exhortation in Doctrine and Covenants

128:22 captures the idea that, ultimately, triumph will be the Lord's, "for the prisoners shall go free." So we see that the challenges in families like Andrea's, as well as disheartening examples such as those of Steven and thousands of others, need not be an end but rather can be a beginning. If we let them, our trials can be serious obstacles to our keeping the promises we make as earthly parents to accept a loving God's will and continue in faith to the end. Regardless of the nature of the trials faced in mortality, there is no greater comfort than the knowledge that the Savior's Atonement is for all humankind who will accept Him.

Satan's efforts to turn away the hearts of as many as possible have been intensified in these closing days of the last dispensation. However, through sacred covenants made in holy temples, God has provided a way that His promises can be realized. We often speak of the Lord's plan and of the path that He has shown us that leads to eternal happiness. We progress on this path through righteous participation in and commitment to covenants. These covenants are the Lord's way of giving us far more than is asked in return. Through covenants we partake of the mercy of a loving God, willing to bring us back into His presence if we do our comparatively small part. In the words of Elder D. Todd Christofferson:

> I urge each one to qualify for and receive all the priesthood ordinances you can and then faithfully keep the promises you have made by covenant. In times of distress, let your covenants be paramount and let your obedience be exact. Then you can ask in faith, nothing wavering, according to your need, and God will answer. He will sustain you as you work and watch. In His own time and way He will stretch forth his hand to you, saying, "Here am I" (2009, p. 22).

We will forever give praise to a loving God for the blessing of the temple sealing ordinance that binds families for eternity. Through covenants made between God and His children, His purposes may be fulfilled in this life or the next. "And this is life eternal, that they might know thee the only true God, and Jesus Christ, whom thou hast sent" (John 17:3). "For behold, this is my work and my glory—to bring to pass the immortality and eternal life of man" (Moses 1:39).

Kyle L. Pehrson *is a retired professor of social work at Brigham Young University. He and his wife, Edyth, have seven adult children and they have twenty-one grandchildren.* Ron Cook *and his wife, Kelly, are the parents of nine children.* Nancy L. Madsen *is a recent graduate of the School of Family Life at Brigham Young University. She and her late husband, Kent, are the parents of four daughters and they have six grandchildren.*

References

Carmack, J. K. (1997, February). When our children go astray. *Ensign, 27*, 7–13.

Christofferson, D. Todd. (2009, May). The power of covenants. *Ensign, 39*, 19–23.

Eyring, H. B. (2009, November). Our perfect example. *Ensign, 39*, 70–73.

Faust, J. E. (2003, May), Dear are the sheep that have wandered. *Ensign, 33*, 61.

McConkie, B. R. (1955). *Doctrines of salvation* (vol. 2). Salt Lake City: Bookcraft, 90.

Packer, B. K. (1992, May). Our moral environment. *Ensign, 22*, 66–68.

Packer, B. K. (2008, February 9). *Worldwide leadership training meeting: Building up a righteous posterity,* 4–9.

Smith, J. F. (Ed.) (1976). *Teachings of the Prophet Joseph Smith.* Salt Lake City: Deseret Book, 321.

Whitney, O. F. (1929). Ninety-ninth Semi-Annual General Conference of The Church of Jesus Christ of Latter-day Saints (p. 110). Salt Lake City: The Church of Jesus Christ of Latter-day Saints, 1897–1964.

CHAPTER 17

Supporting Families across Generations

Richard B Miller and Jeremy B. Yorgason

Extended families should lend support when needed.

DISCUSSIONS ABOUT FAMILY LIFE TYPICALLY FOCUS on the nuclear family, which includes parents and their young or adolescent children. However, because people are living longer today than ever before, family relationships are increasingly extending into mid- and later life. These adult child–parent and grandchild–grandparent relationships provide satisfying emotional bonds, as well as tangible help and assistance between generations.

In 1900, the average life expectancy in the United States was 49 years; today it is 77, with baby boys being born today expecting to live 75 years and baby girls expecting to live 80 years. Looking at longevity from another perspective, a male born in 1900 had a 39 percent chance of living to the age of 65, while a male born today has a 79 percent probability of living that long. For females, the probability has increased from 43 percent to 87 percent (Arias, Rostron, & Tejada-Vera, 2010). In both cases, the probability of living to 65 has doubled.

As a result, intergenerational relationships are lasting longer. Sociologist Peter Uhlenberg (1996) has observed that in 1900, less than 40 percent of 50-year-olds in the United States still had a living parent; that percentage has increased to 80 percent. In fact, 44 percent of 60-year-olds currently have a parent who is still living. In addition, grandparents and grandchildren are able to enjoy their relationship for an unprecedented number of years. In earlier times, most grandparents died before or shortly after their grandchildren were born and it was unusual to have more than one living grandparent when a grandchild was an adolescent. However, today 97 percent of 20-year-old grandchildren have at least one grandparent still alive and 76 percent still have a living grandparent when they are 30 years old. Stated another way, 20-year-old young adults in the United States today are more likely to have a grandmother still living (91 percent) than were 20-year-olds in 1900 to have their mothers still alive (83 percent).

Relationships between Adult Children and their Parents

What are relationships like between adult children and their parents? Family scholars during the first half of the 20th century predicted that dramatic societal changes would have severe detrimental effects on adult child–parent relationships. Their fear was that, consistent with the societal trend during that time of moving from rural to urban areas, children would leave home when they reached young adulthood and move to cities. They would find jobs, marry, and raise families in these urban areas and rarely have contact with their aging parents and extended families. Thus, they would become disconnected from them. Talcott Parsons (1943), a famous sociologist at the time, termed this new family type the "isolated nuclear family." But extensive subsequent research has exposed this notion as a myth. Research shows that the vast majority of adult children visit their parents regularly and maintain close emotional relationships with them (Lye, 1996). For example, one study found that more than half of adult children live within a one-hour drive of their parents, and more than two thirds of adult children have at least weekly contact with their parents, including 20 percent who have daily contact with them (Lawton, Silverstein, & Bengtson,

1994a). Similarly, the vast majority of adult children report having close emotional relationships with their parents (Lye, 1996). A national sample of adult children and parents in the United States found that about 80 percent of the children reported feeling very close to their parents (Lawton, Silverstein, & Bengtson, 1994b). In a large study conducted in the Netherlands, researchers found that more than 90 percent of adult children reported very little conflict with their parents on issues such as money, politics, and values, and 93 percent reported having little conflict in the adult child–parent relationship at all (Van Gaalen & Dykstra, 2006).

One characteristic of adult child–parent relationships is that the relationships are usually tilted toward females. Adult children are more likely to feel closest to their mothers (Silverstein & Bengtson, 1997), and daughters and mothers generally have the closest relationship (Lye, 1996). Indeed, female family members are often the "kin keepers" that maintain connections with other family members, benefiting males and females alike.

The divorce of parents often has a negative impact on adult child–parent relationships. Although a parent becoming a widow does not have a negative effect on the parent–child relationship, adult children with divorced parents (compared to adult children whose parents' marriages are intact) visit either parent less often, make fewer telephone calls, usually live further away from their parents, and experience less emotional closeness in the relationship (Lye, 1996). However, most of this research has been conducted with adult children whose parents divorced while they were children or adolescents. When specifically looking at the effect of parental divorce after the child has left home, research indicates that divorce does not have a negative impact on adult children's relationship with their mothers, but it has a dramatic detrimental influence on their contact and perceived closeness to the father (Booth & Amato, 1994; Silverstein & Bengtson, 1997).

The Role of Grandparents in Extended Families

Grandparenting has become a more prominent role in modern society. As mentioned, adults are living longer than ever before, which gives them the opportunity to enjoy relationships with their grandchildren for many years. In addition, they are more likely to be active and healthy during the period of time when their grandchildren are young. Much of grandparenting occurs when the grandparents are middle-aged, not elderly.

In addition, the trend toward families having fewer children has made the grandparent role more distinct. In earlier times when parents often had eight to twelve children, it was common for parents to become grandparents while still having young children of their own. In fact, it was not uncommon for the first grandchild to be older than the youngest child. Consequently, the grandparent and parenting roles were often blurred. With today's parents having fewer children, most parents are finished with their day-to-day parenting responsibilities before they become grandparents. Consequently, the grandparenting role has become more salient as grandparents are able to focus considerable attention on their grandchildren. For example, a national study found that 80 percent of grandparents in the United States reported that the role of grandparenthood was extremely important to them (Silverstein & Marenco, 2001).

Grandparents are usually actively involved in the lives of their grandchildren. A national study of grandparents in the United States found that more than half of them visited with a grandchild at least weekly and two thirds of them talked to a grandchild at least weekly (Silverstein & Marenco, 2001). More than 85 percent of them reported feeling very or extremely close to their grandchildren.

Grandparents are important in their grandchildren's lives. President Boyd K. Packer (2003, p. 82) taught: "We must teach our youth to draw close to the elderly grandpas and grandmas." Children's perceptions of emotional closeness to their grandparents is related to reduced acting-out behaviors, such as sexual promiscuity, drug abuse, and delinquency (Henderson, Hayslip, Sanders, & Louden, 2009), and fewer symptoms of depression (Ruiz & Silverstein, 2007). Grandparent involvement is also related to grandchildren's prosocial behaviors, such as wanting to help others (Yorgason, Padilla-Walker, & Jackson, 2011). These positive consequences of grandparent involvement are especially true among single-parent families and African American families (Attar-Schwartz, Tan, Buchanan, Flouri, & Griggs, 2009).

Extended Family Support: Help from the Grandparent Generation

Grandparents provide valuable support to their adult children and grandchildren. The most common types of support that older parents give are emotional support and advice, and research shows that parents give high levels of both to their adult children (Fingerman, Miller, Birditt, & Zarit, 2009). Babysitting grandchildren is another frequent way that grandparents help their adult children.

"The Family National Guard." Sometimes family circumstances make it necessary for the grandparent generation to provide more substantial assistance to their adult children and grandchildren. Grandparents have been called "the Family National Guard" (Hagestad, 1985). Elder Neal A. Maxwell echoed this idea when he called grandparents the "strategic reserve" in extended families (1997, p. 146). When times are normal, grandparents are careful not to interfere in the lives of their children and grandchildren. They foster relationships with them, while maintaining appropriate boundaries and letting their adult children live their own lives and lead their young families. But in times of major family stress, grandparents change their role, put on their "uniforms," and actively provide help and assistance. Emergencies that may necessitate help from extended family could include a health problem, death, unemployment, or divorce. The help can be simple, such as helping prepare some meals, cleaning the house, or taking the grandchildren for a few days. In other cases, the assistance may be more substantial. For example, it is not uncommon for adult children experiencing a crisis to return home to live with their parents for a time. In fact, the incidence of children returning home to the "nest" is increasing (Ward & Spitze, 2004).

Once the crisis or emergency is over, though, the grandparents again adjust roles. They change back into their "civilian" clothes and resume a more typical relationship with their children and grandchildren. Although grandparents in their role as the Family National Guard do not frequently go on "active duty" (Silverstein & Marenco, 2001), they provide great strength and stability to families by being available to help when needed. This anchor provides a sense of security to adult children, knowing that their parents are there to help if they are needed.

Custodial grandparents. For some grandparents, caring for their grandchildren becomes a full-time responsibility. The number of grandparents who have assumed custodial care of their grandchildren has increased in recent years (Landry-Meyer, Gerard, & Guzell, 2005), with approximately 2.4 million grandparents currently raising grandchildren (Hayslip & Kaminski, 2005). A national study found that 15 percent of grandmothers had experienced raising a grandchild for at least six months (Fuller-Thomson & Minkler, 2000). In most cases, the grandparents have assumed custodial care of their grandchildren because the courts have taken away the parents' rights (for example, in cases of child abuse or neglect) or the parents are in prison. In other cases, teenage or young adult parents are unable or unwilling to continue the parenting role and leave their children in the care of their grandparents rather than placing them in foster care. These noble grandparents have accepted the day-to-day responsibility of caring for their grandchildren.

These custodial grandparents are a great blessing to their grandchildren. Children being raised by their grandparents experience improved academic performance and fewer delinquent behaviors, compared to the time when they were in the custody of their poorly functioning parents (Hayslip & Kaminski, 2005). However, full-time parenting is stressful for grandparents. The demands of caring for young children and adolescents on a daily basis take a toll on these grandparents, more than 25 percent of whom are over age 65 (Hayslip & Kaminski, 2005). These custodial grandparents are more likely to suffer depression and have health problems, compared to other grandparents their same age who are not caring for grandchildren (Landry-Meyer et al., 2005).

Despite the demands and stresses of caring for grandchildren, custodial grandparents report many rewards associated with the responsibility. They enjoy having close relationships with their grandchildren, and they see themselves as having a "second chance" at parenting (Hayslip & Kaminski, 2005). This is important to some of the grandparents because they believe that they were at least partially responsible for the failings of their children, and they see the custodial grandparenting role as an opportunity to "redeem themselves" by providing quality care to their grandchildren.

Extended Family Support: Help for the Elderly

Through most of their adult years, the exchange of help between generations is fairly reciprocal, with adult children and parents providing emotional and practical support to each other (Van Gallen & Dykstra, 2006).

However, there comes a time when the health of aging parents fails and they are no longer able to care for themselves. The unfortunate reality is that increased years of life expectancy over the past century have been accompanied by longer periods of disability (Pinquart & Sörensen, 2003). Consequently, there is an increasing need to care for the frail elderly.

LDS Church leaders have made it clear that family members should provide care for disabled family members. Elder Dallin H. Oaks (1991) taught that caring for elderly parents is an important aspect of the Lord's commandment to "honor thy father and thy mother" (Exodus 20:12). President Ezra Taft Benson (1989, pp. 6, 7) said,

> We encourage families to give their elderly parents and grandparents the love, care, and attention they deserve. Let us remember the scriptural command that we must care for those of our own house lest we be found "worse than an infidel" (1 Timothy 5:8). . . . If they become less able to live independently, then family, Church, and community resources may be needed to help them. When the elderly become unable to care for themselves, even with supplemental aid, care can be provided in the home of a family member when possible.

Research suggests that our society is actually doing fairly well in caring for elderly parents. Between 80 percent and 85 percent of all care to disabled elderly persons is provided by family members (Pinquart & Sörensen, 2003). These caregivers provide assistance with shopping, transportation, household tasks, financial management, personal care (like grooming, bathing, and eating), and administration of medicine. Family caregivers provide an average of 30 hours a week of assistance to their disabled family member (Wolff & Kasper, 2006); more than one fourth of them spend at least 40 hours a week performing caregiving duties. An adult child, typically a daughter, is the most likely family member to be a caregiver, with the spouse the second most likely caregiver (Wolff & Kasper, 2006). Other family members, such as siblings, nieces, and grandchildren sometimes become caregivers as well.

Caregiving is usually stressful. Caregivers are more likely to suffer from depression than comparable non-caregivers; they are also more likely to suffer health problems (Pinquart & Sörensen, 2003). The level of the elderly person's physical disability, the level of cognitive impairment that is associated with Alzheimer's disease and other types of dementia, and the frequency of behavioral problems (such as hostility, anger, and wandering) are all associated with greater caregiver stress. In addition, the amount of care that the caregiver provides is associated with increased stress.

Family relationships can also influence the well-being of a primary caregiver, who is generally an adult child who steps forward to provide the bulk of care for aging parents. When an adult child cares for her parents, her relationships with her siblings become more salient. Ideally, siblings can provide encouragement and practical support to the primary caregiver. Indeed, social support, especially from siblings, can substantially reduce caregiver stress (Suitor & Pillemer, 1993). A phone call from a sibling expressing appreciation for all of the work that the sister does to help their mother can bring welcome encouragement to an exhausted caregiver. Unfortunately, the opposite can also be true. The sting of criticism from a sibling to a frazzled caregiver can hurt deeply. One study found that 40 percent of adult child caregivers reported substantial conflict with a family member, typically a sibling, over caregiving issues (Strawbridge & Wallhagen, 1991). Perceived criticism and feelings of resentment felt by caregivers is actually a leading cause of caregiver stress (Semple, 1992), and family conflict is a significant predictor of placing the care recipient in a nursing home, indicating that the caregiver is no longer able to adequately care for the family member (Fisher & Lieberman, 1999).

Consequently, it is important for adult children to cooperate and work together in providing care to a frail mother or father. When one adult child assumes primary caregiving responsibilities, it is important that the other family members provide the caregiver with encouragement and tangible assistance. Elder Dallin H. Oaks counseled, "When a parent lives with one child, the other children should make arrangements to share the burdens and blessings of this arrangement" (1991, p. 16). And President Benson said, "The role of the care-giver is vital. There is great need for support and help to be given to such a person" (1989, p. 7).

Although not always possible, it is ideal for aging parents to let their wishes be known to all of their children regarding how they would like to be cared for, if needed. It is often difficult to know whether to admit a family member to a nursing home, or whether to extend life through artificial means, such as life support. When a parent's desires are expressed to all adult children, choices made during critical times become less of a burden for adult children, and arguments between siblings about what would be best are likely to be diminished. Often, aging parents make these wishes known through a living will, durable power of attorney, or advance directive, forms for which can be accessed on the Internet or through local health care providers.

Despite the stresses of caregiving, the experience of providing extensive care to a disabled older family member can also bring substantial benefits. President Boyd K. Packer said, "My wife and I have seen our grandparents and then our parents leave us. Some experiences that we first thought to be burdens or trouble have long since been reclassified as blessings" (2003, p. 83–84). Indeed, most caregivers report that the caregiving experience, though often stressful, has positive aspects, as well. The experience helped them feel close to their family member who was receiving the care, it helped them feel useful, and it gave them confidence in handling stressful situations (Kramer, 1997). One study found that the majority of caregivers reported that the experience helped them feel more compassionate toward others and more aware of other peoples' needs (Ott, Sanders, & Kelber, 2007).

Conclusion

People in modern society are living longer than ever before, which is giving family members unprecedented opportunities to experience and enjoy extended family relationships. Despite dire predictions to the contrary, adult children and their parents typically stay connected with each other and provide support to each other. Grandparents, the "Family National Guard," are valuable resources in providing assistance to their adult children and grandchildren when needed. As their health eventually fails, most aging parents will need help from their family members, and Church leaders have taught that families have the responsibility to care for their older family members. In doing so, it is important that family members work together and support each other. Despite the demands of caregiving, this labor of love also brings significant blessings.

Richard B Miller *is professor and director of the School of Family Life at Brigham Young University. He and his wife, Mary, are the parents of six children.* Jeremy B. Yorgason *is an assistant professor in the School of Family Life at Brigham Young University. He and his wife, Cheri, are the parents of four daughters.*

References

Arias, E., Rostron, B. L., & Tejada-Vera, B. S. (2010). United States life tables, 2005. *National vital statistics reports, 58*(10). Hyattsville, MD: National Center for Health Statistics.

Attar-Schwartz, S., Tan, J., Buchanan, A., Flouri, E., & Griggs, J. (2009). Grandparenting and adolescent adjustment in two-parent biological, one-parent, and step-families. *Journal of Family Psychology, 23,* 67–75.

Benson, E. T. (1989, November). To the elderly in the Church. *Ensign, 19,* 4–8.

Booth, A., & Amato, P. R. (1994). Parental marital quality, parental divorce, and relations with parents. *Journal of Marriage and the Family, 56,* 21–34.

Fingerman, K., Miller, L., Birditt, K., & Zarit, S. (2009). Giving to the good and the needy: Parental support of grown children. *Journal of Marriage and Family, 71,* 1220–1233.

Fisher, L., & Lieberman, M. A. (1999). A longitudinal study of predictors of nursing home placement for patients with dementia: The contribution of family characteristics. *Gerontologist, 39*(6), 677–686.

Fuller-Thomson, E., & Minkler, M. (2000). The mental and physical health of grandmothers who are raising their grandchildren. *Journal of Mental Health and Aging, 6,* 311–323.

Hagestad, G. O. (1985). Continuity and connectedness. In V. L. Bengtson & J. F. Robertson (Eds.), *Grandparenthood* (pp. 31–48). Beverly Hills, CA: Sage Publications.

Hayslip, B. Jr., & Kaminski, P. L. (2005). Grandparents raising their grandchildren: A review of the literature and suggestions for practice. *Gerontologist, 45*(2), 262–269.

Henderson, C. E., Hayslip, B. Jr., Sanders, L. M., & Louden, L. (2009). Grandmother–grandchild relationship quality predicts psychological adjustment among youth from divorced families. *Journal of Family Issues, 30,* 1245–1264.

Kramer, B. J. (1997). Gain in the caregiving experience: Where are we? What next? *Gerontologist, 37,* 218–232.

Landry-Meyer, L., Gerard, J. M., & Guzell, J. R. (2005). Caregiver stress among grandparents raising grandchildren: The functional role of social support. *Marriage and Family Review, 37* (1/2), 171–190.

Lawton, L., Silverstein, M., & Bengtson, V. L. (1994a). Solidarity between generations in families. In V. L. Bengtson & R. A. Harootyan (Eds.), *Intergenerational linkages: Hidden connections in American society* (pp. 19–42). New York: Springer.

Lawton, L., Silverstein, M., & Bengtson, V. (1994b). Affection, social contact, and geographic distance between adult children and their parents. *Journal of Marriage and the Family, 56,* 57–68.

Lye, D. N. (1996). Adult child–parent relationships. *Annual Review of Sociology, 22,* 79–102.

Maxwell, C. H. (Ed.). (1997). *The Neal A. Maxwell quote book.* Salt Lake City: Bookcraft.

Oaks, D. H. (1991, May). Honour thy father and thy mother. *Ensign, 21,* 14–17.

Ott, C. H., Sanders, S., & Kelber, S. T. (2007). Grief and personal growth experience of spouses and adult-child caregivers of individuals with Alzheimer's disease and related dementias. *Gerontologist, 47,* 798–809.

Packer, B. K. (2003, May). The golden years. *Ensign, 33,* 82–84.

Parsons, T. (1943). The kinship system of the contemporary United States. *American Anthropologist, 45,* 22–38.

Pinquart, M., & Sörensen, S. (2003). Associations of stressors and uplifts of caregiving with caregiver burden and depressive mood: A meta-analysis. *Journals of Gerontology: Psychological Sciences, 58B,* P112–P128.

Ruiz, S. A., & Silverstein, M. (2007). Relationships with grandparents and the emotional well-being of late adolescent and young adult grandchildren. *Journal of Social Issues, 63,* 793–808.

Semple, S. J. (1992). Conflict in Alzheimer's caregiving families: Its dimensions and consequences. *Gerontologist, 32*(5), 648–655.

Silverstein, M., & Bengtson, V. L. (1997). Intergenerational solidarity and the structure of adult child–parent relationships in American families. *American Journal of Sociology, 103*(2), 429–460.

Silverstein, M., & Marenco, A. (2001). How Americans enact the grandparent role across the family life course. *Journal of Family Issues, 22*(4), 493–522.

Strawbridge, W. J., & Wallhagen, M. I. (1991). Impact of family conflict on adult child caregivers. *Gerontologist, 31*(6), 770–777.

Suitor, J. J., & Pillemer, K. (1993). Support and interpersonal stress in the social networks of married daughters caring for parents with dementia. *Journal of Gerontology: Social Sciences, 48,* S1–S8.

Uhlenberg, P. (1996). Mortality decline in the twentieth century and supply of kin over the life course. *Gerontologist, 36*(5), 681–685.

Van Gaalen, R. I., & Dykstra, P. A. (2006). Solidarity and conflict between adult children and parents: A latent class analysis. *Journal of Marriage and Family, 68,* 947–960.

Ward, R. A., & Spitze, G. D. (2004). Marital implications of parent–adult child coresidence: A longitudinal view. *Journals of Gerontology: Social Sciences, 59B,* S2–S8.

Wolff, J. L., & Kasper, J. D. (2006). Caregivers of frail elders: Updating a national profile. *Gerontologist, 46*(3), 344–356.

Yorgason, J. B., & Padilla-Walker, L. M., & Jackson, J. (2011). Non-residential grandparents' financial and emotional involvement in relation to early adolescent grandchild outcomes. *Journal of Research on Adolescence, 21,* 552–558.

Section III:
Proclamation Principles and
Research on Successful Family Processes

CHAPTER 18

Faith in Family Life

Loren D. Marks, David C. Dollahite, and Joanna Jacob Freeman

Successful marriages and families are established and maintained on principles of faith [and] prayer.

In *Lectures on Faith*, Joseph Smith defined faith not only as belief but as "the principle of action in all intelligent beings" (1835/1985, p. 6). He further emphasized in the fourth article of faith that the first principle of the gospel is "faith in the Lord Jesus Christ." In "The Family: A Proclamation to the World," faith (as a principle of action and power) leads the list of nine foundational principles upon which "successful marriages and families are established and maintained" (¶ 7). Prayer is the second foundational principle mentioned in the proclamation and is defined, in part, in the LDS Bible Dictionary as "the process by which the will of the father and the will of the child are brought into correspondence with each other" (752–753). Such prayer is, like faith, a principle of action.

Our central purpose in this chapter is to examine the connection between faith and successful marriages and families, based on the social science record. As part of this examination, we briefly explore a central element of faith—prayer—and its connections to successful marriages and families. The chapter on prayer (chapter 19, this volume) explores this important principle in greater depth. Readers should be aware that it is difficult, perhaps impossible, for social science to "prove" that faith "causes" stronger marriages or other family outcomes. It is reasonable to conclude, for example, that persons in a healthy marriage are more likely to want to attend church together than a couple who are facing divorce. So, does faith influence family or does family influence faith? The answer is almost certainly both—but in terms of social science, the best we can usually do is to discover and examine correlations, or relationships, between ideas such as faith and the quality of family life. This chapter, then, is not infallible proof, but a series of hints and connections that work together to create a sketch that becomes both clearer and more complex as our study of the record progresses—not unlike faith itself. We now turn to the social scientific record on faith.

The broader record includes more than 800 studies that examine the connections between different aspects of faith and individual—not couple or family—physical and mental health (Koenig, McCullough, & Larson, 2001). Among these, perhaps the most striking finding was the discovery of a 7.6-year difference in longevity among persons who attended worship services more than once a week compared with non-attendees—a figure that nearly doubled to 13.7 years among African Americans (Hummer, Rogers, Nam, & Ellison, 1999). However, as interesting as these and several other individual-level findings are, our focus in this chapter is on marriages and families. Employing a three-dimensional framework of *religious community*, *religious practices*, and *religious beliefs*, we now address the research-based connection between faith and family.

Dimension One: Religious Community and Family

There's an old [African] adage, "It takes a village to raise a child." Our congregation is the [village] that we have chosen to focus our energies on. . . . When we work with people, it helps us to keep our own struggles in a better perspective and they don't become a burden, just a part of life. . . .

[Also], I personally believe that people are at their happiest when they're serving others. . . . Service in the Church . . . is based on doing things for other people, [going] outside yourself.
—William, Latter-day Saint father of six
(Marks, 2002)

The dimension of religious community encompasses and includes "support, involvement, and relationships grounded in a congregation or less formal religious group" (Dollahite, Marks, & Goodman, 2004, p. 413). We have mentioned the increase in life expectancy among persons who attend worship services more than once a week. We now turn to the question of whether those who faithfully attend also have higher marital stability and quality.

Religious community and marital fidelity. One recent study reported "that with the exception of two religious groups (nontraditional conservatives and non-Christian faiths), holding any religious affiliation is associated with reduced odds of marital infidelity compared to those with no religious affiliation" (Burdette, Ellison, Sherkat, & Gore, 2007, p. 1571). However, the same study also noted substantial denominational variation in the odds of marital fidelity, particularly among those who strongly affiliate with their religious group. In another study of 1,439 currently married participants, Atkins and Kessel (2008) concluded that church attendance was significantly related to issues of fidelity and infidelity. However, measures of faith, nearness to God, prayer, and other religious attributes were not. In fact, data indicated that individuals who had reported "high religious importance" but low church attendance were more likely to have had an affair than those in many other categories. In sum, going to church together was what mattered, not more abstract reports regarding faith, importance of religion, or nearness to God. In an even larger previous study on fidelity involving approximately 3,000 couples, the same lead researcher measured marital satisfaction, opportunities of spouses to interact with other men and women (such as in workplaces), age at first marriage, previous divorces, socioeconomic background, and religious affiliation and attendance (Atkins, Baucom, & Jacobson, 2001). This study also found that religious involvement appears to protect against infidelity, but only among those who were reportedly satisfied in their marital relationship.

Atkins and colleagues (2001) concluded, "Couples who are not happy in their relationship might believe that participating in organized religious activities can help safeguard their marriages." Based on their study, however, "only people who were in happy marriages and were involved in frequent religious activities were less likely to engage in infidelity" (p. 747). It seems that the combination of marital satisfaction and shared religious involvement may work together to provide an effective preventive maintenance program for marital fidelity.

Religious community and avoidance of pornography, violence, and conflict. A recent study addressed Internet pornography, a growing concern because of its negative effects on the marital relationship and family ties, and found that greater church attendance was related to lower rates of pornography use (Stack, Wasserman, & Kern, 2004). Similarly, Ellison, Bartkowski, and Anderson (1999) found that regular attendance at religious services was related to lower rates of domestic violence for men and women. However, rates of abuse tend to escalate in situations in which "the men attend religious services much more often than their wives or partners" (p. 98). Indeed, differences in religious involvement seem to portend higher rates of both marital conflict and failure. A remarried mother in a recent interview-based study reflected:

I've been married before, and my first husband was not saved, and he wasn't interested. That goes back to what the Lord said about being equally yoked. I was at the church, but there was not a lot of [support] there [from him], because as a nonbeliever he thought I was giving too much time. . . . We weren't serving together, we weren't going together, and we would always feel some type of rift (Marks, Dollahite, & Baumgartner, 2010, p. 446).

While the above example focuses on marriage, another remarried mother from the same study discussed a parental hardship of being "unequally yoked."

[If a faith is shared, then children] see that the parents are doing it [going to church] . . . but if a house has a parent that's *not* going . . . that causes the child to have a misunderstanding of what you're really supposed to do. So it's really beneficial . . . to be worshiping in the same church. The benefits . . . carry through . . . in the lives of your children (Author Data).

Consistent with the two preceding reflections, Curtis and Ellison (2002) found—based on national data from 2,945 first-time married couples—that not only are religious differences linked with increased religion-oriented disputes, but there also appears to be something of a spillover effect. When men attend church with their wives there are fewer disputes, not only over faith, but also over housework, money, how time is spent, and sex. Conversely, significant religious differences among spouses have also been linked to increased risk of violence and contention (Ellison et al., 1999). In summary, high levels of religious involvement—when dissimilar or unshared—may contribute to instability and volatility instead of marital satisfaction, stability, and durability.

Religious community and the importance of being "equally yoked." Differences in religious attendance also relate to increased conflict around parenting, as well as other domains of life. Research conducted by Bartkowski, Xu, and Levin (2008) explored the religious effects over time on psychological and social development and adjustment of children during early childhood and found that parental, couple, and familial religious involvement were all linked with more positive behavioral outcomes in children. However, these same researchers also report that religion often seems to undermine child development when it is a source of conflict in families (Bartkowski et al., 2008). Phrased differently, faith involvement can be a unifying blessing or a contentious curse. It has been nearly 30 years since Bahr's (1981) published finding that "same-faith marriages are much more stable than interfaith marriages" (p. 260)—but it is a finding that has been convincingly corroborated. Indeed, religious commitments that reportedly help bind marriages when shared often produce tension and conflict when these commitments are unshared. This is especially true of faiths that require significant sacrifices of time and money. Sociologists Lehrer and Chiswick (1993) found, based on five-year findings, that Latter-day Saint interfaith marriages were more than three times as likely to end in divorce as LDS-to-LDS marriages. LDS-to-LDS marriages were classified by the researchers as "remarkably stable" (13 percent dissolution rate), while LDS-to-non-LDS marriages had an "extremely high" rate of dissolution

(40 percent) during the five-year time frame of the study. Not only was the increase in the divorce rate from same-faith to interfaith marriages higher among the Latter-day Saint sample than that of any other faith, but no other faith was even close. The 27-point increase was double or nearly double that of most faiths. Why?

Perhaps part of the explanation is found in the significant demands placed on faithful Latter-day Saints. Research by Carroll and colleagues (2000) has found that "highly religious Latter-day Saints are less likely to engage in pre-marital sex, are more likely to support a traditional division of labor in marriage, [and] are more likely to desire a large family" (p. 202). These ideals are all proclamation-centered but they also tend to be (from a non-LDS perspective) expensive. They "cost" significant time, discipline, energy, sacrifice, status, money, and an array of opportunity costs (Marks, Dollahite, & Dew, 2009). Indeed, when a spouse is called to serve in a time-intensive Church position, there can be significant costs to the family. The demands of fully consecrated commitment to the LDS Church are best borne by married couples who are equally yoked and covenanted. By extension, the greatest blessings the faith has to offer in time and eternity are to be enjoyed by married couples who have jointly made and kept covenants of consecration.

Religious community and mothering. We now shift from a marital to a parental focus. Perhaps the first key research finding relative to religious community and the parent–child relationship is that women who are involved in a faith community (as measured by reported attendance) are significantly more likely to have children. Pearce's (2002) work emphasizes a mutual relationship in the religiosity–childbearing connection—namely, that the importance of religion in a woman's life appears to shape childbearing attitudes and behaviors, and that family situation (such as the presence of children) also seems to influence religiosity. This finding holds for some men as well (Palkovitz, 2002). The above findings were both confirmed and extended in work by Abma and Martinez (2006) who, based on a national sample of 4,032 women, ages 35 to 44, concluded that being voluntarily childless is linked with lower levels of religious involvement at every survey point beginning in 1982.

Research indicates that religious involvement and engagement influence family-related decisions (like the type of marriage, timing of marriage, and fertility), and that family decisions (for example, divorce or voluntary childlessness) can negatively influence religious involvement. Further, family structure is associated with the level of benefits families receive from the religious community when they are religiously involved. Namely, unwed, divorced, and separated mothers tend to receive less social support from their faith communities than do widows (Sorenson, Grindstaff, & Turner, 1995). Findings like these contextualize Dollahite and colleagues' (2004) conclusion that a "key challenge for [many] American churches in the 21st century will be to find a balance between supporting the standard of marriage-based families that is idealized . . . [while] addressing the pluralistic family realities that confront them" (p. 414). This balance remains an especially important one in Latter-day Saint congregations due to "a veritable [Latter-day Saint] 'theology of the family'" (Jarvis, 2000, p. 245)—a theology that presents a challenge to those whose family structure does not meet the temple-marriage-based ideal, as well as a high standard for those whose family processes and interactions fall short of the celestial ideal—in other words, all of us.

Religious community and fathering. Nock's (1998) work has emphasized that a man is known and respected in his religious community for filling his responsibilities, including his responsibilities to his children. A central responsibility-related wrestle for many fathers is maintaining a balance between work and home life (Palkovitz, 2002), and recent work indicates that religious involvement seems to factor into these decisions for many men. Ammons and Edgell (2007) note, "Work-family strategies . . . [often involve] making sacrifices, hard choices, or accommodations . . . [and] religious involvement and religious subculture [often] shape [pro-family] trade-offs" (p. 794). This high priority of fatherhood is reflected by the following father:

> Fatherhood is the greatest thing I could attain. If I were president of the United States, if I were CEO of a major corporation—that would end. The time would come that I would be voted out of office or I would resign and retire. Yet I will *always* be the father of my children (Marks & Palkovitz, 2007, p. 209).

This ideal is reflected in an extensive review of literature by Dollahite and Thatcher (2007), who summarized

that a man with serious religious commitment and involvement, on average, is more likely than one with little or no religious involvement to:

- remain sexually chaste before marriage and faithful to his marriage vows and thus not endanger his wife and children with sexually transmitted diseases nor father a child out of wedlock;
- be and remain committed to marriage and children even during times of difficulty and thus not bring the trials and challenges of divorce upon his wife and children;
- be highly involved in the lives of his children and parent with higher degrees of emotional warmth;
- practice kindness and mercy in his relationship with his children and be less likely to abuse his children;
- remain involved with his children in the face of challenging circumstances such as dissolution of marriage or disability of a child;
- avoid practices that harm family relationships such as substance abuse, crime, violence, child abuse, pornography, gambling, and idleness (p. 431).

Dollahite and Thatcher concluded that "based on the evidence of the research we [have] cited, it may be that [religious involvement] provides the strongest force available to reverse the powerful trends that are breaking fathers and children apart" (p. 431).

Having discussed how shared involvement in a religious community links with marital, familial, and parental outcomes, we turn to the dimension of religious practices.

Dimension Two: Religious Practices and Family

Praying together as a family and reading the scriptures . . . together is probably the best [thing we do to pull us toward Heavenly Father and each other]. . . . It feels right. It feels good. . . . I'm grateful to . . . be able to do that. If my family that I grew up with ever would have done that . . . it would have been a fond memory that I would have held, but we never did. [Our family now] should pray more, but when we kneel together and hold hands as a family, it brings the Spirit in[to our home] and makes the children feel right . . . and [teaches them] that this is what they need to do with their families—and I'm sure they'll remember it. It's special (Marks, 2002, p. 81).

—Shana, Latter-day Saint mother

Religious practices are "outward, observable expressions of faith such as prayer, scripture study, rituals, traditions, or less overtly sacred practice or abstinence that is religiously grounded" (Dollahite et al., 2004, p. 413). This definition captures both the proscriptions (or "thou shalt nots") and prescriptions (or "thou shalts") of religious practice.

The religious practice of prayer in marriage. Over the past 15 years, prayer has received increased attention in connection with marriage. A qualitative study by Butler and colleagues (1998) produced several findings that were substantiated and supported in a quantitative follow-up study with 217 religious spouses (Butler, Stout, & Gardner, 2002). These findings included participants' statements of belief that prayer enhanced experiences of emotional validation; promoted accountability toward deity; de-escalated negative interactions, contempt, hostility, and emotional reactivity; enhanced relationship behavior; facilitated partner empathy; increased self-change focus; encouraged reconciliation and problem-solving; and promoted a sense of guidance from God (Butler et al., 2002).

Although several positive outcomes have been associated with prayer, certain types of accusative or blaming prayer can also be "red flags" that reflect negative coping (Pargament et al., 1998). One recent study also indicated that one-sided prayer attempts indicate that "imbalances of anxiety, distress, and/or power may exist in a couple relationship [that] need to be addressed" (Gardner, Butler, & Seedall, 2008, p. 163). There can be diametric differences between a prayer where a marital couple seeks shared guidance from God throughout a difficulty (Butler et al., 2002), compared with blaming, resentment-filled prayer. Framed within a marital context, praying to God and stating "If you want my marriage to work, help my spouse to not be such an aggravating jerk" is far less active and facilitative than praying to Him and pleading, "Please soften our hearts and help us to be more patient and understanding with each other" (Marks, 2008, p. 682). Negatively focused prayer is associated with ill, not good. Conversely,

humble, charity-filled, true prayer often helps with conflict resolution and promotes a sense of relational responsibility (Butler et al., 2002). A Christian mother in a recent qualitative study explained:

We have disagreements [in our marriage], we have things we don't see the same sometimes, and faith is a source of help. We can pray about things together and the Lord can help us work things out. Sometimes one person has to give in and accept the other person's point of view [and] it helps to be able to pray about things. The Lord, He's the best counselor you could ever have (Dollahite & Marks, 2009, p. 381).

The religious practice of family rituals. While prayer is reportedly helpful for the above couple and others like them, it is not the only influential religious practice. Fiese and Tomcho's (2001) work with a primarily Catholic sample linked shared, meaningful religious holiday rituals with higher levels of marital satisfaction. Lee, Rice, and Gillespie (1997) similarly linked home-based family worship with higher marital satisfaction. Even so, the study by Lee and colleagues also found that, in some cases, rigid, compulsory family worship was more detrimental for children than no family worship at all.

Research on Jewish families indicates that certain rituals, including the celebration of the Sabbath (for example, the lighting of the candles, the *Shabbat* meal, and sacred prayers and blessings), can serve as family-strengthening practices (Kaufman, 1993). Such rituals are often intended to prompt a deliberate turning from the mundane or even profane to the sacred (Eliade, 1959), which includes a renewal of relationships with spouse and children. A Jewish mother of two in one study explained:

When we take the time out, when we light the [Sabbath] candles Friday night, that's a time that I feel really close to (my children). . . . I always say a prayer of thanks for my children. . . . When we sit across the table from each other, my husband and I, and the Sabbath candles are lit, and I see the kids, there is something I get from that that is *so deep*. It's just a feeling that [all is right in the world] . . . it doesn't matter what else is going on. Right in that circle . . . it's awe-inspiring (Dollahite & Marks, 2009, p. 381, italics added).

Recent qualitative work examining devout Christian, Jewish, and Muslim families has revealed that these Abrahamic faiths include practices that reportedly promote a sense of familial closeness with each other and with God (Dollahite & Marks, 2009). Such practices include saying grace before meals for Protestants, offering novenas (prayers centered on gratitude) for Catholics, family home evening for Latter-day Saints, the *Shabbat* meal and accompanying rituals for Jewish families, and the Ramadan fast for Muslims. In most cases, these rituals and practices were reportedly meaningful (and sometimes deeply or transcendently so) for both fathers and mothers.

Religious practices and the parent–child bond. Rituals can be powerful, but sometimes simple conversation can be salient as well. Boyatzis and Janicki's (2003) study based on surveys and diaries found that most Christian mothers in their study frequently engaged in discussions with their children regarding matters of faith—a practice that has been reported to be influential, even years later in children's lives (Wuthnow, 1999). Pearce and Axinn (1998) found that "various dimensions of family religious life [including religious practices] have *positive* enduring effects on mothers' and children's perceptions of the quality of the mother–child relationship" (p. 810). Kind, loving behavior by parents seems to facilitate the ability of a child to conceive of (and believe in) a loving God, while hostile parental practices seem to dispel a child's faith in a benevolent supreme being (Dollahite, 1998). A positive illustration of this principle was offered by a Christian mother, who said of her husband:

> He loves the Lord and wants to do what pleases Him [by] modeling what he sees as being valuable for the kids to see. . . . A lot of our understanding of who God is comes through fathers, because God is presented as a father in the Bible. If a kid grows up having a father who is loving and kind and supportive and strong . . . I think it is easier for them to understand God and who He is (Marks & Dollahite, 2007, p. 340).

Fathers were the primary focus of early research on children's God images, but mothers are now studied as well, with some research indicating that, in some respects, "parenting [practices] by mothers *more than [by] fathers*

predicts youths' images of God" (Hertel & Donahue, 1995, p. 196). On a related note, Brelsford and Mahoney's (2009) work, based on college students and their mothers, found that mutual disclosure and discussion about religion and spirituality is a good indicator of the quality of the mother–child relationship.

A related series of findings from the National Study of Youth and Religion (NYSR) show that the greatest evidence of religious practice and involvement influencing youth's lives for the better can be seen when comparing the lives of the most religious youth, the "devoted" (8 percent of American youth), with the lives of the average American youth (Smith & Denton, 2005). Devoted youth report that their religion is "very or extremely important in [their] everyday life" and that they feel "very or extremely close to God"; they pray, read scriptures more, and attend religious services more than other American teens (p. 220). In their family relationships, the devoted group of highly religious youth reported having the highest quality of parent–child relationships in every area studied, including levels of honesty, acceptance, and understanding; getting along; and feeling loved by and close to their parents. These findings seem to indicate a strong, two-way connection between religious practice and family relationships.

We began our discussion of the dimension of religious practices by defining them as engaging in the "thou shalts" and avoiding the "thou shalt nots." It seems significant to us that several studies on adolescent outcomes indicate that a central key to helping our children, youth, and young adults avoid dangerous "thou shalt nots" (like alcohol, drugs, and premarital sex) seems to be high levels of participation in the "thou shalts" of religious practice (Carroll et al., 2000; Chadwick & Top, 1998; Laird, Marrero, & Marks, 2009). On this note, based on his national study, Smith (2005) offered two overarching conclusions: (a) "highly religious teenagers appear to be doing much better in life than less religious teenagers" (p. 263); however, (b) "a modest amount of religion . . . does not appear to make a consistent difference in the lives of U.S. teenagers; . . . only the more serious religious teens" seem to benefit (p. 233). In addition to "serious religious" practice, a second recurring key in promoting a wide array of positive outcomes is the sharing of meaningful family time (Chadwick & Top, 1998; Doherty & Carlson, 2002). For Latter-day Saint families, these two keys of religious practice and family unity can be synergistically integrated in family prayer, family home evening, and family scripture study.

We now turn from the dimension of religious practices to the third dimension of religious beliefs.

Dimension Three: Religious Beliefs and Family

There's something that . . . when as a family your hearts are pointed together toward the same thing, and it's God, then parenting and economics and space and food and disagreements and hassles and joys and celebrations and all that other stuff . . . it works different, it seems different, it feels different. . . . Our family is all oriented in the same way. Christ is king, He's the center, He's what it's all about. . . . Our faith informs our relationships and everything about us.

—Joseph, non-denominational Christian father
(Marks, 2003, p. 10)

As we begin our discussion of the third dimension of religious beliefs, we note its close relationship with the second dimension of religious practices—particularly in connection with marriage and family life. Myers (2006) summarized:

Research in the past 50 years routinely finds a positive association between a couple's religious beliefs and behaviors [practices] and the quality of their marriage. . . . The extent to which husbands and wives hold similar religious beliefs and participate jointly in religious practices . . . appears to be one of the stronger religious predictor[s] of marital quality (p. 292).

Myers's repeated emphasis on the combination of belief and practice is apt. Indeed, neither belief nor practice carries much meaning without the other's animating influence.

Religious beliefs include "personal, internal beliefs, framings, meanings, [and] perspectives," which can, and often do, influence family life (Dollahite et al., 2004, p. 413). Over the past two decades, religious belief has received more rigorous, balanced, and comprehensive treatment in connection with family relationships than ever before (Koenig et al., 2001; Marks, 2006). Polls

and surveys have indicated that 95 percent of all married couples and parents in the United States report a religious affiliation (Mahoney et al., 2001), and religion is "the single most important influence" in life for "a substantial minority" of Americans (Miller & Thoresen, 2003, p. 25). In this section we will not focus on the pervasiveness of religious belief but on the ways it seems to influence and be influenced by family life.

Religious beliefs and parenting. Studies indicate that mothers in more positive mother–child relationships are more likely to transmit their religious beliefs to their adolescent children (Bao, Whitbeck, Hoyt, & Conger, 1999), and that agreement between mothers and their children on religious issues protects against child depression (Miller, Warner, Wickramaratne, & Weissman, 1997). These studies mesh with an extensive review of 64 studies, 60 of which reported linkages between higher religious involvement and lower depression (Koenig et al., 2001). Parental mental health is often a significant benefit to children, who appear to reap secondary benefits. Benefits of mental health extend to (and perhaps from) healthy marriages as well (Waite & Gallagher, 2000).

Research from the past decade or so has linked religious beliefs with higher levels of fathers' care for and commitment to children, as well as increased father involvement (Christiansen & Palkovitz, 1998; Wilcox, 2002). In a related study, King (2003) concluded,

The influence of religiousness [including religious beliefs] on father involvement is generally modest and should not be overstated. . . . Nevertheless, certain aspects of father involvement are more frequent among the more religious, including better quality relationships . . . and stronger feelings of obligation for contact with children (p. 392).

Qualitative work with fathers, including fathers of children with special needs, has underscored and supported this connection between religious belief and a sense of sacred obligation. One Latter-day Saint father, reflecting on his beliefs about fatherhood, stated, "I learned that I would die for this person. . . . We will be linked forever. [I know that] this child is my responsibility forever, to guide, to direct, and to nurture" (Dollahite, Marks, & Olson, 1998, p. 84). This connection between faith in God and the responsibility to care for a child is, perhaps, never tested or strained more than when parents see their child struggling for his or her life. In an in-depth interview, a Latter-day Saint father named Tom shared the following experience surrounding his 6-year-old daughter Megan's bout with leukemia:

> We did our best to make sure we got through it [Megan's leukemia] well. We weren't going to say, "Why me?" and that is something I spent very little time on. I still wondered from time to time why she had to go through this, but I didn't spend any time being mad at God. I decided early on that we were going to tackle this with faith and determination, and we were going to make it. We were going to come out being in love with God and not hating Him (Dollahite, Marks, & Olson, 2002, p. 282).

However, as discussed earlier, beliefs need the embodiment of practices to become real. Tom was tested to not only believe, but to act. He went on to relate:

> I have just about spent my life caring for and nurturing Megan, when I wasn't at work. Maybe the hospital is the part we like to forget but can't. When her pain got to the point that she couldn't [get up to] go to the bathroom, I was the one that got her bedpans for her. She would only let me do it; I was the one that did that. . . . I would get the bedpan as best as I could under her bottom without hurting her. Moving the sheets hurt her. It was not a good thing. But she let me do that for her, and I was able to take care of her needs, and it helped me that I was the only one she'd let do it. . . . You wouldn't expect bedpan shuffling to be a wonderful memory, but it was. She trusted me to do my best job not to hurt her, and that was special to me that she let me do that (Dollahite et al., 1998, p. 79).

In terms of mortal life, Megan lost her fight with leukemia, but she and her family won their struggle to "come out being in love with God." Of the more than 200 total studies focused on both faith and mental health, roughly 80 percent indicate greater hope or optimism, greater well-being, a greater sense of purpose and meaning in life, lower depression, less anxiety

and fear, and less negative coping among those who are religious (Koenig et al., 2001). These numbers and percentage points represent personal and family lives like Megan's and Tom's.

Religious beliefs and marriage. As we indicated at length earlier, statistical (and real-world) differences in marriage tend to emerge when we compare spouses who share religious involvement with those who do not. Indeed, religious beliefs can impact marriage at ideological levels as well, including the very definitions of marriage. After interviewing 57 highly religious couples, Dollahite and Lambert (2007) reported, "The most prevalent finding in these data was that religious involvement 'sanctified' marriage by giving marriage a sacred, spiritual, or religious character" (p. 294). A highly religious mother in another study similarly stated:

> "What God hath put together, let no man put asunder." I don't believe in divorce. . . . God has engrained my marriage in me so deeply. . . . [Some] women might say, "I don't care if he [my husband] is mad or not." Or "I don't care if I spend all the money up." But in my mind I'm thinking . . . I've got to get myself together and give [God and my husband] the honor of what this relationship means (Marks, 2002, p. 101).

Such views contrast sharply with the privatized and contractual view of marriage that family scholar and therapist Bill Doherty (2000) disparagingly refers to as "commitment-as-long-as . . . things are working out for me" (p. 21). Comparatively, quantitative research has shown connections between religious belief and involvement and higher marital satisfaction, stability, duration, and increased commitment and fidelity (Dollahite et al., 2004)—as well as a "greater likelihood of future marital happiness" (Clements, Stanley, & Markman, 2004, p. 622). A qualitative study that examined potential reasons these positive marital differences tend to emerge among the more highly religious reported "insider" explanations, including pro-marriage/anti-divorce beliefs, shared religious beliefs, and faith in God as a marital support (Marks, 2005).

Conclusion

An in-depth U.S. study with nearly 200 diverse highly religious families clearly indicates that these marriages and families have their share of challenges and problems—including some that are related to or exacerbated by their faith involvement (Marks et al., 2009). Religious community, practices, and beliefs do not unite to form a panacea. With this said, the social science research base (including myriad quantitative and qualitative studies) indicates that marriage-based families in which the parents share religious involvement seem to fare comparatively well. Many of these families may be fortunate enough to avoid some of the forces that threaten and destroy marriages and families. Whether this is the case or not, the multi-dimensional resources of faith seem to serve as valuable coping resources that help families of faith to navigate the challenges that inevitably find us all. In the words of one African American father, "When you believe in God . . . yes, the boat still gets to rockin' but [God] says, 'In me you can weather the storm'" (Marks et al., 2008, p. 179). Social science evidence suggests that shared faith appears to be a principle upon which "successful marriages and families are established and maintained," even during the storm.

Loren D. Marks *holds the Kathryn Norwood and Claude Fussell Alumni Professorship in the Louisiana State University School of Human Ecology. He and his wife, Sandra, are the parents of five children.* **David C. Dollahite** *is a professor in the School of Family Life at Brigham Young University. He and his wife, Mary, are the parents of seven children and they have two grandchildren.* **Joanna Jacob Freeman** *is a recent graduate of Brigham Young University in marriage and family studies. She is married to Nathaniel Freeman.*

References

Abma, J. C., & Martinez, G. M. (2006). Childlessness among older women in the United States: Trends and profiles. *Journal of Marriage and Family, 68,* 1045–1056.

Ammons, S. K., & Edgell, P. (2007). Religious influences on work-family trade-offs. *Journal of Family Issues, 28,* 794–826.

Atkins, D. C., Baucom, D. H., & Jacobson, N. S. (2001). Understanding infidelity: Correlates in a national random sample. *Journal of Family Psychology, 15,* 735–749.

Atkins, D. C., & Kessel, D. E. (2008). Religiousness and infidelity: Attendance, but not faith and prayer, predict marital fidelity. *Journal of Marriage and Family, 70,* 407–418.

Bahr, H. M. (1981). Religious intermarriage and divorce in Utah and the mountain states. *Journal for the Scientific Study of Religion, 20,* 251–261.

Bao, W., Whitbeck, L. B., Hoyt, D. R., & Conger, R. D. (1999). Perceived parental acceptance as a moderator of religious transmission among adolescent boys and girls. *Journal of Marriage and the Family, 61,* 362–374.

Bartkowski, J. P., Xu, X., & Levin, M. L. (2008). Religion and child development: Evidence from the early childhood longitudinal study. *Social Science Research, 37,* 18–36.

Boyatzis, C. J., & Janicki, D. L. (2003). Parent-child communication about religion: Survey and diary data on unilateral transmission and bi-directional reciprocity styles. *Review of Religious Research, 44,* 252–270.

Brelsford, G. M., & Mahoney, A. (2009). Relying on God to resolve conflict: Theistic mediation and triangulation in relationships between college students and mothers. *The Journal of Psychology and Christianity, 28,* 291–301.

Burdette, A. M., Ellison, C. G., Sherkat, D. E., & Gore, K. A. (2007). Are there religious variations in marital infidelity? *Journal of Family Issues, 28,* 1553–1581.

Butler, M. H., Gardner, B. C., & Bird, M. H. (1998). Not just a time-out: Change dynamics of prayer for religious couples in conflict situations. *Family Process, 37,* 451–478.

Butler, M. H., Stout, J. A., & Gardner, B. C. (2002). Prayer as a conflict resolution ritual: Clinical implications of religious couples' report of relationship softening, healing perspective, and change responsibility. *The American Journal of Family Therapy, 30,* 19–37.

Carroll, J. S., Linford, S. T., Holman, T. B., & Busby, D. M. (2000). Marital and family orientations among highly religious young adults: Comparing Latter-day Saints with traditional Christians. *Review of Religious Research, 42,* 193–205.

Chadwick, B. A., & Top, B. L. (1998). Religiosity and delinquency among LDS adolescents. In J. T. Duke (Ed.), *Latter-day Saint social life: Social research on the LDS Church and its members* (pp. 499–523). Provo, UT: Brigham Young University Press.

Christiansen, S. L., & Palkovitz, R. (1998). Exploring Erikson's psychosocial theory of development: Generativity and its relationship to paternal identity, intimacy, and involvement in childcare. *The Journal of Men's Studies, 7,* 133–156.

Clements, M. L., Stanley, S. M., & Markman, H. J. (2004). Before they said "I do": Discriminating among marital outcomes over 13 years. *Journal of Marriage and Family, 66,* 613–626.

Curtis, K. T., & Ellison, C. G. (2002). Religious heterogamy and marital conflict. *Journal of Family Issues, 23,* 551–576.

Doherty, W. J. (2000). *Take back your marriage: Sticking together in a world that pulls us apart.* New York: Guilford.

Doherty, W. J., & Carlson, B. Z. (2002). *Putting family first: Successful strategies for reclaiming family life in a hurry-up world.* New York: Owl Books.

Dollahite, D. C. (1998). Origins and highlights of the special issue on fathering, faith, and spirituality. *The Journal of Men's Studies, 7,* 1–2.

Dollahite, D. C., & Lambert, N. M. (2007). Forsaking all others: How religious involvement promotes marital fidelity in Christian, Jewish, and Muslim couples. *Review of Religious Research, 48,* 290–307.

Dollahite, D. C., & Marks, L. D. (2009). A conceptual model of family and religious processes in highly religious families. *Review of Religious Research, 50,* 373–391.

Dollahite, D. C., Marks, L. D., & Goodman, M. A. (2004). Families and religious beliefs, practices, and communities: Linkages in a diverse and dynamic cultural context. In M. Coleman & L. H. Ganong (Eds.), *The handbook of contemporary families: Considering the past, contemplating the future.* (pp. 411–431). Thousand Oaks, CA: Sage.

Dollahite, D. C., Marks, L. D., & Olson, M. M. (1998). Faithful fathering in trying times: Religious beliefs and practices of Latter-day Saint fathers of children with special needs. *The Journal of Men's Studies, 7,* 71–93.

Dollahite, D. C., Marks, L. D., & Olson, M. M. (2002). Fathering, faith, and family therapy: Generative narrative therapy with religious fathers. *Journal of Family Psychotherapy, 13,* 259–290.

Dollahite, D. C., & Thatcher, J. Y. (2007). How family religious involvement benefits adults, youth, and children and strengthens families. In L. D. Wardle & C. S. Williams (Eds.) *Family law: Balancing interests and pursuing priorities* (pp. 427–436). Buffalo, NY: W. S. Hein & Company.

Eliade, M. (1959). *The sacred and the profane: The nature of religion.* New York: Harcourt Brace Jovanovich.

Ellison, C. G., Bartkowski, J. P., & Anderson, K. L. (1999). Are there religious variations in domestic violence? *Journal of Family Issues, 20,* 87–113.

Fiese, B. H., & Tomcho, T. J. (2001). Finding meaning in religious practices: The relation between religious holiday rituals and marital satisfaction. *Journal of Family Psychology, 15,* 597–609.

Gardner, B. C., Butler, M. H., & Seedall, R. B. (2008). En-gendering the couple-deity relationship: Clinical implications of power and process. *Contemporary Family Therapy, 30,* 152–166.

Hertel, B. R., & Donahue, M. J. (1995). Parental influences on god images among children: Testing Durkheim's metaphoric parallelism. *The Journal for the Scientific Study of Religion, 34,* 186–199.

Hummer, R. A., Rogers, R. G., Nam, C. B., & Ellison, C. G. (1999). Religious involvement and U.S. adult mortality. *Demography, 36,* 273–285.

Jarvis, J. (2000). Mormonism in France: The family as a universal value in a globalizing religion. In S. K. Houseknecht & J. G. Pankhurst (Eds.), *Family, religion, and social change in diverse societies* (pp. 237–266). New York: Oxford.

Kaufman, D. R. (1993). *Rachel's daughters.* New Brunswick, NJ: Rutgers University.

King, V. (2003). The influence of religion on fathers' relationships with their children. *Journal of Marriage and Family, 65,* 382–395.

Koenig, H. G., McCullough, M. E., & Larson, D. B. (Eds.) (2001). *Handbook of religion and health.* New York: Oxford.

Laird, R. D., Marrero, M. D., & Marks, L. D. (2009). Adolescent religiosity as a protective factor for delinquency: Review of evidence and a conceptual framework for future research. In O. Sahin & J. Maier (Eds.), *Delinquency: Causes, reduction, and prevention* (pp. 157–176). Hauppage, NY: Nova Science.

Lee, J. W., Rice, G. T., & Gillespie, V. B. (1997). Family worship patterns and their correlation with adolescent behavior and beliefs. *Journal for the Scientific Study of Religion, 36,* 372–381.

Lehrer, E. L., & Chiswick, C. U. (1993). Religion as a determinant of marital stability. *Demography, 30,* 385–403.

Mahoney, A., Pargament, K. I., Tarakeshwar, N., & Swank, A. B. (2001). Religion in the home in the

1980s and 1990s: A meta-analytic review and conceptual analysis of links between religion, marriage, and parenting. *Journal of Family Psychology, 15,* 559–596.

Marks, L. D. (2002). Illuminating the interface between faith and highly involved families. Unpublished doctoral dissertation, University of Delaware, Newark.

Marks, L. D. (2003). The effects of religious beliefs in marriage and family. *Marriage and Families, 12,* 2–10.

Marks, L. D. (2005). How does religion influence marriage? Christian, Jewish, Mormon, and Muslim perspectives. *Marriage and Family Review, 38,* 85–111.

Marks, L. D. (2006). Religion and family relational health: An overview and conceptual model. *Journal of Religion and Health, 45,* 603–618.

Marks, L. D. (2008). Prayer and marital intervention: Asking for divine help . . . or professional trouble? *Journal of Social and Clinical Psychology, 27,* 678–685.

Marks, L. D., & Dollahite, D. C. (2007). Turning the hearts of fathers to their children: Why religious involvement can make a difference. In S. E. Brotherson & J. M. White (Eds.), *Why fathers count* (pp. 335–351). Harriman, TN: Men's Studies.

Marks, L. D., Dollahite, D. C., & Baumgartner, J. (2010). In God we trust: Qualitative findings on finances, family, and faith from a diverse sample of U.S. families. *Family Relations, 59,* 439–452.

Marks, L. D., Dollahite, D. C., & Dew, J. P. (2009). Enhancing cultural competence in financial counseling and planning: Understanding why families make religious contributions. *Financial Counseling and Planning, 20,* 14–26.

Marks, L. D., Hopkins, K., Chaney, C., Monroe, P. A., Nesteruk, O., & Sasser, D. D. (2008). "Together, we are strong": A qualitative study of happy, enduring African American marriages. *Family Relations, 57,* 172–184.

Marks, L. D., & Palkovitz, R. (2007). Fathers as spiritual guides: Making the transcendent pragmatic. In S. E. Brotherson & J. M. White (Eds.), *Why fathers count: The importance of fathers and their involvement with children* (pp. 209–223). Harriman, TN: Men's Studies.

Miller, L., Warner, V., Wickramaratne, P., & Weissman, M. (1997). Religiosity and depression: Ten-year follow-up of depressed mothers and offspring.

Journal of the American Academy of Child and Adolescent Psychiatry, 36, 1416–1425.

Miller, W. R., & Thoresen, C. E. (2003). Spirituality, religion, and health: An emerging research field. *American Psychologist, 58,* 24–35.

Myers, S. M. (2006). Religious homogamy and marital quality: Historical and generational patterns, 1980–1997. *Journal of Marriage and Family, 68,* 292–304.

Nock, S. L. (1998). *Marriage in men's lives.* New York: Oxford University Press.

Palkovitz, R. (2002). *Involved fathering and men's adult development: Provisional balances.* Mahwah, NJ: Lawrence Erlbaum Associates.

Pargament, K. I., Zinnbauer, B. J., Scott, A. B., Butter, E. M., Zerowin, J., & Stanik, P. (1998). Red flags and religious coping: Identifying some religious warning signs among people in crisis. *Journal of Clinical Psychology, 54,* 77–89.

Pearce, L. D. (2002). The influence of early life course religious exposure on young adults' dispositions toward childbearing. *Journal for the Scientific Study of Religion, 41,* 325–340.

Pearce, L. D., & Axinn, W. G. (1998). The impact of family religious life on the quality of mother–child relations. *American Sociological Review, 63,* 810–828.

Smith, C. (with Denton, M. L.) (2005). *Soul searching: The religious and spiritual lives of American teenagers.* New York: Oxford.

Smith, J. (1835/1985). *Lectures on faith.* Salt Lake City: Deseret Book.

Sorenson, A. M., Grindstaff, C. F., & Turner, R. J. (1995). Religious involvement among unmarried adolescent mothers: A source of emotional support? *Sociology of Religion, 56,* 71–81.

Stack, S., Wasserman, I., & Kern, R. (2004). Adult social bonds and use of Internet pornography. *Social Science Quarterly, 85,* 75–88.

Waite, L. J., & Gallagher, M. (2000). *The case for marriage: Why married people are happier, healthier, and better off financially.* New York: Doubleday.

Wilcox, W. B. (2002). Religion, convention, and parental involvement. *Journal of Marriage and Family, 64,* 780–792.

Wuthnow, R. (1999). *Growing up religious: Christians and Jews and their journeys of faith.* Boston: Beacon.

CHAPTER 19

Sanctification and Cooperation:
How Prayer Helps Strengthen Relationships in Good Times and Heal Relationships in Bad Times

Nathan M. Lambert

Successful marriages . . . are established and maintained on principles of . . . prayer.

IN HIS TALK ABOUT HALLMARKS OF A HAPPY HOME, President Thomas S. Monson describes the counsel he received from his sealer at the marriage altar on his wedding day:

> May I offer you newlyweds a formula which will ensure that any disagreement you may have will last no longer than one day? Every night kneel by the side of your bed. One night, Brother Monson, you offer the prayer, aloud, on bended knee. The next night you, Sister Monson, offer the prayer, aloud, on bended knee. I can then assure you that any misunderstanding that develops during the day will vanish as you pray. You simply can't pray together and retain any but the best of feelings toward one another (Monson, 2001, p. 4).

Drawing on the powers of heaven through prayer is a powerful resource available to couples that can make a good relationship better and can heal a faltering marriage. Prayer is included as a key principle for building a successful marriage and family in "The Family: A Proclamation to the World." The objective of this brief chapter is to describe two models in the social science literature that depict how prayer can strengthen a relationship when things are going well or restore love and unity during conflict: sanctification and cooperative goals.

Prayer and Sanctification of Marriage

When people perceive something as sacred, it changes the way they treat it. For example, workers who defined their work as a "calling" reported missing fewer days

than those who defined it as a "job" or a "career" (Wrzesniewski, McCauley, Rozin, & Schwartz, 1997). Also, Mahoney and colleagues (2005) reported that those who viewed their bodies as sacred placed a higher priority on daily physical exercise.

Mahoney and colleagues (1999) introduced the idea of "sanctification of marriage" as perceiving one's marriage as being holy and sacred. They defined sanctification of marriage as a process by which secular aspects of one's relationship are perceived as having spiritual significance (Mahoney, Pargament, Murray-Swank, & Murray-Swank, 2003). For example, a wedding ring in the secular world represents commitment, but a sanctified view of the wedding ring could symbolize an eternal union between a man and a woman. A "sanctified" relationship ought to be a happy relationship as people go to great lengths to protect and preserve that which they perceive to be sacred (Pargament & Mahoney, 2005). In fact, Mahoney and colleagues (1999) found that the perception of marriage as holy and sacred was related to greater global marital adjustment, more perceived benefits from marriage, fewer communication problems, and less overall conflict. Other researchers have found that perception of the relationship as being sacred was related to enhanced fidelity for married couples (Dollahite & Lambert, 2007) as well as for young adult romantic relationships (Fincham, Lambert, & Beach, 2010).

A key aspect of coming to view a relationship as sacred is to first include God as an active member of the relationship. Ecclesiastes 4:12 refers to a type of "threefold cord" bond that is established when God is included in the partnership when it states, "A threefold cord is not quickly broken." Many couples report such an inclusion of God in their relationship. Butler and Harper (1994) found that for some religious couples, God is more involved in the marriage than any mortal individual. Other couples described God as a "crucial family member" (Griffith, 1986) with whom the couple has a personal and often a daily relationship (Butler & Harper, 1994). In one study, highly religious couples reported that including God in their marriage enhanced and stabilized marital commitment (Lambert & Dollahite, 2008). Thus, several studies support the hypothesis that religious individuals tend to include God in their marriage, but what might couples do to include God in their relationship and how might doing so affect how they view their relationship?

Prayer is the means by which individuals may invite God to play an active role in their relationship. Including God in a relationship as one of the "threefold cords" through praying for one's partner should imbue the relationship with perceived sacredness. As individuals pray specifically for the well-being of their partner, they come to perceive their relationship with this person as being holy and sacred (Fincham et al., 2010). For example, when Jim petitions God to help him understand Jenny's feelings, Jim may come to see Jenny as God sees Jenny and will hence perceive his relationship with Jenny differently (and more sacredly) as a result.

This idea has been empirically tested through an experiment in which religious individuals were randomly assigned to pray for their romantic partner every day for four weeks or to complete a control activity such as thinking positive thoughts about their partner every day. Those who prayed for their partner during the four weeks came to perceive their relationship as more holy and sacred than those in the control group. Also, perceiving the relationship as sacred had important implications, as this perception led to lower levels of sexual infidelity (Fincham et al., 2010). In another study, highly religious couples suggested that their perception of the relationship as sacred helped them to resist the tendency to divorce (Lambert & Dollahite, 2008).

Thus, prayer can be a key component in coming to perceive a marriage relationship as sacred. Coming to view the relationship in this way can be a protective factor, buffering the marriage against certain challenges (such as infidelity) that can diminish or destroy

a marriage. Christ advised his Apostles to "watch and pray, that ye enter not into temptation: the spirit indeed is willing, but the flesh is weak" (Matthew 26:41). Hence, praying is one way that we can defend ourselves against the temptations that can tear a marriage apart. The next section describes in more detail how prayer can facilitate healing during times of conflict.

Prayer and Restoring Cooperative Goals

Conflict is a universal part of marriage. For many, unresolved contention eventually leads to the dissolution of the marriage. Prayer, however, can help protect couples from divorce by healing the relationship and restoring harmony to the marriage. Elder Dallin H. Oaks (2007, p. 72) advised:

> If you are already descending into the low state of marriage-in-name-only, please join hands, kneel together, and prayerfully plead for help and the healing power of the Atonement. Your humble and united pleadings will bring you closer to the Lord and to each other and will help you in the hard climb back to marital harmony.

Many people report praying during times of conflict. In a sample of 20 religious denominations, Abbott, Berry, and Meredith (1990) found that 63 percent of their married sample reported frequently asking for help from God about difficulties in their family, and more than 29 percent reported almost always receiving guidance and inspiration from God in relation to family problems. In another study, 81 percent of happy couples reported praying frequently or extensively as a means of addressing marital problems (Gruner, 1985). Butler, Stout, and Gardner (2002) asked couples if they prayed during a conflict. Among couples in their study, 31 percent indicated almost always praying during conflict, while 42 percent reported that they sometimes prayed during conflict. Thus, many religious couples turn to prayer during times of conflict. Yet how may praying in such situations facilitate marital harmony?

According to Goal Theory (Fincham & Beach, 1999), two primary goals exist in any relationship: cooperative goals and emergent goals. Cooperative goals reflect a win–win mentality in which couples are actively helping each other to succeed. Conversely, emergent goals reflect a win–lose mentality and commonly surface during times of conflict. For example, rather than focus on generating a solution to the problem at hand, partners locked in conflict may find themselves focused on getting their way—or at least focused on not getting proved wrong or losing the argument to the other partner. Prayer may be a medium that transforms emergent goals and restores cooperative goals to the relationship.

Prayer and de-escalation during conflict. Some preliminary research suggests that prayer has a transformative effect on goals by de-escalating conflict. For instance, Butler, Gardner, and Bird (1998) interviewed several couples who reported that prayer invoked a couple–God system, or partnership with God, that helped them during situations of conflict. For instance, couples reported that including God in their marriage through prayer appeared to be a "softening" event that facilitated problem-solving and reconciliation. This couple–God system mentioned by Butler and colleagues is similar to the "threefold cord" metaphor mentioned previously.

A qualitative study found that religious practices such as prayer helped couples to manage their anger during marital conflict (Marsh & Dallos, 2001). Furthermore, couples in another study reported that prayer alleviated tension and facilitated open communication during conflict situations (Lambert & Dollahite, 2006). Results from these studies indicate that prayer can help couples manage the escalation of emotions typically experienced during conflict, suggesting that emergent goals are mitigated by prayer. However, given that all of these studies relied on retrospective reports of the helpfulness of prayers, they could be biased (for example, religious couples wanting to make a case for beneficial effects of their religion). The next section describes a set of studies that did not rely on retrospective reports but rather tested the theoretical model more directly.

Partner-focused prayer, cooperative goals, and forgiveness. Elder Russell M. Nelson (2006, p. 38) said, "Good communication is also enhanced by prayer. To pray with specific mention of a spouse's good deed (or need) nurtures a marriage." Thus, according to Elder Nelson, praying specifically for a partner's well-being is especially good for communication. A research team that I have been a part of examined this type of prayer in a series of studies. Given that feelings are often hurt during conflict, necessitating forgiveness, we hypothesized that praying for a partner would increase forgiveness. Also, in these studies we examined not just any kind

of prayer, but specifically the impact of praying for a partner's well-being (Lambert, Fincham, DeWall, Pond, & Beach, under review).

In the first study, participants reported how much they prayed for their romantic partner's well-being. Three weeks later they came to our research lab and were told to discuss something their partner had done to annoy or upset them. Objective coders, blind to study hypotheses, rated how vengeful participants acted toward their partner as they talked about the upsetting incident. Consistent with our hypothesis, participants who prayed the most for their romantic partner were rated as being the least vengeful during their interactions, indicating that praying for a partner seemed to facilitate forgiveness.

In the second study, participants were randomly assigned to one of two conditions: partner-focused prayer or partner-focused positive thought. Participants were required to engage in their assigned activity every day for four weeks and to report their compliance twice a week in an online log. Meanwhile, the romantic partners of the participants completed a forgiveness measure about the participants before and after they engaged in their assigned four-week activity. We predicted that praying for one's romantic partner, compared to simply thinking positive thoughts about one's partner, would generate behavioral change with respect to forgiveness that would be evident to romantic partners. As hypothesized, the partners of participants who had engaged in partner-focused prayer noticed increased forgiveness in their partners relative to the partners of participants who were assigned to think positive thoughts about their partner.

In the third study, we wanted to examine how praying for one's partner would affect cooperation during the heat of an argument. Participants arrived at the research lab together with their partner and were put in separate rooms. Each received a blank piece of paper and was instructed to complete a drawing that would be rated for creativity by their partner. The research assistant took participants' drawings as if to give them to the partners to rate, but did not actually show the partner the drawing. A few minutes later, the research assistant returned with an envelope containing a false rating sheet with the number "1—not at all creative" ostensibly circled by the partner. By random assignment, they were then instructed to either pray for their partner or to answer a philosophical question about God.

Finally, participants completed a game that they thought they were playing with their partner. In this game they could choose to cooperate with or antagonize their partner to win differing amounts of points depending on their choice. We were especially interested in how participants responded toward their partner right after their partner seemed to have behaved in an insulting manner. We found that compared to participants who contemplated a philosophical question related to God, participants who prayed for their partner cooperated more often during the game.

In the final study, we tested whether cooperative goals would mediate the relationship between partner-focused prayer and forgiveness. Participants reported their partner-focused prayer, cooperation with their partner, and forgiveness of their partner three times a week for three weeks. We found that on days when there was conflict in the relationship, participants who prayed for their partner reported higher cooperation with and forgiveness of their partner. As predicted, reported cooperative tendencies mediated the association between partner-focused prayer and forgiveness. In other words, prayer for a partner predicted more cooperation with that partner, which predicted more forgiveness of that person.

These studies suggest that, consistent with Goal Theory, partner-focused prayer transformed relationship goals, even in the heat of an insult or conflict, and that this transformation of goals facilitated forgiveness (Lambert et al., under review). Inviting God into the relationship through prayer can alleviate anger and restore harmony and cooperative goals to a relationship. Satan strives to "[stir] up the hearts of men to contend with anger, one with another" (3 Nephi 11:29), to disrupt the holy union of marriage in a blatant attempt to make us "miserable like unto himself" (2 Nephi 2:27). However, when contention occurs, prayer can heal hearts and unite couples in love and harmony.

Summary and Conclusion

The growing literature on prayer provides scientific support for President Monson's suggestion that couple prayer is one of the hallmarks of a happy home. Indeed, prayer helps couples in good times and bad times. During the good times, including God in the relationship through prayer helps people to view their partner through God's eyes and come to view the relationship

as holy and sacred. This outlook can protect a couple from the fiery darts that the adversary throws at relationships (D&C 27:17; Ephesians 6:16).

Prayer can also be helpful during the bad times or times of conflict. Goal Theory suggests that couples typically demonstrate cooperative (win–win) or emergent (win–lose) goals in their relationship. During times of conflict, when emergent goals typically prevail, prayer can restore harmony and promote a greater desire to work together. Prayer can aid us in both strengthening and mending our eternally important relationships.

Nathan M. Lambert *is a professor in the School of Family Life at Brigham Young University. He and his wife, Olya, are the parents of three children.*

References

Abbott, D. A., Berry, M., & Meredith, W. H. (1990). Religious belief and practice: A potential asset in helping families. *Family Relations, 39,* 443–448.

Butler, M. H., Gardner, B. C., & Bird, M. H. (1998). Not just a time out: Change dynamics of prayer for religious couples in conflict situations. *Family Process, 37,* 451–478.

Butler, M. H., & Harper, J. M. (1994). The divine triangle: God in the marital system of religious couples. *Family Process, 33,* 277–286.

Butler, M. H., Stout, J. A., & Gardner, B. C. (2002). Prayer as a conflict resolution ritual: Clinical implications of religious couples' report of relationship softening, healing perspective, and change responsibility. *American Journal of Family Therapy, 30,* 19–37.

Dollahite, D. C., & Lambert, N. M. (2007). Forsaking all others: How religious involvement promotes marital fidelity in Christian, Jewish, and Muslim couples. *Review of Religious Research, 48,* 290–307.

Fincham, F. D., & Beach, S. R. H. (1999). Conflict in marriage: Implications for working with couples. *Annual Review of Psychology, 50,* 47–77.

Fincham, F. D., Lambert, N. M., & Beach, S. R. H. (2010). Faith and unfaithfulness: Can praying for your partner reduce infidelity? *Journal of Personality and Social Psychology, 99,* 649–659.

Griffith, J. L. (1986). Employing the God–family relationship in therapy with religious families. *Family Process, 25,* 609–618.

Gruner, L. (1985). The correlation of private, religious devotional practices and marital adjustment. *Journal of Comparative Family Studies, 16,* 47–59.

Lambert, N. M., & Dollahite, D. C. (2006). How religiosity helps couples prevent, resolve, and overcome marital conflict. *Family Relations, 55,* 439–449.

Lambert, N. M., & Dollahite, D. C. (2008). The three-fold cord: Marital commitment in religious couples. *Journal of Family Issues, 29,* 592–614.

Lambert, N. M., Fincham, F. D., DeWall, C. N., Pond, R. S. Jr., & Beach, S. R. H. (under review). Shifting towards cooperative goals: How partner-focused prayer facilitates forgiveness. Manuscript submitted for publication.

Mahoney, A., Carels, R. A., Pargament, K. I., Wachholtz, A., Edwards Leeper, L., Kaplar, M., & Frutchey, R. (2005). The sanctification of the body and behavioral health patterns of college students. *The International Journal for the Psychology of Religion, 15,* 221–238.

Mahoney, A., Pargament, K. I., Jewell, T., Swank, A. B., Scott, E., Emery, E., & Rye, M. (1999). Marriage and the spiritual realm: The role of proximal and distal religious constructs in marital functioning. *Journal of Family Psychology, 13,* 321–338.

Mahoney, A., Pargament, K. I., Murray-Swank, A., & Murray-Swank, N. (2003). Religion and the sanctification of family relationships. *Review of Religious Research, 44,* 220–236.

Marsh, R. D., & Dallos, R. (2001). Roman Catholic couples: Wrath and religion. *Family Process, 40*(3), 343–360.

Monson, T. S. (2001, October). Hallmarks of a happy home. *Ensign, 31,* 2–8.

Nelson, R. S. (2006, May). Nurturing marriage. *Ensign, 36,* 36–38.

Oaks, D. H. (2007, May). Divorce. *Ensign, 37,* 36–38.

Pargament, K. I., & Mahoney, A. (2005). Sacred matters: Sanctification as a vital topic for the psychology of religion. *The International Journal for the Psychology of Religion, 15,* 179–198.

Wrzesniewski, A., McCauley, C., Rozin, P., & Schwartz, B. (1997). Jobs, careers, and callings: People's relations to their work. *Journal of Research in Personality, 31,* 21–33.

CHAPTER 20

Repentance and Forgiveness in Family Life

Elaine Walton and Hilary M. Hendricks

Successful marriages and families are established and maintained on principles of . . . repentance [and] forgiveness.

ROBERT TOOK CARE OF HIS DISABLED MOTHER FOR several years. Despite the demands of his large family and their small home, he made room for his mother, and the family pitched in to take care of her. After ten years of this devoted service, the mother died without a will. Robert's sister, Mary, never married and was a practicing attorney. She didn't think the years of caring for their mother should make a difference in dividing the estate and, in Robert's view, used her expertise to "cheat" him out of tens of thousands of dollars. Disheartened by the loss and troubled by his own financial concerns, Robert vowed never to speak to his sister again.

Linda was sexually abused by her father over a period of several years as she was growing up. The abuse had a crippling effect on her self-esteem and probably contributed to the fact that she married and divorced three times. As a teenager, she had disclosed the abuse to her bishop, but the bishop believed her father's denial. Nothing was ever done to make her father accountable or to help her overcome the emotional injury. As she grew older, she became increasingly bitter and, blaming the bishop for not coming to her defense, she left the Church.

Interpersonal transgressions are common occurrences in all families. They range from misunderstandings and minor mistakes, such as forgetting to take out the garbage, to more substantive disagreements, such as Robert's altercation with his sister, and grievous sins, such as the abuse perpetrated on Linda. In most families, where there are almost daily interpersonal transgressions, repentance and forgiveness need to be ongoing. The purpose of this chapter is to help families achieve repentance and forgiveness, especially with major offenses, in a way that promotes healing and personal growth.

Repentance and Forgiveness: An Interactive Process

Repentance and forgiveness are two sides of the same coin and are frequently addressed together. For example, apologies facilitate forgiveness, and forgiveness motivates repentance (Holeman, 2008). In families, repentance and forgiveness blend into an interactive process that is strengthened by family members' commitment to each other (Finkel, Rusbult, Kumashiro, & Hannon, 2002). The term "interpersonal transgression" implies the involvement of a victim and an offender who are, at the time of the offense, connected through an ongoing relationship.

Although the process of repentance and forgiveness is interpersonal, successful outcomes are profoundly intrapersonal—experienced individually, apart from or in addition to any interpersonal interaction. The noted forgiveness researcher Worthington (2006) wrote, "Forgiveness does not occur in a relationship. It occurs within the forgiver" (p. 20). He posited that this was true, even in intimate relationships.

Factors Associated with Forgiveness

The interactive nature of repentance and forgiveness is evident in the work of Mullet, Neto, and Rivière (2005). They found three factors that influence the victim's decision to forgive:

(a) *situational factors*, [such as] intention of harm, repetition of offense, severity of the consequences, cancellation or not of the consequences, presence of apologies, and/or compensation from the offender; (b) *relational factors*, [such as the] offender's identity and his or her proximity with the victim, his or her hierarchical status, his or her attitude after the offense, and environmental pressures; and (c) [the victim's] *personality factors* (p. 159; italics added).

Likeliness to forgive was associated with the victim's agreeableness, emotional empathy, extraversion, interdependence, dutifulness, conscientiousness, and religiousness. On the other hand, victim personality factors negatively associated with forgiveness were anger, neuroticism, and rumination (p. 168).

Types of interpersonal forgiveness. Three kinds of forgiveness will be discussed in this chapter. By implication, the repentance/forgiveness scenario involves an offender and a victim. However, in the first type of forgiveness, the interpersonal transgressions are such that both parties are at fault and the roles of victim and offender are shared. In this case, the resulting process is mutual forgiveness. By contrast, bilateral forgiveness—the second type of forgiveness—presumes there has been wrongdoing on only one side, and forgiveness comes in response to apology and repentance. In the third case, the offender will not or cannot participate in this type of healing, and therefore unilateral, or one-way, forgiveness can be achieved by the victim, without the offender's apology or repentance (Govier, 2002).

Situations that necessitate forgiveness. Battle and Miller (2005) found a wide range of situations and events within families that necessitate forgiveness:

In addition to infidelity and abuse, many other types of transgressions are reported as important. . . . These include (a) unequal treatment of siblings by one or both parents, (b) failure of a parent to protect a child from harm, (c) hurt feelings from divorce and/or remarriage, (d) lack of parental acceptance of a spouse or romantic partner (particularly in interracial or same-sex relationships), (e) irresponsible or dishonest financial decisions made by a family member, (f) problems associated with a family member's addiction or mental illness, (g) inequitable distribution of household tasks, (h) repeated instances of broken family commitments or prolonged absences, (i) disagreements

regarding care of an ill or elderly relative, and (j) disputes regarding funerals and estate settlement (p. 233).

Repairing the damage caused by such occurrences in families is hard work for all involved. However, the well-established benefits of repentance and forgiveness make those efforts worthwhile.

Why Repent and Forgive?

Repentance and forgiveness have historically been regarded by social scientists as religious issues only. However, since the 1990s, repentance and forgiveness have become increasingly prominent in professional literature. Mental health experts acknowledge that it is impossible to address emotional and physical well-being without considering the relevance of repentance and forgiveness. Likewise, the words of ancient and modern prophets affirm that repentance and forgiveness are central to the gospel plan.

Doctrinal implications. From a religious perspective, the need for repentance is clear. Hundreds of years before Christ's birth, King Benjamin taught that "salvation cometh to none . . . except it be through repentance and faith on the Lord Jesus Christ" (Mosiah 3:12). President David O. McKay (1953. p. 13) stated that no "principle or ordinance of the gospel" is "more essential to the salvation of the human family than the divine and eternally operative principle [of] repentance." Elder Dallin H. Oaks (2003) identified the instruction to repent as the gospel's "most frequent message" and defined repentance as transformation:

The gospel of Jesus Christ challenges us to change. . . . Repenting means giving up all of our practices—personal, family, ethnic, and national—that are contrary to the commandments of God. The purpose of the gospel is to transform common creatures into celestial citizens, and that requires change (p. 37).

Similarly, divine mandate is one reason many Latter-day Saints seek to forgive. Christ taught that forgiving is prerequisite to being forgiven:

And when ye stand praying, forgive, if ye have ought against any: that your Father also which is in heaven may forgive you your trespasses. But if ye do not forgive, neither will your Father which is in heaven forgive your trespasses (Mark 11:25–26).

For victims of serious offenses, Elder Richard G. Scott (2004, p. 16) recommended forgiveness—although it is "most difficult"—as "the sure path to peace and healing." And President Gordon B. Hinckley (2005, p. 81) emphasized that forgiveness "may be the greatest virtue on earth, and certainly the most needed."

Benefits to families and individuals. Interpersonal repentance and forgiveness have obvious benefits in repairing or mediating damaged family relationships (Enright & Fitzgibbons, 2000). In addition, individuals and families who are able to forgive important transgressions are likely to have better emotional and physical health (Battle & Miller, 2005), and positive emotions improve health in a variety of ways (Harris & Thoresen, 2005). Numerous studies have demonstrated a relationship between forgiveness and well-being (e.g., Thoresen, Harris, & Luskin, 2000).

By contrast, not forgiving can lead to harm. "Unforgiveness" is considered a stress reaction in response to a perceived threat (Worthington, 2006), and the emotions associated with unforgiveness, such as resentment, hostility, blame, and fear, have been linked to health risks (Harris & Thoresen, 2005).

Cautions in Conceptualizing Forgiveness

A number of myths surround the conceptualization of forgiveness. Some writers are uncomfortable with forgiveness because empowerment of the victim, not reconciliation between the abuser and victim, is usually the therapeutic goal for victims of family abuse (Bass & Davis, 1988). And there is a perception that Western culture unfairly targets women as the ones who are expected to forgive (Norlock, 2009). In summarizing the work of several authors, Rye and Pargament (2002) noted that forgiveness should not be confused with legal pardon, condoning, or forgetting. It is also distinct from reconciliation. These are not necessary for forgiveness and its attendant benefits for the victim to be obtained. Rye and Pargament argued that "conceptualizing forgiveness using these distinctions allows people to forgive without compromising their safety or their right to pursue social justice" (p. 420). But without some sort of deliberate action, whether interpersonal or intrapersonal, actual forgiveness does not take place.

It is natural to be angry and even vindictive when one has been wronged. Sometimes victims are uncomfortable with these emotions and try to skip straight to reconciliation, without adequately acknowledging the wrong or allowing time for meaningful repentance and forgiveness to take place. But forgiveness demands recognition of wrongful behavior.

Murphy (2005, p. 33) warned of this superficial forgiveness, or "cheap grace," explaining that "hasty forgiveness can . . . undermine self-respect, respect for the moral order, respect for the wrongdoer, and even respect for forgiveness." Elaborating, Murphy explained that resentment legitimizes the wrongness and empowers the victim to seek redress: "Just as indignation over the mistreatment of others stands as emotional testimony that we care about them and their rights, so does resentment stand as emotional testimony that we care about ourselves and our rights" (p. 35).

Malcolm, Warwar, and Greenberg (2005) warned of "short-circuiting" anger, such that the victim inappropriately condones hurtful behavior or ends up taking responsibility for the injury. They explained that anger provides a self-protective mechanism. Indeed, there is evidence that some forms of anger (such as "constructive anger," which focuses our energies on ways of rectifying the situation) may actually improve health (Davidson, MacGregor, Stuhr, Dixon, & MacLean, 2000). Such constructive anger can even reduce or moderate an unforgiving attitude. Clearly, the problem with resentment is not in having it but in being dominated by it and stuck in it. An understanding of what forgiveness is—and is not—will help both victims and offenders as they attempt the complicated processes described next.

Repenting after Interpersonal Transgression

Repentance is a process of enhancing internal awareness and interpersonal accountability (Holeman, 2008). Outwardly, the offender not only acknowledges wrongdoing but also makes reparation. Inwardly, repentance is achieved through humility and empathy, making it possible for the offenders to see themselves and those they wounded with a new perspective that is refreshing and motivating.

Humility is the opposite of arrogance, narcissism, or pride. Transgressors who are truly contrite are able to admit their mistake and make every effort to accept the consequences and conditions desired by the offended party without blaming others or justifying their actions. However, seeking forgiveness should not be confused with submissiveness, nonassertiveness, or inappropriate responsibility (Sandage, Worthington, Hight, & Berry, 2000), such as child victims of abuse who try to make sense of injury by reasoning that a parent who loves them wouldn't hurt them unless they deserved it in some way.

Empathy is the ability to understand the deep feelings of another person. While humility helps transgressors see themselves differently, empathy helps them see their victim differently (Holeman, 2008). True empathy is experienced as a feeling, not merely as a cognition. It is not enough to say, "I know I hurt you." With empathy, the offender can know how it feels to be the offended person. For example, empathy helps a transgressing spouse respond to the following question: "What if something strange happened, and you were suddenly transformed into your partner? Knowing how you treated [him or her], how would you feel? What would it be like being in an intimate partnership with you?" (Jory, Anderson, & Greer, 1997, p. 408).

The scholarly concept of empathy meshes well with Elder Neal A. Maxwell's (2002, p. 58) explanation of the change of perspective that comes through repentance. Drawing from the Bible Dictionary, Elder Maxwell taught that repentance is "a Greek word which means 'a change of mind,' such as changing one's view of himself, God, the universe, life, others, and so on." In attempting to repent, said Elder Maxwell (2001, p. 10), "we are actually progressing toward what Paul called 'the mind of Christ' (1 Corinthians 2:16)."

Guilt or shame? With the offender's newfound perspective may come feelings of guilt or shame. Shame involves a painful focus on self—feeling small, worthless, or unworthy: "I am a bad person." However, guilt is more likely to be associated with a particular act: "I did a bad thing" (Tangney, Boone, & Dearing, 2005). Guilt involves tension, remorse, and regret—emotions that can motivate repentance. Elder Richard G. Scott (2004) explained that guilt can be constructive: "The ability to have an unsettled conscience is a gift of God to help you succeed in this mortal life" (p. 15). On the other hand, feelings of shame often result in defensive behavior that inhibits the repentance process.

Guilt or shame that serves only to generate feelings of unworthiness without instigating change is counterproductive. Alma counseled his wayward son, "Let these things trouble you no more, and only let your sins trouble you, with that trouble which shall bring you down unto repentance" (Alma 42:29). Excessive feelings of guilt or shame may require the intervention of a professional or a spiritual leader in order to transform these feelings into positive changes in behavior.

Apology and change. There are many ways for offenders to acknowledge their wrongdoing and express remorse. According to Lazare (2004), a successful apology includes several parts: (a) an accurate acknowledgment of the offense; (b) an appropriate expression of regret, remorse, or sorrow; (c) a suitable offer of repayment or restitution; and (d) a pledge for behavior reform to ensure that the offense is not repeated. The apology will fail if any of the steps is missing or inadequate. For example, wrongdoers may minimize the offense or not recognize the injury suffered by the victim, resulting in a less-than-authentic apology (see Holeman, 2004). Regardless, victims may find inadequate apologies better than none.

Apologies are essential for reconciliation (Lazare, 2004). However, in the case of severe interpersonal transgressions, it takes more than apology to restore love and trustworthiness. It takes genuine repentance. Repentance implies that a sin has been committed and involves an acknowledgement of the damage done to the offender's relationship to God as well as to the victim. Holeman (2004, p. 238) defined repentance as

> a decisive turning away from thoughts, words, and deeds that have betrayed love and trust, and a wholehearted turning toward attitudes and activities that can restore love and trust to the relationship. [It] includes confession and a commitment to consistent changed behavior over time.

The steps of repentance as outlined next are similar to the steps of apology as discussed by Lazare (2004). However, repentance is more than apology. It is a humbling, all-encompassing experience. It requires offenders to see themselves through the eyes of the injured party as well as through the eyes of God. For members of The Church of Jesus Christ of Latter-day Saints, the repentance process is explained in the manual *Gospel Principles* (The Church of Jesus Christ of Latter-day Saints, 2009), and includes the following:

1. *Recognize the sin.* We admit to ourselves that we have done something wrong.
2. *Feel sorrow for the sin.* Feeling sorrowful, we are humble and submissive before God, and we come to Him with a broken heart and contrite spirit.
3. *Forsake the sin.* We stop committing the sin and pledge to never do it again.
4. *Confess.* We should confess all our sins to the Lord. In addition, we must confess serious sins that might affect our standing in the Church to the proper ecclesiastical authority.
5. *Make restitution.* Insofar as possible, we make right any wrong that we have done.

Of course, the process will vary depending on the type and seriousness of the sin. Some are sins against society with legal implications. Some are sins that require confession to Church leaders. Repentance for less serious sins may be accomplished privately between spouses or within the family, but all five steps are still needed.

The offender bears the burden of change in order to restore trust and repair relationships. However, repentance does not necessarily elicit forgiveness or result in reconciliation. If repentance has been sincere and appropriate changes have been maintained over time without forgiveness from the victim, the offender may benefit by apologizing or making restitution to a surrogate, perhaps a family member or friend who stands in for the victim. This is particularly meaningful in cases where the confession has been delayed and the victim is deceased or refuses contact. The offender is not entirely dependent upon forgiveness from the victim in order to experience the cleansing, healing, and renewing power of repentance. After true repentance, if forgiveness is not forthcoming, self-forgiveness can facilitate healing for the transgressor (Hall & Fincham, 2005). Ultimately, offenders must forgive themselves in order to restore self-respect or complete the process of reconciliation where reconciliation is possible (Dillon, 2001).

Forgiving an Interpersonal Transgression

Victims of serious offenses sometimes take one of two opposing views. Either they are reluctant to forgive because they fear that the process will leave them with even less power and will allow them to be hurt again, or they are intimidated by a religious mandate and know

they must forgive but don't know how (Walton, 1998). The first view leaves victims hardened. No amount of justice seems adequate, and the concept of forgiving is laughable. Victims with the second view may be passive, with minimal understanding of both the injury and the forgiveness process because they deal with it only superficially, complying with a religious mandate without making an effort to fully understand it. In such a case they cannot figure out why they are still unable to take control of their lives or feel joy. Neither response provides a clear understanding of what forgiveness really is.

For victims, forgiveness means being released from anger and developing empathy for the offender (Gordon, Hughes, Tomcik, Dixon, & Litzinger, 2009). This implies a change of heart and a change in expectations—there will be no later recriminations or paybacks (Walton, 2005). Being able to say "I forgive you" means that the feeling of injury no longer supports resentment, though the definition of forgiveness does not specify how the injured person arrives at this change of heart. The change may happen through the victim's realizing that resentment was a mistake (for example, no wrong was done), or the harm may be excusable, such as an honest misunderstanding. Another possibility may be that the victim recognizes that feeding resentment and dwelling on injuries is a bad idea, with negative implications for health or a valued relationship.

Genuine forgiveness is a process, not a product. It is hard work and it takes time. It is a voluntary act that gives meaning to the wound and frees the injured person from the ills of bitterness and resentment.

Releasing from Debt

Forgiveness has been compared to cancelling a debt (Exline & Baumeister, 2000). Metaphorically, if that debt were a financial loan that was not likely to be repaid, the victim (lender) would have to weigh the benefit of being free of the hassle and bad feelings against the benefit of having a vague hope of repayment in the future and being able to hold the debtor forever responsible for the victim's own financial needs.

Forgiveness might come as an altruistic gift (Worthington, 2001), not because the debtor somehow deserved the money but rather because the lender chose to be gracious. Alternatively, forgiveness might be granted simply as a way of freeing the lender from the entanglement of the relationship. It would be a way for the victim to be empowered and to go on without the burden. However, in choosing to forgive, the victim now takes responsibility: he or she can no longer use the unpaid debt as an excuse for his or her own financial ills (Walton, 2005).

Such forgiveness involves multiple processes. Cognitively, the lender no longer thinks about the debt. Affectively, or emotionally, the lender no longer feels angry about the debt. And behaviorally, he or she decides not to seek repayment or punishment for the debt (Exline & Baumeister, 2000). This does not necessarily mean that the victim does not seek legal recourse. Crimes against society, including sexual or physical abuse, must be reported to law enforcement authorities. In such cases, Elder Richard G. Scott (2004, p. 17) advised, "leave [discipline] to the Church and civil authorities. Don't burden your own life with thoughts of retribution."

The victim should not prematurely try to erase, or cover up, the memory of the wrong. Rather, the metaphorical forgiving of the debt means that the victim is able to stop dwelling on the wrong. He or she has worked through the feelings of resentment and is ready to let them go. Freed from the negative emotions and cognitions, the offended person is transformed from victim to survivor—a change perhaps as meaningful as the change experienced by the offender who repents.

How to Forgive?

Several models of forgiveness have been examined in the scholarly literature (Worthington, 2006). Some are interpersonal models with reconciliation as the goal. Others are intrapersonal with a cognitive, behavioral, emotive, or process-oriented approach. For this chapter, we chose to focus on Worthington's (2001) cognitive–behavioral, five-step process, which is summarized below:

1. *Recall the hurt.* It is human nature to try to protect ourselves from pain. Too often we try to deny or forget the pain of the offense and avoid the discomfort associated with addressing that offense in an interpersonal relationship. In order to forgive, we have to be clear about the wrongdoing and acknowledge the injury.
2. *Empathize.* Empathy involves borrowing the lens of another person so we see something from their point of view. In order to forgive, it is important to understand the transgressor's feelings. Was the

offense committed knowingly or was it an honest mistake? What were the pressures that influenced the offender to commit the offense? Is there an understandable reason for the offender to disagree with the victim regarding the seriousness of the offense? In what ways may the offender have been victimized in the past? What pain might the offender be experiencing associated with guilt and remorse?

3. *Offer the altruistic gift of forgiveness.* Forgiving with altruism is easier when the victim is humbled by an awareness of his or her own shortcomings and offenses, with special gratitude for those occasions when he or she was freely forgiven.
4. *Commit publicly to forgive.* The victim has a better chance of successful forgiveness if he or she verbalizes the forgiveness commitment to another person (for example, telling a friend or counselor about the decision). Some victims have formalized their decision by writing a letter, making a journal entry, or creating a certificate of forgiveness.
5. *Hold on to forgiveness.* After completing the forgiveness process, victims may still be haunted on occasion by the pain of the offense. During this stage it is important to move forward. When thoughts revert to the painful injury, the victim is reminded that the decision to forgive has already been made. He or she does not have to repeat that process. Also, it is important for the victim to remember that having forgiven, he or she has promised that there will be no paybacks or grudges. Although painful memories are not necessarily replaced by forgiveness, the pain should be a reminder to move forward with one's life instead of revisiting the transgression committed against him or her. Deliberate efforts to stop unwanted thoughts are often unsuccessful. Instead, when victims have successfully reframed their thought processes, it is probably because they have *replaced* the unwanted thoughts with something more meaningful or important.

Scholars do not know exactly how forgiveness takes place, but when genuine forgiveness is achieved, thoughts, emotions, motivations, and behaviors are changed. Worthington (2006) suggested that change is a process of "emotional replacement" wherein the complex negative emotions of unforgiveness are replaced with positive ones.

The case of Cathy. Cathy is a Latter-day Saint woman whose husband was unfaithful. The effects of that betrayal were many. She began to doubt her own worth and desirability as a woman and her self-esteem reached an all-time low. The functioning of the family deteriorated and the children's needs took a backseat to the tension and strain all too evident in their parents' faces. Finances were increasingly tight with separate households to manage. When it became clear that divorce was inevitable, Cathy, who had for more than a decade been a stay-at-home wife and mother, had to figure out how to provide for her children. A longtime stalwart member of the Church, she now felt uncomfortable facing ward members. She believed she had been transformed from being part of the backbone of the ward to a charity case.

As Cathy's dreams for her family faded away, her heart was filled with anger and bitterness. Sermons from the pulpit, which had once been inspiring, now seemed hollow. How could she be expected to forgive the man who not only made her life miserable but also compromised the eternal welfare of her children?

Now in survival mode, she found the day-to-day demands of life her only priority, and she didn't have the luxury of spending time feeling sorry for herself. For practical reasons, she "cancelled the debt" owed by her estranged husband—not because she forgave him but rather because she was forced to take responsibility for her life in a new way and realized that waiting for him to make restitution would only bring heartache and disappointment.

Life was difficult. In comparison to previous times, Cathy had twice the responsibility with only half the resources. But she was determined to make her life work. She found an opportunity to launch a new career. She worked tirelessly to address the needs of her children—trying to compensate for being outside the home during the day and a single parent at night. Eventually, by any measure, Cathy was successful. However, "cancelling the debt" was only part of the healing process. It allowed her to move forward with her life, but true forgiveness was elusive. She tried to conceal her feelings of anger and bitterness, but they were still there—buried deep.

Cathy didn't like feeling bitter. It dulled life and made it difficult for her to feel real joy. Also, she had that recurring pang of guilt every time she read a scripture or heard a talk that reminded her that she was required to forgive—up to seventy times seven if necessary. She wondered, "How could anyone be expected to be forgiven 490 times?"

There was a blessing associated with Cathy's losses, however. In being humbled financially, socially, and emotionally—completely stripped of pride—she actually became free. She was freed from the state of constant comparison with her neighbors, and she realized that there is no fast track to the celestial kingdom. Her heart had been broken, but not her spirit. And fortunately her broken heart was not a crushed heart. Rather, it was a heart broken open, ready to receive help and wisdom.

Her prayers became more lengthy and heartfelt. In her desire to overcome the darkness inside, she found herself not only praying for help in managing her increasingly difficult life, but also she remembered her husband in her prayers. She wanted to know how Heavenly Father viewed him. She prayed to be able to see her husband through His eyes. After many such prayers, she began to think and feel differently. She realized that her husband was a beloved child of God. Yes, Heavenly Father was unhappy with some of his choices—just as He was unhappy with some of her choices. But He didn't stop loving.

She also gained an enhanced understanding of the power of the Atonement. She was thankful all over again for the ways she had been forgiven of her past transgressions. Her mistakes were perhaps less grievous than those of her husband, but forgiveness was no less important. Recognizing the blessing of forgiveness in her own life, she was overwhelmed with gratitude. Perhaps even more poignant, she recognized that through the Atonement, Christ had paid for her husband's betrayal. She still believes her husband made a grievous mistake, but she became comfortable leaving judgment to God. Her job was to be grateful for the bounties she received and to press forward in doing the best she could.

Appreciating the Atonement. Central to Cathy's ability to forgive was her growing understanding of the Atonement of Jesus Christ. Elder Richard G. Scott (2008, p. 42) explained how faith in Christ brings about the ultimate healing:

The beginning of healing requires childlike faith in the unalterable fact that Father in Heaven loves you and has supplied a way to heal. His Beloved Son, Jesus Christ, laid down His life to provide that healing. But there is no magic solution, no simple balm to provide healing, nor is there an easy path to the complete remedy. The cure requires profound faith in Jesus Christ and in His infinite capacity to heal.

The most meaningful and growth-promoting repentance and forgiveness require a relationship with the Lord—the willingness and humility to be taught by the Spirit. The process is about reconciliation with God first and foremost. That is the reconciliation that makes reconciliation with family members possible. Healthy guilt and godly sorrow are gifts that motivate repentance. And remembering the graciousness of God in forgiving our sins makes it easier to forgive the sins of others. Cathy moved toward forgiveness as she prayed, like the publican in Luke 18:13, "God be merciful to me a sinner."

Reconciliation: To Reconcile or Not?

Reconciliation is often, but not always, the desired result of repentance and forgiveness (Worthington, 2001). Park and Enright (2000) conceptualized the process of resolving an interpersonal transgression as a series of possibilities in which forgiveness may be achieved with or without reconciliation and reconciliation achieved with or without repentance.

As previously mentioned, in some cases reconciliation is not possible. Perhaps the offender is deceased, in prison, or has moved far away. In some cases, reconciliation may not be prudent. Reopening a strained relationship may be uncomfortable and awkward in addition to painful. For those victims who have moved on, the pain and risk may not be worth it. In other cases, reconciliation may not be desirable. It might be unhealthy or unsafe for a victim to put him- or herself back in harm's way. For example, a child who has been sexually abused should be protected from the abuser and should not be pressured to communicate with him or her. Reconciliation requires a restoration of trust and a willingness to have ongoing contact. If that trust and willingness are not achievable, reconciliation is not wise.

People generally work at reconciliation because they have invested a lot in the relationship and do not like to accept failure (Worthington, 2001). In addition, they are likely to still value the other person and the relationship, and they recognize that if nothing is done to mend the relationship, it is likely to worsen.

Reconciliation is a give-and-take process wherein the parties gradually move closer to each other. For example, victims are more likely to reconcile with offenders who have repented, and offenders are more likely to confess and apologize to victims whom they believe will forgive them. However, false starts and missteps are common, and there are barriers to overcome. Offenders may disagree with the charge, or they may be afraid of punishment or restrictions associated with confession. Victims may be reluctant to give up the leverage associated with victim status (Exline & Baumeister, 2000), or they may fear appearing weak and being hurt anew. Courage and humility are required for both parties in order to repair the injury—especially because in most cases of interpersonal transgression there is neither a "pure victim" nor a "pure villain" (Holeman, 2008).

Strategies for Reconciliation

Although explicit acknowledgement is essential in cases of serious offenses, victims should not disregard or devalue other reconciliation tactics too quickly. Waldron and Kelley (2008, p. 112) identified a number of strategies typically used in the process of reconciliation, not all of which are direct. For example, when the offender is fearful that an acknowledgement and apology may not be accepted, the use of humor or gift-giving may be a way of postponing explicit acknowledgement while testing the other party's receptiveness. Waldron and Kelley (p. 116) suggested that "self-deprecating humor in particular may signal that the offender is now willing to take responsibility." Other indirect strategies may include nonverbal assurance (for example, a hug), compensation (like giving a gift), or simply giving explanations about the offense.

Nonverbal assurance, such as eye contact and touch, provides verification of the sincerity of an apology or evidence of acceptance on the part of the victim. Also, explanations and discussions are part of the clarifying process. Offenders need an opportunity to share, without inappropriate justification, their side of the story along with motives or reasons surrounding the infraction. Waldron and Kelley (2008, p. 115) state that "explanation may help the offender save face but it also helps the wounded partner interpret the transgression and assess its seriousness." Reconciliation is a process of renegotiating the rules of the relationship, reframing shared memories and, in the case of couples, starting over again with a second courtship. At some point, future planning will be an essential component in the process. When partners or family members collectively plan activities or set mutual goals, they are imagining a future together and moving away from a painful past (Waldron & Kelley, 2008).

In the case of Robert, mentioned at the outset, who cut off relations with his attorney sister after feeling cheated in the settlement of their mother's estate, reconciliation was eventually achieved through the mediating efforts of a relative. A caring aunt spent time individually with both siblings, helping them develop greater understanding and empathy for each other. Eventually, they both agreed to attend a reunion of the extended family, which led to light-hearted reminiscence, which led to a serious discussion of the painful situation. With increased understanding, the sister was able to acknowledge with gratitude the service provided by Robert and his family during their mother's final years. She also came to appreciate the financial situation of her brother and the imminent need that had precipitated his anger. Likewise, Robert was able to recognize that his sister was operating out of a professional, rather than personal, business model and was only behaving as she would in any estate settlement case. He also became aware of some deep-seated feelings of loneliness on her part, which increased his empathy for her. Once their feelings and behaviors were understood by each other, they renegotiated a more equitable estate settlement, and they made plans for celebrating Thanksgiving together.

One-Way Forgiveness

For victims whose offenders cannot or will not repent, forgiveness is understandably more difficult. Although reconciliation may not be feasible or even desirable, forgiveness is still an important part of the healing process. All victims need to be relieved of the burden of resentment and the entanglements of a painful relationship. Govier (2002, p. 63) asserted that "no victim will benefit, psychologically or morally from clinging to a resentful sense of her own victimhood and dwelling on the past."

One way to conceptualize the one-way, or unilateral, forgiveness process is to repent on behalf of the offender (Walton, 2005). "On behalf of" does not imply that the victim is taking the burden of repentance away from the offender. That is not possible—the responsibility will forever remain with the offender. "On behalf of" means that the victim can accomplish for him- or herself what

might be accomplished if the offender were to sincerely repent. The victim can experience the validation, freedom, and healing that come with apology and contrition even though the offender is not remorseful or is not available (for example, deceased). To envision this possibility, the five-step repentance process is revisited:

1. *Recognize the offense.* The offender is not the only one who is responsible for recognizing the wrongdoing. The victim must be willing to name the offense and claim the injury. What moral or civil laws were broken? How did the betraying event break those rules? What injury was sustained and what were the consequences? What is the meaning of the injury—how was the victim's belief system changed, and how is he or she different?

2. *Sorrow for the offense.* Obviously the offender should feel sorrow because of transgression. But grieving is also an essential element for the victim in the healing process. For many victims, sorrow has been averted or camouflaged by anger, and in giving up the anger, they must be willing to feel the sadness that gave rise to the anger. Sorrow is a natural response to loss and will come as the victim is able to name the offense and claim the injury, identifying and grieving all the accompanying losses. However, sorrow should be temporary—one step in the healing process, not a perpetual state of being.

3. *Disclose.* The offender's unwillingness or inability to confess does not stop the victim from disclosing the offense. The victim confesses on behalf of the offender as he or she breaks the silence and shares the details of the offense with someone—perhaps a confidante, therapist, legal authority, or religious leader. By disclosing, the victim moves out of a world of confusion and shame and is now ready to place the blame where it belongs. Blaming is prerequisite to forgiving. If there is no blame, there is no need to forgive. In order to forgive, the victim must recognize that something was wrong and someone was at fault. Once that is established, the process of forgiving and healing can proceed.

4. *Avoid the offending behavior.* In the repentance process, offenders are expected to commit never to engage in the sinful behavior again. Victims cannot force offenders to change their behavior, but

they can take responsibility for protecting themselves and others from further victimization. During this stage, victims take responsibility for their happiness and safety. They establish boundaries and make important decisions about the people they want in their lives and how they want to be treated by them. Victims who have suffered serious abuse by a family member may choose not to have any contact with that relative—at least for a time. Or they may choose to attend family gatherings, but on their own terms. During this stage, victims develop guidelines for determining a person's trustworthiness and establish commonsense rules of conduct for themselves in order not to place themselves at risk.

5. *Make restitution.* Restitution is essential in restoring order and wholeness to the life of the injured person. Another way to think of restitution is "balancing the scales." Balance is destroyed when one person takes choice away from another while at the same time increasing his or her own choices. Balance is restored to uneven scales by either taking away from the heavier side or adding to the lighter side. Likewise, in dealing with serious offenses, balance is restored by punishing the offender or by loading resources to the depleted reserves of the victim. During this stage, the victim may take legal steps to bring about justice. However, desire for retribution may play out in ways that are counterproductive or even self-destructive. Instead of expending energy on retaliation, the victim can find ways to replenish his or her own depleted reserves. Some possibilities might include (a) joining a support group, (b) obtaining additional education or training, (c) seeking a better job, (d) rejuvenating one's social life, (e) starting a new hobby, or (f) exploring new self-nurturing activities.

Through these steps, the injured party is able to move from victim to survivor—accomplishing for him or herself what would be accomplished if the offender were truly contrite and had sincerely repented. During the process, it is natural for the victim to begin to view the offender with more compassion and empathy. Compassion may help to facilitate the process, but it is not the primary goal. Ultimately, forgiveness is for the benefit of the victim. It is also important to reiterate that forgiveness is not a simple process and the victim should not feel hurried. Working through painful memories and grieving significant losses require time and considerable emotional energy.

In the case of Linda, who had been sexually abused by her father, forgiveness was a long time coming. With the help of a counselor, she was finally able to recognize that her anger and bitterness were impeding her progress and making it impossible for her to find real joy in life. The counselor helped her validate the pain she had endured, identifying the specific injuries, particularly injuries to her self-esteem. The validation made it possible for her to take responsibility for her own happiness.

After "cancelling the debt," Linda was able to focus on healing, and she also found meaning by helping others in the same situation to heal. Instead of being stuck in bitterness and anger, she moved forward with her life. She went back to school and with additional credentials was able to obtain employment she enjoyed. She worked on developing and maintaining good friendships. Eventually, she counseled with her bishop—a bishop who believed her story and sensitively helped her back into Church activity. She chose not to reconcile with her father, but she was eventually able to see the abuse from his perspective. She found out that he himself had been severely abused as a child, and the abuse resulted in a mental disorder that made it difficult for him to perceive abusive situations accurately.

Conclusion

Repentance and forgiveness are divine expectations that are particularly relevant to family life. The question is not if forgiveness should take place, but how? When the offense is associated with a simple misunderstanding, forgiveness can be almost immediate. But with deep betrayal and serious injury, the process is lengthy and painful, and there is no shortcut. True healing comes only through experiencing the pain of loss and completing the tasks associated with repentance and forgiveness.

In the end, sincere repentance and genuine forgiveness are gifts from God made possible through the Atonement of Christ. With enhanced humility and empathy, the offender can gain new perspectives—that of the victim and of Jesus Christ, who atoned for that transgression. Likewise, victims also achieve forgiveness through sharing Heavenly Father's perspective—infinite love for all His children.

Elaine Walton *recently retired from the faculty of the School of Social Work at Brigham Young University. She and her husband, Wendel, have a blended family of 10 children, 29 grandchildren, and 6 great-grandchildren.* Hilary M. Hendricks *edits faculty manuscripts at Brigham Young University. She and her husband, Todd, are the parents of Hannah, Eli, and Asher.*

References

Bass, E., & Davis, L. (1988). *The courage to heal: A guide for women survivors of child sexual abuse.* New York: Harper & Row.

Battle, C. L., & Miller, I. W. (2005). Families and forgiveness. In E. L. Worthington Jr. (Ed.), *Handbook of forgiveness* (pp. 227–241). New York: Routledge.

The Church of Jesus Christ of Latter-day Saints. (2009). *Gospel Principles.* Salt Lake City: Author.

Davidson, K., MacGregor, M. W., Stuhr, J., Dixon, K., & MacLean, D. (2000). Constructive anger verbal behavior predicts blood pressure in a population-based sample. *Health Psychology, 19,* 55–64.

Dillon, R. S. (2001, October). Self-forgiveness and self-respect. *Ethics, 112,* 53–83.

Enright, R. D., & Fitzgibbons, R. P. (2000). *Helping clients forgive: An empirical guide for resolving anger and restoring hope.* Washington DC: American Psychological Association.

Exline, J. J., & Baumeister, R. F. (2000). Expressing forgiveness and repentance: Benefits and barriers. In M. E. McCullough, K. I. Pargament, & C. E. Thoresen (Eds.), *Forgiveness: Theory, research, and practice* (pp. 133–155). New York: Guilford Press.

Finkel, E. J., Rusbult, C. E., Kumashiro, M., & Hannon, P. A. (2002). Dealing with betrayal in close relationships: Does commitment promote forgiveness? *Journal of Personality and Social Psychology, 82,* 956–974.

Gordon, K. C., Hughes, F. M., Tomcik, N. D., Dixon, L. J., & Litzinger, S. C. (2009). Widening spheres of impact: The role of forgiveness in marital and family functioning. *Journal of Family Psychology, 23*(1), 1–13.

Govier, T. (2002). *Forgiveness and revenge.* New York: Routledge.

Hall, J. H., & Fincham, F. D. (2005). Self-forgiveness: The stepchild of forgiveness research. *Journal of Social and Clinical Psychology, 24,* 621–637.

Harris, A. H. S., & Thoresen, C. E. (2005). Forgiveness, unforgiveness, health, and disease. In E. L. Worthington, Jr. (Ed.), *Handbook of forgiveness* (pp. 321–333). New York: Routledge.

Hinckley, G. B. (2005, November). Forgiveness. *Ensign, 35,* 81–84.

Holeman, V. T. (2004). *Reconcilable differences: Hope and healing for troubled marriages.* Downers Grove, IL: InterVarsity Press.

Holeman, V. T. (2008). Repentance in intimate relationships. In W. Malcolm, N. DeCourville, & K. Belicki (Eds.), *Women's reflections on the complexities of forgiveness.* New York: Routledge.

Jory, B., Anderson, D., & Greer, C. (1997). Intimate justice: Confronting issues of accountability, respect, and freedom in treatment for abuse and violence. *Journal of Marital and Family Therapy, 23,* 399–419.

Lazare, A. (2004). *On apology.* New York: Oxford University Press.

Malcolm, W., Warwar, S., & Greenberg, L. (2005). Facilitating forgiveness in individual therapy as an approach to resolving interpersonal injuries. In E. L. Worthington Jr. (Ed.), *Handbook of forgiveness* (pp. 379–391). New York: Routledge.

Maxwell, N. A. (2001, October). Testifying of the great and glorious Atonement. *Ensign, 31,* 10–15.

Maxwell, N. A. (2002, July). The Holy Ghost: Glorifying Christ. *Ensign, 32,* 56–61.

McKay, D. O. (1953). *Gospel ideals: Selections from the discourses of David O. McKay.* Salt Lake City: Improvement Era.

Mullet, E., Neto, F., & Rivière, S. (2005). Personality and its effects on resentment, revenge, forgiveness, and self-forgiveness. In E. L. Worthington Jr. (Ed.), *Handbook of forgiveness* (pp. 159–181). New York: Routledge.

Murphy, J. G. (2005). Forgiveness, self-respect, and the value of resentment. In E. L. Worthington Jr. (Ed.), *Handbook of forgiveness* (pp. 33–40). New York: Routledge.

Norlock, K. (2009). *Forgiveness from a feminist perspective.* New York: Lexington Books.

Oaks, D. H. (2003, November). Repentance and change, *Ensign 33,* 37–40.

Park, S. R., & Enright, R. D. (2000). The evolution and development of morality. In F. Aureli & F. B. M. de Waal (Eds.), *Natural conflict resolution* (pp. 359–361). Berkeley, CA: University of California Press.

Rye, M. S., & Pargament, K. I. (2002). Forgiveness and romantic relationships in college: Can it heal the wounded heart? *Journal of Clinical Psychology, 58*(4), 419–441.

Sandage, S. J., Worthington, E. L. Jr., Hight, T. L., & Berry, J. W. (2000). Seeking forgiveness: Theoretical context and an initial empirical study. *Journal of Psychology and Theology, 28*, 21–35.

Scott, R. G. (2004, November). Peace of conscience and peace of mind. *Ensign, 34*, 15–18.

Scott, R. G. (2008, May). To heal the shattering consequences of abuse. *Ensign, 38*, 40–43.

Tangney, J. P., Boone, A. L., & Dearing, R. (2005). Forgiving the self: Conceptual issues and empirical findings. In E. L. Worthington Jr. (Ed.), *Handbook of forgiveness* (pp. 143–158). New York: Routledge.

Thoresen, C. E., Harris, A. H. S., & Luskin, F. (2000). Forgiveness and health: An unanswered question. In M. E. McCullough, K. I. Pargament, & C. E. Thoresen (Eds.), *Forgiveness: Theory, research, and practice* (pp. 254–280). New York: Guilford Press.

Waldron, V. R., & Kelley, D. L. (2008). *Communicating forgiveness*. Thousand Oaks, CA: Sage.

Walton, E. (1998). The role of forgiveness in healing intimate wounds: A model for LDS psychotherapists. *AMCAP Journal, 23*, 71–95.

Walton, E. (2005). Therapeutic forgiveness: Developing a model for empowering victims of sexual abuse. *Clinical Social Work Journal, 33*, 193–207.

Worthington, E. (2001). *Five steps to forgiveness: The art and science of forgiving*. New York: Crown Publishers.

Worthington, E. L. Jr. (2006). *Forgiveness and reconciliation: Theory and application*. New York: Routledge.

CHAPTER 21

The Meanings and Blessings of Family Work

Kathleen Slaugh Bahr, Kristine Manwaring, Cheri Loveless, and Erika Bailey Bahr

Successful marriages and families are established and maintained on principles of . . . work.

ONE DAY A WEEK WE DEEP CLEAN THE HOUSE together. My parents divide us into teams. We hate this. They force us to work together. We get along much better when we aren't working so closely together. Usually it ends up in a yelling match, and then my parents freak out. My mom starts crying because we aren't getting along, and therefore we aren't righteous enough and she's failed as a mother. Then my dad gets upset because Mom is upset. The result: We are forced to spend more time with each other to prepare us for eternal life as a family. Cleaning the house is a miserable experience for everyone (Smith, 1996, n.p.).

So wrote one university student, and her feelings are not uncommon. While hard work in other contexts is generally regarded as a virtue, family work—the necessary, hands-on labor of sustaining life by feeding, clothing, and sheltering a family—has become the work no one wants to do. Housework is also a major source of contention between the sexes. One study found that six months into marriage, disagreement over allocation of household chores was the top source of conflict between husband and wife, and it remained so after five years (Cox, 1996).

In contrast, "The Family: A Proclamation to the World" describes caring for spouse and children as a "solemn responsibility." It calls providing for the physical needs of children a "sacred duty," and it lists work among principles like faith, prayer, repentance, and compassion, principles upon which "successful marriages and families are established and maintained" (¶¶ 6, 7). President

Gordon B. Hinckley listed families working together as one of four things that could "in a generation or two" turn society's "moral values" around (1996, p. 7).

Is family work a God-ordained necessary evil? Or do we ignore its true nature? In fact, ordinary household work that is often considered a waste of time can be a time of closeness and fun that strengthens family bonds and develops Christlike virtues.

We Must Leave the Ease of Eden to Follow the Savior

When Adam and Eve left the garden, they exchanged an existence sustained without effort for a life grounded in hard work. Some Old Testament readers may think of labor as a curse, but a close reading reveals that God cursed *the ground* to bring forth thorns and thistles, which in turn forced Adam to labor "*for [his] sake.*" In other words, Adam's hard work of obtaining bread "by the sweat of [his] face" can be a blessing (Moses 4:23, 25). The Apostle Paul connects childbearing (and childrearing) to the salvation of both Adam and Eve (1 Timothy 2:15, footnote a; from Joseph Smith Translation).

The reason family-centered work brings blessings and salvation is so obvious in common experience that it has become obscure: Family work provides endless opportunities to recognize and fill others' needs. It thus teaches us to love and serve one another, inviting us to be like Jesus Christ. Elder Neal A. Maxwell observed, "The divine attributes of love, mercy, patience, submissiveness, meekness, purity . . . cannot be developed in the abstract. These require the clinical experiences. . . . Nor can these attributes be developed in a hurry" (1998,

p. 7). Family work can become the clinical experience that over time shapes us toward divinity.

When family members work together in the right spirit, a foundation of caring and commitment grows out of their shared experience. The most ordinary tasks, like fixing meals or doing laundry, hold great potential for connecting us to those we serve and with whom we serve. Among student comments we collected in a course focusing on family work, we found this one:

> I never realized why my older brother and I were such good friends. When we were in our early teens, we helped my dad build our house, install the sprinklers, landscape the yard, and do all sorts of odds-and-ends jobs. I remember many times when we would have to cooperate to accomplish many of our work goals. . . . Now that we are older, there is a bond that we share because we worked side by side in our developing years.

Jesus was consistently concerned with others' physical needs as He set the perfect example of a spiritual life. When He prepared the Apostles for His imminent death and instructed them on becoming one, He established the sacred ordinance of washing feet, based on a daily task ordinarily done by the most humble of servants:

> [Jesus] riseth from supper, and laid aside his garments; and took a towel, and girded himself. After that he poureth water into a basin, and began to wash the disciples' feet, and to wipe them with the towel wherewith he was girded (John 13:4–5).

Peter objected, protesting that such work was beneath Jesus' stature. In response, Jesus clarified its importance: "If I wash thee not, thou hast no part with me" (John 13:8). Then he taught: "If I then, your Lord and Master, have washed your feet; ye also ought to wash one another's feet. For I have given you an example, that ye should do as I have done to you" (John 13:14–15). Thus Christ suggests that humble, serving work is central, truly *for our sakes.*

Prosaic Work
Connects People and Changes Hearts

Family work is prosaic work—commonplace, even tedious or dull. But these small, everyday events combine to form the character of a week, a month, a year, and eventually a lifetime. Literary critic Gary Saul Morson chose the term *prosaics* to describe "a way of thinking about human events that focuses on the ordinary, messy, quotidian facts of daily life" (1988, p. 516). He observed that "grand drama and ecstatic moments do not make a life good. Life is an everyday affair, and the sum total of unremarkable, daily happenings defines its quality. . . . Many can perform heroic actions in the sight of all, but few possess the courage to do small things right without recognition" (2007, pp. 28–29).

Ancient prophets understood the power of prosaics. Nephi noted that "by small means the Lord can bring about great things" (1 Nephi 16:29), and Alma observed that "by small and simple things are great things brought to pass; and small means in many instances doth confound the wise" (Alma 37:6). Modern scripture also emphasizes the power of seemingly small events: "Out of small things proceedeth that which is great" (D&C 64:33).

Elder Neal A. Maxwell said, "We must look carefully, therefore, not only at life's large defining moments but also at the seemingly small moments. Even small acts and brief conversations count, if only incrementally, in the constant shaping of souls" (1998, p. 8). Few things in life are as small, simple, or of seemingly little value as the everyday tasks we do for family members.

Plus family work, though essential, can still seem burdensome. Why does running a household, even with modern conveniences, take such inordinate chunks of time and displace other activities we consider important? If cooperating as a family is the ideal, why is it often easier to work alone than to involve children or a spouse? To answer such questions, we must reach beyond personal experience to view family work outside of our cultural mindset.

A common notion in Western culture, for instance, is that an ideal life is work-free. This idea directly conflicts with central gospel themes. The first commandments given to Adam and Eve were to till the soil and to bear and care for children. However, in the West, the more distant a man's work from the fields and the more removed from home and children a woman's work, the more they are admired. We prefer life's bounties at minimal cost, without the so-called interruptions of children. In other words, we long for the life Adam and Eve left behind in the Garden of Eden.

Yet Adam and Eve found joy in leaving the garden to face the labors of this life (Moses 5:11). Only by doing so could they grow toward godhood (see 2 Nephi 2:22–25).

As their posterity, shall we turn back toward Eden or press forward toward Zion, where all people are "of one heart and one mind" (Moses 7:18)?

Modern culture also encourages a dislike for characteristics of family work that may offer great possibilities for fostering growth and nurturing relationships. For instance, we consider chores that require little mental effort mindless. But from a spiritual perspective, work done with a minimum of concentration leaves our minds free to focus on one another as we labor. Unlike play, which often involves significant mental activity, sharing an everyday task can dissolve feelings of hierarchy, inviting light-hearted or intimate conversation that binds us together.

One student wrote, "Some of the best times with my dad were when I would help him do yard work. . . . We'd have some of our best talks about life as we raked leaves or hauled wood." Another stated, "I think picking strawberries and string beans was especially productive as a family because the work was long and mundane. The quiet, almost mentally effortless work is fertile soil for conversation. I sometimes miss those days."

Of course, prosaic work may also engender complaints and conflict, and sometimes does not build solidarity. Yet even stressful interaction, annoying in the short term, can gradually stimulate growth and build relationships. We observed a 12-year-old boy, asked to watch the baby while father and sisters weeded the garden, protest, argue, tease his sisters, and whine about the baby's runny nose. Yet, when left to care for her, he lovingly wiped her face and sang to her.

Another objection is that household work is menial. Like servant's work, it requires so little skill as to be seen by some as beneath the dignity of well-educated people. Menial tasks, however, allow small children to make meaningful contributions as they fold laundry, wash walls, or sort silverware with sufficient skill to feel value as part of the family. Since daily tasks range from the simple (chopping, folding, scrubbing) to the complex (prioritizing, organizing, training others), participants at every level can feel competent yet challenged, including parents with the overall responsibility for coordinating tasks, people, and projects into a cooperative, working whole.

A third bothersome aspect of family work is its entropic nature. Once accomplished, it is quickly undone: meals labored over are soon eaten; bathrooms cleaned are soon dirty. Such work proverbially is never done, requiring some tasks to be repeated several times a day.

A positive aspect of such repetition is that it facilitates learning. Quarrelsome, reluctant helpers one day can practice working together again the next day. Some chores may become daily rituals that teach love and forge family ties, building family identity moment by moment amidst talking, teasing, singing, and storytelling. A young man from a family that had "never gone on vacation together nor ever once had family home evening" fondly remembered cooking together:

> The most fun thing we would prepare together was enchiladas. It was definitely a group project because we would always form an assembly line. My dad would prepare the tortillas, and next, someone would be in charge of dipping them in the sauce. . . . Down the line we had people in charge of cheese, olives, and the rolling and putting them in the pan. There was a job for everybody, and we spent more time talking and laughing than preparing food (Smith, 1996, n.p.).

Family members may not notice the cumulative impact of these small moments, but the daily repetition of words and actions that accompany such work help form basic character, virtues, and beliefs.

Culturally, family work is also considered demeaning, as it can involve cleaning up after others in the most personal way. In so doing, we glimpse our mortality in another's vulnerability. We are reminded that when we are fed, we could be hungry; when we are clean, we could be dirty; when we are healthy and strong, we could be feeble and dependent. Family work is humbling, helping us to acknowledge our unavoidable interdependence and encouraging us to sacrifice self for the welfare of others in the pattern of the Savior.

Family work thus reveals a profound potential to strengthen and heal relationships. Performing mundane yet essential tasks for those who cannot do so for themselves can create, in the absence of pride, a precious connection between giver and receiver. As we figuratively touch each other at the simple level of everyday need, routine acts of service begin to mend feelings and foster unity. A mother of four related:

> When my mother was twelve, her mother abandoned her and left her with an alcoholic, abusive father. My mother knew why my grandmother

left, but still felt cheated. . . . Their relationship had been strained for years when my grandmother was diagnosed with terminal cancer. But my mother decided to care for her. . . . At first, she resented her mother's constant demands. She had to say a silent prayer at the door of Granny's bedroom every time she entered. But something happened during the five months that my mother gave round-the-clock service to my grandmother. My mother came to deeply love her mother. She later explained to me, "When I took care of her, I could see who she was. When I would bathe her or see her in a vulnerable moment, my whole body would fill with love and warmth, and I would just feel for her. . . . I got back more than I gave."

The daily work of feeding, clothing, and sheltering others has the power to transform us spiritually as we transform others physically. Said Elder Russell M. Nelson: "The home is the great laboratory of love. There the raw chemicals of selfishness and greed are melded in the crucible of cooperation to yield compassionate concern and love one for another" (1999, p. 40).

Prosaic Work Was Once the Norm

Is it possible for families to enjoy, or at least appreciate, such work? Yes! Most societies, including our own, have not always viewed family work negatively. Working together to sustain life was once what families naturally did all day, often at a pace they enjoyed. "How I would love to go with my father when he would hook up the old ox team and go to get sage brush for wood," wrote Florence Slaugh Willes (1874–1954), remembering how she picked flowers and played in the sand while her good-natured father loaded the wagon (n.d.).

Like most children in the United States in the early 1900s, Florence grew up in a home dependent upon her hands-on labor to help keep the family alive. Their household work was strenuous and required everyone's participation for most of each day. Still, there seems to have been little desire to get the work out of the way so that everyone could get on with life. Work *was* life— so much so that in Florence's account, work is sometimes difficult to distinguish from play as she describes "corn husking bees, the apple cuttings, and washing each other's faces in apple and peach peelings. Oh! I can feel the sticky mess now!" (Willes, n.d.).

Though we cannot and do not need to restore the non-technological lifestyle of Florence's girlhood, we can learn much from the more relaxed approach to work and the blending of work with play that was then the norm. Over the century that separates us, events combined to reverse the positive concept of family work in the United States. With industrialization, many families abandoned the physical labor of farm life to seek more dependable work in factories. The resulting inner-city squalor motivated reformers to seek "scientific solutions" to "home problems" (Richards, 1910), and scientific expertise began to replace traditional family authority. As daily work lost its tie to the earth, homes began to consume more than they produced, and men's and women's work spheres became separated.

The changing work of fathers. Before industrialization, most men learned the trade of their fathers and took pride in doing well the work they felt called to do. Indeed, *vocation* is derived from *vocatio*, the Latin term for *calling*. As workers came to earn their wages away from the household, the notion of work as a calling nearly disappeared. Where a son once had forged ties with his father by working beside him, he now followed his father's example by distancing himself from the daily work of the household. Providing for one's family came to mean bringing home a paycheck to purchase goods and services (Cowan, 1983) rather than performing physical tasks of feeding, clothing, and sheltering family members. Historian John Demos notes:

> The wrenching apart of work and home-life is one of the great themes in social history. And for fathers, in particular, the consequences can hardly be overestimated. . . . Fathers had always been involved in the provision of goods and services to their families; but before the nineteenth century such activity was embedded in a larger matrix of domestic sharing. . . . Now, for the first time, the central activity of fatherhood was sited outside one's immediate household. Now, being fully a father meant being separated from one's children for a considerable part of every working day (1986, pp. 51–52).

By the 1950s, fathers had so fully left the domestic circle that they became guests in their own homes. The natural connection between fathers and children was said to be preserved and strengthened through play. However, play, like work, also changed over the course of the century, becoming more structured, costly, and less interactive. "It could well be argued," said Demos, "that men's experience of domestic life has changed more deeply than that of all the other [family members] combined" (1986, p. 41).

The changing work of mothers. While the family work mothers did remained much the same, *how* that work was carried out changed drastically. In 1912, Frank B. Gilbreth told readers of the *Journal of Home Economics,* "It would seem that principles that have proved of use in the scientific management of commercial industries might have an application to the business of housekeeping" (p. 438). The fact that goals of industry, such as increased production and profit, might not fit the purpose of homes seemed not to concern those who encouraged housewives to organize, sterilize, and modernize.

Women were told that applying methods of factory and business management at home would ease their burdens and raise the status of their work by "professionalizing" it. Surprisingly, the proposed innovations did neither. Machines tended to replace tasks once performed by husbands and older children who were now at work and school. Left alone to care for the home and young children, a mother actually experienced a longer workday (Cowan, 1983). Also, houses and wardrobes expanded, standards for cleanliness heightened, and modern appliances encouraged more elaborate meal preparation. New tasks like shopping and driving children to activities were added. Work, once enjoyed alongside family and friends, began to feel lonely, boring, and monotonous.

Experts also urged women to replace hands-on labor with the work of the mind, reducing the value of work done by hand. A leading home economics educator declared, "The woman who today makes her own soap instead of taking advantage of machinery for its production enslaves herself to ignorance by limiting her time for study" (Hunt, 1901, pp. 3–4). Nurturing and housework, unpaid in the market economy, declined in public esteem. Later efforts to raise their status by calculating the monetary value of homemaking tasks inadvertently fed a growing concept that time is money, further pushing the demanding nurture side of family work toward near invisibility. Thus, the perceived difficulty and importance of a woman's family work began

to differ enormously from the actual experience of running a home.

The changing work of children. As homes shifted from centers of production to centers of consumption, the role of children reversed. Prior to modernization, children shared much of the hard work of family life, laboring with their parents. Work was considered good for them, part of education for adulthood. When children began to accompany parents to factories, profit-driven manufacturers saw them as a cheap source of labor. It became more common for children than mothers to provide additional family income. Sometimes children could even find work when their fathers could not. Lacking parental supervision at the workplace, they were subject to abuses, giving rise to the child labor movements that aimed to protect the "thousands of boys and girls once employed in sweat shops and factories" from "the grasping greed of business" (McKeever, 1913, p. 137).

Child labor laws, designed to end abuse, nearly ended all child labor (Zelizer, 1985). As expectations for children's employment diminished, new fashions in childrearing dictated that children should have their own money and be trained to spend it wisely. The economic role of children shifted from worker to pampered consumer. By the early 1900s, childcare experts advised that the only legitimate reason to require work from children was educational, and even then it should have a play-like quality (Zelizer, 1985). Soon play was deemed a child's "work." By 1970 the report of the Carnegie Council on Children stated that "today . . . children rarely work at all" (Keniston & Carnegie Council on Children, 1977, p. 14). Recent time-use studies show that today's children do minimal household work, and the little they do is mostly for themselves, such as cleaning their own rooms or doing their own laundry (Stearns, 2003).

Combined, these changes promoted a new ideal where family members were physically isolated from one another much of the day—father working away from home, mother (whether in the workforce or not) efficiently running the home, and children at school or at play. Unfortunately, when family members no longer cooperate for their mutual care, individual growth may be compromised and opportunities to love and serve one another may be diminished. A significant contemporary challenge for families is to find ways to cooperate in meaningful family work.

Managing Our Homes Like Businesses May Be a Faulty Ideal

We interviewed parents of adult children about how they had coordinated family work when their children were growing up. Most spoke of trying several ways to structure and reward chores. Typically, each system broke down after a few weeks or months, prompting parents to reorganize according to a new plan that promised better results. As time passed, the new plan would yield yet another failure. Not even the most competent and organized families found a way for family work to remain consistently structured, convenient, and conflict-free.

Parents tended to blame themselves for these failures. However, family work, by design, defies a systematic approach. First, as noted earlier, family work places us in situations that require reliance on divine attributes we do not yet have—love, mercy, patience, submissiveness, and a willingness to sacrifice for others. Also, family work does not fit neatly into many accepted notions about motivating and managing people.

Nowadays we are encouraged to apply rational economic principles everywhere, including at home. We are taught to seek measurable results (a spotless home), to use resources efficiently (no wasting time or money), and to manage people by maintaining control (reward good workers, penalize shirkers). Money as the bottom line guides much decision-making. Considering the dollar value of a mother's time, why spend time making a dress when we can buy one or cooking a meal when convenience foods are faster? Indeed, operating entirely by the criterion of economic efficiency, parents should not work or play with their children when others whose time is worth less can be hired to do it for them (Carver, 1913; Galbraith, 1973).

While the economic model values efficiency, independence, and profit, the Lord teaches longsuffering, humility, and love unfeigned. Family work organized exclusively by economic principles loses its power to strengthen families and develop Christ-centered virtues. President Kimball addressed this point:

> I hope that we understand that, while having a garden, for instance, is often useful in reducing food costs and making available delicious fresh fruits and vegetables, it does much more than this. Who can gauge the value of that special chat between daughter and Dad as they weed or water the garden? . . . And how do we measure the family togetherness and cooperating that must accompany successful canning? (1977, p. 78).

In an eternal perspective, the purposes of home—fostering growth, forging unity, and learning charity—far exceed economic advantage or efficiency criteria. Occasionally economic principles may apply, but as daily *modus operandi* they fall short. Consider scheduling. Before modernization, deadlines imposed on family work were rarely contrived. Work was done in response to the natural demands of life: cows had to be milked, eggs gathered, stoves fired up. Most of these tasks did not lend themselves to haste, and the slower pace of work enhanced opportunities for interaction. A Navajo woman recalls learning to cook by watching her grandmother: "She cut me a little dough and tell me to make it like this and I try my best to make it. And there was a hot coal under it, and when it bubbled up I turned it over and I just do that and that is how I learned how to cook" (Bahr & Bahr, 1993, p. 360). With no sense of hurry, the work was allowed to proceed at the pace of the child.

In contrast, by the 1950s, textbooks for high school home economics were advising, "A home should be managed as smoothly and as well as any factory or business. The profitable business is one which has a definite routine and permits only a minimum of waste" (Van Duzer, Andrix, Bobenmyer, Hawkins, Hemmersbaugh, & Page, 1951, p. 424). Most components of family life, from laundry to infant feedings, became subject to the clock. Events and needs that defied advance planning—an illness, a child's curiosity, or a friend stopping by—became interruptions. Inviting a child to help make bread was devalued, for it would slow the process. Besides, homemakers were advised to buy bread to save time.

Planning ahead, following a schedule, and learning to work efficiently have their place. Parents sometimes appropriately encourage a child to meet high standards or impose short-term goals to create a product that takes precedence over the process. But plans too easily become ends rather than means, with end products overshadowing the shared creative process that produced them. A loving family atmosphere reflects the rhythms of daily life rather than the artificial demands of planner and clock. Too much emphasis on efficiency and scheduling precludes experiences like this one described by a college student:

> My favorite [work experience] is singing at the top of our lungs with my sisters while we do the dishes. We sing all the songs we know and sometimes teach each other new ones. We sing in parts: soprano, alto, tenor, and whatever else we can make up. It probably takes longer to do dishes that way, but it sure is fun!

Parents Do Not Need a Perfect System for Doing Chores

Family work is a lifelong opportunity, essential to the process of becoming like our heavenly parents. It was not meant to be consistently easy, convenient, or well-managed. Even parents who appreciate the value of family work get discouraged on the days it seems fraught with tedium and turmoil. Children quarrel, refuse to help, or must be cajoled and persuaded. Parents tire of cleaning the same messes, listening to the same arguments, and folding the same towels day after day after day. No wonder families seek a system that will remove these problems once and for all.

Work that unifies hearts is "not after the manner of men." We cannot describe any systems that guarantee meaningful experiences with family work. Individuals and families, with diligence and through inspiration, can discover better ways to solve their earthly challenges than anything a leader or so-called expert could impose. Each family can prayerfully evaluate their family work practices and in light of gospel principles make changes that will eventually bring great joy.

When Nephi's family was told to build a ship to carry them to a promised land, Nephi went to the mount often in prayer and received specific instructions regarding "timbers of curious workmanship" and other aspects of construction "not after the manner of men" (1 Nephi 18:2). Today's parents, bombarded with expert advice, must also be willing to seek guidance from the Lord—not man—as they negotiate between living in the world without being of the world (John 17:15–16). Answers pertaining to family work will vary in detail from household to household and will often diverge from "the manner of [well-accepted theories among] men."

One popular pattern, for example, is to pay children to participate in family work. Grace Weinstein cautions parents that this approach "soon develops complicated emotional connotations":

> "We pay the children for all the chores they do around the house," says one couple. "They get paid for walking the dog, babysitting each other, and not fighting when they're alone in the house. It seems to work." It probably does, on the surface. Yet if their parents had demanded it, these children would have done all these things anyway. Not always joyously, perhaps—but they're not always ecstatic about doing chores even when they're paid in cash. And they're certainly not developing much sense of responsibility for the family. Unless you want your children to think of you as an employer and of themselves not as family members but as employees, you should think long and hard about introducing money as a motivational force. Money distorts family feeling and weakens the members' mutual support (1985, p. 107).

Parents should seek an approach based on "attentive love." King Benjamin admonishes parents to teach their children to love one another and serve one another (Mosiah 4:15). Indeed, the commandment to "love one another" does not carry the caveat, "if you feel like it." Even though many families today associate housework more often with conflict than with love and service, that is no excuse to yield to societal pressures. Much research shows that joint activity in meaningful tasks is associated with solidarity and emotional bonding (Doherty, 1999; Lee, 1959; Sherif & Sherif, 1953). Parents who seek spiritual guidance can discover how to use family work to link and heal.

Philosopher, mother, and feminist Sara Ruddick writes that love, "the love of children," at any rate, "is not only the most intense of attachments, but it is also a detachment, a giving up, a letting grow" (1984, p. 224). She describes this quality of love as "attentive love," a careful attention to another's needs for growth seen through "the patient eye of love."

Parents may be easily convinced to fall back on recipes for childrearing: A child who refuses to pick up his toys goes to time-out; a child who remembers to make her bed is rewarded with a quarter. Even when such recipes work, they may be short-circuiting attention to the child's real needs. Attentive love asks,

"What is the child telling me through this behavior?" and "How can I help my child so that he is pulled closer to the family, so that she is not pushed away?" Such questions may be answered with family work's potential to link those who labor together. Helping a child pick up toys, then cuddling with her, connects her to the family; requiring him to clean his room alone isolates him.

Parents are also tempted to use methods that yield quick results because in the short term they demand less parental effort. In contrast, attentive love requires parents to seek deeper, more long-term results: "Does my child need to learn to sacrifice self-centered interests for the good of others?" Chats with mom while folding the family laundry together may open the right door, or yield insights about the child's true needs.

Ruddick identifies the enemy of attentive love as "the greedy organism of the self," with its self-focused aims and purposes (1984, p. 223). Parents and children, participating together in family work, plant seeds of Zion where "every man [seeks] the interest of his neighbor and [does] all things with an eye single to the glory of God" (D&C 82:19). Family members cooperating on a mundane task day after day can literally become "of one heart and one mind" (Moses 7:18) as they progress through a range of experiences that lead them to know each other's hearts and learn from one another.

Of course, in any household, loving feelings run up and down, but caring parents can strive to manifest love as the expected norm. "There is nothing so stretching as mothering," states one young mother, amazed that even when feelings of inadequacy tempt her to "just walk out the door," she soon remembers that "the joy of family life is very real and sweeter than anything I have known" (Personal correspondence, 2010).

Essayist Wendell Berry tells how our daily habits of caring and serving eventually carry us beyond the difficulties of life into a manifestation of love:

> Our marriages, kinships, friendships, neighborhoods, and all our forms and acts of homemaking are the rites by which we solemnize and enact our union with the universe. . . . They give the word "love" its only chance to mean, for only they can give it a history, a community, and a place. Only in such ways can love become flesh and do its worldly work (1987, p. 118).

Note that non-family relationships also are strengthened by sharing essential work. One student wrote that "family work ideas work with roommates, too." She offered to help her roommates as they did their apartment cleaning assignments. At first each roommate was suspicious of her offer, certain she must have some ulterior motive. "They told me later . . . that they felt as if I was trying to help them out of pity. . . . After we got over this barrier, I found that we were actually enjoying working together." She reported growing closer to each roommate with whom she worked.

President Henry B. Eyring has promised that if we seek opportunities to work in behalf of others, "the Atonement working in our lives will produce in us the love and tenderness we need" (Eyring, 1986, p. 75). Once when he and his wife were "both under pressure" and rushing to get out the door, he was struck by the thought that serving others is the purpose of all God-given gifts. So he asked his wife if there was anything he could do to help. He writes:

> There was—I made the bed. It was such a small thing that I'm sure it doesn't sound very impressive to you, and it probably wasn't very impressive to her either. I could have done more. But as I did that simple little thing . . . when I gave of my time in a way I thought the Savior would want me to for my wife, not only did my love for her increase—I also felt *his* love for her. I promise you that if you'll use your gifts to serve someone else, you'll feel the Lord's love for that person (Eyring, 1997, pp. 87–88).

All Family Members Are Vital to Family Work

How, then, do parents lovingly include children in family work? Young children want to help, and working with them can be fun. But as they mature and become more capable, they are influenced by the wider culture to avoid family work. Teenagers, perhaps skilled and mature enough to see a need and do the job, are often too busy. Even so, President Thomas S. Monson counsels, "Mothers, share household duties. It is often easier to do everything yourself than to persuade your children to help, but it is so essential for them to learn the importance of doing their share" (2005, p. 20).

Children can learn to take responsibility for family work. To succeed, parents must have faith that the inevitable conflicts involved in helping children participate in family work will, in the long run, bless the children. Interestingly, among the families we interviewed, those who felt most successful were parents who had learned to enjoy family work. They did not waste energy complaining about the workload, wishing it would go away, or punishing children for less than adequate performance.

Today it is politically correct to believe that children should freely choose what they want to do, that parents have little right to insist on participation in family work. Yet the Lord teaches us that we have an obligation to see the needs of others and respond to them in loving ways. The Lord has high expectations, for He knows our capabilities. Similarly, parents should have high expectations for their children.

We can establish these expectations in caring ways, but children need to know their participation in family work is not optional. Laman and Lemuel, after being reminded of their duty to family and God, still refused to help build the ship, but Nephi insisted that lack of support was not an option. Guided by inspiration, he insisted that "neither should they withhold their labor from me" (1 Nephi 17:49) because the Lord had commanded them to participate. To insist that children help when they would rather do their own thing does not damage self-esteem; it aids the discovery of true worth. Such insistence says, "I need you. You are an essential member of our family. We cannot get along without you or your help."

At every age, children respond best when working alongside parents or other children, but even when they work alone, they benefit from the experience. Canadian scholars who compared children who do "self-care tasks" (making own beds, cleaning own messes) with children who participate in "family-care tasks" (setting the table, washing family dishes, folding family laundry) found "an overall pattern of results suggesting that beneficial effects of household work occur . . . when that work involves assistance to others, when it is required on a routine or self-regulating basis, and when the outcome variable is concern for others revealed in the family context" (Grusec, Goodnow, & Cohen, 1996, p. 1006). In other words, children learn to care for others by doing work that helps them think about others.

Mothers set the household tone for family work. Most parents want children to work in order to develop a work ethic, in anticipation of the child's future employment. However, sociologist Robert Bellah and his colleagues

caution, "The problem is not so much the presence or absence of a 'work ethic' as [it is] the meaning of work and the ways it links, or fails to link, individuals to one another" (Bellah, Madsen, Sullivan, Swidler, & Tipton, 1985, p. 56). Such linking has less to do with what is accomplished than with how work is done—alone or together, for self or others, grudgingly or with joy. Guiding family work toward a context that connects family members is an important aspect of mothers' work, because they usually spend the most time with both the relevant chores and the children. The subtle difference between a mother who emphasizes how work is done and one who emphasizes what work is done yields startling results, as noted by anthropologist Dorothy Lee:

> We have built homes as if they were backgrounds to set off our imaginatively selected furniture and fabrics, our artistic arrangements and color combinations. . . . Somehow we forgot to build a home for a zestful, boisterous, untidy existence; full of the opportunity and invitation to real talk and quarreling and anguish and absorbing spontaneous activities. . . . Does my kitchen invite a rush of noisy feet to find out what is cooking, to batter me with excited accounts of the day's happenings or even with offers of help? Or have I planned it so successfully, with such step-saving, muscle-bound efficiency, that it freezes out my husband and my children? (1964, p. 45).

One young mother recalls pondering during scripture study why family work constantly requires every hour of every day. While reading about the law of Moses, she realized that "just as the law was designed to remind the people of the Lord, our family work has been designed to point our hearts toward the central reason we are here on the earth—to build a family." If children were never underfoot and only had to be fed once a day, parents would get distracted. "But because they are spitting up on us, whining to us, dumping cereal on our floors, and saying 'Mommy?' all day, there's no way we can forget [where] our focus needs to be" (Personal correspondence, 2010).

Obviously, commitment to the meaningfulness of family work does not make a mother's experience easy in a culture where women no longer share everyday family work with their extended family and neighbors.

Especially with preschoolers, progress may be barely measurable. A mother who began working with her children when they were very young told of eventual unexpected rewards:

> I had four surgeries last year, and I spent months recovering. On days that were really hard, my children would send me to bed, and they would clean the whole downstairs for me. My 6-year-old likes to polish the wood table . . . , my 7-year-old can do the dishes . . . and my 10-year-old can manage the other two children, take out trash, and put things in their places. . . . I would go downstairs and say, "Oh! How did the house get so clean?" And then they would walk me around, showing me everything they did. It brings tears to my eyes just to think about it (Personal correspondence, 2010).

Award-winning journalist Jeannette Batz describes the extremes in attitude a mother can experience and the importance of goodwill in performing family work:

> Housework fail[ed] to interest me. I shirked most of its chores for years, studiously shunning marriage until I found someone who didn't expect me to retrieve and launder his socks. Then, as irony would have it, I began to enjoy washing his socks. I started collecting 1950s cookbooks and asking older ladies whether mayonnaise really removes white rings from wood tables. Either I was turning into my mother or this realm was more powerful than I'd thought. Banking on the latter, I plotted out a doctoral dissertation and began researching the symbolic and spiritual meanings of housework. What I learned convinced me that the chores I'd branded oppressive and mundane are creative and profound, bringing us closer to the earth, to each other and to God. At least, that's true when they're done with love. Freshly laundered sheets tucked with care can symbolize and reinforce family stability, keeping home a haven from a cold, confusing world. The same sheets, stained and crumpled and flung angrily across the bed, can undermine that security (Batz, 2007, pp. 78–79).

Fathers set the example for participation in household chores. The scriptures repeatedly teach the importance of daily labor and the dangers of idleness or seeking ease. Nephi, King Benjamin, and the prophet Alma taught that even high priests and kings should labor with their own hands (2 Nephi 5:17, Mosiah 2:14, Alma 27:4), and Paul, as an apostle and missionary, did the same (Acts 20:34; 2 Thessalonians 3:8–10). Fathers sometimes have difficulty accepting responsibility for family work traditionally associated with women. Jesse Crosby, a neighbor to Joseph Smith, recorded the following:

> Some of the home habits of the Prophet—such as building kitchen fires, carrying out ashes, carrying in wood and water, assisting in the care of the children, etc.—were not in accord with my idea of a great man's self-respect. [An occasion when] the Prophet [returned a] sack of flour gave me the opportunity to give him some corrective advice which I had desired to do for a long time. I reminded him of every phase of his greatness and called to his mind the multitude of tasks he performed that were too menial for such as he. . . . The Prophet listened quietly to all I had to say, then made his answer in these words: "If there be humiliation in a man's house, who but the head of that house should or could bear that humiliation?" . . . Thinking to give the Prophet some light on home management, I said to him, "Brother Joseph, my wife does much more hard work than does your wife." Brother Joseph replied by telling me that if a man cannot learn in this life to appreciate a wife and do his duty by her, in properly taking care of her, he need not expect to be given one in the hereafter. His words shut my mouth as tight as a clam. I took them as terrible reproof. After that I tried to do better by the good wife I had and tried to lighten her labors (2004, p. 141).

Fathers' actions influence their children's attitudes toward family work. A father who assumes responsibility for a single significant daily task, such as washing dishes, and actively gathers his children to help him, is a powerful example of partnership and service within his home. Author Orson Scott Card advises:

> Your household is a 24-hour-a-day enterprise. You do a part of your work at the office or shop or school or on the road, but that's not the end of

your working day. The good thing is: When you get home, you get to do the rest of your day's work in the company of, or in support of, the person you love most in all the world (2010, p. 3).

He goes on to suggest that new husbands learn three things: "1. Your wife may become a mother, but you are not one of her children. . . . 2. There is no job so hard or disgusting that your wife can do it and you can't. . . . 3. If you do it now, she won't have to do it later" (p. 1).

Other benefits may accrue as well. Sociologists Scott Coltrane and Michele Adams found that school-aged children who do chores with their fathers are more likely to get along with their peers and have more friends, and they are less likely to disobey teachers, make trouble at school, or be depressed or withdrawn. Coltrane and others reported that wives see domestic contributions by husbands as evidence of love and caring and are therefore more sexually attracted to their spouses (Coltrane, 2010).

Family Work Becomes a Joyful Blessing When Not Seen as a Burden

The daily rituals of family work are the Lord's gift and blessing to all people and cultures, providing daily opportunities for parents to teach while working alongside their children, for husbands to draw closer to their wives, and for siblings to bond while they work together to serve the family. Daily rituals of cooking, packing lunches, washing dishes, making beds, folding laundry, weeding gardens, sweeping floors, and countless other prosaic tasks are the invisible glue that can bind families together. Instead of asking how to make such work go away, parents should ask how to use it to increase love and joy in their families.

Jesus Christ taught that our willingness to perform these life-sustaining tasks will separate the sheep from the goats at the time of judgment: "For I was an hungered, and ye gave me meat: I was thirsty, and ye gave me drink: I was a stranger, and ye took me in: Naked, and ye clothed me: I was sick, and ye visited me: I was in prison, and ye came unto me." Answering the query of the righteous as to when they had done so, the Savior responded, "Verily I say unto you, Inasmuch as ye have done it unto one of the least of these my brethren, ye have done it unto me" (Matthew 25:35–36, 40). In a world that now rewards and glorifies the work we

do outside of the home and minimizes the value of humble work within our homes, perhaps it is appropriate to include within the Savior's meaning of the "least of these" the caring for our children, sisters, brothers, spouses, and parents in our own homes.

Kathleen Slaugh Bahr *is a retired associate professor in the School of Family Life at Brigham Young University. She and her husband, Howard, are the parents of five sons.* **Kristine Manwaring** *has a master's degree in sociology from Brigham Young University and has taught in the School of Family Life at BYU. She and her husband, Todd, are the parents of four children.* **Cheri Loveless** *is an at-home mother, author, professional editor, and civic activist. She and her husband, Scott, have eight children and eleven grandchildren.* **Erika Bailey Bahr** *graduated from BYU in communications. She is married to Alden Bahr. She is working as a rich media associate producer with lds.org.*

References

Bahr, K. S., & Bahr, H. M. (1993). Autonomy, community, and the mediation of value: Comments on Apachean grandmothering, cultural change, and the media. *Family Perspective, 27*(4), 347–374.

Batz, J. (2007). The joys of housework: Late have I loved it. In A. Peck (Ed.), *Next to godliness: Finding the sacred in housekeeping* (pp. 78–81). Woodstock, VT: Skylight Paths Publishing.

Bellah, R. N., Madsen, R., Sullivan, W. M., Swidler, A., & Tipton, S. M. (1985). *Habits of the heart: Individualism and commitment in American Life.* Berkeley: University of California Press.

Berry, W. (1987). Men and women in search of common ground. In *Home Economics: Fourteen Essays* (pp. 112–122). New York: North Point Press.

Card, O. S. (2010, May 27). Husbands need to pick up the slack. *MormonTimes.com.* Retrieved from http://www.mormontimes.com/article/13599/Husbands-need-to-pick-up

Carver, T. N. (1913). Home economics from a man's point of view. *Journal of Home Economics, 5,* 291–300.

Coltrane, S. (2010). Personal communication with Kathleen Slaugh Bahr.

Cowan, R. S. (1983). *More work for mother: The ironies of household technology from the open hearth to the microwave.* New York: Basic Books.

Cox, F. D. (1996). *Human intimacy: Marriage, the family, and its meaning* (6th ed.). St. Paul, MN: West Publishing.

Crosby, J. W. (2004). Jesse W. Crosby. In H. L. Andrus & H. M. Andrus, *They knew the prophet: Personal accounts from over 100 people who knew Joseph Smith* (pp. 144–145). American Fork, UT: Covenant Communications.

Demos, J. (1986). The changing faces of fatherhood. In *Past, present, and personal: The family and the life course in American history* (pp. 41–67). New York: Oxford University Press.

Doherty, W. J. (1999). *The intentional family: Simple rituals to strengthen family ties*. New York: Avon Paperbacks.

Eyring, H. B. (1986, November). The spark of faith. *Ensign, 16,* 74–75.

Eyring, H. B. (1997). *To draw closer to God: A collection of discourses*. Salt Lake City: Deseret Book.

Galbraith, J. K. (1973, August). The economics of the American housewife. *Atlantic Monthly, 232*(2), 78–83.

Gilbreth, F. B. (1912, November). Scientific management in the household. *Journal of Home Economics, 4,* 438–447.

Grusec, J. E., Goodnow, J. J., & Cohen, L. (1996). Household work and the development of concern for others. *Developmental Psychology, 32,* 999–1007.

Hinckley, G. B. (1996, September). First presidency message: Four simple things to help our families and our nations. *Ensign, 26,* 2–8.

Hunt, C. L. (1901, June–July). Revaluations. Paper presented at the Third Annual Conference on Home Economics, Lake Placid, NY.

Keniston, K., & Carnegie Council on Children (1977). *All our children: the American family under pressure*. New York: Harcourt Brace Jovanovich.

Kimball, S. W. (1977, November). Welfare services: the gospel in action. *Ensign, 7,* 76–79.

Lee, D. (1959). *Freedom and culture*. New Jersey: Prentice-Hall.

Lee, D. (1964, Spring/Summer). Home economics in a changing world. *Penney's Fashion and Fabrics, 13,* 45.

Maxwell, N. A. (1998, September). The pathway of discipleship. *Ensign, 28,* 6–8.

McKeever, W. A. (1913, April). The new child labor movement. *Journal of Home Economics, 5,* 137–139.

Monson, T. S. (2005, May). Constant truths for changing times. *Ensign, 35,* 19–22.

Morson, G. S. (1988, Autumn). Prosaics: An approach to the humanities. *American Scholar, 57,* 515–528.

Morson, G. S. (2007). *Anna Karenina in our time: Seeing more wisely*. New Haven, CT: Yale University Press.

Nelson, R. M. (1999, May). Our sacred duty to honor women. *Ensign, 29,* 38–40.

Richards, E. H. (1910). The outlook in home economics. *Journal of Home Economics, 2,* 17–18.

Ruddick, S. (1984). Maternal thinking. In J. Trebilcot (Ed.) *Mothering: Essays in feminist theory* (pp. 213–230). Totowa, NJ: Rowman & Allanheld.

Sherif, M., & Sherif, C. W. (1953). *Groups in harmony and tension: An integration of Studies of Intergroup Relations*. New York: Harper & Brothers.

Smith, D. E. (1996). *Investigating playfulness in family process.* Unpublished data gathered for Ph.D. dissertation, Brigham Young University. On file with Kathleen Slaugh Bahr, not paginated.

Stearns, P. N. (2003). *Anxious parents: A history of modern childrearing in America*. New York: New York University Press.

Van Duzer, A. L., Andrix, E. M., Bobenmyer, E. L., Hawkins, E. M., Hemmersbaugh, M. E., & Page, E. P. (1951). *The girl's daily life*. Chicago: J. B. Lippincott.

Weinstein, G. W. (1985, August). Money games parents play. *Redbook,* 106–107, 138–139.

Willes, F. M. S. (n.d.). *The story of my life* (pp. 1–14). Unpublished typed manuscript. On file with Kathleen Slaugh Bahr.

Zelizer, V. A. (1985). *Pricing the priceless child: The changing social value of children*. New York: Basic Books.

CHAPTER 22

Wholesome Family Recreation: Building Strong Families

Mark A. Widmer and Stacy T. Taniguchi

Successful marriages and families are established and maintained on principles of
faith, prayer, repentance, forgiveness, respect, love, compassion, work, and wholesome recreational activities.

RECREATION CAN BE EASY. WE ALL KNOW HOW TO find fun things to do. In our current world, we are immersed in a plethora of entertaining technology. We have access to a variety of television programming; we have myriad interactive video games. If we are on the go, we have smart phones that access the digital airways. Opportunities to recreate surround us. The choices are endless. But we must consider the implications of these different recreation choices for the quality of our lives and families.

In many developed countries around the world, people tend to make poor choices regarding the use of discretionary time. Our free time should be used wisely to create the best possible life, to promote individual growth and strengthen families. Meaningful recreation does not just happen; it must be prepared for, cultivated, and privately defended (Csikszentmihályi, 1990). In general, we spend an inordinate amount of time with electronic media and, as a result, become disconnected from one another (Putnam, 2000; Rideout, Foehr, & Roberts, 2010). We have lost vital and nourishing connections to nature; many of us do not exercise, are overweight, and work too much (Aldana, 2005; De Graaf, 2003; Louv, 2005). We suffer from depression, anxiety, and discontent. Wholesome family recreation can help us strengthen our relationships and reduce negative emotional and spiritual consequences. Wholesome recreation strengthens families.

The purpose of this chapter is to explore how our recreation choices directly influence quality of life for both individuals and families. Problems associated with seeking contemporary happiness are identified. This chapter will provide insights and principles from theory and research about what forms of recreation lead to a good life, and why it is important to understand how to choose free-time activities that truly are "wholesome recreation" (¶ 7). In the context of recent admonitions by modern-day prophets, specific parallels between revealed truth and research are identified. This information can help readers reflect on their own recreation and understand how to create wholesome recreation in the family.

The Failure of Contemporary Happiness

Psychologists and social philosophers describe *contemporary happiness* as transient states of feeling well (Hudson, 1992). In practical terms, contemporary happiness is characterized by the pursuit of comfort, pleasure, and wealth in the form of material goods. Acquisition of these values is often a personal or solitary pursuit, not conducive to family well-being because family members are not a part of these pursuits. For example, coauthor Stacy loves to play golf. Yet his family has no interest in golf. His pursuit of golf takes him away from his wife and children. In moderation, this might not be a problem, and Stacy is certainly a responsible father. But many of us have seen a pattern of behavior where a parent, hoping to find individual comfort or pleasure, engages obsessively in recreation apart from family. As a result, such an excessive obsession for a recreational activity may cause discord and disunity amongst family members rather than achieving the goal to strengthen family ties.

Pleasure and comfort as means to happiness. Pleasure, when sought for its own sake and as an end in and of itself, is not useful in finding happiness. Pleasurable experiences are characterized by strong positive emotions. Although these strong positive emotions are highly desired, they are often short lived. You eat a great meal and soon it is forgotten. You come in chilled and aching from hours in cold weather and it feels great to stand by the fire. An hour later, standing by the fire may become uncomfortably warm. We may believe we will be happier if we get a beautiful new house with all the modern comforts, or if we can go on cruises in the Caribbean and lie on white sandy beaches in the sun. Research suggests seeking more comfortable or pleasurable circumstances is likely to only bring temporary happiness. This is because, as Lyubomirsky (2008) suggests, "human beings are remarkably adept at becoming rapidly accustomed to sensory or physiologic changes" (p. 48). Psychologists refer to this as hedonic adaptation or the hedonic treadmill. We seek pleasure or comfort, thinking it will make us happy, but soon become accustomed to the new pleasure or comfort and then continue to seek something more appealing. Pleasure, when sought as an ultimate good, appears to have little or no positive influence on mental health or development (Lyubomirsky, Sheldon, & Schkade, 2005; Seligman, 2002).

In contrast, activities requiring concerted effort can be considered less pleasurable than relaxing activities, and such less-pleasurable activities are not accompanied by a separable stream of positive emotion like most pleasurable activities. Rather, these activities often consist of total engagement and loss of self-consciousness. Research suggests that feelings arising from overcoming challenges are rated as much more meaningful than pleasurable activities, such as watching television, which pale by comparison (Seligman, 2002).

Lyubomirsky (2008) differentiates between experiences of gratification due to personal effort and experiences of pleasure that are provided by the environment (like watching TV or eating pizza). This is a key distinction. Gratification results when we invest rather than consume. For example, when we spend our free time interacting with our families by reading to our children, teaching them to ride a bike, playing a board game, gardening together, or going backpacking, we build knowledge, relationships, memories, and skills. These forms of family recreation promote social and psychological growth. On the other hand, pleasure often involves consuming—like tasting chocolate, buying new clothes, or getting a massage. These experiences do not build higher levels of social knowledge, relationships, or skills, but simply satiate basic biological needs and desires.

The following example from research illustrates this distinction and the different outcomes related to these two different types of experiences. Researchers gathered data from two large groups of teenagers (Seligman, 2002). They measured variables related to quality of life and psychological well-being. One group, called the "Mall Kids," went to the mall after school to hang out, flirt, play video games, and do what mall kids do. The other group, called the "Chore Kids," typically went home to do homework and chores or stayed after school to engage in extracurricular activities like sports, music, or art. When asked, the Chore Kids said the Mall Kids were having more fun. Yet, the Chore Kids scored higher on measures of quality of life and subjective well-being. Here again is an example of the difference between pleasurable, consumptive activities and constructive activities requiring psychological and physical investment. Activities that appear to be fun or pleasurable do not necessarily lead to a good life. The challenge and adversity in the Chore Kids' lives provided structure, required self-discipline, and resulted in a sense of accomplishment and identity.

Consider the contrast between a family going on a cruise for vacation and a family going to a developing country to work in an orphanage. The cruise (a consumptive activity) would certainly provide pleasure, comfort, and memories. The orphanage experience (an investment activity) may not be pleasurable or comfortable, but it is more likely to produce stronger family relationships, compassion, skills, knowledge, and more valuable memories than the cruise. Coauthor Mark and his family are avid mountain bikers. Even when the kids were as young as 7 years old, they went to Canyonlands National Park and spent three days riding the 100-mile White Rim Trail. Because this activity required each family member to invest him- or herself physically and mentally in the efforts required to stay together and finish the ride together, this mountain biking experience provided great memories, a feeling of accomplishment, and a sense of identity for both the individuals and the family. Today, the kids still love to ride, and Mark and his sons enjoy competing in bike races. The investment involved in this pursuit has resulted in great dividends.

Wealth and material goods as means to happiness. Advertisers spend their time finding ways to convince us we need what they are selling in order to find happiness.

The media portray happiness as wealth, status, and ostentatious possessions, such as a large beautiful home with a pool and a boat. These misleading expectations leave us feeling like we need more, bigger, better, and faster things. Parents often use their discretionary funds to buy recreation toys. Next time you drive down the freeway, look at the number of expensive ski boats, ATVs, and RVs. Unfortunately, many families go into significant debt to buy these toys that they believe will bring happiness. Skiing, wake boarding, and mountain biking can be excellent family activities, but the expense of the toys required to participate in these activities must be reasonably considered. The quest for bigger and better things is like the quest for pleasure and can easily defeat the important reasons for participating in recreational activities as a family. The pursuit of toys can become like running on a treadmill going nowhere.

As it happens, little or no meaningful relationship exists between wealth and happiness among people above the poverty level (Lyubomirsky, 2008). Although strong relationships are reported between the wealth of nations and happiness, the correlations tend to disappear when looking at individual income and happiness of people above the poverty level. People who place high importance on material goods over values like family relationships and community are likely to be unhappy (Deci & Flaste, 1996; Diener & Biswas-Diener, 2002). Marriage, family, education, and other forms of social capital are better predictors of subjective well-being than money (Helliwell & Putnam, 2004). Money cannot buy happiness. Philosophers and religious leaders have warned societies for centuries, and psychologists now agree: the pursuit of money as a means of happiness is misguided.

Beyond individual happiness, the pursuit of money and material goods often creates difficulty and stress within marriages and families. Elder Joseph B. Wirthlin (2004, p. 42) said:

> Brothers and sisters, beware of covetousness. It is one of the great afflictions of these latter days. It creates greed and resentment. Often it leads to bondage, heartbreak, and crushing, grinding debt. The number of marriages that have been shattered over money issues is staggering. The amount of heartbreak is great. The stress that comes from worry over money has burdened families, caused sickness, depression, and even premature death.

If Happiness Is Not the Answer, What Is?

Research on the effect of extrinsically and intrinsically motivated aspirations found that people who focus on pleasure, wealth, and material goods are likely to experience poorer mental health—reflected in higher levels of anxiety and depression and poor social functioning. In contrast, people who "focus on developing satisfying personal relationships, growing as individuals, and contributing to their community" are among the healthiest in society (Deci & Flaste, 1996, p. 129; Kasser & Ryan, 1993; Kasser & Ryan, 1996).

If pleasure, wealth, material goods, and beauty do not lead to happiness, what will? Or perhaps we are asking the wrong question. Do we really want to be happy? Apparently not; at least not all the time. This answer may be surprising at first. Deci and Flaste wrote:

> In truth, happiness is not all that it's cracked up to be, and most people don't really want to be happy all the time anyway. People often choose to go to movies or operas that are very unsettling—that terrify, sadden, disgust, or anger them. There is something about experiencing these emotions, whether in the safe and comfortable context of a theater or at a dangerous mountain pass in the Himalayas that is appealing to many people. . . . *The true meaning of being alive is not just to feel happy, but to experience the full range of human emotions* (1996, p.192, italics in original).

They continue, "Happy is simply the wrong concept for what it is that is natural to people, for what it is that they seek and what it is that promotes human development" (p. 192). So, do we really want to be happy? Not if happiness is characterized by superficial sources and ephemeral moments of enjoyment. Instead, what we seek is really found in "the great plan of happiness" (Alma 42:8); we seek fulfillment and gratification.

One perspective on activities that bring fulfillment is identified in the work of Csikszentmihályi (1997), who began a quest to understand what leads to our best experiences, which he called *optimal experiences*. Many years of research found that optimal experiences have common features. By gathering data about daily experiences from people across the world, researchers found that people become bored when their activities lack challenge. When they engage in activities exceeding their skill level, they experience anxiety or frustration. Between boredom and anxiety is an area of experience called "flow." Flow, or optimal experience, occurs when our skill level is matched by the challenge. People identify these experiences as the most meaningful in their lives (Csikszentmihályi, 1997). These experiences have eight common elements: We are (a) confronting tasks that we have a chance of completing; (b) we are able to concentrate on what we are doing; (c) we have clear goals; (d) we receive immediate feedback; (e) we act with deep awareness, but have effortless involvement, forgetting our cares and worries; (f) the experience allows us to exercise a sense of control; and (g) our concern for self disappears, yet the sense of self becomes stronger after the experience. Finally, and perhaps most noticeable, (h) the sense of duration of time is altered (Csikszentmihályi, 1997).

Failure of contemporary happiness may stem from our misguided assumption that we can make ourselves happy by seeking wealth and possessions that give us comfort and pleasure. Instead, we should intentionally create experiences that provide opportunities for challenge and growth for ourselves and our families.

Contemporary Constraints on Family Recreation

Life is complicated and full of demands. The expectation to experience wholesome recreation while we travel down life's road does not make life any easier. Recognizing the potholes along the way and the probable consequences if we step in them can help us avoid them, making the journey easier. Barriers restricting our recreation participation are called constraints. Constraints are factors assumed to "limit the formation of leisure preferences and/or to inhibit or prohibit participation and enjoyment of leisure" (Jackson, 2000, p. 62). Common constraints include the lack of time, lack of skills and abilities, the cost of participating, or even social isolation.

Perhaps the most influential constraint directly influencing wholesome family recreation is time. During the end of the 20th century, the annual workload of the average American worker increased about 16 percent, or almost five weeks of work (Golden, 2009). In an average U.S. household, the paid hours of work for both the husband and wife increased 388 hours per year (Schor, 2003).

In Europe, the average worker earns about six weeks of paid vacation each year, while Americans are lucky to get two. Overwork directly affects the family, adding stress and reducing opportunities for positive interaction. Parents work more, kids have more schoolwork and more opportunities to participate in sports and extracurricular activities, and, generally, more demands on their already busy lives. Competition to get on teams or get into college requires greater commitment and more time to prepare. The result is less time together as families for wholesome family recreation, including eating meals together, and even going on vacations together. Choices about how we use our time become limited. In reference to a research study on time, Elder Dallin H. Oaks (2007, p. 105) said,

> Family experts have warned against what they call "the overscheduling of children" (Anderson & Doherty, 2005). . . . Among many measures of this disturbing trend are the reports that structured sports time has doubled, but children's free time has declined by 12 hours per week and unstructured outdoor activities have fallen by 50 percent. The number of those who reported that their "whole family usually eats dinner together" has declined 33 percent. . . . There is inspired wisdom in this advice to parents: what your children really want for dinner is you.

As we experience this time crunch, we are more likely to engage in recreation that provides a sense of escape. Escapist recreation is easily accessed and does not require interaction with other humans; therefore, it is convenient. It includes activities like surfing the Internet, texting, watching television, and playing video games. We have multiple televisions in our homes, personal computers at work and home, digital music players in our pockets that plug into our ears, and cell phones within easy reach (Roberts & Foehr, 2008). We seem to be connected to the whole world electronically, yet disconnected to those closest to us. Some of these activities generally organize our consciousness for us and do not require much mental or physical effort. All of these escapist activities tend to isolate us from other family members. They may provide great relaxation, which sometimes is needed, but are not nearly as valuable in promoting family growth and development. The time crunch not only leads to escapist recreation, but also makes it less likely we will engage in some of the more meaningful recreation experiences that are more difficult to access, such as attending arts events, giving service, and enjoying nature.

Another constraint to wholesome family recreation is our addiction to escapist forms of entertainment. We are tied to our mobile phones, iPods, and the Internet. We text, Tweet, and look at Facebook during many of our waking hours. As a result, children and their parents are spending little if any time together or out in nature. This movement away from wholesome family recreation such as hiking, camping, and simply spending time in our backyards may hold negative consequences for children and families.

In his book, *Last Child in the Woods*, Richard Louv (2005) argues that individuals and families have become disconnected from nature and consequently are suffering from what he calls Nature Deficit Disorder (NDD). Parents and grandparents of today's youth grew up outdoors, working and playing together with friends, neighbors, and family. Today, families are increasingly spending large amounts of leisure time indoors, usually spending that time with electronic media (Rideout et al., 2010). In general, research suggests that nature plays an important role in promoting health and well-being (Maller, Townsend, Pryor, Brown, & St Leger, 2006). Louv reports that nature experiences have a direct influence on physical health; simple contact with nature, such as watching fish in an aquarium, owning a pet, working in a garden, or having a view of nature through a window can reduce blood pressure, increase survival after heart attacks, and increase speed of recovery after surgery. Stress-reducing contact with nature can influence mental and emotional well-being; children are more likely to be depressed or have a low sense of self-worth and to be less creative and resilient under high levels of stress. Adults, as well, experience reduced stress in the presence of nature. And for children, some evidence suggests that nature can attenuate attention deficit hyperactivity disorder (ADHD) (Louv, 2005).

While outdoor family activities are not the only forms of wholesome family recreation, our research suggests that as families participate in challenging outdoor adventure activities together, communication patterns are strengthened (Huff, Widmer, McCoy, & Hill, 2003). When families are together for an extended time in the outdoors, they are able to reconnect with each other. The absence of cell phones, Internet, and television allows family members to interact. When families take the time and make the effort to go hiking, camping, and backpacking, and engage in other outdoor pursuits, they learn to cope with new and diverse environments as a family. These types of wholesome family recreational experiences promote family members' beliefs in their ability to resolve conflicts at home (Wells, Widmer, & McCoy, 2004). Nevertheless, planning and engaging in these forms of recreation can be time-consuming and difficult. Most families are packing in so many activities that adding experiences in nature may feel more like another burden than a joy. It is just easier to watch nature shows on TV, play video games, or surf the Internet in our free time. The concern with the trend toward spending far less time in nature, in part, is that it leads to spending less time together as a family. Even families who spend time together in their homes may struggle with the isolation created by the use of technology.

The time and effort required to engage in wholesome recreation, whether it involves taking part in a play or going camping, is well worth the effort. For example, a few years ago, a group of families joined our research team in a remote area of northern Arizona. The parents each had faced challenges with their children, such as substance abuse, depression, and failure in school. They came to take part in a four-day survival experience we were conducting as part of our research program. With limited equipment and food, the families hiked and climbed across dry and rugged desert mountains. They drank water out of standing pools filled with bugs and other interesting floating objects and slept on the ground with only a wool blanket. They learned how to build fires without matches. On the third evening, after a long, difficult, hot day, the families each selected a campsite on the top of a mesa. Tired and hungry, they tried to build fires using bow drills, a somewhat difficult task for the inexperienced. One family, with two teenage daughters who had struggled with substance abuse over a long period of time, settled in to build a fire. The father held the bow drill tightly in his hand, with the base plate under one foot and the other hand pushing down on the spindle with a rock. The daughters sat across from him. One daughter anxiously held a nest of dried grass and bark to start the fire once the father created a burning coal. Near the father, the mother also sat on the ground, legs folded, waiting patiently.

The father began to push the bow back and forth to spin the spindle. After one or two strokes, the spindle would pop out and fly away. He would get up, walk over, pick it up, come back, and try again. This scenario repeated itself for about 10 minutes. During that time, in the dark of night, you could hear other families across the mesa yelling with excitement as they lit a coal and started their fires. The daughters grew visibly impatient as their father struggled, without success, to light a coal. He began sweating and continued to wipe beads of sweat off his bald head with his shirtsleeve. After six or seven attempts, the spindle flew out again, landing about 12 feet from the circled family. One of the daughters got up, walked over, picked up the spindle, and brought it back to her father. She then sat down next to him. As he got the bow drill ready to go, she put her foot next to his on the base plate and then put her hand over her father's to add pressure to the rock holding the top of the spindle. Together, they pushed the bow back and forth. For the first time, the spindle stayed in place, and in a few seconds smoke began rising from the base plate. They continued until they had a bright red coal, which the father took and carefully placed in the nest held by the other daughter. Holding the nest like a precious baby, she blew softly on the coal until a flame erupted from the nest. Overcome with relief and excitement, they all began screaming and hugging each other.

A day later, at the closing of the experience, the families gathered as a group. The father of these teenage girls recounted their bow drill fire experience of the previous night. As he described his daughter picking up the spindle, coming back, and giving it to him, his voice slowed and cracked as he choked up. Then he told the entire group that for years he had seen his daughter, her drug abuse, her lies, and her terrible behaviors as one big problem. He had felt nothing but frustration, anger, and contempt for her. He then told them how she helped him by bringing the spindle back to him, and how when she put her hand on his hand to help hold the spindle, he felt a flow of love from her hand to his, to his whole being. He felt again the love that had been lost in their conflicts over the past few years. When he closed his story, his daughter, now holding his hand, told her story, and how she, too, had through this experience come to appreciate and love her father again. She had seen him as a controlling religious zealot who was trying to force her into a lifestyle she wanted to escape. The family adventure

in the wilderness created a shared experience requiring the family members to work together in order to be successful. The experience also allowed this family to leave behind the technology and problems of home and create new relationships in a quiet, peaceful setting in nature. This example involves extreme circumstances that not all families would need or want to face, but it shows that participation together away from the usual distractions—even in a less rigorous setting, such as having a digital-free evening at home to play family games, make treats, or serve others—can help family members improve communication and see each other in a new light.

The constraints of time and place are not all-inclusive, but they exemplify how easily wholesome family recreation can be diminished or enhanced by the choices we make.

Building the Best Family Experiences: Principles of Wholesome Recreation

Research in the area of family recreation provides evidence-based principles to help us make wise recreational choices. Studies in the areas of marriage, child development, adolescent development, and positive psychology make important contributions to our understanding of wholesome recreation.

Wholesome recreation and marriage. You might think the secret to a great marriage is finding a spouse who loves the same recreational activities that you do. Marital satisfaction and stability, however, do not depend on similar recreational interests. For example, research suggests participating in activities both partners enjoy is only moderately related to the husband's marital satisfaction (Crawford, Houts, Huston, & George, 2002).

We must consider forms of recreation. Orthner and Mancini (1990) described three types of leisure: (a) parallel, (b) joint, and (c) independent. Parallel activities involve multiple members of the family doing the same thing but not interacting with each other very much. Watching movies and television are examples of parallel recreation. Joint recreational activities involve high levels of communication and interdependence. Examples include canoeing, tennis, chess, and rock climbing. Independent activities are those undertaken alone by individuals.

Research suggests that joint activities lead to the highest marital satisfaction (Holman & Jacquart, 1988; Orthner, 1975). Parallel activities have a small positive effect on marital satisfaction, while independent activities may have a negative effect, especially for wives (Orthner & Mancini, 1990). Joint activities strengthen relationships by promoting interaction, communication, and cooperation. Increased interaction in joint activities may also lead to more conflict than parallel activities, but when resolved in a healthy manner, conflict can help relationships grow and improve. Conflicts provide parents with opportunities to model appropriate conflict resolution skills for their children.

Often it is not possible to participate in joint activities, so spouses should support each other's individual activity choices. A study by Baldwin, Ellis, and Baldwin (1999) found spousal support of individual partners' leisure pursuits to be a key predictor of marital satisfaction. Shared activities can be rewarding and valuable in building a healthy marriage, but when spousal support of individual leisure interests wanes, marital satisfaction may be negatively affected. A study by Goff, Fick, and Oppliger (1997) also supports these findings. They found that when one spouse becomes a serious leisure participant (for example, racing triathlons), a lack of spousal support is linked to marital conflict. Serious leisure pursuits like competitive baseball or participating in a musical group may take inordinate time away from the other spouse and family. If the spouse or children feel neglected or that they are carrying an inappropriate share of family responsibility, conflict and low satisfaction result. Placing a priority on family recreation over individual pursuits can be rewarding and will moderate the risk of problems associated with serious leisure and spousal support.

Wholesome recreation and children. Csíkszentmihályi (1990) argued that the habits children develop early in their lives stay with them and are difficult to change. Wiersma and Fifer (2008) found that youth observe their parents' behavior in sports programs and often mimic the behavior when they engage in sports programs on their own. Parents interested in helping their children become flexible and curious should spend quality playtime with them and model good sportsmanship, kindness, and fair play. Time spent playing with children also helps them become more secure and independent (Belsky, Garduque, & Hrncir, 1984; Slade, 1987).

Variation, novelty, and choices are crucial in maintaining a playful attitude and promoting growth in children. Parents who push children to do just one activity, like baseball or dance, may limit opportunities for their children to grow and play. Play is reported as one of life's most enjoyable experiences by fathers, not because of the activity, but because of the joy of being together (Dollahite, Marks, & Olson, 1998). It is a powerful tool to facilitate parent–child connection because it allows the parents to interact on the child's level. Young children love to play not only because it is fun, but also because it makes them feel loved.

Wholesome recreation and adolescents. With the onset of adolescence, many children have less interest in recreation with parents and more interest in being with friends. As teenagers struggle to become independent, a variety of conflicts may naturally arise. Family recreation can create a positive home environment where adolescents feel comfortable discussing conflicts and personal issues. Family recreation can also promote healthy identity development (Hauser, Powers, Noam, Jacobson, Weiss, & Follansbee, 1984; Duerden, Widmer, Taniguchi, & McCoy, 2009).

As adolescents develop their own identities, they evaluate personal experiences, interests, and skills (Erikson, 1963). Varied, diverse, fun, and non-threatening recreational experiences help adolescents identify activities they enjoy. This process allows teens to see how their interests and skills are interrelated. It also gives them a sense of personal uniqueness as they differentiate their interests from those of their parents, siblings, and friends. As they engage in specific activities and develop higher levels of skill, the activities and skills become integrated into their identities. For example, teenagers who study and learn music begin to see themselves as musical. Differentiation and integration are important processes associated with identity development. Research indicates that varied and meaningful recreation promotes positive identity development (Munson & Widmer, 1997). Parents should consider the value of providing varied recreation experiences for their children.

Our own research demonstrates that engaging in challenging outdoor adventures, like learning to rock climb, backpack, fly fish, and mountain bike, promotes healthy adolescent identity development (Duerden et al., 2009). Healthy identity development moderates the risk of delinquent behaviors. In other words, adolescents who develop healthy identities are less likely to be influenced by peers or the media to engage in substance abuse, truancy, theft, and other problematic behaviors. Wholesome family recreation can play an important role in promoting healthy adolescent development and in moderating risky behaviors.

Positive psychology and positive youth development. The focus for many psychologists has shifted from the causes of mental illness in adults to what makes a good life for adults *(positive psychology),* and from cause of juvenile delinquency in adolescents to what leads to positive development in youth *(positive youth development)* (Larson, 2000; Peterson & Seligman, 2004; Seligman, Steen, Park, & Peterson, 2005). Both of these movements provide useful perspectives on how to make recreation wholesome.

Seligman (2002) identifies 24 character strengths possessed by people who report high levels of overall well-being. Examples of these include creativity, curiosity, love of learning, persistence, integrity, kindness, citizenship, forgiveness, humility, gratitude, and spirituality. The possession of character strengths buffers the negative effects of stress and trauma. These strengths are associated with a number of positive outcomes, including success in school, leadership, the ability to delay gratification, and a desire to help others, especially within the family unit (Park, 2004).

Leisure time provides an opportunity to promote positive development in adolescents. But the contrasting controlled environment of school and unstructured free time found after school leaves a void (Larson, 2000, pp. 173–174; Lehto, Choi, Lin, & MacDermid, 2009, pp. 173–174).

> The great majority of adolescents' time is spent in two opposite experiential situations. In schoolwork, they experience concentration and challenge without being intrinsically motivated. In most leisure, including watching TV and interacting with friends, they experience intrinsic motivation but not in a context of concentration and challenge. Neither provides the combination of both of these elements necessary for the experience and development of initiative.

Consequently, Larson suggests, many middle-class youth are bored, alienated, and disconnected. As indicated in the research we cited earlier, leisure time

boredom is linked to drug use, lower academic motivation, dropping out of school, premature sexual involvement, and delinquency (Larson, 2000; Wegner, Flisher, Chikobvu, Lombard, & King, 2008; Widmer, Ellis, & Munson, 2003). This boredom appears, at least in part, to be a result of a lack of engagement with family members in wholesome recreation. It is also likely due to constraints to leisure or the inability to access meaningful activities. As discussed previously, the lack of time, resources, and skills and abilities, as well as social isolation, present barriers to participation in wholesome recreation. Parents might consider each of these constraints and assist their teenagers in finding ways to successfully negotiate the constraints they face.

Wholesome recreation often should include service learning or volunteering opportunities, like tutoring peers, cleaning up the local environment, and helping the elderly. Church programs, Boy Scouts, and after-school programs provide opportunities to serve. Researchers suggest that these programs produce positive outcomes, such as increased academic performance, positive self-concept, and reduced teen pregnancy, delinquency, and academic failure (Catalano, Berglund, Ryan, Lonczak, & Hawkins, 2002). These types of activities can be low cost and often are easily accessible.

Family Recreation: Benefits and Challenges for Families

As the previous section demonstrated, most of the recent literature suggests that family recreation provides a variety of important benefits. Research has shown that family satisfaction with current levels of leisure involvement is a strong predictor of overall satisfaction with family life, even when accounting for income, marital status, age, and history of divorce (Agate, Zabriskie, Agate, & Poff, 2009). Holman and Epperson (1984) suggest that recreational activities involving the family are central to families of every kind. They found a positive relationship between the quality of family relationships and a family's participation in outdoor recreational activities. Other literature cites specific benefits such as enhanced communication, interaction, satisfaction, problem solving, trust, and love (Kugath, 1997; Nelson, Capple, & Adkins, 1995).

Wells and colleagues (2004) found that families who increased their belief in their ability to do outdoor recreation increased their belief in their ability to collectively solve problems at home. Recent unpublished research by the same authors suggests the higher the perceived challenge, the greater the positive changes in communication and conflict resolution.

Studies using the Core and Balance Model have consistently reported direct positive relationships between family leisure involvement and levels of family functioning (Zabriskie & McCormick, 2003). Families who regularly engage in core leisure activities "depicted by common everyday, low-cost, relatively accessible, and often home-based activities that many families do frequently," such as playing board games or playing catch in the yard (Zabriskie & McCormick, p. 168), have higher levels of family cohesiveness than those families who do not regularly engage in such activities. Families who participate in balanced leisure activities, "depicted through activities that are generally less common, less frequent, more out of the ordinary, and usually not home based thus providing novel experiences" (Zabriskie & McCormick, p. 168), such as going to Disneyland or on a cruise, have been found to have higher levels of adaptability than families who do not engage in such activities. Research conducted by Lehto, Choi, Lin, and MacDermid (2009) is among the first studies to find empirical evidence that family vacations, a common example of a balanced activity, are positively correlated with family communication, bonding, and solidarity.

Not all family recreation, however, is bliss and joy. According to Shaw (1997), family recreation should be studied without assuming it is always a positive experience with beneficial outcomes and pure intrinsic motivation. Different family members will have different experiences in the same activity. Added physical and emotional burdens can arise for mothers or other family members who carry the responsibility for preparation and implementation. Families should consider the burdens and responsibilities of each member, making efforts to help everyone enjoy the experience. In a more recent study on family recreation, Shaw (2008) suggests that family leisure has become a responsibility for parents and is not always considered enjoyable, especially for the mother. Many parents, however, feel family leisure is essential for children's positive development and that children can learn life lessons for future success. Shaw argues that family leisure is a responsibility requiring thought, attention, time, and commitment.

Family rituals and celebrations, such as religious rituals, birthdays, or Christmas, may be labor-intensive for some members of the family. But even though such rituals may be challenging, none were noted for having negative influences (Loser, Hill, Klein, & Dollahite, 2009). "Familial benefits of religious rituals included strengthened relationships, more family togetherness and unity, increased communication, less contention and more kindness, [and] better parenting" (p. 345). The effort to create these experiences, although difficult, appears to hold meaningful rewards.

Family meals, a traditional family ritual, have also been found to be beneficial for families. Professional literature relates positive outcomes to family meals: family communication, family cohesiveness, healthy eating patterns, improved literacy, better academic performance, and better mental health of adolescents (Hamilton & Wilson, 2009).

In summary, wholesome family recreation has been shown to provide benefits to marriages and families across the lifespan. Parents should carefully consider how they choose to spend their individual and family time. They should thoughtfully plan in order to create meaningful, memorable, and strengthening experiences for their families.

Conclusion

We live in a world full of opportunities to engage in wholesome family recreation, if we know where to look for them. Wholesome recreation is an intentional process. It can serve to promote positive development in our children, strengthen our marriages, and build strong families. We must know, however, what constitutes wholesome recreation and purposefully seek opportunities for our families to meaningfully recreate together. The components to wholesome recreation include opportunities to verbally communicate, develop skills, face challenges, create memories, share traditions and beliefs, and spend time together in the family setting.

If we are drawn to seek wealth, material goods, and pleasure in the pursuit of happiness, we are likely to miss important opportunities for wholesome family recreation. We may find ourselves struggling with emotional and social difficulties. A truly good life is one characterized by a wide range of emotions. It is a tapestry woven by our struggles as well as our joys. Seeking wholesome family recreation requires each of us to think about happiness and what is truly important to us: family and living in a way that we could stand with confidence before God.

We hope this discussion about flow, nature, time, electronic media, escapist recreation, positive psychology, and positive youth development will provide families with insights about what leads to wholesome family recreation and will help families make wise choices. We believe thoughtful, prayerful consideration and intentional action will help families avoid meaningless leisure and pursue more wholesome recreation.

Mark A. Widmer *is a professor in the Department of Recreation Management in the Marriott School of Management at Brigham Young University. He and his wife, Suzy, are the parents of four children.* Stacy T. Taniguchi *is an assistant professor in the Department of Recreation Management and Youth Leadership in the Marriott School of Management at Brigham Young University. He and his wife, LuAnn, are the parents of four children and they have five grandchildren.*

References

Agate, J. R., Zabriskie, R. B., Agate, S. T., & Poff, R. (2009). Family leisure satisfaction and satisfaction with family life. *Journal of Leisure Research, 41,* 205–223.

Aldana, S. G. (2005). *The culprit and the cure: Why lifestyle is the culprit behind America's poor health and how transforming that lifestyle can be the cure.* Mapleton, UT: Maple Mountain Press.

Anderson, J. R., & Doherty, W. J. (2005) Democratic community initiatives: The case of overscheduled children. *Family Relations, 54,* 654–665.

Baldwin, J. H., Ellis, G. D., & Baldwin, B. M. (1999). Marital satisfaction: An examination of its relationship to spouse support and congruence of commitment among runners. *Leisure Sciences, 21,* 117–131.

Belsky, J., Garduque, L., & Hrncir, E. (1984). Assessing performance, competence, and executive capacity in infant play: Relations to home environment and security of attachment. *Developmental Psychology, 20,* 406–417.

Catalano, R. F., Berglund, M. L., Ryan, J. A. M., Lonczak, H. S., & Hawkins, J. D. (2002). Positive youth development in the United States: Research findings on evaluations of positive youth development programs. *Prevention and Treatment, 5,* 1–117.

Crawford, D. W., Houts, R. M., Huston, T. L., & George, L. J. (2002). Compatibility, leisure, and satisfaction in marital relationships. *Journal of Marriage and Family, 64,* 433–449.

Csikszentmihályi, M. (1990). *Flow: The psychology of optimal experience.* New York: Harper Perennial.

Csikszentmihályi, M. (1997). *Finding flow: The psychology of engagement with everyday life.* New York: Basic Books.

Deci, E. L., & Flaste, R. (1996). *Why we do what we do: Understanding self-motivation.* New York: Penguin Books.

De Graaf, J. (Ed.). (2003). *Take back your time: Fighting overwork and time poverty in America.* San Francisco: Berrett-Koehler Publishers.

Diener, E., & Biswas-Diener, R. (2002). Will money increase subjective well-being? A literature review and guide to needed research. *Social Indicators Research, 57,* 119–169.

Dollahite, D. C., Marks, L. D., & Olson, M. M. (1998). Faithful fathering in trying times: Religious beliefs and practices of Latter-day Saint fathers of children with special needs. *Journal of Men's Studies, 7,* 71–93.

Duerden, M. D., Widmer, M., Taniguchi, S., & McCoy, J. K. (2009). Adventures in identity development: The impact of adventure recreation on adolescent identity development. *Identity, 9,* 341–359.

Erikson, E. H. (1963). *Childhood and society.* New York: W. W. Norton & Co.

Goff, S. J., Fick, D. S., & Oppliger, R. A. (1997). The moderating effect of spouse support on the relation between serious leisure and spouses' perceived leisure–family conflict. *Journal of Leisure Research, 29,* 47–60.

Golden, L. (2009). A brief history of long work time and the contemporary sources of overwork. *Journal of Business Ethics, 84,* 217–227.

Hamilton, S. K., & Wilson, J. H. (2009). Family mealtimes: Worth the effort? *ICAN: Infant, Child, and Adolescent Nutrition, 1,* 346–350.

Hauser, S. T., Powers, S. I., Noam, G. G., Jacobson, A. M., Weiss, B., & Follansbee, D. J. (1984). Familial contexts of adolescent ego development. *Child Development, 55,* 195–213.

Helliwell, J. F., & Putnam, R. D. (2004). The social context of well-being. *Philosophical Transactions of the Royal Society B: Biological Sciences, 359,* 1435–1446.

Holman, T. B., & Epperson, A. (1984). Family and leisure: A review of the literature with research recommendations. *Journal of Leisure Research, 16*(4), 277–294.

Holman, T. B., & Jacquart, M. (1988). Leisure-activity patterns and marital satisfaction: A further test. *Journal of Marriage and the Family, 50,* 69–77.

Hudson, S. (1992). Contemporary views of happiness. In M. J. Adler (Ed.), *The great ideas today: 1992.* Chicago: Encyclopedia Britannica, Inc. 170–216.

Huff, C., Widmer, M., McCoy, K., & Hill, B. (2003). The influence of challenging outdoor recreation on parent–adolescent communication. *Therapeutic Recreation Journal, 37,* 18–37.

Jackson, E. L. (2000). Will research on leisure constraints still be relevant to the twenty-first century? *Journal of Leisure Research, 32,* 62–68.

Kasser, T., & Ryan, R. M. (1996, March). Further examining the American dream: Differential correlates of intrinsic and extrinsic goals. *Personality and Social Psychology 22,* 280–287.

Kasser, T., & Ryan, R. (1993, August). A dark side of the American dream: Correlates of financial success as a central life aspiration. *Journal of Personality and Social Psychology, 65,* 410–422.

Kugath, S. D. (1997). The effects of family participation in an outdoor adventure program. *Back to the Basics: Proceedings of the International Conference on Outdoor Recreation and Education,* 105–124.

Larson, R. W. (2000). Toward a psychology of positive youth development. *American Psychologist, 55,* 170–183.

Lehto, X. Y., Choi, S., Lin, Y. C., & MacDermid, S. M. (2009). Vacation and family functioning. *Annals of Tourism Research, 36,* 459–479.

Loser, R. W., Hill, E. J., Klein, S. R., & Dollahite, D. C. (2009). Perceived benefits of religious rituals in the Latter-Day Saint home. *Review of Religious Research, 50,* 345–362.

Louv, R. (2005). *Last child in the woods.* Chapel Hill, NC: Algonquin Books of Chapel Hill.

Lyubomirsky, S. (2008). *The how of happiness: A scientific approach to getting the life you want.* New York: The Penguin Group.

Lyubomirsky, S., Sheldon, K. M., & Schkade, D. (2005). Pursuing happiness: The architecture of sustainable change. *Review of General Psychology, 9,* 111–131.

Maller, C., Townsend, M., Pryor, A., Brown, P., & St Leger, L. (2006, March). Healthy nature healthy people: "Contact with nature" as an upstream health promotion intervention for populations. *Health Promotion International, 21*(1), 45–54.

Munson, W. W., & Widmer, M. A. (1997). Leisure behavior and occupational identity in university students. *Career Development Quarterly, 46,* 190–198.

Nelson, D. A., Capple, M. L., & Adkins, D. (1995, June). Strengthening families through recreation: Family outdoor recreation activities provide opportunities for skill development and socialization. *Parks and Recreation, 30*(6), 44–47.

Oaks, D. (2007, November). Good, better, best. *Ensign, 37,* 104–108.

Orthner, D. K. (1975). Leisure activity patterns and marital satisfaction over the marital career. *Journal of Marriage and the Family, 37,* 91–102.

Orthner, D. K., & Mancini, J. A. (1990). Leisure impacts on family-interaction and cohesion. *Journal of Leisure Research, 22*(2), 125–137.

Park, N. (2004). Character strengths and positive youth development. *Annals of the American Academy of Political and Social Science, 591,* 40–54.

Peterson, C., & Seligman, M. E. P. (2004). *Character strengths and virtues: A handbook and classification.* Cary, NC: Oxford University.

Putnam, R. D. (2000). Technology and mass media. In *Bowling alone: The collapse and revival of American community* (pp. 216–246). New York: Simon & Schuster.

Rideout, V. J., Foehr, U. G., & Roberts, D. F. (2010). *GENERATION M2: Media in the lives of 8- to 18-year-olds.* Menlo Park, CA: Kaiser Family Foundation.

Roberts, D. F., & Foehr, U. G. (2008). Trends in media use. *The Future of Children, 18*(1), 11–37.

Schor, J. (2003). The (even more) overworked American. In J. De Graaf (Ed.), *Take back your time: Fighting overwork and time poverty in America* (pp. 6–11). San Francisco: Berrett-Koehler Publishers.

Seligman, M. E. P. (2002). *Authentic happiness: Using the new positive psychology to realize your potential for lasting fulfillment.* New York: Free Press.

Seligman, M. E. P., Steen, T. A., Park, N., & Peterson, C. (2005). Positive psychology progress: Empirical validation of interventions. *American Psychologist, 60*(5), 410–421.

Shaw, S. M. (1997). Controversies and contradictions in family leisure: An analysis of conflicting paradigms. *Journal of Leisure Research, 29*(1), 98–112.

Shaw, S. M. (2008). Family leisure and changing ideologies of parenthood. *Sociology Compass, 2*(2), 688–703.

Slade, A. (1987). A longitudinal study of maternal involvement and symbolic play during the toddler period. *Child Development, 58,* 367–375.

Wegner, L., Flisher, A. J., Chikobvu, P., Lombard, C., & King, G. (2008). Leisure boredom and high school dropout in Cape Town, South Africa. *Journal of Adolescence, 31,* 421–431.

Wells, M. S., Widmer, M. A., & McCoy, J. K. (2004). Grubs and grasshoppers: Challenge-based recreation and the collective efficacy of families with at-risk youth. *Family Relations, 53*(3), 326–333.

Widmer, M. A., Ellis, G. D., & Munson, W. W. (2003). Development of the Aristotelian ethical behavior in leisure scale short form. *Therapeutic Recreation Journal, 37*(3), 256–274.

Wiersma, L. D., & Fifer, A. M. (2008). "The schedule has been tough but we think it's worth it": The joys, challenges, and recommendations of youth sport parents. *Journal of Leisure Research, 40*(4), 505–530.

Wirthlin, J. B. (2004, May). Earthly debts, heavenly debts, *Ensign, 34,* 40–43.

Zabriskie, R. B., & McCormick, B. P. (2003). Parent and child perspectives of family leisure involvement and satisfaction with family life. *Journal of Leisure Research, 35*(2), 163–189.

CHAPTER 23

Crucibles and Healing:
Illness, Loss, Death, and Bereavement

W. David Robinson, Jason S. Carroll, and Elaine Sorensen Marshall

In the premortal realm, spirit sons and daughters . . . accepted [God's] plan
by which his children could obtain a physical body and gain earthly experience to progress toward perfection. . . .
The divine plan of happiness enables family relationships to be perpetuated beyond the grave.

THE PROCLAMATION TEACHES THAT IT IS ESSENtial to our Eternal Father's plan that His children "obtain a physical body and gain earthly experience" (¶ 3). The experience of being human in a flawed mortal realm brings both joy and sorrow, with many of life's most difficult challenges occurring as a result of the temporal condition of our bodies. To experience earth life is to know suffering at various times. This suffering involves enduring physical, psychological, and spiritual distress as well as emotional struggles with feelings of loss, grief, loneliness, and despair (Cowling, 2004; Edwards, 2003; Marshall, 2008). The meaning and purpose of suffering have confounded philosophers, theologians, health care professionals, and family scholars through the ages (see Edwards, 2003; Johnston & Scholler-Jaquish, 2007). Profound loss is associated with suffering and comes in many forms: illness as loss of health, disability as loss of independence, infertility as loss of hope of having a child, and bereavement as the mortal loss of a loved one in death. Though these experiences are physical, their influence extends far beyond the temporal aspects of our lives.

Both scholars and spiritual leaders have referred to such experiences as "crucibles" of human experience (Robinson, Carroll, & Watson, 2005; Romney, 1969). A crucible is a furnace-like vessel that endures intense heat that refines and transfigures raw materials into a new, stronger substance. The crucible purges away impurities and unifies elements into an entirely new final product. In industry, crucibles produce high-grade steel and alloys of unusual strength that are actually different in

quality from the original ingredients. The crucible is a metaphor for life-changing challenges, adversities, and losses that have a refining effect on a person or an entire family. Crucible experiences have the potential to change how we view ourselves, our relationships with others, and our relationship with God, thus transforming our very natures. The Lord's prophets have called such experiences the refiner's fire (Isaiah 48:10; 1 Nephi 20:10). President James E. Faust explained:

Into every life there come the painful, despairing days of adversity and buffeting. There seems to be a full measure of anguish, sorrow, and often heartbreak for everyone, including those who earnestly seek to do right and be faithful. The thorns that prick, that stick in the flesh, that hurt, often change lives which seem robbed of significance and hope. This change comes about through a refining process which often seems cruel and hard. In this way the soul can become like soft clay in the hands of the Master in building lives of faith, usefulness, beauty, and strength. For some, the refiner's fire causes a loss of belief and faith in God, but those with eternal perspective understand that such refining is part of the perfection process (1979, p. 53).

Adversities such as illness or disability, death and bereavement, and other losses are unavoidable parts of earthly experience and may become spiritual crucibles with the potential to transform individuals and families. For some families, these life-altering experiences tear at relationships and drown family members in feelings of heartache, injustice, and bitterness. For others, these unexpected challenges serve as "emotional crucibles" (Robinson, et al, 2005) that enhance relationships among family members, renew appreciation for significant aspects of life, and inspire faith in the wisdom and grace of God. These challenges and the complex relationship patterns that surround them become defining experiences in family life.

The purpose of this chapter is to discuss how shared experiences of adversity influence families. At the outset, it is important to note that crucibles in families are not confined to the topics addressed in this chapter. The primary goal of this chapter is to explore and come to appreciate the perspective of the restored gospel in dealing with family crucibles in our own lives and in the lives of others.

The Importance of Perspective and Meaning

When illness, loss, or other trials touch families, the first questions are often, "Why is this happening to me?" "Why must she suffer?" "If God loves us, why did He allow the person I love to die?" "Am I not righteous enough?" How families answer these questions has a profound influence on how adversity affects their lives. Our perspective often determines how we define and respond to such situations. The term *perspective* refers to one's worldview or way of making meaning out of life experiences. Perspective is "our frame of reference, our beginning assumptions, our way of seeing, or our way of thinking" (Burr, Day, & Bahr, 1993, p. 8). A specific perspective may be held by a single individual or family, or it can be shared by larger groups of people in communities or nations.

In modern society, personal and collective perspectives influence how family members and professionals deal with illness and loss in families. Scholars have identified viewpoints for understanding family experiences with illness or disability, bereavement, and other challenges. In contrast to early theory and research that focused on how families become disrupted and incapacitated by stress (Boss, 1988; Patterson & Garwick, 1994), a crucible perspective highlights the potential for adversity to promote strength and resilience. Rather than assuming that the stressors of life's most difficult

challenges are always harmful, crucible-oriented perspectives focus on how some aspects of managing adversity may promote growth, strength, and positive adaptation. Pauline Boss, a prominent family stress scholar, noted that families have "the potential to grow and learn from a crisis" (Boss, 1988, p. 51), and while recovering from stressful experiences they often reorganize above past levels of functioning.

The gospel of Jesus Christ offers an eternal perspective that helps families to understand that there may be significant purposes to the adversities of this life. President Spencer W. Kimball comforted us when he said:

> If we looked at mortality as the whole of existence, then pain, sorrow, failure, and short life could be a calamity. But if we look upon life as an eternal thing stretching far into the premortal past and on into the eternal post-death future, then all happenings may be put in proper perspective (1972, p. 97).

Nevertheless, it is natural in crisis to have moments of doubt, fear, and uncertainty as families strive to cope (Sorensen, 1992). The truths of the gospel offer spiritual comfort and a widening perspective that invites the potential for growth and development, in contrast to a perspective that is solely oriented toward coping with crisis. In recent studies, scholars have begun to recognize how experiences with chronic illness or disability can promote resilience and spirituality among family members (see Cattich & Knudson-Martin, 2009; Cox, Marshall, Mandleco, & Olsen, 2003; Marshall, Olsen, Allred, Mandleco, Dyches, & Sansom, 2003).

Expanding Perspectives

The proclamation teaches that the cumulative purpose of all experiences in this life is to help us "progress toward perfection" (¶ 3) and realize our "destiny as heirs of eternal life." Having faith in God and in His "divine plan of happiness" (¶ 3) is the first principle of a perspective that recognizes meaning and growth as coming from life's crucibles. Similar to a wide-angle lens on a camera, this perspective expands the frame of reference and helps individuals better understand and ultimately appreciate aspects of experiences with adversity and loss. There are several perceptual expansions that are fundamental to understanding and enduring adversity and loss as a family crucible. They require expansion from one viewpoint to another perspective endowed with greater meaning and purpose.

From crisis to crucible. It is natural to view adversity as a crisis. Life is difficult, and certainly not fair. It is natural to suffer and it is normal to feel alone and perhaps even abandoned at times. But we can feel the sorrow and loss while also eventually acknowledging the potential for personal growth, enhancement of family relationships, and the companionship of the Spirit of the Lord. Most important, such an expanding perspective is not merely a positive outlook that denies or glosses over the hurt and loss that come with serious illness, disability, or death; rather, it frames the inescapable sorrow and suffering that accompany adversity as pathways toward refining spiritual development personally and in family relationships. Some growth occurs because of pain, not in spite of it. As a member of the Seventy, Elder Bruce C. Hafen (1989, p. 5) wrote:

> Our understanding of the Atonement is hardly a shield against sorrow; rather, it is a rich source of strength to deal productively with the disappointments and heartbreaks that form the deliberate fabric of mortal life. The gospel helps us to heal our pain, not necessarily to prevent it.

Expanding the perspective from crisis to crucible, the reality of sore trials is not avoided; rather, afflictions are experienced in ways that give purpose to pain and developmental guidance for growth.

From individual to family. The proclamation teaches "that the family is central to the Creator's plan for the eternal destiny of His children" (¶ 1). We learn from this principle that our Father in Heaven intends for life experiences to be shared within families. Illness, disability, and death are best understood as experiences that are shared by all members of the family. Indeed, scholars in the health and social sciences have begun to develop models to recognize the entire family perspective of managing illness and disability (see Knafl & Deatrick, 2006; Rolland, 2005; Wiegand, Deatrick, & Knafl, 2008). Because such experiences may begin with an individual, it is sometimes easy to attribute the trial to that particular family member. For example, we say that "John has multiple sclerosis" or "Sarah is infertile." Sometimes we do not think of such situations as family issues; however, when a mother has cancer, to a significant degree all members of the family suffer from the illness (Robinson et al., 2005). When a child is ill, the entire family needs to learn how to live with the illness (Neil & Clarke, 2010). Parents, siblings, grandparents, and extended family grieve the loss of a child (Hoppes, 2005). By appreciating the relational component of these experiences, we expand our perspective and can become more sensitive to all who need care and concern.

From temporal to spiritual. Because physical illness and disability are usually visible to others, it is common to view them primarily through a biological or temporal lens. This viewpoint is supported by the physical manner in which illness is diagnosed and treated in modern cultures. Nevertheless, there has been considerable recent expansion to a focus on the spiritual and emotional aspects of illness (Koenig, 2000; Prest & Robinson, 2006). Though specific physical problems may have common signs and symptoms, individuals and families create their own personal and spiritual meaning from such experiences. Marshall (2008, p. 260) noted, "Suffering takes a person to the borders of the sense of identity, of life and its purpose, toward metaphysical realms of meaning, and often to a personal sense of the sacred." In recent studies, scholars have explored how human suffering leads to personal meaning and purpose that includes a powerful sense of the sacred (Black, 2006; Sacks & Nelson, 2007). Through this meaning-making process, illness and disability have the potential to become defining factors in how family members view themselves and their relationships with others and with God.

Opposition and Crucibles

In many ways, the principle of opposition is an important part of the crucible experience. Many of life's experiences are oppositional in nature and involve learning through contrast and comparison. In counseling his son Jacob, the Book of Mormon prophet Lehi taught, "For it must needs be, that there is an opposition in all things. If not so . . . righteousness could not be brought to pass, neither wickedness, neither holiness nor misery, neither good nor bad" (2 Nephi 2:11). Why must there be opposition? The Lord taught Adam that opposition is needed in this life so that the children of God can "taste the bitter, that they may know to prize the good" (Moses 6:55). While imprisoned in Liberty Jail, the Prophet Joseph Smith learned a similar principle when the Lord revealed,

"Know thou, my son, that all these things shall give thee experience, and shall be for thy good" (D&C 122:7). To find meaning from adversity in our lives, it is important to understand vital lessons that may be learned from an appreciation of our own oppositional experiences. Elder Bruce C. Hafen (1989, p. 79) observed:

Somehow, our joyful experiences mean more when we are fully conscious of the alternatives and the contrasts that surround us. We prize the sweet more when we have tasted the bitter. We appreciate our health when we see sickness. . . . These contrasts do not deter our idealism. Properly understood, they only make the moments of the true joy worth waiting for.

Scholars in family and health sciences have explored the oppositions and paradoxes of illness experiences, noting the "emotional roller-coaster ride that is both draining and empowering" (McDaniel, Hepworth, & Doherty, 1997, p. 3). There are at least three important opposites that often contribute to the sense of crucible in experiences of temporal adversity.

Isolation and connection. One of the most distressing polarities that families and individual family members feel is isolation versus connection (McDaniel et al., 1997; Robinson et al., 2005). Suffering is lonely and, at their core, adversity and healing are private (Marshall, 2002). Elder Neal A. Maxwell (1979, p. 43) reminded:

There is, in the suffering of the highest order, a point that is reached—a point of aloneness—when the individual (as did the Savior on a much grander scale) must bear it . . . alone. Even the faithful may wonder if they can take any more or if they are in some way forsaken. Those who . . . stand at the foot of the cross often can do so little to help absorb the pain and the anguish. It is something we must bear ourselves in order that our triumph can be complete.

A sense of isolation may be intensified as individual family members each struggle with his or her personal experiences and responses. At the same time, the entire family may feel isolated from others as life seems to go on normally in the outside world while inside the family is crashing.

Paradoxically, suffering can also have a profound bonding influence in families. It can bring family members closer to each other as they come closer to their mutual sense of spirituality, and indeed closer to the veil. Lingering contentions can become resolved through the process of pulling together in a time of need. Eternal perspectives can become clearer as families distinguish the important from the trivial. In the midst of crisis, families can turn to the essential activities for family survival and let go, at least temporarily, of non-essentials.

Senselessness and meaning. The search for meaning is one of the most common themes in research of experiences of adversity and loss (Robinson, et al., 2005). Human beings have a natural need to find meaning in life and to make sense of painful experiences. At first, it is natural to question the apparent senselessness and futility of adversity. However, in time there is typically a desire to find meaning and explanation for our struggles. For some families, the search for meaning "takes the form of a spiritual quest" that may lead to a "heightened awareness of life's gifts" (McDaniel et al., 1997, p. 8). Such awareness may involve increased appreciation for the prosaic gifts of life, like spending time with loved ones, enjoying the sunset, or simple acts of service.

Old world and new. The proclamation advises, "Disability, death, or other circumstances may necessitate individual adaptation" (¶ 7). This counsel presents at least two important considerations for families. First, successful adaptation to difficult circumstances may require change of habits, change of attitudes, change of ways of living, and even sometimes a change of heart. It requires the marshaling of resources to cope. Second, we are well advised to avoid judging others. We are not aware of private challenges that have provoked change and adaptation in family roles, routines, and responsibilities in the lives of others.

Robinson, Carroll, and Watson (2005) outlined a model that highlights the journey families take from their old world to the uncertain new landscape of living with a chronic illness or tragedy. Like immigrants in an unfamiliar land, families confronting such changes often feel as if they have been pushed into a new world where many things that were once taken for granted are now changed or missing altogether. The challenges associated with adapting to the new world are compounded when family members have differing views about how to continue old patterns of living and interacting versus how much must change. At the other extreme is the family that embraces an illness-saturated worldview, where the experience becomes a "cause" that pervades every aspect of their lives. In this view, family routines, activities, and relationships with the outside world become centered on the illness or the person with the condition as the overriding theme of the family. In this situation, relationships can become strained by guilt or resentment of the ever-present condition.

It is natural to linger in one world or the other for a time. Honoring the history and traditions of their familiar world is a source of healing for families as they strive to forge a new life of meaning and face needs for change in activities and even relationships. Families must realize that different individuals may be in different places emotionally and spiritually, and nearly everyone moves back and forth among such dynamic aspects of crucible experiences.

The next two sections will use the concept of family crucibles as a guiding lens through which to explore some specific experiences of illness, disability, death, infertility, and bereavement (see also Marshall & Crane, 2005). Of course, this is only a sampling of crucibles that families experience. Since there is no way to determine the impact of a stressor on a family, crucibles are defined by the families themselves. What is a crucible experience for one family may be easily managed by another. The subjective lived experience of the family is what determines the impact of the stressor. Also, it is important to remember that the crucible experiences discussed here have important elements that are universal as well as aspects that may differ across families and cultures (Callister, 2005; in press).

Illness and Disability

"In the narrative of every human life and every family, illness is a prominent character. Even if we have avoided serious illness ourselves, we cannot escape its reach into our family lives and our friendship circles" (McDaniel et al., 1997, p. 1). Because of its wide-reaching effects on families, physical or mental illness or disability will affect all of us at one time or another. Therefore, it is important to develop an understanding of their effects on families so that we can respond in helpful and meaningful ways. Issues addressed here include the family life cycle, issues of caregiving, and shared experiences of illness and disability.

The family life cycle. The concept of the individual life cycle began with developmental theorists such as Erikson (1950). Duvall (1977) expanded the concept to include transitional stages in families, such as marriage, birth and raising children, launching children, retirement, and death. Rolland (1987) stated that it is critical to consider chronic illness and disability of a family member within the context of the life cycle of the entire family. The family's capacity to deal with illness or disability is likely to be affected by milestones in the family life cycle. Issues may be more difficult related to timing of the illness or disability and interference with normative family transitions.

Timing. Illness may occur at an age when most people would not expect it, such as cancer in a child or a heart ailment in a young adult. While almost all illnesses and disabilities take families by surprise, the assault may seem more unfair when such challenges seem to strike prematurely. Adversities such as illness and death impose different meanings at different stages in the process of life. A family is more likely to feel unfairly ambushed by the death of a young child than in the loss of an elderly parent who has lived a long and productive life. Such process and developmental considerations are important in understanding how life challenges may influence particular families.

Interference. It is also difficult when illness or disability interferes or overlaps with normative family transitions because family members may already be dealing with the stress of adapting to new roles and responsibilities (Shuman, 1996). The obligations placed on families during such transitions can disrupt, delay, or stop normative progression through life stages. Examples include leaving school to care for an ill parent or postponing marriage because of life-threatening illness.

Issues of caregiving. Caregiving is a key issue for families confronted with chronic illness or disability. Depending upon the condition, caregiving can range from minimal adaptation of daily routines to complete lifestyle change. As much of health care has moved from hospital to home, stress associated with family caregiving is an important matter to consider. Caregiver burden is well-documented among both women and men as caregivers for family members (Brazil, Bedard, Willison, & Hode, 2003; Deeken, Taylor, Mangan, Yabroff, & Ingham, 2003). In some cases, the physical and emotional toll on the family caregiver can be enormous, including the fear of doing something wrong, lack of personal time, and losing energy for other roles such as employment, other home-related work, childcare, or involvement in other relationships. The degree of burden depends upon the stage and severity of the ill person's condition, the stage in the family life cycle, and resources available to the family. Caregiver burden has been shown to be especially high in caring for family members with dementia (Mittelman, Roth, Clay, & Haley, 2007; Tremont, Davis, & Bishop, 2006), mental illness (Awad & Voruganti, 2008), and enduring debilitating chronic illness that invokes a sense of loss of the affected person who was once healthy (Kouzoupis, Paparrigopoulos, Soldatos, & Papadimitriou, 2010; Mutch, 2010).

Guilt may be associated with caregiving for both the recipient of care and the caregiver. For the recipient, guilt can emerge from feeling responsible for placing demands on the caregiver. For the caregiver, guilt can arise because there may be times when caring for a loved one becomes overwhelming. Nevertheless, research has shown that caregiving relationships can promote personal growth and closer family ties (Conger & Marshall, 1998), wherein difficulty and growth can be part of the same shared experience.

Shared experience of illness. Although the illness or disability of one family member affects all family members, family members do not have identical experiences. Though there are elements of the experience that are collectively shared among family members, it is common for each individual to have distinct ways of interpreting and living through the crucible. When confronted by adversity, each family member experiences a personal sense of loss. But the entire family shares the experience of suffering as a unit. Herein lies another paradoxical characteristic of families' experiences with illness and disability. As families recognize and appreciate that their personal experiences are different from one another's, their collective experience as a family becomes *more shared*. In other words, the validation of difference within the unit brings unity.

Individuals feel most supported when their personal experiences are valued and included. By disclosing feelings and concerns and appreciating each person's individual ways of thinking and responding, family members are able to build connections with one another, develop empathy, adapt to challenges in ways that benefit everyone involved, and develop the family story.

Indeed, an effective way to recognize and promote the shared family experience of illness is to share personal stories in order to create a shared family narrative (see Garden, 2010).

Death, Infertility, and Bereavement

Death. The proclamation notes that as "spirit sons and daughters [we] knew and worshipped God as [our] Eternal Father and accepted His plan . . . [to] obtain a physical body" and that "the divine plan of happiness enables family relationships to be perpetuated beyond the grave." Sacred temple ordinances "make it possible for individuals to return to the presence of God and for families to be united eternally" (¶ 3). Elder Russell M. Nelson (1992a, April 11) said:

> We need not look upon death as an enemy. With full understanding and preparation, faith supplants fear. Hope displaces despair. The Lord said, "Fear not even unto death; for in this world your joy is not full, but in me your joy is full" (D&C 101:36). . . . [An] eternal perspective eases [the] pangs of death.

But even with the marvelous comforting perspective of the gospel, among the most difficult of life's crucibles is the loss of a loved one to death or facing one's own imminent passing.

Medical advances that have extended life even with a chronic or terminal illness have provoked consideration and choices about how to live at the end of life (Wrubel, Acree, Goodman, & Folkman, 2009). Increasingly, family members are able to make decisions about their own care at the end of life. Families should openly discuss individual and family wishes. Family members need clear guidance regarding the desires of an individual. Consider if an illness or accident left you in a coma. What measures, if any, would you want to prolong your life? Family members should prepare advance directives, which may be in the form of a living will or health care power of attorney. By such documents, the family member may direct desires regarding such treatments as resuscitation measures, dialysis or breathing machines, or tube feedings. Families should also discuss who and how one might care for another whether at home or in an extended care facility. It is helpful for families to discuss plans, hopes, and desires regarding the end of life to facilitate, wherever possible, a comforting death experience for all family members (Oppenheim, Bos, Heim, Menkin, & Porter, 2010; Shield, Wetle, Teno, Miller, & Welch, 2010).

Elder Russell M. Nelson (1992b, May, p. 72) observed, "Even when the elderly or infirm have been afforded merciful relief, their loved ones are rarely ready to let go. The only length of life that seems to satisfy the longings of the human heart is life everlasting." The death of a young parent or spouse causes not only the loss of a father or mother, wife or husband, but also the loss of an entire way of living for surviving family members.

Death by suicide is among the most difficult of tragedies. Not only do family members experience the terrible loss, but they are also often faced with associated stigma (Feigelman, Gorman, & Jordan, 2009). Family members may blame themselves for not preventing the loss (Maple, Edwards, Plummer, & Minichiello, 2009). When the victim is a parent, the effects on children are especially devastating (Hung & Rabin, 2009). Latter-day Saint families may wonder about the eternal salvation of the deceased. Elder M. Russell Ballard counseled:

> Suicide is a sin—a very grievous one, yet the Lord will not judge the person who commits that sin strictly by the act itself. The Lord will look at that person's circumstances and the degree of his accountability at the time of the act (1987, p. 8).

The death of a child is among the most intense and profound adversities for a family, where parents and others wrestle with their loss of not only the present, but also the anticipated future earthly experiences with the child and the future promise of who the child might have become. Moments of mourning often resurface as "would have been" milestones are marked by other children.

The loss of a child before birth creates a tragic mourning situation as family expectations turn from joy to despair. Perinatal loss, such as having a miscarriage or stillborn child, includes the loss of the creation of a new life, the loss of the anticipated child, the loss of the dream and hopes for parenthood, and the loss of an extension of both parents (Callister, 2006, 2010). Societal acknowledgements of perinatal loss are noticeably absent. There is often no memorial service and no respite from the usual life and work expectations of family members.

The experience of perinatal loss can further complicate subsequent pregnancies by possible emotional distress or a return of grief experiences (Armstrong, Hutti, & Myers, 2009), or vigilance and safety concerns regarding the next expected child (Lamb, 2002). The influence of perinatal loss on family life cannot be overstated. The development of a lifelong grief response to the loss, filled with comfort and coupled with sorrow, may be more realistic and fulfilling than the myth that parents should just "get over it." Families often need to tell their story (Forhan, 2010; St. John, Cooke, & Goopy, 2006). Those who discover a sense of meaning in such adversity are often able to find bittersweet resolution and can be helpful to others who experience such challenges.

Infertility. Infertility is another form of loss that can be emotionally, physically, and financially exhausting for couples, yet it is often a silent crucible born in loneliness because it is neither expected, visible, life-threatening, nor disabling. The variety of treatments for infertility available today, each involving physical, ethical, and economic concerns, can cause confusion, tension, and burdens on couples. Couples frequently report high levels of stress, loss of hope, and feelings of frustration due to the long trail of complex technology, medicalizing of intimacy, invasive procedures, surgeries, and potent drugs with problematic side effects. Further, when a couple decides on a treatment option and invests significant resources, hope, time, and effort without the result of a baby, the grief can be devastating (Lee, Wang, Kuo, Kuo, Lee, & Lee, 2010). Couples struggling with becoming pregnant often deal with well-meaning family and friends who may perpetuate myths that couples simply need to relax or that infertility is only a female problem. Others may assume that childlessness is by choice. Leaders of the Church have long taught that decisions about the number and timing of children are left to each couple and the Lord, and not to be judged by others (see chapter 14).

To mourn with those that mourn. One may easily feel powerless, not knowing what to say or how to help families who are grieving. We are admonished as a covenant people to "mourn with those that mourn" and "comfort those that stand in need of comfort" (Mosiah 18:9). Elder Nelson (1992b, May, p. 72) said:

> Mourning is one of the deepest expressions of pure love. It is a natural response in complete

accord with divine commandment: "Thou shalt live together in love, insomuch that thou shalt weep for the loss of them that die" (D&C 42:45). . . . The only way to take sorrow out of death is to take love out of life.

The grieving individual must learn to focus on the love they have for the person who died, not get stuck on the last few days of the individual's life. Missing the individual and remembering the good times are profoundly effective ways to grieve. Pain can be eased by sharing with others.

When attempting to comfort another, the most helpful thing to do is simply to be present. The simple words, "I am sorry," accompanied by a willingness to listen, are more helpful than possibly unwelcome clichés such as, "It's God's will," "She's no longer suffering," or "He's in a better place." Empathetic presence allows the grieving person to feel supported without needing to respond. It is also often comforting to share positive memories of the person or to give concrete help such as childcare, housecleaning, or car-washing.

Comfort through grief comes according to individual and family needs and time. There is no typical time frame for recovery, nor are there specific chronological stages of grief (Friedman & James, 1998a, 1998b). Surges of pain, numbness, anger, guilt, and relief may come and go, and then return in unexpected ambushes. Tangible reminders of the person, such as photographs or belongings, may be comforting. Do not assume that because the survivor does not mention the deceased person that he or she is not constantly thinking of the loved one. Talking about the deceased person is often comforting; one should not avoid saying his or her name, as if the person never lived or does not continue to exist. Anniversaries and holidays, such as birthdays, the date of the death, or Christmas, may be especially difficult. People who have lost beloved family members report that the ache is always present to some degree and that they eventually learn to live with the loss as a constant companion.

Healing: The Perspective of the Restored Gospel

Healing is both a temporal and spiritual concept. It is the process of growing and learning from the crucibles of adverse life experiences. Though medicine appears to be a healing profession, scholars have noted that it "has neither an operational definition of healing nor an explanation of its mechanisms beyond the physiological processes related to curing" (Egnew, 2005, p. 255). Healing is not cure. It may be "as simple as the union of a wound for restoration of tissue integrity or as complex as the achievement of serenity and harmony among mind, body, and spirit" (Marshall, 2008, p. 259). It is a lifelong "process of restoring and becoming whole" (Marshall, 2002). It is born of suffering, "whether from a simple physical injury or from the most intense assault to the soul" (Marshall, 2008, p. 260). It is an active process of recovery that requires time and support. One scholar has defined healing as "the personal experience of the transcendence of suffering" (Egnew, 2005, p. 255).

Transcendence implies effort. Social scientists and health care scholars are beginning to explore specific elements of transcendence (Marshall, 2008). Such elements include forgiveness (Reed & Enright, 2006; Worthington, Vanoyen, Lerner, & Scherer, 2005). Marshall (2008, p. 261) asserted, "Forgiveness and healing happen when one gives up hoping the past did not happen. Instead, life experience is claimed and integrated and we ask, 'What lesson was learned?'" Another element of healing or transcendence is sacrifice (Florczak, 2004). Van Hooft (1998) stated that when we suffer for a cause or give up something for a greater good, even if it means accepting experiences of adversity in order to find deeper meaning, we sacrifice.

As we view life's experiences with illness and disability, death and bereavement, and the myriad other challenges as crucibles from which we can emerge stronger in our path toward eternal development, we allow ourselves to benefit more fully from the principles of healing found within the gospel of Jesus Christ. Knowledge of the Eternal Father's plan can ease the losses associated with adversity and provide needed guidance along the unpredictable journey toward healing. While the specific steps in the process are individual to each person, the gospel of Jesus Christ provides a clear directional course for families to follow as they move along their own personal pathways to healing.

There are a few principles upon which the Lord's divine healing process is predicated. The term *healing* is important. The scriptures record numerous occasions where faithful individuals were physically healed from their illnesses and disabilities, even raised from the dead.

Although such miracles are part of our Lord's plan and such signs "follow them that believe" (Mark 16:14–20), the use of healing on such occasions also has a spiritual interpretation. Elder Richard G. Scott (1994, p. 7) explained:

> It is important to understand that [the Lord's] healing can mean being cured, or having your burdens eased, or even coming to realize that it is worth it to endure to the end patiently, for God needs brave sons and daughters who are willing to be polished when in His wisdom that is His will.

From this perspective, the concept of healing is appropriately considered as a process of supported growth and refinement as well as a relief from suffering. Healing happens over time as we seek to understand the Lord's divine purposes in our lives. Elder Scott (1994, p. 9) further noted that the surest, most effective path to healing comes through an application of the teachings of Jesus Christ in our lives. He noted that such a path "begins with an understanding of and appreciation for the principles of . . . the Atonement of Jesus Christ," which "leads to faith in Him and obedience to His commandments."

The prophet Alma provided critical insight into the nature of the Atonement and Christ's healing power when he addressed the people of Gideon. Referring to the Savior, Alma taught,

> And he shall go forth, suffering pains and afflictions and temptations of every kind; and this that the word might be fulfilled which saith he will take upon him the pains and the sicknesses of his people. . . . and he will take upon him their infirmities, that his bowels may be filled with mercy, . . . that he may know according to the flesh how to succor his people (Alma 7:11–12).

From this scripture, we learn two important truths. First, the Atonement's healing power is not only for overcoming the effects of sin, but also extends to the entire range of mortal suffering and adversity (Hafen, 1989). Elder Neal A. Maxwell (2008, p. 54) noted, "Since not all human sorrow and pain is connected to sin, the full intensiveness of the Atonement involved bearing our pains, infirmities, and sicknesses, as well as our sins."

The second truth we learn from Alma's words is that because the Savior experienced the complete range of human suffering and loss, He is uniquely able to comprehend our pain and succor us in our times of personal suffering. As a member of the Seventy, Elder Merrill J. Bateman (1995, p. 14) counseled,

> The Savior's Atonement in the garden and on the cross is intimate as well as infinite. Infinite in that it spans the eternities. Intimate in that the Savior felt each person's pains, sufferings, and sicknesses. Consequently, He knows how to carry our sorrows and relieve our burdens that we might be healed from within, made whole persons, and receive everlasting joy in His kingdom.

As we realize that the blessings of the Atonement extend to all of life's suffering and that the Lord truly understands our personal situations, we can more fully turn to the Savior in times of illness or death and accept His invitation: "Come unto me, all ye that labour and are heavy laden, and I will give you rest. Take my yoke upon you, and learn of me; for I am meek and lowly in heart: and ye shall find rest unto your souls" (Matthew 11:28–29).

Healing is also found in the believer's hope for the promised gift of resurrection. The proclamation states that our Eternal Father's "divine plan of happiness enables family relationships to be perpetuated beyond the grave." The comfort provided by a knowledge of the resurrection and the potential for families to be united eternally can be the balm of Gilead (Genesis 37:25) that eases the losses associated with death and provides hope to family members on both sides of the veil. As grieving family members have faith in the Savior and His atoning sacrifice, "death's sting is softened as Jesus bears the believers' grief and comforts them through the Holy Spirit" (Bateman, 1995, p. 13).

A family crucible perspective grounded in the restored gospel provides a guiding lens through which we can more fully understand and appreciate how individuals and families are influenced and transformed by experiences with illness and disability, death and bereavement, and other profound experiences with adversity and loss. Such expanded understanding helps us to realize more fully the two greatest resources of healing in this life: the gospel of Jesus Christ and our families.

W. David Robinson is an associate professor in the Department of Family Medicine at the University of Nebraska Medical Center. He and his wife, Jamie, are the parents of five children. **Jason S. Carroll** *is an associate professor in the School of Family Life at Brigham Young University. He and his wife, Stefani, are the parents of five children.* **Elaine Sorensen Marshall** *is Professor and Bulloch Healthcare Endowed Chair at Georgia Southern University. She is married to Dr. John Marshall. They have a blended family of nine children and are the grandparents of many grandchildren.*

References

Armstrong, D. S., Hutti, M. H., & Myers, J. (2009). The influence of prior perinatal loss on parents' psychological distress after the birth of a subsequent healthy infant. *Journal of Obstetrical, Gynecologic, and Neonatal Nursing, 38,* 654–666.

Awad, A. G., & Voruganti, L. N. P. (2008). The burden of schizophrenia on caregivers: A review. *Pharmacoeconomics, 26*(2), 149–162.

Ballard, M. R. (1987, October). Suicide: Some things we know, and some we do not. *Ensign, 17,* 6–9.

Bateman, M. J. (1995, May). The power to heal from within. *Ensign, 25,* 13–14.

Black, H. K. (2006). The sacred self: Suffering narratives in old age. *Omega: Journal of Death and Dying, 53*(1/2), 69–85.

Boss, Pauline (1988). *Family stress management.* Newbury Park, CA: Sage.

Brazil, K., Bedard, M., Willison, K., & Hode, M. (2003). Caregiving and its impact on families of the terminally ill. *Aging and Mental Health, 7*(5), 376–382.

Burr, W. R., Day, R. D., & Bahr, K. S. (1993). *Family science.* Pacific Grove, CA: Brooks/Cole.

Callister, L. C. (2005). What has the literature taught us about culturally competent care of women and children? *MCN: The American Journal of Maternal Child Nursing, 30*(6), 380–388.

Callister, L. C. (2006). Perinatal loss: A family perspective. *Journal of Perinatal and Neonatal Nursing, 20*(3), 227–234.

Callister, L. C. (2010). Global infertility: Are we caring yet? *MCN: The American Journal of Maternal Child Nursing, 35*(3), 174.

Cattich, J., & Knudson-Martin, C. (2009). Spirituality and relationship: A holistic analysis of how couples cope with diabetes. *Journal of Marital and Family Therapy, 35*(1), 111–124.

Conger, C. O., & Marshall, E. S. (1998). Recreating life: Toward a theory of relationship development in acute home care. *Qualitative Health Research, 8,* 526–546.

Cowling, W. R. (2004). Despair: A unitary appreciative inquiry. *Advances in Nursing Science, 27*(4), 287–300.

Cox, A. H., Marshall, E. S., Mandleco, B., & Olsen, S. F. (2003). Coping responses to daily life stressors of children who have a sibling with a disability. *Journal of Family Nursing, 9*(4), 397–413.

Deeken, J. F., Taylor, K. L., Mangan, P., Yabroff, K. R., & Ingham, J. M. (2003). Care for the caregivers: A review of self-report instruments developed to measure the burden, needs, and quality of life of informal caregivers. *Journal of Pain and Symptom Management, 26*(4), 922–953.

Duvall, E. M. (1977). *Marriage and family development* (5th ed.). Philadelphia, PA: J. B. Lippincott.

Edwards, S. D. (2003). Three concepts of suffering. *Medicine, Health Care, and Philosophy, 6,* 59–66.

Egnew, T. R. (2005). The meaning of healing: Transcending suffering. *Annals of Family Medicine, 3*(3), 255–262.

Erikson, E. H. (1950). *Childhood and society.* New York: W. W. Norton & Company.

Faust, J. E. (1979, May). The refiner's fire. *Ensign, 9,* 53–59.

Feigelman, W., Gorman, B. S., & Jordan, J. R. (2009). Stigmatization and suicide bereavement. *Death Studies, 33*(7), 591–608.

Florczak, K. L. (2004). An exploration of the concept of sacrifice. *Nursing Science Quarterly, 17*(3), 195–200.

Forhan, M. (2010). Doing, being, and becoming: A family's journey through perinatal loss. *American Journal of Occupational Therapy, 64*(1), 142–151.

Friedman, R., & James, J. (1998a). The myth of the stages of dying, death, and grief. *Skeptic, 14*(2), 37–41.

Friedman, R., & James, J. (1998b). *The grief recovery handbook: The action program for moving beyond death, divorce, and other losses.* New York: HarperPerennial.

Garden, R. (2010). Telling stories about illness and disability: The limits and lessons of narrative. *Perspectives in Biology and Medicine, 53*(1), 121–135.

Hafen, B. C. (1989). *The broken heart: Applying the Atonement to life's experiences.* Salt Lake City: Deseret Book.

Hoppes, S. (2005). When a child dies the world should stop spinning: An autoethnography exploring the impact of family loss on occupation. *American Journal of Occupational Therapy, 59*(1), 78–87.

Hung, N. C., & Rabin, L. A. (2009). Comprehending childhood bereavement by parental suicide: A critical review of research on outcomes, grief processes, and interventions. *Death Studies, 33*, 781–814.

Johnston, N. E., & Scholler-Jaquish, A. (2007). *Meaning in suffering: Caring practices in the health professions.* Madison: University of Wisconsin Press.

Kimball, S. W. (1972). *Faith precedes the miracle.* Salt Lake City: Deseret Book.

Koenig, H. G. (2000). Religion, spirituality, and medicine: Application to clinical practice. *Journal of the American Medical Association, 284*, 1708.

Knafl, K. A., & Deatrick, J. A. (2006). Family management style and the challenge of moving from conceptualization to measurement. *Journal of Pediatric Oncology Nursing, 23*(1), 12–18.

Kouzoupis, A. B., Paparrigopoulos, T., Soldatos, M., & Papadimitriou, G. N. (2010). The family of the multiple sclerosis patient: A psychosocial perspective. *International Review of Psychiatry, 22*(1), 83–89.

Lamb, E. H. (2002). The impact of previous perinatal loss on subsequent pregnancy and parenting. *Journal of Perinatal Education, 11*(2), 33–40.

Lee, S., Wang, S., Kuo, C., Kuo, P., Lee, M., & Lee, M. (2010). Grief responses and coping strategies among infertile women after failed *in vitro* fertilization treatment. *Scandinavian Journal of Caring Sciences, 24*, 507–513.

Maple, M., Edwards, H., Plummer, D., & Minichiello, V. (2009). Silenced voices: Hearing the stories of parents bereaved through the suicide death of a young adult child. *Health and Social Care in the Community, 18*(3), 241–248.

Marshall, E. S. (2002). Learning the healer's art. BYU Devotional Address. Retrieved from http://speeches.byu.edu/reader/reader.php?id=533&x=59&y=2

Marshall, E. S. (2008). Home as place for healing. *Advances in Nursing Science, 31*(3), 259–267.

Marshall, E. S., & Crane, D. R. (2005). Chronic illness, death, and grieving: Pathways to healing. In C. H. Hart, L. D. Newell, E. Walton, & D. C. Dollahite (Eds.). *Helping and healing our families* (pp. 283–287). Salt Lake City: Deseret Book.

Marshall, E. S., Olsen, S. F., Mandleco, B. L., Dyches, T. T., Allred, K. W., & Sansom, N. (2003). "This is a spiritual experience": Perspectives of Latter-day Saint families living with a child with disabilities. *Qualitative Health Research, 13*(1), 57–76.

Maxwell, N. A. (1979). *All these things shall give thee experience.* Salt Lake City: Deseret Book.

Maxwell, N. A. (2008). *Not my will, but thine.* Salt Lake City: Deseret Book.

McDaniel, S. H., Hepworth, J., & Doherty, W. J. (Eds.). (1997). *The shared experience of illness: Stories of patients, families, and their therapists.* New York: Basic Books.

Mittelman, M. S., Roth, D. L., Clay, O. J., & Haley, W. E. (2007). Preserving health of Alzheimer caregivers: Impact of a spouse caregiver intervention. *American Journal of Geriatric Psychiatry, 15*(9), 780–789.

Mutch, K. (2010). In sickness and in health: Experience of caring for a spouse with MS. *British Journal of Nursing, 19*(4), 214–219.

Neil, L., & Clarke, S. (2010). Learning to live with childhood cancer: A literature review of the parental perspective. *International Journal of Palliative Nursing, 16*(3), 110–119.

Nelson, R. M. (1992a, April 11). Eternal perspective eases pangs of death. *Church News.* Salt Lake City: Deseret News Publishing Company.

Nelson, R. M. (1992b, May). Doors of death. *Ensign, 22,* 72–74.

Oppenheim, S., Bos, C., Heim, P., Menkin, E., & Porter, D. (2010). Developing guidelines for life-support therapy withdrawal in the home. *Journal of Palliative Medicine, 13*(5), 491–492.

Patterson, J. M., & Garwick, A. W. (1994). Levels of meaning in family stress theory. *Family Process, 33,* 287–303.

Prest, L. A., & Robinson, W. D. (2006). Exploring spirituality within the crucible of illness and healing. New York: Haworth Press.

Reed, G. L., & Enright, R. D. (2006). The effects of forgiveness therapy on depression, anxiety, and post-traumatic stress for women after spousal emotional abuse. *Journal of Consulting and Clinical Psychology, 74*(5), 920–929.

Robinson, W. D., Carroll, J. S., & Watson, W. L. (2005). Shared experience building around the family crucible of cancer. *Families, Systems, and Health, 23*(2), 131–147.

Rolland, J. S. (1987). Chronic illness and the family: An overview. In L. M. Wright & M. Leahey

(Eds.) *Families and chronic illness.* Springhouse, PA: Springhouse.

Rolland, J. S. (2005). Cancer and the family: An integrative model. *Cancer, 104*(11 Supp.), 2584–2595.

Romney, M. G. (1969, December). The crucible of adversity and affliction. *Improvement Era, 72,* 66–69.

Sacks, J. L., & Nelson, J. P. (2007). A theory of nonphysical suffering and trust in hospice patients. *Qualitative Health Research, 17*(5), 675–689.

Scott, R. G. (1994, May). To be healed. *Ensign, 24,* 7–9.

Shield, R. R., Wetle, T., Teno, J., Miller, S. C., & Welch, L. C. (2010). Vigilant at the end of life: Family advocacy in the nursing home. *Journal of Palliative Medicine, 13*(5), 573–579.

Shuman, R. (1996). *The psychology of chronic illness.* New York: Basic Books.

Sorensen, Elaine S. (1992). Seeds of faith: A follower's view of Alma 32. In M. S. Nyman & C. D. Tate, Jr. (Eds.), *The Book of Mormon: Alma, the testimony of the Word* (pp. 129–139). Provo, UT: Brigham Young University.

St. John, A., Cooke, M., & Goopy, S. (2006). Shrouds of silence: Three women's stories of prenatal loss. *Australian Journal of Advanced Nursing, 23*(3), 8–12.

Tremont, G., Davis, J. D., & Bishop, D. S. (2006). Unique contribution of family functioning in caregivers of patients with mild to moderate dementia. *Dementia and Geriatric Cognition Disorders, 21*(3), 170–174.

Van Hooft, S. (1998). The meanings of suffering. *The Hastings Center Report 28*(5), 13–19.

Wiegand, D. L., Deatrick, J. A., & Knafl, K. (2008). Family management styles related to withdrawal of life-sustaining therapy from adults who are acutely ill or injured. *Journal of Family Nursing, 14*(1), 16–32.

Worthington, E. L. Jr., Witvliet, C. V., Lerner, A. J., & Scherer, M. (2005). Forgiveness in health research and medical practice. *Explore, 1*(3), 169–176.

Wrubel, J., Acree, M., Goodman, S., & Folkman, S. (2009). End of living: Maintaining a lifeworld during terminal illness. *Psychology and Health, 24*(10), 1229–1243.

CHAPTER 24

Understanding Abuse in Family Life

Kay Bradford and Jason B. Whiting

We warn that individuals who . . . abuse spouse or offspring . . . will one day stand accountable before God.

I HAVE IN MY OFFICE A FILE OF LETTERS RECEIVED from women who cry out over the treatment they receive from their husbands in their homes. They . . . tell of husbands who lose their tempers and shout at their wives and children. They tell of men who demand offensive intimate relations. They tell of men who demean them and put them down and of fathers who seem to know little of the meaning of patience and forbearance with reference to their children.

—President Gordon B. Hinckley (1990, p. 52)

There are few things so completely contrary to the plan of our Heavenly Father than the problem of abuse. Abuse involves hurting, demeaning, and controlling others, and often the worst types of abuse take place within families. Abuse comes in many forms, has many causes, is common, and can have profound consequences. This subject may be difficult to understand or uncomfortable to consider, particularly for those who have suffered abuse. However, because abuse affects so many, it is important for Church leaders and members to understand. In this chapter we will define and describe types of abusive behaviors. Then we will address what can be done to identify and prevent them. We review scholarship on abuse in families, but frame this information within a gospel context. Using our own research, we include quotes from individuals who have been affected by abuse (names have been changed).[1]

The topics in this chapter are far too broad to cover in depth, but we hope that the material spurs the reader to greater awareness and commitment to recognize, prevent, and alleviate maltreatment of all types.

Abuse in the family is not new. Cain murdered his brother Abel (Genesis 4:8), and in the days of Noah "the earth [was] filled with violence" (Genesis 6:13). Throughout history, family members have hurt each other, and often these abuses have remained hidden from others. Not until the early 1800s was child abuse initially recognized in the United States; since the 1960s there has been a marked increase in scholarly attention to abuse in the family. In the year 2002, the World Health Organization identified violence between family members as a global health problem (World Health Organization [WHO], 2002).

Abuse—What Is It?

Taking the telephone to work was not just him being mean, but that was him showing control, his control over me, saying, "Well you're not going to be able to talk with anybody."

—Jill, age 55

Abuse consists of actions or attitudes that are intended to hurt or control. It can include many different types of behaviors, from subtle verbal criticisms to the severest forms of physical or sexual violence. Church leaders have been given this definition: "Abuse is the physical, emotional, sexual, or spiritual mistreatment of others. It may not only harm the body, but it can deeply affect the mind and spirit, destroying faith and

---

1. Quotes are from individuals interviewed for several studies, including Whiting & Lee, 2003; Whiting, 2010; Whiting, Oka, & Fife, manuscript submitted for publication; and Whiting, Smith, Oka, & Karakurt, manuscript submitted for publication.

causing confusion, doubt, mistrust, guilt, and fear" (The Church of Jesus Christ of Latter-day Saints, 1995, p. 1). It is important to recognize differences in severity. The term *maltreatment* is sometimes used to identify relatively mild to moderate harm, whereas the term *abuse* denotes more serious harm (Barnett, Miller-Perrin, & Perrin, 2011). Such distinctions are important so that relatively minor acts are taken seriously but seen as different from severe abuse, such as battering. The context is important as well. For example, grabbing or pushing in a sibling relationship is different from such behaviors in a couple relationship.

We will first review types and prevalence of child maltreatment. This includes harm to a child physically, psychologically, emotionally, or sexually, as well as child neglect, defined as deficits in meeting a child's needs for care, supervision, and safety. We will then discuss domestic or intimate partner violence (IPV), which usually includes a pattern of abusive behaviors (such as physical and psychological attacks, economic coercion, or manipulation) that adults use against a spouse or intimate partner. We will discuss types of IPV, some of which are characterized by one partner's coercive control of the other, while others include patterns of poor self-management and emotions.

Child Abuse and Neglect

"My mom's boyfriend . . . he would beat us and stuff, . . . beat us. Tie us up and beat us. Yeah, when I would be in trouble, when [he] would beat me, I would cry and cry."

—Junius, age 8

Prevalence. Any maltreatment is abhorrent, particularly in the family where relationships have precious and eternal potential, but child abuse is all the more egregious due to the special status of children in the eyes of the Creator. "Who is the greatest in the kingdom of heaven?" asked Jesus' disciples. "And Jesus called a little child unto him, and set him in the midst of them" (Matthew 18:1–2). In modern scripture, the Savior further explained, "But little children are holy, being sanctified through the atonement of Jesus Christ" (D&C 74:7).

The term *child maltreatment* encompasses child neglect and child abuse in their various forms. Estimating the prevalence of child maltreatment is complex due

not only to its multiple manifestations (physical abuse, emotional and mental abuse, child neglect, and child sexual abuse), but also because it is impossible to know how much maltreatment goes unreported. Worldwide, younger children tend to be more vulnerable to physical abuse, and pubescent and adolescent children are at relatively higher risk for sexual abuse (WHO, 2002). A national survey in the United States found that during a one-year span of time, one in seven children between ages 2 and 17 were victims of maltreatment, including physical, sexual, or psychological/emotional abuse, child neglect, and custodial interference or family abduction (Centers for Disease Control and Prevention [CDC], 2009). Parents or adult caregivers are responsible for child maltreatment in about 80 percent of cases (Holden & Barker, 2004). More than some forms of violence, child abuse is often hidden from those in the community and even in the family. Nevertheless, revelation states that, in time, these insidious acts will eventually be brought to light (D&C 1:3).

Risk factors for child abuse. Certain demographic, parental, and child variables have been found to be associated with child maltreatment (note that these are linkages, not necessarily causes). In a 17-year study, poverty was found to be linked to child neglect, but not to child sexual abuse (Brown, Cohen, Johnson, & Salzinger, 1998). Other characteristics that may increase the risk for child maltreatment included poor parent–child relationships, low parental involvement, low parental warmth, an authoritarian parenting style, single parenthood, poor marital quality, dissatisfaction with the child, unrealistic expectations of children, stress, and low impulse control (Brown et al., 1998). Child traits associated with maltreatment include perinatal problems (such as low birth weight), child disability (for example, low IQ), and maladaptive personality traits (like a difficult temperament). In one study, the rate of child maltreatment was 3 percent where there were no risk factors, but increased to 24 percent when four or more risk factors were present (Brown et al., 1998).

Frequently, abusers have themselves been victims. One study found that about half of sex offenders had themselves been abused (Craissati, McClurg, & Browne, 2002), and in general, those who have witnessed or experienced physical abuse as children are more likely to have violence in their relationships as adults (Whiting, Simmons, Havens, Smith, & Oka, 2009). In part, this is because children tend to learn behaviors and attitudes from their parents and other important adults around them, including attitudes about how to act in relationships, and how to view others and themselves. Still, transmission of violence may not be as common as once thought and is a complex process that is affected by a number of factors (Ertem, Leventhal, & Dobbs, 2000). Notably, most individuals who are exposed to abuse as children do not grow up to become abusive (Barnett et al., 2011). Many who experience abusive childhoods are able to learn healthy relationship skills and succeed brilliantly as parents.

Despite contextual influences and other risk factors that may make abuse more likely, individuals still choose how to react to others, even in stressful situations. This is a primary tenet of most abuse treatment programs (see, for example, Stith, Smith, Penn, Ward, & Tritt, 2004), and is consistent with what we know about agency. Elder Richard G. Scott (2008) stated that moral agency is at the center of God's plan of happiness. However, the Savior taught that those who use their agency to abuse others will suffer: "Whoso shall offend one of these little ones . . . , it were better for him that a millstone were hanged about his neck, and that he were drowned in the depth of the sea" (Matthew 18:6). To abusers, Elder Scott (2008) emphasized the importance of taking responsibility for overcoming abusive behavior and seeking professional help.

Child Physical Abuse

My mommy hit me with an extension cord on my face, and . . . I went to church like that, my face was all swollen . . . and they say what happened to you? And I [can't tell them].

—Cherise, age 7

Like, she would be mean in the morning, like all the time, and then she had this man and he used to beat us. . . . Yeah, you know like a piece of a table, the leg, it had nails in it and he used to beat us with that.

—Juan, age 12

The offense of child physical abuse is increasingly recognized and denounced by society, but is all the more serious in light of key doctrines regarding the sanctity of our physical bodies. We are asked, "Seest thou that ye are created after mine own image?" (Ether 3:15), and "know ye not that your body is the temple of the Holy Ghost . . . ?" (1 Corinthians 6:19). Child physical abuse was initially defined as observable bodily harm to a child, but the definition has been expanded to include substantial risk for injury or endangerment (Miller-Perrin & Perrin, 2007).

With regard to physical abuse in the United States, research suggests that at least three fourths of parents have used some form of physical discipline at some point in their parenting (such as spanking), and more than one half have used tactics such as hitting with fists, striking children with sticks or belts, kicking, pushing, or even throwing children (Barnett et al., 2011). International data on child physical abuse is scant, but the World Health Organization reports that in a study in Korea, 45 percent of parents self-reported beating or kicking their children, and in a study from Ethiopia, 21 percent of urban children and 64 percent of rural children reported bruises resulting from their parents' punishment (WHO, 2002). Fathers or father figures are implicated in abuse in the United States in 28.2 percent of cases, and mothers in 32.1 percent of cases (Holden & Barker, 2004). This is perhaps not surprising, considering that mothers typically spend considerably more time with children than do fathers. However, men—often fathers or boyfriends—are typically responsible for more severe forms of maltreatment, and boys are victims of physical abuse and beating more often than are girls (Edleson, 1999).

Spanking children has long been accepted in the United States as an appropriate practice. Nevertheless, frequent, reflexive, and thoughtless spanking becomes less effective over time. As a child guidance tool, spanking may teach something about what not to do, but it does not teach what the child should do. The child still needs positive instruction, logical consequences for poor choices, and coaching toward better behavior. Over the years, many professionals have expressed the view that spanking teaches children that hitting is an appropriate way of interacting with others (Straus, 1994). As Steinberg (2004, p. 149) stated, "The main side effect of physical punishment is excessive aggression." Children who are punished physically (versus those who are not) are more likely to fight other children, use aggression to solve problems, and to bully (Straus,

1994). But the expressed concerns seldom address the appropriate limits of nonaggression in an imperfect world. Important distinctions have recently been made between normative versus severe physical punishment. Findings from a longitudinal study (preschool age to adolescence) using such refined distinctions point to "no significant effects, either detrimental or beneficial, of normative physical punishment (spanking)" (Baumrind, Larzelere, & Owens, 2010, p. 187). Results from another study suggest that the adverse effects previously found to be linked to antisocial behavior (Straus, Sugarman, & Giles-Sims, 1997) may be statistical artifacts when potentially confounding variables were controlled for (Larzelere, Cox, & Smith, 2010). Perhaps most importantly, recent scholarship suggests that the potential for negative side effects depends on how punishment is used; for example, whether punishment is aversive rather than abusive (Baumrind et al., 2010; Larzelere et al., 2010).

Brigham Young said,

Bring up your children in the love and fear of the Lord; study their dispositions and their temperaments, and deal with them accordingly, never allowing yourself to correct them in the heat of passion; teach them to love you rather than to fear you (Widtsoe, 1977, p. 207).

The scientific research on parenting confirms that methods consistent with the gospel are best for children: abiding love, clear guidelines, and moral autonomy (Steinberg, 2004).

Sexual Abuse

My dad sexually abused me, and my mom had to come back because he threatened to kill me.
—Brian, age 11

The sacred power of procreation is an act of partnership with God. Elder Jeffrey R. Holland (1988) explained that the sanctity of sex can only be understood in the context of the doctrine of the body and spirit as the soul, ransomed by Christ. He described appropriate sexuality between husband and wife as a symbol of their total union—of their hearts, hopes, lives, and family. Speaking of inappropriate sexual relations, he said:

In trivializing the soul of another (please include the word *body* there), we trivialize the Atonement that saved that soul and guaranteed its continued existence. And when one toys with the Son of Righteousness, the Day Star himself, one toys with white heat and a flame hotter and holier than the noonday sun. You cannot do so and not be burned (p. 2).

Sexual abuse is a violation of sacred moral agency and, for the perpetrator, is a particular atrocity because it is a violation of the soul and the sacred God-given power of procreation. Those who are vulnerable are its victims, and it has the potential to cause later difficulties to the sexual—and symbolic—union between husband and wife.

Sexual abuse is often the most hidden and secretive form of maltreatment. Child sexual abuse can vary widely in its range of problems and severity, but it includes abuse inside and outside the family, as well as contact offenses and non-contact offenses (such as exposure to pornography). It also includes sexual exploitation of a vulnerable individual and the advantage of age or physical maturity or both of the perpetrator over the victim (Miller-Perrin & Perrin, 2007). Accurate numbers of sufferers are unknown, but existing data suggests that worldwide, approximately 20 percent of women and 5 to 10 percent of men were sexually abused as children (WHO, 2002). A U.S. retrospective study of a randomized general population sample of adults found that child sexual abuse had occurred to 14 percent of men and 32 percent of women (Briere & Elliott, 2003). In another study of a nationally representative sample of children and youth, 1 in 12 had experienced sexual victimization in the study year, ranging from relatively mild to severe offenses (Finkelhor, Ormrod, Turner, & Hamby, 2005). Rates of reported child sexual abuse in North America increased in the 1980s (Sedlak & Broadhurst, 1996), but actually declined in the 1990s and in the early 2000s (Barnett et al., 2011). Culture and attitudes have an impact: perpetration of sexual abuse is more likely to occur in nations and contexts where other types of violence are prevalent, and men are more likely to sexually abuse if they have strong attitudes of male sexual entitlement and rigid gender roles (WHO, 2002). Most sex abusers are male (at least 75 percent) and most who abuse sexually have developed deviant sexual interest by age 18 (Miller-Perrin & Perrin, 2007). Although about one half of this type of abuse is perpetrated by someone other than a parent or caregiver, the consequences tend to be most serious when a birth parent abuses, which is in about one fourth of cases (Sedlak & Broadhurst, 1996). The World Health Organization also reports that most sexual violence is perpetrated by men against women and girls, but scholars tend to agree that sexual abuse is underreported, especially among male victims.

Perpetrators tend to be relatively younger than perpetrators of other forms of abuse, with about 22 percent under the age of 26, many of them teenagers (Sedlak & Broadhurst, 1996). As with physical abuse, some who sexually abuse were themselves victimized as children. One study found that approximately one half of sexual abusers were also victims of abuse, and, compared to sex offenders who had not been abused, these perpetrators had higher levels of psychosexual difficulties, deviant attitudes, and recidivism (Craissati et al., 2002). Other abuse survivors become intergenerational buffers and break the cycle. Children of virtually all ages are victimized, but sufferers of sexual abuse are on average 9 to 11 years old (Miller-Perrin & Perrin, 2007), and girls are abused up to three times more often than are boys (Sedlak & Broadhurst, 1996). The consequences of sexual abuse, discussed later, bear similarities to consequences of other types of abuse. For abuse survivors, being believed and supported upon disclosure and cultivating positive cognitive appraisals (for example, the ability to recognize it was not their fault) can aid in recovery.

Child Psychological Abuse

Psychological abuse of children was previously seen as a side effect of other types of abuse, but is now recognized as maltreatment in its own right. It consists of degrading or rejecting a child, threatening harm to a child, exploiting or corrupting a child, ignoring a child's emotional needs, or isolating a child from appropriate interaction (Barnett et al., 2011).

Although psychological abuse tends to happen in tandem with other maltreatment, its consequences can be as harmful as or even more harmful than physical abuse (CDC, 2009). Sometimes referred to as emotional and verbal abuse, psychological abuse is inherent to any form of abuse. At its heart is a repeated pattern of demeaning, devaluing, and conveying to a person that he or she is unlovable, worthless, or unwanted (Miller-Perrin & Perrin, 2007). Children learn from the important adults in their lives how to think about themselves and others. Psychological abuse is insidious because of the negative outcomes to a child's self-image and subsequent behavior. "For as he thinketh in his heart, so is he" (Proverbs 23:7). Children come to believe what important others consistently tell them, and these beliefs also help to shape their conceptualizations of people and the world around them.

There are gradations to any type of abuse. In this regard, any parent can become upset and lash out verbally, fail to meet a need, become critical, or any number of things later regretted. Psychological abuse is characterized by more frequent, intense, and negative patterns of such behavior. Perhaps it is the most difficult type of maltreatment to define and may be the least reported. Estimates from a variety of reporting agencies indicate that 3 to 28 percent of the reported cases of child maltreatment are identified primarily as psychological and emotional abuse (Miller-Perrin & Perrin, 2007). Psychological abuse happens in the majority of physical abuse cases, and it overlaps with sexual abuse also, and so it might be considered as the most common form of child maltreatment. Compared with physical abuse, psychological abuse more strongly predicts a range of problems, including social impairment and low self-esteem, suicidal thoughts, problems in social interactions, and acting-out behaviors, including delinquency and substance abuse (Kaplan, Pelcovitz, & Labruna, 1999). Data suggest that parents are responsible for 90 percent of the reported cases of emotional abuse, and that characteristics of parents who abuse emotionally often include social and interpersonal problems, lack of support network, relatively higher rates of mental health problems (for example, depression or aggression), as well as social anxiety, low self-esteem, and substance abuse disorders (Barnett et al., 2011).

Child Neglect and Deprivation

Inside [our house] there was rats and roaches . . . and the basement was flooded so we couldn't take a bath . . . yeah, and the toilet was filled with rats, and so we had to go outside to use it.

—Cherise, age 7

Neglect is the most common form of child maltreatment, but may receive the least attention. Neglect, or deficiency of appropriate care, may not include abusive actions, but it still can have significant impact on children. It includes physical neglect (inattention or delay in care regarding physical needs and hygiene, inadequate supervision, inattention or delay in health care, or abandonment), neglect of emotional and social nurturing (lack of parental warmth or appropriate social support and interaction), and educational neglect (Schumacher, Slep, & Heyman, 2001). Context matters: for example, a parent may fail to give a child a necessary medication due to poverty, not disregard. Thus, the U.S. National Incidence Study (Sedlak & Broadhurst, 1996) distinguished between parents' lack of provision when options are available or unavailable. Gradation is also important to defining this type of abuse: for example, leaving a toddler in the care of a school-aged child for five minutes is different from doing the same for several hours, several days, or at regular intervals. The majority of neglected children tend to be quite young, and risk for neglect decreases with age (Barnett et al., 2011).

Poverty is perhaps the most important risk factor for neglect. Sedlak and Broadhurst (1996) found that in households with incomes of $15,000 or less compared to those with $30,000 or above, children were 22 times more likely to suffer maltreatment of some kind and 44 times more likely to suffer neglect. Other risk factors of neglecting children include being a single parent, having a lack of developmental knowledge, poor judgment, high stress, low social support, and problems with self-motivation (Schumacher et al., 2001). Substance abuse is another prominent risk factor, and in terms of family risk, single-parent families, less cohesive families, and larger families are at relatively higher risk for child neglect (Schumacher et al., 2001). Women are more often held responsible for cases of neglect than men, but this is due to women most often being identified as primary caregivers.

Consequences of Child Abuse

I am in special ed because of my behavior. . . . I am ADHD. . . . I am really bad in everything. . . . I went to [a group home] and [a worker] . . . threatened to tie me up with a rope . . . and then I left because the people couldn't deal with me. I kept

going into the hospital because of my behavior. If I was bad there they would give me a shot in the butt . . . and I got one too.

—Carlos, age 12

Maltreatment during childhood is particularly harmful because children are vulnerable and in "need of much nourishment" (1 Nephi 18:19), and childhood experiences have important impact on a person's well-being during adolescence and adulthood. Broadly, the consequences of physical abuse are often manifest in externalizing problems (such as delinquency or aggression); the consequences of sexual abuse are often manifest in internalizing behaviors (such as depression, anxiety, or low self-esteem). The consequences of abuse can differ, ranging from mild to severe and from short term to long term, and the consequences can manifest in diverse ways—physically, psychologically, behaviorally, and in interpersonal relationships. Important factors include the child's age, developmental stage, and the type of abuse, as well as its frequency and severity.

Physical abuse. Physical abuse of children often results in physical, behavioral, and emotional problems that manifest in childhood but that can continue into adulthood. In addition to bruises and injuries, physical abuse creates risk for impaired brain and cognitive functioning, poor perceptual and motor skills, and poor academic achievement (Miller-Perrin & Perrin, 2007). It is linked to anxiety, depression, irritability, dissociation, and impaired self-image (Briere & Elliott, 2003). Interpersonally, physical abuse is associated with attachment problems, impaired social skills, and peer rejection. Not surprisingly, such abuse can lead to symptoms of posttraumatic stress disorder (PTSD), such as hyperarousal and hypervigilance, since the child may be faced with the prospect of further assault (Ford et al., 2000). Exposure to trauma may also increase the likelihood of oppositional defiant disorder (ODD) and attention-deficit disorder (ADHD) (Ford et al., 2000). In adulthood, those abused as children are more prone to engage in criminal and violent behavior, to abuse intimate partners, to abuse alcohol and other substances, and to have emotional problems (Barnett et al., 2011).

Sexual abuse. Data suggest that sexual abuse can have more extensive and longer-lasting negative consequences than child physical abuse (Briere & Elliott, 2003). Like physical abuse, the harms that result from sexual abuse are manifest in multiple areas, including physical and reproductive health problems, and, in adulthood, difficulties in maintaining a healthy sexual relationship (Briere & Elliott, 2003). Other possible consequences of sexual abuse include sexually transmitted infections; mental health issues, such as self-blame and shame; negative and avoidant ways of coping; and interpersonal problems, which are in turn associated with emotional distress, insomnia, feelings of helplessness in avoiding victimization, and substance use to dull the pain (Whiffen & MacIntosh, 2005; WHO, 2008).

Psychological abuse and neglect. Psychological maltreatment can result in emotional problems, intellectual deficits, shame and guilt, and insecure attachment. It also can increase anger and aggression, disruptive behavior, and difficulty in making and keeping friends (Miller-Perrin & Perrin, 2007). These problems can continue into adolescence and adulthood, but can become complicated with other problems, such as negative life views, depression and suicidal ideation, and personality disorders. Relatively less is known about the consequences of neglect, but like other types of maltreatment, it can lead to social, cognitive, behavioral, and academic difficulties; emotional problems; and even physical dysfunction. These outcomes can be long term, but they vary depending on the type, severity, and frequency of neglect.

Characteristics of the child and the child's environment can have a positive effect toward recovery, including the child's self-esteem, optimism, and creativity; their independence and courage; and the ways in which the child thinks about the abuse. The child's safety; access to support; and a social network of trusted people, including peers, teachers, or other important adults, are important protective factors that help promote recovery (Fraser & Terzian, 2005).

Link between Child Abuse and Intimate Partner Violence

Child maltreatment and intimate partner violence are often examined and discussed as separate issues, with little attention given to their potential overlap. However, if one form of maltreatment exists in a family (such as child abuse), there is a 30 to 60 percent likelihood that another form of maltreatment also is present (such as intimate partner violence; Edleson, 1999). For example, frequent, intense conflict between parents has a negative impact on children's emotional security and is associated with negative outcomes, such as depression, and

externalizing behaviors, such as delinquency (Bradford & Barber, 2005; Cummings & Davies, 2002). Witnessing domestic violence can lead to developmental and emotional problems similar to those found in children who are directly abused, and accordingly, approximately 21 states and Puerto Rico have legislation regarding child witnesses of abuse to a cohabitant in the home (Child Welfare Information Gateway [CWIG], 2009). Therefore, adult violence in the presence of children is typically considered a type of child abuse and is often reportable to child protective services along with other types of child abuse.

Intimate Partner Violence

[My friends and family] would think I was stupid for putting up with it. Shoot, I'm embarrassed. At least if it's on my arm or my legs, I can cover it up. I've walked around with black eyes or fat lips. . . . I'm just getting over a fat lip here. . . . They know and make me feel like an idiot because I stay with him. Nobody can figure it out.

—Janet, age 32

Intimate partner violence (IPV) is a public health problem, human rights issue, and clinical challenge (Saltzman, 2004). Rates of IPV are difficult to assess accurately and vary greatly, depending on sample and methods used. The National Coalition Against Domestic Violence (2005) gives the following estimates on rates of intimate partner violence in the United States: (a) Approximately one in every four women will experience physical violence by an intimate partner at least once in her life; (b) Almost one third of female homicide victims reported in police records are killed by an intimate partner (see also Johnson, 2008); (c) About 1.3 million women are raped or physically assaulted or both by their intimate partners every year; (d) Intimate partner violence results in more than 18.5 million mental health care visits each year (www.ncadv.org). Although these numbers are specific to the United States, a recent worldwide study confirms that this problem is indeed global.

World Health Organization researchers found that women throughout the world suffer physical and sexual violence by intimate partners at rates usually between 29 and 62 percent (Garcia-Moreno, Jansen, Ellsberg, Heise, & Watts, 2006). Much of this violence is severe and continuous. To find this information, a trained group of more than 500 female interviewers met with more than 24,000 15- to 49-year-old women at 15 sites in 10 countries. Women were randomly selected to be interviewed in the area they lived, and care was taken to keep the interviews completely private. For example, the interviewers had alternate questionnaires in case a husband or partner showed up. Sometimes an interviewer would hold a "fake" interview with male household members to keep them busy while the woman participated in the study. Many of these women (20 to 60 percent) had never spoken of this problem with anyone, which illustrates not only the fear that violence can instill, but also its underreported nature. Even though many different cultures and languages were part of this study, violence was prevalent and hidden in every country visited. As members of a worldwide church, Latter-day Saints should be aware that violence crosses cultures and is also found within the families of Church members.

Gender and Patterns of Violence

I would start off small, grabbing her arm as she's trying to walk away, not put too much force behind my actions, to instigate her to go even further so that I could justify going a little bit further myself. When she pushes me too hard . . . in my mind I say, "Thank you for giving me what I wanted, pushing me. You hit me hard so I'm gonna come back and I'm gonna hit you just as hard or even harder." So I'd push back, I'd do whatever I wanted. . . . It's like the sting of the slap is making me grin . . . it's like . . . "You don't know what the heck you just did, it's just what I wanted . . . thank you." Now I can take it a step further myself and I'll lash out on her [with] all the anger, frustration I'm feeling at the moment.

—Jacob, age 28

This quote, by a Latter-day Saint man, illustrates how differences in power between the sexes can sometimes be used to provoke, threaten, and control the process of high intensity dynamics in relationships. The quote also illustrates how couples can engage in patterns of aggression and violence that can sometimes be mutual. Although it is difficult to disentangle the roles and responsibilities of those who contribute to violence, it is important to look at how violence may be experienced differently by men and women.

When we discuss violence in professional settings, it is common for some to object to the gendered nature of our discussion. Some ask, "Isn't it true that men are commonly victims of violence? What about women who are violent?" These are good questions. Both women and men can be victims of intimate partner violence, and some types of physical aggression are as commonly perpetrated by women as by men (Johnson, 2008). Nevertheless, women are at far greater danger for physical and emotional trauma than are men (Clements & Sawhney, 2000; Sleutel, 1998). Also, men cause more injury than do women, and female victims express more fear than do male victims (Felson & Cares, 2005). The physical differences between most men and women put women at a disadvantage when things spiral out of control. As Lisa, age 27, said:

I think that men might not understand the impact of a raised voice, that type of thing. . . . I don't think I am threatening even if I am speaking in an angry tone. Whereas the 6′3″ guy can be threatening if he is speaking in an angry tone.

Although women can become very physically violent (more on that below), it is unusual for a man to become terrorized by his wife's violence in the same way that a woman might be fearful of her husband. Another issue is that women's violence may be reactive in the face of male violence, although occasionally it can consist of more severe violence and control (Johnson, 2006).

Typologies of Violence

Not only is partner violence prevalent, it is also multifaceted, multicausal, and complex. There are many types and patterns of violence in intimate relationships, with varying degrees of intensity and risk. For example, one influential typology distinguishes between traditional battering (intimate terrorism) and non-controlling or situational couple violence (Johnson, 2008). Intimate terrorism is usually characterized by a strong, controlling, and dominating male, who uses physical violence in addition to other tactics. These may include behaviors that terrorize, manipulate, humiliate, blame, and wear down an intimate partner. This is the type of violence most often reported to authorities, and these victims (nearly always women) are more likely to seek social and health services as well as legal protections.

In contrast, situational couple violence is more bi-directional and tends to occur when an angry argument escalates into verbal and physical aggression (Johnson & Leone, 2005). This type of violence is common in community and agency samples, is not characterized by domination and control, and is less likely to result in serious injury. When reports of similar rates of IPV between men and women are given, it is usually this type of violence. While not as severe as intimate terrorism, situational couple violence is still a significant problem.

Adult Sexual Violence

> He would come in and throw himself on top of me, hold me down, hold me by the neck and threaten me and tell me that he was going to do whatever he wanted to do to me and there wasn't anything that anybody could do about it.
>
> —Beth, age 56

When people hear the term *adult sexual violence,* they may think of rape, which indeed is a terrifying and traumatic event, with many potential consequences (Briere & Scott, 2006). However, people may not necessarily think of marital rape, although it is much more common than stranger assault, and also has significant consequences. Although a full discussion of this type of abuse is beyond the scope of this chapter, it is important to know that sexual coercion in intimate partnerships exists, and may occur along with other types of violence, especially as a form of domination and control (Logan, Walker, Jordan & Leukefeld, 2006).

Psychological Abuse

> [I would do] anything that I could think of: physical, emotional things that I could say; put her down in every way that I possibly could; say everything that I possibly could to hurt her; make her cry.
>
> —Lars, age 30

Psychological abuse (sometimes referred to as emotional or verbal abuse) includes a repeated pattern of demeaning, devaluing, and conveying to a person that he or she is unlovable, worthless, or unwanted (Miller-Perrin & Perrin, 2007). Victims of abuse will often say that this type of abuse is even more damaging than physical abuse since it frequently leaves the victim struggling with low self-worth and feelings of inadequacy (Whiting, Oka, & Fife, manuscript submitted for publication). Psychological abuse is always present with physical violence, but often occurs in nonviolent relationships as well (Straus & Field, 2003). It can range from severe shaming and demeaning to more subtle forms of criticizing and contempt, all of which are damaging to relationships and individuals (Gottman, 1999).

The Joseph Smith Translation of Ephesians 4:26 reads, "Can ye be angry, and not sin?" Similarly, Jesus warned against the dangers of letting strong emotions control relational behavior: "He that hath the spirit of contention is not of me, but is of the devil, who is the father of contention, and he stirreth up the hearts of men to contend with anger" (3 Nephi 11:29).

Why Do They Stay?

> I was powerless. I felt trapped and I felt like I was paralyzed, I couldn't get out of it and I started struggling with moral issues and spiritual issues and feeling like I wanted to get out of it but honestly I was so terrified of the process and the aftermath of what that would mean . . . it was easier to just stay in that situation and deal with [it] than to make things worse by getting out.
>
> —Joanie, age 26

As illustrated by this woman's experience, leaving abuse is not usually a simple matter. Although many people who suffer abuse ultimately do leave abusive relationships, this may take a long time, and many want to stay and just have the abuse stop (Sleutel, 1998). Sometimes people blame a victim for staying in an abusive relationship because of their own strong feelings of shock or anger, but this is a complex decision that can carry great risk. Many women are threatened if they leave, and indeed this is a time that rates of violence and even homicides spike (Morton, Runyan, Moracco, & Butts, 1998). Women may also fear for their children, who may have been threatened, and they may have few options or resources to draw upon if they do leave.

Dating Violence

Although it may be easy to think of violence as only a marital or cohabitation problem, it occurs with similar frequencies in dating relationships. In fact, women who are between the ages of 20 and 24, which includes many college students, are at the highest risk of violence (Catalano, 2007). Dating violence, like most forms of abuse, is difficult to define and measure, but awareness of this problem has increased in recent years as college and even high school campuses are addressing the issue. Physical and verbal aggression is common between partners who are committed, casually dating, or may not know each other well at all. Another form of dating violence is date rape and sexual assault, which may involve the use of drugs (for example, GHB or Rohypnol) that can impair a person's ability to consent to sexual relations or even remember them (Schwartz, Milteer, & LeBeau, 2000). Also, stalking is a common dating-violence issue, involving unwanted communication, pursuing, or harassing of another person that causes fear (Sheridan, Blaauw, & Davies, 2003).

Risk Factors for IPV

His father was that way [controlling], so I think his perception is that the man is always in charge and the man takes control, and the woman is to be submissive, and of course that's the way I thought I was supposed to be . . . not just because of what I saw growing up. . . . You know, well, I'm supposed to do what he said, or even hearing that religiously . . . the woman is to follow the man, he is to be the head of the house.

—Kathy, age 48

Researchers have identified a number of possible risk factors that may contribute to the likelihood of intimate partner violence. These include substance abuse, alcohol abuse, male partner isolation, living in an economically disadvantaged neighborhood, witnessing or experiencing violence in one's family of origin, child maltreatment, stress, gender inequality, and psychopathology (Coker, Smith, McKeown, & King, 2000; DeMaris, Benson, Fox, Hill, & Van Wyk, 2003; Fox, Benson, DeMaris, & Van Wyk, 2002; Holtzworth-Munroe & Stuart, 1994; Straus, 1991). Although these are contributing factors, it is important to know that violence is

a multifaceted phenomenon that is found in all sectors of society, affecting those of varying marital status, socioeconomic status, ethnicity, nationality, sexual orientation, and gender (Barnett et al., 2011; Michalski, 2004; Valente, 2002). It is notable that cohabiting relationships are found to be more likely to be violent than marital relationships (Kenney & McLanahan, 2006).

Consequences of Intimate Partner Violence

One day I went to the mall and I had no idea what I liked anymore, nothing. And that's when I realized you just totally lose your whole person.

—Rosa, age 33

Violence towards women has been found to correlate with symptoms of PTSD, depression, stress, low self-esteem, substance abuse, limited problem-solving skills, low social support, and limited material resources (Logan, et al., 2006). Abuse is also associated with many adverse health outcomes for female victims, such as chronic pain, arthritis, disability, migraines, frequent headaches, stomach ulcers, spastic colon, and other illnesses (Coker et al., 2000; Logan, et al., 2006). And of course, abuse is extremely spiritually damaging for both victims and perpetrators.

Other Abuse in the Family

A thorough treatment of subtypes of family maltreatment is beyond the scope of this chapter, but below we briefly address the topics of elder abuse and sibling abuse.

Elder Abuse

"How tragic it is, how absolutely revolting is abuse of the elderly" (President Gordon B. Hinckley, 2002a, May, p. 54).

Elder abuse is typically defined as being perpetrated by a caregiver or other trusted person who causes injury, confinement, physical or psychological harm, or deprivation of care (Gorbien & Eisenstein, 2005). Like other maltreatment, elder abuse can be the infliction of physical, sexual, and psychological harm or neglect, but it can also include misuse of the elder's assets or exploitation of funds. The most common setting is the home, but it also occurs in hospitals, nursing homes, and assisted-care centers. The few available survey studies suggest that between 4 and 6 percent of elders are abused at home, and that abuse in care centers and institutions may be more prevalent than once thought (WHO, 2002). Views on elder abuse differ greatly by culture and nation, and cultural practices may have an impact. For example, poverty and female dependency in India tend to leave elderly Indian women relatively vulnerable, whereas proximity in multigenerational households in Poland may play a part in the psychological abuse and neglect of the elderly (Barnett et al., 2011). Conversely, younger respondents in a study in China were less likely than older respondents to view victims as provoking their own abuse (Malley-Morrison, Nolido, & Chawla, 2006). In the United States, it is estimated that 2 million senior people (32 per 1000 adults) are abused each year (Gorbien & Eisenstein, 2005).

This type of abuse can be complex because abusers may be at least somewhat dependent on the elder for housing or other support, and the abuser may have some form of impairment in social, emotional, or financial functioning. Risk factors of elder abuse include a shared living situation (increasing the possibility for contact), social isolation, strained family relationships, low education, dementia, and functional impairment (Gorbien & Eisenstein, 2005). There is comparatively higher risk for maltreatment in institutional settings when standards of care are low, when staff is poorly trained, and there are deficiencies in the physical environment (WHO, 2002).

Sibling Abuse
Sibling abuse is difficult to define due to the complexity of differentiating normal developmental behaviors from abuse. Like most forms of maltreatment, sibling abuse can be physical, emotional, or sexual. Mild physical abuse among siblings is common. For example, a recent U.S. study found sibling violence to be highly prevalent, but most in the study did not identify it as problematic or as violence (Kettrey & Emery, 2006). The severity, intent, and frequency of aggression should be considered; also, the hierarchy between siblings may be equal or very disparate. Regardless, severe actions typically qualify as abuse, such as intense and frequent ridicule or intimidation; destroying possessions; extreme violence, such as punching or kicking; hitting

with an object; stabbing; sexual advances; or forcing a sibling to view pornography. The outcomes for victims of sibling abuse are similar to other types of abuse (such as internalizing and externalizing problems), and the correlates are similar (for example, violence in dating relationships among perpetrators; Kiselica & Morrill-Richards, 2007).

What Can We Do?

If you give way to your angry feelings, it sets on fire the whole course of nature . . . and you are then apt to set those on fire who are contending with you.
—Brigham Young (Widtsoe, 1977, p. 269).

Prevention and intervention. The cultural lens through which maltreatment is viewed has important impact on the response. Family violence is viewed by some cultures as largely a private affair in which authorities should not be involved, and in some countries the victims of sexual abuse may be silenced, constrained to marry an abuser, or even killed by relatives in the name of family honor (WHO, 2002). Fortunately, maltreatment is gaining recognition and is increasingly denounced. One encouraging trend is a decrease in rates of child abuse, at least in some Western countries. Substantiated cases of child sexual abuse decreased 41 percent from 1992 to 2000 in the United States and 49 percent between 1993 and 1998 in Ontario, Canada, with similar declines found in a 2003 study in Australia and a 2002 study in Ireland (see Crooks & Baur, 2005). Some experts believe the progress is in part due to better public awareness and improved prevention and intervention programs.

There are many ways to help decrease the prevalence and impact of child abuse. Some of these include condemning the cultural acceptance of violence and considering its detrimental effects (for example, media violence and culturally accepted family violence). Individuals can advocate for public policies that support the prevention as well as the treatment of child maltreatment (Miller-Perrin & Perrin, 2007). Other methods include supporting local and national agencies that address abuse, including programs that address related causes (poverty, unemployment, housing issues, family life education). Individuals can volunteer for agencies or as court-appointed special advocates (CASA) or even become foster or adoptive parents (Barnett et al., 2011). Efforts in various parts of the world have been effective in reducing the risk of child maltreatment. For example, where risk factors for abuse exist (multiple stressors such as teen parenthood, or impoverished single parent households), parent education has helped reduce rates of physical abuse (WHO, 2008). A parent who had been court-ordered to receive treatment stated after completing the program, "Five months ago we felt like a broken toy that everybody wanted to fix. All we really needed was our battery replaced . . . we got some good ideas and information to be better parents. And that's a good thing!" (Egbert, 2006, p. 1).

Interventions are beginning to focus on prevention of abuse and not just treatment once abuse has occurred. The results of a meta-analytic study of 56 programs found that strengths-based programs with proactive, empowerment-based approaches and social support components had better efficacy and longer positive impact, while the gains made in "reactive" treatment programs (once abuse has occurred) were not as large nor as long lasting (MacLeod & Nelson, 2000). The authors of the study concluded that although part of the difference in outcome may be attributed to population (meaning participants who had not maltreated versus those who had), the children of those in preventative interventions were generally younger (infants or young children), and the children of those in the reactive interventions were generally older (school-aged children and teens). The facilitation of positive habits in parent–child interactions and early intervention where needed is more effective in alleviating child maltreatment than is reactive treatment (MacLeod & Nelson, 2000). Kofi Annan, winner of the 2001 Nobel Peace Prize, stated:

> Men and women everywhere have the right to live their lives and raise their children free from the fear of violence. We must help them enjoy that right by making it clearly understood that violence is preventable, and by working together to identify and address its underlying causes (WHO, 2002, p. 45).

Regarding the prevention of child sexual abuse, specialists recommend the following suggestions for parents, caregivers, and educators: (a) provide prevention-oriented material to children, (b) present simple, developmentally appropriate information, (c) equip the child with tools so she or he can be proactive and competent, rather than fearful, (d) define good touch (like hugs or pats) versus bad touch (contact that hurts, touch in "bathing suit" areas, or touch that creates discomfort or confusion), (e) encourage children to talk to trusted adults about bad touch and discuss strategies for how to handle such situations (Crooks & Baur, 2005).

Reporting Abuse

All states in the United States and its territories mandate that professionals report child maltreatment (CWIG, 2008); reporting laws vary by state. In 18 states and Puerto Rico, any person who suspects child abuse, not just a professional or an agent, is required to report the suspected abuse. In many states, a report must be made if a person suspects or has reason to believe that a child is being abused or neglected—proof is not required. State laws vary regarding when a communication is privileged—that is, privacy of communication between a patient or client and a professional or clergy member (CWIG, 2008)—either affirming confidentiality or denying it. Most states protect the confidentiality of reporters, but often find it helpful to know the identity of reporters. Most states do not mandate the reporting of intimate partner violence, but most do mandate the reporting of injuries related to IPV (Scalzo, 2006). All states in the United States have laws in place for the reporting of elder abuse (Gorbien & Eisenstein, 2005).

Church Response

> Any form of physical or mental abuse to any woman is not worthy of any priesthood holder. . . . This, of course, means verbal as well as physical abuse (President James E. Faust, 1988, p. 37).

> When we undertake to . . . exercise control or dominion or compulsions upon the souls of the children of men, in any degree of unrighteousness, behold, the heavens withdraw themselves; the Spirit of the Lord is grieved; and when it is withdrawn, Amen to the priesthood or the authority of that man (D&C 121:37).

The Church of Jesus Christ of Latter-day Saints was among the first churches to recognize the problem of abuse and has issued an official statement regarding child abuse. In the early 1980s, President Gordon B. Hinckley, then second counselor in the First Presidency, denounced child abuse: "The exploitation of children . . . for the satisfaction of sadistic desires is sin of the darkest hue" (The Church of Jesus Christ of Latter-day Saints Newsroom, 2009). Confirming Church policy, he later stated, "We cannot tolerate it. We will not tolerate it. Anyone who abuses a child may expect Church discipline as well as possible legal action" (Hinckley, 2002b, November, p. 59). The Church has taken several steps to address abuse. For example, men are required to have a co-instructor when teaching children and are not permitted to teach alone. To support the lay clergy, the Church has developed training materials and videos to educate leaders, and a 24-hour help line is available, giving lay clergy access to professional counselors who provide support and advice on specific issues. The Church has published 50 articles since 1976 that condemn abuse and educate members about child abuse, and the Church includes the topic of abuse for study during Sunday meetings. Convicted sex offenders are excommunicated, and as of 1995, a confidential annotation is placed on the membership record of the one who abused. Even if an offender repents and comes back into fellowship with the Church, the annotation remains on the record (and follows the record through any move), alerting clergy not to place the person in situations with children. In dealing with reports of child abuse, bishops are instructed that they must first protect the victim and second hold the perpetrator responsible. The Church defers to the laws of the state within which clergy reside: some states mandate the confidentiality of a confession and other states mandate reporting the abuse. Regardless, bishops are instructed to "do all they can to prevent further abuse" (The Church of Jesus Christ of Latter-day Saints Newsroom, 2009).

Healing

Recovery from abuse is possible. The process of healing can be facilitated with help from mental health professionals as well as trusted family members, friends, and ecclesiastical leaders. In addition, reliable information is available online from sources such as the National Child Traumatic Stress Network (www.nctsnet.org),

the National Institutes of Health (health.nih.gov/topic/ChildAbuse), and the American Academy of Pediatrics (www.aap.org/sections/childabuseneglect/). The first step in recovery, of course, is to do everything possible to ensure a safe environment and prevent further harm. Although early treatment may increase the likelihood of its success, in some cases it is only later that symptoms are recognized. Treatment can be effective even when it occurs long after the abuse happened.

Several aspects should be considered with regard to treatment. Perhaps most important, treatment should be matched with the severity of abuse and should address the unique set of problems that result from abuse. One's age at treatment as well as the circumstances that lead to treatment should also be considered, along with any coexisting conditions. Appropriate diagnoses can help in focusing treatment on key issues, but diagnosis may be difficult because symptoms stemming from abuse (which often are manifest as posttraumatic stress disorder or acute stress disorder) can overlap significantly with a range of other related symptoms, such as bipolar disorder (for example, hypomania), sleep disorders, anxiety, or oppositional–defiant disorder due to re-enactment of abuse, such as aggression (Cohen et al., 2010). Abuse is a global problem, and treatment requires understanding of cultural characteristics and culturally appropriate diagnostic and treatment methods (for example, sensitivity to societal and community definitions and accepted practices).

Treatment may include individual and group formats, family intervention, and even community-focused prevention. Individual treatment often includes cognitive restructuring, relaxation skills, self-esteem building, and problem-solving. A common curative component of therapeutic treatment is to help the sufferer to recognize, re-experience, and reprocess thoughts and feelings about the trauma in a relatively gentle and safe way, such that the distress is eventually lessened. Treatment may also include interpersonal components to help the sufferer interact with important others in adaptive ways. Family therapy may include parent coaching and stress reduction. Group therapy often includes social skills training, sharing experiences, and anger management.

Those seeking treatment should know that research suggests that therapies specifically targeting abuse-related trauma are considered to be more effective than general or nondirective therapies. According to guidelines put forth by the American Academy of Child and Adolescent Psychiatry, best practices include the following components: (a) the therapy directly addresses trauma, (b) as appropriate, parents or other significant persons are included as agents of change, and (c) the therapy focuses on enhancement of functioning as well as symptom reduction (Cohen et al., 2010). These same guidelines state that treatment may include components represented by the acronym PRACTICE: *psychoeducation* about abuse and its prevalence, *parenting skills*, *relaxation skills* (such as progressive relaxation), *affective modulation* (for example, feeling identification), *cognitive coping and processing* (such as changing inaccurate or unhelpful thoughts), *trauma narrative* (creating a narrative and correcting cognitive distortions about the experiences), *in vivo mastery of trauma reminders* (gradual exposure to problematic memories), *conjoint child–parent sessions,* and *enhancing safety and development* (creating safety and facilitating a return to normal development).

Not all who have suffered abuse need treatment. However, there are treatments that have been shown to be effective in reducing symptoms and improving well-being. For example, Multisystemic Therapy for Child Abuse and Neglect (MST–CAN) was found to reduce adolescent mental health symptoms and parents' psychiatric distress and behaviors linked to maltreatment (Swenson, Schaeffer, Henggeler, Faldowski, & Mayhew, 2010). MST–CAN includes a safety plan, identifies strengths and needs (including peers, school, and social support network), prioritizes intervention (for example, to improve parenting skills or anxiety management), and provides cognitive–behavioral interventions for individuals and families. Another study tested two commonly used therapies in the treatment of trauma from child abuse: trauma-focused cognitive–behavioral therapy (TF–CBT) and eye movement desensitization and reprocessing (EMDR) (Seidler & Wagner, 2006). TF–CBT uses stimulus confrontation (recalling and challenging problem-laden responses) and cognitive restructuring (examining and re-forming thought patterns). Conversely, in EMDR, the person focuses on disturbing images and memories, during which time the therapist performs bilateral stimulation (the use of auditory or tactile stimuli, such as the therapist moving two fingers back and forth as the client follows them with the eyes). Findings from this meta-analytic study suggest that both treatments are equally effective (Seidler & Wagner, 2006).

An increasingly prominent approach in psychotherapy in general is acceptance and commitment therapy (ACT). This therapeutic model facilitates psychological flexibility, encouraging acceptance of experience and action in keeping with one's values (Ruiz, 2010). ACT includes exposure exercises, but unlike the classical goals of extinguishing discomfort, the purpose is to help the individual to increase the ability to be more fully present. Available data suggest that ACT is effective for addressing a wide range of psychological problems (Ruiz, 2010), but further study is needed regarding the efficacy of ACT on reducing symptoms of trauma related to past abuse.

In some cases, medications are used in treatment, typically prescribed by a psychiatrist who has specialized medical training in the use of psychotropic medications. SSRI antidepressant medications may be prescribed and are best used in conjunction with psychotherapy. Although SSRIs are approved for adult use, some studies indicate they may also be used to reduce symptoms of posttraumatic stress disorder in children; but other studies suggest a strong placebo effect (Cohen et al., 2010). Non–SSRI antidepressants and other psychotropic medications may also be prescribed, such as dopamine-blocking agents to counteract potentially elevated levels of dopamine found among some survivors of abuse, or adrenergic-blocking agents, due to increased adrenergic tone (linked to adrenaline) in some survivors (Cohen et al., 2010).

Maltreatment ranges widely in terms of its types and subtypes. It is blatant in some cases and can be difficult to recognize in other cases, but it has at the foundation the unrighteous exercise of agency that causes harm to another. Because our Father in Heaven is just and loves us deeply, He can help individuals overcome the consequences of abuse. Elder Richard G. Scott (2008) urged abuse survivors to study the Atonement, exercise faith in Christ's power to heal, and begin to place the burden on Him. Elder Scott emphasized the importance of hope, as well as the realization that sources of help are available and healing is possible. He stated that damaged abilities to form close, trusting relationships can be overcome in the realization of our divine nature and through the love and support of loved ones and trusted leaders. Finally, Elder Scott urged those who have suffered from abuse to find the courage to seek help. A survivor spoke of the long, difficult process of healing, a process of more than 20 years:

> I had never really understood the *healing* power of the Atonement. I had no idea how personal and penetrating it could be, no idea that it could heal my broken heart and take away the pain and hurt and anger and bitterness that I had been feeling for so many years (Name withheld, 2009, p. 54).

The consequences of abuse vary enormously according to the frequency, type, and severity of abuse. It is crucial to note that healing is possible, through the support of caring Church leaders, competent professionals, and close loved ones, but ultimately through the healing power of the Savior, whose love is deep, personal, and constant.

Kay Bradford is an associate professor in the department of Family, Consumer, and Human Development at Utah State University, and a licensed family therapist. He and his wife, Glenna, have one son. Jason B. Whiting *is an associate professor in the Marriage and Family Therapy Program at Texas Tech University. He and his wife, April, are the parents of six children.*

References

Barber, B., Stolz, H., & Olsen, J. (2005). Parental support, psychological control, and behavioral control: Assessing relevance across time, culture, and method. *Monographs of the Society for Research in Child Development, 70*, 1–137.

Barnett, O. W., Miller-Perrin, C. L., & Perrin, R. D. (2011). *Family violence across the lifespan: An introduction* (3rd ed.). Thousand Oaks, CA: Sage.

Baumrind, D., Larzelere, R. E., & Owens, E. B. (2010). Effects of preschool parents' power assertive patterns and practices on adolescent development. *Parenting, 10*, 157–201.

Bradford, K., & Barber, B. K. (2005). Interparental conflict as intrusive family process. *Journal of Emotional Abuse, 5*, 143–167.

Briere, J., & Elliott, D. M. (2003). Prevalence and psychological sequelae of self-reported childhood physical and sexual abuse in a general population sample of men and women. *Child Abuse and Neglect, 27*, 1205–1222.

Briere, J., & Scott, C. (2006). *Principles of trauma therapy: A guide to symptoms, evaluation, and treatment.* Thousand Oaks, CA: Sage.

Brown, J., Cohen, P., Johnson, J. G., & Salzinger, S. (1998). A longitudinal analysis of risk factors for child maltreatment: Findings of a 17-year prospective study of officially recorded and self-reported child abuse and neglect. *Child Abuse and Neglect, 22*, 1065–1078.

Catalano, S. (2007). *Intimate partner violence in the U.S.* Washington D.C.: U.S. Dept of Justice Bureau of Justice Statistics. Retrieved from http://bjs.ojp.usdoj.gov/content/pub/pdf/ipvus.pdf

Centers for Disease Control and Prevention. (2009). Child maltreatment: Consequences. Retrieved from http://www.cdc.gov/ViolencePrevention/childmaltreatment/consequences.html

Child Welfare Information Gateway. (2009). Child witnesses to domestic violence: Summary of state laws. Washington, DC: U.S. Department of Health and Human Services. Retrieved from http://www.childwelfare.gov/systemwide/laws_policies/statutes/witnessdvall.pdf

Child Welfare Information Gateway. (2008). Mandatory reporters of child abuse and neglect. Washington, DC: U.S. Department of Health and Human Services. Retrieved from http://www.childwelfare.gov/systemwide/laws_policies/statutes/manda.cfm

The Church of Jesus Christ of Latter-day Saints. (1995). Responding to abuse: Helps for ecclesiastical leaders. Salt Lake City: Author.

The Church of Jesus Christ of Latter-day Saints Newsroom. (2009). Public issues: Child abuse. Retrieved from http://newsroom.lds.org/ldsnewsroom/eng/public-issues/child-abuse

Clements, C. M., & Sawhney, D. K. (2000). Coping with domestic violence: Control attributions, dysphoria, and hopelessness. *Journal of Traumatic Stress, 13*, 219–240.

Cohen, J. A., Bukstein, O., Walter, H., Benson, R. S., Chrisman, A., Farchione, T. R., . . . Medicus, J. (2010). Practice parameter for the assessment and treatment of children and adolescents with posttraumatic stress disorder. *Journal of the American Academy of Child and Adolescent Psychiatry, 49*, 414–430.

Coker, A. L., Smith, P. H., McKeown, R. E., & King, M. J. (2000). Frequency and correlates of intimate partner violence by type: Physical, sexual, and psychological battering. *American Journal of Public Health, 90*, 553–559.

Craissati, J., McClurg, G., & Browne, K. (2002). Characteristics of perpetrators of child sexual abuse who have been sexually victimized as children. *Sexual Abuse: A Journal of Research and Treatment, 14*, 225–239.

Crooks, R., & Baur, K. (2005). *Our sexuality* (9th ed.). Belmont, CA: Thomson Wadsworth.

Cummings, E. M., & Davies, P. T. (2002). Effects of marital conflict on children: Recent advances and emerging themes in process-oriented research. *Journal of Child Psychology and Psychiatry, 43*, 31–63.

DeMaris, A., Benson, M. L., Fox, G. L., Hill, T., & Van Wyk, J. (2003). Distal and proximal factors in domestic violence: A test of an integrated model. *Journal of Marriage and Family, 65*, 652–667.

Edleson, J. L. (1999). The overlap between child maltreatment and woman battering. *Violence Against Women, 5*, 134–154.

Egbert, S. C. (2006). Child abuse prevention in Utah: A process evaluation. Retrieved from http://www.socwk.utah.edu/pdf/childabusepreventionevaluation.pdf

Ertem, I. O., Leventhal, J. M., & Dobbs, S. (2000). Intergenerational continuity of child physical abuse: How good is the evidence? *Lancet, 356*, 814–819.

Faust, J. E. (1988, May). The highest place of honor, *Ensign, 18*, 36–39.

Felson, R. B., & Cares, A. C. (2005). Gender and the seriousness of assaults on intimate partners and other victims. *Journal of Marriage and Family, 67*, 1182–1195.

Finkelhor, D., Ormrod, R., Turner, H., & Hamby, S. L. (2005). The victimization of children and youth: A comprehensive, national survey. *Child Maltreatment, 10*, 5–25.

Ford, J. D., Racusin, R., Ellis, C. G., Daviss, W. B., Reiser, J., Fleischer, A., et al. (2000). Child maltreatment, other trauma exposure, and posttraumatic symptomatology among children with oppositional defiant and attention deficit hyperactivity disorders. *Child Maltreatment, 5*, 205–217.

Fox, G. L., Benson, M. L., DeMaris, A. A., & Van Wyk, J. V. (2002). Economic distress and intimate violence: Testing family stress and resources theories. *Journal of Marriage and Family, 64*, 793–807.

Fraser, M. W., & Terzian, M. A. (2005). Risk and resilience in child development: Principles and strategies of practice. In G. P. Mallon & P. M. Hess (Eds.), *Child welfare for the twenty-first century: A handbook of practices, policies, and programs* (pp. 55–71). New York: Columbia University Press.

Garcia-Moreno, C., Jansen, H., Ellsberg, M., Heise, L., & Watts, C. H. (2006). Prevalence of intimate partner violence: Findings from the WHO multi-country study on women's health and domestic violence. *Lancet, 368*, 1260–1269.

Gorbien, M. J., & Eisenstein, A. R. (2005). Elder abuse and neglect: an overview. *Clinics in Geriatric Medicine, 21*, 279–292.

Gottman, J. M. (1999). *The marriage clinic: A scientifically based marital therapy.* New York: W. W. Norton & Company.

Hinckley, G. B. (1990, May). Keeping the temple holy. *Ensign, 20*, 49–53.

Hinckley, G. B. (2002a, May). Personal worthiness to exercise the priesthood. *Ensign, 32*, 52–59.

Hinckley, G. B. (2002b, November). To men of the priesthood. *Ensign, 32*, 56–59.

Holden, G. W., & Barker, T. (2004). Fathers in violent homes. In M. E. Lamb (Ed.), *The role of the father in child development* (4th ed., pp. 417–445). New York: Wiley.

Holland, J. R. (1988, January 12). Of souls, symbols, and sacraments. Brigham Young University devotional address. Retrieved from http://emp.byui.edu/SATTERFIELDB/PDF/Chastity/SymbSac2.pdf

Holtzworth-Munroe, A., & Stuart, G. (1994). The relationship standards and assumptions of violent versus nonviolent husbands. *Cognitive Therapy and Research, 18*, 87–103.

Johnson, M. P. (2006). Conflict and control: Gender symmetry and asymmetry in domestic violence. *Violence Against Women, 12*, 1003–1018.

Johnson, M. P. (2008). *A typology of domestic violence: Intimate terrorism, violent resistance, and situational couple violence.* Lebanon, NH: Northeastern University Press (University Press of New England).

Johnson, M. P., & Leone, J. M. (2005). The differential effects of intimate terrorism and situational couple violence: Findings from the national violence against women survey. *Journal of Family Issues, 26,* 322–349.

Kaplan, S. J., Pelcovitz, D., & Labruna, V. (1999). Child and adolescent abuse and neglect research: A review of the past 10 years. Part I: Physical and emotional abuse and neglect. *Journal of the American Academy of Child and Adolescent Psychiatry, 38,* 1214–1222.

Kenney, C. T., & McLanahan, S. S. (2006). Why are cohabiting relationships more violent than marriages? *Demography, 43,* 127–140.

Kettrey, H. H., & Emery, B. C. (2006). The discourse of sibling violence. *Journal of Family Violence, 21,* 407–416.

Kiselica, M. S., & Morrill-Richards, M. (2007). Sibling maltreatment: The forgotten abuse. *Journal of Counseling and Development, 85,* 148–160.

Larzelere, R. E., Cox, R. B., & Smith, G. L. (2010). Do nonphysical punishments reduce antisocial behavior more than spanking? A comparison using the strongest previous causal evidence against spanking. *BMC Pediatrics, 10*(10), n.p.

Logan, T. K., Walker, R., Jordan, C. E., & Leukefeld, C. G. (2006). *Women and victimization: Contributing factors, interventions and implications.* Washington, DC: American Psychological Association.

MacLeod, J., & Nelson, G. (2000). Programs for the promotion of family wellness and the prevention of child maltreatment: A meta-analytic review. *Child Abuse and Neglect, 24,* 1127–1149.

Malley-Morrison, K., Nolido, N. E.-V., & Chawla, S. (2006). International perspectives on elder abuse: Five case studies. *Educational Gerontology, 32,* 1–11.

Michalski, J. H. (2004). Making sociological sense out of trends in intimate partner violence: The social structure of violence against women. *Violence Against Women, 10,* 652–675.

Miller-Perrin, C. L., & Perrin, R. D. (2007). *Child maltreatment: an introduction* (2nd ed). Thousand Oaks, CA: Sage.

Morton, E., Runyan, C. W., Moracco, K., & Butts, J. (1998). Partner homicide–suicide involving female homicide victims: A population based study in North Carolina, 1988–1992. *Violence and Victims, 13,* 91–106.

Name withheld. (2009, July). A longing for peace. *Ensign, 39,* 52–57.

National coalition against domestic violence. (2005). Retrieved from http://www.ncadv.org

Ruiz, F. J. (2010). A review of Acceptance and Commitment Therapy (ACT) empirical evidence: Correlational, experimental psychopathology, component and outcome studies. *International Journal of Psychology and Psychological Therapy, 10,* 125–162.

Saltzman, L. E. (2004). Definitional and methodological issues related to transnational research on intimate partner violence. *Violence Against Women, 10,* 812–830.

Scalzo, T. P. (2006). Reporting requirements for competent adult victims of domestic violence. The National Center for the Prosecution of Violence Against Women: America Prosecutors Research Institute. Retrieved from http://www.usmc-mccs.org/famadv/restrictedreporting/National%20Rape%20Reporting%20Requirements%206.15.06.pdf

Schumacher, J. A., Slep, A. M. S., & Heyman, R. E. (2001). Risk factors for child neglect. *Aggression and Violent Behavior, 6,* 231–254.

Schwartz, R. H., Milteer, R., & LeBeau, M. A. (2000). Drug-facilitated sexual assault ("date rape"). *Southern Medical Journal, 93,* 558–561.

Scott, R. G. (2008, May). To heal the shattering consequences of abuse. *Ensign, 38,* 40–43.

Sedlak, A. J., & Broadhurst, D. D. (1996). Executive summary of the Third National Incidence Study of Child Abuse and Neglect. Washington, D.C.: U.S. Department of Health and Human Services. Retrieved from http://www.childwelfare.gov/pubs/statsinfo/nis3.cfm

Seidler, G. H., & Wagner, F. E. (2006). Comparing the efficacy of EMDR and trauma-focused cognitive–behavioral therapy in the treatment of PTSD: A meta-analytic study. *Psychological Medicine, 36,* 1515–1522.

Sheridan, L. P., Blaauw, E., & Davies, G. M. (2003). Stalking: Knowns and unknowns. *Trauma, Violence, and Abuse, 4,* 148–162.

Sleutel, M. R. (1998). Women's experiences of abuse: A review of qualitative research. *Issues in Mental Health Nursing, 19,* 525–539.

Steinberg, L. (2004). *The ten basic principles of good parenting.* New York: Simon & Schuster.

Stith, S. M., Smith, D. B., Penn, C. E., Ward, D. B., & Tritt, D. (2004). Intimate partner physical abuse perpetration and victimization risk factors: A meta-analytic review. *Aggression and Violent Behavior, 10,* 65–98.

Straus, M. A. (1991). Discipline and deviance: Physical punishment of children and violence and other crime in adulthood. *Social Problems, 38,* 133–154.

Straus, M. A. (1994). Ten myths about spanking children. Durham, NH: University of New Hampshire. Retrieved from http://eric.ed.gov/PDFS/ED 377989.pdf

Straus, M. A., & Field, C. J. (2003). Psychological aggression by American parents: National data on prevalence, chronicity, and severity. *Journal of Marriage and Family, 65,* 795–808.

Straus, M. A., Sugarman, D. B., & Giles-Sims, J. (1997). Spanking by parents and subsequent antisocial behavior of children. *Archives of Pediatrics and Adolescent Medicine, 151,* 761–767.

Swenson, C. C., Schaeffer, C. M., Henggeler, S.W., Faldowski, R., & Mayhew, A. M. (2010). Multisystemic therapy for child abuse and neglect: A randomized effectiveness trial. *Journal of Family Psychology, 24,* 497–507.

Valente, S. M. (2002). Evaluating intimate partner violence. *Journal of the American Academy of Nurse Practitioners, 14,* 505–514.

Whiffen, V. E., & MacIntosh, H. B. (2005). Mediators of the link between childhood sexual abuse and emotional distress: A critical review. *Trauma, Violence, and Abuse, 6,* 24–39.

Whiting, J. B. (2010, June). Intimate partner violence: A guide for professionals. Retrieved from http://www .ttuhsc.edu/Health.edu

Whiting, J. B., & Lee, R. E. (2003). Voices from the system: A qualitative study of foster children's stories. *Family Relations, 52,* 288–295.

Whiting, J. B., Oka, M., & Fife, S. T. (Manuscript in submission). Appraisal distortions and intimate partner violence: Gender, power and denial.

Whiting, J. B., Simmons, L. A., Havens, J. R., Smith, D. B., & Oka, M. (2009). Intergenerational transmission of violence: The influence of self-appraisals, mental disorders and substance abuse. *Journal of Family Violence, 24,* 639–648.

Whiting, J. B., Smith, D. B., Oka, M., & Karakurt, G. (Manuscript in submission). Safety in intimate partnerships: The role of appraisals and threat.

Widtsoe, J. A. (Ed.). (1977). *Discourses of Brigham Young.* Salt Lake City: Deseret Book.

World Health Organization. (2002). World report on violence and health: summary. Geneva: Author.

World Health Organization. (2008, March 12). Ten facts on injuries and violence. Retrieved from http:// www.who.int/features/factfiles/injuries/facts/en/ index2.html

Section IV:
Advocating Public Policies for Successful Marriages and Families

CHAPTER 25

A Public Policy Agenda to
Help Couples Form and Sustain Healthy, Stable Marriages

Alan J. Hawkins

Marriage between a man and a woman is ordained of God. . . .
We call upon responsible citizens and officers of government everywhere
to promote those measures designed to maintain and strengthen the family as the fundamental unit of society.

FOCUSING ON OUR OWN MARRIAGES IS IMPORTANT. We need to establish them on a firm foundation for success and then work daily to keep them strong. Yet the family proclamation asks for more: "We call upon responsible citizens and officers of government everywhere to promote those measures designed to maintain and strengthen the family as the fundamental unit of society" (¶ 9). I have spent much time thinking about the laws and policies government officials could promote that would be an effective response to this prophetic call. I am convinced that promoting strong marriages is the best way to strengthen the family. Laws and government policies to strengthen marriages can be difficult to pass and implement because there is so much political controversy these days surrounding the institution of marriage as well as the proper role and limits of government. Nevertheless, we all have a stake in the quality of intimate unions formed; there are substantial public costs to the private problems of family dissolution (Scafidi, 2008). My involvement in federal and state law and policy debates has taught me that conservatives, liberals, and moderates alike are interested in strengthening the institution of marriage but struggle to know what to do. All sides acknowledge that a stronger institution of marriage will significantly improve children's well-being and reduce poverty. Nevertheless, both conservatives and liberals doubt that government can or should intrude into private behavior in ways intended to strengthen marriages.

The point of greatest convergence in the debate may be a widespread acknowledgement that too many young

peoples' paths to marriage portend problems down the road (Cahn & Carbone, 2010; Cherlin, 2009); relationship and family formation behavior among many youth and emerging adults creates a sandy foundation for a future of marital success. I think the most valuable focus for law and public policy would be to help more young people get to marriage with less relationship baggage and provide them better skills for maintaining a healthy relationship. And I believe there are feasible policies that can be implemented to help young people form healthy marriages. While effective parental teaching (and modeling) and quality religious instruction may be the best means of helping young people learn how to form a healthy marriage, many are not blessed with these advantages. I believe the state can do more to help youth learn how to form and sustain a healthy marriage, which is an important component of promoting the general welfare of individuals and society (Waite & Gallagher, 2000).

Perhaps the need for such teaching has never been greater. For youth and young adults, the pathways to a healthy, stable marriage are increasingly convoluted and challenging to walk. The large majority of young people participate in sexual activity before marriage (Finer, 2007) and most form cohabiting relationships before marriage (Wilcox, 2009). Most wait until they are in their mid- to late twenties to marry (National Center for Family & Marriage Research, 2009). Divorce is common (Bramlett & Mosher, 2001) and family formation outside of marriage is widespread—more than 40 percent of children are born to unmarried parents

(Ventura, 2009). Cherlin (2009) argues that the institutional boundaries of marriage have shrunk; marriage no longer effectively governs intimate associations before or outside of marriage nor structures "proper" pathways to the desired goal of a healthy, stable marriage. Personal development and individual emotions—rather than societal expectations and religious and civil norms—are at the core of modern marriage (Cherlin, 2009; Coontz, 2005). All of this suggests that contemporary youth and young adults face a more complex passage to marriage. Hymowitz (2006) argues that, especially for disadvantaged youth, marriage is no longer a core cultural institution that orders their lives; young adults have a thin "life script" to help them achieve their family ideals.

From an empirical perspective, there are a number of known risk factors that impede forming and sustaining healthy marriages, such as many premarital sexual partners (Teachman, 2003), premarital parenthood (Amato & Booth, 2001), pre-engagement cohabitation (Rhoades, Stanley, & Markman, 2009), and premarital relationship violence (Jackson, 2009). Yet it is probably not too much of a stretch to summarize the 21st century ABCs of marriage preparation as follows: (a) early, prolonged, self-interested sexual exploration followed by (b) finding a "soul mate," then (c) living together to test the relationship, and then (d) deciding to get married when the "time is right." But this is not a reliable basis for marital success. Leaving youth and young adults on their own to try to figure out how they can achieve their hopes for a healthy, stable marriage seems a heartless and counterproductive strategy.

As a society, how can we help young people find safer and more effective pathways to healthy marriages? In this chapter, I set forth a modest public policy agenda to address this question. The agenda stresses the availability of a series of educational opportunities, including: (a) school-based relationship literacy for youth; (b) positive relationship formation education for young adults; and (c) effective premarital education for engaged couples, as well as ongoing relationship enrichment education in the early years of marriage to help couples learn the needed skills for a healthy marriage. I stress feasible policies that make voluntary and inexpensive education more available and take advantage of existing service delivery infrastructures. I provide brief examples of ongoing efforts to illustrate the feasibility of these initiatives. I draw these examples almost exclusively from the

United States because few other nations have explored such policies to a comparable extent. In addition, I place a significant emphasis on services for disadvantaged youth and young adults who are at greater risk for problematic pathways to marriage (Ooms & Wilson, 2004).

Before proceeding, however, I raise several important issues. First, I do not address the issue of same-sex marriage here. While this is an important issue, I focus on marriage as traditionally defined between a man and a woman. Indeed, media attention with regard to law and policy about marriage is dominated by a focus on same-sex marriages and relationships. I seek to balance that focus with needed attention to heterosexual marriage.

Second, I will focus here on governmental measures to help young adults form healthy, stable marriages. I do so because of the family proclamation's specific call to "officers of government everywhere to promote those measures designed to maintain and strengthen the family as the fundamental unit of society." Of course, there are other collective measures that can be taken. For instance, voluntary citizen initiatives in a community can strengthen marriages (Doherty & Carroll, 2002); workplace human resource policies and programs could be more supportive of forming and sustaining healthy marriages (Turvey & Olson, 2006); and religious organizations will play a key role in helping youth find their path to successful marriages.

Third, while there is ongoing debate about whether and how government should be involved in individuals' personal decisions about family formation (Amato, 2004; Cahn & Carbone, 2010; Gallagher, 2004; Haskins & Sawhill, 2009), most acknowledge that youth and young adults across class, race, and ethnicity still highly value marriage and desire a healthy, lifelong marriage for themselves (Wilcox, 2009). In addition, most understand that there are significant societal costs when healthy relationships dissolve or fail to form, especially when children are involved (Cherlin, 2009). Accordingly, while this debate continues, I believe it is wise to proceed with rigorous thinking about potential public policy efforts that could help youth and young adults achieve their aspirations, especially when the public benefits of successful marriages are well documented (Wilcox, Doherty, Glenn, & Waite, 2005).

Fourth, it is important to understand that simply passing legislation intended to strengthen marriage is not enough. There is ample evidence already that laws can be passed but implementation can be so poor that intended effects are virtually impossible (Nock, Sanchez, & Wright, 2008). Thus, I advocate here not only for legislation and policy initiatives with the potential to help young people form healthy, stable marriages, but also for ongoing mechanisms to monitor implementation, evaluate outcomes, and make needed adjustments.

Finally, I acknowledge the need for this marriage-strengthening policy agenda to be attached to a broader agenda of coterminous social and economic policy. A robust economy and the ability to gain a good education and improve job skills support individuals' attempts to build healthy, stable marriages (Haskins & Sawhill, 2009). Similarly, social policy that helps to prevent unwanted pregnancies, reduce domestic violence and substance abuse, and support responsible fatherhood will make it easier for couples to form and sustain healthy relationships (Fagan, Palkovitz, Roy, & Farrie, 2009; Ooms et al., 2006; Wilson, 2002). I believe governmental efforts to help young adults form and sustain healthy marriages enhance, rather than supplant, these other efforts.

Helping Youth Learn about Healthy Relationships

The period of the life course between adolescence and first marriage has increased substantially, such that for most young adults there will be nearly a decade between high school graduation and a wedding (Arnett, 2000). In the meantime, there is a prolonged period of sexual and relationship exploration relatively unconnected to the ultimate goal of marriage shared by most youth (Carroll, Willoughby, Badger, Barry, & Madsen, 2007). In addition, high divorce rates—and high rates of nonmarital family formation and dissolution—among parents mean that many contemporary youth cannot rely on the social modeling of their parents to find a pathway to their own healthy marriages. In some disadvantaged communities, healthy marriages are nearly extinct and youth may not even have a clear concept of what a healthy marriage or relationship is (Hymowitz, 2006). And through the media, youth are exposed to a dizzying array of models of romantic relationships (Kunkel, Eyal, Finnerty, Biely, & Donnerstein, 2005). Accordingly, I believe it is incumbent on a responsible society to help youth become "relationship literate" in order to better handle the choices that may impact their present

lives, future relationships, and eventual marriages. Even when marriage seems a long time away for youth, there is still interest in learning positive relationship skills and ways to form healthy relationships.

Relationship literacy, while it may encompass basic sex education, is broader because it pays significant attention to the relational and familial contexts of sexuality (Whitehead & Pearson, 2006). Furthermore, relationship literacy gives significant attention to basic communication and problem-solving skills that undergird forming and sustaining healthy romantic relationships. It also clarifies what a healthy relationship is (and is not), including addressing the problem of relationship aggression and violence (Lewis & Fremouw, 2001). And increasingly, youth relationship programs outline the research on how sexual partnering and cohabitation may affect the prospects for marital success.

Recently, marriage and relationship educators have given more attention to developing youth relationship literacy, including programs targeted to at-risk, disadvantaged youth. (For a description of several current programs, see www.dibblefund.org.) Because increased efforts to promote relationship literacy for youth are recent, the body of evaluation research examining the effectiveness of these programs is limited. The early, emerging research, however, is interesting. For instance, Gardner, Giese, and Parrott (2004) evaluated a curriculum with a mostly middle-class sample and found modest, short-term, positive effects on healthy relationship knowledge, decreased dating violence, decreased risk for teen pregnancy, and positive attitudes about marital success. In a four-year follow-up of this study, however, most of the positive effects diminished, although importantly there was still a significant effect for decreased dating and relationship violence (Gardner & Boellaard, 2007). In another study with a large, predominantly low-income and diverse group of Alabama youth, Kerpelman and her colleagues (2010) found that, one year after the program, relationship literacy education significantly reduced youths' faulty beliefs about relationships and marriage and increased their positive relationship skills. Moreover, these effects generally were seen across socioeconomic and racial groups. These studies provide only preliminary results; much more evaluation research is needed, especially studies that follow youth over a longer period of time to ascertain whether relationship literacy programs actually help youth establish healthier romantic relationships in their young adult years and result in more positive marital outcomes.

An effective educational infrastructure to deliver relationship literacy programs to youth is already in place, of course, in secondary education. Teachers with backgrounds in the behavioral sciences, such as family and consumer sciences, psychology, sociology, and health sciences, are well situated to deliver this education. The state of Oklahoma has used public funds to train public school educators in a scientifically based relationship literacy program, "Connections." From 2004 to 2010, 100,000 high school students have received this course. With a federal grant for support, Alabama has also made youth relationship education widely available. In Utah, a course on relationship literacy was merged with a state-mandated course on financial literacy to create a year-long course option that has been popular with students and increased the number of students receiving relationship literacy education. These kinds of initiatives can be supported within regular funding channels, making their implementation more feasible.

Helping Young Adults Chart a Safer Course to Marital Success

Even if youth relationship literacy education achieves its objective of helping more youth get on track to a healthy marriage, it still may be unrealistic to think that it can sustain that positive effect for nearly a decade between high school and the average age of marriage. Moreover, young adults will engage in more serious romantic and cohabiting relationships that provide proximate challenges to building a positive foundation for marriage. For instance, serial sexual partnerships appear to be a risk for maintaining stable marriages (Heaton, 2002; Teachman, 2003). Cohabitation before engagement also increases the risk factor for eventual divorce (Jose, O'Leary, & Moyer, 2010; Rhoades et al., 2009). Premarital parenthood, especially having children with multiple partners (McLanahan, 2009; Meyer, Cancian, & Cook, 2005), lowers the chances of future relationship and marriage success (Heaton, 2002; Jackson, 2009). And relationship violence in dating and cohabiting relationships continues to be a problem in the young adult years (Wood, McConnell, Moore, Clarkwest, & Hsueh, 2010) and can affect later marital success (Jackson, 2009).

Cohabiting young adult couples may be an especially important target for preventative intervention. Rhoades and her colleagues (2009) have begun to explore the issues facing cohabiting couples and their implications for relationship education. Perhaps the most prominent issue they explore is commitment. Cohabiting couples can have different levels of commitment and different notions of where the relationship is headed. These scholars note how many couples *slide* into a marriage rather than *decide* to marry with a firm commitment to the long-term future of the relationship. Such issues have important consequences for the health and stability of a potential marriage.

Hence, I believe early exposure to youth relationship literacy will need to be supplemented with positive relationship formation education targeted to the unique issues and concerns of young adults, with special attention to disadvantaged young adults. The term *disadvantaged* includes more than those who have grown up in economically impoverished circumstances; it also includes, for instance, those with poor role models of a healthy marriage growing up or those who inherit incorrect notions about marriage from their culture.

Relationship education for young adults who are dating, in serious relationships, or living together is probably the newest category of relationship education. Until the last few years, young adulthood, or emerging adulthood, has been viewed as a period of "marital latency" (Carroll et al., 2007), a period of time unconnected to future marital outcomes. But this is changing because we know that relationship behaviors in young adulthood impact future marital options and some young adults will cohabit long term and rear children together.

In response to these contemporary issues, marriage and relationship educators are beginning to develop and implement positive relationship programs for young adults who are single, dating, or cohabiting. Research is beginning to emerge on the effectiveness of positive relationship formation education for young adults, with more research in the pipeline. Interestingly, in contrast to most marriage and relationship education programs, these emerging educational efforts for young adults appear to be targeted primarily toward lower-income couples and individuals. In addition, they focus on couples who have already had children together outside of marriage, putting them at greater risk for unstable relationships. Still, this emerging research suggests some reasons for early optimism (Hawkins & Fackrell, 2010). For instance, Cox and Shirer (2009) evaluated a program with low-income parents of young children, finding significant effects for communication and problem-solving skills and greater positive co-parenting attitudes and behaviors. Cowan, Cowan, Pruett, Pruett, and Wong (2009) studied a program delivered to a large, diverse sample of low-income cohabiting and married parents, finding a modest increase in relationship quality more than a year after the program, regardless of marital status, as well as increases in father involvement. The strongest evidence to date of the potential of couple education for low-income cohabiting couples comes from the Building Strong Families (BSF) study, a rigorous, multi-site, U.S. federally funded study of 5,000 low-income, new-parent couples randomly assigned either to a relationship education intervention or a control group (Wood et al., 2010). At about one year after the intervention, the results were mixed. Overall, a rigorous examination of the effects found little evidence to support the effectiveness of the intervention on the couple relationship. However, further analyses revealed a pattern of significant, positive couple relationship and father involvement effects for African American couples. In addition, one site (Oklahoma City) revealed an overall pattern of positive couple relationship and father involvement effects. This site had by far the highest level of full participation in the intervention. The results of this BSF study indicate that we still have much to learn about effective relationship education for young, romantically involved, unmarried parents, but the potential for positive influence exists.

One of the challenges of delivering relationship education to young adults will be finding the right infrastructures to deliver these services. Social service agencies that work regularly with disadvantaged young adults could be a good source for delivering relationship education, although it will take some time and effort to help them see that this kind of service is appropriate to their organizations, which traditionally have been focused on working with single mothers (Palm & Fagan, 2008). U.S. federal Healthy Marriage Initiative grants issued in the late 2000s have been used to stimulate more outreach to disadvantaged young adult couples in community settings. Community colleges

and universities also may be effective settings for reaching young adults. Anecdotally, I have observed an increasing number of course offerings at U.S. colleges and universities focused not just on the institutional aspects of marriage but also on the personal aspects of dating, cohabitation, marriage, sexual relationships, and relationship skills.

Oklahoma has taken seriously the need to reach young adults with tailored programs delivered in many different settings, including traditional social service delivery organizations that work regularly with single parents. No doubt creative web-based delivery of services will play an important role in delivering relationship education to young adults given the omnipresence of the Internet in their lives. (See www.twoofus.org for an example of a website targeting young adults with healthy marriage and relationship information.)

Helping Engaged Couples Build a Stronger Foundation for Marriage

Whatever path they have taken through their youth and young adult years, when couples make the decision to marry, they may be more open to receiving programmatic help to build a stronger foundation for their marriage. While the temptation exists for engaged couples to think about marriage preparation in terms of wedding dresses, floral arrangements, and exotic honeymoons, we need to encourage engaged couples to focus more on preparing for a marriage rather than a wedding. Individuals who have experienced the divorce of their parents may be especially in need of formal preparation as they are two to three times more at risk of experiencing their own divorce (Wolfinger, 2005).

Formal premarital education has a long tradition (Stanley, 2001). It emphasizes building better communication and problem-solving skills to deal with the inevitable challenges of married life. It also usually addresses a wide range of issues that influence marital quality, from money management to the division of household labor to in-law relationships. A study that reviewed the large body of evaluation research shows that premarital education for engaged couples is moderately effective at increasing couples' communication skills (Fawcett, Hawkins, Blanchard, & Carroll, 2010). And there is some evidence that couples who invest in formal premarital education are less likely to divorce in the early years of marriage (Nock et al., 2008; Stanley,

Amato, Johnson, & Markman, 2006). Also, researchers have observed that 10 to 15 percent of couples taking premarital education classes call off the wedding because they come to believe that the relationship will not succeed (Stanley, 2001); this may prevent divorces in the making. Unfortunately, research has not yet confirmed that premarital education for lower-income engaged couples is effective.

In the United States, a large majority of weddings take place in religious rather than civil settings. Many clergy offer or even require couples they perform ceremonies for to attend a formal premarital education program. Research suggests that premarital education delivered by clergy or their designees in religious settings can be as effective as those programs delivered by trained family life educators or clinicians in secular settings (Stanley et al., 2001). Thus, there is a ready-made infrastructure for delivery of premarital education to engaged couples that requires no public support. However, public funds could be used to facilitate greater use of these services, which several U.S. states are doing, including Oklahoma, Texas, and Utah. Utah invested in a five-year media campaign to promote premarital education. In addition, six states (Florida, Maryland, Minnesota, Oklahoma, Tennessee, and Texas) provide financial incentives to take premarital education by discounting the cost of a marriage license for those couples who invest in educational services that meet legislated standards. (Services from religious organizations that meet the standards are acceptable.)

Some couples, however, will prefer secular options. These couples could be reached through various means, including the Cooperative Extension Service of the U.S. land-grant universities (Futris, 2007). Every county in every state has a Cooperative Extension Service that delivers research-based educational services to its population. Virtually all have extension agents trained to deliver family life education. In addition, social service agencies that serve disadvantaged young adults with other kinds of support services, such as employment services, may be a prime venue for reaching lower-income couples with premarital education.

In Australia, the federal government recently funded Family Relationship Centres in all areas of the country with the mission to strengthen marriage and family relationships. The centers are staffed by well-qualified family professionals. Many services are free or offered on a sliding scale. While most of the resources of these centers apparently are devoted to helping families navigate family break-up in less conflictual ways, their mission also includes trying to support educational services for couples forming families. With a slight shift in orientation and modest increase in funding, this existing infrastructure could do more to provide helpful educational services to engaged couples.

Unfortunately, even if couples invest in formal premarital education, there is no guarantee that smooth marital sailing is ahead. Accordingly, I think it is wise to extend the conceptualization of premarital education to encompass early marital enrichment as well. There is a need for continuing efforts to help newly married couples improve their relationship skills.

A large body of evaluation research on marriage enrichment programs has been directed mostly at couples in the early years of marriage. Comprehensive review studies suggest that these programs can modestly improve communication skills and enhance relationship quality (Blanchard, Hawkins, Baldwin, & Fawcett, 2009; Hawkins, Blanchard, Baldwin, & Fawcett, 2008). A recent study documented an 11-year follow up of a sample of couples who were randomly assigned to a marriage enrichment program or a control group that did not receive the program (Hahlweg & Richter, 2010). This study found a significantly lower divorce rate in the treatment group that received the enrichment program. The few studies of enrichment programs for more disadvantaged married couples suggest some modest potential, as well (Cowan et al., 2009; Hawkins & Fackrell, 2010; Stanley, Allen, Markman, Rhoades, & Prentice, 2010), although more research is needed.

Again, religious organizations may be a natural educational infrastructure to deliver early-marriage enrichment programs to couples, especially if the couples also took a premarital education class in a religious setting. Marriage and parenthood tend to draw young people into religious organizations (Nock, 1998). But non-religious, community-based services should be strengthened as well. Several U.S. states have statewide initiatives to develop marriage enrichment services. Oklahoma has gone the farthest to date. Public funds have trained more than 2,500 instructors. Free classes based on the well-researched PREP curriculum (Markman, Stanley, & Blumberg, 2010) are widely advertised and run in community settings all over the state. These classes are widely available in Spanish as well as English. In states that have not invested so thoroughly in a statewide healthy marriage initiative, the presence of Cooperative Extension Service family life educators in virtually every county of every U.S. state provides a ready infrastructure for the delivery of marriage enrichment education. Also, recent U.S. federal grants to a small number of Head Start programs that help disadvantaged preschool children and their parents have explored the feasibility of offering healthy marriage and relationship programs to the parents. These venues have a history of providing parenting education; if these healthy marriage and relationship demonstration programs prove effective, perhaps marriage-strengthening curricula could be added to many more Head Start programs to reach many young, lower-income couples.

Summary and Conclusion

The social policy agenda I have proposed to help more youth and young adults establish positive pathways to a healthy and stable marriage is hardly dramatic. I have emphasized feasible policies to promote delivery of educational services using existing infrastructures. Admittedly, this agenda puts much faith in the power of education. Voluntary educational interventions may seem weak in the face of powerful historical and cultural forces working against individual hopes for lifelong marriage (Coontz, 2005). But past and emerging research points to the modest potential of youth relationship literacy; relationship education for single, dating, and cohabiting young adults; premarital education; and early-marital enrichment. Certainly, there are knowledgeable scholars who doubt the ability of government efforts to effect change in how we form and sustain marriage in our societies. For instance, the prominent sociologist James Q. Wilson argues that restoring the value of marriage "is not something that can be done by public policy" (2002, p. 221). Broad cultural change is needed, he asserts, but this must be done "retail, not wholesale, by families and churches and neighborhoods and the media" (p. 221). When he thinks about policy, however, he seems focused on such things as tax breaks and government subsidies; he does not seem to consider the possibility that extensive educational efforts supported by modest public funding could help shift the cultural current and bring youth and young adults along in its wake.

I believe this is a reasonable possibility. The merit in the policy agenda I have proposed to help youth and young adults find a safer path to achieving their marital aspirations—and avoid the detours that put those aspirations at risk—derives from its specifics, its political and financial feasibility, and the emerging evidence that relationship and marriage education can improve prospects. Research to date has examined the effectiveness of specific programs. What remains unexamined to date, however, is the value of a string of educational opportunities beginning in adolescence and stretching through the young adult years, engagement, and the early years of marriage. The accumulation of modest educational effects in the early life course may provide significant help for young people; repeated, timely exposure to research-based information and relationship skills may help guide many more youth from adolescence to quality relationships, healthy marriages, and stable family life.

Of course, there is much room for debate about whether the policies I have suggested here ultimately would be effective and whether other kinds of efforts would yield better fruit. Whatever the outcome of that debate—a debate I welcome—I believe that the family proclamation places a responsibility upon government officials everywhere to try to find feasible ways to strengthen marriages. Furthermore, the proclamation calls upon each of us as responsible citizens to support those efforts that we deem will best strengthen the family as the fundamental unit of society.

Alan J. Hawkins *is a professor in the School of Family Life at Brigham Young University. He and his wife, Lisa, are the parents of two children and they have two grandchildren.*

References

Amato, P. R. (2004). Tension between institutional and individual views of marriage. *Journal of Marriage and Family, 66,* 959–965.

Amato, P. R., & Booth, A. (2001). The legacy of parents' marital discord: Consequences for children's marital quality. *Journal of Personality and Social Psychology, 81,* 627–638.

Arnett, J. (2000). Emerging adulthood: A theory of development from the late teens through the twenties. *American Psychologist, 55*, 469–480.

Blanchard, V. L., Hawkins, A. J., Baldwin, S. A., & Fawcett, E. B. (2009). Investigating the effects of marriage and relationship education on couples' communication skills: A meta-analytic study. *Journal of Family Psychology, 23*, 203–214.

Bramlett, M. D., & Mosher, W. D. (2001). First marriage dissolution, divorce, and remarriage: United States. *Advanced Data from Vital and Health Statistics, no. 323.* Hyattsville, MD: National Center for Health Statistics.

Cahn, N., & Carbone, J. (2010). *Red families v. blue families: Legal polarization and the creation of culture.* New York: Oxford University.

Carroll, J. A., Willoughby, B., Badger, S., Barry, C. M., & Madsen, S. D. (2007). So close, yet so far away: The impact of varying marital horizons on emerging adulthood. *Journal of Adolescent Research, 22*, 219–247.

Cherlin, A. J. (2009). *The marriage-go-round.* New York: Alfred A. Knopf.

Coontz, S. (2005). *Marriage, a history: From obedience to intimacy, or how love conquered marriage.* New York: Viking.

Cowan, P. A., Cowan, C. P., Pruett, M. K., Pruett, K., & Wong, J. J. (2009). Promoting fathers' engagement with children: Preventive interventions for low-income families. *Journal of Marriage and Family, 71*, 663–679.

Cox, R. B., Jr., & Shirer, K. A. (2009). Caring for my family: A pilot study of a relationship and marriage education program for low-income unmarried parents. *Journal of Couple and Relationship Therapy, 8*, 343–364.

Doherty, W. J., & Carroll, J. S. (2002). The families and democracy project. *Family Process, 41*, 579–590.

Fagan, J., Palkovitz, R., Roy, K., & Farrie, D. (2009). Pathways to paternal engagement: longitudinal effects of risk and resilience on nonresident fathers. *Developmental Psychology, 45*, 1389–1405.

Fawcett, E. B., Hawkins, A. J., Blanchard, V. L., & Carroll, J. S. (2010). Do premarital education programs really work? A meta-analytic study. *Family Relations, 59*, 232–239.

Finer, L. B. (2007, January-February). Trends in premarital sex in the United States, 1954–2003. *Public Health Reports, 122*, 73–78.

Futris, T. G. (2007). Cultivating healthy couple and marital relationships: Introduction from the guest editor. *Forum for Family and Consumer Issues, 12* (1). Retrieved from http://ncsu.edu/ffci/publications/2007/v12-n1 -2007-spring/futris-1/fa-2-futris-1.php

Gallagher, M. (2004). *Can government strengthen marriage? Evidence from the social sciences.* New York: Institute for American Values. Retrieved from http:// www.americanvalues.org/pdfs/cangovernment.pdf

Gardner, S. P., & Boellaard, R. (2007). Does youth relationship education continue to work after a high school class? A longitudinal study. *Family Relations, 56*, 490–500.

Gardner, S. P., Giese, K., & Parrott, S. M. (2004). Evaluation of the connections: Relationships and marriage curriculum. *Family Relations, 53*, 521–527.

Hahlweg, K., & Richter, D. (2010). Prevention of marital instability and distress: Results of an 11-year longitudinal follow-up study. *Behaviour Research and Therapy, 48*, 377–383.

Haskins, R., & Sawhill, I. (2009). *Creating an opportunity society.* Washington, DC: Brookings Institution.

Hawkins, A. J., Blanchard, V. L., Baldwin, S. A., & Fawcett, E. B. (2008). Does marriage and relationship education work? A meta-analytic study. *Journal of Consulting and Clinical Psychology, 76*, 723–734.

Hawkins, A. J., & Fackrell, T. A. (2010). Does relationship and marriage education for lower-income couples work? A meta-analytic study of emerging research. *Journal of Couple and Relationship Therapy, 9*, 181–191.

Heaton, T. B. (2002). Factors contributing to increasing marital stability in the United States. *Journal of Family Issues, 23*, 392–409.

Hymowitz, K. S. (2006). *Marriage and caste in America: Separate and unequal families in a post-marriage age.* Chicago: Ivan R. Dee.

Jackson, J. B. (2009). Premarital couple predictors of marital relationship quality and stability: A meta-analytic study. Unpublished doctoral dissertation, Brigham Young University, Provo, Utah.

Jose, A., O'Leary, K. D., & Moyer, A. (2010). Does premarital cohabitation predict subsequent marital stability and marital quality? A meta-analysis. *Journal of Marriage and Family, 72*, 105–116.

Kerpelman, J. L., Pittman, J. F., Adler-Baeder, F., Stringer, K. J., Eryigit, S., Cadely, H. S., & Harrell-Levy, M. K.

(2010). What adolescents bring to and learn from relationship education classes: Does social address matter? *Journal of Couple and Relationship Therapy, 9,* 95–112.

Kunkel, D., Eyal, K., Finnerty, K., Biely, E., & Donnerstein, E. (2005). *Sex on TV, 2005.* Menlo Park, CA: Kaiser Family Foundation. Retrieved from http://www.kff.org/entmedia/upload/Sex-on-TV-4-Full-Report.pdf

Lewis, S. F., & Fremouw, W. J. (2001). Dating violence: A critical review of the literature. *Clinical Psychology Review, 21,*105–127.

Markman, H. J., Stanley, S. M., & Blumberg, S. L. (2010). *Fighting for your marriage: A deluxe revised edition of the classic best seller for enhancing marriage and preventing divorce* (3rd ed.). San Francisco: Jossey-Bass.

McLanahan, S. (2009). Fragile families and the reproduction of poverty. *The ANNALS of the American Academy of Political and Social Science, 621,* 111–131.

Meyer, D. R., Cancian, M., & Cook, S. T. (2005). Multiple-partner fertility: Incidence and implications for child support policy. *Social Science Review, 79,* 577–601.

National Center for Family & Marriage Research. (2009). Median age at first marriage in the U.S., 2008. Retrieved from http://ncfmr.bgsu.edu/pdf/family_profiles/file78895.pdf

Nock, S. L. (1998). *Marriage in men's lives.* New York: Oxford University.

Nock, S. L., Sanchez, L. A., & Wright, J. D. (2008). *Covenant marriage: The movement to reclaim tradition in America.* New Brunswick, NJ: Rutgers University.

Ooms, T., Boggess, J., Menard, A., Myrick, M., Roberts, P., Tweedie, J., & Wilson, P. (2006). *Building bridges between healthy marriage, responsible fatherhood, and domestic violence programs: A preliminary guide.* Washington, DC and Denver, CO: Center for Law and Social Policy and the National Conference on State Legislators.

Ooms, T., & Wilson, P. (2004). The challenges of offering relationship and marriage education to low-income populations. *Family Relations, 53,* 440–447.

Palm, G., & Fagan, J. (2008). Father involvement in early childhood programs: review of the literature. *Early Child Development and Care, 178,* 745–759.

Rhoades, G. K., Stanley, S. M., & Markman, H. J. (2009). Working with cohabitation in relationship

education and therapy. *Journal of Couple and Relationship Therapy, 8,* 95–112.

Scafidi, B. (2008). *The taxpayer costs of divorce and unwed childbearing: First-ever estimates for the nation and all fifty states.* New York: Institute for American Values. Retrieved from http://www.americanvalues.org/pdf_dl.php?name=COFF

Stanley, S. M. (2001). Making a case for premarital education. *Family Relations, 50,* 272–280.

Stanley, S. M., Amato, P. R., Johnson, C. A., & Markman, H. J. (2006). Premarital education, marital quality, and marital stability: Findings from a large, random household survey. *Journal of Family Psychology, 20,* 117–126.

Stanley, S. M., Markman, H. J., Prado, L. M., Olmos-Gallo, P. A., Tonelli, L., St. Peters, M., Leber, B. D., Bobulinski, M., Cordova, A., & Whitton, S. W. (2001). Community-based premarital prevention: Clergy and lay leaders on the front lines. *Family Relations, 50,* 67–76.

Stanley, S. M., Allen, E. S., Markman, H. J., Rhoades, G. K., & Prentice, D. L. (2010). Decreasing divorce in U.S. Army couples: Results from a randomized controlled trial using PREP for Strong Bonds. *Journal of Couple and Relationship Therapy, 9,* 149–160.

Teachman, J. (2003). Premarital sex, premarital cohabitation, and the risk of subsequent marital dissolution among women. *Journal of Marriage and Family, 65,* 444–455.

Turvey, M. D., & Olson, D. H. (2006). *Marriage and family wellness: Corporate America's business?* Minneapolis, MN: The Marriage CoMission.

Ventura, S. J. (2009, May). Changing patterns of non-marital childbearing in the United States. *NCHS Data Brief, No. 18.* Hyattsville, MD: National Center for Health Statistics. Retrieved from http://www.cdc.gov/nchs/data/databriefs/db18.pdf

Waite, L. J., & Gallagher, M. (2000). *The case for marriage: Why married people are happier, healthier, and better off financially.* New York: Doubleday.

Whitehead, B. D., & Pearson, M. (2006). *Making a love connection: Teen relationships, pregnancy, and marriage.* Washington, DC: The National Campaign to Prevent Teen Pregnancy.

Wilcox, W. B. (2009). *The state of our unions: Marriage in America 2009: Money and marriage.* Charlottesville, VA, & New York: The National Marriage Project and the Institute for American Values. Retrieved from http://

www.virginia.edu/marriageproject/pdfs/Union_11_25_09.pdf

Wilcox, W. B., Doherty, W., Glenn, N., & Waite, L. J. (2005). *Why marriage matters, second edition: Twenty-six conclusions from the social sciences.* New York: Institute for American Values.

Wilson, J. Q. (2002). *The marriage problem: How our culture has weakened families.* New York: HarperCollins.

Wolfinger, N. H. (2005). *Understanding the divorce cycle: The children of divorce in their own marriages.* New York: Cambridge University.

Wood, R. G., McConnell, S., Moore, Q., Clarkwest, A., & Hsueh, J. (2010). *The Building Strong Families project: Strengthening unmarried parents' relationships: The early impacts of Building Strong Families.* Princeton, NJ: Mathematica Policy Research. Retrieved from http://www.mathematica-pr.com/publications/pdfs/family_support/BSF_impact_finalrpt.pdf

CHAPTER 26

An LDS Family Law Professor's Perspectives on Same-Sex Marriage

Lynn D. Wardle

Marriage between a man and a woman is ordained of God.

Introduction:
The Defining Issue of Our Generation

FUTURE HISTORIANS WILL LIKELY IDENTIFY THE public policy controversies of the past two decades concerning the legal definition of marriage as the defining social issue for this generation of Americans.[1] This chapter provides an overview of the history of recognition of the importance of marriage and marital families; offers current insights about the importance of marriage for individuals, families, and society generally; reviews the history of the movement to legalize same-sex marriage; notes the relevance of "The Family: A Proclamation to the World" for these and related family policy issues; suggests some ways that people can appropriately exercise their influence as citizens concerning these public policy issues; and briefly outlines some arguments that may help to raise the quality of discourse about these issues.

The Critical Importance of Marriage for Individuals, Families, and Society

The debate about whether marriage should be redefined in the law to allow same-sex couples to marry is an entirely novel public policy issue. Before the Netherlands legalized same-sex marriage in 2000, same-sex unions had never been given the legal status of marriage in any legal system in world history. However, underlying the current debate about same-sex marriage are some social concerns that are as old as society.

The importance of marriage and marriage regulation has long been recognized. For example, Aristotle famously taught that marriage is "the foundation of the republic and the prototype of friendship," and both Plato and Aristotle prescribed a set of laws governing the ideal ages, qualities, and duties of husband and wife to each other and to their children "to ensure that marital couples would remain bonded together for the sake of their children" (Witte, 2001, p. 1023-24). Aristotle also reasoned that it was the "first duty" of wise legislators to establish rules regulating marriage (Aristotle, pp. 1334–1335).

The regulation of marriage in Western civilization reflected profoundly Christian teachings about the importance of marriage (Witte & Nichols, 2008, pp. 595–615). St. Augustine

> called marriage a "faithful and sincere fellowship," "the seedbed . . . of a city," [and] the "foundation of domestic peace." . . . [H]is Greek contemporary, St. John Chrysostom ([A.D.] 345–407), [wrote:] "The love of husband and wife is the force that welds society together. . . . Because when harmony prevails, the children are raised well, the household is kept in order, and neighbors and relatives praise the result. Great benefits, both for families and states, are thus produced" (Witte, 2001, p. 1030).

The axiom that stable marriages and families are essential to the survival, stability, flourishing, and happiness of the larger communities of church, state, and civil society is deeply rooted in and throughout millennia of Western thought (Witte, 2001, pp. 1070–1071).

1. Parts of the following discussion are extracted from longer discussions of these issues; see Wardle, 2006b, 2007, 2008b. See also Hafen & Hafen, 1994, pp. 21–40.

Marriage is the well-spring of social capital—those intangible resources that contribute to a strong society, economy, and nation—in any community or *polis*. Economists emphasize the importance of trust that facilitates exchange, while sociologists and others note the importance of social engagement, willingness to serve, and charity (see Allen & Reed, 2006, p. 88; Putnam, 1995, p. 671).

In these times of increasing individualism, isolation, and alienation in post-industrial societies, family bonds and relations are waning (Hafen, 1991, pp. 17–21, 31–34; Putnam, 2000; Putnam 1993; Shapiro 2002, 99–126). Robert Putnam has noted that the time that families spend together eating family meals has dramatically declined in modern America, as has family attendance at religious services and even family television watching together (Putnam, 2000, pp. 100–101). More seriously, family integrity has declined as centrifugal forces such as child-bearing out of wedlock, nonmarital cohabitation, and divorce have increased, fragmenting families (Wardle, 2003a, 189–236). The decline in family integrity is accompanied by and associated with decline in civic participation and community life (Putnam, 2000). The relationship between family disintegration and loss of civic commitment is complex (McLean, 2002, p. 155; Putnam, 2000, p. 279), but undeniably there is a significant relationship (Hafen, 1991; Hafen & Hafen, 1994, pp. 255–257).

Families not only generate but also distribute social capital (Furstenberg, 2005, p. 809). "Marriage generates 'social capital'—interfamily and intergenerational bonds that embed married couples and their children within larger social networks and direct their efforts to the good of all" (Storrow, 2006, p. 352). The married union of mother and father "provides children with increased social capital and leads to increased educational achievement and security" (Michael, 2004, p. 1467). Conjugal "marriage is a powerful creator and sustainer of human and social capital for adults as well as children, about as important as education when it comes to promoting the health, wealth, and well-being of adults and communities" (Gallagher, 2000, n.p.). This is due to the nature and qualities of marriage, not the label.

It is widely recognized that the marital family—the legal union of man and woman—is the foundational institution for the most promising, most potentially beneficial of family forms. Most people in the world see the family as the unit of society in which relationships, patterns of behavior, and values are first, and most firmly, inculcated and acquired. The highest judicial authorities have described the marital family as the initial and most significant source of our ideas of morality, moral order, and moral acting. The U.S. Supreme Court long has noted that marriage "giv[es] character to our whole civil polity" (*Maynard v. Hill,* 1888, p. 213, quoting *Noel v. Ewing,* 9 Indiana, 37, 49–50), and that marriage "is the foundation of the family and of society, without which there would be neither civilization nor progress" (*Maynard v. Hill,* 1888, p. 211). In more recent years, the Supreme Court has re-emphasized that the "institution of marriage is of peculiar importance to the people of the States," because it relates to the States' interest in "the stability of their social order, . . . the good morals of all their citizens, and . . . the needs of children from broken homes. The States, therefore, have particular interests in the kinds of laws regulating their citizens when they enter into, maintain, and dissolve marriages" (*Boddie v. Connecticut,* 1971, p. 11).

The family transmits the most critical virtues that are essential to a republican (liberal democratic) society, especially service and commitment to the common good (Wardle, 2003b), for as children are raised so will they become responsible or irresponsible citizens. In families, children acquire their first and most deeply imbedded identity, their kinship identity. Families are a principal source of what distinguished BYU anthropologist Merlin Myers called "root paradigms" to explain how society prepares and guides its members to live and cope with life crises (1983). Root paradigms crystallize the formative validity beliefs of an individual, family, and society. Families inculcate root paradigms in individuals and transmit core values from one generation to the next.

Over the course of civilization, marital families have been the most secure, effective, successful form of families, producing the most valuable, long-lasting benefits for the members of the particular family and for society. The marriage-based family has "contributed enormously to the ultimate purposes of a democratic society by providing the stability and the structure that are essential to sustaining individual liberty over the long term" (Hafen, 1983, p. 473). "[M]arriage has become 'an enormously important element in the rise of stable political systems and dynamic economies'" (p. 485, quoting Johnson, The family as an emblem of freedom, p. 2 (Am. Fam. Inst., 1980, on file with the Michigan Law Review)).

Anthropologist David W. Murray has noted: "Marriage is a society's cultural infrastructure" (1994, p. 9). All communities are built upon an infrastructure that consists of the basic institutions on which the preservation and functioning of the community are dependent. Marriage and marital families are part of the substructure, the foundation for social relations. Societies and communities with weak and unstable marriages and families have weak and unstable (typically corrupt and dysfunctional) economic, social, and political relations, as well, and, concomitantly, significant impediments to growth and development.

Legal historian Charles Reid has shown how ecclesiastical teachings have influenced both family law and social values about families (2004). For example, he cites the Catechism of the Catholic Church, which states:

The family is the original cell of social life. It is the natural society in which husband and wife are called to give themselves in love and in the gift of life. Authority, stability, and a life of relationships within the family constitute the foundation for freedom, security, and fraternity within society. The family is the community in which, from childhood, one can learn moral values, begin to honor God, and make good use of freedom. Family life is an initiation into life in society (Catechism of the Catholic Church, 2000, ¶ 2207, quoted in Reid, 2004, p. 525).

Legal scholar John Witte concludes, "A breakdown of marriage and the family will eventually have devastating consequences on these larger social institutions" (2001, p. 1070). When the institution of marriage disintegrates, the transmission and inculcation of the root paradigms and core values of a society also disintegrate. Great religious leaders have emphasized this causal connection. Pope John Paul II famously said: "As the family goes, so goes the nation, and so goes the whole world in which we live" (1986, n.p.). LDS Church President Gordon B. Hinckley likewise declared: "A nation will rise no higher than the strength of its homes. If you want to reform a nation, you begin with families" (1996, pp. 48–49). Likewise, Elder Neal A. Maxwell warned more than a decade ago:

As parenting declines, the need for policing increases. There will always be a shortage of police if there is a shortage of effective parents! Likewise, there will not be enough prisons if there are not enough good homes.

. . . How can a nation nurture family values without consistently valuing and protecting the family in its public policies? How can we value the family without valuing parenting? And how can we value parenting if we do not value marriage? How can there be "love at home" without love in marriage? (1994, p. 89).

Evidence for Elder Maxwell's observations is undeniable. One recent study by a business school professor published by the Institute for American Values and the Institute for Marriage and Public Policy reports that the public costs—costs to American taxpayers—of marital family non-formation (nonmarital childbearing) and break-up in the United States total at least $112 billion each year for American taxpayers, $70 billion in federal tax dollars and $42 billion in state and local tax dollars each year (Institute for American Values et al., 2008, pp. 5–6, 17–21). So there is a huge public interest in protecting and strengthening the institution of marriage. There is also a substantial fiscal danger in legalizing same-sex marriage if it weakens the institution of marriage.

For important reasons, marriage as the union of male and female is the oldest highly preferred legal relationship. Not all intimate relationships are equal; not all provide the same benefits for adults or the same advantages for children. Marriage, the legal union of a man and a woman, creates a uniquely powerful and positive family relationship that benefits not only those members of the relationship and their family, but all of society. Mere legal positivism in the form of calling other relationships "marriages" does not magically transform them into real marriages or change their nature, characteristics, or qualities into those of dual-gender marriages. Marriage, the union of a man and a woman, is recognized as a fundamental human right, and the legal and policy battle to preserve and protect that critical social institution is a civil rights battle of enormous consequence. Marriage is the oldest legal institution to recognize gender equal rights (one man and one woman are required, not two men or two women) in the composition of the institution, and casting aside that definition of marriage will therefore have undesirable negative implications for women's equal rights. Because marriage is of such critical importance in and to religion, the legalization of same-sex marriage raises serious issues about religious liberty; there already have been numerous incidents of harassment, persecution, and denial of civil rights of churches, clergy, and persons of faith seeking to live according to the tenets of their faith (Laycock, Picarello, & Wilson, 2008).

The Movement to Legalize Same-Sex Marriage in the Unites States and the World

Today, perhaps as a consequence of significant recent social devaluation of marital and family relations (evidenced by the historic rates of divorce, nonmarital cohabitation, and child-bearing out of wedlock in recent times), efforts to deconstruct and redefine marriage and family relations have developed. A "leveling" of all intimate relationships has taken place in society and the law. The most radical deconstruction and redefinition of marriage is presented by the global movement to legalize same-sex marriage and marriage-equivalent domestic relations.

The Status of the Legality of Same-Sex Marriage and Equivalent Unions

As late as 2000, same-sex marriage was not legal (and never had been legal) in any nation on earth. As of August 1, 2011, however, same-sex marriage is legal in the United States in six (12 percent) of the states (Connecticut, Iowa, Massachusetts, New Hampshire, Vermont, and New York) and the District of Columbia ("Same-Sex Marriage," 2011). (Same-sex marriage was briefly legalized in California, after the state supreme court mandated legalization of same-sex marriage on May 15, 2008, but less than five months later California voters passed an amendment to the state constitution providing that "[o]nly a marriage between a man and a woman is valid or recognized in California" [*Strauss v. Horton*, 2009, p. 59]. Court battles to impose same-sex marriage by judicial decree continue in California and other states.) Legislators in Maine also voted to allow same-sex marriage but under a unique Maine populist constitutional process that allows the people to vote on whether to override the law before it takes effect, the

voters in Maine in November 2009 passed a "peoples' veto" of a bill passed by the legislature a few months earlier to legalize same-sex marriage (Falcone, 2009).

In nine other states (18 percent), new legal domestic status relationships for same-sex couples that are equivalent to marriage but called something else (usually "civil unions") have been adopted.[2] Four other states (8 percent) have extended some specific, limited relational rights and benefits to same-sex couples (often called "domestic partner" or particular benefits or registries) that are not marriage-equivalent in legal status or total benefits.[3] In summary, in 38 percent of the states, some legal benefits or domestic status are given to same-sex relationship: in six of the states, same-sex couples are allowed to marry; in another nine, they may register for marriage-equivalent rights and status, and in another four states, narrowly tailored packages of some specific rights (not equivalent to marriage) are available.

Because of the constitutional allocation of power between the states and the national government (called *federalism*), the regulation of domestic relations is a matter of state, not national, authority. However, when state and federal laws conflict, the Supremacy Clause (art. VI, ¶ 2) of the U.S. Constitution mandates that federal law pre-empts state law. Thus, advocates of same-sex marriage have tried for decades, since 1970 or earlier, to expand various federal constitutional doctrines in order to compel states to recognize same-sex marriage (*Baker*, 1971). No federal court had ever accepted such doctrines until the dubious ruling of a federal court in California in 2010 that Proposition 8, the amendment to the California state constitution passed by voters in 2009 and barring same-sex marriage, is unconstitutional (*Perry v. Schwarzenegger*, 2010). Since the U.S. Constitution is supreme in all the states, the implications of the interpretation of the Constitution in *Perry* and similar cases are of national importance.

Internationally, there also is a small and slowly growing movement for same-sex marriage. Of the 193 sovereign nations recognized by the United Nations, only

---

2. The states are California, Delaware, Hawaii, Illinois, Nevada, New Hampshire, New Jersey, Oregon, Rhode Island, and Washington. See "Status of Same-Sex Relationship," 2011, Goodnough, 2011.

3. The states are Alaska, Colorado, Hawaii, Maine, Maryland, and Wisconsin. (Goodnough, 2011.)

nine nations (4.7 percent) allow same-sex marriage.[4] Fifteen additional nations (7.8 percent) provide legal benefits to same-sex couples that are largely equivalent to legal benefits provided to married couples (and some nations allow both same-sex marriage and civil unions).[5] At least nine nations (4.7 percent) provide some limited benefits to same-sex couples.[6] In summary, only 12.5 percent of all sovereign nations (mostly western European nations or former colonies) give same-sex couples marital or marriage-equivalent legal status, and nearly 83 percent of the sovereign nations in the world give no significant benefits or status to same-sex couples. In the vast majority of nations, homosexual relationships have no legal status or significant domestic relations benefits.

The Status of Laws Prohibiting
Same-Sex Marriage and Equivalent Unions

Despite the serious dangers of the global movement to legalize same-sex marriage, we also see signs of a renaissance of interest in protecting traditional marriage. There is a much stronger, broader, and deeper national and international marriage protectoin movement in America and globally than the movement to legalize same-sex marriage or equivalent unions. In the past decade, 30 states (that is, 60 percent of all American states) have passed constitutional amendments protecting marriage as the union of husband and wife,[7] including 19 state constitutional amendments that also prohibit the legal recognition of marriage-equivalent same-sex civil unions. Most states have passed their own "defense of marriage" policies by statute, constitutional amendment, or both. Such "defense of marriage" policies effectively prohibit courts in those states from recognizing same-sex marriages performed in other jurisdictions and also express strong public policy in the states barring same-sex marriage recognition.[8] Most (more than 40) American states have explicitly and unequivocally rejected allowing either marriage or any marriagelike legal status or marital benefits for same-sex couples by statute, constitutional provision, or both. Forty-four American states (88 percent) now recognize marriage as the union between a man and a woman only[9]; most by explicit statutory or constitutional provisions,[10] and several others by judicial interpretation of existing statutes (see *Chambers v. Ormiston*, 2007; *Hernandez v. Robles*, 2006; *Lewis v. Harris*, 2006). Nerly two-thirds of the states do not give statewide special legal status or benefits to same-gender couples.

Internationally, legal rejection of same-sex marriage is the prevailing rule and growing trend of constitutional marriage law. Forty-six nations—24 percent of 193 sovereign nations recognized by the United Nations—have constitutional provisions that define marriage as the union of man and woman (Wardle, 2007, p. 1391). This is a recent, modern trend—all but one of these national constitutions have been adopted since 1970.[11] By contrast, no language in a national constitution expressly protects or explicitly requires same-sex marriage (though South Africa's and Canada's constitutions were so interpreted by appellate courts). Additionally, same-sex marriage is prohibited by statute, common law, or binding legal custom in most nations that do not explicitly forbid same-sex marriage in their constitutions (Wardle, 2008a, pp. 443–446). The overwhelming global rejection of same-sex unions comes as no surprise to students of comparative family law. Since World War II, explicit constitutional protection of male-female marital families has been considered one of the foundations for the nurturing and protection

---

4. The nations are Argentina, Belgium, Canada, Iceland, The Netherlands, Norway, Portugal, South Africa, Spain, and Sweden.

5. The nations are Andorra, Austria, Denmark, Finland, France, Germany, Luxembourg, New Zealand, Slovenia, Switzerland, and the United Kingdom.

6. The nations are Argentina, Colombia, Croatia, Czech Republic, Hungary, Israel, and Portugal.

7. The states are Alabama, Alaska, Arkansas, Arizona, California, Colorado, Florida, Georgia, Hawaii (structural provision), Idaho, Kansas, Kentucky, Louisiana, Michigan, Mississippi, Missouri, Montana, Nebraska, Nevada, North Dakota, Ohio, Oklahoma, Oregon, South Carolina, South Dakota, Tennessee, Texas, Utah, Virginia, and Wisconsin.

8. This includes the 30 marriage-amendment states (note 7, above), plus Delaware, Illinois, Indiana, Maryland, New Hampshire, North Carolina, Pennsylvania, West Virginia, and Wyoming.

9. The only states that do not bar same-sex marriage by positive law or judicial decision are Connecticut, Iowa, Maine, Massachusetts, and Vermont.

10. See notes 7 and 8. Additionally, some states have other statutory or judicial language that appears to recognize marriage as the union of husband and wife.

11. The other nation with a constitutional provision limiting marriage to male-female couples is Japan, whose constitution was adopted in 1947.

of human rights. For example, the Universal Declaration of Human Rights (1948, Article 16(3)) recognizes that "[t]he family is the natural and fundamental group unit of society and is entitled to protection by society and the State." Similar statements about the foundational importance and specially protected role of families are found in dozens of other international conventions, compacts, and instruments (Wardle, 2006, p. 483). While this area of law is dynamic, the consistent, overwhelming rejection of same-sex marriage is clearly the dominant policy and trend globally.

Same-sex marriage issues are very controversial, social values are in flux, and the laws are changing. Further changes will occur in the foreseeable future. So it is a good idea to regularly check reliable resources (such as those listed in Box 26.1) for updates on the status of the law.

"The Family: A Proclamation to the World"

Since the days of Joseph Smith, The Church of Jesus Christ of Latter-day Saints has given special emphasis to family relations. The Doctrine and Covenants contains much divine admonition and counsel and many commandments regarding families, family relations, and family duties (for example, see D&C 19:34; 20:47, 51; 42:22; 49:15–16; 83:2, 4; 90:40–43).

The most comprehensive recent example of this family emphasis by the Church is "The Family: A Proclamation to the World," first presented by President Gordon B. Hinckley on September 23, 1995, in a general Relief Society meeting. It is a declaration by "the First Presidency and the Council of the Twelve Apostles of The Church of Jesus Christ of Latter-day Saints," all of whom are sustained by Church members as prophets, seers, and revelators. Thus, the proclamation unequivocally presents itself (and has been accepted by the members of the Church) as a prophetic statement about the importance and purposes of families and the principles governing happy and successful living in families.

The proclamation addresses many specific issues responsible for the confusion, ambiguity, and instability of modern families. It declares that there is a direct relationship between family health and stability and the stability and well-being of any given people or community. The proclamation takes clear positions on some controversial issues regarding family relations, family structure, and family composition. Salient to this paper

> **BOX 26.1**
> **RESOURCES ON SAME-SEX MARRIAGE ISSUES**
> Many sources to keep you informed, pro and con, are available online, such as:
> * Alliance Defense Fund, DOMA watch, at http://222.domatch.org
> * Doha International Institute for Family Studies & Development, at http://www.fsd.org.qa/
> * Family Research Council, at http://www.frc.org/
> * Heritage Foundation, at http://www.heritage.org/
> * Human Rights Campaign, at http://www.hrc.org /
> * Institute for American Values, at http://www.americanvalues.org/
> * Marriage & Family Law Research Project, at http://www.law2.byu.edu/organizations/marriage_family/index.php
> * National Organization for Marriage, at http://www.nationformarriage.org/
> * Ruth Institute, at http://www.ruthinstitute.org/

and the debate over same-sex marriage are these five declarations: (1) "marriage between a man and a woman is ordained of God"; (2) "Gender is an essential characteristic of individual premortal, mortal, and eternal identity and purpose"; (3) "Children are entitled to birth within the bonds of matrimony"; (4) "Children are entitled . . . to be reared by a father and a mother"; and (5) "the disintegration of the family will bring upon individuals, communities, and nations the calamities foretold by ancient and modern prophets."

Thus, the spiritual and moral principles presented in the proclamation have clear social and public policy implications. That is not merely coincidental, for the proclamation concludes with an explicit call for citizen activity to achieve public policy reforms: "We call upon responsible citizens and officers of government everywhere to promote those measures designed to maintain and strengthen the family as the fundamental unit of society."

Some Basic Principles to Consider in Marriage Policy Discussions

It is important to participate in the public policy discussion regarding the definition and protection of marriage, and to do so using appropriate public language and arguments. (Since most citizens do not share Mormons'—or any other specific church community's—religious views, religious language and perspectives may not be very persuasive in this context.) Some issues arise regularly, and some principles are generally relevant. For example:

It's about Marriage

The issue raised by proposals to *legalize* same-sex marriage is whether the basic social institution of marriage should be radically redefined *in law*. It is not about homosexual relations per se, which have long existed without being called "marriages." It is not about same-sex attraction or nature-vs.-nurture or a vague idea of equality for individuals with any or all sexual orientations. It is not about homosexuality or respect for homosexuals. (Most people have close friends or family members who consider themselves gay or lesbian or have at some time lived LGBT lifestyles. This battle is not about them or their lifestyles or sexualities.) The legal issue is whether a core social institution should be profoundly altered from a gender-integrating union by allowing same-sex couples to be "married" also. The legal issue is solely about whether we should continue to protect in the law the institution of marriage as the union of a man and a woman. This issue of defining marriage should not be confused with other issues about LGBT persons, practices, rights, or relations.

Marriage Is an Extremely Important Core Social Institution

Like all significant social institutions, marriage reflects and shapes the shared understanding of society about what marriage is and about what the institution of marriage means. "[M]arriage, like all social institutions, is constituted by a web of shared public meanings; . . . these meanings teach, form, and transform individuals; and . . . in this way, these meanings provide vital social goods" (Stewart, 2006, p. 1). To redefine marriage in such a radical way as to include gender-segregated adult sexual unions will unavoidably have profound social consequences that change the root paradigms of society in revolutionary ways. As legal analyst Monte Stewart has explained, same-sex "marriage is a radically different institution than man/woman marriage, as evidenced by the large divergence in the nature of their respective social goods; and . . . society can have at any time only one of those two institutions denominated marriage" (p. 1). The last time a significant (but perhaps less conceptually profound) change of marriage policy was considered was when unilateral divorce-on-demand was widely adopted in the 1970s, in the belief that it would have no or only minor harmful social consequences. Today, it is widely recognized that unilateral no-fault divorce, which legally erased the concept of marital permanence, has had some severely detrimental social consequences, especially for children of divorce (Cherlin, 2009). Likewise, children will suffer in the new social laboratory experiment of same-sex marriage.

Protection of the Institution of Male-Female Marriage Is a Profoundly Important Civil Rights Movement

Advocates of traditional male-female marriage seek to preserve one of the oldest and most important civil rights—the right of all adults to enter into the social institution of marriage between a man and woman—and to maintain civil rights protection for the core social unit of society. Legalization of same-sex marriage will transform the institution of marriage in many ways and effectively eliminate the unique and uniquely important status and protections in law accorded the union of man-and-woman as marriage. Resulting consequences will lead to a significant loss of civil rights for married men and women and for the rising generation. Preservation of marriage should be seen as a civil rights cause of the highest importance to all of society.

To Legalize Same-Sex Marriage Will Radically Change the Institution of Marriage and Drain It of Essential Qualities That Have Given It Its Unique Value and Meaning

Those changes will effectively eliminate by redefinition the institution of marriage. That is dangerously risky and inappropriate, especially for the judiciary. Its likely effects would fall heaviest on the young. The consequences for society of weakening marriage are far-reaching. One need only look to what happened in Russia in the two decades following the Bolshevik Revolution of 1917, when the new Marxist government attempted to implement measures to encourage the "withering away" of marriage (by prohibiting religious marriages, allowing postcard divorces, legitimizing cohabitation, etc.). "The failure of those radical family law policies was spectacular and the consequences devastating for individuals, families, and for the nation," and after less than two decades of social breakdown, parentless children, and unstable family relations, Russian family law policy "underwent a profound upheaval" and returned to strongly supporting marriage and marital parenting with the fervor of a religious convert (Wardle, 2004, pp. 470, 473).

Legalizing Same-Sex Marriages Will Harm All of Society, Just as Legalizing Child Marriages, Incestuous Marriages, and Bigamous Marriages Would Harm All of Society

It is not just the adults who enter into such unions (same-sex or child-marriages, for example) who are affected. The usurpation of this social institution deprives all who are married or who would marry of a substantial part of the value of the institution and affects their lives, their families, and future generations. The nature and meaning of the institution of marriage would be radically changed by the transformative power of inclusion. For example, as a 2010 *New York Times* article admitted, it is an "open secret" that gay married couples generally have different standards regarding promiscuity, infidelity, and multiple sexual partners (nearly half of married gay couples in California had agreements allowing for sex outside of the marital relationship) (James, 2010). That diverges sharply from the norms of monogamy and sexual fidelity that are fostered by and characteristic of male-female marriages. Similarly, a study by Dutch AIDS researchers reported on the number of partners among Amsterdam's homosexual population (Xiridou, Geskus, de Wit, Coutinho, & Kretzschmar, 2003). They found: (a) 86 percent of new HIV/AIDS infections in gay men were in men who had steady partners; (b) gay men with steady partners engaged in more risky sexual behaviors than gays without steady partners; (c) gay men with steady partners had eight other sex partners ("casual partners") per year, on average; (d) the average duration of committed relationships among gay steady partners was 1.5 years. That was the nature of sexual fidelity among committed gay couples in the most gay-friendly, gay-supportive nation on earth. So the sexual

mores and expectations of marriage will be transformed as the relations of same-sex couples who engage widely in those practices are denominated *marriages* and as there typical behaviors become more regularized.

Legalizing Same-Sex Marriage also Impacts Public Education and Religious Liberty

Legalizing same-sex marriage impacts what and how our children are taught in public schools, as well as religious liberty. It affects who can or must marry, cohabit, live in dorms, and who must be treated as married by private persons, as numerous cases have shown. For example, children in public schools have been required to be exposed to information designed to "normalize" and foster acceptance of same-sex relationships as marriages; parents have been denied prior notice and opportunity to withdraw their children; public schools have adopted "cross-dressing" days; children have been taken on field trips to observe same-sex weddings; students have been shouted down and ridiculed for expressing their viewpoint that marriage is between a man and a woman; college teachers have been terminated for expressing perspectives critical of homosexuality or about the etiology of homosexuality; college students have been dismissed from graduate counseling programs for declining, on religious grounds, to counsel gay or lesbian couples—to name a few examples (Wardle, 2011).

Marriage Is the Only Social Institution That Exists to Link Biological Parents to Their Children in Order to Foster and Link Responsible Sexuality with Responsible Procreation and Parenting

To legally redefine marriage into an institution defined by adult sexual interests alone, detached from the actual or symbolic procreative potential of a dual-gender union, devalues the importance of responsible procreation and responsible, dual-gender parenting. Marriage contains the script for parenting. Legalizing same-sex marriage profoundly edits that script of marital life in a way that moves children from the center to the margins of the relationship. Indicators warn that children will pay for this social experiment.

Racial Equality Principles Do Not Support Same-Sex Marriage

As the Rev. Walter Fauntroy, who marched and worked with the Rev. Martin Luther King Jr., put it: "I am one of gay rights' strongest advocates . . . [b]ut . . . it's a serious mistake to redefine marriage as anything other than an institution between a man and a woman" (Wright, 2007, p. A1). The U.S. Supreme Court held that race (interracial union) is unrelated to any legitimate state interest in regulating marriage (*Loving v. Virginia*, 1967). On the other hand, sexual relations go to the very core reason for regulating marriage. Likewise, General Colin Powell described the difference between black civil rights claims for equality and gay rights claims for equality: "Skin color is a benign, non-behavioral characteristic; sexual orientation is perhaps the most profound of human behavioral characteristics. Comparison of the two is a convenient but invalid argument" (Wardle & Oliphant, 2007, p. 146).

Gender-Equality Principles Strongly Support Protection of Dual-Gender Marriage

The legal requirement that marriage consist of the gender-integrating union of a man and a woman is the oldest gender-equality institution in the world. For centuries in Anglo American common law, both a man and a woman were indispensible to create the legal institution of marriage. Even at times when the common law did not treat women as equal to men in many other respects, it insisted that two men or two women was not sufficient to create marriage, but only the union of a man and woman. If the law accepts the notion that gender is irrelevant to marriage and repudiates this historic rule of gender equality for the basic institution of society, can gender equality be required in other institutions (such as business, education, or the professions)? A substantial body of relational feminist literature celebrates the differences between women and men and the requirement of one man and one woman for marriage; it expresses the belief in the equal necessity of men and women in creating the core social institution, and of the equal importance of their gender-differentiated contributions to the institution of marriage.

The Legal Redefinition and Manipulation of Marriage to Promote Other Social Goals Is Inappropriate

That is how laws forbidding interracial marriage became widespread; in the nineteenth century, racial eugenicists successfully "captured" the institution of marriage and redefined marriage to prohibit interracial marriage in order to promote their social ideology of "white supremacy." That tactic was wrong then, and it is wrong now to redefine marriage to promote LGBT ideology and agenda. The legalization of same-sex marriage will greatly "privatize" a public institution, turning marriage into a mechanism for expression of almost any private romantic preferences rather than the assumption of a public trust.

Conclusion: The Need for a Renaissance of Recognition of the Value of Marriage and Marital Parenting

There is a need for a renaissance of the institutions of marriage and marital parenting, and in public support of marriage and marital families in the United States and the world today. On the one hand, there is a strong and influential movement to redefine marriage to include unions of same-sex couples and to redefine adoptive parenting to include same-sex partners. On the other hand, however, there is a counter-movement for the revitalization of the institution of marriage in many countries. In many nations there are promising indications of growing public recognition of the importance of marriage and marital parenting—stirrings of a vibrant reawakening.

The fate of such defining and strongly contested political issues depends in large part upon the commitment of those who learn and know the truth. This is not a cause for summer soldiers or fair-weather warriors. It will take a long time for all of the changes to occur that are needed to revitalize the social institutions of marriage and marital families. There will be many issues, elections, and public policy decisions that will arise and that need our attention and effort for many years. As President Gordon B. Hinckley admonished:

> The evils of the world will continue to escalate unless there is an underlying acknowledgement, even a strong and fervent conviction, that the family is an instrument of the Almighty. It is His creation. It is also the most fundamental and basic unit of society. And it deserves—no, it *demands*—our combined focus and attention.
>
> We go to great lengths to preserve historical buildings and sites in our cities. We need to apply the same fervor to preserving the most ancient and sacred of institutions—the family!

We cannot effect a turnaround in a day or a month or a year. But with enough effort, we can begin a turnaround within a generation, and accomplish wonders within two generations—a period of time that is not very long in the history of humanity (2000, pp. 169–170).

Lynn D. Wardle *is the Bruce C. Hafen Professor of Law at Brigham Young University. He and his wife, Marian, are the parents of two children and six grandchildren.*

References

Allen, D. W. & Reed, C. G. (2006). The duel of honor: Screening for unobservable social capital. *American Law and Economics Review, 8,* 81–115.

Aristotle, *Politica* (W. D. Ross ed., Oxford University Press, 1921).

Baker v. Nelson, 191 N.W.2d 185 (Minn. 1971).

Boddie v. Connecticut, 401 U.S. 371 (1971).

Chambers v. Ormiston, 935 A.2d 956 (R.I. 2007).

Cherlin, A. J. (2009). *The marriage-go-round: The state of marriage and family in America today.* New York: Alfred A. Knopf.

Falcone, M. (2009, November 4). Maine vote repeals gay marriage law. *Politico.* Available at: http://www.politico.com/news/stories/1109/29119.html

First Presidency & Council of the Twelve Apostles (1995, November). The family: A proclamation to the world, *Ensign, 25,* 102.

Furstenberg, F. F. (2005). Banking on families: How families generate and distribute social capital. *Journal of Marriage and Family, 67,* 809–821.

Gallagher, M. (2000, Autumn). Why marriage is good for you. *CITY Journal.* Retrieved from http://www.city-journal.org/html/10_4_why_marriage_is.html

Goodnough, Abby. (2011, June 29). Rhode Island lawmakers approve civil unions. *New York Times.* Retrieved from http://www.nytimes.com/2011/06/30/us/30unions.html?_r=1

Hafen, B. C. (1983). The constitutional status of marriage, kinship, and sexual privacy—Balancing the individual and social interests. *Michigan Law Review, 81,* 463–574.

Hafen, B. C. (1991). Individualism and autonomy in family law: The waning of belonging. *Brigham Young University Law Review, 1991,* 1–43.

Hafen B. C. & Hafen M. K. (1994). *The belonging heart: The Atonement and relationships with God and family.* Salt Lake City: Deseret Book.

Hernandez v. Robles, 855 N.E.2d 1 (N.Y. 2006).

Hinckley, G. B. (1996, November). "This thing was not done in a corner," *Ensign, 26,* 48–51.

Hinckley, G. B. (2000). *Standing for something: 10 neglected virtues that will heal our hearts and homes.* New York: Three Rivers Press.

Institute for American Values, Institute for Marriage & Public Policy, Georgia Family Council, & Families Northwest (2008). *The taxpayer costs of divorce and unwed childbearing.* Available at: http://www.americanvalues.org/html/coff_mediaadvisory.htm

James, S. (2010, January 28). Many successful gay marriages share an open secret. *New York Times,* Bay Area Blog. Available at: http://www.nytimes.com/2010/01/29/us/29sfmetro.html?_r=1

Laycock, D., Picarello, A. R., & Wilson R. F. (2008). *Same-sex marriage and religious liberty: Emerging conflicts.* Lanham, MD: Rowman & Littlefield.

Lewis v. Harris, 908 A.2d 196 (N.J. 2006).

Loving v. Virginia, 388 U.S. 1 (1967).

Maxwell, N. A. (1994, May). Take especial care of your family. *Ensign, 24,* 88–90.

Maynard v. Hill, 125 U.S. 190 (1888).

McLean, S. L. (2002). Patriotism, generational change, and the politics of sacrifice. In S. L. McLean, D. A. Schultz, & M. B. Steger (Eds.), *Social capital: Critical perspectives on community and "bowling alone"* (pp. 147–166). New York: New York University Press.

Michael, E. (2004). Note: Approaching same-sex marriage: How second parent adoption cases can help courts achieve the "best interests of the same sex family." *Connecticut Law Review, 36,* 1439–1473.

Murray, D. W. (1994, Spring). Poor suffering bastards: An anthropologist looks at illegitimacy. *Policy Review, 68,* 9–15.

Myers, M. G. (1983). *The morality of kinship.* Virginia F. Cutler Lecture, College of Family, Home, and Social Sciences, Brigham Young University, Provo, UT, November 15.

Perry v. Schwarzenegger, 704 F.Supp.2d 921, (N.D. Cal. 2010).

Pope John Paul II. (1986, November 30). *Homily of John Paul II.* Available at: http://www.vatican.va/holy_father/john_paul_ii/homilies/1986/documents/hf_jp-ii_hom_19861130_perth-australia_en.html

Putnam, R. D. (1993). *Making democracy work: Civic traditions in modern Italy.* Princeton, NJ: Princeton University Press.

Putnam, R. D. (1995). Tuning in, tuning out: The strange disappearance of social capital in America. *Political Science and Politics, 28,* 664–683.

Putnam, R. D. (2000). *Bowling alone: The collapse and revival of American community.* New York: Simon & Schuster.

Reid, C. (2004). The unavoidable influence of religion upon the law of marriage. *Quinnipiac Law Review, 23,* 493–528.

Same-sex marriage, civil unions, and domestic partnerships." (2011, June 30). *New York Times.* Retrieved from http://topics.nytimes.com/top/reference/times topics/subjects/s/same_sex_marriage/index.html

Shapiro, M. J. (2002). Post-liberal civil society and the worlds of neo-Tocquevillean social theory. In S. L. McLean, D. A. Schultz, & M. B. Steger (Eds.), *Social capital: Critical perspectives on community and "bowling alone"* (pp. 99–126). New York: New York University Press.

Status of same-sex relationship nationwide. (2011, June 29). *Lambda Legal.* Retrieved from http://www.lambdalegal.org/publications/articles/nationwide-status-same-sex-relationships.html

Stewart, M. N. (2006). Genderless marriage, institutional realities, and judicial elision. *Duke Journal of Constitutional Law & Public Policy, 1,* 1–78.

Storrow, R. F. (2006). Rescuing children from the marriage movement: The case against marital status discrimination in adoption and assisted reproduction. *University of California Davis Law Review, 39,* 305–370.

Strauss v. Horton, 207 P.3d 48 (Cal. 2009).

Universal Declaration of Human Rights (UDHR). (2010). Available at: http://www.un.org/en/documents/udhr/index.shtml

Wardle, L. D. (2003a). Is marriage obsolete? *Michigan Journal of Gender & Law, 10,* 189–236.

Wardle, L. D. (2003b). The bonds of matrimony and the bonds of constitutional democracy. *Hofstra Law Review, 32,* 349–377.

Wardle, L. D. (2004). The "withering away" of marriage: Some lessons from the Bolshevik family law reforms, 1917–1926. *Georgetown Journal of Law & Public Policy, 2,* 469–521.

Wardle, L. D. (2006). Federal constitutional protection for marriage: Why and how. *BYU Journal of Public Law, 20,* 439–486.

Wardle, L. D. (2007). The attack on marriage as the union of a man and a woman. *North Dakota Law Review, 83,* 1365–1391.

Wardle, L. D. (2008a). A response to the "conservative case" for same-sex marriage: Same-sex marriage and "the tragedy of the commons." *BYU Journal of Public Law, 22,* 441–474.

Wardle, L. D. (2008b). The morality of marriage and the transformative power of inclusion. In L. D. Wardle (Ed.), *What's the harm? Does legalizing same-sex marriage really harm individuals, families, or society?* Lanham, MD: University Press of America.

Wardle, L. D. (2011). The impacts on education of legalizing same-sex marriage and lessons from abortion jurisprudence. *Education & Law Journal, 2011,* 593–645.

Wardle, L. D., & Oliphant, L. C. (2007). In praise of *Loving*: Reflections on the "*Loving* analogy" for same-sex marriage, *Howard Law Journal, 51,* 117–186.

Witte, J. Jr. (2001). The goods and goals of marriage. *Notre Dame Law Review, 76,* 1019–1071.

Witte, J., Jr., & Nichols, J. A. (2008). Marriage, religion, and the role of the civil state: More than a mere contract: Marriage as contract and covenant in law and theology, *University of St. Thomas Law Journal, 5,* 595–615.

Wright, J. (2007, January 16). Debate: The Baptist minister will meet members of gay community. *The Register Guard* (Eugene, OR), A1.

Xiridou, M., Geskus, R., de Wit, J., Coutinho, R., & Kretzschmar, M. (2003). The contribution of steady and casual partnerships to the incidence of HIV infection among homosexual men in Amsterdam. *AIDS (Ovid SP, Lippincott, Williams, & Wilkins), 17,* 1029–1038.

CHAPTER 27

Defending the Sanctity of Human Life

Cynthia L. Hallen

We affirm the sanctity of life and its importance in God's eternal plan.

IN ACADEMIC CIRCLES AND PUBLIC FORUMS, THE phrase "sanctity of life" is used by people who have concerns about life-related issues such as abortion on demand, birth control, capital punishment, and euthanasia. When leaders of The Church of Jesus Christ of Latter-day Saints speak about the sanctity of life in conference talks, Church magazine articles, and official statements, they usually focus on the issue of elective abortion. For example, as Young Women general president, Susan W. Tanner identified abortion as one of the weapons in "Satan's attack on families" and showed how the family proclamation succinctly takes a stand on the issue (2005, p. 23). Other life-related topics are also addressed in Church materials, including issues such as abuse, addiction, adoption, chastity, cohabitation, fidelity, pornography, purity, teen pregnancy, virtue, and the unwillingness of some married couples to bear and rear children. This chapter focuses mainly on what Elder Russell M. Nelson calls the global "war on the unborn," a war that kills approximately 40 million voiceless and defenseless unborn babies each year (2008, p. 32).

In 1991, the First Presidency (1991, p. 78) issued a comprehensive statement on abortion, reaffirming the "sanctity of human life":

> In view of the widespread public interest in the issue of abortion, we reaffirm that The Church of Jesus Christ of Latter-day Saints has consistently opposed elective abortion. More than a century ago, the First Presidency of the Church warned against this evil. We have repeatedly counseled people everywhere to turn from the devastating practice of abortion for personal or social convenience.

> The Church recognizes that there may be rare cases in which abortion may be justified—cases involving pregnancy by incest or rape; when the life or health of the woman is adjudged by competent medical authority to be in serious jeopardy; or when the fetus is known by competent medical authority to have severe defects that will not allow the baby to survive beyond birth. But these are not automatic reasons for abortion. Even in these cases, the couple should consider abortion only after consulting with each other, and their bishop, and receiving divine confirmation through prayer. The practice of elective abortion is fundamentally contrary to the Lord's injunction, "Thou shalt not steal; neither commit adultery, nor kill, nor do anything like unto it" (D&C 59:6). We urge all to preserve the sanctity of human life and thereby realize the happiness promised to those who keep the commandments of the Lord.

> The Church of Jesus Christ of Latter-day Saints as an institution has not favored or opposed specific legislative proposals or public demonstrations concerning abortion.

> Inasmuch as this issue is likely to arise in all states in the United States of America and in many other nations of the world in which the Church is established, it is impractical for the Church to take a position on specific legislative proposals on this important subject. However, we continue to encourage our members as citizens to let their

voices be heard in appropriate and legal ways that will evidence their belief in the sacredness of life.

The introduction of a brain-extraction (D&X) abortion method, used on partially delivered babies, prompted further comment from Church leaders in a 1997 statement:

The Church of Jesus Christ of Latter-day Saints declares the sanctity of human life. We deplore the practice of partial-birth abortion which destroys innocent life, and we condemn and oppose it as one of the most revolting and sinful practices of our day. It is abhorrent to God and is fundamentally contrary to his injunction, "Thou shalt not kill . . . nor do anything like unto it" (D&C 59:6) (Davidson, L., 1997).

When President Gordon B. Hinckley presented the proclamation at the general Relief Society meeting in 1995, he reaffirmed "the sanctity of life and of its importance in God's eternal plan" (¶ 5). A careful look at the language of such teachings can help us understand why life is so sacred and so important.

What Is Life? Why Is Life Sacred? Why Is Life Important in God's Eternal Plan?

Life. The etymology of the Old English word for *life* includes meanings such as "body" and "person," or that which "remains" and "continues" (OED, 1989, *s.v., life*). Life can be defined as a condition of sustained regenerative activity, energy, expression, or power that human beings and other animate creatures experience. Emily Dickinson said, "To be alive—is Power" (Franklin, 1998). Her definition suggests that life is empowerment, in spite of the risks and difficulties that human beings may experience in mortality. Respect for the sanctity of life increases when we remember that "the life" is one of the titles by which Jesus identifies himself: "I am the way, the truth, and the life: no man cometh unto the Father, but by me" (John 14:6).

Sacred. The earliest meanings of the word *sacred* in English have to do with the consecration of the body and blood of Christ in the sacrament (OED, 1989, *s.v., sacred*). Life is sacred because Jesus Christ is the ultimate source or fountain of life through His work in the Creation and through His sacrifice in the Atonement. Human life is sacred because human bodies are temples

(1 Corinthians 3:16), and all flesh is in the Lord's hands (D&C 101:16). Our bodies belong to the Lord:

What? know ye not that your body is the temple of the Holy Ghost which is in you, which ye have of God, and ye are not your own? For ye are bought with a price: therefore glorify God in your body, and in your spirit, which are God's (1 Corinthians 6:19–20).

Each individual is sacred because each one reflects the divine image of the Creator (Genesis 1:26–27; Colossians 1:13–16; Moses 2:27). The proclamation confirms that "all human beings—male and female—are created in the image of God" (¶ 2). While a member of the Seventy, Elder Lynn A. Mickelsen elaborated on the importance of this principle:

We are created in the image of God. The union of the flesh with the spirit can bring us a fulness of joy. Teach your children to respect the sanctity of human life, to revere it and cherish it. Human life is the precious stepping-stone to eternal life, and we must jealously guard it from the moment of conception (1995, p. 79).

From conception to resurrection, mortal life is a gift from God (Job 33:4; Acts 17:25; Alma 40:11). Elder Russell M. Nelson explains why we should have respect for the gift of life:

As sons and daughters of God, we cherish life as a gift from him. . . . Life comes from life. It is a gift from our Heavenly Father. It is eternal, as he is eternal. Innocent life is not sent by him to be destroyed! This doctrine is not of me, but is that of the living God and of his divine Son (Nelson, 1985, pp. 11, 14).

Each human being, no matter how young or how small, is a "beloved spirit son or daughter of heavenly parents, and, as such, each has a divine nature and destiny" (¶ 2). Welcoming children into our lives is one of the most important ways to follow Christ, who invited little children to come unto him (Luke 18:16). Elder Russell M. Nelson testifies of the value of a child's life: "Yes, life is precious! No one can cuddle a cherished newborn baby, look into those beautiful eyes, feel the little fingers, and caress that miraculous creation without deepening reverence for life and for our Creator" (1985, p. 14).

What Is Abortion?

The English word *abort* comes from the Latin *ab,* which means "off, away," and the Latin *or-ri,* which means to "arise, appear, come into being." To abort literally means to "cut off the existence of someone" or to "cause someone to disappear" (OED, 1989, *s.v., abortion*). Abortion can generally be defined as the natural or deliberate termination of the life of an unborn or partially born child.

To better understand public attitudes and Church policies on abortion, it is useful to distinguish between two types of abortion: (a) spontaneous or natural abortion, and (b) nonspontaneous or induced abortion. The phrase "spontaneous abortion" is a synonym for miscarriage: the premature, involuntary expulsion of a fetus from its mother by natural causes. While a miscarriage may cause significant grief for the mother and family members, spontaneous abortions are not considered a moral issue.

Nonspontaneous or induced abortion can be divided into two subcategories: (a) emergency abortion, and (b) elective abortion. The more advanced a pregnancy is, the greater the danger to the mother who undergoes an emergency or elective abortion. Methods of abortion correspond to various stages of fetal development in order to reduce risk factors for women who abort their pregnancies. All methods of induced abortion involve the violent destruction of at least one human life—the life of a child. All methods of abortion pose at least some potential health risks to the mother, such as infertility, bleeding, increased susceptibility to breast cancer, problem pregnancies, and sometimes death. Whether legal or illegal, an elective abortion may also be fatal to the mother. John Willke, M.D., and his wife Barbara Willke, R.N. (1997), provide further information about the methods and risks of abortion in a handbook titled, *Why Not Love Them Both? Questions and Answers about Abortion.*

The term *emergency abortion* refers to cases in which a fetus is intentionally expelled from the womb of its mother because of critical circumstances attending the mother, the child, or both. Such "hard cases" include serious health problems for the mother and severe health problems for the baby (Torres & Forrest, 1988). For example, in medical emergencies such as ectopic or tubal pregnancy, the life of the unborn child is taken because the child and possibly the mother would die if the pregnancy were to continue (Willke & Willke, 1997).

In other cases, a pregnant mother may consider aborting a child conceived as a result of incest or rape because of the severe trauma that she has already experienced as a victim. However, the mother may not wish to experience aborting the child because she may see it as an extension or reenactment of the trauma she experienced as a victim of rape or incest (Willke & Willke, 1997, pp. 234–246).

Although emergency abortions raise moral questions, they are not at the heart of the abortion debate in society, because the number of emergency abortions is very low in comparison to the vast number of nonemergency elective abortions performed each year.

The phrase "elective abortion" is synonymous with terms such as "nontherapeutic abortion" or "abortion on demand." Elective abortion is the voluntary destruction of the fetus in the womb of its mother for nonemergency purposes or nonmedical reasons: "Most abortions are performed on demand to deal with unwanted pregnancies. These abortions are simply a form of birth control" (Nelson, 2008, p. 34). Elective abortion is a serious moral problem because it pits the social, emotional, personal, psychological, or financial concerns of adults against the innocent lives of unborn children. Women cite financial trouble and pregnancy outside of marriage as the most frequent reasons for having an elective abortion (Reardon, 1992, p. 35).

In 1971, the United States Supreme Court upheld a law that prohibited all abortions except for "those necessary for the preservation of the mother's life" (Wardle, 2007, quoting *United States v. Vuitch,* 402 U.S. at 70). But in January 1973, the U.S. Supreme Court legalized elective abortion in the *Roe v. Wade* decision, overriding all previous state laws that had protected the sanctity of unborn life. Since then, federal and state courts have wrestled with numerous abortion-related issues, including clinic malpractice, informed consent, parental consent, parental notification, 48-hour notification, spousal notification, post-viability restrictions, pro-life protests, public funding, partial-birth abortion, and the rights of unborn victims who experience other forms of violence resulting in injury or death.

Due to increasingly broad judicial interpretations of the U.S. Supreme Court's 1973 decision in *Roe v. Wade,* it is now legal for a woman to abort her child for almost any reason at almost any time. *Roe v. Wade* judicially created a federal abortion "law" that was unlike the laws of the states, most of which tended to protect the unborn child, with exceptions for health emergencies. In a handful of states, a woman could obtain an abortion for reasons that did not rise to the level of an emergency, but often the law required her to obtain permission from a doctor who felt her reasons were justified. Some of these consultations were, for the most part, a matter of form.

Under *Roe v. Wade*'s trimester system, the states could not interfere with the abortion decision during the first three months of pregnancy. During the fourth, fifth, and sixth months—the second trimester—the states could regulate abortion in the interest of maternal health. For example, laws could require people performing abortions to be licensed appropriately. Finally, when the unborn child was "potentially viable"—able to live outside the mother's womb, with or without assistance (*Roe*, 410 U. S. 113), the state could regulate or prevent abortion unless a doctor found the mother's life or health to be in danger (Wardle & Wood, 1982, pp. 52–53).

Roe's trimester system created problems, and later cases aggravated them. First, *Roe*'s trimester system did not allow for advances in medical science. "Potential viability" has medically moved from about 30 weeks' gestation to almost 20 weeks. But the legal definition remains unchanged. As the medical definition of viability continues its progress back to earlier and earlier stages of prenatal development, the difference between the legal and medical definitions is increasing. Furthermore, improvements in ultrasound technology are giving parents and medical personnel a clearer window into the status of preborn babies as human beings and legal persons before the time of viability.

Second, the difference between legal and medical definitions of "potential viability" creates a situation where babies are aborted alive, meaning the baby survives an abortion attempt, is born alive, and is left to die from the abortion's effects, even though it could survive with medical help. Most methods used for pre-viability abortion make survival impossible, but some post-viability methods result in babies surviving abortion attempts and being born alive. Before 2002, the U.S. Supreme Court had ruled that a state could not require a doctor to care for a baby aborted alive as he or she would care for a baby that had been born, not aborted (*Colautti v. Franklin*, 1979). However, the 2002

Born-Alive Infants Protection Act was passed by Congress and signed into law to protect babies who survive abortion. Although such instances are rare, the law recognizes the personhood of a baby who is still breathing or still has a heartbeat after expulsion from the mother in an abortion procedure. The law also enables physicians and other medical attendants to care for abortion survivors, instead of discarding them as mere abortion complications. The law is unclear about who has ongoing responsibility for the abortion survivor.

Finally, the *Roe* system was undermined by its companion decision, *Doe v. Bolton*, which was decided the same day. *Roe* provided an exception for the mother's life and health to a state's prohibiting abortion in the third trimester. But *Doe* defined *health* loosely as "all factors—physical, emotional, psychological, familial, and the woman's age—relevant to the wellbeing of the patient" (410 U.S. at 192).

The result was a barely regulated industry that essentially provided abortion on demand (at almost any time during a pregnancy for nearly any reason). The realistic limits on elective abortion in the United States are geography and money. If a pregnant woman desires an abortion and has money to travel, she can find clinics and doctors willing to provide it. A woman of limited means, living in a rural area, may have a more difficult time. In the Midwest and Intermountain West, outside of large cities, abortion clinics and doctors willing to perform elective abortions are less common.

The number of abortions performed in the United States since 1973 increased dramatically, to more than 1.5 million per year during the 1980s and 1990s (Wardle & Wood, 1982, p. 7; Willke & Willke, 1997, p. 112). In the 1990s and early 2000s the rate and number of abortions has decreased somewhat, although they remain tragically high, with 22 percent of pregnancies in the United States ending in abortion (Guttmacher Institute, 2011). The 1989 *Webster* (Wardle, 1989) and the 1992 *Casey* U.S. Supreme Court decisions reinstated the right of states to place some limitations on the practice of abortion (*Planned Parenthood v. Casey*, 1992).

States continue to work on laws that provide informed consent for women, parental notification for minors, abortion clinic safety regulations, limits on fetal-tissue experimentation, adoption education, and bans on the partial-birth abortion method (Willke & Willke, 1997, p. 41). Abortion rates have dropped significantly in states where informed consent laws have enabled women to obtain information about fetal development, adoption, and the risks of abortion.

Notwithstanding some setbacks, efforts to uphold the sanctity of life for unborn children are slowly but surely increasing. These efforts include abortion public funding restrictions, abstinence education support, funding for crisis pregnancy programs, the 2002 Born Alive Infants Protection Act, the 2003 partial-birth abortion ban, and the 2004 Unborn Victims of Violence Act.

Just as chattel slavery fell through the efforts of abolitionists, authors, church leaders, and others in the 19th century, advocates for the sanctity of life are gaining moral and legal ground in the 21st century. Today's abortion-rights arguments have parallels to 19th-century pro-slavery arguments. Many Southerners argued that slavery was protected by the U.S. Constitution, just as *Roe v. Wade* proponents argue that abortion is protected by the Constitution. Slavery advocates insisted that popular sovereignty and the right to privacy guaranteed the right to hold slaves; pro-choice supporters insist that the right to privacy guarantees the right to have an abortion. In his 1856 Kansas speech, Senator Alexander H. Stephens "defended slavery as a form of free choice" (Duffy & Halford, 1987, p. 352); now free choice is the appeal of those who defend abortion. Slave-holders said, "These slaves are my property; they're not people." Abortion advocates say, "It's my body; it's not a baby."

Appropriate and Legal Ways to Support the Sacredness of Life

The proclamation concludes with a call to action: "We call upon responsible citizens and officers of government everywhere to promote those measures designed to maintain and strengthen the family" (¶ 9). Although the Church maintains strict neutrality with regard to candidates and political parties, Elder Joseph B. Wirthlin affirms that the Church has a right to speak out on moral issues such as abortion and to support public policy that coincides with moral beliefs (1992). An *Ensign* article on "Preparing Children for Their Community Roles" lists opposition to abortion as a valid contribution to community service:

In recent years the First Presidency has frequently urged Church members *as citizens* to join with their neighbors in vigorously opposing such evils as pornography, abortion, and the availability of liquor to youth. Acting as concerned citizens (*not* as Church representatives) members have in many cases helped achieve tighter abortion laws (1988, p. 60, italics in original).

Latter-day Saints share a reverence for human life with people of many other faiths. Perhaps the best-known champion for unborn children was Mother Teresa, the beloved Catholic humanitarian and Nobel Peace Prize recipient, who said:

Many people are deeply concerned with the children of India, with the children of Africa where quite a few die of hunger. Many people are also concerned about all the violence in this great country of the United States. These concerns are very good. But often these same people are not concerned with the millions who are being killed by the deliberate decision of their own mothers. And this is what is the greatest destroyer of peace today—abortion, which brings people to such blindness.

By abortion, the mother kills even her own child to solve her problems. And, by abortion, the father is told that he does not have to take any responsibility at all for the child he has brought into the world. That father is likely to put other women into the same trouble. So abortion leads to abortion. Any country that accepts abortion is not teaching its people to love but to use violence to get what they want. This is why the greatest destroyer of love and peace is abortion (Mother Teresa, 1996, p. 313, 371).

The 1991 First Presidency statement on abortion encourages Church members as citizens "to let their voices be heard in appropriate and legal ways that will evidence their belief in the sacredness of life" (p. 78). The following are a few suggestions for preserving and defending the sanctity of life in legal and appropriate ways.

1. Maintain and promote chastity and fidelity. Since unwed pregnancy is one of the chief motives behind elective abortion, the most important thing anyone can do to uphold the sanctity of life is to maintain sexual chastity before marriage and marital fidelity after marriage: "Marriage between man and woman is essential to [God's] eternal plan" (¶ 7). Supporting measures that help individuals make and keep commitments to sexual chastity will help promote the sanctity of life. For example, the Young Women general presidency invited mothers and daughters all over the world to uphold the golden banner of virtue (Dalton, 2009). The principle and practice of virtue protects all of God's children everywhere, born and unborn.

2. Help provide for unwed parents. Since financial problems are another common motive for elective abortion, another important way to protect the sanctity of life is to provide help for people who face parenthood out of wedlock. The United States has approximately 4,000 crisis pregnancy agencies (Willke & Willke, 1998, p. 7). These nonprofit organizations help women and their partners choose constructive solutions, such as adoption, when a problem pregnancy occurs. LDS Family Services provides such aid for unwed parents and their families regardless of religious affiliation or economic status. (See Chapter 15.)

3. Become better informed. We can also help by becoming better informed about life-related issues. Research on the topic of elective abortion enables us to build persuasive arguments for promoting the sacredness of life. Latter-day Saint legal scholars have published many useful studies on this topic from the perspective of family law (Wardle & Wood, 1982; Wilkins, Sherlock, & Clark, 1991). Professional organizations such as Americans United for Life (AUL; http://www.united forlife.org), Feminists for Life of America (FLA; http://www.serve.com/fem4life), and University Faculty for Life (UFL; http://www.marquette.edu/ufl/) can also be a source of helpful information on abortion and other issues surrounding the sanctity of life.

4. Discuss the sanctity of life accurately and appropriately. Members of the Church must not condone violent or illegal means for opposing elective abortion. Just mentioning the topic of abortion can stir up controversy because the issue has become so sensitive and volatile in modern society. Therefore, Latter-day Saints should seek the Spirit in order to discuss the sanctity of life in ways that will help others gain accurate information about elective abortion and its consequences. The vast majority of people who oppose abortion use peaceful means to express their concern. In a few highly publicized

incidents, some individuals have chosen to fight abortion on demand with terrorist tactics. Elder Neal A. Maxwell has warned that "violence to an unborn child does not justify other violence" (1993, May, p. 76). All reputable "pro-life" advocates and organizations are opposed to the use of violence to end the violence of abortion.

5. Recognize the consequences of abortion. We need to recognize the grief and psychological pain that may come to women, men, and families who have been affected by elective abortion. Through "Project Rachel" workshops (http://www.hopeafterabortion.com/), the Catholic Church has made great strides in addressing post-abortion trauma and the effects of abortion on individuals and families. Women Exploited by Abortion (WEBA; http://www.abortionfacts.com/reardon/statistics.asp) provides support for the living victims of the abortion industry. Other groups help men deal with abortion-related grief issues.

6. Strengthen our testimonies of the sanctity of life. Latter-day Saints should prayerfully strive to strengthen their testimonies of the sanctity of life, their resolve to oppose elective abortion, and their ability to articulate and defend gospel principles relating to the sanctity of life. Box 27.1 provides prophetic responses to the common arguments used to justify legal elective abortion.

Upholding the sanctity of life is not only a defense for unborn children but also a shelter for individuals and families whose lives might otherwise be devastated by elective abortion. The proclamation invites us to counteract the violence of abortion by peacefully upholding the sanctity of life.

Cynthia L. Hallen *is an associate professor of linguistics and English language at Brigham Young University. She has two nieces, one nephew, one great-niece, and one great-nephew.*

References

Born-Alive Infants Protection Act of 2002, Pub. L. 107-207, 116 Stat. 926 (2002). Retrieved from http://en.wikisource.org/wiki/Born-Alive_Infants_Protection_Act_of_2002

Colautti v. Franklin, 439 U.S. 379 (1979); see Wood, M. A., & Hawkins, L. B. (1980). State regulation of late abortion and the physician's duty of care to the viable fetus. *Missouri Law Review 45,* 394–422.

Dalton, E. S. (2009, May). Come let us go up to the mountain of the Lord. *Ensign, 39,* 120–122.

Davidson, L. (1997, April 12) "Partial-birth" abortions condemned. *Deseret News,* E8. Retrieved from http://www.deseretnews.com/article/554509/Partial-birth-abortions-condemned.html

Doe v. Bolton, 410 U. S. 179 (1973).

Duffy, B. K., & Halford, R. R. (Eds.). (1987). *American orators before 1900.* Westport, CT: Greenwood.

Faust, J. E. (1995, September). Serving the Lord and resisting the devil. *Ensign, 25,* 2–7.

First Presidency, The Church of Jesus Christ of Latter-day Saints. (1991, March). Church issues statement on abortion. *Ensign, 21,* 78.

Franklin, R. W. (Ed.). (1998). The poems of Emily Dickinson: Reading edition. Cambridge: President and Fellows of Harvard College. Poem No. 876.

Guttmacher Institute. (2011, January). *Facts on induced abortion in the United States.* Retrieved from http://www.guttmacher.org/pubs/fb_induced_abortion.html

Hinckley, G. B. (1994, November). Save the children. *Ensign, 24,* 52–54.

Hinckley, G. B. (1998, November). What are people asking about us? *Ensign, 28,* 70–72.

Maxwell, N. A. (1993, April). The inexhaustible gospel. *Ensign, 23,* 68–73.

Maxwell, N. A. (1993, May). "Behold, the enemy is combined" (D&C 38:12). *Ensign, 23,* 76–79.

Mickelsen, L. A. (1995, November). Eternal laws of happiness. *Ensign, 25,* 78–80.

Mother Teresa. (1996). *The joy in loving: A guide to daily living with Mother Teresa.* J. Chaliha and E. Le Joly (Eds.) New York: Viking.

Nelson, R. M. (1985, May). Reverence for life. *Ensign, 15,* 11–14.

Nelson. R. M. (1987, November). Lessons from Eve. *Ensign, 17,* 86–89.

Nelson, R. M. (2008, October). Abortion: An assault on the defenseless. *Ensign, 38,* 32–37.

Oaks, D. H. (1993, November). "The great plan of happiness." *Ensign, 23,* 72–75.

Oaks, D. H. (1999, February 9). Weightier matters. BYU Devotional Address. Retrieved from http://speeches.byu.edu/?act=browse&speaker=Oaks%2C+Dallin+H.&topic=&type=&year=1999&x=11&y=7

Oxford English dictionary [OED]. (1989). (CD-ROM ed.). Clarendon, UK: Oxford University Press.

Packer, B. K. (1986, November). Little children. *Ensign, 16,* 16–18.

Packer, B. K. (1990, November). Covenants. *Ensign, 20,* 84–86.

Packer, B. K. (1992, March 29). The fountain of life. BYU Devotional Address. Retrieved from http://www.byub.org/talks/Talk.aspx?id=713

Packer, B. K. (1992, May). Our moral environment. *Ensign 22,* 66–68.

Planned Parenthood v. Casey, 505 U.S. 833 (1992).

Preparing children for their community roles. (1988, August). *Ensign, 18,* 59–60.

Reardon, D. C. (1992). *Life stories.* Wheaton, IL: Crossway Books.

Roe v. Wade, 410 U.S. 113 (1973).

Tanner, S. W. (2005, June). Strengthening future mothers. *Ensign, 35,* 20–24.

Torres, A., & Forrest, J. D. (1988, July/August). Why do women have abortions? *Family Planning Perspectives, 20*(4), 169–176.

Unborn Victims of Violence Act of 2004, 18 U.S.C. § 1841; 10 U.S.C. (UCMJ) § 919a (2006).

United States v. Vuitch, 402 U.S. 62 (1971).

Wardle, L. D. (1994, Summer). Thomas Jefferson v. Casey. *Human Life Review, 20*(3), 49–58.

Wardle, L. D. (1989). "Time enough": *Webster v. Reproductive Health Services* and the prudent pace of justice. *Florida Law Review, 41,* 882–986.

Wardle, L. D. (2007). Major U.S. Supreme Court abortion decisions: A summary. Unpublished document, Brigham Young University (not paginated).

Wardle, L. D., & Wood, M. A. Q. (1982). *A lawyer looks at abortion.* Provo, UT: Brigham Young University Press.

Webster v. Reproductive Health Services, 492 U.S. 490 (1989).

Willke, J. C., and Willke, B. H. (1998, June). Why can't we love them both? In J. W. Koterski (Ed.), *Life and learning VII: Proceedings of the Seventh University Faculty for Life Conference,* Loyola [University Maryland]. Washington, DC: Georgetown University.

Willke, J. C., & Willke, B. H. (1997). *Why not love them both? Questions and answers about abortion.* Cincinnati, OH: Hayes Publishing.

Wilkins, R. G., Sherlock, R., & Clark, S. (1991). Mediating the polar extremes: A guide to post-*Webster* abortion policy. *Brigham Young University Law Review, 1,* 403–488.

Wirthlin, J. B. (1992, May). Seeking the good. *Ensign, 22,* 86–88.

BOX 27.1
UPHOLDING THE SANCTITY OF LIFE:
COMMON BELIEFS ABOUT ABORTION
AND STATEMENTS FROM CHURCH LEADERS

1. Abortion is an option if the pregnancy affects the health of the mother; health may be defined in personal, physical, mental, emotional, social, or financial terms.

When deemed by competent medical authorities that the life of one must be terminated in order to save the life of the other, many agree that it is better to spare the mother. But these circumstances are rare (Nelson, 1985, p. 12).

2. Abortion is an option if the pregnancy is the result of rape or incest.

Abortion is an ugly thing, a debasing thing. . . . While we denounce it, we make allowance in such circumstances as when pregnancy is the result of incest or rape. . . . But such instances are rare, and there is only a negligible probability of their occurring. In these circumstances those who face the question are asked to consult with their local ecclesiastical leaders and to pray in great earnestness, receiving a confirmation through prayer before proceeding (Hinckley, 1998, p. 71).

3. Abortion is an option if the child will be born with a physical disability or a mental deficiency.

If one is to be deprived of life because of potential for developing physical problems, consistency would dictate that those who already have such deficiencies should likewise be terminated . . . those who are either infirm, incompetent, or inconvenient should be eliminated by those in power. Such irreverence for life is unthinkable! (Nelson, 1985, p. 13).

4. A woman should be free to choose what she does with her own body: Although I would not have an abortion, I believe others should have freedom to choose abortion.

The woman's choice for her own body does not validate choice for the body of another. . . . The consequence of terminating the fetus therein involves the body and very life of another. These two individuals have separate brains, separate hearts, and separate circulatory systems. To pretend that there is no child and no life there is to deny reality (Nelson, 1985, p. 13).

I have been fascinated with how cleverly those who sought and now defend legalized abortion on demand have moved the issue away from a debate on the moral, ethical, and medical pros and cons of legal restrictions on abortion and focused the debate on the slogan or issue of choice. . . . Pro-choice slogans have been particularly seductive to Latter-day Saints because we know that moral agency, which can be described as the power of choice, is a fundamental necessity in the gospel plan. . . . Choice is a method, not the ultimate goal. . . . We are not true to our teachings if we are merely pro-choice. We must stand up for the *right* choice. Those who persist in refusing to think beyond slogans and sound bites like pro-choice wander from the goals they pretend to espouse and wind up giving their support to results they might not support if those results were presented without disguise. . . . If we say we are anti-abortion in our personal life but pro-choice in public policy, we are saying that we will not use our influence to establish public policies that encourage righteous choices on matters God's servants have defined as serious sins. I urge Latter-day Saints who have taken that position to ask themselves which other grievous sins should be decriminalized or smiled on by the law. . . . Should we decriminalize or lighten the legal consequences of child abuse? (Oaks, 1999, pp. 3, 4).

5. Abortion is an option because we do not know exactly when life begins or when the spirit enters the body.

It is not a question of when "meaningful life" begins or when the spirit "quickens" the body. In the biological sciences, it is known that life begins when two germ cells unite to become one cell, bringing together twenty-three chromosomes from both the father and from the mother. . . . A continuum of growth results in a new human being. . . . At twenty-six days the circulation of blood begins. Scripture declares that the "life of the flesh is in the blood" (Leviticus 17:11). Abortion sheds that innocent blood (Nelson, 1985, p. 13).

We do not know all about when a spirit enters the body, but we do know that life, in any form, is very precious. While we are given the power to generate life and commanded to do so, we have no license to destroy it (Packer, 1992, March 29, p. 3).

Abortion, which has increased enormously, causes one to ask, "Have we strayed so far from God's second great commandment—love thy neighbor—that a baby in a womb no longer qualifies to be loved—at least as a mother's neighbor?" (Maxwell, 1993, May, p. 76).

Our attitude toward abortion is not based on revealed knowledge of when mortal life begins for legal purposes. It is fixed by our knowledge that according to an eternal plan all of the spirit children of God must come to this earth for a glorious purpose, and that individual identity began long before conception and will continue for all the eternities to come (Oaks, 1993, p. 74).

6. Abortion should be used to reduce the number of people born because the earth is over-populated. Abortion is necessary to stop poverty and to protect the environment.

Many in developing nations unknowingly ascribe their lack of prosperity to overpopulation. While they grovel in ignorance of God and his commandments, they may worship objects of their own creation (or nothing at all), while unsuccessfully attempting to limit their population by the rampant practice of abortion (Nelson, 1985, p. 13).

Today I speak to members of the Church as an environmentalist. . . . The deliberate pollution

of the fountain of life now clouds our moral environment. The gift of mortal life and the capacity to kindle other lives is a supernal blessing. . . . While we pass laws to reduce pollution of the earth, any proposal to protect the moral and spiritual environment is shouted down and marched against as infringing upon liberty, agency, freedom, the right to choose (Packer, 1992, May, p. 66).

(See also chapter 14 of this volume.)

7. Abortion is a means of empowering women; abortion improves the status of women.

For the wrath of God is provoked by governments that sponsor gambling, condone pornography, or legalize abortion. These forces serve to denigrate women now, just as they did in the days of Sodom and Gomorrah (Nelson, 1987, p. 89).

8. Reproductive freedom through abortion is a fundamental human right.

The rights of any individual bump up against the rights of another. And the simple truth is that we cannot be happy, nor saved, nor exalted, without one another. . . . Nowhere is the right of choice defended with more vigor than with abortion. . . . In or out of marriage, abortion is not an individual choice. At a minimum, three lives are involved (Packer, 1990, pp. 84, 85).

9. Abortion is a moral issue; morality cannot be legislated.

Life is a moral issue. When morality is involved, we have both the *right* and the *obligation* to raise a warning voice (Packer, 1992, May, p. 67).

Some reach the pro-choice position by saying we should not legislate morality. Those who take this position should realize that the law of crimes legislates nothing but morality. Should we repeal all laws with a moral basis so our government will not punish any choices some persons consider immoral? Such an action would wipe out virtually all of the laws against crimes (Oaks, 1999).

10. Abortion is now legal. Abortion is "politically correct."

Whatever the laws of man may come to tolerate, the misuse of the power of procreation, the destroying of innocent life through abortion, and the abuse of little children are transgressions of enormous proportion (Packer, 1986, p. 18).

Hence we view pornography as an awful and enslaving thing. We cannot feel otherwise concerning such practices as abortion and pornography, even if practices such as abortion and pornography are legally and politically protected (Maxwell, 1993, April, p. 72).

During a prayer breakfast in Washington on 3 February 1994, Mother Teresa gave the most honest and powerful proclamation of truth on this subject I have ever heard.... Mother Teresa had tied abortion to growing violence and murder in the streets by saying, 'If we accept that a mother can kill even her own child, how can we tell other people not to kill each other? . . . Any country that accepts abortion is not teaching its people to love, but to use any violence to get what they want.' . . . What consummate spiritual courage this remarkable aged woman [Mother Teresa] demonstrated. How the devil must have been offended! Her remarkable declaration, however, was not generally picked up by the press or the editorial writers. Perhaps they felt more comfortable being politically or socially correct. After all, they can justify their stance by asserting that everyone does it or that it is legal. Fortunately the scriptures and the message of the prophets cannot be so revised (Faust, 1995, p. 4).

11. Abortion is a solution for teen pregnancy and unwed parents.

There will be those who . . . discover to their shock and dismay that they are to become parents, while they are scarcely older than children themselves. Abortion is not the answer. This only compounds the problem. It is an evil and repulsive escape that will someday bring regret and remorse. . . . When marriage is not possible, experience has shown that adoption, difficult though this may be for the young mother, may afford a greater opportunity for the child to live a life of happiness (Hinckley, 1994, p. 53).

Mother Teresa pled for pregnant women who don't want their children to give them to her. She said, "I am willing to accept any child who would be aborted and to give that child to a married couple who will love the child and be loved by the child" (Faust, 1995, p. 4).

CHAPTER 28

Social Policies to Assist and Bless Families and Children

Michael M. Seipel

Parents have a sacred duty to rear their children in love and righteousness, to provide for their physical and spiritual needs.
. . . We call upon responsible citizens and officers of government everywhere
to promote those measures designed to maintain and strengthen the family as the fundamental unit of society.

FAMILIES ARE VITAL TO INDIVIDUALS AND SOCIETY. Families typically provide group identity. They generate economic resources, address the health and emotional needs of family members, and enforce moral codes and norms of behavior (Baker, 2006; Bogenschneider, 2002; Briar-Lawson, Lawson, Hennon, & Jones, 2001; Cheal, 2008). In my opinion, however, other social institutions—religious organizations, corporations, non-profit organizations, and governments—could do much more than they presently do to make it possible for parents, especially in poor families, to provide for their families' needs and to rear children in love and righteousness. This chapter explores current policies and suggests policies and other means by which the U.S. government, especially, could support needy families as they work to fulfill sacred purposes.

Government Policies and the Family

The family is by far the most effective way to provide social, emotional, spiritual, and economic security. Some argue that when families are supported by pro-family government polices, families become stronger and problems are prevented (Bogenschneider, 2002). Some developed countries, such as France, provide direct benefits to families in order to support childrearing. Conversely, others argue that the government should not get involved in family matters. They see the government's intervention as unwise because they fear government will eventually strip the family of its power and influence (Baker, 2006; Mann, 1998). They also fear that any government involvement in the private choices made by families may create a public burden in the form of increased taxes (Baker, 2006; Mann, 1998). Nevertheless, the well-being of families is important to society as a whole.

Regardless of one's philosophy of government and family relationships, it is difficult to find ways in which the United States government has directly promoted and supported families (Briar-Lawson, et al., 2001). Jacobs, Little, and Alemeida (1993) note that it was not until 1981 that the word *family* first appeared in the title of a subcommittee of the U.S. Congress. Since then, public discourse on the family has increased significantly. In recent years, there has been an increase in the number of government programs and policy proposals that affect family life (Cheal, 2008). Family researchers and policymakers are now collaborating to identify factors that influence family formation, living arrangements, marriage, and family relations (Moynihan, Smeeding, & Rainwater, 2004).

Obviously, policy evaluation is difficult work and we cannot always ensure that public policies will have a positive effect on parents and families. Some public policies have provided needed help to families but have created unintended consequences. Social Security, for example, was never meant to be a comprehensive pension program, but many workers did not save money for retirement, believing that Social Security would provide a full retirement income for them (Diamond & Orszag, 2004). In addition, some companies used the same reasoning as an excuse to abolish their employee pension plans. Improved medical care, resulting in increased longevity, and lower birth rates, resulting in fewer workers to support recipients of Social Security, also placed unanticipated stresses on the Social Security system. Those who craft government policies must be careful and foresighted in order to minimize such unintended consequences.

In order to better help parents meet the needs of their families, government should work in partnership with employers and nonprofit organizations. Government can provide Social Security, health care, and related services, while corporations and employers can offer pensions, health insurance, and other benefits. Churches and non-profit organizations also can contribute to family welfare by giving spiritual guidance, counseling, food, shelter, clothing, and other necessities. In order to provide the comprehensive social service needs of families, these three groups must become partners. They each have a role to play in helping families. While this paper will focus mainly on the importance of government policies, the government cannot and should not try to meet all the needs of the people. Nevertheless, the government can be an important source of help for poor families.

Families Under Stress

Some believe that the case for greater government support of families is strengthened by the realization that, over the last two decades, American families and families all over the world are experiencing elevated levels of stress. One key factor is economic pressure. A U.S. Department of Labor, Bureau of Labor Statistics (2009), report shows that in 2007, of 146 million workers in the labor force in the United States, 11.9 percent of part-time workers earned at or below poverty wages while 3.6 percent of full-time workers earned at or below poverty wages. Millions do not have sufficient income to support their families, and the minimal, unrealistic definition of the poverty line means that even more families are unable to provide adequately for themselves.

Working and near-poor families are particularly affected by recent socio-economic conditions. For instance, more low-income people lack access to health insurance. In 2007, about 25 percent of people who earned less than $24,000 a year did not have health insurance, while less than 10 percent of the people who earned more than $75,000 had none (DeNavas-Walt, Proctor, & Smith, 2009). Furthermore, low-income families face increased financial risk from credit card debt. In 2008, the total consumer debt reached

$2.57 trillion and the number of low-income households with credit card debt increased by 18 percent, the largest increase of any income group (Mintz, 2008). Also, more families are declaring bankruptcy. Han and Li (2009) report that there were 3.6 bankruptcies per thousand in 1980, but the rate jumped to 14 per thousand in 2000. In 2009, there were almost 1.5 million bankruptcy filings, an increase of 31.9 percent, from 2008 (United States Courts, 2009).

While reasonable people may differ in their opinions about how involved government should be in family life, as a Latter-day Saint social work scholar I believe that supporting low-income working American families should be a priority of this nation. American workers keep the economy thriving, but up-and-down economic cycles have made millions of workers vulnerable to poverty and dependency. To make matters worse, public policies have largely failed to protect low-wage workers from economic insecurity. This affects the ability of parents to care for their families adequately. Well-crafted policies are needed to help workers increase their wealth and become active participants in the mainstream economic life of America. Consequently, families will be lifted out of poverty and parents will have the resources they need to provide the physical necessities of life. They will also be relieved from the worries and cares of poverty, and thus better able to meet the spiritual needs of their families. When families are blessed with sufficient resources, they will be able to focus more time and means on developing the individual talents of their children and helping them develop spiritually to achieve their full potential.

Throughout the ages, the Lord has importuned his people to care for the poor. Sodom was destroyed in part because its citizens did not look after the poor (Ezekiel 16:49–50). King Benjamin told the Nephites that they could not walk guiltless before God unless they took care of the poor and needy (Mosiah 4:26). King Benjamin taught that it is a serious sin to refuse to help the poor because we think they have brought their troubles upon themselves (Mosiah 4:17–21). In the meridian of time, Jesus declared, "Inasmuch as ye have done it unto one of the least of these my brethren, ye have done it unto me" (Matthew 25:40). In the latter days, His message is the same. The Lord has often instructed his people to care for the poor. He commanded Vincent Knight (and all of us), "Let him lift up his voice long and loud, in the midst of the people, to plead the cause of the poor and the needy; and let him not fail, neither let his heart faint" (D&C 124:75; see also D&C 42:30–31; D&C 104:18). Today President Thomas S. Monson (2009, p. F-2) continues the message of compassion toward the poor. He said:

When we have eyes that see and ears that hear and hearts that know and feel, we will recognize needs of our fellow beings who cry out for help. How do they eat—without food? How do they keep warm—without clothing? without shelter? How do they live—without means? How do they get well—without doctors, medicines, and hospitals?

Strengthening Needy Families

Effective public policies can help us to fulfill our religious duty to care for the poor, especially since not all people and organizations accept or are able to fulfill this commandment. For example, The Church of Jesus Christ of Latter-day Saints does not have the resources to support all the needy of the world, or even of the Church. And yet, as the Savior taught, the poor are always with us (Mark 14:7). In addition to the efforts of individuals, corporations, and non-profit organizations, I believe that government programs and public policies to enable workers to obtain and keep more income, support a more fair tax structure, and strengthen social provisions will best achieve economic blessings for low-income families. In the remainder of this chapter I outline specific policy recommendations that I believe will strengthen needy families.

Income Security Policies

Living wage law. Minimum wage policy has largely failed to lift low-wage workers from poverty through increased earning. Contrary to the expectations of some advocates, since its enactment in 1938, the purchasing power of the minimum wage has not kept up with the cost of living, and increasingly, minimum-wage workers are unable to support their families. Since its enactment, the U.S. Congress has not adjusted the minimum wage in a timely manner to help low-wage workers climb out of poverty (Pollin, Brenner, Wicks-Lim, & Luce, 2008; Stoker, 2006). With the current minimum wage ($7.25 per hour), for instance, full-time workers working all year long will earn $13,920—far short of the $18,310

federal poverty guideline for a family of three (U.S. Department of Health and Human Services, Assistant Secretary for Planning and Evaluation, 2009).

Since minimum wage work is unlikely to provide sufficient income, I believe an important strategy to improve the earning power of low-income workers is through adoption of a living wage law. The purpose of this law is to raise the income of low-wage workers high enough that they are able to support their families above the poverty level (Luce, 2002; Waltman, 2004; Pollin et al., 2008). The living wage policy was first advocated in the United States by trade union groups in the early part of the 20th century—known then as "family wage" (Ciscel, 2000). Advocates argued that the wage should be sufficient to cover the cost of running a household, paying for health care, and raising children. Today, this policy idea is becoming more politically acceptable for three reasons. First, the wages and salaries of low-wage workers are stagnant or are losing ground even as real per capita income for most has been growing. Second, many municipalities are outsourcing work that in the past was done by civil servants. The wages and benefits paid to workers by the private sector that receive these work contracts are lower than those paid by the municipalities. Third, service sector wages are typically lower than manufacturing sector wages and hence more effort must be made to boost the income of service industry jobs (Ciscel, 2000).

The empirical and political support for the living wage movement has been gaining momentum. Baltimore first passed its living wage ordinance in 1994 (Pollin et al., 2008). Since then, more than 140 cities have passed living wage laws. Studies from San Francisco, Los Angeles, New Haven, Boston, and Hartford all showed that these laws have benefited low-wage workers without causing a significant hardship for employers. The feared massive increase in operating costs, job eliminations, and the like has not materialized (Brenner & Luce, 2005; Reich, Hall, & Jacobs, 2005; Fairris, 2005).

Pension reform. Another way to provide greater income security for low-wage workers is through strengthening pension plans. The traditional pension plan has been important to workers. This plan provided retirees with a guaranteed modest income from retirement to death, but due to manipulation of laws and regulations, many employers have been able to break or change retirement obligations (Wolff & Weller, 2005;

Economic Policy Institute, 2006). By 2004, the number of people receiving traditional pension plans fell to 37 percent from 88 percent in 1983 (Economic Policy Institute, 2006). As a cost-saving measure, some employers implemented various forms of "pension freezes," others declared bankruptcy, and still others switched traditional benefit plans to defined-contribution plans—more often known as 401(k) plans (Pension Rights Center, 2009). Subsequently, 401(k) plans became de facto retirement plans for many workers. Although there are some positive features in these kinds of plans, such as encouraging workers to save, 401(k) plans mostly benefit employers and higher-income earners (who are able to save more) but eliminate the security of a guaranteed pension for low-income workers. Under the traditional pension plan, employers contribute to the pension fund an amount equal to about 7 percent of the employee's wages, but under 401(k) plans, participating employers typically contribute only about 3 percent. Since these plans are voluntary, not all employers contribute to the plans and many low-income workers do not contribute anything to the matching fund even if their employers do participate in the 401(k)-type plans. More than 21 percent of 401(k) plan–eligible workers do not participate, and less than 1 percent of lower- to moderate-income workers make a maximum contribution. As a consequence, the median annual 401(k) household pension in 2004 was only $40,000 (Munnell & Sundén, 2006; Wolff & Weller, 2005).

An analysis of the national retirement risk index shows that increasing numbers of retirees, particularly among low-income workers, will face significant economic challenges in their old age (Munnell, Webb, & Delorme, 2006). There is little hope that the current 401(k)-types of approaches will solve the problem. They are fraught with inequalities, risks, and uncertainties.

I believe a real solution to the current insecurity must be based on universal coverage and a policy that guarantees lifelong retirement benefits. Unlike traditional pension or 401(k) plans, Ghilarducci's (2007) Guaranteed Retirement Account (GRA) has great potential for meaningful reform. GRA calls for workers who are not in traditional pension plans to enroll in an alternative plan. This alternative plan will be jointly financed by worker and employer contributions of up to 5 percent of the worker's income, and workers will receive a government-guaranteed and inflation-adjusted return

on investment. At retirement, funds will be converted to life annuities so that retirees will never run out of benefits. There are at least four reasons why this approach is desirable and workable. First, GRA is a more equitable financial arrangement because employers, workers, and government all share the financial responsibilities. Second, since government guarantees these plans, retirees will have greater peace of mind even if investments perform poorly. Third, due to greater economies of scale and efficient administration, the cost of running the program will be smaller. The projected cost of running the program is about 5 percent of the total operating cost, compared to 23 percent for 401(k)-type plans. Fourth, GRA plans will not increase the federal deficit since the plan's subsidy is structured around uniform refundable tax credits for all, rather than tax deferrals, as in 401(k) plans (Ghilarducci, 2007).

Asset-development policy. Income security for low-income families can be strengthened through adoption of asset-development policies. In his groundbreaking work on assets and the poor, Sherraden (1991, 2008) observed that while the past spending-and-consumption–based welfare policies (such as food stamps and supplemental security income) did lessen hardship, they rarely alleviated poverty. Thus, he calls for policies that promote savings, investment, and asset accumulation. He believes that working toward obtaining tangible and intangible assets such as housing, education, real property, jewelry, tools, savings, and bonds will help create real wealth and help safeguard against contingencies. Asset-development policies have helped many middle- and upper-income families to build assets. They benefited from the Homestead Act and GI Bill of earlier years, and currently benefit from college savings plans, medical savings accounts, the home mortgage interest deduction, a variety of retirement accounts, and other policies. Though these programs are important to building assets for many families and individuals, they are not always available to low-income families.

Given the success of asset-building programs for middle-income families, universal and progressive asset-building programs should also be extended to low-income families. While there are several options, Individual Development Accounts (IDAs) have been found to be effective for building assets for the poor. IDAs offer matching funds, typically at a three to one rate, from government and community organizations.

They encourage low-income families to save for education, home ownership, business capitalization, and retirement. Early research evidence shows that those who participate in the program increase home ownership and other assets and have better outcomes in economic, social, and psychological well-being (Sherraden, 2008; Schreiner & Sherraden, 2007).

Supportive Tax Structures

Earned Income Tax Credit. The Earned Income Tax Credit (EITC) legislation of 1975 has been one of the most effective anti-poverty tools used to increase income for low-wage workers. With a timely adjustment, this policy could alleviate economic hardship for many more low-income families (Levitis, 2007). EITC supports low-wage workers in three important ways. First, it reduces the tax burden on workers through refundable tax credits. Though many low-wage workers may not have federal tax liabilities, they pay state and local taxes and especially burdensome payroll taxes. Second, EITC creates an incentive for workers to stay in the labor market rather than turning to welfare programs. Third, it helps low-income families take care of the necessities of life and also accumulate assets (Blank, Danziger, & Schoeni, 2006; Center on Budget and Policy Priorities, 2008; Koulish & Levitis, 2008; Stoker, 2006).

All low-wage workers qualify for the program. The value of EITC that a family receives depends on the family's income and size. The benefits increase as earnings rise until they reach an income of $12,060 for a couple with two children ($8,580 for a couple with one child). At that point, the maximum benefit is attained. The benefits begin to diminish as a worker's income rises. For example, a married couple with two children receives a maximum benefit of $4,824 as their income reaches $12,060. Once the worker's income exceeds that level, the benefits begin to decline and are phased out completely as they reach a maximum income of $41,646 for a couple with two children ($36,995 for a couple with one child). Thus the program encourages people to earn as much as they can without fear of losing all benefits (Center on Budget and Policy Priorities, 2008).

EITC has been an effective program and has received strong political support from both liberals and conservatives. Liberals support it because they view EITC as a fair and simple way to redistribute societal resources from the affluent to the poor without creating large bureaucracies or class struggle. Conservatives support it because benefits are tied to work, and it encourages the poor to stay in the labor market (Plotnic, 1997). Despite its usefulness, some adjustments to the EITC are needed. First, states should enact their own EITC programs to give the poor relief from state taxes. Already 24 states have enacted an EITC and found it to be beneficial (Koulish & Levitis, 2008). Next, more generous benefits should be given to individuals and couples who are without children in the home, because some of these workers are noncustodial parents who pay child support and have other financial responsibilities toward children (Koulish & Levitis, 2008).

Tax reform. I believe tax codes must be reformed. Based on analysis of the tax systems in all 50 states, Davis and his associates (2009) concluded that almost all states tax low-to-moderate income earners more than other income groups. The report shows that the tax rate (income tax, property tax, and sales tax) for the most affluent 1 percent of families was 5.2 percent, whereas the tax rate for the middle 20 percent of families was 9.4 percent. The average tax rate for the lowest 20 percent of families was highest at 10.9 percent—more than twice the rate of the most affluent families. Despite some efforts to make state tax codes fairer in recent years, low-to-moderate income tax payers still carry unfair tax burdens.

Some states currently tax families in poverty, thereby creating increased economic hardship and further pushing families out of economic self-reliance. In 2007, 18 states levied income taxes on families in poverty. Of those 18 states, 9—Alabama, Georgia, Hawaii, Illinois, Indiana, Michigan, Montana, Ohio, and West Virginia—even taxed families that lived below 75 percent of the poverty line. Another 26 states collected income taxes from families that earned just above the poverty line (Levitis & Nicholas, 2008).

I believe the following measures would effectively provide relief to the poor from inequitable tax policies. First, personal exemptions and standard deductions should be updated to reflect inflation; when such measures are in place, more poor people will be below taxable income brackets altogether. Second, state Earned Income Tax Credits should be adopted and the credit should be refundable so that cash benefits are given to low-income workers, even if they do not owe taxes. Third, taxes should be raised on the highest income earners.

Raising income tax on a small number of high earners by even 1 percent would be enough to generate the revenue needed to offset the tax revenue lost by not taxing the poor. Wealthy taxpayers can recoup much of their state taxes since state income tax can be deducted on the federal tax.

Further, low-income families need relief from property taxes. Property taxes are an effective way for states to generate tax revenue, but are generally regressive because they are essentially a wealth tax—and homes represent the largest source of wealth for poor and moderate-income families, whereas a home is only a small part of the overall wealth of the affluent. An Institute on Taxation and Economic Policy (2005) report showed that low-income families in 2002 paid 3 percent of their income on property tax; middle-income families paid 2.4 percent; while the most affluent families paid only 0.8 percent.

There are several ways to reduce tax liability for low- to moderate-income families. First, implement a homestead exemption. This approach sets aside a certain amount of a home's value to be free from property taxes so that taxes are not levied on the total value of the home. Second, a circuit-breaker program needs to be implemented in every state. This measure is designed to offer tax relief to low-income families when their property tax bill exceeds a certain percentage of personal income. It buffers families from tax "overload," like an electric circuit breaker. Third, a "split roll" would help low-income families. Unlike a traditional property tax, which taxes all real property at the same rate, under a split roll a certain class of property is taxed at a different rate. For example, Utah assesses all residential property at 55 percent of its value, but all other properties are valued at 100 percent of their value under a split roll system (Institute on Taxation and Economic Policy, 2005).

Sales tax relief is also needed. Since the poor pay the same rate of sales tax as the rich, a higher percentage of their income is subjected to taxation. On the whole, low-income families spend three-quarters of their income on the consumption of goods, compared to about half for middle-income families and about one-sixth for the wealthiest families. In other words, low-income families pay 1.5 times more consumption or sales taxes than middle-income families (as a proportion of their income) and about 4.5 times more than the wealthiest families. Certainly wealthy families spend more on consumer goods and consequently pay more taxes, but those taxes are relatively small when compared to their overall income (Institute on Taxation and Economic Policy, 2005).

To make it more fair, sales tax must be made less regressive by reducing taxes on goods that the poor consume. The most important way to reduce this regressive tax is by eliminating taxes for groceries purchased for home consumption. This is especially important to low-income families since they spend a higher percentage of their income on food. Thus far the District of Columbia and 31 states out of the 45 that levy sales taxes have eliminated sales tax on groceries completely. While this effort is desirable, more must be done to fully eliminate sales taxes on groceries without creating economic hardships to states and local communities (Center on Budget and Policy Priorities, 2007).

Given the importance of this tax to state revenue formation, the loss of grocery taxes may create economic challenges for some state and local jurisdictions, but states can help low-income families and still raise sufficient revenue by broadening their tax base. Taxing legal services, accounting services, and even haircuts and other similar professional services are all feasible ways to raise revenues with limited impact on low-income families, since they do not often use these services.

Strengthening Social Service Provisions

Family and Medical Leave Act. Darrah, Freeman, and English-Lueck (2007) noted that American families are busier than ever, and increased demands from their jobs and other obligations have overwhelmed workers' ability to manage family life effectively. But since the passage of the Family and Medical Leave Act (FMLA) in 1993, more than 50 million workers have taken a temporary leave of absence from work to take care of family matters without fear of losing their jobs. This was particularly beneficial to low-income families because their employment offers little or no flexibility for balancing work obligations and family life (National Partnership for Women and Families, 2005).

The FMLA is available to private sector employees in organizations with more than 50 workers, all state and local government employees, and some federal employees. Under FMLA provisions, workers are entitled to take up to 12 weeks of unpaid leave with their regular benefits, and upon return to work, they must be given the same or equivalent job with similar pay and benefits. Covered workers are granted leave for the following reasons: the birth and care of a newborn child, the care or placement of an adopted or foster care child, to obtain medical attention when an employee has a serious health condition, or to care for immediate family members (spouse, child, or parent) with a serious health condition. A 26-week unpaid leave is allowed to care for a military family member (U.S. Department of Labor Employment Standards Administration, Wage and Hour Division, 2009).

Even though the FMLA has benefited families, many low-income workers are not taking advantage of this policy because they cannot afford to take time off without pay. Changing federal unpaid FMLA to a paid system would help. Although other steps can be taken to strengthen the FMLA policy, I believe making it into a universal paid system is a good first move. In other industrialized countries, workers enjoy generous family leave benefits. As a case in point, Canadian parents are allowed 35 weeks combined parental leave at 55 percent pay plus benefits (Service Canada, 2010). The United States is one of only four countries (also including Papua New Guinea, Swaziland, and Liberia) out of more than 170 studied that, by law, does not even offer leave for new mothers. California, New Jersey, New York, Puerto Rico, and Washington do offer state- (or commonwealth-) paid family leave, but it is somewhat disjointed and benefits are minimal (U.S. House of Representatives, Committee on Education and Labor, 2008). Being forced to choose between work and family responsibilities is no choice for many low-income workers because they cannot afford unpaid leave.

I believe every effort must be made to help workers take care of both work and family responsibilities with limited hardships. There are several benefits to consider for helping families to balance between work and family responsibilities. A study shows longer maternity leaves help mothers to recover more fully from childbirth and have better health outcomes (Chatterji & Markowitz, 2005). Moreover, when workers are given paid leave of absence, they are more likely to stay on the job and display increased loyalty toward their employers. Supporting these kinds of family policies could be accomplished with minimal costs. Only about $33 per employee was needed to implement paid family leave in California and New Jersey (U.S. House of Representatives, Committee on Education and Labor, 2008).

Health insurance. Low-income families find it increasingly difficult to obtain health insurance. In 2007, those who earned less than 200 percent of the poverty level made up just one-quarter of all workers, but they made up half of all uninsured workers (Kaiser Family Foundation, Health Research & Educational Trust, & National Opinion Research Center, 2009). Although most workers are covered under employer-sponsored insurance (ESI), more and more people are being locked out of such insurance benefits. Cunningham, Artiga, and Schwartz (2008) report that overall employer-based health insurance coverage declined steadily from 80.4 percent in 2000 to 2001 to 75.7 percent in 2007. However, for families with income less than 200 percent of the poverty level during the same time period, the decrease was steepest, with coverage falling from 53 percent to 40.8 percent. Robinson and Ginsburg (2009) argue that the consumer-driven health care system and its performance have largely failed.

Living without health insurance can lead to grave consequences. Those who lack health insurance are not likely to receive timely care, or any care. Delayed care often results in serious illness, which ends up costing far more, or even death. It is estimated that about 27,000 deaths in 2006 could have been prevented if the deceased had health insurance (Rowland, Hoffman, & McGinn-Shapiro, 2009). Also, lack of health insurance can lead to bankruptcy because of high medical bills. Himmelstein, Thorne, Warren, and Woolhandler (2009) found in their national study that 62.1 percent of all bankruptcies resulted from medical bills. Lack of health insurance also creates burdens on society. All too often, uninsured people seek primary care from public hospitals and clinics supported by tax dollars, which are spending about $100 billion annually to care for the uninsured (Cohen & Levin, 2007; Marquis & Kapur, 2003; Waddoups, 2006).

I believe a policy that creates universal health care for all Americans with a simple administrative structure is highly desirable, but given the current political reality this may not take place anytime soon. However, with the current health care reform, more people will obtain health insurance if all aspects of the law are upheld. While the law makes it possible for more people to acquire health insurance either on their own or from their employers, the law needs more incentives and enforcement mechanisms.

Conclusion

Contrary to popular belief, most low-income families work hard and play by the rules, but they are falling further behind. Societal efforts to relieve the economic challenges faced by working poor families have been inadequate. Finding ways to help them into economic self-sufficiency is a desirable goal for the nation and requires policies that promote and reward work. The current "safety net" was created to address crises rather than prevent future problems or strengthen families and communities. Policies must be restructured to more fully address the needs of poor families. Public policies that enable workers to obtain and keep more income, support a more fair tax structure, and strengthen social provisions should be enacted. Work-based polices that promote more fair and just ways to distribute societal wealth are paramount to the well-being of families and society. Such policies would also help to fulfill the commandment that we assist the poor and needy.

Michael M. Seipel *is a professor in the School of Social Work at Brigham Young University. He and his wife, Verla, are the parents of three children. This paper is a compilation of his previous work: Promoting American families: The role of state legislation,* Families in Society *(2008), 89(2), 174–182, and Silver rights legislation: An economic justice for low-income workers,* Journal of Poverty *(2009), 13(4), 384–401.*

References

Baker, M. (2006). *Restructuring family policies: Convergences and divergences.* Toronto: University of Toronto Press.

Blank, R. M., Danziger, S. H., & Schoeni, R. F. (Eds.). (2006). *Working and poor: How economic and policy changes are affecting low-wage workers.* New York: Russell Sage Foundation.

Bogenschneider, K. (2002). *Family policy matters: How policymaking affects families and what professionals can do.* Mahwah, NJ: Lawrence Erlbaum Associates.

Brenner, M. D., & Luce, S. (2005). *Living wage laws in practice: The Boston, New Haven and Hartford experiences.* Amherst, MA: Political Economy Research Institute.

Briar-Lawson, K., Lawson, H. A., Hennon. C. B., & Jones, A. R. (2001). *Family-centered policies and practices: International implications.* New York: Columbia University Press.

Center on Budget and Policy Priorities. (2007). Which states tax the sale of food for home consumption in 2009? Washington, DC: Author. Retrieved from http://www.cbpp.org/cms/index.cfm?fa=view&id=1230

Center on Budget and Policy Priorities. (2008). *Policy basics: The earned income tax credit.* Washington, DC: Author. Retrieved from http://www.cbpp.org/cms/?fa=view&id=2505

Chatterji, P., & Markowitz, S. (2005). Does the length of maternity leave affect maternal health? *Southern Economic Journal, 72,* 16–41.

Cheal, D. (2008). *Families in today's world: A comparative approach.* New York: Routledge.

Ciscel, D. H. (2000). The living wage movement: Building a political link from market wages to social institutions. *Journal of Economic Issues, 34,* 527–535.

Cohen, E., & Levin, Y. (2007). Health care in three acts. *Commentary, 123*(2), 46–52.

Cunningham, P., Artiga, S., & Schwartz, K. (2008). The fraying link between work and health insurance: Trends in employer-sponsored insurance for employees, 2000–2007. Washington, DC: Kaiser Family Foundation. Retrieved from http://www.kff.org/uninsured/upload/7840.pdf

Darrah, C. N., Freeman, J. M., & English-Lueck, J. A. (2007). *Busier than ever! Why American families can't slow down.* Stanford, CA: Stanford University Press.

Davis, C., Davis K., Gardner, M., McIntyre, R. S., McLynch, J., & Sapozhnikova, A. (2009). Who pays? A distributional analysis of the tax systems in all 50 states (3rd ed.). Washington, DC: Institute on Taxation and Economic Policy. Retrieved from http://www.itepnet.org/whopays3.pdf

DeNavas-Walt, C., Proctor, B. D., & Smith, J. C. (2009). Income, poverty, and health insurance coverage in the United States: 2007. Washington, DC: U.S. Government Printing Office. Retrieved from http://www.census.gov/prod/2008pubs/p60-235.pdf

Diamond, P. A., & Orszag, P. R. (2004). *Saving Social Security: A balanced approach.* Washington, DC: Brookings Institution Press.

Economic Policy Institute. (2006). Retirement Security: facts at a glance. Washington, DC: Author. Retrieved from http://www.epi.org/index.php/phpee/redirect/issueguides_minwage_minwagefacts

Fairris, D. (2005). The impact of living wages on employ-ers: A control group analysis of the Los Angeles ordinance. *Industrial Relations, 44,* 85–105.

Ghilarducci, T. (2007). Guaranteed retirement accounts: Toward retirement income security. EPI Briefing Paper #204. Washington, DC: Economic Policy Insti-tute. Retrieved from http://www.sharedprosperity.org/bp204.html

Han, S., & Li, G. (2009). Household borrowing after per-sonal bankruptcy. Finance and Economic Discussion Series: 2009-17. Washington, DC: Federal Reserve System Online. Retrieved from http://www.federal reserve.gov/pubs/feds/2009/200917/200917pap.pdf

Himmelstein, D. U., Thorne, D., Warren, E., & Wool-handler, S. (2009). Medical bankruptcy in the United States, 2007: Results of a national study. *American Journal of Medicine, 122*(8), 741–746.

Institute on Taxation and Economic Policy (ITEP) (2005). The ITEP guide to fair state and local taxes. Washington, DC: Author. Retrieved from http://www.itepnet.org/pdf/guide.pdf

Jacobs, F., Little, P. M. D., & Alemeida, C. (1993). Sup-porting family life: A survey of homeless shelters. *Journal of Social Distress and the Homeless, 2,* 269–288.

Kaiser Family Foundation, Health Research & Edu-cational Trust, & National Opinion Research Cen-ter (2009). Employer health benefits: 2008 annual survey. Menlo Park, CA: Kaiser Family Foundation. Retrieved from http://ehbs.kff.org/2009.html

Koulish, J., & Levitis, J. (2008). State earned income tax credits: 2008 legislative update. Washington, DC: Center on Budget and Policy Priorities. Retrieved from http://www.cbpp.org/cms/?fa=view&id=462

Levitis, J. (2007). A state EITC is a cost-effective way to ease Hawaii's high income tax burden on the poor. Washington, DC: Center on Budget and Policy Pri-orities. Retrieved from http://www.cbpp.org/cms/index.cfm?fa=view&id=1061

Levitis, J. A., & Nicholas, A. C. (2008). The impact of state income taxes on low-income families in 2007. Washington, DC: Center on Budget and Policy Pri-orities. Retrieved from http://www.cbpp.org/cms/index.cfm?fa=view&id=788

Luce, S. (2002). "The full fruits of our labor": The rebirth of the living wage movement. *Labor History, 43,* 401–409.

Mann, T. E. (1998). Is the era of big government over? *Public Perspective, 9*(2), 27–29.

Marquis, M. S., & Kapur, K. (2003). Employment tran-sitions and continuity of health insurance: Implica-tions for premium assistance programs. *Health Affairs, 22*(5), 198–209.

Mintz, J. (2008). The New York City department of con-sumer affairs' comment on docket no. R-1286, truth in lending, submitted to the Federal Reserve System. New York: New York City Department of Consumer Affairs. Retrieved from http://home2.nyc.gov/html/dca/downloads/pdf/Regulation_Z_Comments.pdf

Monson, T. S. (2009, June). How many people can we help? *Liahona, 33,* F2–F3.

Moynihan, D. P., Smeeding, T. M., & Rainwater, L. (Eds.). (2004). *The future of the family.* New York: Russell Sage Foundation.

Munnell, A. H., & Sundén, A. (2006). 401(k) plans are still coming up short. Issue Brief 43. Chest-nut Hill, MA: Center for Retirement Research at Boston College. Retrieved from http://crr.bc.edu/images/stories/Briefs/ib_43.pdf?phpMyAdmin=43ac483c4de9t51d9eb41

Munnell, A. H., Webb, A., & Delorme, L. F. (2006). Retirements at risk: A new national retirement risk index. Chestnut Hill, MA: Center for Retirement Research at Boston College. Retrieved from http://crr.bc.edu/images/stories/NRRI_Files/NRRI.pdf?phpMyAdmin=43ac483c4de9t51d9eb41

National Partnership for Women and Families (2005). Family and medical leave at risk: Millions of Ameri-cans could lose access to leave if Bush administration revises regulations, Ness warns. Washington, DC: Author.

Pension Rights Center (2009). Pension Freezes. *Pen-sion Publications.* Retrieved from http://www.pension rights.org/publications/fact-sheet/pension-freezes

Plotnic, R. D. (1997). Child poverty can be reduced. *Children and Poverty, 7,* 72–87.

Pollin, R., Brenner, M., Wicks-Lim, J., & Luce, S. (2008). *A measure of fairness: The economics of living wages and minimum wages in the United States.* Ithaca, NY: ILR Press.

Reich, M., Hall, P., & Jacobs, K. (2005). Living wage pol-icies at the San Francisco Airport: Impacts on work-ers and businesses. *Industrial Relations, 44,* 106–138.

Robinson, J. C., & Ginsburg, P. B. (2009). Consumer-driven health care: Promise and performance. *Health Affairs, 28,* 272–281.

Rowland, D., Hoffman, C., & McGinn-Shapiro, M. (2009). Health care and the middle class: More costs and less coverage. Focus on Health Reform. Menlo Park, CA: Henry J. Kaiser Family Foundation. Retrieved from http://www.kff.org/healthreform/upload/7951.pdf

Schreiner, M., & Sherraden, M. (2007). *Can the poor save? Saving and asset building in individual development accounts.* New Brunswick: Transaction.

Service Canada. (2010). Employment insurance (EI) and maternity, parental and sickness benefits. Retrieved from http://www.servicecanada.gc.ca/eng/ei/types/special.shtml#much (amount of benefit); http://www.servicecanada.gc.ca/eng/ei/types/special.shtml#Parental3 (length of benefit).

Sherraden, M. (1991). *Assets and the poor: A new American welfare policy.* Armonk, NY: M. E. Sharpe.

Sherraden, M. (2008). IDAs and asset-building policy: Lessons and directions (CSD Working Papers No. 08-12). St. Louis, MO: Center for Social Development, Retrieved from http://csd.wustl.edu/Publications/Documents/WP08-12.pdf

Stoker, R. P. (2006). *When work is not enough: State and federal policies to support needy workers.* Washington, DC: Brookings Institution Press.

U.S. Department of Health and Human Services, Assistant Secretary for Planning and Evaluation. (2009). The 2009 HHS poverty guidelines: One version of the [U.S.] federal poverty measure. Retrieved from http://aspe.hhs.gov/poverty/09poverty.shtml

U.S. Department of Labor, Bureau of Labor Statistics. (2009). A profile of working poor, 2007. U.S. Bureau of Labor Statistics (Report 1012). Washington, DC: Author. Retrieved from http://www.bls.gov/cps/cpswp2007.pdf

U.S. Department of Labor Employment Standards Administration, Wage and Hour Division. (2009). Fact sheet #28: The Family and Medical Leave Act of 1993. Washington, DC: Author. Retrieved from http://www.dol.gov/whd/regs/compliance/whdfs28.pdf

U.S. House of Representatives, Committee on Education and Labor. (2008, June). Family-friendly leave policies: Improving how workers balance home and family. Field hearing before the Subcommittee on Workforce Protections, June 9, 2008. Opening statement of the Honorable Lynn Woolsey (chairwoman). Retrieved from http://frwebgate.access.gpo.gov/cgi-bin/getdoc.cgi?dbname=110_house_hearings&docid=f:42727.pdf

United States Courts. (2009). Bankruptcy statistics. Washington, DC: Author. Retrieved from http://www.uscourts.gov/uscourts/Statistics/BankruptcyStatistics/BankruptcyFilings/2009/1209_f2.pdf (2009 statistics); http://www.uscourts.gov/uscourts/Statistics/BankruptcyStatistics/BankruptcyFilings/2009/1209_f.pdf (2009–2008 comparison).

Waddoups, C. J. (2006). Public subsidies of low-wage employment: The case of uncompensated health care. *Journal of Economic Issues, 40,* 813–824.

Waltman, J. L. (2004). *The case for the living wage.* New York: Algora Publishing.

Wolff, E. N., & Weller, C. E. (2005). *Retirement income: The crucial role of Social Security.* Washington, DC: Economic Policy Institute.

Section V:
Perspectives on the Proclamation

CHAPTER 29

The Proclamation:
A Guide, a Banner, and a
Doctrinal Summary of the Church's Emphasis on the Family

Lloyd D. Newell

THE FAMILY: A PROCLAMATION TO THE WORLD" has been used wisely and widely since President Gordon B. Hinckley first announced it on September 23, 1995, at the annual general Relief Society meeting. As the name suggests, it is addressed to all the world: all nations, all faiths, all families. It continues to be a light in a darkening world and a bulwark in defense of the family. Elder M. Russell Ballard (2005) called the proclamation "a clarion call to protect and strengthen families and a stern warning in a world where declining values and misplaced priorities threaten to destroy society by undermining its basic unit" (p. 41). He continued:

> I call upon members of the Church and on committed parents, grandparents, and extended family members everywhere to hold fast to this great proclamation, to make it a banner not unlike General Moroni's "title of liberty," and to commit ourselves to live by its precepts. As we are all part of a family, the proclamation applies to everyone (p. 42).

The proclamation has served as a guide for individuals and families, a banner to communities and nations, and a doctrinal summary of the Church's emphasis on the family.

A Guide for Individuals and Families

More than ever, families are under attack. A culture of throwaway relationships; familial apathy and permissive values; and secularism, selfishness, and immorality has made the responsibility to build strong families more challenging and more important. The eternal truths in

the proclamation counteract this culture and provide individuals and families with a guide and a standard, a kind of Liahona or compass to chart their course.

For example, President Henry B. Eyring (1998) explained that the proclamation provides an eternal perspective to help us understand the value of family relations: "A child hearing and believing the words of the proclamation regarding families united eternally would begin a lifetime of looking for a holy temple where ordinances and covenants perpetuate family relationships beyond the grave" (p. 13). Truly, understanding and internalizing the principles in the proclamation changes our perspective, our goals, and our entire approach to family life.

Elder David B. Haight (2000) spoke in general conference about the Goodrich family, whose teenage daughter, Chelsea, memorized the proclamation and told Elder Haight how it blessed her life:

> As I think of the statements in that proclamation, and as I understand more of our responsibility as a family and our responsibility for the way we live and the way we should conduct our lives, the proclamation becomes a new guideline for me. As I associate with other people and when I start dating, I can think of those phrases and those sentences in the proclamation on the family. It will give me a yardstick which will help guide me. It will give me the strength that I need (p. 20).

Personal strength is just one of the many blessings that families and individuals reap when they internalize the proclamation and live by its truths. Virna Rodríguez of Guatemala said that the proclamation has blessed her family with clarity in a world of confusion. She explained, "It has helped us prioritize our activities, know our responsibilities, and recognize our blessings" (Seymour, 2005, p. 127). Similarly, Lee Mei Chen Ho from Taiwan said the proclamation has helped her see how divine characteristics such as faith, patience, and love are developed in the home. "When I try to improve myself according to the proclamation," she said, "I can experience real happiness" (Seymour, 2005, p. 127).

Countless individuals and families across the world are choosing to make the proclamation a part of their lives in a variety of ways. The proclamation has been set to music, interpreted and performed in dance, and presented in various forms in homes and chapels across the world. Some families have memorized the proclamation, as Chelsea Goodrich did. One family worked at it every Monday evening for family home evening. The mother recalls:

> It took almost a year, but we memorized the entire family proclamation together. Although this might not be possible for every family, it has proven a blessing for ours. . . . Our children have been exposed to activities, debates, and friends that do not support the Lord's view of the family. I am so grateful to know that they have the words of the Lord's chosen servants when needed (Johnson, 2009, p. 12).

Over the past decade, I have taught a course on the proclamation at Brigham Young University. I have asked scores of students about ways they and their families have brought the proclamation into their hearts and homes. In their responses, which I have collected over the years, I have sensed their love for the proclamation and their desire to make it a more meaningful part of their lives. One student, Stephanie, explained that the proclamation helped her clarify her beliefs and articulate them to others:

> I always keep a proclamation posted by my desk with a picture of my family so I can remember to follow it. . . . Whenever questioned with why I want to be a mom, I can proudly say because that is my divine role. A loving Heavenly Father gave this divine role to me. He will entrust me with his children to raise them in righteousness in the gospel.[1]

Another student, Jonathan, recalled how memorizing the proclamation with his family unified and strengthened them:

> When I was 16, our stake president challenged the entire stake to memorize the family proclamation. He asked us to work together as families to accomplish this goal. My family began reading and memorizing it in our family home evenings and around our home. I remember well having multiple copies of the family proclamation pamphlet in our van. We would quiz each other and practice on car trips. As we worked together to accomplish this, we grew together.

Reed, another student, and his family did not memorize the proclamation, but they referred to it often: "My parents would refer to it as we discussed relevant issues in the news, or gospel principles, or extended family concerns. The proclamation was just always there." Amelia wrote that her family used the proclamation to guide their family home evenings: "My parents . . . would take a phrase or a sentence or two and build a lesson around it." Similarly, Daniel explained that as the family home evening group leader in his student ward, he and his group leader partner used the proclamation as a framework for their lessons for an entire semester. He elaborated:

> We've encouraged those who have been assigned to teach a lesson from one of the paragraphs to pick a particular point and base their lesson around that point rather than gloss over the entirety of the paragraph. This, for myself and hopefully for other members of the group, has led to some powerful insights, understanding, and practical applications of the document.

The proclamation continues to make a meaningful difference in the lives of countless individuals and families. The real test of the proclamation's impact is how it

---

1. All student statements are in possession of the author.

clarifies our understanding and beliefs, how it changes our associations and interactions, and how it guides us to choices that strengthen our faith and our eternal relationships. Many Latter-day Saint families around the world have a copy of the proclamation hanging on the walls of their homes, but even more important, they have its precepts in their hearts and minds to influence their attitudes and behavior.

A Banner to Communities and Nations

The proclamation has been translated into more than 80 languages and distributed to thousands of citizens and leaders around the world. In it the First Presidency and Quorum of the Twelve Apostles extend this charge: "We call upon responsible citizens and officers of government everywhere to promote those measures designed to maintain and strengthen the family as the fundamental unit of society" (¶ 9). As members of the Church who have entered a covenant with Christ, we are not only "fellowcitizens with the saints" (Ephesians 2:19), but we are also called to be "responsible citizens" who can share principles found in the proclamation with others in our communities and nations. We can do this as we converse with neighbors and associates, communicate with civic leaders, get involved in our communities and attend political and legislative forums and debates, and let our voices be heard in exercising our right to vote.

David Dollahite, a professor at Brigham Young University, says that several profamily organizations have been established since the proclamation was first introduced, and a number of those have used the proclamation "as the basis or at least as one of the sources of language or ideas to craft statements that support marriage and family life" (Seymour, 2005, p. 127). For example, the Doha Declaration, which was recognized by the United Nations General Assembly on December 6, 2004, contains many of the proclamation's central teachings, including the concepts that marriage is between man and woman and that husband and wife are equal partners (Seymour, 2005). And Bonnie D. Parkin, former Relief Society general president, relied heavily on statements from the proclamation in her speech at the European Regional Dialogue Conference on the Family in Geneva, Switzerland, in August 2004 (Seymour, 2005). All such efforts illustrate a point that Elder Merrill J. Bateman made as a member of the Seventy. Regarding the proclamation's power to influence

scholarship and world policy, he said, "The proclamation serves not only as a handbook for family living, but also as a compass for family research and advocacy" (Seymour, 2005, p. 128).

Kendel Christensen, a BYU graduate and founding member of a profamily conference at BYU, says he has come to realize how badly the world needs the proclamation: "I had no idea growing up that the world would so seriously question the value of children, the importance of gender, and the meaning of marriage."[2] He now views the proclamation as a banner to the world that inspires the outreach efforts of the Stand for the Family Club. "We used the proclamation in our mission statement," he says, "because we know that it is the only way for families and societies to flourish." A journalist once interviewed him and asked why Latter-day Saints have such clear views about marriage and family while others seem confused. He gave credit to the proclamation and referred the journalist to a Church web site where she could find a copy. She was impressed that the proclamation was written in 1995, well before much of the current debate about the nature of marriage and family. Christensen explained to her that "the Church's position on marriage and family wasn't a 'response' to any specific political policy, but an established doctrine." Christensen also used the proclamation at a 2010 conference sponsored by the Ruth Institute and at another hosted by the Love and Fidelity Network at Princeton University. He recounts:

The Church's stance on marriage was well-known by all the students because of the Church's involvement in Proposition 8 [a 2008 California ballot initiative to recognize only marriages between a man and a woman], and as a result, they had many questions about our faith. During those discussions . . . I was able to share many copies of the proclamation. . . . To many members of other faiths, the proclamation was a very powerful statement of truth with which they agreed.

Church leaders have also used the proclamation to promote the importance of families to non–Latter-day Saint audiences. At the fifth World Congress of Families in Amsterdam during the summer of 2009, Elder

2. Personal communication, March 3, 2010.

Russell M. Nelson (*Church News*, 2009a) drew on principles from the proclamation in his address on the importance of children to families and nations. He said:

> History and contemporary studies have shown that marriage of a husband and a wife, with both contributing their distinctive natural traits to the family, provides the ideal context within which to rear productive, compassionate, and moral individuals. . . . Individuals and groups who would overthrow the traditional concept of marriage and family would first mutate and then mutilate these long-established, time-tested social norms. The consequences of such changes would have far-reaching implications (p. 4).

He referred to the proclamation as "a document that supports the development of happy children who are morally strong" (p. 4). He quoted extensively from the proclamation, offered free copies to conference attendees, and explained how to download the text from the Internet.

When Church officers meet with leaders from around the world, the proclamation is frequently given as a gift and memento of the visit. For example, when Elder Nelson and President Thomas S. Monson visited Brazil's vice president, José Alencar, on June 2, 2008, the Church leaders presented him with a framed copy of the proclamation (Avant, 2008). Similarly, the Caribbean Area Presidency welcomed Dominican Republic President Leonel Fernandez Reyna on May 8, 2008, and presented him with a copy of the proclamation as a token of friendship (*Church News*, 2008).

Following the example of the General Authorities, Church members have been creative in sharing the proclamation within their communities. For example, in June 1999, the *Ensign* reported on a project launched by members in the United States in the Waynesboro Virginia Stake; their goal was for each of the 9 units in the stake to present 10 framed copies of the proclamation to friends, associates, and community leaders. They exceeded their goal, ultimately presenting more than 100 framed proclamations and an additional 180 unframed copies throughout the area. They personalized the frames for a variety of individuals, "from CEOs to pediatricians, from local and state government leaders to radio announcers, and from fire fighters to school principals" (Sexton & Skeen, 1999, p. 69). Copies

were presented in a variety of formal and informal settings: at the close of a service project, at a banquet, and at an appreciation dinner for fire and rescue workers. "In every case," the article reported, "the proclamation has been warmly received by men and women from different backgrounds, occupations, and nationalities, and the recipients have discovered that the givers share a high regard for the family unit" (p. 69). One sister in this stake told of an experience in which the youth presented a copy of the proclamation to the mayor of Charlottesville, Virginia, on a Monday night:

> At that particular meeting . . . a controversial subject was scheduled to be discussed. The large room was filled to capacity, with even the aisles being filled. The meeting was also being televised live. The first order of business was our young men and young women making a presentation to the mayor and city council of the family proclamation. The room seemed charged with tension, which dissipated as a parade of smiling youth approached the podium and made the presentation. The youth then explained that inasmuch as it was Monday evening, that this was family home evening for members of our Church and asked their families to stand. The positive response was indicated by two ovations! The following day many favorable comments were made by people who had watched the broadcast (p. 69).

In El Salvador, Church members, in partnership with school administrators throughout the country, use the proclamation to teach lessons on families to schoolchildren. One of the teachers, after hearing these lessons, decided to learn more about the Church: "I have seen the change in my students' lives, and I said to myself, 'I will go to see if I can find something to help my own family,'" she said. "After visiting the presentations, I think the only thing I have to do is to make the decision to change. I want to receive the missionaries because I need help for my children" (Seymour, 2005, p. 128).

I have found that as I travel and converse with others not of our faith, the proclamation is an effective missionary tool. Returned missionaries report having shared the proclamation with people as they taught investigators and as they interacted with people in the community. Church members are also finding ways to share the proclamation with their families and friends of other faiths. Jonathan, a BYU student who was planning a wedding, said:

> My mother suggested placing a framed family proclamation with other pictures on a table at our wedding reception. I was immediately excited! The family proclamation is an integral part of who I am. Since my mother is a convert to the Church, I look forward to sharing my testimony on the family though the proclamation with those relatives.

Another BYU student told of giving copies of the proclamation to guests as they left her wedding reception. She considered the proclamation the best and most appropriate gift she could give to the many non-LDS family members, friends, and neighbors who came to wish her well. Other families have shared the proclamation with non-LDS friends and family as Christmas gifts, in family newsletters and birthday cards, and in family and neighborhood parties and open houses.

A Doctrinal Summary of the Church's Emphasis on the Family

The Church, which is led by those we sustain as prophets, seers, and revelators, is at the forefront of efforts to strengthen and promote happy family life. The proclamation provides a clear and concise statement of the doctrinal foundation of such efforts.

Dan Roberts, a former bishop from the Alpine Utah North Stake, said:

> While serving as a bishop I continually referred to the proclamation in my talks, in my meetings with the adults and youth, and in my counseling with ward members. I always felt that if I could just get our members to really internalize the principles of the proclamation, they would have the answers they needed and the pathway to a happy family life. The proclamation is truth, and I've seen its truth and power change lives.[3]

In addition, the proclamation serves as a building block for greater Church emphasis and outreach on the family. The proclamation is available free at Church distribution centers. It is available in more than 80 languages at the Church's website (lds.org); it has been quoted from and referenced in countless conference and sacrament meeting talks, as well as Church classes and lessons; it has been cited in innumerable articles and books and is the basis for two in-depth textbooks and a foundational family course at BYU–Provo and BYU–Idaho.

The proclamation has influenced many other Church programs and publications. For example, the theme for the Church's 2009 Primary sharing time and the children's sacrament meeting presentation, "My Eternal Family," came from the proclamation: "Happiness in family life is most likely to be achieved when founded upon the teachings of the Lord Jesus Christ" (¶ 7). Reproductions of the proclamation appear in publications such as *For the Strength of Youth*, *True to the Faith*, the Young Women Personal Progress book, the Aaronic Priesthood Duty to God book, Church handbooks and guidebooks, family home evening manuals, seminary and institute manuals, Sunday School manuals, and many others. It has also been placed in temple and chapel cornerstone boxes since it was first issued in 1995 (*Church News*, 2009b).

Conclusion

Although over the past years the proclamation has become more broadly known and referenced, it has yet to be brought fully out of obscurity; there are so many hearts and homes around the world it has not reached. In some sense, though progress has been made, we have just scratched the surface of its potential impact. Just as General Authorities of the Church share the proclamation with citizens and leaders around the world, so can we. People across the globe love their families, as we do. They worry about their children and care about the strength and well-being of their families, but some may have become confused about certain vital principles of happy family life. The proclamation speaks to the hearts and minds of our neighbors, friends, and those who care about the strength of the family as it declares the sacredness of family life and calls upon us to maintain and strengthen the family as the fundamental unit of society.

The impact, power, and influence of the proclamation are found in the lived experience of quality family life—in husbands and wives who "love and care for each other and for their children" (¶ 6) and "help one another as equal partners" (¶ 7), in children who grow up with the understanding that "marriage between a man and

---

3. Personal communication, February 10, 2010.

a woman is ordained of God" (¶ 1), in families who find true happiness through "faith, prayer, repentance, forgiveness, respect, love, compassion, work, and wholesome recreational activities" (¶ 7).

In ever-widening ripples—like those that silently spread after a rock is thrown into a still pond—the influence of the proclamation will expand in every direction, blessing individuals, marriages, families, communities, and nations.

Lloyd D. Newell is a professor of religious education at Brigham Young University. He and his wife, Karmel, are the parents of four children.

References

Avant, G. (2008, June 7). Courtesy call on Brazil's vice president. *Church News*, 6.

Ballard, R. M. (2005, November). What matters most is what lasts longest. *Ensign, 35,* 41–44.

Church News. (2009a, August 15). Children matter to families and nations alike, 4.

Church News. (2009b, March 28). Cornerstone contents, 13.

Church News. (2008, May 17). Visit from nation's president, 7.

Eyring, H. B. (1998, February). The family. *Ensign, 28,* 10–18.

Haight, D. B. (2000, November). Be a strong link. *Ensign, 30,* 19–21.

Johnson, M. (2009, July). Fortifying our family. *Ensign, 39,* 12–13.

Seymour, N. (2005, November). "The Family: A Proclamation to the World" reaches 10-year milestone. *Ensign, 35,* 126–128.

Sexton, D., & Skeen, T. K. (1999, June). A proclamation to the world. *Ensign, 29,* 68–69.

CHAPTER 30

A Guide to Using Social Science in Discussions about the Family

Thomas W. Draper

Happiness in family life is most likely to be achieved when founded upon the teachings of the Lord Jesus Christ.

A BROAD CULTURAL DISCUSSION IS GOING ON ABOUT the meaning of marriage and family. "The Family: A Proclamation to the World" is relevant to this discussion. One attempt to defeat the "great plan of happiness" (Alma 42:8) as it is taught in the proclamation involves redefining marriage and the family. If humankind can be persuaded to pursue the right thing in the wrong way, our chances of finding happiness will be diminished.

Much of the broad discussion is being conducted with social science data and interpretations of data (e.g., Armour & Haynie, 2007; Harden, Mendle, Hill, Turkheimer, & Emery, 2008; Orth, Trzesniewski, & Robins, 2010; Twenge, 2006). One may or may not appreciate the social sciences, but if one wants to join the discussion, some knowledge about how the social sciences are used may be helpful. Gaining that knowledge is one of the reasons there is a university class on the proclamation at Brigham Young University.

Social science is that part of science that looks at human attributes, traits, attitudes, beliefs, behaviors, and relationships. It is generally thought to cover the disciplines of anthropology, clinical psychology, economics, family science, geography, human development, family therapy, political science, psychology, social work, and sociology. But it is much larger than that. Any time scientists study human attitudes, beliefs, behaviors, and relationships, they are likely doing social science, regardless of the official name of their disciplines. Advertising, biology, business, communications, education, history, law, medicine, organizational behavior, psychiatry, religious studies, and testing all conduct some social science. I recently attended an academic symposium at one of the top scientific organizations in the world. The symposium had been organized by mathematicians (Farley et al., 2010). Nevertheless, much of the symposium dealt with human attributes, traits, attitudes, beliefs, behaviors, and relationships, and was in fact social science.

Mathematicians, biologists, and physicists turn to opinion polls for the same reasons social scientists do. Pressing questions need to be answered, and people cannot think of any better way to get a tentative answer. Everyone has elusive questions they would like answered, and virtually everyone engages in social science–like activities, though often without availing themselves of the best techniques the social sciences have to offer.

That said, most thoughtful people have some concerns about the ambiguities and uncertainties of the social sciences. For example, the tobacco companies got away with selling unhealthy products for decades because the correlations between self-reported tobacco use and poor health were ambiguous. The findings always could be interpreted in more than one way. The tobacco companies could always call top scientists to testify that it was unclear whether smoking was unhealthy or whether smoking and premature death were both manifestations of some other factor, such as a genetic propensity to seek stimulants and take risks. Incidentally, people may have thought those tobacco studies were purely medical studies, but the common self-reports of behaviors used in them make them partly social science. That is, even if a scientist has direct physiological measurements in one part of a study, if he or she is correlating that data with individual reports of beliefs, behaviors, or attitudes, the study is open to the thoughtful concerns associated with the social sciences.

People often express concerns about social science measurement. Unease about the validity of intelligence or achievement tests are two examples. Some people who score very well on such tests do not seem to have much practical sense. Some of those with middling scores turn out to be great achievers. Others question the ambiguity of studies that report findings such as "children with learning disabilities are more likely to have frustrated parents." They rightfully ask if this is a cause-and-effect relationship, and if so, in which direction does the "effect" flow—parent to child, child to parent, or some of both. Educated readers also want to know if the findings of particular studies can be generalized beyond the particular individuals studied to the reader or other individuals. As we shall see, questions about the ambiguities of correlation studies; the validity of self-reported data, psychological measures, cause and effect, direction of effect, and size of effect; and the adequacy of the sample are questions that should always be asked of any social science, or social science–like, research report.

In the remainder of this chapter, I will list twelve issues that readers ought to consider as they participate in any discussion where social science research is being used. This list is neither complete nor definitive, but it is a good start. But in making this list I do not wish to discourage students about the value of the social sciences. Though social science findings are often weak, probabilistic, and ambiguous, taken in aggregate, they can often serve as guides to the "best guess" about what course to pursue when a decision needs to be made and all of the choices contain uncertainties.

1. Moral Agency

Some people doubt the value of the social sciences because the findings seem to suggest that many important choices are simply the product of one's environment or biological makeup. The importance of moral choices in the plan of happiness cannot be overstated. Moral agency is central to our progression. Many choices are implied in the proclamation.

Social scientists typically do not say much about that which is sovereign and divine within us. They cannot. Social science is about explaining human phenomena that can be explained. Social scientists study the outward manifestations of behavior, the inner workings of the mind, and the contexts in which beliefs, attitudes, and behaviors are forged. The observation that much human behavior appears to be following predictable scripts does not obviate agency. The predictable scripts social scientists study are nothing more than behavioral summaries of what most people will do in a given situation most of the time. For example, I know, by observation, what time I need to leave home in the morning in order to get a covered parking space at BYU. I'm a moral agent. All of the other members of the BYU community seeking parking spaces are moral agents. But I can still make accurate predictions about when many drivers will arrive in the morning so I can arrive five minutes earlier.

Most thoughtful people, including most social scientists, recognize that there are often moral choices by which they may elect to depart from their familiar predictable behavioral scripts. For example, one morning I came across a crying toddler inexplicably in the middle of the road on a dangerous curve. I did what you would do. I ceased pursuing a parking spot, got the baby out of the street, and found his parents. But even some moral choices can be predictable. My actions were the sort of thing one would expect of a mostly good person.

When we are not being morally called away from our routines by the needful "face of the other" (Levinas, 1991, pp. 187–201), there are many meaningful patterns that can be predicted from social science's empirical scripts. For example, if a child is struggling to read, one can consult the research literature on learning disabilities or a therapist who has consulted the literature and find procedures that might help solve the problem. In many ways the orderly application of so-called deterministic knowledge can increase agency by increasing choices. Using the scripts to solve the problem so that the child knows how to read increases the child's choices, including the choice to read the scriptures and great literature, and to otherwise become well-educated.

2. Truth

In some discussions about the family, people may make allegations of "proof" from the social sciences. Sometimes these allegations go contrary to proclamation principles. For this reason, it is useful to take a look at the nature of truth in the social sciences. Like many academic disciplines, the social sciences deal with truth that is constructed according to rules. The rules for constructing social science truth are the common ones for publishing peer-reviewed research (Salkind, 2009). When a research paper is finally published, it becomes a weak social science truth. But, because of the nature of social science variables, everything important needs replication. For example, some years ago a paper was published by a good scientist announcing the discovery of the "gay gene" (Hamer, Hu, Magnuson, Hu, & Pattatucci, 1993). However, attempts to replicate the study failed (Rice, Anderson, Risch, & Ebers, 1999). Hence, the "gay gene" finding lost its standing as a weak truth and science moved on to something else.

Once again, the possibility of a gay gene may seem like it was biological science since it involved the examination of genetic markers. The thing that makes it social science is the self-reported dependent variable, "gayness." The main way to know if someone is gay is that he or she says so. Defining oneself as something that is not materially verifiable moves the claim into the realm of self-reported attitudes and beliefs, or in other words, social science.

3. Development

The proclamation notes the importance of parents in guiding and nurturing children. There was a time when people believed that many complex behaviors were established at the time of conception. Current thinking is that many biogenetic behaviors are the result of parental, environmental, prior genetic, social, or other influences—including choices—activating and deactivating elements of each individual's genetic code (Allis, Jenuwein, Reinberg, & Caparros, 2007). The activation and deactivation processes and how they are chemically mediated is one of the more exciting areas of epigenetic research (Tahiliani et al., 2009). This differentiation can begin in monozygotic twins before they are born. The older identical twins are, the greater the differences in the way elements of their identical genetic codes are expressed. One well-known group of behavioral geneticists said it this way: "Causal genetic influences are thus intimately bound to causal environmental circumstances. . . . Moreover, even highly heritable traits can be strongly manipulated by the environment, so heritability has little if anything to do with controllability" (Johnson, Turkheimer, Gottesman, & Bouchard, 2009, p. 218).

Developmental theories have long held that certain behavioral tendencies were put in place by key environmental events that occur during sensitive periods

of individual development (Gottlieb, 1997). Science's ability to observe changes in DNA markers yields a potential improvement over the early developmental theories because some of the latter hypotheses are more materially testable. Much scientific work remains to be done to determine which complex behaviors rely on incarnate chains of genetic material that were activated and deactivated by environmental, prior genetic, social, or other influences, including choices. Saying that a complex behavior was the inevitable result of one's genetic makeup must be regarded as only one of several diminishing hypotheses.

For example, it has long been known that one can make equally good cases that alcoholism, one's political temperament, and one's sexual preference all have a behavioral genetic basis (Goodwin, 1976; Settle, Dawes, Hatemi, Christakis, & Fowler, 2010; Scarr & Weinberg, 1981). But genetic proclivity is always interwoven with the potential to be activated or deactivated by nongenetic events. For example, I had a grandfather and two uncles who, at times, drank more alcoholic beverages than was wise. I may have been born with a genetic potential to become an alcoholic. But my parents effectively taught me to live the Word of Wisdom (D&C 89). Because of the social influence of that parenting, and my own choices in a wide variety of situations, any hereditary potential I may have toward alcoholism is, so far, irrelevant. Nothing has turned on that likely part of my biogenetic makeup. Nevertheless, at any time I could choose to make different choices and follow a different script. One of my uncles gave up drinking in his early 80s and spent the next ten years as an Alcoholics Anonymous sponsor for others who were struggling with the same problem.

Similarly, considering sexual orientation, a hypothetical young man might be born with a potential for a high degree of social awareness of or even an affinity for other males. As this heightened awareness grows, the young man may decline to participate in some of the destructive or insensitive activities conducted by his peer group. This may lead to some peer-group estrangement and the establishment of ties with other like-minded individuals. But the behavioral scripts those individuals follow and the social identities they forge may depend on the scripts that are available and the encouragement present in their subculture. Who they become may depend on how their gifts are defined, what they choose, and how they are labeled. Notably, the above scenarios do not provide evidence that developmental phenomena are fully chosen by the individual, and they take no position on the reversibility of every type of activated proclivity. Not every alcoholic who tries recovers. Questions about the reversibility of traits are still being answered.

Developmental phenomena can make moral responsibility difficult to assign. In the Book of Mormon, when the prophet Lehi blesses the children of his sons Laman and Lemuel, he fully recognizes that some of his grandchildren are following scripts they did not choose and are not likely to change (2 Nephi 4:9). Undoubtedly, this is common in many developmental scenarios. In such cases, choice, and therefore moral responsibility, become tricky. Adolescents with a hereditary social sensitivity would be most likely to choose to follow the dominant scripts and labeling of their culture. Those promoting destructive scripts may be more morally culpable than those who follow them. Helping to determine what scripts dominate and are offered to children during sensitive periods of genetic awakening may be an inescapable moral duty of those who live in any society.

In the coming years, the whole developmental field is going to be rethought, taking behavioral–genetic findings into account. In the meantime, statements like, "The majority of biogenetic scientists accept that _____ [fill in the blank with any complex behavior] is genetic" should always be tempered with a developmental caveat. And no one, including me, should attempt to close off scientific inquiry and research with presupposition.

4. Politics

In the proclamation, responsible citizens are asked to engage in political processes and support measures that will "maintain and strengthen the family as the fundamental unit of society" (¶ 9). Rarely do both sides of a political discussion start out on equal footing. One side or the other, depending on the particular context for the discussion, is initially presumed to be more correct. Individuals representing a viewpoint that is in the minority will almost always have to make a better presentation than the side representing the majority viewpoint. In the social sciences, the majority point of view is often different from the principles put forward in the proclamation. These political points of view can be present in (a) the selection of the research topic, (b) the interpretations that are made of the data, and

(c) the decisions as to which articles get published or rejected. Even the mostly helpful *Publication Manual of the American Psychological Association* (2010), which is the style guide for most of the social sciences, jumps in with a forced interpretation on an issue that is far from settled. In the section on sexual orientation, we find: "The term *sexual orientation* should be used rather than *sexual preference*. For a person having a bisexual orientation, the orientation is not chosen even though the sex of the partner may be a choice" (p. 74, italics in original). What this means, in practice, is that if researchers wanted to interpret their same-gender attraction data, even in part, as being due to a complex developmental phenomenon, they might have a harder time publishing their work than a scientist who treats sexual orientation as biologically determined at conception. With such forces in play, one should not marvel if literature reviews of scientific research on politically sensitive topics seem one-sided. Often it is easier for one side of the discussion to get their research and interpretations published than it is for another.

Fortunately, science, through the process of replication, is a self-correcting enterprise. But when political opinions are strong, the self-correction can take a long time. For example, the notion that human embryos had gills persisted in biological textbooks for more than 100 years after it was discredited (Richardson, 1998). For morally important issues, it may be perilous to wait for science to correct itself.

5. Faint Signals

By using the word *likely* in the phrase, "Happiness in family life is most likely to be achieved when founded upon the teachings of the Lord Jesus Christ" (¶ 7), the authors of the proclamation remind us that while those who do good "shall in nowise lose their reward" (D&C 58:28), in this life there are no absolute guarantees of a perfect outcome in family life. Some outcomes in family life are probabilistic. The social sciences can help parents understand some of the ways that they can give their marriage and their children the best opportunities. However, one should be careful not to read too much into useful social science findings. Often the applied value of a study will be small. Often it will not be applicable to a given family's situation.

As a child, I used to sit on top of my parents' home, trying to pull in radio stations with a crystal radio I had made in Cub Scouts. There was a lot of static and occasionally something intelligible. Similarly, social scientists often deal in faint signals that exist in a sea of static. The faint signals are the findings we report, and the sea of static is the ever-present variation that accompanies all of our inferential studies. Some of this seemingly random variation is due to studying moral agents who can choose to go "off script." Some comes from the variety of different social scripts that are available for people to follow. Some comes from studying the most complex and unique beings in the universe. Some stems from the influences of variables we do not know how to measure or forgot to include in our studies. Some may even be random.

Most statistics contain ratios of signal (the phenomenon being studied) to "static" (the unexplained variation that is present along with the event being studied). For example, the correlation coefficient, one of the most used statistics in the social sciences, is simply a ratio between the orderly variation that is present between two variables divided by a weighted average of the total variation that is present in the two variables (Salkind, 2011). In the social sciences, studies can disagree and correlations tend to be small. For example, a .30 correlation between couples divorcing and having had one or both sets of their parents divorce allows one to predict intergenerational divorce 9 percent better than chance guessing (.30 x .30 = 9 percent). That small prediction is something, but it's not much; 91 percent of divorce would be unexplained or predicted by choice and other variables. In some larger and more complex multivariable inferential studies, it often appears that a much higher degree of influence has been accounted for. But remember, these higher figures are the percentage of the variation in the constrained world specified by the variables that were included in the study, not the unconstrained and more complex world that is often referred to as "real life." The bottom line is that when you hear reports of social science research, most often the results will not pertain to most people, most of the time, in most situations. If they do pertain, they will usually do so in a modest and contextualized way. Of course, occasional findings may have high relevance for a specific individual or group of individuals. But most will not. Knowing which reports you should attend to and which ones you need not worry about involves education, discernment, and common sense.

6. Declarative Style

A related issue that tends to make social science predictions seem more likely to be important than they actually are is that social scientists are taught to write with "declarative style" (Salkind, 2009). It sounds better and more convincing to write, "There is a relationship between whether or not a couple divorces and their parents' marital status" than to write in a way that appropriately conveys all of the uncertainty and ambiguities in our data: "There is a kind of, sort of, sometimes, hopefully, but faint, probabilistic and ambiguous relationship between . . . ." You get the idea. The certitude in social science speaking and writing often goes beyond what is justified by the observations. One problem with the constant drumbeat of inflated trivial findings is that, over time, a repeated and exaggerated emphasis on the evanescent can obscure the more substantive issues that would best be attended to. A large part of being wise in today's world is simply knowing what ideas deserve our attention and what ideas we should ignore.

Similarly, the strong claims made by some researchers sometimes belie small effects. For example, if treatment A helped one afflicted person in 1,000 and treatment B helped two afflicted people in 1,000, the headline might read, "Treatment B is twice as effective as treatment A." The headline is technically true, but the observation that neither treatment was effective for most people might get glossed over in the media report. It is always important to know what social scientists call "effect size" in order to assess the overall importance of a reported study.

7. The Premature Assumption (or Non-Assumption) of Causation

The term *likely* is often interpreted to mean "helps to cause." Yet, social scientists mostly analyze their data using correlation coefficients. Most everyone who has had a basic statistics class has heard the quip, "Correlation does not imply causation." The quip is correct. But neither does correlation, of necessity, imply the lack of causation (remember the tobacco studies). The presence or lack of causation in correlation studies is usually unknown. Sometimes interpreters of social science make or imply the causal statements they want rather than the ones that are appropriate given their research design. For example, a conservative political organization might release a study showing that young adults who attend college are more liberal in their political outlook than are young adults who do not attend college. From this study, they might argue that the difference is due to those darned liberal college professors. That might be a possibility, but it is not the only one. An alternate hypothesis for the same data is that families who value and support the education of their children tend to score higher on tests of political liberalism because there is a built-in assumption in some of the political measures that those who are well-read are more liberal. Attributing causation, or the lack thereof, to the results of any correlation-based study usually represents an underlying assumption.

8. No Difference

On occasion, social science studies may report a comparison that seems to contradict proclamation principles. Most of the time when social scientists compare two groups, there are two possible outcomes: (a) the groups are different, or (b) the researcher was unable to tell whether the groups were different (Salkind, 2011). Group comparison statistics are set up to detect differences between groups with 95 percent confidence so that we will not say there is a difference when there is not one. The failure to demonstrate such a difference between two groups does not mean the two groups are the same. If, after the statistical analysis, a social scientist's data suggests that there was only a 90 percent certainty that the two groups were different, then by the rules for constructing social science truth, the scientist would most often say, "There was no difference between the groups." Consequently, if a study reported that two groups were not different, for example, that gay parents were no different from straight parents, that would not necessarily mean that the two types of parenting had similar impact and produced similar outcomes. But when the finding gets reported in the popular press, that is the way it would sound. This error was made in a recent state supreme court ruling on the constitutionality of denying marriage licenses to same-sex couples. The judges were presented in testimony with two opinions about the "effects" of same-sex parenting on children. One respected scholar testified that there were multiple studies that had concluded that there were no meaningful differences in outcomes for children raised by same-sex parents as compared to opposite-sex parents. A second scholar accurately testified that the body of social science literature on this question was still too

weak to provide the courts with a reliable answer to the question. The court ignored the correct argument presented by the latter scholar in favor of the easier-to-grasp "no differences" argument of the first scholar (see *Varnum v. Brien*, 2009).

9. Measurement Error

Social science demonstrations of what is "likely" and what is not rests on social science measures. The biggest question people have about such measures is, "Do they actually measure what they profess to measure?" The answer is, "At best, partially." The Stanford–Binet IQ test is much criticized. But it is one of the best measures ever developed for predicting behavioral outcomes. This ability is called "predictive validity." Pointing out that the predictive validity of an IQ test is relatively high is not to say that IQ tests are good. Rather, it is a means of noting that pretty much every other measuring scale used by social scientists (for example personality or marital satisfaction measures) is more problematic in terms of predictive validity than the IQ test.

Nevertheless, in spite of the limitations of social science measures, when combined as a battery of multiple measures, their predictive validity usually increases. For example, the ACT achievement test is used in combination with high school GPA and other measures as part of the BYU admissions process. Together these measures may predict about 25 percent of success in college. When compared to admitting applicants to a university randomly, the inclusion of the social science test and variables leads to a greater likelihood that the admitted students will be the ones who would benefit most from a college education, 62.5 percent accuracy versus 50 percent accuracy (assuming, for simplicity's sake, twice as many applicants as vacancies to fill). That 12.5 percent gain in accuracy may not seem like much, but it illustrates why the social sciences persist. By using them, one can make better predictions than by not using them. The predictions are far from perfect, and far from just, but no one has yet thought of a better way to approach many problems where decisions must be made in the face of uncertainty, or in the case of BYU admissions, where demand exceeds supply.

10. Sampling Error

In general, national pollsters can predict elections 95 percent of the time within plus or minus 4 percent.

On a day that I was writing this chapter, I consulted the website realclearpolitics.com (2010) and found seven different national polls that asked American voters their opinions of the job performance of the president of the United States. All of the polls had been completed during the same two-week period. Three polls had the president's approval rating at plus 3 percent (47 percent approve minus 44 percent who disapprove, with 9 percent uncertain). Three of the polls had the president's approval rating at minus 3 percent. One poll had the president at minus 5 percent.

Possibly the president's approval rating shifted up and down and up 6 to 8 percent in two weeks. But it is more likely that the differences were simply due to sampling error, since six of the seven polls were within plus or minus 4 percent. Also instructive is that two of the polls that had the president at plus 3 percent were CBS and CNN, and the one that had him at minus 5 percent was Fox News. Not to accuse any of the networks of bias, but if a pollster is biased, there are innocent-looking ways of sampling and asking questions that can nudge the results. For example, the poll numbers for "likely voters" are usually different from those for "eligible voters."

Some of the more egregious examples of sampling error occur not in national polls but in everyday social science research. I once hosted a family research conference. One of the presenters claimed to have a set of measures that could predict the success or failure of a romantic relationship with more than 95 percent accuracy. Given moral agency, the complexity of a lifetime of living with another person, and the "slings and arrows of outrageous fortune" (Shakespeare, *Hamlet*, act 3, scene 1), such predictive power from a short one-time assessment is highly suspect. I offered to help the researcher find the error in his data analysis. He was unwilling to let me look at the data and he never sent in his chapter for the book that was published based on the conference (Draper & Marcos, 1990).

Predicting relationship success with 95 percent certainty would be virtually impossible with a nationally representative sample. But it would be easy and trivial with some clinical samples. Consider an oncologist who limited her practice to only the most severe and advanced cases of liver cancer. She likely would be able to predict a with 95 percent accuracy or higher which patients would live and which patients would die during the next five years simply by predicting that they all

would die. Or, if she used a sample of teenagers who had just passed a thorough physical exam, she could predict with 95 percent accuracy or higher that none of them would die of liver cancer during the next five years. Sometimes individuals mistakenly believe that if a clinical finding has been replicated over and over in different locales with different samples, then it must be correct for the whole population. This can sometimes be the case. But such replications with the two hypothetical clinical samples just mentioned would still be trivial.

In general, one should be careful with any percentage estimate derived from any type of nonrepresentative sample. Therapists, in particular, often only see the most problematic behaviors, and this limits their ability to extend their findings—what social scientists call generalizing—to the population as a whole.

11. Included and Excluded Variables

When confronting studies that seem to contradict proclamation principles, one should examine the independent as well as the dependent variables. Here are the results of four well conducted national polls. The citizens of Utah have (a) the highest sense of personal well-being and happiness in the nation (Gallup Poll, 2009), (b) the lowest levels of neuroticism (Rentfrow, Gosling, & Potter, 2008), (c) the highest levels of depression (Mark, Shern, Bagalman, & Cao, 2007), and (d) the fifth highest suicide rate (Centers for Disease Control and Prevention, 2009).

These paradoxical observations might be due to sampling error, measurement error, or false consciousness (a term Karl Marx coined to describe such things as slaves saying they are happy in slavery). Or they might be due to a real phenomenon wherein some professedly happy people are actually committing suicide at a faster rate than the professedly unhappy people.

Since this is state-level data, the paradox does not have to exist within the same individuals. Possibly a happy, insensitive, and intolerant majority could be driving some minority groups to depression and destruction. That is, it may not be easy to be an Athenian in Sparta, or a Spartan in Athens.

I did a state-level correlation study using these four data sets and some others in an attempt to provide a "best guess" about the precursors of the observed paradox. Since Utah is an exemplar of the paradox, almost everyone who hears about it immediately wants to know if religion plays a role in the outcome. But there is a problem. Many of the variables that might influence the paradox are themselves intercorrelated. For example, religiosity, membership in the Republican party, gender, and gun ownership are all correlated with each other and likely predict some of the same outcomes.

This turned out to be the case. If I enter all four of these variables, along with five others, into my analysis, religiosity played no role in the most parsimonious statistical model of the paradox. By the rules of social science truth, I could say that religiosity made no difference. That is, everything religion would account for is better explained by the other variables. But, if I excluded only one variable, gender, from the analysis (in both cases a stepwise multiple regression), then religiosity became the single most important variable related to the paradox. So as a social scientist, I could pretty much say whatever I wanted to say about religion and the paradox depending on which variables I included and excluded in the analysis.

This example is not an isolated or rare case. The variables social scientists choose to include and exclude in their analyses can influence the results obtained and the interpretations made. One ought always to ask, "What other relevant variables could have been included in this study that might change its findings?" When research is offered in support of "hot" political topics, one should also ask how many different ways the data were analyzed before the results that supported what the researcher wanted to say were obtained. While it is not appropriate, it is not uncommon for researchers to "massage" the data and to do multiple analyses until preferred results are obtained. The old maxim, "I wouldn't have seen it if I hadn't believed it," is alive and well on all sides in the broad discussions on the family.

12. Normative Morality

The authors of the proclamation speak with a solid, principled voice befitting modern-day prophets. However, in the grand discussion on the family, right and wrong are most often put forward using one of two approaches. The discussants may base their views on consistency with accepted foundational principles or in accordance with normative standards. In the normative approach to morality, the true and the good are likely to be defined as what most people believe or do. From the time of the ancient Greeks (Jowett, 2009), the normative approach

to morality has made people uneasy, and for good reason. Essentially, "voting with behavior" on what is right or wrong violates nearly everyone's foundational principles. But it is in this area of normative morality that the social sciences have some of their strongest influences in the broad discussions. Documenting that the majority of people or experts hold a particular opinion or that certain practices are fairly common or produce valued normative benefits can be a step in arguing that some attitudes, beliefs, or behaviors are normal or even better than others.

We do this as members of The Church of Jesus Christ of Latter-day Saints when we point out that faithful Latter-day Saints live longer, have better health, have more enduring marriages, have kinder teenagers, and that those teenagers are having less unwed sex than teenagers in other comparable groups (Enstrom & Breslow, 2008; Smith, 2005). But, of course, from a principled point of view, none of those outcomes, of necessity, make a church true. Consider the early Christian Saints who were stoned or thrown to the lions because of their beliefs. The negative outcomes associated with their beliefs are insufficient arguments for the incorrectness of their beliefs. Nevertheless, Latter-day Saints are fond of normative, "by their fruits ye shall know them" (Matthew 7:20), points from the social sciences. During the course of a general conference, there are occasional appeals to social science research to further emphasize principled truths (see, for example, Hales, 2010; Uchtdorf, 2010).

Right and wrong in our legal system is partially based on the consensus of a jury. Writing for the majority in a decision released in May 2010, Justice Kennedy of the U.S. Supreme Court explained that the first task in making a Supreme Court ruling is to look for consensus in the legislation of the states (*Graham v. Florida*, 2010). Note, the court was not looking for principles as a first priority, but for consensus. Consensus as a moral principle is playing an ever-increasing role in the political and social decisions that are being made as part of the discussions about the family. But remember Noah (Genesis 7)—correct principles are always superior to normative morality.

Conclusion

When my students leave the fall semester research class I teach and go home for Christmas, I, tongue-in-cheek, tell them that when their families ask them what they have learned in their social science majors, the correct answer is, "Nothing for sure." That is an inescapably true statement. That said, the social sciences have a definite place as a secondary witness to some important proclamation truths and as a diffuse guiding light on some important family issues. Though social science research is often ambiguous and probabilistic, I have no trouble offering my witness that by the persistent application of social science's small, probabilistic findings, coupled with spiritual discretion, great and useful things can come to light and aid one's family. In applying the findings, one should not expect success all the time. And some findings should simply be ignored. If the Spirit says something is wrong, don't do it—no matter what the social sciences say. Remember "Article of Belief 8¾ths": "We believe the social sciences insofar as they are interpreted correctly." Also, remember Las Vegas. Those gargantuan hotels and casinos on the Strip are monuments to evil's relentless application of a small probabilistic advantage. The house may only win 52 percent of the time, but that is more than enough to build a Babylon in the desert. Our task is to employ everything virtuous, lovely, praiseworthy, and of good report (including the social sciences when appropriate) to build an intergenerational structure in the hearts of families that will be there long after the dark monuments of the inappropriate and false pursuit of happiness have crumbled and are blowing in the desert like the rest of the sand.

Trying to live and raise a family by only attending to social science findings is a recipe for disaster. But pondering the secondary witness of the social sciences and receiving confirmation of one's best guesses about what will make family life better within one's stewardship can be invaluable. We must be humble skeptics as we winnow through the chaff for that which is good and worthwhile.

For better and for worse, in spite of its insufficient philosophical grounding and many problems and detractors, social science is being persuasively employed in the grand discussions that are defining marriage and family in our culture. Many people who are in positions to make and change social policy at various levels are being swayed by social science. Those cultural discussions and the social science claims made within some of them are important for shaping the futures of our

children and families, as well as our neighborhoods and states. Rather than waiting for social sciences to solve all of their problems and resolve all of their ambiguities, I believe it is best to enter the discussions now, informed by a knowledge of the strengths and weakness of the type of knowledge influential policymakers are finding persuasive. In doing this, it will at times be necessary to "deconstruct" some of the weak social science points that are being made. I hope this chapter is useful for this purpose. In dealing with good individuals who have begun to make up their minds based on ambiguous information, but who cannot follow the arguments contained herein, one may be left with little more than the curious move of saying, "Well, if you found that (weak) social science argument to be persuasive, here is an equal argument that should give you pause in your decision making." Either way, waiting for perfect arguments to answer those who would use social science to lead the world in good-hearted but wrong-headed directions simply cedes too much, too soon.

Thomas W. Draper *is a professor in the School of Family Life at Brigham Young University. He and his wife, Linda, are the parents of four children and they have nine grandchildren.*

References

Allis, C. D., Jenuwein, T., Reinberg, D., & Caparros, M. (2007). *Epigenetics.* Cold Spring Harbor, NY: Cold Spring Harbor Laboratory Press.

Armour, S., & Haynie, D. L. (2007). Adolescent sexual debut and later delinquency. *Journal of Youth and Adolescence, 36,* 141–152.

Centers for Disease Control and Prevention. (2009). Suicide prevention. Retrieved from http://www.cdc.gov/ViolencePrevention/suicide/index.html

Draper, T. W., & Marcos, A. C. (Eds.). (1990). *Family variables: Conceptualization, measurement, and use.* Sage: Newbury Park, CA.

Enstrom, J. E., & Breslow, L. (2008). Lifestyle and reduced mortality among active California Mormons, 1980–2004. *Preventative Medicine, 46*(2), 133–136.

Farley, J. D. (Chair), Horton, S., Cliff, C., Woo, G., Brase, J., Tanenbaum, P., & Lefebvre, V. (2010, February). Real numbers: Mathematical technologies for counterterrorism and border security. Annual meeting of the American Association for the Advancement of Science, San Diego, CA.

Gallup Poll. (2009, March 10). Wellbeing rankings reveal state strengths and weaknesses. Retrieved from http://www.gallup.com/poll/116497/rankings-reveal-state-strengths-weaknesses.aspx

Goodwin, D. (1976). *Is alcoholism hereditary?* New York: Oxford University Press.

Gottlieb, G. (1997). *Synthesizing nature–nurture: Prenatal roots of instinctive behavior.* Mahwah, NJ: Lawrence Erlbaum Associates.

Graham v. Florida, No. 08-7412 U.S. Supreme Court (May 17, 2010, modified July 6, 2010).

Hales, R. D. (2010, May). Our duty to God: The mission of parents and leaders to the rising generation. *Ensign, 40,* 95–97.

Hamer, D. H., Hu, S., Magnuson, V. L., Hu, N., & Pattatucci, A. M. L. (1993). A linkage between DNA markers on the X chromosome and male sexual orientation. *Science, 261* (5119), 321–327.

Harden, K. P., Mendle, J., Hill, J. E., Turkheimer, E., & Emery, R. E. (2008). Rethinking timing of first sex and delinquency. *Journal of Youth and Adolescence, 37,* 373–385.

Johnson, W., Turkheimer, E., Gottesman, I. I., & Bouchard, T. J. Jr. (2009). Beyond heritability: Twin studies in behavioral research. *Current Directions in Psychological Science, 18*(4), 217–220.

Jowett, B. (Trans.). (2009). *Plato's Protagoras.* Rockville, MD: Serenity Publishers.

Levinas, E. (1991). *Totality and infinity.* Norwell, MA: Kluwer Academic Publishers.

Mark, T. L., Shern, D. L., Bagalman, J. E., & Cao, Z. (2007, December 11). Ranking America's mental health: An analysis of depression across the states. Alexandria, VA: Mental Health America. Retrieved from http://www.mentalhealthamerica.net/files/Ranking_Americas_Mental_Health.pdf

Orth, U., Trzesniewski, K. H., & Robins, R. W. (2010). Self-esteem development from young adulthood to old age: a cohort-sequential longitudinal study. *Journal of Personality and Social Psychology, 98*(4), 645–658.

Publication manual of the American Psychological Association (6th ed.). (2010). Washington, DC: American Psychological Association.

RealClearPolitics.com. (2010, March 19). President Obama job approval. Retrieved from http://www.realclearpolitics.com/epolls/other/president_obama_job_approval-1044.html

Rentfrow, P. J., Gosling, S. D., & Potter, J. (2008). A theory of the emergence, persistence, and expression of geographic variation in psychological characteristics. *Perspectives on Psychological Science, 3*(5), 339–352.

Rice G., Anderson C., Risch N., & Ebers, G. (1999). Male homosexuality: Absence of linkage to microsatellite markers at Xq28. *Science, 284,* 665–667.

Richardson, M. K. [letter]. (1998). Haeckel's embryos, continued. *Science, 281*(5381), 1285.

Salkind, N. J. (2009). *Exploring research* (7th ed.). Upper Saddle River, NJ: Pearson/Prentice Hall.

Salkind, N. J. (2011). *Statistics for people who think they hate statistics* (3rd ed.). Thousand Oaks, CA: Sage.

Scarr, S., & Weinberg, R. (1981). The transmission of authoritarianism in families: Genetic resemblance. In S. Scarr (Ed.) *Social–political attitudes in race, social class, and individual difference* (pp. 299–347). Hillsdale, NJ: Erlbaum.

Settle, J. E., Dawes, C. T., Hatemi, P. K., Christakis, N. A., & Fowler, J. H. (2010). Friendships moderate an association between a dopamine gene variant and political ideology. *Journal of Politics, 72,* 1189–1198.

Smith, C. (2005). *Soul searching: the religious and spiritual lives of American teenagers.* New York: Oxford University Press.

Tahiliani, M., Koh, K. P., Shen, Y., Pastor, W. A., Bandukwala, H., Brudno, Y., . . . Rao, A. (2009). Conversion of 5-methylcytosine to 5-hydroxymethylcytosine in mammalian DNA by MLL partner TET1. *Science, 324,* 930–935.

Twenge, J. M. (2006). *Generation me.* NY: Simon & Schuster.

Uchtdorf, D. F. (2010, May). Continue in patience. *Ensign, 40,* 56–59.

Varnum v. Brien, 763 N.W.2d 862 (Iowa 2009).

CHAPTER 31

Some Linguistic Observations on "The Family: A Proclamation to the World"

Dallin D. Oaks and Evelyn S. Stanley

We, the First Presidency and the Council of the Twelve Apostles of
The Church of Jesus Christ of Latter-day Saints, solemnly proclaim . . . .

A LINGUISTIC CONSIDERATION OF THE FAMILY proclamation instantly presents a vast landscape for examination. Because language is the immediately apparent medium by which the proclamation is conveyed to most of us (the spiritual dimension being more significant but not so easily described and discussed), the proclamation provides us with a multitude of language features that could be noted and described. And if we are not careful, we could soon find ourselves in the proverbial predicament of the person who can't see the forest because of the trees. Indeed, if we are not careful, we could describe many language features in the proclamation and yet fail to provide much insight into the actual nature and significance of the document.

So how should we approach an analysis of the very medium by which the proclamation is conveyed? The best solution, in our opinion, is to look at the proclamation from the perspective of significant linguistic choices that have been made in the preparation of the document, especially when another available option would have conveyed the same basic meaning, without some of the resulting effects of the selected form. In doing so, we will not attempt to identify why a particular choice was made, but we will often note a result of the particular linguistic choice. These resulting effects can be shown to be significant, even though we may not always know the motivation behind the choice.

Let's consider, for a moment, one example of a linguistic choice in the proclamation. One of the more highly charged words in the proclamation is *calamities,* which we encounter near the end of the proclamation, where we are told that "the disintegration of the family will bring upon individuals, communities, and nations the calamities foretold by ancient and modern prophets" (¶ 8). The word *calamities* grabs our attention, not only for its directness, but also for its strength of expression. The authors could have conveyed the same essential meaning by referring to destructive or terrible events of the future. Or they could have used a euphemistic or less direct expression such as "challenging times." The directness of the word *calamities,* however, demands our attention and signals the seriousness and significance of our circumstances and the terrible consequences for ignoring the message of the proclamation. The word is also scripturally appropriate as the Lord Himself used this word to refer to our day. In an address on the proclamation, President Boyd K. Packer quotes the following from the first section of the Doctrine and Covenants:

> Wherefore, I the Lord, knowing the calamity which should come upon the inhabitants of the earth, called upon my servant Joseph Smith, Jun., and spake unto him from heaven, and gave him commandments (D&C 1:17) (Packer, 2008b, p. 4).

Our discussion of the word *calamities* illustrates the kind of approach we will take towards the language of the proclamation as we consider the choice of particular forms and structures and what their consequences might be. Of course, even in this regard, we may only note just a few of the significant linguistic features of the proclamation. Other linguists and language specialists might call attention to a different set of features. We will focus our attention on three linguistic aspects of the proclamation: the use of an instructive religious register, the syntactic validation of key concepts, and the prominent use of performative verbs.

Before proceeding, we should also remember that our observations about characteristics and features of specific linguistic forms have particular application to the English language. But because English is the language in which the First Presidency and Quorum of the Twelve have spoken and from which the document is translated into various languages, our analysis of the significance of particular choices still has a potential relevance that may extend into subsequent languages as translators make choices about not only how to translate the meaning of the various words and sentences but perhaps also their linguistic effect.

An Instructive Religious Register

One of the significant linguistic features of the proclamation is its use of an instructive religious register. When we communicate, we have different choices available to us as far as the particular variety of our language, or register, we wish to use. We must choose, for example, whether the language we use will be formal, informal, clinical, specialized, general, religious, or some combination of these. More often than not, our choices are not between good and bad language but rather about which type of language would be most appropriate for a given situation. In the proclamation, as with all carefully prepared documents, the language is appropriate to the subject matter or purpose of the document as well as the identity of the originators and its intended audience. These considerations relate to how a document is to be fashioned, as well as to how it should be interpreted. In a 1998 article, President Henry B. Eyring said the following about the title of the proclamation: "Three things about the title are worth our careful reflection. First, the subject: the family. Second, the audience, which is the whole world. And third, those proclaiming it are those we sustain as prophets, seers, and revelators" (p. 10). We would like to give additional consideration here to the second and third factors mentioned by President Eyring, applying his statement to how the identity of those issuing the proclamation relates to its form and interpretation.

Even though the proclamation addresses a topic, the family, which could also be of interest to those working in the social sciences, the language of the proclamation is religious rather than academic. For instance, the kind of clinical descriptions and terminology that are found in the social sciences are largely absent in the proclamation. Its language is different because its origins and the authority behind it are different. The proclamation was prepared and issued by the First Presidency and Quorum of the Twelve Apostles of The Church of Jesus Christ of Latter-day Saints, who were divinely inspired and guided in its preparation. President Boyd K. Packer has described the proclamation as being "akin to scripture" (2008a, p. 278) and "revelatory" (2008b, p. 5).

We can note several examples where the language of the proclamation resonates with scriptural phrases and religious expressions rather than the language of the social sciences. For example, we see expressions such as "the image of God," "heirs of eternal life," "multiply and replenish the earth," "rear their children in love and righteousness," "commandments of God," "held accountable before God," "teachings of the Lord Jesus Christ," and "sacred powers of procreation" (not "reproductive abilities"). At the end of the document, as we reenter the realm of policy and laws after the scriptural teachings have been given, the proclamation transitions into language perhaps more indicative of the social sciences when it says, "We call upon responsible citizens and officers of government everywhere to promote those measures designed to maintain and strengthen the family as the fundamental unit of society" (¶ 9). But the language of the proclamation is predominantly religious. In the only instance where an outside authoritative source is invoked in the proclamation, it is a verse from the Old Testament book of Psalms.

With regard to the language of the proclamation, BYU professor Terrance D. Olson (2000) notes the difference between "the language of the world" in discussing morality and "the language of the Lord" (p. 50). More specifically, in commenting on how procreative powers are discussed in secular versus sacred discourse, he notes:

> We live in a world that does not talk about sacred powers, but about sex. The language of the world stands in contrast to the language of the Lord in these matters and is symbolic of a chasm between the sacred principles upon which the Proclamation is based and the secular philosophies that guide worldly views (p. 50).

Another feature of the language of the proclamation that we will note here in relation to its register is its preference for instructive rather than mandative (or commanding) forms. Indeed, although the proclamation provides clear direction for our behavior and conduct, it primarily does so in language that lays out doctrines and principles rather than presenting a series of rules and commandments. It is reminiscent of Joseph Smith's comment when he said, "I teach them correct principles, and they govern themselves" (quoted by John Taylor in the *Millennial Star*, Nov. 15, 1851, p. 339, as cited in Hart, Newell, & Haupt, 2008, p. 64). For example, we may note that on the matter of having children, the proclamation does not issue a directive that specifically commands each set of parents to have children and then prescribes how many. Instead, the proclamation declares that "God's commandment for His children to multiply and replenish the earth remains in force" (¶ 4). The guidance provided by the proclamation is quite clear in this and other matters, but the guidance is general rather than specific, encouraging self-governance. And because the direction given in the proclamation is presented in such a way as to tie it to an underlying doctrinal foundation, its potential influence on people's behavior can be increased. As President Boyd K. Packer (1986, p. 17) has noted:

> True doctrine, understood, changes attitudes and behavior. The study of the doctrines of the gospel will improve behavior quicker than a study of behavior will improve behavior. Preoccupation with unworthy behavior can lead to unworthy behavior. That is why we stress so forcefully the study of the doctrines of the gospel.

Despite the near absence of mandative language, an awareness of the identity of those issuing the proclamation can influence people's responses to the document, including their desire to evaluate and modify their own personal conduct in relation to the instruction given. For members of the Church, any instructions originating from the First Presidency and Quorum of the Twelve Apostles, as this document shows itself to be in its opening lines, are immediately accorded great significance since these men are revered as prophets, seers, and revelators, receiving direction from the Lord himself. Members of the Church also generally understand the importance of identifying the implications that doctrinal instruction has for their own individual behavior. For these members, the language of the proclamation need not be phrased mandatively in order for them to use it to help modify or correct their own behavior.

Because the proclamation is written to "the world," we should also consider the significance of the use of instructive rather than mandative language for a larger audience who are not members of the Church. For them, the direction given by the proclamation is still clear. And even though they are not as likely to recognize the authority of the Church leadership, they still may be more inclined to reconsider aspects of their own behavior through a document that is instructive rather than one that overtly tells them what to do.

The Syntactic Validation of Key Concepts

Within the proclamation, some syntax, that is, the ordering of grammatical structures, affirms or reinforces key concepts. We shall begin our syntactic consideration by noting that careful writers often structure their clauses and sentences to maintain what can be called "the given-new distinction." This given-new distinction is commonly signaled through a general pattern in which the given, or already known, information is presented at the beginning of a sentence or clause and the newer information is presented closer to the end. This expectation about how careful writers often structure their presentation of information is strong enough that Martha Kolln (2007), a prominent grammarian, has referred to it as the "known-new contract" (pp. 68–71). So, for example, consider the following three sentences in which the ending of one sentence (the new information) serves as the old or given information that begins the subsequent sentence:

> My family traveled to Yellowstone Park last summer.

> The park was full of tourists.

> They came from all over the country and even from abroad.

This placement of information, by which the older, or given, information occurs before the new information is not essential for conveying information. It is merely a stylistic difference, but it is one that enhances the readability of a text. In the passage above, we could have said, "My family traveled to Yellowstone Park last summer. Tourists were everywhere in the park. Various countries were represented in the park." In this latter revision, the meaning hasn't changed, but the revision has made the semantic content of the paragraph less readily transparent. This difference in emphasis and style can also signal a slight difference in how the information is to be regarded. We assume that information that begins a sentence or clause is established, agreed upon, or unnecessary, even if only from its having been introduced in the previous sentence. Interestingly enough, in the proclamation, the first mention of the idea of marriage as being between a man and a woman is not introduced at the end of a sentence or clause, the position where new information is usually introduced, but rather at the beginning of a clause. The proclamation begins: "We, the First Presidency and the Council of the Twelve Apostles of The Church of Jesus Christ of Latter-day Saints, solemnly proclaim *that marriage between a man and a woman is ordained of God*" (¶ 1, italics added). Notice that the embedded clause, the part of the sentence beginning with "that marriage," where they actually state what they are proclaiming, places the idea of marriage between a man and a woman in the given or established information slot and uses the new information slot to assert that such marriages are "ordained of God." A possible consequence of this syntactic positioning of information is that the structure of the sentence seems to establish the necessity of heterosexual marriage, and it does so without appearing to introduce that idea as a new claim or assertion; structuring the sentence differently might more easily invite disagreement or contradiction regarding marriage as a heterosexual institution. Notice the slight difference in emphasis and rhetorical effect that would have occurred if the document had read, "God has ordained that marriage be between a man and a woman." If this latter phrasing had been used, the heterosexual nature of marriage would be presented as a new claim that some might feel invited to challenge. Later in the document, another direct reference to heterosexual marriage is also found in the given information portion of the sentence: "Marriage between man and woman is essential to His eternal plan" (¶ 7).

Elsewhere in the document we do find a reference to marriage between a man and a woman, where the concept is mentioned outside the given or established information slot, but in this case the idea of heterosexual marriage is additional, though important, information in a sentence where the main focus is on how "the sacred powers of procreation are to be employed only between man and woman, lawfully wedded as husband and wife" (¶ 4). Even in this syntactic setting, however, the idea of heterosexual marriage is still provided with grammatical support by a preceding performative verb, *declare* ("We further declare . . . man and woman, lawfully wedded as husband and wife"). More will be said about this type of verb later.

Related to the given-new distinction is the use of presuppositions, which we can also see in the document. Presuppositions are commonly used for information that is generally agreed upon or understood. Thus, if we were to ask someone, "When did you eat breakfast this morning?" the question presupposes that the person ate breakfast this morning. The fact that he ate breakfast is understood or agreed upon, and we may focus the question on when that occurred. If for some reason the listener doesn't agree with the presupposition that he ate breakfast, then he can correct us by saying, "Actually, I didn't eat breakfast this morning." Presuppositions are common in our speech and can be used to make our expressions more concise. If we had to establish particular facts before we said anything and couldn't take certain kinds of information and assumptions for granted, our communication could be lengthy indeed.

The English language has a large set of syntactic forms that can set up presuppositions, more forms than we can address in this article. Levinson (1983, pp. 181–185) provides a useful list of such "presupposition-triggers." One of these triggers is what is called a "*wh*-question." We previously saw an example of a presupposition involving a *wh*-question (a question using words such as *why*, *who*, or *when*) in the earlier example, "When did you eat breakfast this morning?" Another important structure that we think can appropriately be added to the list of presupposition triggers is the set of possessive forms (see Yule, 1996, p. 26). When we say something like "We want to see Jim's house," we presuppose that Jim in fact has a house. The power of presuppositions is at least partly demonstrated in the fact that even when we negate a sentence, a presupposition generally remains intact (see Yule, 1996, pp. 26–27; Levinson, 1983, pp. 178–179). Thus, whether we say, "We want to see Jim's house," or whether we say, "We don't want to see Jim's house," the same presupposition remains: Jim has a house. This is different from what happens when we negate a sentence like "Jim has a house." If we say, "Jim doesn't have a house," then the understanding that Jim has a house has been removed.

In the proclamation, the first two references to the plan of salvation occur as presuppositions in possessive structures ("Creator's plan" and "His plan"). Once the existence of the plan has been established, the third reference to the plan is not found within a possessive structure, but nonetheless uses a definite structure ("The divine plan of happiness"), which refers to something whose identity has already been established either through prior reference or through a shared understanding of what it refers to. The final two references to the plan are once again in possessive structures ("God's eternal plan" and "His eternal plan"). Thus at least four of the five references in the proclamation to the plan of salvation, including the first two references, occur within presuppositions.

On first glance this might not appear to be unusual. But when we consider that the audience for the proclamation is not limited to members of the Church—indeed, that it is intended to go out to the world—this placement may merit some particular consideration. We might have expected that the first reference in the proclamation to the plan of salvation may have been positioned within a new information slot (such as saying, "God has a plan"), accompanied by a brief explanation of that plan. This is not the case. The placement of the references to the plan in presuppositions has at least two resulting consequences. First, as mentioned before, it maintains a certain economy of expression. But perhaps more significantly, particularly with regard to the first occurrence in the proclamation, it introduces the crucial notion of the divine plan in such a way as to possibly suggest that its existence is accepted or established information. By introducing the idea through presuppositions, the references to the plan become less vulnerable to direct challenges or doctrinal sparring from critics wishing to detract from the proclamation's message. The proclamation is not presented as a doctrinal exposition for people to debate or challenge. It is a proclamation. And the use of presuppositions provides a certain insularity and protection to such a crucial concept as the plan. The plan is, after all, what makes it possible for us to return to our heavenly home and live eternally as families. Of course, the placement of a fact or claim in the kind of structure we have identified does not prevent a person from attacking that fact or claim, but it would take a more calculated effort to do so. One couldn't merely contradict it by saying something like "No, it doesn't" or "No, it isn't."

We shall now consider another type of presupposition-trigger that is placed around references to the plan. Levinson (1983) notes that "definite descriptions" may serve as presupposition-triggers. The rather unusual example he provides to illustrate this type of trigger is "John saw/didn't see *the man with two heads*" (p. 181). In this example, as Levinson shows, the italicized information, *the man with two heads*, presupposes that there exists a man with two heads. This presupposition remains whether the sentence is cast positively ("John saw . . .") or negatively ("John didn't see . . .") (p. 181). The term "definite descriptions" isn't used for just any kind of description but rather one that in specifying or describing its referent (what it refers to) seems to confirm the reality of its referent. Thus in the example "John saw [or didn't see] the man with two heads," there is no question that such a man exists. If we argue against the sentence by saying, "No, he didn't," we still seem to accept the notion that such a man exists; we merely challenge whether John saw him. Notice that if the sentence had used an indefinite expression such as "*a* man with two heads," and we challenge the sentence with "No, he didn't," then unlike what we saw with a definite description, we could seem to be challenging the notion of whether such a man exists. Definite descriptions don't have to involve the definite article *the*. Some expressions can be definite in the way they specify something, even without a definite article. A possessive, for example, could be part of a definite description. Note the following five phrases from the proclamation, all of which contain definite descriptions (shown in italics) that presuppose important information about the Lord's plan for us:

the Creator's **plan** *for the eternal destiny of His children*

His **plan** *by which His children could obtain a physical body and gain earthly experience to progress toward perfection and ultimately realize their divine destiny as heirs of eternal life*

The divine **plan** *of happiness*

God's eternal **plan**

His eternal **plan**

The significant power of these definite descriptions to establish the truth of what they have integrated into their structure can be especially evident when we view them within the larger structures containing them. Let's look at the second of the above-listed phrases about the plan and place it within the larger syntactic setting in which it is found. As we do so, we shall once again use italics to highlight the definite description structure:

> In the premortal realm, spirit sons and daughters knew and worshipped God as their Eternal Father and accepted *His* **plan** *by which His children could obtain a physical body and gain earthly experience to progress toward perfection and ultimately realize their divine destiny as heirs of eternal life* (¶ 3).

Notice that a simply phrased challenge to this statement would leave the presupposed information in the italics untouched. If, for example, someone were to argue against this sentence merely by saying something like "No, they didn't," the only information that would be challenged is in the first part of the sentence, where it is explained that the spirit sons and daughters worshipped God and accepted His plan. But the portion mentioning the existence of God's plan and continuing with the description of that plan would still remain unchallenged. Unless a critic wants to unpack the information contained in the rest of the sentence and address it more specifically or express a general disagreement with the entire sentence, the information in the rest of the sentence remains as established information. And that established information is crucial, since it not only tells us that the Lord has a plan for us but also that the plan involves our obtaining a physical body, gaining earthly experience, and eventually being able to be perfected and receive eternal life. The same kind of analysis would apply to the other definite descriptions listed above, whose structures also involve presuppositions that are somewhat insulated from challenges and that assert the eternal and joyful nature of the plan. The proclamation also contains other definite descriptions besides those that refer directly to the plan, and these likewise introduce important presuppositions. For example, we see such expressions as "these sacred responsibilities" and "the calamities foretold by ancient and modern prophets." Regardless of how these particular definite descriptions are placed within larger structures, they would still convey the fact that the responsibilities are sacred and that ancient and modern prophets have foretold calamities.

The Prominent Use of Performative Verbs

We shall conclude by considering what may be the most striking linguistic feature of this document: its heavy use of performative verbs. Performative verbs can serve two powerful roles. First, like the syntactic structures that trigger presuppositions, they can help invest some statements with a measure of insularity or protection from attack. Second, they can unambiguously identify the intended function of what is said. In what follows, we shall briefly explore these two roles. But first we need to introduce some preliminary information related to performative verbs.

Close linguistic analysis of texts commonly involves identifying speech acts. Speech acts are those things we do with language (Fromkin, Rodman, & Hyams, 2011, p. 215). As we communicate and interpret messages, we realize that the meaning of an utterance is not merely the combined sense and referential aspects of its various words. Each utterance is performing some kind of function, whether it is promising, complimenting, explaining, or apologizing. For example, if someone says to us, "I have a great social planned for Friday night. Will you be around?" we probably wouldn't interpret his question as merely a curious inquiry about our whereabouts for that evening, or in other words, a speech act of eliciting information. Instead we are more likely to interpret the question as a speech act in which the speaker has extended an invitation. If we interpret this as an invitation, we may indicate our acceptance of the invitation by saying, "We would love to be there." The original speaker would then probably interpret our utterance as the speech act of "accepting an invitation," even though its surface form could alternatively, though less likely, represent a speech act that merely expresses hypothetical information.

Some verbs, known as "performative verbs," carry a special power in completing particular speech acts (see Fromkin et al., 2011, pp. 215–216). This verb set includes verbs such as *promise, nominate, apologize,* and *warn.* As Hurford, Heasley, and Smith (2007) show, when a performative verb is expressed by speakers (or writers) and when appropriate surrounding linguistic and contextual factors are present, a speech act identified by the verb itself is completed through the uttering of the verb (see pp. 263–265 and 282–287). Thus, if there is a situation in which people are to be nominated and I say, "I nominate Fred," my use of the verb *nominate* essentially completes the act of nominating him. This power of performative verbs is so well understood that it seems almost ridiculous to argue with them. If I say, "I nominate Fred," it would be odd for someone else to counter by saying, "No, you don't." By my having said, "I nominate Fred," I have just nominated him. The speech act of nominating has been completed. Someone may wonder whether I am wise to nominate Fred, or they may question his viability as a candidate, but they can't challenge whether I have nominated him. This feature of performative verbs makes them special. Note that if I use a non-performative verb, I don't get the same result. If I say, "I hereby walk to school," I haven't walked to school just by virtue of having used the verb *walk*. But with performative verbs, the utterance can complete the act that the verb encompasses.

One further observation we could make about performative verbs is that not only are they more resistant to being challenged, but so are the propositions they introduce. Thus, if someone says, "I warn you that the bridge will fall," it isn't just that we can't directly challenge the fact that we have been warned. We also have some difficulty challenging the claim about the bridge itself.

Now let's return to the two roles we mentioned with regard to the use of performative verbs in the proclamation. First, we shall look at their ability to insulate a particular claim. We have observed that it is more difficult to argue directly against both the performative verb as well as whatever proposition it introduces. Performative verbs such as *proclaim*, *declare*, *affirm*, and *warn* are used throughout the proclamation. When the proclamation begins with the statement from the Church's leaders that they "solemnly proclaim that marriage between a man and a woman is ordained of God and that the family is central to the Creator's plan for the eternal destiny of His children" (¶ 1), the statement can't be directly challenged.[1] One can't respond to the main verb of the sentence (*proclaim*) and contradict it by simply saying, "No, you don't." By virtue of using the verb *proclaim* before their statement, the leaders have proclaimed something. The inability to directly challenge the performative verb also helps insulate the proposition it introduces about marriage and families. Once again, someone could still

challenge what is said by unpacking the information that follows the performative verb and taking issue with it, but the grammatical burden is on those who would challenge the statement. This same linguistic situation applies to most of the other performative verbs and the information they introduce.

We shall now look at the important role that performative verbs have in clearly signaling an intended speech act. Many, in fact most, speech acts can be completed without using a performative verb. We can promise things without saying the word *promise*, we can apologize without saying the word *apologize*, and we can warn people without saying the word *warn*. But sometimes there can be ambiguity about what an utterance is intended to do. One of the valuable features of performative verbs is that they not only complete a speech act as they are expressed, but they also clearly identify what the intended speech act is (see Hurford et al., 2007, p. 263). As this applies to the proclamation, we could observe that the proclamation uses a variety of performative verbs that serve both to complete certain speech act goals as well as to label those speech acts as they perform them. When the proclamation says, "We declare," we know that the brethren have declared something to us. When the proclamation says, "We call upon responsible citizens and officers of government everywhere" (¶ 9), those people know that they have been called upon to do something. And most sobering of all, when the proclamation uses the performative verb *warn*, which it does twice near the end of the document, we know, in the clearest language, that we have been warned. In this regard, it is perhaps also instructive to consider the words of the Book of Mormon prophets who took seriously their duty to instruct the people in righteousness in order for themselves to be spotless from sin at the last day. We see this concern, for example, in the words of Jacob as well as those of King Benjamin. Note in particular Jacob's words:

> And we did magnify our office unto the Lord, taking upon us the responsibility, answering the sins of the people upon our own heads if we did not teach them the word of God with all diligence; wherefore, by laboring with our might their blood might not come upon our garments; otherwise their blood would come upon our garments, and we would not be found spotless at the last day (Jacob 1:19). (Compare Mosiah 2:27–28.)

---

1. In an unpublished paper about the proclamation, Matt Larsen, a former student of one of the authors, provides this very example from the proclamation and notes the ability of performative verbs to introduce presupposed propositions.

We can imagine some future judgment day when people may wish to claim that they didn't know that the family proclamation was warning them. But the document bears witness against them, for not only does it warn them, but it clearly signals such an intent, using the unmistakable performative verb *warn*. To the people who will be guilty of sins of omission as they failed to take appropriate action to "maintain and strengthen the family," the document will also bring condemnation, for it clearly calls upon them to do something, which they failed to do. And it uses the unambiguous performative verb *call upon*. They can hardly claim that they thought it was an invitation or a suggestion. Similar observations can be made about the other performative verbs in the document. When we consider that the proclamation serves not only as a declaration or clarification of doctrine, a warning, and a call to action, but perhaps also serves to clear the modern-day prophets from responsibility for the evils and wickedness of the world in our day, the proclamation is a sobering document indeed.

Conclusion

Our consideration of the linguistic features of the proclamation certainly hasn't addressed every significant linguistic feature that might have been examined. We might, for example, have considered at greater length the possible significance of the use of the definite article *the* in the title's reference to "the family." Such a use of the definite article in the document's initial reference to the family could allow us to consider whether "the family" not only refers to families in general but also to a specific family we all connect with: the family of God.

The religious and dignified nature of the language in the proclamation is consistent with and can serve to remind us of both the significance of the topic that is addressed as well as the position and authority of the document's originators. Those proclaiming the message of this document hold sacred priesthood keys or authorities, including the authority to "seal" people within family bonds that may, depending upon the worthiness of the individuals involved, last into eternity. The proclamation also effectively employs language that provides some of its central concepts a measure of protection from contentious challenges by critics. And the proclamation at times clearly signals the function of some of its pronouncements through the use of distinctive verbs.

Of course, the message and direction of the proclamation is more important than the language forms it uses to convey its message. But we hope to have shown that a careful consideration of some of the language of the proclamation also yields significant insights into this important document.

Dallin D. Oaks *is an associate professor of English linguistics at BYU. He and his wife, Marleen, are the parents of six children.* **Evelyn S. Stanley** *is a homemaker, writer, and songwriter. She and her husband, J. Robert, are the parents of four children and they have seventeen grandchildren.*

References

Eyring, H. B. (1998, February). The Family. *Ensign, 28,* 10–18.

Fromkin, V., Rodman, R., & Hyams, N. (2011). *An introduction to language* (9th ed.). Boston: Wadsworth.

Hart, C. H., Newell, L. D., & Haupt, J. H. (2008, August). Love, limits, and latitude. *Ensign, 38,* 60–65.

Hurford, J. R., Heasley, B., & Smith, M. B. (2007). *Semantics: A coursebook* (2nd ed.). Cambridge, UK: Cambridge University Press.

Kolln, M. (2007). *Rhetorical grammar: Grammatical choices, rhetorical effects* (5th ed.). New York: Pearson Education.

Levinson, S. C. (1983). *Pragmatics.* Cambridge, UK: Cambridge University Press.

Olson, T. D. (2000). Chastity and fidelity in marriage and family relationships. In D. C. Dollahite (Ed.), *Strengthening our families: An in-depth look at the proclamation on the family* (pp. 50–59). [Provo, UT]: School of Family Life, Brigham Young University.

Packer, B. K. (1986, November). Little children. *Ensign, 16,* 16–18.

Packer, B. K. (2008a). *Mine errand from the Lord: Selections from the sermons and writings of Boyd K. Packer.* Salt Lake City: Deseret Book.

Packer, B. K. (2008b, February 9). The proclamation on the family. *Worldwide leadership training meeting: Building up a righteous posterity.* Salt Lake City: The Church of Jesus Christ of Latter-day Saints, 4–9.

Yule, G. (1996). *Pragmatics.* Oxford, UK: Oxford University Press.

CHAPTER 32

The Eternal Family:
A Plain and Precious Part of the Plan of Salvation

Daniel K Judd

The family is central to the creator's plan for the eternal destiny of his children. . . .
In the premortal realm, spirit sons and daughters knew and worshiped God as their Eternal Father
and accepted His plan by which His children could obtain a physical body and gain earthly experience
to progress toward perfection and ultimately realize their divine destiny as heirs of eternal life.

FROM THE BEGINNING, GOD ORGANIZED THE HUMAN family and revealed that marriage and family relationships are intended to be eternal. Latter-day prophets have taught that while Adam and Eve were sealed in marriage for time and all eternity, the time would come when the doctrine of the eternal family would be lost to mankind. President Spencer W. Kimball observed, "Eternal marriage was known to Adam and others of the prophets, but the knowledge was lost from the earth for many centuries" (Kimball, 1964, pp. 25). The prophet Isaiah, writing in the eighth century before the birth of Jesus Christ, described these periods of apostasy when he recorded, "The earth also is defiled under the inhabitants thereof; because they have transgressed the laws, changed the ordinance, broken the everlasting covenant" (Isaiah 24:5; see also D&C 84:19–27). In a prophetic description of the centuries of doctrinal darkness that would follow the death of Jesus Christ, the Book of Mormon prophet Nephi envisioned:

> They have taken away from the gospel of the Lamb many parts which are plain and most precious; and also many covenants of the Lord have they taken away. And all this have they done that they might pervert the right ways of the Lord, that they might blind the eyes and harden the hearts of the children of men (1 Nephi 13:26–27).

Nephi also added that "because of these things which are taken away out of the gospel of the Lamb, an exceedingly great many do stumble, yea, insomuch that Satan hath great power over them" (1 Nephi 13:29). The distortion and eventual loss of the doctrine of the eternal family is no doubt a part of what the Prophet Joseph Smith was describing when he observed, "Our Father in Heaven organized the human family, but they are all disorganized and in great confusion" (Watson, 1971, p. 530). The loss of the doctrine and covenant of eternal marriage has confused the great majority of the inhabitants of the world concerning the eternal nature of the family and has led many to believe that such relationships are not part of God's plan for the salvation and eternal destiny of His children.

Beginning with the teachings of Joseph Smith, latter-day prophets have proclaimed to the world that God's holy priesthood and the sacred keys that allow marriages and families to be sealed together for time and all eternity have been restored to the earth. The Prophet Joseph Smith taught, "It is in the order of heavenly things that God should always send a new dispensation into the world when men have apostatized from the truth and lost the priesthood" (Roberts, 1965, p. 478–479).

In 1995, President Gordon B. Hinckley reiterated the doctrine of The Church of Jesus Christ of Latter-day Saints concerning eternal marriages and families when he taught in the proclamation that

> the divine plan of happiness enables family relationships to be perpetuated beyond the grave. Sacred ordinances and covenants available in

holy temples make it possible for individuals to return to the presence of God and for families to be united eternally (¶ 3).

President Hinckley also described the central role of the family in God's plan for the salvation of His children, when he stated:

> We, the First Presidency and the Council of the Twelve Apostles of The Church of Jesus Christ of Latter-day Saints, solemnly proclaim that marriage between a man and a woman is ordained of God and that the family is central to the Creator's plan for the eternal destiny of His children (¶ 1).

The major purpose of this chapter is to help the reader comprehend the significance of the restoration of the doctrine of the eternal family. It also provides a doctrinal framework designed to help the reader better understand the gospel principles regarding the plan of salvation and applications found in "The Family: A Proclamation to the World." This chapter begins with a discussion of the premortal origin of the plan of salvation, and then follows with doctrines of the Creation of man, the Fall of Adam and Eve, and the Atonement of Jesus Christ, and their applications to marriage and family relationships.

The Plan of Salvation

Not only was the doctrine of the eternal family lost to mankind in the centuries following the deaths of Jesus Christ and His Apostles, but the doctrine of the premortal existence of the soul was also taken from the earth. The doctrine of premortal existence was restored through the Prophet Joseph Smith, affirming that prior to mortal birth each person born on earth first existed as a spirit son or daughter of heavenly parents (¶ 2; see also Abraham 2:22–23, Jeremiah 1:5; John 1:1–8). President Joseph F. Smith taught, "Man, as a spirit, was begotten and born of heavenly parents, and reared to maturity in the eternal mansions of the Father prior to coming upon the earth in a temporal body" (Smith, Winder, & Lund, 1909, p. 80). During this premortal period, a grand council was held where God, our Heavenly Father, presented "the plan of salvation" (Moses 6:62) to all of His children (see Abraham 3:21–28 and Moses 4:1–4). The plan presented by our Father included many of the doctrines involved in the plan of salvation, including

the doctrine of eternal families and the Atonement of Jesus Christ. In this council, we learned that "the plan of redemption" (Alma 12:25) required a Savior to "take upon him the pains and the sicknesses of his people" (Alma 7:11) as well as "the sins of his people" (Alma 7:13), thus allowing those who would live and die, sin and repent, to eventually return and dwell in the presence of God. Lucifer, another of God's spirit children, made a selfish and vain attempt to usurp the role of savior, but it was Jesus Christ, the Firstborn of the Father's spirit children (Colossians 1:15; D&C 93:21), who was chosen to carry out God's plan.

At some point, those who supported "the great plan of the Eternal God" (Alma 34:9) were promised that they would have the opportunity and responsibility to live in and perpetuate family relationships. We also learned that each of us would have missions to perform, such as being a son, daughter, sister, brother, husband, wife, mother, or father. We learned that understanding and fulfilling these roles was a part of our divine destiny. President Joseph F. Smith reminded us:

> To do well those things which God ordained to be the common lot of all man-kind, is the truest greatness. To be a successful father or a successful mother is greater than to be a successful general or a successful statesman. One is universal and eternal greatness, the other is ephemeral (Smith, 1986, pp. 285).

Creation, Fall, and Atonement

"The great plan of happiness" (Alma 42:8) presented by our Heavenly Father in the premortal council was and is divinely designed "to bring to pass the immortality and eternal life of man" (Moses 1:39). While containing the whole of the gospel, "the plan of redemption" (Alma 12:25) is founded upon three major doctrines: (a) The Creation of the earth and of all mankind, (b) the Fall of Adam, Eve, and their posterity, and (c) the Atonement of Jesus Christ. As a member of the Seventy, Elder Merrill J. Bateman stated the following in summarizing the familial nature of the Father's plan:

> The creation of the earth, the fall of Adam, and the atonement of Christ are essential elements or pillars in the Father's plan for the progression and development of his children—both as individuals

and as families. . . . These three doctrinal pillars of the plan of salvation are intimately involved in the creation of new eternal families and their extension into the eternities (Bateman, 1998, p. 26).

In addition to the Creation, Fall, and Atonement being literal, historic events, each are doctrines that have direct application to our personal lives. We each have experienced the Creation both spiritually and physically. Our heavenly parents created our spirit bodies in the premortal realm (¶ 2; see also Abraham 2:22–23). Our earthly parents provided our physical bodies and we were born into mortality (see Moses 3:5–7). Each of us experiences the Fall as we are born into a fallen world and are separated from God's presence (Alma 12:22). We also experience the Fall as we face the realities of our fallen natures and suffer the consequences of our own sins and mistakes, as well as those of others (D&C 93:38–39). We learn of and receive the blessings of the Atonement of Jesus Christ as we repent of our sins, are healed from our infirmities, and eventually experience the resurrection of our physical bodies (Alma 7:11–12, 1 Corinthians 15:21–22).

The doctrines of the Creation, Fall, and Atonement can also serve as metaphors as each can have interpretive application to many of the significant events in our lives. Each of us experiences periods of creation, such as the beginning of a marriage, the birth of a child, beginning a new school year or semester, receiving a new Church calling, starting a new job, or beginning any other important process. These periods of creation are generally times when we are optimistic and hopeful concerning the future. Times of creation are generally followed by times when we experience a "fall" as we are confronted with adversity, affliction, and opposition. Our optimistic idealism about the future often turns into recognition of the difficult reality of the present. It is important to remember that these difficult times of fallenness can be followed by experiences of healing and reconciliation as we come to understand our need for a Savior and embrace the Atonement of Jesus Christ.

Consider the example of a young couple in the beginning of their relationship, when they are experiencing a Garden of Eden–like existence. In a metaphorical sense, the grass is green, the water is clear, and the sky is blue—everything in their relationship appears to be idyllic. At some point in their relationship, however, they (like Adam and Eve) are destined to experience opposition. It is a part of the Lord's plan for them to experience the Fall as opposition and adversity comes and affliction follows. Their challenge and opportunity then becomes, as individuals and as a couple, to actively seek reconciliation and healing through the Atonement of Jesus Christ (Judd, 1998, pp. 121–147).

Social scientists have also recognized that marriages, families, and most relationships often pass through stages of growth in their development. Miller, Wackman, Nunally, and Miller acknowledged, "The important relationships we have in life go through transitions" (1988, p. 239). This group of marriage and family scholars coined the term *visionary* to describe the beginning, or what has been termed in this chapter as the creation, of a relationship. They used the term *adversarial* to describe the times of disillusionment, or what this chapter describes as the fall that is commonly experienced in marriages and families. *Vital* is the term they use to describe what this chapter terms as atonement to describe how a couple or others can learn to reconcile their differences.

The Creation and Our Divine Origins and Destiny

The scriptures clearly teach that all human beings are created in the image of God (see Moses 2:26–27 and Genesis 1:26–27). As stated in the proclamation, "each is a beloved spirit son or daughter of heavenly parents, and as such, each has a divine nature and destiny" (¶ 2). From this brief statement, we learn several profound truths: We were created by God; we were created in the image of God; we have heavenly parents—a Father and a Mother; we are literally the spirit offspring of God; our spirit creation includes identity as male or female; we have a divine destiny.

While there is much we do not know about the specifics of the Creation, latter-day prophets have taught that we have both divine origin and divine potential. In 1909, President Joseph F. Smith and his counselors in the First Presidency, John R. Winder and Anthon H. Lund, issued a statement that included the following:

Man is the child of God, formed in the divine image and endowed with divine attributes, and even as the infant son of an earthly father and mother is capable in due time of becoming a man, so the undeveloped offspring of celestial parentage is capable, by experience through ages and aeons, of evolving into a God (Smith, Winder, & Lund, 1909, p. 81).

As mentioned, many doctrines were lost to the earth through apostasy, including the eternal nature of the family and the premortal existence of the human family. In addition, the doctrine of the divine destiny of mankind was also one of the "plain and precious things" (1 Nephi 13:40) lost in the generations following the death of Christ. President Lorenzo Snow taught, "As man now is, God once was; as God now is, man may be" (1892, 404). This statement reveals the potential found in each of the sons and daughters of God. While the doctrine of the divine destiny of man is seen by some as being unique to the teachings of The Church of Jesus Christ of Latter-day Saints, both ancient and contemporary clerics and scholars have taught a very similar doctrine. St. Athanasius, a fourth-century bishop of Alexandria, taught, "God made himself a man in order that man might be able to become God" (Schönborn, 1995, p. 41). The celebrated scholar C. S. Lewis wrote:

> The command *Be ye perfect* is not idealistic gas. Nor is it a command to do the impossible. He is going to make us into creatures that can obey that command. He said (in the Bible) that we were "gods" and He is going to make good His words. If we let Him—for we can prevent Him, if we choose—He will make the feeblest and filthiest of us into a god or goddess, a dazzling, radiant, immortal creature, pulsating all through with such energy and joy and wisdom and love as we cannot now imagine, a bright stainless mirror which reflects back to God perfectly (though, of course, on a smaller scale) His own boundless power and delight and goodness. The process will be long and in parts very painful, but that is what we are in for. Nothing less. He meant what He said (1943, pp. 174–175).

Understanding that we are literally children of heavenly parents in whose image we are created is necessary if we are to understand that we may indeed become like them. The Prophet Joseph Smith taught, "If men do not comprehend the character of God, they do not comprehend themselves" (1961, p. 343).

Marriage, Families, and the Fall

The doctrine of the Fall provides an additional key to understanding our earthly existence. The proclamation teaches that we came to earth to "obtain a physical body and gain earthly experience to progress toward perfection" (¶ 3). Birth into a family was the way God chose to send His spirit children to earth. Marriage and family relationships are the central means He has prepared to achieve His purposes. We best learn the lessons of life, not in a Garden of Eden–like existence, but in a context where we face challenge, opposition, hardship, and temptation (2 Nephi 2:11). The "great plan of happiness" is designed to include adversity and sorrow, "for if [we] never should have bitter [we] could not know the sweet" (D&C 29:39).

Unlike traditional Christianity, Latter-day Saints believe the Fall was a necessary part of the Lord's plan for us: "Adam fell that men might be; and men are, that they might have joy" (2 Nephi 2:25). While much of traditional Christianity views the Fall of Adam and Eve as a necessary evil at best, or an avoidable abomination at worst, there is evidence that some of the early Christian fathers embraced views more consistent with Latter-day Saint theology. In the fourth century AD, St. Ambrose, one of the most influential leaders of the early Catholic Church, wrote that the Fall of Adam and Eve "has brought more benefit to us than harm" (Lovejoy, 1948, pp. 287). Pope Gregory the Great, living in the years 540–604 AD, stated:

> And certainly, unless Adam had sinned, it would not have behooved our Redeemer to take on our flesh. Almighty God saw beforehand that from that evil because of which men were to die, He would bring about a good which would overcome that evil (Lovejoy, 1948, pp. 288–289).

The Fall of Adam and Eve allowed the Lord's plan for marriages and family to continue forward by making it possible for Adam and Eve to "have an increase" (D&C 131:4) as they added children to their family. The proclamation states: "The first commandment that God gave to Adam and Eve pertained to their potential for parenthood as husband and wife. We declare that God's commandment for His children to multiply and replenish the earth remains in force" (¶ 4).

The Book of Mormon prophet Lehi explained that if Adam and Eve had not partaken of the fruit of the tree of knowledge of good and evil, they would not have been able to fulfill the commandment God had given them to multiply and replenish the earth. The prophet Lehi taught:

> And now, behold, if Adam had not transgressed he would not have fallen, but he would have remained in the Garden of Eden. And all things which were created must have remained in the same state in which they were after they were created; and they must have remained forever, and had no end. And they would have had no children; wherefore they would have remained in a state of innocence, having no joy, for they knew no misery; doing no good, for they knew no sin (2 Nephi 2:22–23).

Therefore, rather than being merely a necessary evil, the Fall, "whatever its nature, was formally a transgression but eternally a glorious necessity to open the doorway toward eternal life" (Oaks, 1993, p. 73).

The Atonement of Jesus Christ and Eternal Families

Understanding the doctrines of the Creation and the Fall are essential if we are to comprehend who we are and the purposes of challenges in life. However, understanding these particular doctrines alone is not sufficient. As profound and meaningful as the doctrine of the eternal family is, this precious doctrine cannot bring joy to individuals and families in this life or eternal life in the world to come. There is one doctrine "which is of more importance than they all" (Alma 7:7), and that is the doctrine of the Atonement of Jesus Christ. The Book of Mormon prophet Helaman taught:

> Remember, remember that it is upon the rock of our Redeemer, who is Christ, the Son of God, that ye must build your foundation; that when the devil shall send forth his mighty winds, yea, his shafts in the whirlwind, yea, when all his hail and his mighty storm shall beat upon you, it shall have no power over you to drag you down to the gulf of misery and endless wo, because of the rock upon which ye are built, which is a sure foundation, a foundation whereon if men build they cannot fall (Helaman 5:12).

Not only does the Atonement of Jesus Christ make forgiveness of sins, the resurrection of our bodies, and eternal family relationships possible, but the Savior is also the very embodiment of the ways of living and being by which we are to live our lives. There is no other way or means by which individuals, couples, families, communities, or even nations may be saved (see Mosiah 3:17). Latter-day Saints need to especially be aware of the danger of placing the family before the Savior. This concern is dramatically illustrated in the following story from Elder Russell M. Nelson:

> Years ago when Sister Nelson and I had several teen-aged daughters, we took our family on a vacation far away from telephones and boyfriends. We went on a raft trip down the Colorado River through the Grand Canyon. As we started our journey, we had no idea how dangerous this trip could be.
>
> The first day was beautiful. But on the second day, when we approached Horn Creek rapids and saw that precipitous drop ahead, I was terrified. Floating on a rubber raft, our precious family was about to plunge over a waterfall! Instinctively I put one arm around my wife and the other around our youngest daughter. To protect them, I tried to hold them close to me. But as we reached the precipice, the bended raft became a giant sling and shot me into the air. I landed into the roiling rapids of the river. I had a hard time coming up. Each time I tried to find air, I hit the underside of the raft. My family couldn't see me, but I could hear them shouting, "Daddy! Where's Daddy?" I finally found the side of the raft and rose to the surface. The family pulled my nearly drowned body out of the water. . . .
>
> Brothers and sisters, I nearly lost my life learning a lesson that I now give to you. As we go through life, even through very rough waters, a father's instinctive impulse to cling tightly to his wife or to his children may not be the best way to accomplish his objective. Instead, if he will lovingly cling to the Savior and the iron rod of the gospel, his family will want to cling to him and to the Savior.
>
> This lesson is surely not limited to fathers. Regardless of gender, marital status, or age, individuals can choose to link themselves directly to the Savior, hold fast to the rod of His truth, and lead by the light of that truth. By so doing, they become examples of righteousness to whom others will want to cling (2001, p. 69).

The Savior taught:

And thou shalt love the Lord thy God with all thy heart, and with all thy soul, and with all thy mind, and with all thy strength: this is the first commandment. And the second is like, namely this, Thou shalt love thy neighbour as thyself. There is none other commandment greater than these (Mark 12:30–31).

As we truly learn to love God and He who atoned for our families, we are best able to love others, especially members of our own family.

The Atonement of Jesus Christ has special relevance for marriages and families in crisis. While there is much to be gained from learning the principles of effectively functioning families, there are times when the healing power that a family requires is beyond what any mortal can provide. President Howard W. Hunter taught: "Whatever Jesus lays his hands upon lives. If Jesus lays his hands upon a marriage, it lives. If he is allowed to lay his hands on the family, it lives" (1979, p. 65). This is especially important for Latter-day Saints who know that marriage and family relationships can be eternal. The Atonement of Jesus Christ makes possible "eternal lives" (D&C 132:24), or life with our families in the presence of God. In order to do so, He leads families along the path—from making available sealing ordinances in the temple to healing hearts and bridging gaps for families in crisis. God's work and glory is to unite couples and families together for time and eternity, and only through the Atonement of Christ is this possible.

The Atonement of Jesus Christ also allows each of us to grow and progress by repenting, being forgiven, and being worthy of the guiding influence of the Holy Ghost. The prophet Mormon taught his son Moroni:

And the remission of sins bringeth meekness, and lowliness of heart; and because of meekness and lowliness of heart cometh the visitation of the Holy Ghost, which Comforter filleth with hope and perfect love, which love endureth by diligence unto prayer, until the end shall come, when all the saints shall dwell with God (Moroni 8:26).

Jesus Christ took upon Himself the sins of the world, and it is only through faith in Him and obedience to the laws and ordinances of His gospel that salvation and exaltation are possible. Without the Atonement, no one could live in God's presence, inherit all He has, or be sealed for eternity as families.

Eternal Life is Familial

Eternal life is more than just living forever. President Henry B. Eyring stated, "Eternal life means to become like the Father and to live in families in happiness and joy forever" (1998, p. 10). The ecclesiastical structure of the Lord's Church is designed to bring the benefits of the eternal sealing powers of the temple to marriage and family relationships, so those relationships can endure throughout eternity. Elder M. Russell Ballard taught, "The family is where the foundation of personal, spiritual growth is built and nurtured; the Church, then, is the scaffolding that helps support and strengthen the family" (1996, p. 81).

As stated earlier, the doctrine that eternal life includes life in family relationships is one of the unique teachings of the restored gospel. These teachings have brought joy and consolation to millions of souls. Many people from all faiths, even though their religion does not teach this principle, personally hope and anticipate that their lifelong and deeply cherished relationships with spouse and family members will continue beyond the grave. Only the teachings and temple ordinances of The Church of Jesus Christ of Latter-day Saints can provide the realization of these blessings for all of Heavenly Father's children.

The Doctrine of Eternal Families— A Blessing of the Restoration

Soon after learning of the doctrine of eternal families from the Prophet Joseph Smith, Elder Parley P. Pratt, a member of the Quorum of the Twelve Apostles in the early days of the Church, described his feelings as follows:

It was Joseph Smith who taught me how to prize the endearing relationships of father and mother, husband and wife, of brother and sister, son and daughter. It was from him that I learned that the wife of my bosom might be secured to me for time and all eternity; and that the refined sympathies and affections which endeared us to each other emanated from the fountain of divine eternal love . . .

the true dignity and destiny of a son of God, clothed with an eternal priesthood, as the patriarch and sovereign of his countless offspring . . . that the highest dignity of womanhood was, to stand as a queen and priestess to her husband, and to reign for ever and ever as the queen mother of her numerous and still increasing offspring. I had loved before, but I knew not why. But now I loved—with a pureness—an intensity of elevated, exalted feeling, which would lift my soul from the transitory things of this groveling sphere and expand it as the ocean. I felt that God was my heavenly father indeed; that Jesus was my brother, and that the wife of my bosom was an immortal, eternal companion; a kind ministering angel . . . a crown of glory for ever and ever (1968, pp. 297–298).

The power to seal families that was restored through the prophet Joseph Smith was given anciently by the Savior to Peter (Matthew 16:19) and is held by all presidents of the Church today, who in turn bestow this authority on others, who then perform these sacred ordinances in the holy temples. Pertaining to these ordinances, Elder A. Theodore Tuttle of the Seventy taught:

Frequently we perform marriages in the temple. These marriages are properly called celestial marriages, temple sealings, or eternal marriages. . . . The family is the most important relationship in this life. In reality, the bride and groom are called to assignments in the family from which they are never released, except by transgression. This is the one eternal unit which can exist in the presence of God (Tuttle, 1969, p. 130).

In speaking of the importance of keeping marriage covenants, President Joseph Fielding Smith said, "Marriage according to the law of the Church is the most holy and sacred ordinance. It will bring to the husband and the wife, if they abide in their covenants, the fullness of exaltation in the kingdom of God" (Smith, 1955, p. 84).

Latter-day scripture and the words of latter-day prophets teach us that not only are covenant marriages intended to last beyond the grave, but so can sibling and family relationships endure across generations. The prophet Mormon recorded:

And the day soon cometh that your mortal must put on immortality . . . and then ye must stand before the judgment-seat of Christ, to be judged according to your works; and if it so be that ye are righteous, *then are ye blessed with your fathers who have gone before you* (Mormon 6:21, italics added).

In the Doctrine and Covenants we read, "And that same sociality which exists among us here will exist among us there, only it will be coupled with eternal glory, which glory we do not now enjoy" (D&C 130:2). The Prophet Joseph Smith saw a vision of the celestial kingdom as it would one day exist and said, "I saw Father Adam and Abraham; and my father and my mother; my brother Alvin, that has long since slept" (D&C 137:5). It is significant that of all the great and noble people Joseph could have named, he mentioned his own parents, who were still living at the time of the vision, and his beloved elder brother, Alvin. Adam, one of our "first parents" (Alma 42:2), and Abraham, the "Father of the Faithful" (Abraham 2:10), have a familial relationship with those who will live with God in the celestial kingdom. The truth that the binding of humanity into eternal families is the whole purpose of the Creation is demonstrated by the prophecy of Malachi:

Behold, I will send you Elijah the prophet before the coming of the great and dreadful day of the Lord: And he shall turn the heart of the fathers to the children, and the heart of the children to their fathers, lest I come and smite the earth with a curse (Malachi 4:5–6).

From modern revelation we learn that Elijah appeared to the prophet Joseph Smith and Oliver Cowdery on April 3, 1836, in the temple at Kirtland, Ohio. Elijah, along with Elias and Moses, bestowed sacred priesthood keys that were a part of the restoration of those keys that had been lost to the earth from previous dispensations. President Joseph F. Smith's vision of the redemption of the dead describes the blessings brought by Elijah:

The Prophet Elijah was to plant in the hearts of the children the promises made to their fathers, foreshadowing the great work to be done in the temples of the Lord in the dispensation of the fulness of times, for the redemption of the dead, and the sealing of the children to their parents, lest the whole earth be smitten with a curse and utterly wasted at his coming (D&C 138:47–48).

The sealing powers restored by Elijah make possible the joy of being sealed to one's immediate family and beyond in a great chain from Adam and Eve to the last woman and man to be born upon the earth (see D&C 128:18). In addition to Elijah, Elias also appeared to Joseph Smith and Oliver Cowdery, restoring the doctrine and the keys of celestial marriage. Elder Bruce R. McConkie explained:

"Elias appeared, and committed the dispensation of the gospel of Abraham," meaning the great commission given to Abraham that he and his seed had a right to the priesthood, the gospel, and eternal life. Accordingly, Elias promised those upon whom these ancient promises were then renewed that in them and in their seed all generations should be blessed. (D&C 110:12–16.) Thus, through the joint ministry of Elijah, who brought the sealing power, and Elias, who restored the marriage discipline of Abraham, the way was prepared for the planting in the hearts of the children of the promises made to the fathers. (D&C 2:2.) These are the promises of eternal life through the priesthood and the gospel and celestial marriage (1985, p. 322).

With the restoration of "the new and everlasting covenant of marriage" (D&C 131:2), the order of the priesthood known as the patriarchal order was reestablished. President Ezra Taft Benson observed that the patriarchal order is

an order of family government where a man and woman enter into a covenant with God—just as did Adam and Eve—to be sealed for eternity, to have posterity, and to do the will and work of God throughout their mortality (1985, p. 9).

The patriarchal order, established in the days of Adam (see D&C 107:40–42), was and is an order of the Melchizedek Priesthood. The patriarchal order began with Adam and Eve and continued through Abraham and Sarah and their righteous descendants until the time Moses was translated, when the keys of the Melchizedek Priesthood were taken from the people (see D&C 84:19–27).

Through the keys and authority brought and bestowed by Elijah and Elias, Joseph Smith was able to officiate in all ordinances necessary for the salvation and exaltation of men and women. Commenting on the restoration of the blessings that would come with the sealings of marriages and families, the Lord Himself stated on this occasion, "Yea the hearts of thousands and tens of thousands shall greatly rejoice in consequence of the blessings which shall be poured out" (D&C 110:9).

Although the exact nature of family relationships after this life has not been fully revealed and we do not fully comprehend what God has prepared for the righteous (1 Corinthians 2:9), the Lord has revealed that marriage is essential for exaltation in the celestial kingdom (see D&C 132:15–16). Each exalted couple will, like God, be involved in the creative process of bringing forth spirit children, who will be privileged to experience mortality for themselves (see D&C 131:4).

Conclusion

God and His plan are eternal. He instituted marriage and family in the beginning. God created the earth, the garden, and our first parents in order to create families for all of His children to be born into and experience mortal life—especially mortal *family* life. The Fall occurred because Adam and Eve chose to obey God's commandment to multiply and replenish the earth and thus create the first family. The Savior completed the Atonement in order to reconcile God's children with the Father and with one another. Thus, the great plan of happiness is God's plan for happiness in time and in eternity.

God commands his children to marry and become one, and the Savior taught that "what therefore God hath joined together, let not man put asunder" (Matthew 19:6, see also 1 Corinthians 11:11). Marriage and family are eternal, and priesthood keys have been given to prophets to seal on earth and in heaven. The Lord told Moses, "Behold this is my work and my glory, to bring to pass the immortality and eternal life of man" (Moses 1:39), and He told the Prophet Joseph Smith that the new and everlasting covenant of marriage "was instituted for the fulness of my glory" (D&C 132:6). The work and glory of God is to assist His children to make and keep sacred covenants designed to allow them to be sealed together eternally to one another and to Him, and thereby enjoy all God enjoys. It should be the work and glory of all Latter-day Saints to make and keep these sacred covenants, to teach these transcendent truths to those who do not yet know of them, and to work in God's holy temples to make these covenants and ordinances available to all the children of God.

The eternal nature of the marriage covenant and the promise of everlasting family association are among the most beautiful and essential doctrines of the restored gospel. In fact, the purpose of the gospel and the Church is to exalt the family. Elder Hugh B. Brown stated:

> The family concept is one of the major and most important of the whole theological doctrine. In fact, our very concept of heaven itself is the projection of the home into eternity. Salvation, then, is essentially a family affair, and full participation in the plan of salvation can be had only in family units (1966, 103).

From the time of Adam and Eve and on to the present day, God's covenant people rejoice in the plain and most precious doctrine of eternal families.

Daniel K Judd *is a professor in the Department of Ancient Scripture at Brigham Young University. He and his wife, Kaye, are the parents of four children and they have five grandchildren.*

References

Ballard, M. R. (1996, May). Feasting at the Lord's table. *Ensign, 26*, 80–82.

Bateman, M. J. (1998). The eternal family. *BYU Magazine, 52*(4), 26.

Benson, E. T. (1985, August). What I hope you will teach your children about the temple. *Ensign, 15*, 6–10.

Brown, H. B. (1966, October). In *Conference Report*, 101–105.

Eyring, H. B. (1998, February). The family. *Ensign, 28*, 10–18.

Hunter, H. W. (1979, November). Reading the scriptures. *Ensign, 9*, 64–65.

Judd, D. K (1998). *The simpleness of the way.* West Valley City, UT: Bookcraft.

Kimball, S. W. (1964, October). In *Conference Report*, 24–26.

Lewis, C. S. (1952). *Mere Christianity.* New York: Harper Collins.

Lovejoy, A. O. (1948). *Essays in the history of ideas.* Baltimore, MD: Johns Hopkins Press.

McConkie, B. R. (1985). *A new witness for the Articles of Faith.* Salt Lake City: Deseret Book.

Miller, S., Wackman, D., Nunally, E., & Miller, P. (1988). *Connecting with self and others.* Littleton, CO: Interpersonal Communications Programs.

Nelson, R. M. (2001, November). "Set in order thy house." *Ensign, 31*, 69–71.

Oaks, D. H. (1993, November). "The great plan of happiness." *Ensign, 23*, 72–75.

Pratt, P. P. (1968). *The autobiography of Parley Parker Pratt.* Salt Lake City: Deseret Book.

Roberts, B. H. (Ed.). (1965). *History of the Church of Jesus Christ of Latter-day Saints: Period I: History of Joseph Smith, the prophet by himself* (vol. 6). Salt Lake City: Deseret Book.

Schönborn, C. (1995). *From death to life: the Christian journey.* San Francisco: Ignatius Press.

Smith, J. (1961). *Teachings of the Prophet Joseph Smith* (J. Fielding Smith, Ed.). Salt Lake City: Deseret. Book.

Smith, J. F., Winder, J. R., & Lund, A. H. (1909, November). The origin of man. *Improvement Era, 13*, 77.

Smith, J. F. (1955). *Doctrines of salvation* (vol. 2, B. R. McConkie, Ed.). Salt Lake City: Bookcraft.

Smith, J. F. (1986). *Gospel doctrine: Selections from the sermons and writings of Joseph F. Smith.* Salt Lake City: Deseret Book.

Snow, L. (1892, June 27). *Latter-day Saints' Millennial Star, 54.*

Tuttle, A. T. (1969, October). In *Conference Report*, 130–132.

Watson, E. J. (Ed.). (1971). *Manuscript history of Brigham Young, 1846–1847.* Salt Lake City: Elden J. Watson.

Section VI:
Applying, Sharing, and Defending Proclamation Principles

Drawing Specific Inspiration from the Proclamation

E. Jeffrey Hill

The Family: A Proclamation to the World . . . is scripture-like in its power. . . .
Read the proclamation . . . and you'll find answers there. And the answers that are there are the answers of the Church.
—President Boyd K. Packer, February 9, 2008, p. 5–6

THE FIRST TIME I HEARD "THE FAMILY: A PROCLA-mation to the World" is indelibly etched in my mind and heart. I had just completed a Ph.D. in family and human development at Utah State University and was serving on the Logan Utah Central Stake high council. As part of my calling, I was asked to attend the general Relief Society broadcast on September 23, 1995.

I sat comfortably in the chapel. It had been a long week and the lights were low. Even though the talks were inspiring and interesting, I found myself gently drifting into sleep on occasion. Then President Hinckley got up to speak, so I rallied my energy to listen to the prophet. He spoke a few words and then announced he would read "The Family: A Proclamation to the World."

Immediately something turned on a brilliant light inside me. I sat up straight and tuned in. Every word President Hinckley spoke resonated with me. Here was the prophet illuminating in clear, understandable words the undefiled principles upon which to build a successful family. Almost audibly, I cheered every pronouncement. Here was gospel truth unfettered by the world.

In the weeks that followed, I couldn't stop thinking about the proclamation. When the *Ensign* containing the text of the proclamation arrived, I pondered and prayed about its words. I wanted the proclamation to become a part of me and my family. I felt impressed to memorize the proclamation. I was 42 years old at the time and it had become much more difficult for me to memorize things than in my younger years, especially long passages. But the impression came again, "Memorize the proclamation!" I made several copies of the proclamation and took it with me wherever I went. As I jogged, I memorized. As I drifted off to sleep in the evening, the words of the proclamation were flowing through my mind. As I waited for my luggage in airports around the country, I had a tattered copy of the proclamation that I was trying to memorize. Although it was difficult, in about a month I could say the complete proclamation almost word for word.

Then came the process for truly digesting and drawing specific inspiration from the proclamation. I am a devout jogger and often have impressions, which I believe are from the Spirit, as I jog. I felt that while jogging I should be open to letting the Spirit use the proclamation as a means to provide inspiration about my family.

Each morning, as I jogged, the Spirit would bring to mind a different paragraph or a different sentence from the proclamation. One morning I was concerned about my teenage daughter and the friends she associated with. As I recited the proclamation in my mind, the Spirit highlighted in my thoughts the sentence that says, "Extended families should lend support when needed" (¶ 7). I paused, and to my mind came a picture of my sister struggling with trials and imminently expecting her seventh child in a distant state. I thought that we, as extended family, should lend our support to her—she definitely needed it. When I got home from jogging, I bought inexpensive plane tickets for my oldest daughter and oldest son to enable them to spend a week serving in my sister's home. As part of that trip, my daughter and sister had many long talks. They were able to talk about things in a way that I had been unable to as a father. My daughter returned from the trip with a clearer perspective and made wise decisions that blessed her life. My sister, her family, and my children were greatly blessed by this experience inspired by the proclamation.

Another time my responsibility to provide for my family seemed very heavy. My job seemed to be draining the life energy right out of me. I had difficulty sleeping. On my morning jog, the Spirit highlighted this portion of the proclamation:

> By divine design, fathers . . . are responsible to provide the necessities of life and protection for their families. Mothers are primarily responsible for the nurture of their children. In these sacred responsibilities, fathers and mothers are obligated to help one another as equal partners (¶ 7).

I recognized that in the frazzle to provide, I had been neglecting the nurture of my children, and that, as the proclamation said, I had an obligation to help my wife, Juanita, in this regard as an equal partner. I asked her what I could do, and she said putting the kids to bed would be the most helpful. So I started being more consistent in reading to the children, helping them brush their teeth, kneeling with them for their prayers, and putting them to bed with a song. These activities, right before I retired for the night, were calming and peaceful. They provided a prelude to joyful rest. With peaceful rest at night, I had more energy to put things in perspective.

Then I wondered how Juanita might help me, as an equal partner, in my responsibility to provide. I felt certain that the Lord did not want this mother of eight to go out and get a job to help out financially. The answer came on another morning jog during another internal recitation of the proclamation. As I went through the "provider" paragraph, the picture of Juanita and me walking and talking came to my mind. Then I realized she could help me by being a sounding board and helping me talk through my work problems and come to solutions. I asked Juanita if she would get up and walk with me in the mornings. She agreed, and we started strolling around the neighborhood to talk about my work problems. Juanita is a very good listener, especially early in the morning, and I found that just talking through my work problems with her enabled me to generate solutions that I had never thought of before. My work pressures got lighter and lighter. When

something frustrating happened during the day, I could think, "Tomorrow morning Juanita and I will talk about it, and we'll figure this out." So then I could go on without feeling frustration.

A pattern was emerging. As I frequently reviewed the words of the proclamation, they formed a conduit through which the Spirit could give my wife and me inspiration to move our family forward. True, most of the inspiration was not as grand as these examples. Most of it came as ideas like "take Hannah on a daddy-daughter date," or "fix dinner tonight," or "listen more to Emily," or "put Seth to bed more often." But the hundreds of little bits of direction added up to a much better family life.

In 2001, Juanita was diagnosed with advanced breast cancer and given a 50 percent chance for five-year survival. Our best option was to pursue an aggressive but very taxing course of chemotherapy, surgery, and radiation. We were discouraged when, after eight weeks of nauseating chemo, the large tumor had not shrunk at all. During this trial, I went jogging and recited the proclamation as loud as I could to relieve the stress I was feeling. It comforted me.

On one jog when I got to the sentence, "Successful marriages and families are established and maintained on principles of faith, prayer" (¶ 7), I stopped. I felt a sense of peace as an impression formed in my mind. It was the Saturday morning before fast Sunday, and I felt inspired to send an email to everyone I knew, inviting them to fast and pray and exercise their faith for Juanita so that the chemotherapy would be effective. We received a great outpouring of support. Even friends of other faiths described powerful experiences with fasting and prayer. Without our asking them to do so, friends in Australia, Japan, Hawaii, Salt Lake City, Boston, Belgium, and South Africa put Juanita's name on the prayer rolls in their temples. The results were miraculous. Immediately our mood and our faith improved. And during the next four weeks of treatments, the tumor almost totally disappeared. Juanita finished the treatment, and no measurable cancer remained.

We were so grateful! But this wasn't the end of our trials or of the continued comfort the proclamation brought us. In early 2004 we were devastated to learn that Juanita's cancer had returned, this time in her lungs. In somber tones, our doctor told us he would try to keep the cancer under control as long as possible, but there was now no possible cure. At first I felt betrayed and hopeless. Juanita and I had righteous desires and plans. What about the missions we were going to serve together? What about the grandchildren we were going to strengthen spiritually? How could this happen to us?

As I went through the proclamation again, this time it was as if someone turned a flashlight on to highlight the words, "Children are entitled to birth within the bonds of matrimony, and to be reared by a father and a mother" (¶ 7), I recognized that my children were entitled to be raised by a father *and a mother*. This statement filled me with hope that, in the face of great medical odds, Juanita would be blessed with a miracle and be healed.

We lived a fairly normal and hopeful life for about six months, but then the cancer began to take its unmistakable toll. Juanita lost weight rapidly and acquired a nearly constant and uncomfortable cough. Even the smallest exertion left her struggling for breath. Things seemed always to get worse and never better. Soon it became apparent that it was not God's will for Juanita to live much longer. I was at a complete loss to explain why God had not stepped forward with the miracle we so badly needed and so sincerely hoped for. But then again, the words of the proclamation provided inspiration and comfort: "Sacred ordinances and covenants available in holy temples make it possible for individuals to return to the presence of God and for families to be united eternally" (¶ 3). Through many tears, my understanding was enlarged to see that Juanita would indeed receive a miraculous healing. Because of the plan of salvation, Juanita would pass from this life into a beautiful place to be greeted by her father, our daughter who had passed away, and the Savior. Because of the Atonement of Jesus Christ, Juanita would be healed and at the resurrection receive a perfect body, free from cancer and any other illness. I could also see that through all eternity our children would have access to her influence as their mother—another miracle.

I also felt impressed that there was much we could yet do in this life to give the children continued access to her wisdom. I received a clear impression that it was time for us to stop focusing our faith on a physical miracle that was not in keeping with God's will and focus instead on learning as much as we could from Juanita in the short time we had left. We needed to be better prepared "to return to the presence of God and for [our family] to be united eternally." In our family testimony

meeting we expressed these feelings poignantly, and their truth washed over us all. Then we went to work.

Juanita wrote her testimony of the restored gospel of Jesus Christ, and I wrote mine as well. We printed and laminated them along with our pictures in a size that would fit in the children's scriptures. Juanita then wrote long letters in her own hand to each of the children, expressing appreciation and offering words of encouragement and advice. We recorded Juanita's sweet voice singing hymns, Primary songs, and childhood lullabies and made CDs for each of the children and for future grandchildren. We also recorded messages to be listened to on special occasions such as going to the temple, leaving on a mission, getting married, or giving birth to a child. Juanita crocheted baby blankets and bibs for future grandchildren. Our lives now became focused and full of activity, and we received great comfort from the Spirit. All this came as a result of inspiration from the proclamation.

Early one morning during this time, I outlined my plans for the day in prayer to God and asked if there might be anything else He would have me do. I do this regularly and generally do not have any specific impressions, usually just sweet feelings of peace—but on this morning I felt a strong impression that I should set aside what I had planned and write an *Ensign* article sharing my experiences with the proclamation. The impression became urgent for me, and I felt like I should write the article that very day. So I left my home, went to my BYU office, and wrote and wrote and wrote. The words came easily. By the end of the day, I emailed my article to the *Ensign*. I didn't expect to hear anything soon. I had published articles in the *Ensign* before and the first one took 14 years before it was in print. So I was very surprised when an editor emailed me the next day to tell me that my article was just what he was looking for, to make a few minor changes, and it would be included in the *Ensign* within a year (Hill, 2006).

All of our children were at Juanita's side when she died, and each had the opportunity to share tender communication with her. She was alert and talked to us until about 10 minutes before she passed away. That's when I told her, "I love you," and she responded in Spanish, *"Lo mismo,"* which means "same to you." Those were her last words. Her passing was sweet. We all knew and the Spirit etched in our hearts that our "family relationships [would be] perpetuated beyond the grave" and that we would "return to the presence of God and . . . be united eternally" (¶ 3).

For the first few weeks after Juanita's death, we received an outpouring of support from both sides of the veil that helped us cope. But then reality set in. Without Juanita, our family was much different. We still had the kids, we still had the work of the home, and I still had my job, but we didn't have Juanita. I learned very clearly the meaning of the sentence, "Disability, death, or other circumstances may necessitate individual adaptation" (¶ 7). Boy, was I adapting!

I had always thought of myself as being a fairly good dad. But as I tried to fill in for Juanita, I found that I was a pretty lousy mother. I found that if being a good mom were reduced to explicit instructions, it would contain a checklist of hundreds or thousands of things. My problem was that I was not only doing a poor job at what I attempted, but also that there were countless things I was not doing that I wasn't even aware of. Let me share an experience to illustrate.

One weekday morning our family was running late. Emily missed her ride to school and informed me I needed to take her to high school immediately. Seth hurried to finish preparing his lunch, and I gathered up materials for my day of teaching at BYU. With haste, we scurried out to the van, and I started to back out of the driveway. Then Seth got a terrified look on his face and cried out.

I looked at him with concern and asked, "What's wrong?"

With alarm in his voice, he said, "I forgot to get dressed!"

I looked at him, and sure enough, he was wearing his pajamas. None of us had noticed. He ran in and got dressed. Seth, Emily, and I were all late to school. I hadn't realized that something I was supposed to do was make sure my child was dressed for school. I started noticing.

Through this and countless other daily disasters, I found that as a mother I always fell short. At first this made me frustrated, sad, angry, and discouraged. No matter how hard I tried, I *always* fell short. There were things to feel guilty about 24 hours a day, 7 days a week, 52 weeks a year. My weaknesses required me to swallow my pride and humbly learn from others. With time, things started to get a little better. I started celebrating small successes month to month. Little did I realize that God was preparing a miracle for me.

On April 11, 2006, Tammy Mulford, a widowed mother with four children, had just put her children to bed and decided to read an *Ensign* article before retiring. She read my article and related to many of the experiences I recounted. During the night, she awakened several times with an impression to send a note to the *Ensign* thanking them for this insightful article. In the morning she set the impression aside, but it kept returning again and again and became urgent. At about 11:00 a.m., she responded to the prompting and emailed a four-line comment to the *Ensign* about my article. About noon that same day, an editor at the *Ensign* felt impressed to forward the comment to me. This was about the one-year anniversary of Juanita's passing, and I was feeling very discouraged. When I read Tammy's comment, it felt like a weight was lifting off my shoulders. Inexplicably, I felt light and bright. That afternoon I emailed Tammy a thank-you note for the comment and its effect on me. The next time she checked her email, she was surprised to have a note from the author of the article she had read the night before. We found we had a lot in common, and she was very helpful as I made adjustments as a single parent. When we started talking on the phone together, I immediately felt as though I was visiting with my best friend. To make a long story short, we emailed prolifically, we talked on the phone extensively, we dated, we enjoyed family outings together, and we became engaged in the Nauvoo Temple. On October 6, 2006, we were married for time in the Bountiful Utah Temple.

We have found the blending of the Hill-Mulford family to be quite an adventure and, frankly, quite challenging. With so many of us, with so many different temperaments, and with grief that still occurs, it is difficult to create a home where everyone feels accepted and where we feel as though we are one family. Still, there is much of peace and joy. The principles of the proclamation have again blessed us as we move forward in our family. A while ago, I was watching Tammy play with our children, both Mulfords and Hills, and the words of the proclamation flowed into my mind: "Children are entitled . . . to be reared by a father and a mother who honor marital vows with complete fidelity" (¶ 7). As I watched the children joking and laughing and enjoying one another with this beautiful woman, tears of gratitude came to my eyes as I understood that my children had been blessed beyond measure. They were indeed claiming their entitlement to be raised by a father *and a mother*. In fact, they are now blessed to have two moms who love them, one from this side of the veil and another from the other side. I am so grateful that Tammy came into our lives.

In conclusion, I have marveled at the numerous specific and personal ways the proclamation has blessed me and my family since that Saturday night about 15 years ago when I first heard it. It has changed our lives forever. It is the word of God, and it can be the basis for great joy and happiness in family life, even in the midst of unfathomable trials. I know by the Spirit that "The Family: A Proclamation to the World" is an inspired document for families today, and if seriously studied, it will open the windows of divine assistance. I invite all serious students of the proclamation to feast upon these inspired words regularly and allow them to bless your family.

E. Jeffrey Hill *is an associate professor in the School of Family Life at Brigham Young University. He and his wife, Tammy, are the parents of twelve children and they have twelve grandchildren.*

References

Hill, E. J. (2006, April). The proclamation: A guide, a comfort, and an inspiration. *Ensign, 36,* 52–56.

Packer, B. K. (2008, February 9). The proclamation on the family. *Worldwide Leadership Training Meeting: Building Up a Righteous Posterity.* Salt Lake City: The Church of Jesus Christ of Latter-day Saints. Retrieved from http://lds.org/library/display/0,4945,8027-1-4404-3,00.html

CHAPTER 34

Sharing and Defending Family Proclamation Principles

Alan J. Hawkins

We call upon responsible citizens . . . everywhere to promote those measures designed to maintain and strengthen the family as the fundamental unit of society.

PRESIDENT SPENCER W. KIMBALL TAUGHT THAT "the time will come when only those who believe deeply and actively in the family will be able to preserve their families in the midst of the gathering evil around us" (Kimball, 1980, p. 4). While our own families are our most important responsibility, every family of the earth is in need of the vital blessings that come from living proclamation principles. I believe, therefore, that a deep and active belief in the principles articulated in "The Family: A Proclamation to the World" should motivate us not only to apply true principles to protect our own families, but it should also move us to share these principles with others. The statement by the prophet Joseph Smith applies here—that when we gain a witness of the truth, we will not be "content with blessing [our] family alone, but [range] through the whole world, anxious to bless the whole human race" (Smith, 1976, p. 227). In the Doctrine and Covenants we are taught, "And the voice of warning shall be unto all people, by the mouth of my disciples, whom I have chosen in these last days" (D&C 1:4). "And let your preaching be the warning voice, every man to his neighbor, in mildness and in meekness" (D&C 38:41). As we share the principles of the proclamation with others, we can fulfill that directive to preach and warn our neighbors, helping them strengthen their families.

Over the past decade, I have been teaching a foundational class at Brigham Young University that explores in depth the family proclamation. One of my goals for this class is to encourage students to share and defend proclamation principles with others near and far, not keep them solely for personal profit. I tell students that

the proclamation is to the world, but that we, as Latter-day Saints, are the messengers that take its truths to our friends, associates, and family members who collectively constitute the "world"; we are that mild and meek warning voice. One thing I do to accomplish this objective is encourage students throughout the semester to initiate "share and defend" experiences with friends, family members, colleagues, and acquaintances both near and far. At the end of the semester they share their experiences with me in a brief report. For some it is just a class exercise, but for many it develops into a sincere effort to reach out. A few students even contact me long after graduation to tell me of their recent share and defend experiences.

In this essay, I will share some of those experiences. I asked and received the students' permission to include their stories in this book, with names and some minor details changed. The first set of student stories involves associates who were not members of the LDS Church. The second set of stories is from students' conversations with family members and friends who belong to the LDS Church and how these conversations blessed lives.

First, however, I will share two of my own experiences. After all, it is best to ask my students to do something that I try to do myself. In sharing these stories, I hope I can motivate readers to seek some of their own share and defend experiences.

My Own Share and Defend Experiences

A reverend's curiosity. A few years ago, I was in a car for a couple of hours traveling from a conference back to the Atlanta airport. The driver, an ordained minister, led a large African American congregation in an eastern state. I don't think he'd had many opportunities to learn directly about Latter-day Saint beliefs. Since the conference we had been attending was about strengthening marriages, he was asking many questions about Mormon beliefs about marriage and family life. I did the best I could to respond to his questions, first with phrases directly from the proclamation. (I have memorized the family proclamation, something also I ask my students to do.) For instance, we discussed the concept of eternal families and the purpose of temples. I quoted from the proclamation:

> The divine plan of happiness enables family relationships to be perpetuated beyond the grave. Sacred ordinances and covenants available in holy temples make it possible for individuals to return to the presence of God and for families to be united eternally (¶ 3).

I sensed he enjoyed the conversation. I promised to send him a copy of the proclamation and did so. He wrote me back expressing appreciation. When I saw him again about a year later at another conference, he thanked me again for sending him the proclamation. I doubt this incident will produce any conversions, but I do not doubt that a man of religious influence will be less susceptible to accept or pass on misinformation about our faith now. "By small and simple things are great things brought to pass" (Alma 37:6).

A Christmas gift. On a number of occasions I have shared the proclamation as a whole, not any specific part. For instance, a few years ago I gave the proclamation as a Christmas gift to colleagues I was working with on a national project to build the National Healthy Marriage Resource Center. The project director called me a few days after she received her copy. It was a gloomy, stressful period in our project when we were uncertain whether the project we had invested so much in was even going to survive the New Year. But her voice was a bit more cheerful as we began our conversation that day. "Thank you so much for sending me that document," she said. "It really brightened my day, and I needed it today." Again, I do not expect that this deeply religious woman will become a member of the LDS Church. But I rejoice in the sweet spirit that accompanies that document; it can inspire people of very different backgrounds across the world.

Students' Share and Defend Experiences with Members of Other Faiths

The cohabitation question. Now I relate some of my students' experiences. One of the most common topics that my students bring up when they are sharing and defending proclamation principles is living together before marriage, what family scholars call cohabitation. In class we talk about how common cohabitation is these days, but we also discuss its association with an *increased* risk of divorce if the couple eventually marries, which many do (see Jose, O'Leary, & Moyer, 2010; Rhoades, Stanley, & Markman, 2009). My students almost seem relieved to learn this. Their faith has taught them right and wrong, but the culture they grew up in has bought into the so-called logic of cohabitation.

One student—I'll call him "Richard"—reached out to a high school friend and initiated a conversation about cohabitation. He had recently joined the Facebook revolution and set up his own social networking site on the Internet. Within a few hours, a good friend from high school he had lost contact with sent him a hello and they were exchanging messages. Richard discovered that his friend, Tom, had just decided to move in with his girlfriend. Tom said he and his girlfriend were hoping to get married someday in the distant future, but there were no formal plans. (This kind of no-firm-marriage-plans cohabitation appears to be the riskiest; Rhoades, Stanley, & Markman, 2009). Richard realized this was an ideal "share and defend" experience for my class assignment, if he could muster the courage. Richard said he knew that Tom was a young man of good character who cared deeply about his girlfriend, and he knew that he wouldn't want to do anything that would hurt her. So Richard shared some concerns about Tom's decision to live with his girlfriend by telling him some of the research on cohabitation he had just learned in class. For instance, he mentioned the research that cohabitation before marriage actually increases the risk of a future divorce if the couple is not engaged first (Rhoades, Stanley, & Markman, 2009). He said he didn't want to offend him, but as a friend, he wanted to share his concerns. He was anxious while anticipating Tom's reply. Tom did reply and sincerely thanked Richard for his concern. Tom said he knew that living together was not the best thing. Despite this, unfortunately, Tom said he was going to do it anyway. Nevertheless, Richard had planted a good seed and had been obedient to the commandment to give warning in mildness and meekness.

But several of my students have had more "success," so to speak, with this issue. One student also bravely dived in when her best friend back home called to tell her the news about deciding to move in with her new boyfriend. Again, in a series of long and sometimes difficult phone conversations, "Natalie" shared with her friend the research on the risks of cohabitation. She also shared her own feelings and faith about marriage as the proper guardian of human sexuality: "Marriage between a man and a woman is ordained of God. . . . [and] God has commanded that the sacred powers of procreation are to be employed only between man and woman, lawfully wedded as husband and wife" (¶¶ 1, 4). Natalie said she got resistance from her friend, first questioning the research, then confessing that she felt some pressure to move in with her boyfriend and really was unsure. Eventually, Natalie's friend expressed appreciation for her concern and support and told Natalie that she had decided against living with her boyfriend. I don't know the end of this story, but I have confidence that a life was blessed by a brave young woman who helped a friend to follow the Light of Christ within her.

Students' Share and Defend Experiences with LDS Family Members and Friends

Valuable experiences sharing the proclamation are not limited to friends and associates who do not share fully our faith. Some of the most inspiring stories my students have shared have been reaching out to Latter-day Saint friends and even to their own family members. Let me share a few of those stories.

Sanctity of life. One young freshman student— "Cindy"—was listening in class one day to the statistics about the large number of abortions, the declining number of adoptions, and prophetic statements about the sanctity of human life. Her thoughts went out to a close friend from her ward in the town in which she grew up. Cindy knew that her friend had made some bad choices and had become pregnant by her boyfriend. Her friend had struggled to know what to do. She received pressure from different directions: abort the child; keep and rear the child herself; give the child up for adoption. Eventually, after pleading in prayer, Cindy's friend gave the child life and then gave her to an overjoyed Latter-day Saint couple. Thinking about

this, after class Cindy called her friend, who had just weeks before given such an unselfish gift to this couple. Cindy shared her feelings about the sanctity of life and how proud she was of her friend. Her friend echoed Cindy's sentiments, and also said how happy she was that the Lord could make something so beautiful out of her mistake. This was a powerful, confirming experience for Cindy of her faith in sacred truths:

> We affirm the sanctity of life and of its importance in God's eternal plan. . . . Children are entitled to birth within the bonds of matrimony and to be reared by a father and a mother who honor marital vows with complete fidelity (¶¶ 5, 7).

One of the most memorable share and defend experiences I have heard came from "Rachel." Rachel had lost track of her best friend growing up when she went off to college. But out of the blue one day, Rachel's childhood friend called her up—somehow getting a hold of her brand new cell phone number—and confessed that she was pregnant by her boyfriend. The unborn child was six months along when Rachel's friend discovered that the baby tested positive for Down's Syndrome. Rachel's friend decided that she was going to end the "mess" by getting an abortion. Rachel summoned her courage to express her feelings about the sacredness of life. And she related to her friend a story shared by a classmate just a day earlier. This classmate, during a discussion of the sacredness of human life, said that she had tested positive for Down's Syndrome prenatally but her parents decided to give her life anyway, a rare occurrence these days. The test was a false positive and she was born perfectly normal. Perhaps as a result of hearing this story, Rachel's friend decided to give her unborn child life rather than abort. In raising a warning voice in mildness and meekness, Rachel helped to preserve a sacred life.

Most of the stories that my students tell me about sharing proclamation principles are not as dramatic as this one. They are on the more prosaic elements of family life, like compassion and forgiveness. But students have related to me powerful experiences conversing about these topics with family members.

Maternal nurturing. For instance, "Mary" told me of a share and defend experience that ended up being more than a class assignment. She was talking for two hours to her younger sister back home who was complaining, as teenagers typically do, about their mother and how she was overbearing, overprotective, and hypercritical. Finally, Mary jumped in. She related to her sister some statistics about how so many mothers feel unappreciated by society for the nurturing work they do. Despite this, they still believe that the most important work they do is in the walls of their own homes (Erickson & Aird, 2005). This holds true even when they work outside the home, as Mary's mother did part time to help support the family. Mary talked to her sister about how mothers sacrifice so much for their families. Mary quoted the proclamation phrase, "Mothers are primarily responsible for the nurture of their children" (¶ 7). She pointed out why mothers sometimes seem overbearing because they care so deeply for the happiness of their children and their God-given responsibility to "rear their children in love and righteousness" (¶ 6). Mary urged her sister to cut their mother a little slack. After a few moments of silence, Mary heard muffled sniffles coming from the other end of the line. Her sister choked a few words out and said she would try harder. They hung up, but a few minutes later, Mary's phone rang and it was her mother on the other end. "Mary, what did you say to your sister?" she asked. Mary recounted to her mother just a few of the things she had said. Her mother simply responded: "Mary, thank you. I don't know everything you said, but it made a huge impact on your sister."

Family compassion. That same semester, "Melissa" recounted a rather touching experience she had trying to urge family members to be compassionate towards another family member. Her mother was visiting her at BYU during general conference weekend. Listening to conference, Melissa noticed that her mother was getting emotional. She also noticed that the emotion was most evident when the talks were focused on family responsibilities. At one point, Melissa's mother began to cry. Melissa asked what was wrong. Her mother then shared with her the heartbreaking news that her brother had become ensnared in the trap of pornography. Her mother sobbed her fears and self-doubt. She also worried that Melissa's father would be harsh and severe with his son and that this would drive him away.

Melissa tried to comfort her mother. Later, Melissa was pondering how she could help. She felt that she should send her father an email letting him know that

she was aware of the family problem. She expressed her support to him in his divine responsibility as a father to "preside over [his family] in love and righteousness" and protect his family (¶ 7). But boldly, and knowing her father the way she did, she encouraged him to use compassion with her brother. I didn't get to hear the end of the story, but Melissa did express confidence that things would be handled differently—with more compassion—in this situation than might have occurred. And she came to understand that sometimes a mild, meek, and sensitive voice of warning is needed within family circles too.

Family forgiveness. Another student, "Anne," took advantage of a difficult family situation to urge forgiveness. Her younger sister, "Maggie," called very upset. Another younger sister, "Trisha," was going through a rebellious time and getting into serious trouble. Maggie had been very compassionate and supportive, trying to do her best to love her troubled little sister, Trisha. Then one night, Trisha stole Maggie's car keys and went for a joy ride. She was underage and didn't have a license and got pulled over for speeding. Because she didn't have a license, she gave the police officer Maggie's name instead of her own. When the speeding ticket arrived in the mail, Maggie quickly figured out what had happened and became furious. That's when she called her older sister, Anne, my student. Maggie said that she was done supporting her ungrateful little sister. She didn't know how she could ever forgive Trisha. Anne then quietly rehearsed to Maggie some of the things we had been learning in class about forgiveness in families. She reminded her that she had a spiritual duty to forgive all and that harboring this anger and resentment would only canker her own soul. Forgiving, as difficult as it can be, would be liberating for her. Maggie was crying and saying how hard it would be, but she said she would try. She went to Trisha and expressed her love and said that she forgave her for stealing her car and the lie she told the police officer. A few weeks later, Anne was home and visited with Trisha, reciting the proclamation for her, and telling her how much she loved her. Again, I don't know if there was a storybook ending; the semester ended before the final chapter of the story. But I know that Anne and Maggie were reaching out in accordance with truth to bless a family member in need.

Hearing these students' stories has been a personal privilege. There is great value in sharing the principles contained in the family proclamation and great fulfillment to be found in doing so. The family proclamation is an inspired document—President Boyd K. Packer (2008, p. 5) called it "revelatory" and "scripturelike in its power"—and it contains timeless truths that will bless not only our lives but also the lives of those around us as we reach out, near and far, to share it.

Alan J. Hawkins is a professor in the School of Family Life at Brigham Young University. He and his wife, Lisa, are the parents of two children and they have two grandchildren.

References

Erickson, M. F., & Aird, E. G. (2005). *The motherhood study: Fresh insights on mothers' attitudes and concerns.* New York: Institute for American Values.

Jose, K., O'Leary, D., & Moyer, A. (2010). Does premarital cohabitation predict subsequent marital stability and marital quality? A meta-analysis. *Journal of Marriage and Family, 72,* 105–116.

Kimball, S. W. (1980, November). Families can be eternal. *Ensign, 10,* 4–5.

Packer, B. K. (2008, February 9). The proclamation on the family (pp. 4–9). *Worldwide leadership training meeting: Building up a righteous posterity.* Salt Lake City: The Church of Jesus Christ of Latter-day Saints.

Rhoades, G. K., Stanley, S. M., & Markman, H. J. (2009). Working with cohabitation in relationship education and therapy. *Journal of Couple and Relationship Therapy, 8,* 95–112.

Smith, J. (1976). *History of the Church of Jesus Christ of Latter-day Saints, Vol. 4.* Salt Lake City: Deseret Book.

Scripture Index

Subject Index